Java 9 Recipes

A Problem-Solution Approach

Third Edition

Josh Juneau

Apress®

Java 9 Recipes: A Problem-Solution Approach

Josh Juneau
Hinckley, Illinois, USA

ISBN-13 (pbk): 978-1-4842-1975-1   ISBN-13 (electronic): 978-1-4842-1976-8
DOI 10.1007/978-1-4842-1976-8

Library of Congress Control Number: 2017943502

Managing Director: Welmoed Spahr
Editorial Director: Todd Green
Acquisitions Editor: Jonathan Gennick
Development Editor: Laura Berendson
Technical Reviewer: Vinay Kumar
Coordinating Editor: Jill Balzano
Copy Editor: Brendan Frost
Compositor: SPi Global
Indexer: SPi Global
Artist: SPi Global

Distributed to the book trade worldwide by Springer Science+Business Media New York, 233 Spring Street, 6th Floor, New York, NY 10013. Phone 1-800-SPRINGER, fax (201) 348-4505, e-mail orders-ny@springer-sbm.com, or visit www.springeronline.com. Apress Media, LLC is a California LLC and the sole member (owner) is Springer Science + Business Media Finance Inc (SSBM Finance Inc). SSBM Finance Inc is a **Delaware** corporation.

For information on translations, please e-mail rights@apress.com, or visit http://www.apress.com/rights-permissions.

Apress titles may be purchased in bulk for academic, corporate, or promotional use. eBook versions and licenses are also available for most titles. For more information, reference our Print and eBook Bulk Sales web page at http://www.apress.com/bulk-sales.

Any source code or other supplementary material referenced by the author in this book is available to readers on GitHub via the book's product page, located at www.apress.com/9781484219751. For more detailed information, please visit http://www.apress.com/source-code.

This book is dedicated to my wife and children.

Contents at a Glance

Contents

About the Author

Josh Juneau has been developing software and enterprise applications since the early days of Java EE. Application and database development have been his focus since the start of his career. He became an Oracle database administrator and adopted the PL/SQL language for performing administrative tasks and developing applications for the Oracle database. In an effort to build more complex solutions, he began to incorporate Java into his PL/SQL applications and later developed stand-alone and web applications with Java. Josh wrote his early Java web applications utilizing JDBC and servlets or JSP to work with back-end databases. Later, he began to incorporate frameworks into his enterprise solutions, such as Java EE and JBoss Seam. Today, he primarily develops enterprise web solutions utilizing Java EE and other technologies. He also includes the use of alternative languages, such as Jython and Groovy, for some of his projects.

Over the years, Josh has dabbled in many different programming languages, including alternative languages for the JVM, in particular. In 2006, Josh began devoting time to the Jython Project as editor and publisher of the *Jython Monthly* newsletter. In late 2008, he began a podcast dedicated to the Jython programming language. Josh was the lead author for *The Definitive Guide to Jython*, *Oracle PL/SQL Recipes*, and *Java 7 Recipes*, and a solo author of *Java EE 7 Recipes* and *Introducing Java EE 7*, which were all published by Apress. He works as an application developer and system analyst at Fermi National Accelerator Laboratory, and he also writes technical articles for Oracle and OTN. He was a member of the JSR 372 and JSR 378 expert groups, and is an active member of the Java Community, helping to lead the Chicago Java User Group's Adopt-a-JSR effort.

When not coding or writing, Josh enjoys spending time with his wonderful wife and five children, especially swimming, fishing, playing ball, and watching movies. To hear more from Josh, follow his blog at http://jj-blogger.blogspot.com. You can also follow him on Twitter at @javajuneau.

About the Technical Reviewer

Vinay Kumar is an Oracle ACE and technology evangelist. He has extensive experience in designing and implementing large-scale projects in Oracle Enterprise Technologies. He has implemented multiple Enterprise Portal on web and intranet using Oracle WebCenter Portal/ADF and open source. He is a technology advisor, trainer, and architect. He loves exploring emerging solutions and applications mainly related to Oracle Middleware and open source. He loves spending his time in mentoring, writing technical blogs (www.techartifact.com), publishing white papers & maintaining dedicated education channel at youtube for Java, ADF/ WebCenter. He also authored a book on Enterprise Portal (WebCenter 12c) of Apress publication.

Find his views at @vinaykuma201.

Acknowledgments

To my wife Angela: As the years pass, I will continue to be amazed by you. I want to thank for being a great wife, mother, and sidekick, always giving your all to me and the children. You've helped me make it through this book and my other projects, and your inspiration always keeps me moving forward. Thanks for always supporting the work I do. It was great to finally have you at JavaOne in 2016, and it was great to spend time away. I love you very much.

To my children, Kaitlyn, Jacob, Matthew, Zachary, and Lucas: I love you all so much and I cherish every moment we have together. You all continue to make me so proud through your schoolwork, Scouting, sports, and the myriad of other things that you achieve. I hate to see you growing up so quickly...sometimes I wish that I could pause time. I hope that you will understand why I've worked so hard at times on the nights and weekends when you read this book some day.

I want to thank my original coauthors of the first edition of this book: Carl Dea, Freddy Guime, John O'Conner, and Mark Beaty. You guys are Java gurus, and your expertise is engrained within the pages of this second edition just as much as the first. I had a great time working with you on the original and hope to do so again in the future.

To the folks at Apress: I thank you for providing me with the chance to share my knowledge with others. I especially thank Jonathan Gennick for the continued support of my work and for providing the continued guidance to produce useful content for our readers. I also thank Jill Balzano for doing a great job coordinating this project. The technical reviewer, Vinay Kumar, has done an excellent job of solidifying the book content. I really thank you for your hard work and expertise. Lastly, I'd like to thank everyone else at Apress who had a hand in this book.

To the Java community: Thanks for continuing to make the Java platform such an innovative and effective platform for application development. We all have the privilege of working with a mature and robust platform, and it would not be successful today if it weren't for everyone's continued contributions to the technology. I thank all of the Oracle and community Java experts. Once again, the roadmap for the future is continuing to look great. I am looking forward to using Java technology for many years to come.

Introduction

The Java programming language was introduced in 1995 by Sun Microsystems. Derived from languages such as C and C++, Java was designed to be more intuitive and easier to use than older languages, specifically due to its simplistic object model and automated facilities such as memory management. At the time, Java drew the interest of developers because of its object-oriented, concurrent architecture; its excellent security and scalability; and because applications developed in the Java language could run on any operating system that contained a Java Virtual Machine (JVM). Since its inception, Java has been described as a language that allows developers to "write once, run everywhere" as code is compiled into class files that contain bytecode, and the resulting class files can run on any compliant JVM. This concept made Java an immediate success for desktop development, which later branched off into different technological solutions over the years, including development of web-based applications and rich Internet applications (RIAs). Today, Java is deployed on a broad range of devices, including mobile phones, printers, medical devices, Blu-ray players, and so on.

The Java platform consists of a hierarchy of components, starting with the Java Development Kit (JDK), which is composed of the Java Runtime Environment (JRE), the Java programming language, and platform tools that are necessary to develop and run Java applications. The JRE contains the JVM, plus the Java application programming interfaces (APIs) and libraries that assist in the development of Java applications. The JVM is the base upon which compiled Java class files run and is responsible for interpreting compiled Java classes and executing the code. Every operating system that is capable of running Java code has its own version of the JVM. To that end, the JRE must be installed on any system that will be running local Java desktop or stand-alone Java applications. Oracle provides JRE implementations for most of the major operating systems. Each operating system can have its own flavor of the JRE. For instance, mobile devices can run a scaled-down version of the full JRE that is optimized to run Java Mobile Edition (ME) and Java SE embedded applications. The Java platform APIs and libraries are a collection of predefined classes that are used by all Java applications. Any application that runs on the JVM makes uses the Java platform APIs and libraries. This allows applications to use the functionality that has been predefined and loaded into the JVM and leaves developers with more time to worry about the details of their specific application. The classes that comprise the Java platform APIs and libraries allow Java applications to use one set of classes in order to communicate with the underlying operating system. As such, the Java platform takes care of interpreting the set of instructions provided by a Java application into operating system commands that are required for the machine on which the application is being executed. This creates a facade for Java developers to write code against so that they can develop applications that can be written once and run on every machine that contains a relevant JVM.

The JVM and the Java platform APIs and libraries play key roles in the life cycle of every Java application. Entire books have been written to explore the platform and JVM. This book focuses on the Java language itself, which is used to develop Java applications, although the JVM and Java platform APIs and libraries are referenced as needed. The Java language is a robust, secure, and modern object-oriented language that can be used to develop applications to run on the JVM. The Java programming language has been refined over several iterations and it becomes more powerful, secure, and modern with each new release. This book covers many features of the Java programming language from those that were introduced in Java 1.0 through those that made their way into the language in Java 9. In 2014, Oracle Corporation released Java 8, which was another milestone release for the Java ecosystem. Not only was Java already the most modern, statically typed, object-oriented language available for development, but Java 8 added important new enhancements to the language, such as lambda expressions, streams processing, and default methods. JavaFX 8 was also released at the same time, advancing desktop Java applications more than ever. JavaFX 8 can be used for developing rich desktop and Internet applications using the Java language, or any other language that runs on the JVM. It provides a rich set of graphical and media user interfaces to develop extraordinary visual applications. This release is another nice update to the JavaFX platform, adding in features such as the Swing node and the Print API. In 2017, Java 9 is released, enhancing the platform with features such as modularity, an updated Process API, and jShell. This book covers the fundamentals of Java development, such as installing the JDK, writing classes, and running applications. It delves into essential topics such as the development of object-oriented constructs, exception handling, unit testing, and localization. The book also provides solutions for desktop application development using the JavaFX, and some web-based and database solutions. It covers JavaFX in depth and is an essential guide for developers beginning to use JavaFX 8+. This book can be used as a guide for solving problems that ordinary Java developers may encounter at some point. A broad range of topics is discussed, and the solutions to the problems that are covered in this book are concise and to the point. If you are a novice Java developer, we hope that this book will help you get started on your journey to working with one of the most advanced and widely used programming languages available today. For those of you who have used the Java language for some time, we hope that this book will provide you with updated material that is new to Java 9, JavaFX, and even some Java web development so that you can further refine your Java development skills. I ensure that advanced Java application developers will also learn a thing or two regarding the new features of the language and perhaps even stumble upon some techniques that were not used in the past. Whatever your skill level, this book is good to have close at hand as a reference for solutions to those problems that you encounter in your daily programming.

Who This Book Is For

This book is intended for all those who are interested in learning the Java programming language and/or already know the language but would like some information regarding the new features included in Java SE 9 and JavaFX. Those who have not yet programmed in the Java language can read this book, and it will allow them to start from scratch to get up and running quickly. Intermediate and advanced Java developers who are looking to update their arsenal with the latest features that Java SE 9 makes available to them can also read the book to quickly update and refresh their skill set. Java desktop programmers will find this book useful for its content on developing desktop applications using the JavaFX API. There is, of course, a myriad of other essential topics that will be useful to Java developers of any type.

How This Book Is Structured

This book is structured such that it does not have to be read from cover to cover. In fact, it is structured so that developers can chose which topics they wish to read about and jump right to them. Each recipe contains a problem to solve, one or more solutions to solve that problem, and a detailed explanation of how the solution works. Although some recipes may build upon concepts that have been discussed in other recipes, they contain the appropriate references so that the developer can find other related recipes that are beneficial to the solution. The book is designed to allow developers to get up and running quickly with a solution so that they can be home in time for dinner.

CHAPTER 1

■ ■ ■

Getting Started with Java 9

In this chapter we present a handful of recipes to help programmers who are new to the Java language, as well as those having experience in other languages, become accustomed to Java 9. You will learn to install Java, and also install an Integrated Development Environment (IDE) from which you'll develop applications and experiment with the solutions provided in this book. You will learn basics of Java such as how to create a class and how to accept keyboard input. Documentation is often overlooked, but in this chapter you will quickly learn how to create great documentation for your Java code.

■ **Note** *Java 9 Recipes* is not intended as a complete tutorial. Rather, it covers key concepts of the Java language. If you are truly new to Java, we recommend buying and reading one of the many *Beginning Java* books that are also published by Apress.

1-1. Creating a Development Environment

Problem

You want to install Java and experiment with the language. You'd also like a reasonable IDE to use with it.

Solution

Install Java Development Kit 9 (JDK. That gives you the language and a compiler. Then install the NetBeans IDE to provide a more productive working environment.

Java Standard Edition (Java SE) is sufficient for most recipes in this book. To download the release, visit the following page on the Oracle Technology Network (OTN):

```
http://www.oracle.com/technetwork/java/javase/overview/index.html
```

Figure 1-1 shows the Downloads tab, and you can see the Java Platform download link and image prominently on the page. Next to that link is an image for the NetBeans IDE, which provides the option of downloading the JDK and NetBeans together. Choose the option that you prefer, download the release for your platform, and run the setup wizard to install. For the purposes of this book, I am using NetBeans IDE 8.2.

© Josh Juneau 2017

J. Juneau, *Java 9 Recipes*, DOI 10.1007/978-1-4842-1976-8_1

Figure 1-1. *Java SE Downloads page on the OTN*

■ **Note**   If you chose to only install the Java Platform (JDK) and not NetBeans, you can download NetBeans at a later time by visiting `netbeans.org`.

How It Works

The name *Java*™ is a trademark owned by Oracle Corporation. The language itself is open source, and its evolution is controlled by a process known as the *Java Community Process* (JCP). You can read more about that process at `www.jcp.org`.

While the language is not owned per se by Oracle Corporation, its core development tends to be steered by that company. It is Oracle Corporation that runs the JCP, and that owns the `jcp.org` domain.

There are many editions of Java, such as the Mobile Edition (ME) and the Enterprise Edition (EE). Java SE is the Standard Edition and represents the heart of the language. We've built the recipes in this book for Java SE programmers. Those interested in the development of embedded applications for devices such as Raspberry Pi may be interested in learning more about Java ME. Similarly, those interested in developing web applications and working with enterprise solutions may be interested in learning more about Java EE.

■ **Note**   Enterprise developers may want to buy and read a copy of *Java EE 7 Recipes* by Josh Juneau (Apress, 2013).

There are several good websites that you can visit to learn more about Java and keep up to date with the latest on the platform. A good place to begin for all things Java is the following page on the OTN:

`http://www.oracle.com/technetwork/java/index.html`

The wealth of resources available from this page can be overwhelming at first, but it's worth your time to look around and get passingly familiar with the many links that are available.

One of the links will be to Java SE, which takes you to the page shown earlier in Figure 1-1. It is from there that you can download Java SE and the NetBeans IDE. Also from there you have access to the official documentation, to community resources such as forums and newsletters, and to training resources designed to help you build knowledge in Java and become certified in the language.

1-2. Getting to "Hello, World"

Problem

You've installed Java SE 9 and the NetBeans IDE. Now you want to run a simple Java program to verify that your installation is working properly.

Solution

Begin by opening the NetBeans IDE. You should see a workspace resembling the one in Figure 1-2. You may see some projects in the left-hand pane if you've already been working on projects within the IDE.

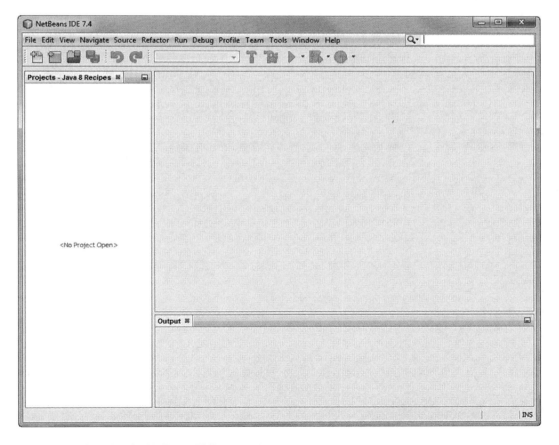

Figure 1-2. *Opening the NetBeans IDE*

Go to the File menu and select New Project. You'll see the dialog in Figure 1-3. Choose the Java category, and then Java Application. Click Next to advance to the dialog shown in Figure 1-4.

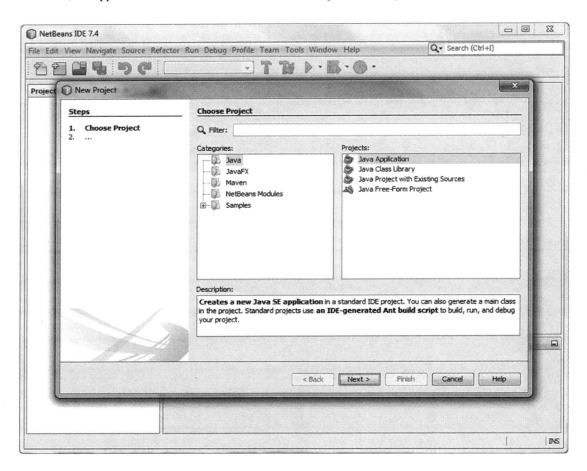

Figure 1-3. *Creating a new Java SE project*

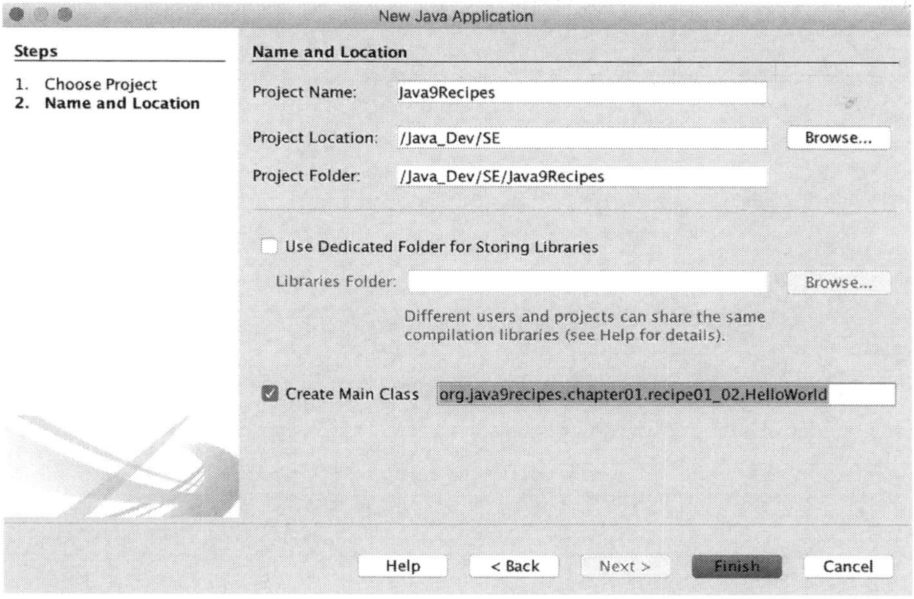

Figure 1-4. *Naming the project*

Give your project a name. For the project related to this book, use the name Java9Recipes. Enter the project name into the Project Name text box at the top of the dialog in Figure 1-4.

Then specify the name of your main class in the Create Main Class text box. Give the following name:

```
org.java9recipes.chapter01.recipe1_02.HelloWorld
```

Be sure to that you've entered the project name and class name just as we provide them here, because the code to follow depends upon your doing so. Make sure the "Project Name" text box specifies Java9Recipes. Make sure the "Create Main Class" text box specifies org.java9recipes.chapter01. recipe1_02.HelloWorld.

■ **Tip**   Pay attention to case; Java is case-sensitive.

Press "Finish" to complete the wizard and create a skeleton project. You should now be looking at a Java source file. Skeleton code is generated for you, and your NetBeans IDE window should resemble the one in Figure 1-5.

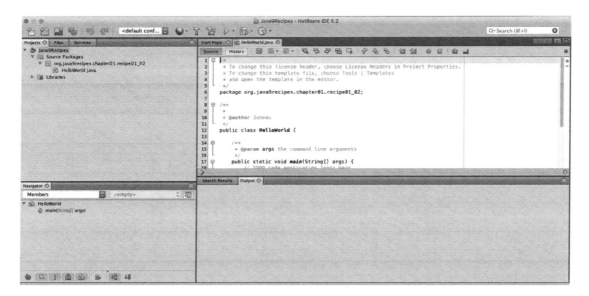

Figure 1-5. *Viewing the skeleton code generated by NetBeans*

Place your cursor anywhere in the source code pane. Press Ctrl-A to select all the skeleton code. Then press Delete to get rid of it. Replace the deleted code with that from Listing 1-1.

You can find the code in Listing 1-1 as part of our example download for the book. There are two files named HelloMessage.java and HelloWorld.java, which reside in a Java package named org.java9recipes.chapter01. recipe1_02. Note that all recipe solutions of substance throughout this book are in that example download.

The first class, HelloMessage, is a container class that is used to hold a String-based message.

Listing 1-1. A "Hello, World" Example

```java
package org.java9recipes.chapter01.recipe1_02;

public class HelloMessage {
    private String message = "";

    public HelloMessage() {
        this.message = "Default Message";
    }

    public void setMessage (String m) {
        this.message = m;
    }

    public String getMessage () {
        return message.toUpperCase();
    }
}
```

The next class is named HelloWorld, and it initiates the program:

```java
public class HelloWorld {
    /* The main method begins in this class */
```

```
public static void main(String[] args) {

    HelloMessage hm;
    hm = new HelloMessage();

    System.out.println(hm.getMessage());

    hm.setMessage("Hello, World");

    System.out.println(hm.getMessage());
  }
}
```

Make sure you have pasted (or typed) the code from Listing 1-1. Compile and run the program, and you should see the following output:

```
run:
DEFAULT MESSAGE
HELLO, WORLD
BUILD SUCCESSFUL (total time: 1 second)
```

This output will appear in a new pane named "Output" that is opened by NetBeans at the bottom of the IDE window.

How It Works

You can run almost all the solutions in this chapter using the same general technique shown in this recipe. We've been painstakingly detailed for that reason, showing the step-by-step screenshots just this one time.

Packages

The solution example begins by creating a Java *package*:

```
package org.java9recipes.chapter01.recipe1_02;
```

Packages are a way of grouping related classes together into a shared namespace. The idea is to achieve universal uniqueness by working your way down your organization's domain name in reverse order. It is also customary to write package names in all lowercase.

NetBeans will create a directory structure to imitate your package path. In this case, NetBeans created the following directory path:

```
C:\Users\JonathanGennick\Documents\NetBeansProjects\
Java9Recipes\src\org\java9recipes\chapter01\recipe1_02
```

Following are some things to notice about this path:

- The front part is `C:\Users\...\NetBeansProjects`. NetBeans creates all projects under a `NetbeansProject` directory unless you specify otherwise, which you can do from the dialog in Figure 1-4. Many developers specify shorter paths.

- Next is the first occurrence of `Java9Recipes`. This occurrence corresponds to the project name you gave when you filled in the Project Name text box from Figure 1-4.

7

- Any source files you create go into the src directory. NetBeans creates other directories at this level. For example, NetBeans creates a build directory, and then underneath it is a classes subdirectory to hold your compiled class files.

- Last are the directories mirroring the package path that you specify, in this case org\java9recipes\chapter01\recipe1_02. When you compile your code, an identical structure is created under the build\classes directory. Note that if using another IDE, you may see differences in the directories that are created.

You do not need to explicitly create a package. If you do not create one, the Java compiler will create one for you, and give it a name that is hidden from you. We prefer to be explicit, and you should too. Being thoughtful and explicit about Java package names is *de rigueur* in the professional setting. Organization, as well as judiciously chosen naming conventions, is important when developing any significant application.

JavaBeans-Style Classes

Next in the solution example you see a class definition following the JavaBeans pattern. The definition of HelloMessage follows a pattern that you'll encounter often in Java programming, and we include it for that reason. The class is a simple one, capable of holding a single, String field named message.

Three methods are defined on the class:

HelloMessage(). This method, also known as the constructor, is named the same as the class. In this case, it takes no arguments. It's automatically invoked whenever you create a new object of the class. Note that this is known as a "no-arg" constructor because it is typed out within the class, and it takes no arguments. If you do not supply a constructor, the JVM will supply a default constructor (also takes no arguments) automatically.

setMessage(String). This accessor method begins with the word set. It takes one parameter. It specifies the message to be returned by the corresponding get method.

getMessage(). This accessor method returns the currently defined message. In our example, we choose to uppercase the message.

▓ **Note**   Accessor methods are used in JavaBeans classes to access any privately declared class members. In this case, the private variable identified as message can be accessed using these methods. Accessor methods are more commonly referred to as "getters" and "setters."

Methods beginning with set and get are termed as *setter* and *getter* methods. The variable message is private to the class, which means you have no direct access to message from outside of the class.

You'll see the keyword this used in the class. It is a special keyword in Java used to reference the current object. Its use is redundant in Listing 1-1, but would be needed if any of the methods happened to create variables of their own that were also named message. It is common practice to make use of the "this" keyword to reference the class members from within the "getter" and "setter" methods.

It is common in Java to mediate access to class variables through setter and getter methods like those in our example. Those methods represent a contract of sorts with other classes and your main program. Their benefit is that you can change the storage implementation of HelloMessage however you like. Other code that depends upon HelloMessage will continue to work properly so long as you maintain the external behavior of setMessage() and getMessage().

The Main Program

The incantation `public static void main(...)` is used from within a public class to denote the entry point of a Java program. That declaration begins an executable method named `main`. You must specify one parameter that is an array of Strings, and typically that parameter is defined as `String[] args`.

When you execute the currently selected class, NetBeans compiles the code to a set of binary files, and then transfers control to the `main()` method. NetBeans can also be configured to recompile on save, which would then cause the transfer of control to the main() method. That method, in turn, does the following:

1. Executes `HelloMessage` to create a variable named `hm` that is capable of holding an instance of the class `HelloMessage`. The variable `hm` is empty at this point.

2. Invokes `new HelloMessage()` to create an object of the class by that name. The no-argument constructor will be executed, and `"Default Message"` is now set as the greeting text. The new object is now stored in the variable `hm`.

3. Makes a call to `System.out.println()` to show that the object's no-argument constructor has indeed executed as expected. The greeting `"DEFAULT MESSAGE"` is displayed in the "Output" pane.

4. Sets the message to be the traditional text `"Hello, World"`.

5. Makes another call to `System.out.println()` to output the new message that has just been set. Now you see the greeting `"HELLO, WORLD"` added to the "Output" pane.

The pattern in the solution is common in Java programming. The `main()` method is where execution begins. Variables are defined, and objects are created using the new operator. Object variables are often set and retrieved using setter and getter methods.

▒ **Tip**　　Command-line apps are passé. System administrators and programmers sometimes write them as utilities, or to batch-process large amounts of data. But in the main, most of today's applications are GUI applications. JavaFX is the way forward in writing standard desktop applications, and you can learn about it in Chapters 14 through 16. Recipe 14-1 provides what is essentially a "Hello, World" application in GUI form. JavaEE offers options for developing web-based applications for the Java Platform, and you can learn more about that in Chapter 17.

1-3. Configuring the CLASSPATH

Problem

You want to execute a Java program, or include an external Java library in the application you are executing.

Solution

Set the `CLASSPATH` variable equal to the directory location of the user-defined Java classes or Java Archive (JAR) files that you need to have access to for executing your application. Let's say that you have a directory named JAVA_DEV located at the root of your OS drive, and all the files your applications needs to access are located in this directory. If this is the case, then you would execute a command such as the following:

```
set CLASSPATH=C:\JAVA_DEV\some-jar.jar
```

Or on Unix and Linux systems:

```
export CLASSPATH=/JAVA_DEV/some-jar.jar
```

Alternately, the javac command provides an option for specifying the location of resources that need to be loaded for an application. On all platforms, setting the CLASSPATH using this technique can be done via the -classpath option as follows:

```
javac -classpath /JAVA_DEV/some-jar.jar
```

Of course, on Microsoft Windows machines the file path will use the backslash (\) instead.

■ **Note** The javac -cp option may be used, rather than specifying the -classpath option.

How It Works

Java implements the concept of a *classpath*. This is a directory search path that you can specify system-wide using the CLASSPATH environment variable. You can also specify the classpath for a specific invocation of the JVM via the java command's -classpath option. (See Recipe 1-4 for an example.)

■ **Note** The CLASSPATH is certainly going to remain important for many Java applications into the future. However, the new module system, introduced in Java 9, replaces the need to use the brittle CLASSPATH for those applications that are built to take advantage of modularization. See Chapter 22 for more information on Java Modularity.

When executing Java programs, the JVM finds and loads classes as needed using the following search order:

1. The classes that are fundamental to the Java platform and are contained in the Java installation directory.

2. Any packages or JAR files that are located within the extension directory of the JDK.

3. Packages, classes, JAR files, and libraries that are loaded somewhere on the specified class path.

You may need to access more than one directory or JAR file for an application. This could be the case if your dependencies are located in more than one location. To do so, simply use the delimiter for your operating system (; or :) as a separator between the locations specified by the CLASSPATH variable. Following is an example of specifying multiple JAR files in the CLASSPATH environment variable on Unix and Linux systems:

```
export CLASSPATH=/JAVA_DEV/some-jar.jar:/JAVA_LIB/myjar.jar
```

Alternatively, you can specify the class path via a command-line option:

```
javac -classpath /JAVA_DEV/some-jar.jar:/JAVA_LIB/myjar.jar
```

When loading the resources for a Java application, the JVM loads all the classes and packages that are specified in the first location, followed by the second, and so on. This is important because the order of loading may make a difference in some instances.

■ **Note**   JAR files are used to package applications and Java libraries into a distributable format. If you have not packaged your application in that manner, you may simply specify the directory or directories in which your `.class` files reside.

Sometimes you'll want to include all JAR files within a specified directory. Do that by specifying the wildcard character (*) after the directory containing the files. For example:

```
javac -classpath /JAVA_DEV/*:/JAVA_LIB/myjar.jar
```

Specifying a wildcard will tell the JVM that it should be loading JAR files only. It will not load class files that are located in a directory specified with the wildcard character. You'll need to specify a separate path entry for the same directory if you also want the class files. For example:

```
javac -classpath /JAVA_DEV/*:/JAVA_DEV
```

Subdirectories within the class path will not be searched. In order to load files that are contained within subdirectories, those subdirectories and/or files must be explicitly listed in the class path. However, Java packages that are equivalent to the subdirectory structure *will* be loaded. Therefore, any Java classes that reside within a Java package that is equivalent to the subdirectory structure will be loaded.

■ **Note**   It is a good idea to organize your code; it is also good to organize where you place your code on the computer. A good practice is to place all your Java projects within the same directory; it can become your workspace. Place all the Java libraries that are contained in JAR files into the same directory for easier management.

1-4. Organizing Code with Packages

Problem

Your application consists of a set of Java classes, interfaces, and other types. You want to organize these source files to make them easier to maintain and avoid potential class-naming conflicts.

Solution

Create Java packages and place source files within them much like a filing system. Java packages can be used to organize logical groups of source files within an application. Packages can help to organize code, reduce naming conflicts among different classes and other Java type files, and provide access control. To create a package, simply create a directory within the root of your application source folder and name it. Packages are usually nested within each other and conform to a standard naming convention. For the purposes of this recipe, assume that the organization is named Juneau and that the organization makes widgets. To organize all the code for the widget application, create a group of nested packages conforming to the following directory structure:

```
/org/juneau
```

Any source files that are placed within a package must contain the package statement as the first line in the source. The package statement lists the name of the package in which the source file is contained. For instance, suppose that the main class for the widget application is named JuneauWidgets.java. To place this class into a package named org.juneau, physically move the source file into a directory named juneau, which resides within the org directory, which in turn resides within the root of the source folder for the application. The directory structure should look like the following:

```
/org/juneau/JuneauWidgets.java
```

The source for JuneauWidgets.java is as follows:

```java
package org.juneau;

/**
 * The main class for the Juneau Widgets application.
 * @author juneau
 */
public class JuneauWidgets {
    public static void main(String[] args){
        System.out println("Welcome to my app!");
    }
}
```

The first line in the source contains the package statement, which lists the name of the package that the source file is located within. The entire package path is listed in the statement, and the names in the path are separated by dots.

■ **Note** A package statement must be the first statement listed within the Java source. However, there may be a comment or Javadoc comment written before the package statement. For more information on comments or Javadoc, please see Recipe 1-12.

An application can consist of any number of packages. If the widget application contains a few classes that represent widget objects, they could be placed within the org.juneau.widget package. The application may have interfaces that can be used to interact with the widget objects. In this case, a package named org.juneau.interfaces may also exist to contain any such interfaces.

How It Works

Java packages are useful for organizing source files, controlling access to different classes, and ensuring that there are no naming conflicts. Packages are represented by a series of physical directories on a file system, and they can contain any number of Java source files. Each source file must contain a package statement before any other statements in the file. This package statement lists the name of the package in which the source file resides. In the solution to this recipe, the source included the following package statement:

```
package org.juneau;
```

This package statement indicates that the source file resides within a directory named juneau, and that directory resides within another directory named org. Package-naming conventions can vary by company or organization. However, it is important that words are in all lowercase so they do not conflict with any Java class file names. Many companies or organizations will use the reverse of their domain name for package naming. However, if a domain name includes hyphens, underscores should be used instead.

▓ **Note**   When a class resides within a Java package, it is no longer referenced by only the class name, but instead the package name is prepended to the class name, which is known as the *fully qualified* name. For instance, because the class that resides within the file JuneauWidgets.java is contained within the org. juneau package, the class is referenced using org.juneau.JuneauWidgets, not simply JuneauWidgets. An identically named class can reside within a different package (for instance, org.java9recipes. JuneauWidgets).

Packages are very useful for establishing levels of security as well as organization. By default, different classes that reside within the same package have access to each other. If a source file resides within a different package than another file that it needs to use, an import statement must be declared at the top of the source file (underneath the package statement) to import that other file for use; otherwise, the fully qualified package.class name must be used within the code. Classes may be imported separately, as demonstrated in the following import statement:

```
import org.juneau.JuneauWidgets;
```

However, it is often likely that all classes and type files that reside within a package need to be used. A single import statement utilizing a wildcard character (*) can import all files within a named package as follows:

```
import org.juneau.*;
```

Although it is possible to import all files, it is not recommended unless absolutely necessary. As a matter of fact, it is considered a poor programming practice to include many import statements that use the wildcard. Instead, classes and type files should be imported individually.

Organizing classes within packages can prove to be very helpful. Suppose that the widget application that was described in the solution to this recipe includes different Java classes for each different widget object. Each of the widget classes could be grouped into a single package named org.juneau.widgets. Similarly, each of the widgets could extend some Java type or interface. All such interfaces could be organized into a package named org.juneau.interfaces.

Any substantial Java application will include packages. Any Java library or Application Programming Interface (API) that you use includes packages. When you import classes or types from those libraries and APIs, you are really importing packages.

1-5. Declaring Variables and Access Modifiers

Problem

You want to create some variables and manipulate data within your program. Furthermore, you wish to make some of the variables available to only the current class, whereas others should be available to all classes, or just the other classes within the current package.

Solution

Java implements eight primitive data types. There is also special support for the String class type. Listing 1-2 shows an example declaration of each. Draw from the example to declare the variables needed in your own application.

Listing 1-2. Declarations for Primitive and String Types

```java
package org.java9recipes.chapter01.recipe1_05;

public class DeclarationsExample {
    public static void main (String[] args) {
        boolean BooleanVal = true;  /* Default is false */

        char charval = 'G';      /* Unicode UTF-16 */
        charval = '\u0490';      /* Ukrainian letter Ghe(Г) */

        byte byteval;        /*  8 bits, -127 to 127 */
        short shortval;      /* 16 bits, -32,768 to 32,768 */
        int intval;          /* 32 bits, -2147483648 to 2147483647 */
        long longval;        /* 64 bits, -(2^64) to 2^64 - 1 */

        float   floatval = 10.123456F; /* 32-bit IEEE 754 */
        double doubleval = 10.12345678987654; /* 64-bit IEEE 754 */

        String message = "Darken the corner where you are!";
        message = message.replace("Darken", "Brighten");
    }
}
```

■ **Note**   If you're curious about the Ukrainian letter in Listing 1-2, it is the Cyrillic letter *Ghe with upturn*. You can read about its history at: http://en.wikipedia.org/wiki/Ghe_with_upturn. You can find its code point value in the chart at http://www.unicode.org/charts/PDF/U0400.pdf. And the URL http://www.unicode.org/charts/ is a good place to start whenever you need to find the code point corresponding to a given character.

Variables are subject to the concept of *visibility*. Those created in Listing 1-2 are visible from the main() method after they have been created, and they are deallocated when the main() method ends. They have no "life" beyond the main() method, and are not accessible from outside of main().

Variables created at the class level are a different story. Such variables can be termed as *class fields or class members*, as in *fields or members of the class*. Use of a member can be restricted to objects of the class in which it is declared, to the package in which it is declared, or it can be accessible from any class in any package. Listing 1-3 shows some of how to control visibility via the `private` and `public` keywords.

Listing 1-3. Visibility and the Concept of Fields

```
package org.java9recipes.chapter01.recipe1_05;

class TestClass {
    private long visibleOnlyInThisClass;
    double visibleFromEntirePackage;
    void setLong (long val) {
        visibleOnlyInThisClass = val;
    }

    long getLong () {
        return visibleOnlyInThisClass;
    }
}

public class VisibilityExample {
    public static void main(String[] args) {
        TestClass tc = new TestClass();
        tc.setLong(32768);
        tc.visibleFromEntirePackage = 3.1415926535;
        System.out.println(tc.getLong());
        System.out.println(tc.visibleFromEntirePackage);
    }
}
```

Output:

```
32768
3.1415926535
```

Members are typically bound to an object of a class. Each object of a class contains an instance of each member in the class. However, you can also define so-called *static* fields that occur just once, and with a single value that is shared by all instances of the given class. Listing 1-4 illustrates the difference.

Listing 1-4. Static Fields

```
package org.java9recipes.chapter01.recipe1_05;

class StaticDemo {
    public static boolean oneValueForAllObjects = false;
}

public class StaticFieldsExample {
    public static void main (String[] args) {
        StaticDemo sd1 = new StaticDemo();
        StaticDemo sd2 = new StaticDemo();
        System.out.println(sd1.oneValueForAllObjects);
```

15

```
        System.out.println(sd2.oneValueForAllObjects);
        sd1.oneValueForAllObjects = true;
        System.out.println(sd1.oneValueForAllObjects);
        System.out.println(sd2.oneValueForAllObjects);
    }

}
```

Listing 1-4 produces the following output:

```
false
false
true
true
```

The field oneValueForAllObjects was set to true only for the class instance named sd1. Yet it is true for instance sd2 also. This is because of the keyword static used in declaring that field. Static fields occur one time for all objects of their class.

How It Works

Listing 1-2 illustrates the basic format of a variable declaration:

```
type variable;
```

It's common to initialize variables when declaring them, so you'll often see:

```
type variable = initialValue;
```

Field declarations can be preceded by modifiers. For example:

```
public static variable = initialValue;
protected variable;
private variable;
```

It's common to put the visibility modifier — public, protected, or private — first, but you are free to list the modifiers in any order you like. Be aware that there are additional modifiers that you will encounter and need to learn about as you get deeper into the language. By default, if no modifier has been specified, the class or member is made package-private, meaning that only other classes within the package have access to the member. If a class member is specified as protected, then it is also package-private, with the exception that any subclass of its class in another package also has access.

The String type is special in Java. It's really a class type, but syntactically you can treat it as a primitive type. Java automatically creates a String object whenever you enclose a String of characters within double quotes ("..."). You aren't required to invoke a constructor, nor to specify the new keyword. Yet String is a class, and there are methods in that class that are available to you. One such method is the replace() method shown at the end of Listing 1-2.

Strings are composed of characters. Java's char type is a two-byte construct for storing a single character in Unicode-s UTF-16 encoding. You can generate literals of the char type in two ways:

- If a character is easy to type, then enclose it within single quotes (e.g.: 'G').

- Otherwise, specify the four-digit UTF-16 *code point* value prefaced by \u (e.g.: '\u0490').

Some Unicode code points require five digits. These cannot be represented in a single char value. See Chapter 12 if you need more information on Unicode and internationalization.

Avoid using any of the primitive types for monetary values. Especially avoid either of the floating-point types for that purpose. Refer instead to Chapter 12 and its recipe on using the Java Money API to calculate monetary amounts (Recipe 12-10). BigDecimal can also be useful anytime you need accurate, fixed-decimal arithmetic.

If you are new to Java, you may be unfamiliar with the String[] array notation, as demonstrated in the examples. Please see Chapter 7 for more information on arrays. It covers enumerations, arrays, and also generic data types. Also in that chapter are examples showing how to write iterative code to work with collections of values such as an array.

1-6. Compiling and Executing from the Command-Line or Terminal Interpreter

Problem

You aren't able to install an IDE, or prefer to use a standard text editor for development. Moreover, you want to compile and execute your Java programs from the command line or terminal so that you have complete control over the environment.

Solution

Compile your programs using the javac command. Then execute them via the java command.

Begin by making sure you have your JDK's bin directory in your execution path. You might need to execute a command such as one of the following.

Windows:

```
setx path "%path%;C:\Program Files\Java\jdk1.9.0\bin"
```

OS X:

```
export PATH=/Library/Java/JavaVirtualMachines/jdk1.9.0.jdk/Contents/Home/bin
```

Then make sure your CLASSPATH environment variable includes the directory containing your Java code. The following is an example of setting the environment variable under Windows:

```
set CLASSPATH=<<path-to-my-Java>>
```

Now change your current working directory to be the one corresponding to your project. Recipe 1-2 had you create a project named Java9Recipes. Change to that project's directory on a Windows system as follows:

```
cd <path-to-project>\Java9Recipes
```

Descend one level into the src subdirectory:

```
cd src
```

From here, you can issue javac commands to compile any classes in your project. Prepend the appropriate package name as part of your path leading to each source file to be compiled. Be sure to include the .java extension after your file name. For example, issue the following command to compile the HelloWorld class from Recipe 1-2.

Windows:

```
javac org\java9recipes\chapter01\recipe1_02\HelloWorld.java
```

OS X:

```
javac org/java9recipes/chapter01/recipe1_02/HelloWorld.java
```

Once the compilation is complete, you will have a .class file in the same directory as your .java file. For example, if you perform a directory listing, you should see four files:

```
dir org\java9recipes\chapter01\recipe1_02
```

```
HelloMessage.class
HelloWorld.class
HelloMessage.java
HelloWorld.java
```

Compilation produces two files. One is for HelloMessage, and the other is for the class named HelloWorld implementing the main() method.

Execute the main() method by issuing the java command to invoke the Java Virtual Machine (JVM). Pass the fully qualified class name as a parameter to the command. Qualify the class name by prepending the package name, but this time use the same dot-notation as used in your source file. For example:

```
java org.java9recipes.chapter1.recipe1_02.HelloWorld
```

Do not specify .class at the end of the command. You are referencing HelloWorld now as a class name, and not as a file name. You should see the same output as from Recipe 1-2.

■ **Tip**   One must compile source code. Source code is kept in files with a .java suffix, so your operating system's file and directory-path notation is appropriate. One executes a class. A class is an abstract concept in the language, so the language's dot-notation becomes appropriate. Keep this distinction in mind to help yourself remember when to use which notation.

How It Works

The first two solution steps are housekeeping steps. You must have the Java compiler and the virtual machine in your execution path. It's also necessary for any classes used by your program to be found somewhere along what is termed the *classpath*. One way to specify the class path is through the CLASSPATH environment variable. See Recipe 1-3 for more information on the classpath.

■ **Note** The Java Modularity system added a couple of options to the javac compiler. Please see Chapter 22 for more information.

The command java with no c at the end is for executing compiled code. Pass as a parameter the qualified name of the class containing your main method. The JVM will interpret and execute the byte-code within that class, beginning from the main method. The JVM will search along the classpath for any additionally required classes such as HelloMessage.

The compiler's default behavior is to place each generated class file into the same directory as holds the corresponding source file. You can override that behavior through the -d option. For example:

```
javac -d "<specify-different-location>" "<path-to-project>
\Java9Recipes\src\org\java9recipes\chapter1\recipe1_02\HelloWorld.java"
```

The -d option in this command designates a directory in our own environment as the target for holding generated class files. The command also specifies the full path and file name of the source file. Thus, the command can be executed with the same result regardless of the current working directory.

■ **Tip** Configure your system so that your command-line environment has the execution path and classpath set correctly by default. The typical approach in Linux- or Unix-based operating systems is to put appropriate commands into your .profile or .bash_profile files. Under Windows you can specify environment variable defaults from the Control Panel window named System, by clicking the Advanced system settings link, and then the Environment Variables button.

There may be times when you need to specify a custom class path for a specific execution of the JVM. You can do that through the -cp parameter, as follows:

```
java -cp ".;<path-to-project>\Java9Recipes\build\classes\org\java9recipes\chapter1\
recipe1_02"
org.java9recipes.chapter1.recipe1_02.HelloWorld
```

This execution will search first in the current working directory (the leading dot in the classpath), and then under the specified package directory corresponding to where NetBeans would place the compiled classes.

■ **Note** See Recipe 1-3 for more on configuring your classpath.

1-7. Developing Within the Interactive jShell

Problem

You wish to write Java code and have it interpreted immediately, so that you can test, prototype, and alter your code quickly, without the need to wait for compilation or the ceremony of writing an entire Java class to perform a trivial task.

Solution

Make use of the interactive jShell, new in Java 9, by opening a command prompt or terminal, and executing the jshell utility. The jshell is located in your JDK home bin directory, just like the java and javac utilities. Assuming that the <JDK>/bin directory is in the CLASSPATH, the jShell can be invoked using as such:

```
jshell
|  Welcome to JShell -- Version 1.9.0
|  Type /help for help

->
```

Once the interpreter has been started, declarations can be defined for the lifetime of the jShell session, expressions and statements can be typed and executed immediately, and so on. The jShell also allows Java developers to write a shorthand version of the language by eliminating superfluous constructs such as semicolons. Listing 1-5 demonstrates some of the basic functionality that is provided by the jShell. Keep in mind that when you are using the interactive shell, if you at any time need assistance, you can type the /help command.

Listing 1-5. Interactive jShell

```
-> System.out.println("Hello World")
Hello World
-> 1 + 1
|  Expression value is: 2
|    assigned to temporary variable $1 of type int
-> System.out.println("Hello Java 9")
Hello Java 9

-> // working with classes

-> class Main {
>>      // Main method
>>      public static void main(String[] args) {
>>          System.out.println("Classes within jShell");
>>          int index = 0;
>>          while(index <= 10){
>>              System.out.println("Looping: " + index);
>>              index++;
>>          }
>>      }
>> }
|  Added class Main

-> // List classes currently loaded in jShell
-> /classes
|      class Main
-> // Execute Class
-> Main.main(null)
Classes within jShell
Looping: 0
Looping: 1
```

```
Looping: 2
Looping: 3
Looping: 4
Looping: 5
Looping: 6
Looping: 7
Looping: 8
Looping: 9
Looping: 10

-> // Reset the state of the jshell
-> /r
|  Resetting state.
-> /classes

-> // Using imports
-> import java.util.ArrayList
-> import java.util.List
-> List<String> colors = new ArrayList<>();
|  Added variable colors of type List<String> with initial value []
-> colors.add("red")
|  Expression value is: true
|    assigned to temporary variable $4 of type boolean
-> colors.add("orange")
|  Expression value is: true
|    assigned to temporary variable $5 of type boolean
-> colors.add("yellow")
|  Expression value is: true
|    assigned to temporary variable $6 of type boolean
-> colors
|  Variable colors of type List<String> has value [red, orange, yellow]

-> // List the current jShell session variables
-> /v
|    List<String> colors = [red, orange, yellow]
|    boolean $4 = true
|    boolean $5 = true
|    boolean $6 = true

-> // List the commands that have been executed
-> /list

    1 : import java.util.ArrayList;
    2 : import java.util.List;
    3 : List<String> colors = new ArrayList<>();
    4 : colors.add("red")
    5 : colors.add("orange")
    6 : colors.add("yellow")
    7 : colors
```

As mentioned previously, one of the boons to having an interactive shell is for prototyping code. In many cases, developers wish to prototype classes and objects. Listing 1-5 demonstrates how to type the code for a class into the jShell, along with some of the commands that can be useful while working with classes. When prototyping, it can oftentimes be helpful to copy code from your favorite editor and paste it into the jShell, then execute commands against it.

How It Works

The jShell provides a Read Evaluate Print Loop (REPL) environment for developers to type or paste in code "snippets" and have them executed immediately. Much like the REPL environments or other languages such as Groovy, Python, and JRuby, the jShell provides an excellent environment for prototyping code, and even for executing stored scripts of Java code on the fly.

The jShell allows one to write abbreviated Java code, otherwise known as snippets. This can be beneficial as it allows one to focus on the logic, rather than the syntax. One of the most used shortcuts is the ability to leave semicolons off the end of a line. To facilitate rapid prototyping, variables can be declared outside of classes, expressions and methods can be typed on the fly outside of classes and interfaces, and expressions leave no side effects. Along with the ability to write code on the fly, the jShell provides a system that facilitates the addition, modification, and removal of code fragments within an active session or instance.

An active session or instance of the jShell environment constitutes a single *JShellState*. An instance of the JShellState includes all previously defined variables, methods, classes, import statements, and so on, that have been made within that same jShell session. Once the jShell instance is terminated, the JShellState is ended, and therefore all declarations are lost.

There are a number of helper commands that can be typed into the jShell to retrieve information regarding the current JShellState. The /classes command lists all of the classes that have been typed into the current JShellState. The /list command lists all of the statements, expressions, classes, methods, imports, and so on, that have been typed into the current JShellState. The /list command provides a line number next to each of the listings, which enables one to easily re-execute that line of code using typing / followed by the line number that you wish to re-execute. Therefore, if you wish to execute line number 2 again, you would type /2 to have that line executed again. Table 1-1 contains a complete listing of the commands available within jShell.

Table 1-1. *jShell Commands*

Command	Description
/l or /list	Lists the sources typed into the current session.
/e or /edit [name or id of source]	Opens JShell Edit Pad. Optionally type the name or id of the source entry to edit.
/d or /drop [name/id of source]	Deletes or drops the source referenced by name or id.
/s or /save [all|history]	Saves sources that have been typed in the current session.
/o or /open	Opens a file of source within the jShell.
/v or /vars	Lists variables that have been declared in the current session along with their current values.
/m or /methods	Lists the methods that have been declared in the current session.
/c or /classes	Lists the classes that have been declared in the current session.
/x or /exit	Exits the current jShell session.
/r or /reset	Resets the JShellState for the current session.

(continued)

Table 1-1. (*continued*)

Command	Description
/f or /feedback [level]	Initiates feedback- options include (off, concise, normal, verbose, default, or ?).
/p or /prompt	Toggles the display of the prompt within the shell.
/cp or /classpath [path]	Adds the typed path to the current CLASSPATH.
/h or /history	Lists the history of the active JShellState.
/setstart [file]	Reads and sets the startup definition file.
/savestart [file]	Saves the current session's definitions to the designated startup file.
/!	Re-executes the last code snippet.
/<n>	Re-executes the nth code snippet.
/-<n>	Re-executes the nth previous code snippet.

If you type the /e command, a scratch pad editor known as "JShell Edit Pad" will open containing the sources that you've entered for the current JShellState, as shown in Figure 1-6. You can edit the sources within this pad and then click the "Accept" button to have those sources evaluated within jShell.

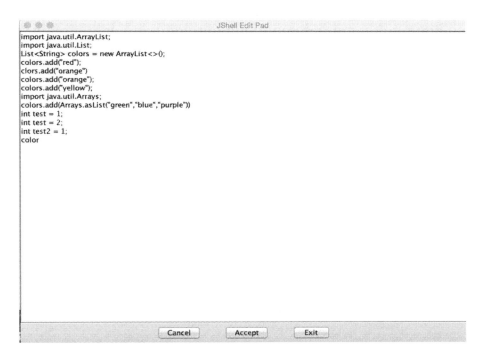

Figure 1-6. *JShell Edit Pad*

Other useful features of the jShell are that you can bring up the previously typed command by pressing the up arrow on your keyboard. The interactive shell also features tab-completion. If you begin typing a statement and then press the Tab key, either the statement will be autocompleted for you or a list of options for the characters currently typed will be displayed. It is also possible to set up a predefined list of imports so that each time a jShell session is started, those imports will occur automatically.

The jShell provides an interactive environment that allows immediate feedback while typing code snippets. This can be beneficial for prototyping or learning the language. Other languages, such as Groovy, Python, and Scala, have similar REPL environments. Now that the jShell is available for Java, it opens the door for a more interactive environment for classroom use and increased developer prototyping productivity.

▓ **Tip** To learn more about the commands available within the jShell, simply type /help once the shell has opened. The help feature displays an extensive listing of the features available in the jShell.

1-8. Converting to and from a String

Problem

You have a value stored within a primitive data type, and you want to represent that value as a human-readable String. Or, you want to go in the other direction by converting a human-readable String into a primitive data type.

Solution

Follow one of the patterns from Listing 1-6. The listing shows conversion from a String to a double-precision floating-point value, and shows two methods for getting back to a String again.

Listing 1-6. General Pattern for String Conversions

```
package org.java9recipes.chapter01.recipe1_08;

public class StringConversion {

    public static void main (String[] args) {
        double pi;
        String strval;

        pi = Double.parseDouble("3.14");
        System.out.println(strval = String.valueOf(pi));
        System.out.println(Double.toString(pi));
    }

}
```

How It Works

The solution illustrates some conversion patterns that work for all the primitive types. First, there is the conversion of a floating-point number from its human-readable representation into the IEEE 754 format used by the Java language for floating-point arithmetic:

```
pi = Double.parseDouble("3.14");
```

Notice the pattern. You can replace Double with Float, or by Long, or by whatever other type is your target data type. Each primitive type has a corresponding wrapper class by the same name but with the initial letter uppercase. The primitive type here is double, and the corresponding wrapper is Double. The wrapper classes implement helper methods such as Double.parseDouble(), Long.parseLong(), Boolean.parseBoolean(), and so forth. These parse methods convert human-readable representations into values of the respective types.

Going the other way, it is often easiest to invoke String.valueOf(). The String class implements this method, and it is overloaded for each of the primitive data types. Alternatively, the wrapper classes also implement toString() methods that you can invoke to convert values of the underlying type into their human-readable forms. It's your own preference as to which approach to take.

Conversions targeting the numeric types require some exception handling to be practical. You generally need to gracefully accommodate a case in which a character-string value is expected to be a valid numeric representation, but it's not. Chapter 9 covers exception handling in detail, and the upcoming Recipe 1-10 provides a simple example to get you started.

■ **Caution** Literals for the Boolean type are "true" and "false". They are case-sensitive. Any value other than these two is silently interpreted as false when converting from a String using the Boolean parseBoolean() conversion method.

1-9. Passing Arguments via Command-Line Execution

Problem

You want to pass values into a Java application that is being invoked via the command line via the *java* utility.

Solution

Run the application using the java utility, and specify the arguments that you want to pass into it after the application name. If you're passing more than one argument, each should be separated by a space. For example, suppose you want to pass the arguments to the class created in Listing 1-7.

Listing 1-7. Example of Accessing Command-Line Arguments

```
package org.java9recipes.chapter01.recipe1_09;

public class PassingArguments {
    public static void main(String[] args){
        if(args.length > 0){
            System.out.println("Arguments that were passed to the program: ");
            for (String arg:args){
                System.out.println(arg);
            }
        } else {
            System.out.println("No arguments passed to the program.");
        }
    }
}
```

First, make sure to compile the program so that you have a `.class` file to execute. You can do that from within NetBeans by right-clicking the file and choosing the "Compile File" option from the context menu, or via the javac utility at the command line or terminal.

Next, open a Command Prompt or terminal window and traverse into the build\classes directory for your project. (See Recipe 1-6 for an extensive discussion of executing from the command line). For example:

```
cd <path-to-project>\Java9Recipes\build\classes
```

Now issue a java command to execute the class, and type some arguments on the command line following the class name. The following example passes two arguments:

```
java org.java9recipes.chapter01.recipe1_09.PassingArguments Upper Peninsula
```

You should see the following output:

```
Arguments that were passed to the program:
Upper
Penninsula
```

Spaces separate arguments. Enclose Strings in double quotes when you want to pass an argument containing spaces or other special characters. For example:

```
java org.java9recipes.chapter01.recipe1_09.PassingArguments "Upper Peninsula"
```

The output now shows just one argument:

```
Arguments that were passed to the program:
Upper Penninsula
```

The double quotes translate the String "Upper Peninsula" into a single argument.

How It Works

All Java classes that are executable from the command line or terminal contain a `main()` method. If you look at the signature for the `main()` method, you can see that it accepts a `String[]` argument. In other words, you can pass an array of `String` objects into the `main()` method. Command-line interpreters such as the Windows Command Prompt and the various Linux and Unix shells build an array of Strings out of your command-line arguments, and pass that array to the `main()` method on your behalf.

The `main()` method in the example displays each argument that is passed. First, the length of the array named args is tested to see whether it is greater than zero. If it is, the method will loop through each of the arguments in the array by executing a for loop, displaying each argument along the way. If there are no arguments passed, the length of the args array will be zero, and a message indicating such will be printed. Otherwise, you see a different message followed by a list of arguments.

Command-line interpreters recognize spaces and sometimes other characters as delimiters. It's generally safe to pass numeric values as arguments delimited by spaces without bothering to enclose each value within quotes. However, you should get into the habit of enclosing character-string arguments in double quotes, as shown in the final solution example. Do that to eliminate any ambiguity over where each argument begins and ends.

> ■ **Note**   All arguments are seen by Java as character Strings. If you pass numeric values as parameters, they enter Java as character Strings in human-readable form. You can convert them into their appropriate numeric types using the conversion methods shown in Recipe 1-8.

1-10. Executing a Script via the jShell

Problem

You wish to write a prototype or script and execute it via the jShell utility from the command line or terminal.

Solution

While the jShell is not intended to provide a new language syntax for Java development, it is possible to save source snippets for execution within the jShell into a file, and then pass the file to the jShell utility for execution. In this solution, we'll save a simple snippet into a file named myScript.java, and execute it with the jShell utility.

To get started, save the following source code into a file named myScript.java, and save it to your file system.

```
System.out.println("Hello from jShell")
/x
```

Execute the script using the following syntax:

```
jShell <path-to-file>/myScript.java
```

Output:

```
Hello from jShell
```

How It Works

Sometimes it can be beneficial to use a text editor or the JShell Edit Pad (see Recipe 1-7) to save sources that can be executed within the jShell environment. This increases the ability to rapidly prototype code, and it also facilitates the ability to develop scripts that can be executed time and time again. This can be useful for development of scheduled tasks or administrative tasks that can be executed by the JVM. As such, sources for the jShell can be stored into a file containing the extension of your choice, and then the file can be passed to the jShell for execution.

In the solution, a simple String is printed as output, and then the jShell environment is exited. Notice that the /x command is placed on a separate line after the sources within the file. The /x command tells the jShell environment to exit upon completion. If exiting upon completion, any variables, method, classes, and so on, that are defined within the file are lost once the sources have run to completion and the jShell environment is closed.

It is not recommended to write applications using the jShell environment for execution. In fact, GUI applications are out of scope for the jShell, and debuggers are also not supported. The environment is clearly intended for educational and prototyping purposes. However, some may find it handy to save snippets of code for execution via the jShell at a later time.

1-11. Accepting Input from the Keyboard

Problem

You are interested in writing a command-line or terminal application that will accept user input from the keyboard.

Solution

Make use of the `java.io.BufferedReader` and `java.io.InputStreamReader` classes to read keyboard entry and store it into local variables. Listing 1-8 shows a program that will keep prompting for input until you enter some characters that represent a valid value of type `long`.

Listing 1-8. Keyboard Input and Exception Handling

```
package org.java9recipes.chapter01.recipe1_11;

import java.io.*;

public class AcceptingInput {
    public static void main(String[] args){
        BufferedReader readIn = new BufferedReader(
                new InputStreamReader(System.in)
        );
        String numberAsString = "";
        long numberAsLong = 0;

        boolean numberIsValid = false;
        do {
            /* Ask the user for a number. */
            System.out.println("Please enter a number: ");
            try {
                numberAsString = readIn.readLine();
                System.out.println("You entered " + numberAsString);
            } catch (IOException ex){
                System.out.println(ex);
            }

            /* Convert the number into binary form. */
            try {
                numberAsLong = Long.parseLong(numberAsString);
                numberIsValid = true;
            } catch (NumberFormatException nfe) {
                System.out.println ("Not a number!");
            }
        } while (numberIsValid == false);
    }
}
```

Following is an example run of this program:

```
Please enter a number:
No
You entered No
Not a number!
Please enter a number:
Yes
You entered Yes
Not a number!
Please enter a number:
42
You entered 42
BUILD SUCCESSFUL (total time: 11 seconds)
```

The first two inputs did not represent valid values in the long data type. The third value was valid, and the run ended.

How It Works

Quite often our applications need to accept user input of some kind. Granted, most applications are not used from the command line or terminal nowadays, but having the ability to create an application that reads input from the command line or terminal helps to lay a good foundation, and may be useful in some applications or scripts. Terminal input can also be useful in developing administrative applications that you or a system administrator may use.

Two helper classes were used in the solution to this recipe. They are java.io.BufferedReader and java.io.InputStreamReader. The early portion of the code that's using those classes is especially important to understand:

```
BufferedReader readIn = new BufferedReader(
        new InputStreamReader(System.in)
);
```

The innermost object in this statement is System.in. It represents the keyboard. You do not need to declare System.in. Java's runtime environment creates the object for you. It is simply available to be used.

System.in provides access to raw bytes of data from the input device, which is the keyboard in our example. It is the job of the InputStreamReader class to take those bytes and convert them into characters in your current character set. System.in is passed to the InputStreamReader() constructor to create an InputStreamReader object.

InputStreamReader knows about characters, but not about lines. It is the BufferedReader class's job to detect line breaks in the input stream, and to enable you to conveniently read a line at a time. BufferedReader also aids efficiency by allowing physical reads from the input device to be done in different-size chunks than by which your application consumes the data. This aspect can make a difference when the input stream is a large file rather than the keyboard.

Following is how the program in Listing 1-8 makes use of an instance (named readIn) of the BufferedReader class to read a line of input from the keyboard:

```
numberAsString = readIn.readLine();
```

Executing this statement triggers the following sequence:

1. `System.in` returns a sequence of bytes.

2. `InputStreamReader` converts those bytes into characters.

3. `BufferedReader` breaks the character stream into lines of input.

4. `readLine()` returns one line of input to the application.

I/O calls must be wrapped in `try-catch` blocks. These blocks are used to catch any exceptions that may occur. The `try` part in the example will fail in the event a conversion is unsuccessful. A failure prevents the `numberIsValid` flag from being set to `true`, which causes the do loop to make another iteration so that the user can try again at entering a valid value. To learn more about catching exceptions, please see Chapter 9.

The following statement at the top of Listing 1-8 deserves some mention:

```
import java.io.*;
```

This statement makes available the classes and methods defined in the `java.io` package. These include `InputStreamReader` and `BufferedReader`. Also included is the `IOException` class used in the first `try-catch` block.

1-12. Documenting Your Code

Problem

You want to document some of your Java classes to assist in future maintenance.

Solution

Use Javadoc to place comments before any class, method, or field that you want to document. To begin such a comment, write the characters /**. Then begin each subsequent line with an asterisk (*). Lastly, close the comment with the characters */ on a line by themselves at the end. Listing 1-9 shows a method commented with Javadoc.

Listing 1-9. Comments Made in Javadoc Form

```
package org.java9recipes.chapter01.recipe1_12;

import java.math.BigInteger;

public class JavadocExample {
    /**
     * Accepts an unlimited number of values and
     * returns the sum.
     *
     * @param nums Must be an array of BigInteger values.
     * @return Sum of all numbers in the array.
     */
```

```
    public static BigInteger addNumbers(BigInteger[] nums) {
        BigInteger result = new BigInteger("0");
        for (BigInteger num:nums){
            result = result.add(num);
        }

        return result;
    }
    /**
    * Test the addNumbers method.
    * @param args not used
    */
    public static void main (String[] args) {
        BigInteger[] someValues = {BigInteger.TEN, BigInteger.ONE};
        System.out.println(addNumbers(someValues));
    }
}
```

Comments can be added to the beginning of classes and fields in the same way. The comments are helpful to you and other programmers maintaining the code, and their specific format enables easy generation of an HTML reference to your code.

Generate the HTML reference by invoking the tool named Javadoc. This is a command-line tool that parses a named Java source file and formulates HTML documentation based upon the defined class elements and Javadoc comments. For example:

```
javadoc JavadocExample.java
```

This command will produce several HTML files containing the documentation for the class, methods, and fields. If no Javadoc comments exist within the source, some default documentation will still be produced. To view the documentation, load the following file into your browser:

```
index.html
```

The file will be in the same directory as the class or package that you are documenting. There will also be an index-all.html file giving a strict alphabetical listing of documented entities.

Keep in mind that the same rules apply when using the Javadoc tool as when using javac. You must reside within the same directory as the source file, or prepend the name of the file with the path to where the file is located.

How It Works

Generating documentation for applications from scratch can be quite tedious. Maintaining documentation can be even more troublesome. The JDK comes packaged with an extensive system for documentation known as Javadoc. Placing some special comments throughout your code source and running a simple command-line tool makes it easy to generate useful documentation and keep it current. Moreover, even if some of the classes, methods, or fields in an application are not commented specifically for the Javadoc utility, default documentation will still be produced for such elements.

Formatting the Documentation

To create a Javadoc comment, begin with the characters /**. Although optional since Java 1.4, a common practice is to include an asterisk as the first character of every subsequent line within the comment. Another good practice is to indent the comment so that it aligns with the code that is being documented. Lastly, close the comment with the characters */.

Javadoc comments should begin with a short description of the class or method. Fields are rarely commented using Javadoc, unless they are declared public static final (constants), in which case it is a good idea to supply a comment. A comment can be several lines in length, and can even contain more than one paragraph. If you want to break comments into paragraphs, then separate those paragraphs using the <p> tag. Comments can include several tags that indicate various details regarding the method or class that is being commented. Javadoc tags begin with an ampersand (@), and some of the common tags are as follows:

```
@param: Name and description of a parameter
@return: What is returned from the method
@see: Reference to another piece of code
```

You may also include inline links within Javadoc to reference URLs. To include an inline link, use the tag {@link My Link}, where link is the actual URL that you want to point at and My Link is the text that you want to have appear. There are also many other tags that can be used within Javadoc comments, including {@literal}, {@code}, {@value org}, and many others. For a complete listing, see the Javadoc reference on the OTN website.

Executing the Tool

The Javadoc tool can also be run against entire packages or source. Simply pass a package name to the Javadoc tool rather than individual source file names. For instance, if an application includes a package named org.juneau.beans, all source files within that package can be documented by running the tool as follows:

```
javadoc org.juneau.beans
```

To generate Javadoc for more than one package at a time, separate the package names with spaces as follows:

```
javadoc org.juneau.beans org.juneau.entity
```

Another option is to specify the path to the source files using the -sourcepath flag. For example:

```
javadoc -sourcepath /java/src
```

By default, the Javadoc tool will generate HTML and place it into the same package as the code being documented. That result can become a cluttered nightmare if you like to have source files separate from documentation. You can instead set up a destination for the generated documentation by passing the -d flag to the Javadoc tool.

1-13. Reading Environment Variables

Problem

The application you are developing needs to make use of some environment variables. You want to read the values that have been set from the operating-system level.

Solution

Make use of the Java System class to retrieve any environment variable values. The System class has a method called getenv(), which accepts a String argument corresponding to the name of a system environment variable. The method will then return the value of the given variable. If no matching environment variable exists, a NULL value will be returned. Listing 1-10 provides an example. The class ReadOneEnvVariable accepts an environment variable name as a parameter, and displays the variable's value that has been set at the operating-system level.

Listing 1-10. Reading an Environment Variable's Value

```
package org.java9recipes.chapter1.recipe1_13;

public class ReadOneEnvVariable {
    public static void main(String[] args) {
        if (args.length > 0) {
            String value = System.getenv(args[0]);
            if (value != null) {
                System.out.println(args[0].toUpperCase() + " = " + value);
            } else {
                System.out.println("No such environment variable exists");
            }
        } else {
            System.out.println("No arguments passed");
        }
    }
}
```

If you are interested in retrieving the entire list of environment variables that is defined on a system, do not pass any arguments to the System.getenv() method. You'll receive back an object of type Map having all the values. You can iterate through them as shown in Listing 1-11.

Listing 1-11. Iterating Through a Map of Environment Variables

```
package org.java9recipes.chapter1.recipe1_13;

import java.util.Map;

public class ReadAllEnvVariables {
    public static void main(String[] args){
        if(args.length > 0){
            String value = System.getenv(args[0]);
        if (value != null) {
            System.out.println(args[0].toUpperCase() + " = " + value);
```

```
        } else {
            System.out.println("No such environment variable exists");
        }
        } else {
            Map<String, String> vars = System.getenv();
            for(String var : vars.keySet()){
                System.out.println(var + " = " + vars.get(var));
            }
        }
    }
}
```

How It Works

The System class contains many different utilities that can aid in application development. One of those is the getenv() method, which will return a value for a given system environment variable.

You can also return the values from all variables, in which case those values are stored in a *map*. A map is a collection of name/value pairs. Chapter 7 provides additional information about maps, including a recipe showing in detail how to iterate over them.

The method invoked to obtain environment variable values in Listings 1-10 and 1-11 is the same. It's been overloaded to handle both cases shown in the solution. Pass the name of a variable as a String if you want to obtain just that variable's value. Pass no argument at all to get back the names and values of all variables that are currently set.

Summary

This chapter included recipes that allow you to get started working with Java quickly. It covered installation of the JDK, to installation and use of the NetBeans IDE. The chapter also covered basics such as declaring variables, compiling code, and documentation. The rest of this book dives deeper into each of the different areas of the Java language, covering a variety of topics from beginner to expert. Refer to this chapter for configuration specifics as you work through the examples in the rest of the book.

CHAPTER 2

Java 9 Enhancements

Each release of the JDK brings forth new enhancements and capability to the Java platform. Each release also carries with it backward compatibility with previous releases. This book includes a number of recipes covering the new features for Java 9, and this chapter showcases a few of the top enhancements to whet your appetite. By no means is this chapter a complete listing of all Java 9 enhancements. Rather, it is a jump start to get you going on some of the hot new features of Java 9.

2-1. Avoiding Redundancy in Interface Code

Problem

You would like to implement two or more default methods within an interface that will contain very similar code. Rather than copying code into each of the different default methods and maintaining each default method separately, you'd like to encapsulate the similar code into its own method for reuse.

Solution

Make use of a private method in an interface to alleviate this issue. Java 9 provides the ability to include private methods within an interface. A private method is only available within that interface, and it cannot be used by any class that implements the interface. However, each default method implementation that is part of the interface can make use of the private method.

The following interface includes two default methods and one private method. The private method encapsulates functionality that can then be used in each of the default method implementations.

```
public interface Pool {

    /**
     * Calculate volume (gal) for a fixed depth square or rectangular pool.
     */
    public default double squareOrRectConstantDepth(double length, double width,
    double depth){
        return volumeCalc(length, width, depth);
    }

    /**
     * Calculate volume (gal) for a variable depth square or rectangular pool.
     */
```

```java
    public default double squareOrRectVariableDepth(double length, double width,
                                                    double shallowDepth, double middleDepth,
                                                    double deepDepth){
        double avgDepth = (shallowDepth + middleDepth + deepDepth) / 3;
        return volumeCalc(length, width, avgDepth);
    }

    /**
     * Standard square or rectangular volume calculation.
     */
    private double volumeCalc(double length, double width, double depth){
        return length * width * depth * 7.5;
    }
}
```

How It Works

Prior to Java 8, it was not possible to include code implementation within a Java interface. An interface is a reference type in Java, similar to a class. However, its original intent only allowed abstract methods, constants, static methods, and nested types. Therefore, classes that implemented an interface must implement each of the abstract methods. In Java 8, that restriction was lifted, and it became possible to include method implementations in the form of default methods. A default method can contain an implementation in the interface, or its implementation could be overridden by an implementing class. Hence, the name default method, meaning that the default method implementation resides in the interface if one is not provided by the implementation class. Private methods were not allowed in interfaces.

Situations have arisen by which multiple default methods within an interface may contain similar code. This code can now be encapsulated within a private method implementation within the interface. The private method implementation cannot be used outside of the interface. It can only be used by any default methods contained within the same interface. In the solution to this recipe, the volumeCalc() method returns the calculated volume of a square or rectangular swimming pool using a standard formula. Each of the default methods within the interface are able to utilize the volumeCalc() method to find the volume. However, the volumeCalc() method will not be available for use outside of the interface.

This seems to be a controversial topic, as interfaces were originally intended for field and method declarations only, but it can also be argued that copying the same code throughout a number of default method implementations would be a bad practice. Take it as you will, this feature makes it easier to reuse code within an interface, thereby reducing the chance for errors and making maintenance much easier.

2-2. Creating Modules for Simplifying and Code Reuse

Problem

You are writing a utility library or a Java application, and you do not wish to rely upon the classpath to manage dependencies with other libraries. Furthermore, you wish to package your library such that it can easily be integrated into other projects.

Solution

Develop your library or application as a module. Creation of modules is quite easy. However, modules can themselves become quite complex. This example will cover the creation of a very simple module that does not depend upon any other modules. No other modules will depend upon the module either. Begin by creating a new directory somewhere on your file system...in this case name it *"recipe2-2."* Create a new folder named src within it, and then create a file named module-info.java, which is the module descriptor, within the src folder. In this file, list the module name as follows:

```
module org.acme {}
```

Next, create a folder named org.acme.wordcount within the src directory that was created previously (Figure 2-1). Next, create a folder named org within the org.acme.wordcount folder. Subsequently, create an acme folder within the org folder, followed by a wordcount folder within the acme folder.

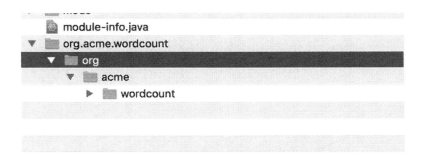

Figure 2-1. *Module folder hierarchy*

Now, create the bulk of the module by adding a new file named WordCount.java inside of the wordcount folder. Place the following code within the WordCount.java file:

```java
package org.acme.wordcount;
public class WordCount {

    public static void main(String[] args) {
        int counter = 0;
        if (args.length > 0){
            for(String arg:args){
                System.out.println("Position " + counter + ": " + arg.length());
                counter++;
            }
        }
    }
}
```

Make use of the javac utility to compile the module by using the command line or terminal and traversing inside of the src directory you created earlier. Issue the javac command, specifying the -d flag to list the folder into which the compiled code will be placed. List each of the source files to be compiled, including the module-info.java descriptor, separating each with a space. The following command compiles the sources that were developed in and places the result into a directory named mods/org.acme.wordcount.

```
javac -d src/mods/org.acme.wordcount src/module-info.java src/org.acme.wordcount/org/acme/
wordcount/WordCount.java
```

Now that the code has been compiled, it is time to execute the module. Use the java executable, specifying the --module-path option, which is new in Java 9, to indicate the path of the module sources. The -m option is used to specify the Main class of the module. Traverse inside of the src directory and issue the following:

```
java --module-path mods -m org.acme.wordcount/org.acme.wordcount.WordCount testing one two
three
```

This example passes the words "testing," "one," "two," "three" to the module to be counted. The output should look as follows:

```
Position 0: 7
Position 1: 3
Position 2: 3
Position 3: 5
```

How It Works

Project Jigsaw brought modules into fruition for the Java platform, finally introducing a means to do away with the classpath of the old, and make use of a newer, more pluggable architecture. The Java 9 module system allows one to package self contained modules of code and make them versatile such that a module can be made to depend upon other modules, or on the other hand, other modules can be made to depend upon it. This modular dependency takes place of the old classpath system, although the classpath is still available for use to accommodate backward compatibility and also for cases where modularity makes little sense.

Creation of a module consists of a module-info.java descriptor file. This file is used to indicate the package containing the module, as well as the dependency contracts that the module shares with other modules. Please see Chapter 22 for more details on the descriptor file.

The self-contained application in this recipe resides within the org.acme.wordcount.WordCount.java file, and it can be compiled with javac, and executed with the java executable, as one would imagine. These two utilities have new options available to support modularity, and the recipe demonstrates the use of these new options for compiling and executing the module. For more details regarding module compilation and execution, see Recipe 22-2.

2-3. Easily Retrieving Information on OS Processes

Problem

You would like the ability to find information regarding operating system processes.

Solution

Make use of the updated Process API in Java 9. The new ProcessHandle interface allows one to easily obtain information regarding operating system processes. In the following code, all operating system processes are listed and printed to the command line.

```
public static void listProcesses(){
    ProcessHandle.allProcesses()
            .forEach(System.out::println);
}
```

However, this is not very helpful, as it simply lists the process number of each operating system process...which is not very useful. To obtain more detail on the process, we need to obtain the ProcessHandle and call upon its helper methods, which is quite easy to do. The following code will print much more information regarding each process, as it prints the ProcessHandle.Info itself.

```
public static void detailListProcesses(){
    ProcessHandle.allProcesses()
            .forEach(h->System.out.println(formattedProcess(h)));
}

public static String formattedProcess(ProcessHandle handle){
        long pid = handle.getPid();
        boolean alive = handle.isAlive();
        Optional<Duration> cpuDuration = handle.info().totalCpuDuration();
        Optional<String> handleName = handle.info().command();
        return pid + " " + alive + " " + handleName + ":"+ cpuDuration;
    }
```

Sample output may look as follows:

```
17584 true Optional[/Library/Java/JavaVirtualMachines/jdk-9.jdk/Contents/Home/bin/
java]:Optional[PT0.250501S]
17581 true Optional[/Library/Java/JavaVirtualMachines/jdk-9.jdk/Contents/Home/bin/
java]:Optional.empty
17576 true Optional.empty:Optional.empty
17575 true Optional.empty:Optional.empty
17574 true Optional.empty:Optional.empty
17364 true Optional[/System/Library/Frameworks/CoreServices.framework/Frameworks/Metadata.
framework/Versions/A/Support/mdworker]:Optional.empty
17247 true Optional[/Applications/Google Chrome.app/Contents/Versions/56.0.2924.87/Google
Chrome Helper.app/Contents/MacOS/Google Chrome Helper]:Optional.empty
```

If you wish to retrieve information pertaining to the user that is running the process, that is easy to do as well.

```
public static void detailListProcessUsers(){
    ProcessHandle.allProcesses()
            .forEach(h->System.out.println(listOsUser(h)));
}

public static String listOsUser(ProcessHandle handle){
    ProcessHandle.Info procInfo = handle.info();
    return handle.getPid() + ": " +procInfo.user();
}
```

Sample output using this technique may look as follows:

```
17584: Optional[Juneau]
17581: Optional[Juneau]
17576: Optional[_postfix]
17575: Optional[_postfix]
17574: Optional[root]
```

How It Works

Prior to the release of Java 9, it was cumbersome to obtain information regarding operating system processes. We had to obtain process IDs using the `ManagementFactory.getRuntimeMXBean()` method and then parse the String that was returned. The `ProcessHandle` interface is introduced in Java 9, making the retrieval of operating system process information a first class citizen of the JDK. Table 2-1 shows the methods that can be called upon within `ProcessInfo` in order to retrieve the desired information.

Table 2-1. *ProcessHandle Interface*

Method	Description
allProcesses()	Snapshot of all processes that are visible to the current process.
children()	Snapshot of the children of the current process.
compareTo(ProcessHandle)	Compare one ProcessHandle to another.
current()	Returns the ProcessHandle for the current process.
descendants()	Snapshot of all descendants of the current process.
destroy()	Requests the process to be killed. Returns a boolean to indicate result.
destroyForcibly()	Requests the process to be killed forcibly. Returns a boolean to indicate result.
equals(Object)	Returns a true if the object passed in is not null, and represents the same system process, otherwise returns a false.
getPid()	Returns the process ID for the process.
hashCode()	Returns hash code value for the process.
info()	Returns `ProcessHandle.Info`, which is a snapshot of information about the current process.
isAlive()	Returns a boolean to indicate whether the process is alive.
of(long)	Returns `Optional<ProcessHandle>` for an existing native process.
onExit()	Returns `CompletableFuture<ProcessHandle>` for the termination of the process. The `CompletableFuture` can then be called upon to determine status.
parent()	Returns `Optional<ProcessHandle>` for the parent of the current process.
supportsNormalTermination()	Returns true if implementation of `destroy()` will terminate the process normally.

2-4. Handling Errors with Ease

Problem

You'd like to easily manage the closing of effectively final variables.

Solution

The try-with-resources construct was introduced in Java 7, and it allows for easy management of resources. In Java 9, it became even easier as there is no need to effectively create a new variable for the sake of the construct. In the following code, the writeFile() method takes a BufferedWriter as an argument, and since it is passed into the method and ready to use, it is effectively final. This means that it can simply be listed in the try-with-resources, rather than creating a new variable.

```
public static void main(String[] args) {
    try {
        writeFile(new BufferedWriter(
                new FileWriter("Easy TryWithResources")),
                "This is easy in Java 9");
    } catch (IOException ioe) {
        System.out.println(ioe);
    }
}

public static void writeFile(BufferedWriter writer, String text) {
    try (writer) {
        writer.write(text);
    } catch (IOException ioe) {
        System.out.println(ioe);
    }
}
```

Prior to Java 9, the writeFile would have looked as follows:

```
public static void writeFile(BufferedWriter writer, String text) {
    try (BufferedWriter w = writer) {
        w.write(text);
    } catch (IOException ioe) {
        System.out.println(ioe);
    }
}
```

This code will create a new file named "Easy TryWithResources" and it will put the text "This is easy in Java 9" into the file.

How It Works

The try-with-resources construct has become even easier with Java 9. The try-with-resources construct was introduced in Java 8, which allows one to handle the opening and closing of resources very easily. If we have a resource, such as a database Connection or a BufferedStream, it is a good idea to manage wisely. In other words, open the resource, then use it accordingly, and finally close the resource when finished to ensure that there are no resource leaks. The try-with-resources construct allows one to open a resource within the try block and have it automatically cleaned up once the block completes.

In the solution, the original way to handle resources is shown, followed by the new way in Java 9. It is now possible to simply begin making use of a resource within a try-with-resources construct if it is passed into a method as an argument or if it is a final field. This means that is no longer necessary to create a placeholder variable for the purposes of utilization within the try-with-resources. While this is not a major language change, it will certainly make handling resources a bit easier, and it certainly makes the try-with-resources block even easier to understand.

2-5. Filtering Data Before and After a Condition with Streams

Problem

You wish to utilize streams for effective manipulation of your collections. While doing so, you wish to filter those streams before and/or after a specified condition occurs. In the end, you want to retrieve all data within the collection before a given predicate condition is met. You also wish to retrieve all data within the collection that is placed after a given predicate condition is met.

Solution

Utilize the new Java 9 takeWhile() and dropWhile() constructs with your stream. Suppose we have the following collection of data, and we wish to retrieve all of the elements prior to the element containing the word "Java."

```
List<String> myLangs = Arrays.asList("Jython is great","Groovy is awesome",
"Scala is functional", "JRuby is productive","Java is streamlined","","Kotlin is
interesting");
```

To retrieve all elements prior to the element containing the String "Java", we could use the takeWhile() construct, as follows:

```
Stream.of("Jython is great","Groovy is awesome","Scala is functional",
          "JRuby is productive","Java is streamlined","","Kotlin is interesting")
          .takeWhile(s -> !s.contains("Java"))
          .forEach(System.out::println);
```

Let's suppose that we wish to retrieve all elements that occur after the element containing the String "Java". We could use the dropWhile() construct, as follows:

```
Stream.of("Jython is great","Groovy is awesome","Scala is functional",
          "JRuby is productive","Java is streamlined","","Kotlin is interesting")
          .dropWhile(s -> !s.contains("Java"))
          .forEach(System.out::println);
```

How It Works

Streams changed the way that we develop code and handle collections of data in Java. The original set of filters that were available for use with streams was fairly generous. However, in Java 8, even more options have been added, making it even easier to refine data with streams. The takeWhile() and dropWhile() constructs allow streams to be parsed, returning a new stream that contains all elements before the first one that fails the specified predicate condition, or returning a new stream containing all elements including and after the first element that fails a specified predicate, respectively.

In the solution to this recipe, the list of Strings is parsed, printing each of the elements to the command line for the first pass. The takeWhile() construct is then applied to the same stream of Strings and the elements from the stream before the element that fails the specified condition will be printed to the command line. The takeWhile() accepts a predicate condition, which it then applies to each of the elements in the stream, and then only those elements that are iterated before the predicate condition is not matched will be returned. All elements that reside in the stream at and after the position where the condition is not met will not be returned.

The opposite result occurs when using the dropWhile() construct. In the solution, all stream elements will be ignored up until the first element upon which the specified condition is no longer met will be returned. Each subsequent element in the stream will also be returned.

The takeWhile and dropWhile constructs are very similar to the filter, with the exception that only one failed condition will cause the remaining elements to be ignored or returned, respectively.

2-6. Developing a Concise HTTP Client

Problem

You wish to develop an HTTP client within a Java application.

Solution

Make use of the updated HTTP/2 client for Java 9. In the following example, the Apress website is parsed and returned via HTTP client code. In the following example, the Apress web page for US is returned as a String.

```
HttpResponse r1;
try {
    r1 = HttpRequest.create(new URI("http://www.apress.com/us/"))
            .GET()
            .response();

    int responseCode = r1.statusCode();
    if(responseCode == 200){
        System.out.println(r1.body(asString()));
    }

 } catch (URISyntaxException|IOException|InterruptedException ex) {
    // Log error
}
```

The output will look something like the following (abbreviated for brevity):

```
<!DOCTYPE html>
<!--[if lt IE 7]> <html lang="en" class="no-js ie6 lt-ie9 lt-ie8"> <![endif]-->
<!--[if IE 7]> <html lang="en" class="no-js ie7 lt-ie9 lt-ie8"> <![endif]-->
<!--[if IE 8]> <html lang="en" class="no-js ie8 lt-ie9"> <![endif]-->
<!--[if IE 9]> <html lang="en" class="no-js ie9"> <![endif]-->
<!--[if gt IE 9]><!--> <html lang="en" class="no-js"> <!--<![endif]-->
<head><meta http-equiv="x-ua-compatible" content="IE=edge">
<script type="text/javascript" src="//static.springer.com/spcom/js/vendor/googleapis/ajax/
libs/jquery/1.9.1/jquery.min.js"></script>
<script type="text/javascript" src="//cdn.optimizely.com/js/8200882355.js"></script>
<script type="text/javascript" id="angular-script" src="//static.springer.com/spcom/js/
vendor/googleapis/ajax/libs/angularjs/1.2.17/angular.min.js"></script>
<script type="text/javascript" id="script--1908162026" src="//static.springer.com/spcom/min/
prod.js?r=201702071421-9"></script>
<link rel="stylesheet" type="text/css" href="//static.springer.com/spcom/min/modern_sprcom-
cms-frontend_apress.css?r=201702071421-9" />
```

```
<!--[if (lt IE 9) & (!IEMobile)]><link rel="stylesheet" type="text/css" href="//static.
springer.com/spcom/min/ielt9_sprcom-cms-frontend_apress.css?r=201702071421-9" media="screen"
/><![endif]-->
<link rel="stylesheet" type="text/css" href="//static.springer.com/spcom/min/print.
css?r=201702071421-9" media="print" />
<link rel="stylesheet" type="text/css" href="/spcom/css/vendor/font-awesome.min.
css?r=201702071421-9" />
<!--[if lt IE 9]><script type="text/javascript" id="ielt9js" charset="utf-8" src="//static.
springer.com/spcom/min/ielt9.js"></script>
```

■ **Note**   This is an excellent example to try out in the Java 9 jShell utility. To start the utility, open a command prompt or terminal and type `jshell –add-modules java.httpclient` to start the shell including the httpclient module. This assumes that the jshell executable utility resides within the PATH.

How It Works

The new `javax.httpclient` module has been added to Java 9, and it comprises of high level HTTP and WebSocket client APIs. The API provides synchronous and asynchronous implementations for the HTTP Client, and asynchronous implementations for WebSocket. The API resides within the `java.net.http` package.

The `HttpClient` is a container for configuration information that is common to the HttpRequests type. An HttpClient is generated by initiating an `HttpRequest.Builder`, passing the URI for the request, and then calling upon the `create()` method. The `create()` method returns an immutable `HttpClient`. As seen in the solution to this recipe, the client can be used to perform a number of activities, both synchronously and asynchronously. Asynchronous requests will return a `CompleteableFuture` object for use. For more details regarding the HTTP and WebSocket clients, please refer to Recipe 21-7 and Recipe 21-8.

2-7. Redirecting Platform Logs

Problem

You wish to filter logs and redirect them to a specific file if they match the specified filtering criteria.

Solution

Utilize the Java 9 Unified Logging API to filter the logs and route accordingly. In the following excerpt from the command line or terminal, the java executable is invoked to execute a class named Recipe02_07. The -Xlog option is specified, passing gc=debug:file=gc.txt:none. This indicates that all log messages tagged with 'gc' using the 'debug' level should be written to the file gc.txt, and no decorations should be used.

```
java -Xlog:gc=debug:file=gc.txt:none Recipe02_07
```

This will result in the creation of a file named gc.txt in the current directory, and all log messages pertaining to the specified –Xlog option will be written to it.

How It Works

The JVM is a complex system, and it can sometimes be difficult to pinpoint the cause of the issue. The Unified JVM Logging system, which was added in Java 9, provides a finer grained solution for helping to find the cause of issues. The new command-line option -Xlog controls this functionality, providing a number of tags, level, decorations, and output options for achieving superior logging. Tags can be specified by name, such as gc, threads, compiler, and so forth. Different logging levels are possible, including error, warning, info, debug, trace, and develop. If the "off" level is specified, then logging will be disabled. Decorators can be specified to provide detailed information regarding the message. Decorators can be specified in a custom ordering, such that the desired results will be logged. Table 2-2 contains a listing of the different decorators that can be used.

Table 2-2. *-Xlog Decorators*

Decorator	Function
Time	Provides current time and date in ISO-8601 format.
uptime	Time that JVM has been up and running (in seconds and milliseconds).
timemillis	Value returned from `System.currentTimeInMillis();`
uptimemillis	Uptime of JVM in milliseconds.
timenanos	Value returned from `System.nanoTime();`
uptimenanos	Uptime of JVM in nanoseconds.
pid	Process identifier.
tid	Thread identifier.
level	Log message level.
tags	Tag-set associated with log message.

Three types of output are supported, those being: stdout, stderr, and text file. Rotation configuration for the output files is possible. When all of these options are specified together, the logging can become extremely detailed. For a complete listing of possible options, please refer to the JEP (`http://openjdk.java.net/jeps/158`).

2-8. Utilizing Factory Methods to Create Immutable Collections

Problem

You wish to generate an immutable Collection of values.

Solution

Utilize the `Collection.of()` construct to generate an immutable collection. In the following example, two Collections are created. The first is an immutable `List<String>`, and the second is an immutable `Map<Integer, String>`.

```
List<String> jvmLanguages = List.of("Java", "Scala", "JRuby", "Groovy", "Jython", "Kotlin");
System.out.println(jvmLanguages);
try {
    jvmLanguages.add("Exception");
} catch (UnsupportedOperationException uoe){
    System.out.println(uoe);
}
Map <Integer, String> players = Map.of(1, "Josh Juneau", 2, "Jonathan Gennick", 3, "Freddy
Guime", 4, "Carl Dea");
System.out.println(players.values());
System.out.println("Player 2: " + players.get(2));
```

The output would look like the following. Note that in the example I have added a try-catch block to catch the UnsupportedOperationException that is thrown when I attempt to modify the List.

```
[Java, Scala, JRuby, Groovy, Jython, Kotlin]
java.lang.UnsupportedOperationException
[Carl Dea, Jonathan Gennick, Freddy Guime, Josh Juneau]
Player 2: Jonathan Gennick
```

How It Works

Java has historically been a verbose language for performing small tasks. In the past, constructing a populated Collection of data took a few lines of code. On the first line, the Collection must be initialized, followed by a line of code for each item that was added to it. Java 9 adds the convenient API for quickly producing an unmodifiable Collection of data, whereby one can now initialize and populate the construct in one line of code.

Factory methods have been added to the List, Set, and Map interfaces for creating such unmodifiable collections of data. The factory methods consist of the of() method, which accepts up to ten values, for quickly creating an immutable collection. The Map factory method accepts up to ten key/value pairs. If more than ten pairs is needed for the Map, then it is possible to call upon the Map.ofEntries() method, passing an arbitrary number of Map.Entry<k,v>. Furthermore, no null values can be used to populate as elements, keys, or values.

Summary

This chapter covered a handful of the new features and enhancements that have been added to Java 9. While certainly not a complete listing of new features, this chapter delved into a few of the most anticipated features, including modularity, Process API, and easy error handling. To gain a more complete knowledge of new features, the entire book should be read through. However, this chapter gave you a taste for what is to come.

CHAPTER 3

Strings

Strings are one of the most commonly used data types in any programming language. They can be used for obtaining text from a keyboard, printing messages to a command line, and much more. Given the fact that Strings are used so often, there have been many features added to the `String` object over time in order to make them easier to work with. After all, a String is an object in Java, so it contains methods that can be used to manipulate the contents of the String. Strings are also *immutable* in Java, which means that their state cannot be changed or altered. This makes them a bit different to work with than some of the mutable, or changeable, data types. It is important to understand how to properly make use of immutable objects, especially when attempting to change or assign different values to them.

This chapter focuses on some of the most commonly used `String` methods and techniques for working with `String` objects. We also cover some useful techniques that are not inherent of `String` objects.

Compact Strings: Java 9 String Enhancements

Since the Java language was introduced, Strings have been stored into an array of type UTF-16 `char`. The char array contains two bytes for each character, which eventually produces a large memory heap since Strings are used so often in our applications. In Java 9, Strings are stored in an array of type byte, and stored characters are encoded either as ISO-8859-1/Latin-1 (one byte per character), or as UTF-16 (two bytes per character). There is also an encoding flag on the char array, which is used to indicate which type of encoding is used for the String. These changes are otherwise known as *compact Strings*.

These changes do not affect the way in which we utilize Strings, nor do they alter the helper methods of the String class in any way. They may, however, significantly decrease the amount of memory used by an application.

3-1. Obtaining a Subsection of a String

Problem

You would like to retrieve a portion of a String.

Solution

Use the `substring()` method to obtain a portion of the String between two different positions. In the solution that follows, a String is created and then various portions of the String are printed out using the `substring()` method.

© Josh Juneau 2017
J. Juneau, *Java 9 Recipes*, DOI 10.1007/978-1-4842-1976-8_3

```
public static void substringExample(){
    String originalString = "This is the original String";
        System.out.println(originalString.substring(0, originalString.length()));
        System.out.println(originalString.substring(5, 20));
        System.out.println(originalString.substring(12));
    }
```

Running this method would yield the following results:

```
This is the original String
is the original
original String
```

How It Works

The String object contains many helper methods. One such method is substring(), which can be used to return portions of the String. There are two variations of the substring() method. One of them accepts a single argument, that being the starting index; and the other accepts two arguments: startingindex and endingindex. Having two variations of the substring() method makes it seem as though the second argument is optional; if it is not specified, the length of the calling String is used in its place. It should be noted that indices begin with zero, so the first position in a String has the index of 0, and so on.

As you can see from the solution to this recipe, the first use of substring() prints out the entire contents of the String. This is because the first argument passed to the substring() method is 0, and the second argument passed is the length of the original String. In the second example of substring(), an index of 5 is used as the first argument, and an index of 20 is used as the second argument. This effectively causes only a portion of the String to be returned, beginning with the character in the String that is located in the sixth position, or index 5 because the first position has an index of 0; and ending with the character in the String that is located in the 20th position, the index of 19. The third example specifies only one argument; therefore, the result will be the original String beginning with the position specified by that argument.

▦ **Note**   The substring() method only accepts positive integer values. If you attempt to pass a negative value, an exception will be thrown.

3-2. Comparing Strings

Problem

An application that you are writing needs to have the ability to compare two or more String values.

Solution

Use the built-in equals(), equalsIgnoreCase(), compareTo(), and compareToIgnoreCase() methods to compare the values contained within the Strings. The following is a series of tests using different String-comparison operations.

As you can see, various if statements are used to print out messages if the comparisons are equal:

```
String one = "one";
String two = "two";

String var1 = "one";
String var2 = "Two";

String pieceone = "o";
String piecetwo = "ne";

// Comparison is equal
if (one.equals(var1)){
    System.out.println ("String one equals var1 using equals");
}

// Comparison is NOT equal
if (one.equals(two)){
    System.out.println ("String one equals two using equals");
}

// Comparison is NOT equal
if (two.equals(var2)){
    System.out.println ("String two equals var2 using equals");
}

// Comparison is equal, but is not directly comparing String values using ==
if (one == var1){
    System.out.println ("String one equals var1 using ==");
}

// Comparison is equal
if (two.equalsIgnoreCase(var2)){
    System.out.println ("String two equals var2 using equalsIgnoreCase");
}

System.out.println("Trying to use == on Strings that are pieced together");

String piecedTogether = pieceone + piecetwo;

// Comparison is equal
if (one.equals(piecedTogether)){
    System.out.println("The Strings contain the same value using equals");
}

// Comparison is NOT equal using ==
if (one == piecedTogether) {
    System.out.println("The String contain the same value using == ");
}
```

```
// Comparison is equal
if (one.compareTo(var1) == 0){
    System.out.println("One is equal to var1 using compareTo()");
}
```

Results in the following output:

```
String one equals var1 using equals
String one equals var1 using ==
String two equals var2 using equalsIgnoreCase
Trying to use == on Strings that are pieced together
The Strings contain the same value using equals
One is equal to var1 using compareTo()
```

How It Works

One of the trickier parts of using a programming language can come when attempting to compare two or more values, particularly String values. In the Java language, comparing Strings can be fairly straightforward, keeping in mind that you should *not* use the == for String comparison. This is because the comparison operator (==) is used to compare references, not values of Strings. One of the most tempting things to do when programming with Strings in Java is to use the comparison operator, but you must not because the results can vary.

■ **Note**   Java uses interning of Strings to speed up performance. This means that the JVM contains a table of interned Strings, and each time the intern() method is called on a String, a lookup is performed on that table to find a match. The interning returns a canonical representation of the String. If no matching String resides within the table, the String is added to the table and a reference is returned. If the String already resides within the table, the reference is returned. Java will automatically intern String literals, and this can cause variation when using the == comparison operator.

In the solution to this recipe, you can see various different techniques for comparing String values. The equals() method is a part of every Java object. The Java String equals() method has been overridden so that it will compare the values contained within the String rather than the object itself. As you can see from the following examples that have been extracted from the solution to this recipe, the equals() method is a safe way to compare Strings.

```
// Comparison is equal
if (one.equals(var1)){
    System.out.println ("String one equals var1 using equals");
}
// Comparison is NOT equal
if (one.equals(two)){
    System.out.println ("String one equals two using equals");
}
```

The equals() method will first check to see whether the Strings reference the same object using the == operator; it will return true if they do. If they do not reference the same object, equals() will compare each String character by character to determine whether the Strings being compared to each other contain exactly the same values. What if one of the Strings has a different case setting than another? Do they still compare equal to each other using equals()? The answer is no, and that is why the equalsIgnoreCase() method was created. Comparing two values using equalsIgnoreCase() will cause each of the characters to be compared without paying attention to the case. The following examples have been extracted from the solution to this recipe:

```
// Comparison is NOT equal
if (two.equals(var2)){
    System.out.println ("String two equals var2 using equals");
}
// Comparison is equal
if (two.equalsIgnoreCase(var2)){
    System.out.println ("String two equals var2 using equalsIgnoreCase");
}
```

The compareTo()and compareToIgnoreCase() methods perform a lexicographical comparison of the Strings. This comparison is based upon the Unicode value of each character contained within the Strings. The result will be a negative integer if the String lexicographically precedes the argument String. The result will be a positive integer if the String lexicographically follows the argument String. The result will be zero if both Strings are lexicographically equal to each other. The following excerpt from the solution to this recipe demonstrates the compareTo() method:

```
// Comparison is equal
if (one.compareTo(var1) == 0){
    System.out.println("One is equal to var1 using compareTo()");
}
```

Inevitably, many applications contain code that must compare Strings at some level. The next time you have an application that requires String comparison, consider the information discussed in this recipe before you write the code.

3-3. Trimming Whitespace

Problem

One of the Strings you are working with contains some whitespace on either end. You would like to get rid of that whitespace.

Solution

Use the String trim() method to eliminate the whitespace. In the following example, a sentence is printed including whitespace on either side. The same sentence is then printed again using the trim() method to remove the whitespace so that the changes can be seen.

```
String myString = " This is a String that contains whitespace.    ";
System.out.println(myString);
System.out.println(myString.trim());
```

The output will print as follows:

```
This is a String that contains whitespace.
This is a String that contains whitespace.
```

How It Works

Regardless of how careful we are, whitespace can always become an issue when working with Strings of text. This is especially the case when comparing Strings against matching values. If a String contains an unexpected whitespace character then that could be disastrous for a pattern-searching program. Luckily, the Java String object contains the trim() method that can be used to automatically remove whitespace from each end of any given String.

The trim() method is very easy to use. In fact, as you can see from the solution to this recipe, all that is required to use the trim() method is a call against any given String. Because Strings are objects, they contain many helper methods, which can make them very easy to work with. After all, Strings are one of the most commonly used data types in any programming language...so they'd better be easy to use! The trim() method returns a copy of the original String with all leading and trailing whitespace removed. If, however, there is no whitespace to be removed, the trim() method returns the original String instance. It does not get much easier than that!

3-4. Changing the Case of a String

Problem

A portion of your application contains case-sensitive String values. You want to change all the Strings to uppercase before they are processed in order to avoid any case sensitivity issues down the road.

Solution

Make use of the toUpperCase() and toLowerCase() methods. The String object provides these two helper methods to assist in performing a case change for all of the characters in a given String.

For example, given the String in the following code, each of the two methods will be called:

```
String str = "This String will change case.";
System.out.println(str.toUpperCase());
System.out.println(str.toLowerCase());
```

The following output will be produced:

```
THIS STRING WILL CHANGE CASE.
this String will change case.
```

How It Works

To ensure that the case of every character within a given String is either upper or lowercase, use the toUpperCase() and toLowerCase() methods, respectively. There are a couple of items to note when using these methods. First, if a given String contains an uppercase letter, and the toUpperCase() method is called against it, the uppercase letter is ignored. The same concept holds true for calling the toLowerCase() method. Any punctuation or numbers contained within the given String are also ignored.

There are two variations for each of these methods. One of the variations does not accept any arguments, while the other accepts an argument pertaining to the locale you wish to use. Calling these methods without any arguments will result in a case conversion using the default locale. If you want to use a different locale, you can pass the desired locale as an argument, using the variation of the method that accepts an argument. For instance, if you want to use an Italian or French locale, you would use the following code:

```
System.out.println(str.toUpperCase(Locale.ITALIAN));
System.out.println(str.toUpperCase(new Locale("it","US")));
System.out.println(str.toLowerCase(new Locale("fr", "CA")));
```

Converting Strings to upper or lowercase using these methods can make life easy. They are also very useful for comparing Strings that are taken as input from an application. Consider the case in which a user is prompted to enter a username, and the result is saved into a String. Now consider that later in the program that String is compared against all the usernames stored within a database to ensure that the username is valid. What happens if the person who entered the username types it with an uppercase first character? What happens if the username is stored within the database in all uppercase? The comparison will never be equal. In such a case, a developer can use the toUpperCase() method to alleviate the problem. Calling this method against the Strings that are being compared will result in a comparison in which the case is the same in both Strings.

3-5. Concatenating Strings

Problem

There are various Strings that you want to combine into one.

Solution 1

If you want to concatenate Strings onto the end of each other, use the concat() method. The following example demonstrates the use of the concat() method:

```
String one = "Hello";
String two = "Java9";
String result = one.concat(" ".concat(two));
```

The result is this:

```
Hello Java9
```

Solution 2

Use the concatenation operator to combine the Strings in a shorthand manner. In the following example, a space character has been placed in between the two Strings:

```
String one = "Hello";
String two = "Java9";
String result = one + " " + two;
```

The result is this:

```
Hello Java9
```

Solution 3

Use `StringBuilder` or `StringBuffer` to combine the Strings. The following example demonstrates the use of `StringBuffer` to concatenate two Strings:

```
String one = "Hello";
String two = "Java9";
StringBuffer buffer = new StringBuffer();
buffer.append(one).append(" ").append(two);
String result = buffer.toString();
System.out.println(result);
```

The result is this:

```
Hello Java9
```

How It Works

The Java language provides a couple of different options for concatenating Strings of text. Although none is better than the others, you may find one or the other to work better in different situations. The `concat()` method is a built-in String helper method. It provides the ability to append one String onto the end of another, as demonstrated by solution 1 to this recipe. The `concat()` method will accept any String value; therefore, you can explicitly type a String value to pass as an argument if you want. As demonstrated in solution 1, simply passing one String as an argument to this method will append it to the end of the String, which the method is called upon. However, if you wanted to add a space character in between the two Strings, you could do so by passing a space character as well as the String you want to append as follows:

```
String result = one.concat(" ".concat(two));
```

As you can see, having the ability to pass any String or combination of Strings to the `concat()` method makes it very useful. Because all of the String helper methods actually return copies of the original String with the helper method functionality applied, you can pass Strings calling other helper methods to `concat()` (or any other String helper method) as well. Consider that you want to display the text `"Hello Java"` rather than `"Hello Java9"`. The following combination of String helper methods would allow you to do just that:

```
String one = "Hello";
String two = "Java9";
String result = one.concat(" ".concat(two.substring(0, two.length()-1)));
```

The concatenation operator (+) can be used to combine any two Strings. It is almost thought of as a shorthand form of the `concat()` method. The last technique that is demonstrated in solution 3 to this example is the use of `StringBuffer`, which is a mutable sequence of characters, much like a String, except that it can be modified through method calls. The `StringBuffer` class contains a number of helper methods for building and manipulating character sequences. In the solution, the `append()` method is used to append two String values. The `append()` method places the String that is passed as an argument at the end of the `StringBuffer`. For more information regarding the use of `StringBuffer`, refer to the online documentation at http://docs.oracle.com/javase/9/docs/api/java/lang/StringBuffer.html.

3-6. Converting Strings to Numeric Values

Problem

You want to have the ability to convert any numeric values that are stored as Strings into integers.

Solution 1

Use the `Integer.valueOf()` helper method to convert Strings to `int` data types. For example:

```
String one = "1";
String two = "2";
int result = Integer.valueOf(one) + Integer.valueOf(two);
```

As you can see, both of the String variables are converted into integer values. After that, they are used to perform an addition calculation and then stored into an `int`.

▓ **Note**   A technique known as *autoboxing* is used in this example. Autoboxing is a feature of the Java language that automates the process of converting primitive values to their appropriate wrapper classes. For instance, this occurs when you assign an `int` value to an Integer. Similarly, *unboxing* automatically occurs when you try to convert in the opposite direction, from a wrapper class to a primitive. For more information on autoboxing, refer to the online documentation at `http://docs.oracle.com/javase/tutorial/java/data/autoboxing.html`.

Solution 2

Use the `Integer.parseInt()` helper method to convert Strings to `int` data types. For example:

```
String one = "1";
String two = "2";
int result = Integer.parseInt(one) + Integer.parseInt(two);
System.out.println(result);
```

How It Works

The Integer class contains the `valueOf()` and `parseInt()` methods, which are used to convert Strings or `int` types into integers. There are two different forms of the Integer class's `valueOf()` type that can be used to convert Strings into integer values. Each of them differs by the number of arguments that they accept. The first `valueOf()` method accepts only a String argument. This String is then parsed as an integer value if possible, and then an integer holding the value of that String is returned. If the String does not convert into an integer correctly, then the method will throw a `NumberFormatException`.

The second version of Integer's `valueOf()` method accepts two arguments: a String argument that will be parsed as an integer and an `int` that represents the radix that is to be used for the conversion.

> ■ **Note**   Many of the Java type classes contain `valueOf()` methods that can be used for converting
> different types into that class's type. Such is the case with the `String` class because it contains many different
> `valueOf()` methods that can be used for conversion. For more information on the different `valueOf()` methods
> that the `String` class or any other type class contains, see the online Java documentation at http://docs.oracle.
> com/javase/9/docs

There are also two different forms of the `Integer` class's `parseInt()` method. One of them accepts one
argument: the String you want to convert into an integer. The other form accepts two arguments: the String
that you want to convert to an integer and the radix. The first format is the most widely used, and it parses
the String argument as a signed decimal integer. A `NumberFormatException` will be thrown if a parsable
unsigned integer is not contained within the String. The second format, which is less widely used, returns
an `Integer` object holding the value that is represented by the String argument in the given radix, given a
parsable unsigned integer is contained within that String.

> ■ **Note**   One of the biggest differences between parseInt() and valueOf() is that parseInt() returns an int and
> valueOf() returns an Integer from the cache.

3-7. Iterating Over the Characters of a String

Problem

You want to iterate over the characters in a String of text so that you can manipulate them at the character
level.

Solution

Use a combination of String helper methods to gain access to the String at a character level. If you use
a String helper method within the context of a loop, you can easily traverse a String by character. In the
following example, the String named `str` is broken down using the `toCharArray()` method.

```
String str = "Break down into chars";
System.out.println(str);
for (char chr:str.toCharArray()){
    System.out.println(chr);
}
```

The same strategy could be used with the traditional version of the for loop. An index could be created
that would allow access to each character of the String using the `charAt()` method.

```
for (int x = 0; x <= str.length()-1; x++){
System.out.println(str.charAt(x));
}
```

Both of these solutions will yield the following result:

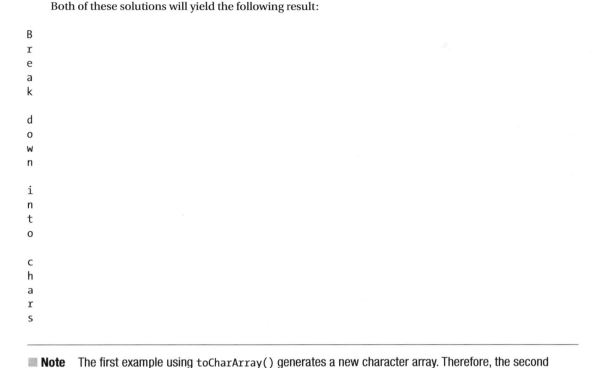

B
r
e
a
k

d
o
w
n

i
n
t
o

c
h
a
r
s

▒ **Note**   The first example using `toCharArray()` generates a new character array. Therefore, the second example, using the traditional `for` loop, might perform faster.

How It Works

String objects contain methods that can be used for performing various tasks. The solution to this recipe demonstrates a number of different `String` methods. The `toCharArray()` method can be called against a String in order to break the String into characters and then store those characters in an array. This method is very powerful and it can save a bit of time when performing this task is required. The result of calling the `toCharArray()` method is a `char[]`, which can then be traversed using an index. Such is the case in the solution to this recipe. An enhanced `for` loop is used to iterate through the contents of the `char[]` and print out each of its elements.

The String `length()` method is used to find the number of characters contained within a String. The result is an `int` value that can be very useful in the context of a `for` loop, as demonstrated in the solution to this recipe. In the second example, the `length()` method is used to find the number of characters in the String so that they can be iterated over using the `charAt()` method. The `charAt()` method accepts an `int` index value as an argument and returns the character that resides at the given index in the String.

Often the combination of two or more String methods can be used to obtain various results. In this case, using the `length()` and `charAt()` methods within the same code block provided the ability to break down a String into characters.

3-8. Finding Text Matches

Problem

You want to search a body of text for a particular sequence of characters.

Solution 1

Make use of regular expressions and the String matches() helper method to determine how many matches exist. To do this, simply pass a String representing a regular expression to the matches() method against any String you are trying to match. In doing so, the String will be compared with the String that matches() is being called upon. Once evaluated, matches() will yield a boolean result, indicating whether it is a match. The following code excerpt contains a series of examples using this technique. The comments contained within the code explain each of the matching tests.

```
String str = "Here is a long String...let's find a match!";
// This will result in a "true" since it is an exact match
boolean result = str.matches("Here is a long String...let's find a match!");
System.out.println(result);
// This will result iin "false" since the entire String does not match
result = str.matches("Here is a long String...");

System.out.println(result);

str = "true";

// This will test against both upper & lower case "T"...this will be TRUE
result = str.matches("[Tt]rue");
System.out.println(result);

// This will test for one or the other
result = str.matches("[Tt]rue|[Ff]alse]");
System.out.println(result);

// This will test to see if any numbers are present, in this case the
// person writing this String would be able to like any Java release!
str = "I love Java 8!";
result = str.matches("I love Java [0-9]!");
System.out.println(result);

// This will test TRUE as well...
str = "I love Java 7!";
result = str.matches("I love Java [0-9]!");
System.out.println(result);

// The following will test TRUE for any language that contains
// only one word for a name. This is because it tests for
// any alphanumeric combination. Notice the space character
// between the numeric sequence...
result = str.matches("I love .*[ 0-9]!");
System.out.println(result);
```

```
// The following String also matches.
str = "I love Jython 2.5.4!";
result = str.matches("I love .*[ 0-9]!");

System.out.println(result);
```

Each of the results printed out in the example will be true, with the exception of the second example because it does not match.

Solution 2

Use the regular expression Pattern and Matcher classes for a better-performing and more versatile matching solution than the String matches() method. Although the matches() method will get the job done most of the time, there are some occasions in which you will require a more flexible way of matching. Using this solution is a three-step process:

1. Compile a pattern into a Pattern object.

2. Construct a Matcher object using the matcher() method on the Pattern.

3. Call the matches() method on the Matcher.

In the following example code, the Pattern and Matcher technique is demonstrated:

```
String str = "I love Java 9!";
boolean result = false;

Pattern pattern = Pattern.compile("I love .*[ 0-9]!");
Matcher matcher = pattern.matcher(str);
result = matcher.matches();

System.out.println(result);
```

The previous example will yield a TRUE value just like its variant that was demonstrated in solution 1.

How It Works

Regular expressions are a great way to find matches because they allow patterns to be defined so that an application does not have to explicitly find an exact String match. They can be very useful when you want to find matches against some text that a user may be typing into your program. However, they could be overkill if you are trying to match Strings against a String constant you have defined in your program because the String class provides many methods that could be used for such tasks. Nevertheless, there will certainly come a time in almost every developer's life when regular expressions can come in handy. They can be found in just about every programming language used today. Java makes them easy to use and understand.

▒ **Note** Although regular expressions are used in many different languages today, the expression syntax for each language varies. For complete information regarding regular expression syntax, see the documentation online at http://docs.oracle.com/javase/9/docs/api/java/util/regex/Pattern.html.

The easiest way to make use of regular expressions is to call the matches() method on the String object. Passing a regular expression to the matches() method will yield a boolean result that indicates whether the String matches the given regular expression pattern or not. At this point, it is useful to know what a regular expression is and how it works.

A *regular expression* is a String pattern can be matched against other Strings in order to determine its contents. Regular expressions can contain a number of different patterns that enable them to be dynamic in that they can have the ability to match many different Strings that contain the same format. For instance, in the solution to this recipe, the following code can match several different Strings:

```
result = str.matches("I love Java [0-9]!");
```

The regular expression String in this example is "I love Java [0-9]!", and it contains the pattern [0-9], which represents any number between 0 and 9. Therefore, any String that reads "I love Java" followed by the numbers 0 through 9 and then an exclamation point will match the regular expression String. To see a listing of all the different patterns that can be used in a regular expression, see the online documentation available at the URL in the previous note.

A combination of Pattern and Matcher objects can also be used to achieve similar results as the String matcher() method. The Pattern object can be used to compile a String into a regular expression pattern. A compiled pattern can provide performance gains to an application if the pattern is used multiple times. You can pass the same String–based regular expressions to the Pattern.compile() method as you would pass to the String matches() method. The result is a compiled Pattern object that can be matched against a String for comparison. A Matcher object can be obtained by calling the Pattern object's matcher() method against a given String. Once a Matcher object is obtained, it can be used to match a given String against a Pattern using any of the following three methods, which each return a boolean value indicating a match. The following three lines of solution 2 could be used as an alternate solution to using the Pattern.matches() method, minus the reusability of the compile pattern:

```
Pattern pattern = Pattern.compile("I love .*[ 0-9]!");
Matcher matcher = pattern.matcher(str);
result = matcher.matches();
```

- The Matcher matches() method attempts to match the entire input String with the pattern.

- The Matcher lookingAt() method attempts to match the input String to the pattern starting at the beginning.

- The Matcher find() method scans the input sequence looking for the next matching sequence in the String.

In the solution to this recipe, the matches() method is called against the Matcher object in order to attempt to match the entire String. In any event, regular expressions can be very useful for matching Strings against patterns. The technique used for working with the regular expressions can vary in different situations, using whichever method works best for the situation.

3-9. Replacing All Text Matches

Problem

You have searched a body of text for a particular sequence of characters, and you are interested in replacing all matches with another String value.

Solution

Use a regular expression pattern to obtain a Matcher object; then use the Matcher object's replaceAll() method to replace all matches with another String value. The example that follows demonstrates this technique:

```
String str = "I love Java 8!  It is my favorite language.  Java 8
 is the "
                    + "8th version of this great programming language.";
Pattern pattern = Pattern.compile("[0-9]");
Matcher matcher = pattern.matcher(str);
System.out.println("Original: " + str);
System.out.println(matcher.matches());
System.out.println("Replacement: " + matcher.replaceAll("9"));
```

This example will yield the following results:

```
Original: I love Java 8! It is my favorite language. Java 8 is the 8th version of this great
programming language.
Replacement: I love Java 9! It is my favorite language. Java 9 is the 9th version of this
great programming language.
```

How It Works

The replaceAll() method of the Matcher object makes it easy to find and replace a String or a portion of String that is contained within a body of text. In order to use the replaceAll() method of the Matcher object, you must first compile a Pattern object by passing a regular expression String pattern to the Pattern. compile() method. Use the resulting Pattern object to obtain a Matcher object by calling its matcher() method. The following lines of code show how this is done:

```
Pattern pattern = Pattern.compile("[0-9]");
Matcher matcher = pattern.matcher(str);
```

Once you have obtained a Matcher object, call its replaceAll() method by passing a String that you want to use to replace all the text that is matched by the compiled pattern. In the solution to this recipe, the String "9" is passed to the replaceAll() method, so it will replace all the areas in the String that match the "[0-9]" pattern.

3-10. Determining Whether a File Suffix Matches a Given String

Problem

You are reading a file from the server and you need to determine what type of file it is in order to read it properly.

Solution

Determine the suffix of the file by using the endsWith() method on a given file name. In the following example, assume that the variable filename contains the name of a given file, and the code is using the endsWith() method to determine whether filename ends with a particular String:

```
if(filename.endsWith(".txt")){
    System.out.println("Text file");
} else if (filename.endsWith(".doc")){
    System.out.println("Document file");
} else if (filename.endsWith(".xls")){
    System.out.println("Excel file");
} else if (filename.endsWith(".java")){
System.out.println("Java source file");
} else {
    System.out.println("Other type of file");
}
```

Given that a file name and its suffix are included in the filename variable, this block of code will read its suffix and determine what type of file the given variable represents.

How It Works

As mentioned previously, the String object contains many helper methods that can be used to perform tasks. The String object's endsWith() method accepts a character sequence and then returns a boolean value representing whether the original String ends with the given sequence. In the case of the solution to this recipe, the endsWith() method is used in an if block. A series of file suffixes is passed to the endsWith() method to determine what type of file is represented by the filename variable. If any of the file name suffixes matches, a line is printed, stating what type of file it is.

3-11. Making a String That Can Contain Dynamic Information

Problem

You would like to generate a String that has the ability to contain a dynamic placeholder such that the String can change depending upon application data variations.

Solution 1

Utilize the String format() built-in method for generating a String containing placeholders for dynamic data. The following example demonstrates a String that contains a dynamic placeholder that allows different data to be inserted into the same String. In the example, as the temperature variable changes, the String is dynamically altered.

```
public static void main(String[] args){
    double temperature = 98.6;
    String temperatureString = "The current temperature is %.1f degrees Farenheit.";

    System.out.println(String.format(temperatureString, temperature));

    temperature = 101.2;

    System.out.println(String.format(temperatureString, temperature));
}
```

Output:

```
The current temperature is 98.6 degrees Farenheit.
The current temperature is 101.2 degrees Farenheit.
```

Solution 2

If you wish to print the contents of the String out, rather than store them for later use, the System. out.printf() method can be used to position dynamic values within a String. The following example demonstrates the same concept as that in solution 1, except this time rather than using the String.format() method, a String is simply printed out, and the placeholders passed to the System.out.printf() method are replaced with the dynamic content at runtime.

```
public static void main(String[] args){
    double temperature = 98.6;
    System.out.printf("The current temperature is %.1f degrees Farenheit.\n", temperature);

    temperature = 101.2;

    System.out.printf("The current temperature is %.1f degrees Farenheit.", temperature);
}
```

Output:

```
The current temperature is 98.6 degrees Farenheit.
The current temperature is 101.2 degrees Farenheit.
```

How It Works

When you require the use of dynamic String content, the format() utility can come in handy. The format() built-in method allows one to position a placeholder within a String, such that the placeholder will be replaced with dynamic content at runtime. The format method accepts a String, along with a series of variables that will be used to displace the placeholders within the String with dynamic content at runtime. The placeholders must be designated specifically for the type of content with which they will be displaced. Table 3-1 contains a list of each placeholder or conversion type for the String.format() function.

Table 3-1. String.format() Conversion Types

Conversion	Content Type
b	boolean
h	hex
s	String
c	Unicode character
d	decimal integer
o	octal integer
x	hexadecimal integer
e	floating point decimal number in computerized scientific notation
f	floating point decimal number
g	floating point using computerized scientific notation or decimal format, depending upon the precision and value after rounding
a	hexadecimal floating-point number with significand and exponent
t	date/time
n	platform-specific line separator

Each placeholder must begin with a % character to denote that it is a placeholder within the String. The placeholder can also contain flags, width, and precision indicators to help format the dynamic value appropriately. The following format should be used to build each placeholder:

```
%[flags][width][.precision]conversion_indicator
```

The second solution demonstrates how to utilize the System.out.printf() method, which accepts the same arguments as the System.format() method. The main difference between the two is that the System.out.printf() method is handy for printing formatted content. If your application requires the need to store a formatted value, you will be more likely to use the String.format() method.

Summary

This chapter covered the basics of working with Strings. Although a String may look like a simple String of characters, it is an object that contains many methods that can be useful for obtaining the required results. Although Strings are immutable objects, many methods within the String class contain a copy of the String, modified to suit the request. This chapter covered a handful of these methods, demonstrating features such as concatenation, how to obtain portions of Strings, trimming whitespace, and replacing portions of a String.

CHAPTER 4

■ ■ ■

Numbers and Dates

Numbers play a significant role in many applications. As such, it is helpful to know how to use them correctly within the context of the work that you are trying to perform. This chapter helps you understand how to perform some of the most basic operations with numbers, and it also provides insight on performing advanced tasks such as working with currency. There are a number of ways to work with currency, and this chapter will focus on a couple of them.

Dates are also important as they can be used for many purposes within an application. In Java 8, the new Date-Time package called `java.time` was introduced. The Date-Time API uses the calendar defined in ISO-8601 as the default. Therefore, the calendar is based on the Gregorian calendar system, and in this chapter, you will learn how to work with date, time, and time zone data. The Date-Time API adheres to several design principles, in that it's clear, fluent, immutable, and extensible. The API uses a clear language that is concise and very well defined. It is also very fluent, so code dealing with date-time data is easy to read and understand. Most of the classes within the Date-Time API are immutable, so in order to alter a date-time object you must create a modified copy of the original. As such, many of the methods in the date-time classes are named accordingly, such as `of()` and `with()`, so that you know you are creating a copy rather than altering the original. Lastly, the new Date-Time API can be extended in many cases, allowing it to be useful in many contexts.

The Date-Time API is made up of a rich set of classes, providing solutions that were rather difficult to achieve in previous APIs. Even though there are many different classes, most of them contain a similar set of methods, so the same principles can be utilized throughout all of the date and time units. Table 4-1 lists the common set of methods that you will find in most of the date-time classes.

Table 4-1. *Date-Time API's Common Methods*

Method	Description
at	Combines one object with another.
format	Applies the specified format to a temporal object, producing a String.
from	Converts input parameters to an instance of the target class.
get	Returns a part of the state of the target object.
is	Queries the target object.
minus	Returns a modified copy of the target object with the specified amount of time subtracted.
of	Creates an instance, using specified input parameters for validation.
parse	Parses an input String to produce an instance of the target class.
plus	Returns a modified copy of the target object with the specified amount of time added.
to	Converts an object to a different type.
with	Returns a modified copy of the target object with the specified element changed (equivalent to a setter).

© Josh Juneau 2017
J. Juneau, *Java 9 Recipes*, DOI 10.1007/978-1-4842-1976-8_4

As mentioned previously, the Date-Time API is fluent; therefore, each of its classes is located in a clearly marked package. Table 4-2 lists the packages that make up the Date-Time API, along with brief descriptions of the classes that can be found in each.

Table 4-2. *Date-Time API Packages*

Package	Description
java.time	The core classes of the API. These classes are used for working with date-time data based on the ISO-8601 standard. These classes are immutable and thread-safe.
java.time.chrono	The API for using calendar systems other than ISO-8601.
java.time.format	Classes for formatting date-time data.
java.time.temporal	Extended API that allows interpolations between date-time classes.
java.time.zone	Classes supporting time zone data.

This chapter presents a brief overview of some commonly used date-time features. If you will be performing significant work with dates and times, you should read the Date-Time API documentation that is available online in addition to this chapter.

4-1. Rounding Float and Double Values to Integers

Problem

You need to be able to round floating-point numbers or doubles in your application to Integer values.

Solution

Use one of the java.lang.Math round() methods to round the number into the format you require. The Math class has two methods that can be used for rounding floating-point numbers or Double values. The following code demonstrates how to use each of these methods:

```
public static int roundFloatToInt(float myFloat){
    return Math.round(myFloat);
}

public static long roundDoubleToLong(double myDouble){
    return Math.round(myDouble);
}
```

The first method, roundFloatToInt(), accepts a floating-point number and uses the java.lang.Math class to round that number to an Integer. The second method, roundDoubleToLong(), accepts a Double value and uses the java.lang.Math class to round that Double to a Long.

How It Works

The java.lang.Math class contains plenty of helper methods to make our lives easier when working with numbers. The round() methods are no exception as they can be used to easily round floating-point or double values. One version of the java.lang.Math round() method accepts a float as an argument. It will round the float to the closest int value, with ties rounding up. If the argument is Not a Number (NaN), then a zero will be returned. When arguments that are positive or negative infinity are passed into round(), a result equal to the value of Integer.MAX_VALUE or Integer.MIN_VALUE, respectively, will be returned. The second version of the java.lang.Math round() method accepts a double value. The double value is rounded to the closest long value, with ties rounding up. Just like the other round(), if the argument is NaN, a zero will be returned. Similarly, when arguments that are positive or negative infinity are passed into round(), a result equal to the value of Long.MAX_VALUE or Long.MIN_VALUE, respectively, will be returned.

■ **Note** NaN, POSITIVE_INFINITY, and NEGATIVE_INFINITY are constant values defined within the Float and Double classes. NaN (Not a Number) is an undefined or unrepresentable value. For example, a NaN value can be produced by dividing 0.0f by 0.0f. The values represented by POSITIVE_INFINITY and NEGATIVE_INFINITY refer to values that are produced by operations that generate such extremely large or negative values of a particular type (floating-point or double) that they cannot be represented normally. For instance, 1.0/0.0 or −1.0/0.0 would produce such values.

4-2. Formatting Double and Long Decimal Values

Problem

You need to be able to format double and long numbers in your application.

Solution

Use the DecimalFormat class to format and round the value to the precision your application requires. In the following method, a double value is accepted and a formatted String value is printed:

```
public static void formatDouble(double myDouble){
    NumberFormat numberFormatter = new DecimalFormat("##.000");
    String result = numberFormatter.format(myDouble);
    System.out.println(result);
}
```

For instance, if the double value passed into the formatDouble() method is 345.9372, the following will be the result:

```
345.937
```

Similarly, if the value .7697 is passed to the method, the following will be the result:

```
.770
```

Each of the results is formatted using the specified pattern and then rounded accordingly.

How It Works

The DecimalFormat class can be used along with the NumberFormat class to round and/or format double or long values. NumberFormat is an abstract class that provides the interface for formatting and parsing numbers. This class provides the ability to format and parse numbers for each locale, and obtain formats for currency, percentage, integers, and numbers. By itself, the NumberFormat class can be very useful as it contains factory methods that can be used to obtain formatted numbers. In fact, little work needs to be done in order to obtain a formatted String. For example, the following code demonstrates calling some factory methods on the NumberFormat class:

```
// Obtains an instance of NumberFormat class
NumberFormat format = NumberFormat.getInstance();

// Format a double value for the current locale
String result = format.format(83.404);
System.out.println(result);

// Format a double value for an Italian locale
result = format.getInstance(Locale.ITALIAN).format(83.404);
System.out.println(result);

// Parse a String into a Number
try {
    Number num = format.parse("75.736");
    System.out.println(num);
} catch (java.text.ParseException ex){
    System.out.println(ex);
}
```

To format using a pattern, the DecimalFormat class can be used along with NumberFormat. In the solution to this recipe, you saw that creating a new DecimalFormat instance by passing a pattern to its constructor would return a NumberFormat type. This is because DecimalFormat extends the NumberFormat class. Because the NumberFormat class is abstract, DecimalFormat contains all the functionality of NumberFormat, plus added functionality for working with patterns. Therefore, it can be used to work with different formats from the locales just as you have seen in the previous demonstration. This provides the ultimate flexibility when working with double or long formatting.

As mentioned previously, the DecimalFormat class can take a String-based pattern in its constructor. You can also use the applyPattern() method to apply a pattern to the Format object after the fact. Each pattern contains a prefix, numeric part, and suffix, which allow you to format a particular decimal value to the required precision and include leading digits and commas as needed. The symbols used to build patterns are displayed in Table 4-3. Each of the patterns also contains a positive and negative subpattern. These two subpatterns are separated by a semicolon (;) and the negative subpattern is optional. If there is no negative subpattern present, the localized minus sign is used. For instance, a complete pattern example would be ###,##0.00;(###,##0.00).

Table 4-3. DecimalFormat Pattern Characters

Character	Description
#	Digit; blank if no digit is present
0	Digit; zero if no digit is present
.	Decimal
-	Minus or negative sign
,	Comma or grouping separator
E	Scientific notation separator
;	Positive and negative subpattern separator

The DecimalFormat class provides enough flexibility to format double and long values for just about every situation.

4-3. Comparing int Values

Problem

You need to compare two or more int values.

Solution 1

Use the comparison operators to compare integer values against one another. In the following example, three int values are compared against each other, demonstrating various comparison operators:

```
int int1 = 1;
int int2 = 10;
int int3 = -5;

System.out.println(int1 == int2);  // Result:  false
System.out.println(int3 == int1);  // Result:  false
System.out.println(int1 == int1);  // Result:  true
System.out.println(int1 > int3);   // Result:  true
System.out.println(int2 < int3);   // Result:  false
```

As you can see, comparison operators will generate a boolean result.

Solution 2

Use the Integer.compare(int,int) method to compare two int values numerically. The following lines could compare the same int values that were declared in the first solution:

```
System.out.println("Compare method -> int3 and int1: " + Integer.compare(int3, int1));
// Result -1
System.out.println("Compare method -> int2 and int1: " + Integer.compare(int2, int1));
// Result 1
```

How It Works

Perhaps the most commonly used numeric comparisons are against two or more int values. The Java language makes it very easy to compare an int using the comparison operators (see Table 4-4).

Table 4-4. *Comparison Operators*

Operator	Function
==	Equal to
!=	Not equal to
>	Greater than
<	Less than
>=	Greater than or equal to
<=	Less than or equal to

The second solution to this recipe demonstrates the integer compare() method that was added to the language in Java 7. This static method accepts two int values and compares them, returning a 1 if the first int is greater than the second, a 0 if the two int values are equal, and a -1 if the first int value is less than the second. To use the Integer.compare() method, pass two int values as demonstrated in the following code:

```
Integer.compare(int3, int1));
Integer.compare(int2, int1));
```

Just like in your math lessons at school, these comparison operators will determine whether the first integer is equal to, greater than, or less than the second integer. Straightforward and easy to use, these comparison operators are most often seen within the context of an if-statement.

4-4. Comparing Floating-Point Numbers

Problem

You need to compare two or more floating-point values in an application.

Solution 1

Use the Float object's compareTo() method to perform a comparison of one float against another. The following example shows the compareTo() method in action:

```
Float float1 = new Float("9.675");
Float float2 = new Float("7.3826");
Float float3 = new Float("23467.373");

System.out.println(float1.compareTo(float3));   // Result: -1
System.out.println(float2.compareTo(float3));   // Result: -1
System.out.println(float1.compareTo(float1));   // Result: 0
System.out.println(float3.compareTo(float2));   // Result: 1
```

The result of calling the compareTo() method is an integer value. A negative result indicates that the first float is less than the float that it is being compared against. A zero indicates that the two float values are equal. Lastly, a positive result indicates that the first float is greater than the float that it is being compared against.

Solution 2

Use the Float class compare() method to perform the comparison. The following example demonstrates the use of the Float.compare(float, float) method.

```
System.out.println(Float.compare(float1, float3)); // Result: -1
System.out.println(Float.compare(float2, float3)); // Result: -1
System.out.println(Float.compare(float1, float1)); // Result: 0
System.out.println(Float.compare(float3, float2)); // Result: 1
```

How It Works

The most useful way to compare two float objects is to use the compareTo() method. This method will perform a numeric comparison against the given float objects. The result will be an integer value indicating whether the first float is numerically greater than, equal to, or less than the float that it is compared against. If a float value is NaN, it is considered to be equal to other NaN values or greater than all other float values. Also, a float value of 0.0f is greater than a float value of -0.0f.

An alternative to using compareTo() is the compare() method, which is also native to the Float class. The compare() method was introduced in Java 1.4, and it is a static method that compares two float values in the same manner as compareTo(). It only makes the code read a bit differently. The format for the compare() method is as follows:

```
Float.compare(primitiveFloat1, primitiveFloat2)
```

The compare() method shown will actually make the following call using compareTo():

```
new Float(float1).compareTo(new Float(float2));
```

In the end, the same results will be returned using either compareTo() or compare().

4-5. Calculating Monetary Values

Problem

You are developing an application that requires the use of monetary values and you are not sure which data type to use for storing and calculating currency values.

Solution 1

Use the BigDecimal data type to perform calculation on monetary values. Format the resulting calculations using the NumberFormat.getCurrencyInstance() helper method. In the following code, three monetary values are calculated using a handful of the methods that are part of the BigDecimal class. The resulting calculations are then converted into double values and formatted using the NumberFormat class. First, take a look at how these values are calculated:

```
BigDecimal currencyOne = new BigDecimal("25.65");
BigDecimal currencyTwo = new BigDecimal("187.32");
BigDecimal currencyThree = new BigDecimal("4.86");
BigDecimal result = null;
String printFormat = null;

// Add all three values
result = currencyOne.add(currencyTwo).add(currencyThree);
// Convert to double and send to formatDollars(), returning a String
printFormat = formatDollars(result.doubleValue());
System.out.println(printFormat);

// Subtract the first currency value from the second
result = currencyTwo.subtract(currencyOne);
printFormat = formatDollars(result.doubleValue());
System.out.println(printFormat);
```

Next, let's take a look at the formatDollars() method that is used in the code. This method accepts a double value and performs formatting on it using the NumberFormat class based on the U.S. locale. It then returns a String value representing currency:

```
public static String formatDollars(double value){
    NumberFormat dollarFormat = NumberFormat.getCurrencyInstance(Locale.US);
    return dollarFormat.format(value);
}
```

As you can see, the NumberFormat class allows for currency to be formatted per the specified locale. This can be very handy if you are working with an application that deals with currency and has an international scope.

```
$217.83
$161.67
```

Solution 2

Utilize the Java Money API, which was the focus of JSR 354, to perform monetary calculations.

■ **Note** The Java Money API was developed under JSR 354 https://jcp.org/en/jsr/detail?id=354. It was originally intended for completion and inclusion with Java 9. However, the JSR was completed quite a bit early, and contains no dependencies on the Java 9 codebase. Therefore, the Java Money API can be used with older versions of Java as well, such as Java 8, and it is available on Github at http://javamoney.github.io/.

The following example demonstrates how to perform currency calculations and formatting using the .Java Money API.

```
MonetaryAmount amount1 =  Money.of(25.65, Monetary.getCurrency("USD"));
MonetaryAmount amount2 =  Money.of(187.32, Monetary.getCurrency("USD"));
MonetaryAmount amount3 =  Money.of(4.86,Monetary.getCurrency("USD"));

MonetaryAmount result = null;
result = amount1.add(amount2).add(amount3);

MonetaryAmountFormat printFormat = MonetaryFormats.getAmountFormat(
    AmountFormatQuery.of(Locale.US));
System.out.println("Sum of all: " + printFormat.format(result));

result = amount2.subtract(amount1);
System.out.println("Subtract amount1 from amount 2: " + printFormat.format(result));
```

How It Works

Many people attempt to use different number formats when working with currency. While it might be possible to use any type of numeric object to work with currency, the BigDecimal class was added to the language in Java 5 to help satisfy the requirements of working with currency values, among other things. We will begin by explaining how to utilize BigDecimal for currency calculations, as it is the classic procedure, and then we'll take a look at the Java Money API.

Perhaps the most useful feature of the BigDecimal class is that it provides control over rounding. This is essentially why such a class is so useful for working with currency values. The BigDecimal class provides an easy API for rounding values, and also makes it easy to convert to double values, as the solution to this recipe demonstrates.

■ **Note**   The use of BigDecimal for working with monetary values is a good practice. However, it can come at some performance expense. Depending on the application and performance requirements, it might be worth using Math.round() to achieve basic rounding if performance becomes an issue.

To provide specific rounding with the BigDecimal class, you should use a MathContext object or the RoundingMode enumeration values. In either case, such precision can be omitted by using a currency-formatting solution such as the one demonstrated in the solution example. BigDecimal objects have mathematical implementations built into them, so performing such operations is an easy task. The arithmetic operations that you can use are described in Table 4-5.

Table 4-5. *BigDecimal Arithmetic Methods*

Method	Description
add()	Adds one BigDecimal object value to another.
subtract()	Subtracts one BigDecimal object value from another.
multiply()	Multiplies the value of one BigDecimal object by another.
abs()	Returns the absolute value of the given BigDecimal object value.
pow(n)	Returns the BigDecimal to the power of n; the power is computed to unlimited precision.

After performing the calculations you require, call the doubleValue() method on the BigInteger object to convert and obtain a double. You can then format the double using the NumberFormat class for currency results.

The Java Money API began as JSR 354, in an effort to make it easier to work with currency in the Java language. The API provides a truly significant change to the language, as it finally allows one to treat currency in a standard manner, rather than utilizing the BigDecimal in various ways. The payoff of using the Java Money API can be huge, since it can make code easier to read and understand, and provide a monetary result rather than a result that must be coerced into a currency value.

In solution 2, the same currency values are used to demonstrate a handful of calculation exercises. The standard types for currency in the API is a MonetaryAmount. In the solution, you can see that there are three MonetaryAmount objects, and each of them represent different values in dollars and cents using the USD currency. To obtain the values that are stored into the MonetaryAmount objects, the Money implementation class is used to parse the value that is given to it, and then return a MonetaryAmount type of the specified currency type. The Money class stores number values using BigDecimal.

The MonetaryAmount interface provides a number of methods that can be utilized for performing operations against the stored value, comparing against other amounts, precision, and so forth. Specifically, in the solution you can see that the add() method accepts another MonetaryAmount, and it is used to add the value passed in to the original MonetaryAmount. Another such method is subtract(), which subtracts the value passed from the original.

The solution also provides information about formatting monetary values. The MonetaryFormats factory can be used to obtain formats specific to a desired locale. The resulting MonetaryAmountFormat pattern can then be applied to a MonetaryAmount to change the presentation of the value accordingly.

4-6. Randomly Generating Values

Problem

An application that you are developing requires the use of randomly generated numbers.

Solution 1

Use the java.util.Random class to help generate the random numbers. The Random class was developed for the purpose of generating random numbers for a handful of the Java numeric data types. This code demonstrates the use of Random to generate such numbers:

```
// Create a new instance of the Random class
Random random = new Random();

// Generates a random Integer
int myInt = random.nextInt();

// Generates a random Double value
double myDouble = random.nextDouble();
```

```
// Generates a random float
float myFloat = random.nextFloat();

// Generates a random Gaussian double
// mean 0.0 and standard deviation 1.0
// from this random number generator's sequence.
double gausDouble = random.nextGaussian();

// Generates a random Long
long myLong = random.nextLong();

// Generates a random boolean
boolean myBoolean = random.nextBoolean();
```

Solution 2

Make use of the `Math.random()` method. This will produce a `double` value that is greater than 0.0, but less than 1.0. The following code demonstrates the use of this method:

```
double rand = Math.random();
```

How It Works

The `java.util.Random` class uses a 48-bit seed to generate a series of pseudorandom values. As you can see from the example in the solution to this recipe, the `Random` class can generate many different types of random number values based on the given seed. By default, the seed is generated based on a calculation derived from the number of milliseconds that the machine has been active. However, the seed can be set manually using the `Random  setSeed()` method. If two `Random` objects have the same seed, they will produce the same results.

It should be noted that there are cases in which the `Random` class might not be the best choice for generating random values. For instance, if you are attempting to use a thread-safe instance of `java.util.Random`, you might run into performance issues if you're working with many threads. In such a case, you might consider using the `ThreadLocalRandom` class instead. To see more information regarding `ThreadLocalRandom`, see the documentation at `http://docs.oracle.com/javase/9/docs/api/java/util/concurrent/ThreadLocalRandom.html`.

Similarly, if you require the use of a cryptographically secure `Random` object, consider the use of SecureRandom. Documentation regarding this class can be found at `http://docs.oracle.com/javase/9/docs/api/java/security/SecureRandom.html`.

The `java.util.Random` class comes in very handy when you need to generate a type-specified random value. Not only is it easy to use but it also provides a wide range of options for return type. Another easy technique is to use the `Math.random()` method, which produces a `double` value that is within the range of 0.0 to 1.0, as demonstrated in solution 2. Both techniques provide a good means of generating random values. However, if you need to generate random numbers of a specific type, `java.util.Random` is the best choice.

4-7. Obtaining the Current Date Without Time

Problem

You are developing an application for which you would like to obtain the current date, not including the time, to display on a form.

Solution

Make use of the Date-Time API to obtain the current date. The LocalDate class represents an ISO calendar in the year-month-day format. The following lines of code capture the current date and display it:

```
LocalDate date = LocalDate.now();
System.out.println("Current Date:" + date);
```

How It Works

The Date-Time API makes it easy to obtain the current date, without including other information such as time. To do so, import the java.time.LocalTime class and call on its now() method. The LocalTime class cannot be instantiated, as it is immutable and thread-safe. A call to the now() method returns another LocalDate object, containing the current date in the year-month-day format.

Another version of the now() method accepts a java.time.Clock object as a parameter and returns the date based on that clock. For instance, the following lines of code demonstrate how to obtain a Clock that represents the system time:

```
Clock clock = Clock.systemUTC();
LocalDate date = LocalDate.now(clock);
```

In previous releases, there were other ways to obtain the current date, but usually the time came with the date and then formatting had to be done to remove the unneeded time digits. The new java.time. LocalDate class makes it possible to work with dates separate from times.

4-8. Obtaining a Date Object Given Date Criteria

Problem

You want to obtain a date object, given a year-month-day specification.

Solution

Invoke the LocalDate.of() method for the year, month, and day for which you want to obtain the object. For example, suppose that you want to obtain a date object for a specified date in November of 2000. You could pass that date criteria to the LocalDate.of() method, as demonstrated in the following lines of code:

```
LocalDate date = LocalDate.of(2000, Month.NOVEMBER, 11);
System.out.println("Date from specified date: " + date);
```

Here's the result:

```
Date from specified date: 2000-11-11
```

How It Works

The LocalDate.of() method accepts three values as parameters. Those parameters represent the year, month, and day. The year parameter is always treated as an int value. The month parameter can be presented as an int value, which corresponds to an enum that represents the month. The Month enum will return an int value for each month, with JANUARY returning a 1 and DECEMBER returning a 12. Therefore, Month.NOVEMBER returns an 11. A Month object could also be passed as the second parameter instead of as an int value. Lastly, the day of the month is specified by passing an int value as the third parameter to the of() method.

▓ **Note**   For more information regarding the Month enum, see the online documentation at http://download.java.net/jdk9/docs/api/java/time/Month.html.

4-9. Obtaining a Year-Month-Day Date Combination

Problem

You would like to obtain the year, year-month, or month of a specified date.

Solution 1

To obtain the year-month of a specified date, use the java.time.YearMonth class. This class is used to represent the month of a specific year. In the following lines of code, the YearMonth object is used to obtain the year and month of the current date and another specified date.

```
YearMonth yearMo = YearMonth.now();
System.out.println("Current Year and month:" + yearMo);
YearMonth specifiedDate = YearMonth.of(2000, Month.NOVEMBER);
System.out.println("Specified Year-Month: " + specifiedDate);
```

Here's the result:

```
Current Year and month:2014-12
Specified Year-Month: 2000-11
```

Solution 2

To obtain the month-day for the current date or a specified date, simply make use of the java.time.MonthDay class. The following lines of code demonstrate how to obtain a month-day combination.

```
MonthDay monthDay = MonthDay.now();
System.out.println("Current month and day: " + monthDay);
```

```
MonthDay specifiedDate = MonthDay.of(Month.NOVEMBER, 11);
System.out.println("Specified Month-Day: " + specifiedDate);
```

Here's the result:

```
Current month and day: --12-14
Specified Month-Day: --11-11
```

Note that by default, MonthDay does not return a very useful format. For more help with formatting, see Recipe 4-17.

How It Works

The Date-Time API includes classes that make it easy to obtain the information that your application requires for a date. Two of those are the YearMonth and MonthDay classes. The YearMonth class is used to obtain the date in year-month format. It contains a few methods that can be used to obtain the year-month combination. As demonstrated in the solution, you can call the now() method to obtain the current year-month combination. Similar to the LocalDate class, YearMonth also contains an of() method that accepts a year in int format, and a number that represents the month of the year. In the solution, the Month enum is used to obtain the month value.

Similar to the YearMonth class, MonthDay obtains the date in a month-day format. It also contains a few different methods for obtaining the month-day combination. Solution 2 demonstrates two such techniques: Obtaining the current month-day combination by calling the now() method and using the of() method to obtain a month-day combination for a specified date. The of() method accepts an int value for the month of the year as its first parameter, and for the second parameter it accepts an int value indicating the day of the month.

4-10. Obtaining and Calculating Times Based on the Current Time

Problem

You would like to obtain the current time so that it can be used to stamp a given record. You would also like to perform calculations based on that time.

Solution

Use the LocalTime class, which is part of the new Date-Time API, to obtain and display the current time. In the following lines of code, the LocalTime class is demonstrated.

```
LocalTime time = LocalTime.now();
System.out.println("Current Time: " + time);
```

Once the time has been obtained, methods can be called against the LocalTime instance to achieve the desired result. In the following lines of code, there are some examples of using the LocalTime methods:

```
// atDate(LocalDate): obtain the local date and time
LocalDateTime ldt = time.atDate(LocalDate.of(2011,Month.NOVEMBER,11));
System.out.println("Local Date Time object: " + ldt);
```

```
// of(int hours, int min): obtain a specific time
LocalTime pastTime = LocalTime.of(1, 10);

// compareTo(LocalTime): compare two times.  Positive
// return value returned if greater
System.out.println("Comparing times: " + time.compareTo(pastTime));

// getHour(): return hour in int value (24-hour format)
int hour = time.getHour();
System.out.println("Hour: " + hour);

// isAfter(LocalTime): return Boolean comparison
System.out.println("Is local time after pastTime? " + time.isAfter(pastTime));

// minusHours(int): Subtract Hours from LocalTime
LocalTime minusHrs = time.minusHours(5);
System.out.println("Time minus 5 hours: " + minusHrs);

// plusMinutes(int): Add minutes to LocalTime
LocalTime plusMins = time.plusMinutes(30);
System.out.println("Time plus 30 mins: " + plusMins);
```

Here are the results:

```
Current Time: 22:21:08.419
Local Date Time object: 2011-11-11T22:21:08.419
Comparing times: 1
Hour: 22
Is local time after pastTime? true
Time minus 5 hours: 17:21:08.419
Time plus 30 mins: 22:51:08.419
```

How It Works

Sometimes it is necessary to obtain the current system time. The LocalTime class can be used to obtain the current time by calling its now() method. Similarly to the LocalDate class, the LocalTime.now() method can be called to return a LocalTime object that is equal to the current time. The LocalTime class also contains several methods that can be utilized to manipulate the time. The examples contained in the solution provide a brief overview of the available methods.

Let's take a look at a handful of examples to provide some context for how the LocalTime methods are invoked. To obtain a LocalTime object set to a specific time, invoke the LocalTime.of(int, int) method, passing int parameters representing the hour and minute.

```
// of(int hours, int min): obtain a specific time
LocalTime pastTime = LocalTime.of(1, 10);
```

The atDate(LocalDate) instance method is used to apply a LocalDate object to a LocalTime instance, returning a LocalDateTime object (for more information, see Recipe 4-11).

```
LocalDateTime ldt = time.atDate(LocalDate.of(2011,Month.NOVEMBER,11));
```

There are several methods that can be used for obtaining portions of the time. For instance, the getHour(), getMinute(), getNano(), and getSecond() methods can be used to return those specified portions of the LocalTime object.

```
int hour = time.getHour();
int min  = time.getMinute();
int nano = time.getNano();
int sec  = time.getSecond();
```

Several comparison methods are also available for use. For example, the compareTo(LocalTime) method can be used to compare one LocalTime object to another. isAfter(LocalTime) can be used to determine if the time is after another, and isBefore(LocalTime) is used to specify the opposite. If calculations are needed, several methods are available, including:

- minus(long amountToSubtract, TemporalUnit unit)
- minus(TemporalAmount amount)
- minusHours(long)
- minusMinutes(long)
- minusNanos(long)
- minusSeconds(long)
- plus(long amountToAdd, TemporalUnit unit)
- plus(TemporalAmount amount)
- plusHours(long)
- plusMinutes(long)
- plusNanos(long)
- plusSeconds(long)

To see all of the methods contained in the LocalTime class, see the online documentation at http://docs.oracle.com/javase/9/docs/api/java/time/LocalTime.html.

4-11. Obtaining and Using the Date and Time Together

Problem

In your application, you want to display not only the current date, but also the current time.

Solution 1

Make use of the LocalDateTime class, which is part of the new Date-Time API, to capture and display the current date and time. The LocalDateTime class contains a method named now(), which can be used to obtain the current date and time together. The following lines of code demonstrate how to do so:

```
LocalDateTime ldt = LocalDateTime.now();
System.out.println("Local Date and Time: " + ldt);
```

The resulting LocalDateTime object contains both the date and time, but no time zone information. The LocalDateTime class also contains additional methods that provide options for working with date-time data. For instance, to return a LocalDateTime object with a specified date and time, pass parameters of int type to the LocalDateTime.of() method, as follows:

```
// Obtain the LocalDateTime object of the date 11/11/2000 at 12:00
LocalDateTime ldt2 = LocalDateTime.of(2000, Month.NOVEMBER, 11, 12, 00);
```

The following examples demonstrate a handful of the methods that are available in a LocalDateTime object:

```
// Obtain the month from LocalDateTime object
Month month = ldt.getMonth();
int monthValue = ldt.getMonthValue();
System.out.println("Month: " + month);
System.out.println("Month Value: " + monthValue);

// Obtain day of Month, Week, and Year
int day = ldt.getDayOfMonth();
DayOfWeek dayWeek = ldt.getDayOfWeek();
int dayOfYr = ldt.getDayOfYear();
System.out.println("Day: " + day);
System.out.println("Day Of Week: " + dayWeek);
System.out.println("Day of Year: " + dayOfYr);

// Obtain year
int year = ldt.getYear();
System.out.println("Date: " + monthValue + "/" + day + "/" + year);

int hour = ldt.getHour();
int minute = ldt.getMinute();
int second = ldt.getSecond();
System.out.println("Current Time: " + hour + ":" + minute + ":" + second);

// Calculation of Months, etc.
LocalDateTime currMinusMonths = ldt.minusMonths(12);
LocalDateTime currMinusHours = ldt.minusHours(10);
LocalDateTime currPlusDays = ldt.plusDays(30);
System.out.println("Current Date and Time Minus 12 Months: " + currMinusMonths);
System.out.println("Current Date and Time MInus 10 Hours: " + currMinusHours);
System.out.println("Current Date and Time Plus 30 Days:" + currPlusDays);
```

Here's the result:

```
Day: 28
Day Of Week: SATURDAY
Day of Year: 332
Date: 11/28/2015
Current Time: 10:23:8
Current Date and Time Minus 12 Months: 2014-11-28T10:23:08.399
Current Date and Time MInus 10 Hours: 2015-11-28T00:23:08.399
Current Date and Time Plus 30 Days:2015-12-28T10:23:08.399
```

Solution 2

If you only need to obtain the current date without going into calendar details, use the java.util.Date class to generate a new Date object. Doing so will generate a new Date object that is equal to the current system date. In the following code, you can see how easy it is to create a new Date object and obtain the current date:

```
Date date = new Date();

System.out.println("Using java.util.Date(): " + date);
System.out.println("Getting time from java.util.Date(): " + date.getTime());
```

The result will be a Date object that contains the current date and time taken from the system that the code is run on, including the time zone information, as shown following listing. The time is the number of milliseconds since January 1, 1970, 00:00:00 GMT.

```
Using java.util.Date(): Sat Nov 28 10:23:08 CST 2015
Getting time from java.util.Date(): 1448727788454
```

Solution 3

If you need to be more precise regarding the calendar, use the java.util.Calendar class. Although working with the Calendar class will make your code longer, the results are more granular than using a java.util.Date. The following code demonstrates just a handful of the capabilities of using this class to obtain the current date:

```
Calendar gCal = Calendar.getInstance();

// Month is based upon a zero index, January is equal to 0,
// so we need to add one to the month for it to be in
// a standard format
int month = gCal.get(Calendar.MONTH) + 1;int day = gCal.get(Calendar.DATE);
int yr = gCal.get(Calendar.YEAR);

String dateStr = month + "/" + day + "/" + yr;
System.out.println(dateStr);

int dayOfWeek = gCal.get(Calendar.DAY_OF_WEEK);

// Print out the integer value for the day of the week
System.out.println(dayOfWeek);

int hour = gCal.get(Calendar.HOUR);
int min  = gCal.get(Calendar.MINUTE);
int sec = gCal.get(Calendar.SECOND);

// Print out the time
System.out.println(hour + ":" + min + ":" + sec);

// Create new DateFormatSymbols instance to obtain the String
// value for dates
DateFormatSymbols symbols = new DateFormatSymbols();
```

```
String[] days = symbols.getWeekdays();
System.out.println(days[dayOfWeek]);

// Get crazy with the date!
int dayOfYear = gCal.get(Calendar.DAY_OF_YEAR);
System.out.println(dayOfYear);

// Print the number of days left in the year
System.out.println("Days left in " + yr + ": " + (365-dayOfYear));

int week = gCal.get(Calendar.WEEK_OF_YEAR);
// Print the week of the year
System.out.println(week);
```

As demonstrated by this code, it is possible to obtain more detailed information regarding the current date when using the Calendar class. The results of running the code will look like the following:

```
11/28/2015
7
10:28:26
Saturday
332
Days left in 2015: 33
48
```

■ **Note**   Although the java.util.Calendar provides a robust technique for obtaining precise Date/Time information, the preferred solution as of Java 8 is to make use of the Java Date-Time API.

How It Works

Many applications require the use of the current calendar date. It is often also necessary to obtain the current time. There are different ways to do that, and the solution to this recipe demonstrates three of them. The Date-Time API includes a LocalDateTime class that enables you to capture the current date and time by invoking its now() method. A specified date and time can be obtained by specifying the corresponding int and Month type parameters when calling LocalDateTime.of(). There are also a multitude of methods available for use via a LocalDateTime instance, such as getHours(), getMinutes(), getNanos(), and getSeconds(), which allow for finer-grained control of the date and time. An instance of LocalDateTime also contains methods for performing calculations, conversions, comparisons, and more. For brevity, all of the methods are not listed here, but for further information; refer to the online documentation at http://docs.oracle.com/javase/9/docs/api/java/time/LocalDateTime.html. Solution 1 to this recipe demonstrates the use of the LocalDateTime, showcasing how to perform calculations and obtain portions of the date and time for further use.

By default, the java.util.Date class can be instantiated with no arguments to return the current date and time. The Date class can also be used to return the current time of day via the getTime() method. As mentioned in the solution, the getTime() method returns the number of milliseconds since January 1, 1970, 00:00:00 GMT, represented by the Date object that is in use. There are several other methods that can be called against a Date object with regard to breaking down the current date and time into more granular intervals. For instance, the Date class has the methods getHours(), getMinutes(), getSeconds(), getMonth(), getDay(), getTimezoneOffset(), and getYear(). However, it is not advisable to use any of these methods, with the exception of getTime(), because each has been deprecated by the use of the java.time. LocalDateTime and the java.util.Calendar get() method. When a method or class is deprecated, that means it should no longer be used because it might be removed in some future release of the Java language. However, a few of the methods contained within the Date class have not been tagged as deprecated, so the Date class will most likely be included in future releases of Java. The methods that were left intact include the comparison methods after(), before(), compareTo(), setTime(), and equals(). Solution 2 to this recipe demonstrates how to instantiate a Date object and print out the current date and time.

As mentioned previously, the Date class has many methods that have become deprecated and should no longer be used. In solution 3 of this recipe, the java.util.Calendar class is demonstrated as one successor for obtaining much of this information. The Calendar class was introduced in JDK 1.1, at which time many of the Date methods were deprecated. As you can see from solution 3, the Calendar class contains all the same functionality that is included in the Date class, except the Calendar class is much more flexible. The Calendar class is actually a class that contains methods that are used for converting between a specific time and date, and manipulating the calendar in various ways. The Calendar, as demonstrated in solution 3, is one such class that extends the Calendar class and therefore provides this functionality. The Calendar class has gained a few new methods in Java 8. The new methods in java.util.Calendar are listed in Table 4-6.

Table 4-6. *New Methods for java.util.Calendar in Java 8*

Method Name	Description
getAvailableCalendarTypes()	Returns unmodifiable set containing all supported calendar types.
getCalendarType()	Returns the calendar type of this calendar.
toInstant()	Converts to an instant.

For some applications, the Date class will work fine. For instance, the Date class can be useful when working with timestamps. However, if the application requires detailed manipulation of dates and times then it is advisable to use a LocalDateTime or the Calendar class, which both include all the functionality of the Date class and more features as well. All solutions to this recipe are technically sound; choose the one that best suits the needs of your application.

4-12. Obtaining a Machine Timestamp

Problem

You need to obtain a machine-based timestamp from the system.

Solution

Utilize an Instant class, which represents the start of a nanosecond on the timeline based on machine time. In the following example, an Instant is used to obtain the system timestamp. The Instant is also utilized in other scenarios, such as when calculating different dates based on the Instant.

```
public static void instants(){
        Instant timestamp = Instant.now();
        System.out.println("The current timestamp: " + timestamp);
```

```
//Now minus three days
Instant minusThree = timestamp.minus(3, ChronoUnit.DAYS);
System.out.println("Now minus three days:" + minusThree);

ZonedDateTime atZone = timestamp.atZone(ZoneId.of("GMT"));
System.out.println(atZone);

Instant yesterday = Instant.now().minus(24, ChronoUnit.HOURS);
System.out.println("Yesterday: " + yesterday);
}
```

Here is the result:

```
The current timestamp: 2015-11-28T16:21:42.197Z
Now minus three days:2015-11-25T16:21:42.197Z
2015-11-28T16:21:42.197Z[GMT]
Yesterday: 2015-11-27T16:21:42.273Z
```

How It Works

The Date-Time API introduces a new class named Instant, which represents the start of a nanosecond on the timeline in machine-based time. Being based on machine time, the value for an Instant counts from the EPOCH (January 1, 1970 00:00:00Z). Any values prior to the EPOCH are negative, and after the EPOCH the values are positive. The Instant class is perfect for obtaining a machine timestamp, as it includes all pertinent date and time information to the nanosecond.

An Instant class is static and immutable, so to obtain the current timestamp, the now() method can be called. Doing so returns a copy of the current Instant. The Instant also includes conversion and calculation methods, each returning copies of the Instant or other types. In the solution, the now() method returns the current timestamp, and then a couple of examples follow, showing how to perform calculations and obtain information on the Instant.

The Instant is an important new feature in Java 8, as it makes it easy to work with current time and date data. The other date and time classes, such as LocalDateTime, are useful as well. However, the Instant is the most accurate timestamp as it's based on nanosecond accuracy.

4-13. Converting Dates and Times Based on the Time Zone

Problem

The application you are developing has the potential to be utilized throughout the world. In some areas of the application, static dates and times need to be displayed, rather than the system date and time. In such cases, those static dates and times need to be converted to suit the particular time zone in which the application user is currently residing.

Solution

The Date-Time API provides the proper utilities for working with time zone data via the Time Zone and Offset classes. In the following scenario, suppose that the application is working with reservations for rental vehicles. You could rent a vehicle in one time zone and return it in another. The following lines of code demonstrate how to print out an individual's reservation in such a scenario. The following method, named scheduleReport, accepts LocalDateTime objects representing check-in and check-out date/time, along with ZoneIds for each. This method could be used by an airline to print time-zone information for a particular flight.

```
public static void scheduleReport(LocalDateTime checkOut, ZoneId checkOutZone,
                         LocalDateTime checkIn, ZoneId checkInZone){

    ZonedDateTime beginTrip = ZonedDateTime.of(checkOut, checkOutZone);
    System.out.println("Trip Begins: " + beginTrip);

    // Get the rules of the check out time zone
    ZoneRules checkOutZoneRules = checkOutZone.getRules();
    System.out.println("Checkout Time Zone Rules: " + checkOutZoneRules);

    //If the trip took 4 days
    ZonedDateTime beginPlus = beginTrip.plusDays(4);
    System.out.println("Four Days Later: " + beginPlus);

    // End of trip in starting time zone
    ZonedDateTime endTripOriginalZone = ZonedDateTime.of(checkIn, checkOutZone);
    ZonedDateTime endTrip = ZonedDateTime.of(checkIn, checkInZone);
    int diff = endTripOriginalZone.compareTo(endTrip);
    String diffStr = (diff >= 0) ? "NO":"YES";
    System.out.println("End trip date/time in original zone: " + endTripOriginalZone);
    System.out.println("End trip date/time in check-in zone: " + endTrip );
    System.out.println("Original Zone Time is less than new zone time? " +
            diffStr );
    ZoneId checkOutZoneId = beginTrip.getZone();
    ZoneOffset checkOutOffset = beginTrip.getOffset();
    ZoneId checkInZoneId = endTrip.getZone();
    ZoneOffset checkInOffset = endTrip.getOffset();

    System.out.println("Check out zone and offset: " + checkOutZoneId + checkOutOffset);
    System.out.println("Check in zone and offset: " + checkInZoneId +  checkInOffset);

}
```

Here is the result:

```
Trip Begins: 2015-12-13T13:00-05:00[US/Eastern]
Checkout Time Zone Rules: ZoneRules[currentStandardOffset=-05:00]
Four Days Later: 2015-12-17T13:00-05:00[US/Eastern]
End trip date/time in original zone: 2015-12-18T10:00-05:00[US/Eastern]
End trip date/time in check-in zone: 2015-12-18T10:00-07:00[US/Mountain]
Original Zone Time is less than new zone time? YES
Check out zone and offset: US/Eastern-05:00
Check in zone and offset: US/Mountain-07:00
```

How It Works

Time zones add yet another challenge for developers, and the Java Date-Time API provides an easy facet for working with them. The Date-Time API includes a `java.time.zone` package, which contains a number of classes that can assist in working with time zone data. These classes provide support for time zone rules, data, and resulting gaps and overlaps in the local timeline that are typically the result of daylight savings conversions. The classes that make up the zone package are outlined in Table 4-7.

Table 4-7. *Time Zone Classes*

Class Name	Description
ZoneId	Specifies zone identifier and is used for conversions.
ZoneOffset	Specifies a time zone offset from Greenwich/UTC time.
ZonedDateTime	A date-time object that also handles the time zone data with time zone offset from Greenwich/UTC time.
ZoneRules	Rules defining how a zone offset varies for a specified time zone.
ZoneRulesProvider	Provider of time zone rules to a particular system.
ZoneOffsetTransition	Transition between two offsets by a discontinuity in the local timeline.
ZoneOffsetTransitionRule	Rules expressing how to create a transition.

Starting with the most fundamental time zone class, `ZoneId`, each time zone contains a particular time zone identifier. This identifier can be useful for assigning a particular time zone to a date-time. In the solution, the `ZoneId` is used to calculate any differences between two time zones. `ZoneId` identifies the rules that should be used for converting, based on a particular offset, either fixed or geographical region-based. For more details on `ZoneId`, see the documentation at `http://docs.oracle.com/javase/9/docs/api/java/time/ZonedDateTime.html`.

`ZonedDateTime` is an immutable class that is utilized for working with date-time and time zone data together. This class represents an object, much like `LocalDateTime`, that includes the `ZoneId`. It can be used to express all facets of a date, including year, month, day, hours, minutes, seconds, nanos, and time zone. The class contains a bevy of methods that are useful for performing calculations, conversions, and so on. For brevity, the methods that are contained in `ZonedDateTime` are not listed here, but you can read about each of them in the documentation at `http://docs.oracle.com/javase/9/docs/api/java/time/ZonedDateTime.html`.

`ZoneOffset` specifies a time zone offset from Greenwich/UTC time. You can find the offset for a particular time zone by invoking the `ZonedDateTime.getOffset()` method. The `ZoneOffset` class includes methods that make it easy to break down an offset into different time units. For instance, the `getTotalSeconds()` method returns the total of hours, minutes, and seconds fields as a single offset that can be added to a time. Refer to the online documentation for more information at `http://docs.oracle.com/javase/9/docs/api/java/time/ZoneOffset.html`.

There are many rules that can be defined for determining how zone offset varies for a single time zone. The `ZoneRules` class is used to define these rules for a zone. For instance, `ZoneRules` can be called on to specify or determine if daylight savings time is a factor. An `Instant` or `LocalDateTime` can also be passed to `ZoneRules` methods such as `getOffset()` and `getTransition()` to return `ZoneOffset` or `ZoneOffsetTransition`. For more information on `ZoneRules`, refer to the online documentation at `http://docs.oracle.com/javase/9/docs/api/java/time/zone/ZoneRules.html`.

Another time zone class that is used often is `ZoneOffsetTransition`. This class models the transition between the spring and autumn offsets as a result of daylight savings time changes. It is used to determine if there is a gap between transitions, obtaining the duration of a transition, and so on. For more information on

ZoneOffsetTransition, see the online documentation at http://docs.oracle.com/javase/9/docs/api/java/time/zone/ZoneOffsetTransition.html.

ZoneRulesProvider, ZoneOffsetTransitionRule, and other classes are typically not utilized as often as others for working with dates and time zones. These classes are useful for managing configuration of time zone rules and transitions.

■ **Note**   The classes within the java.time.zone package are significant, in that there are a multitude of methods that can be invoked on each class. This recipe provides a primer for getting started, with only the basics of time zone usage. For more detailed information, see the online documentation.

4-14. Comparing Two Dates

Problem

You want to determine if one date is greater than another.

Solution

Utilize one of the compareTo() methods that are part of the Date-Time API classes. In the following solution, two LocalDate objects are compared and an appropriate message is displayed.

```
public static void compareDates(LocalDate ldt1,
            LocalDate ldt2) {
        int comparison = ldt1.compareTo(ldt2);
        if (comparison > 0) {
            System.out.println(ldt1 + " is larger than " + ldt2);
        } else if (comparison < 0) {
            System.out.println(ldt1 + " is smaller than " + ldt2);
        } else {
            System.out.println(ldt1 + " is equal to " + ldt2);
        }

    }
```

Similarly, there are convenience methods for use when performing date comparison. Specifically, the methods isAfter(), isBefore(), and isEqual() can be used to compare in the same manner as compareTo(), as seen in the following listing.

```
public static void compareDates2(LocalDate ldt1, LocalDate ldt2){
    if(ldt1.isAfter(ldt2)){
        System.out.println(ldt1 + " is after " + ldt2);
    } else if (ldt1.isBefore(ldt2)){
        System.out.println(ldt1 + " is before " + ldt2);
    } else if (ldt1.isEqual(ldt2)){
        System.out.println(ldt1 + " is equal to " + ldt2);
    }
}
```

How It Works

Many of the Date-Time API classes contain a method that is used to compare two different date-time objects. In the solution to this example, the LocalDate.compareTo() method is used to determine if one LocalDate object is greater than another. The compareTo() method returns a negative int value if the first LocalDate is greater than the second, a zero if they are equal, and a positive number if the second LocalDate is greater than the first.

Each of the date-time classes that contain a compareTo() has the same outcome. That is, an int value is returned indicating if the first object is greater than, less than, or equal to the second. Each of the classes that contains the compareTo() method is listed here:

- Duration
- LocalDate
- LocalDateTime
- LocalTime
- Instant
- MonthDay
- OffsetDateTime
- OffsetTime
- Year
- YearMonth
- ZoneOffset

As seen in the second listing, the isAfter(), isBefore(), and isEqual() methods can also be used for comparison purposes. These methods return a boolean to indicate the comparison results. While the outcome of these methods can be used to perform date comparison in much the same way as compareTo(), they can make code a bit easier to read.

4-15. Finding the Interval Between Dates and Times

Problem

You need to determine how many hours, days, weeks, months, or years have elapsed between two dates or times.

Solution 1

Utilize the Date-Time API to determine the difference between two dates. Specifically, make use of the Period class to determine the period of time, in days, between two dates. The following example demonstrates how to obtain the interval of days, months, and years between two dates.

▨ **Note** This example shows the difference in days, months, and years, but not the cumulative days or months between two dates. To determine the total cumulative days, months, and years between two dates, read on for solutions #2 and #3.

```
LocalDate anniversary = LocalDate.of(2000, Month.NOVEMBER, 11);
LocalDate today = LocalDate.now();
Period period = Period.between(anniversary, today);
System.out.println("Number of Days Difference: " +  period.getDays());
System.out.println("Number of Months Difference: " + period.getMonths());
System.out.println("Number of Years Difference: " + period.getYears());
```

Here is the result:

```
Number of Days Difference: 16
Number of Months Difference: 1
Number of Years Difference: 13
```

Solution 2

Use the java.util.concurrent.TimeUnit enum to perform calculations between given dates. Using this enum, you can obtain the integer values for days, hours, microseconds, milliseconds, minutes, nanoseconds, and seconds. Doing so will allow you to perform the necessary calculations.

```
// Obtain two instances of the Calendar class
Calendar cal1 = Calendar.getInstance();
Calendar cal2 = Calendar.getInstance();

// Set the date to 01/01/2010:12:00
cal2.set(2010,0,1,12,0);
Date date1 = cal2.getTime();
System.out.println(date1);

long mill = Math.abs(cal1.getTimeInMillis() - date1.getTime());
// Convert to hours
long hours = TimeUnit.MILLISECONDS.toHours(mill);
// Convert to days
Long days = TimeUnit.HOURS.toDays(hours);
String diff = String.format("%d hour(s) %d min(s)", hours,
TimeUnit.MILLISECONDS.toMinutes(mill) - TimeUnit.HOURS.toMinutes(hours));
System.out.println(diff);

diff = String.format("%d days", days);
System.out.println(diff);

// Divide the number of days by seven for the weeks
int weeks = days.intValue()/7;
diff = String.format("%d weeks", weeks);
System.out.println(diff);
```

The output of this code will be formatted to display Strings of text that indicate the differences between the current date and the Date object that is created.

Solution 3

To determine the total cumulative difference in days, months, years, or other time unit, use the ChronoUnit class. The following code demonstrates how to utilize the ChronoUnit class to determine the number of days and years between two dates.

```
LocalDate anniversary = LocalDate.of(2000, Month.NOVEMBER, 11);
LocalDate today = LocalDate.now();
long yearsBetween = ChronoUnit.YEARS.between(anniversary, today);
System.out.println("Years between dates: " + yearsBetween);

long daysBetween = ChronoUnit.DAYS.between(anniversary, today);
System.out.println("Days between dates:" + daysBetween);
```

Here are the results:

```
Years between dates: 13
Days between dates:4794
```

How It Works

As with most programmatic techniques, there is more than one way to perform date calculations with Java. The Date-Time API introduced in Java 8 includes a few new techniques for determining time intervals. The Period class is used to determine the period of difference between two units for specified objects. To obtain a Period between two date-time objects, call the Period.between() method, passing the two date-time objects for which you'd like to obtain the Period. The Period has a number of methods that can be used to break down the intervals into different units. For instance, the number of days in the Period of the two date-time objects can be obtained using the getDays() method. Similarly, the getMonths() and getYears() methods can be called to return the number of months or years in the Period.

The Date-Time API also includes a ChronoUnit Enum that can be used to work with calendar systems other than ISO, providing unit-based access to manipulate date and time. Each of the unit values within the Enum contains a number of methods for performing manipulations. One such method is between(), which returns a single unit of time only in the specified unit between the two given date-time objects. In the solution, it is used to return years and days using ChronoUnit.YEARS.between() and ChronoUnit.DAYS.between(), respectively.

One of the most useful techniques is to perform calculations based on the given date's time in milliseconds. This provides the most accurate calculation because it works on the time at a very small interval: milliseconds. The current time in milliseconds can be obtained from a Calendar object by calling the getTimeInMillis() method against it. Likewise, a Date object will return its value represented in milliseconds by calling the getTime() method. As you can see from the solution to this recipe, the first math that is performed is the difference between the given dates in milliseconds. Obtaining that value and then taking its absolute value will provide the base that is needed to perform the date calculations. In order to obtain the absolute value of a number, use the abs() method that is contained in the java.lang.Math class, shown in the following line of code:

```
long mill = Math.abs(cal1. getTimeInMillis() - date1.getTime());
```

The absolute value will be returned in long format. The TimeUnit enum can be used in order to obtain different conversions of the date. It contains a number of static enum constant values that represent different time intervals, similar to those of a Calendar object. Those values are displayed here.

■ **Note**   An *enum type* is a type whose fields consist of a fixed set of constant values. Enum types were welcomed to the Java language in release 1.5.

- DAYS
- HOURS
- MICROSECONDS
- MILLISECONDS
- MINUTES
- NANOSECONDS
- SECONDS

The values speak for themselves with regard to the conversion interval they represent. By calling conversion methods against these enums, long values representing the duration between two dates can be converted. As you can see in the solution to this recipe, first the time unit is established using the enum and then a conversion call is made against that time unit. Take, for instance, the following conversion. First, the time unit of TimeUnit.MILLISECONDS is established. Second, the toHours() method is called against it and a long value that is represented by the mill field is passed as an argument:

```
TimeUnit.MILLISECONDS.toHours(mill)
```

This code can be translated in English as follows: "The contents of the field mill are represented in milliseconds; convert those contents into hours." The result of this call will be the conversion of the value within the mill field into hours. By stacking the calls to TimeUnit, more precise conversions can be made. For instance, the following code converts the contents of the mill field into hours and then into days:

```
TimeUnit.HOURS.toDays(TimeUnit.MILLISECONDS.toHours(mill))
```

Again, the English translation can be read as, "The contents of the field mill are represented in milliseconds. Convert those contents into hours. Next, convert those hours into days."

TimeUnit can make time interval conversion very precise. Combining the precision of the TimeUnit conversions along with mathematics will allow you to convert the difference of two dates into just about any time interval.

4-16. Obtaining Date-Time from a Specified String

Problem

You want to parse a String into a date-time object.

Solution

Utilize the parse() method of a temporal date-time class to parse a String using a predefined or custom format. The following lines of code demonstrate how to parse a String into a date or date-time object using variations of the parse() method.

```
// Parse a String to form a Date-Time object
LocalDate ld = LocalDate.parse("2014-12-28");
LocalDateTime ldt = LocalDateTime.parse("2014-12-28T08:44:00");
System.out.println("Parsed Date: " + ld);
System.out.println("Parsed Date-Time: " + ldt);

// Using a different Parser
LocalDate ld2 = LocalDate.parse("2014-12-28", DateTimeFormatter.ISO_DATE);
System.out.println("Different Parser: " + ld2);

// Custom Parser
String input = "12/28/2013";
try {
    DateTimeFormatter formatter = DateTimeFormatter.ofPattern("MM/dd/yyyy");
    LocalDate ld3 = LocalDate.parse(input, formatter);
    System.out.println("Custom Parsed Date: " + ld3);
} catch (DateTimeParseException ex){
    System.out.println("Not parsable: " + ex);
}
```

Here is the result:

```
Parsed Date: 2014-12-28
Parsed Date-Time: 2014-12-28T08:44
Different Parser: 2014-12-28
Custom Parsed Date: 2014-12-28
```

How It Works

The temporal classes of the Date-Time API include a parse() method, which can be used to parse a given input String using a specified format. By default, the parse() method will format based on the target object's default DateTimeFormatter. For example, to parse the String "2014-01-01", the default LocalDate.parse() method can be called.

```
LocalDate date = LocalDate.parse("2014-01-01");
```

However, another DateTimeFormatter can be specified as a second argument to the parse() method. DateTimeFormatter is a final class used for formatting and printing dates and times. It contains a number of built-in formatters that can be specified to coerce Strings into date-time objects. For example, to parse based on the standard ISO_DATE format without offset, call DateTimeFormatter.ISO_DATE, as demonstrated in the solution to this recipe. For more information regarding DateTimeFormatter, see the online documentation at http://docs.oracle.com/javase/9/docs/api/java/time/format/DateTimeFormatter.html.

Oftentimes, it is necessary to parse Strings of text into date-time objects. Such tasks are made easy with the parse() method being built into many of the core date-time classes.

4-17. Formatting Dates for Display

Problem

Dates need to be displayed by your application using a specific format. You want to define that format once and apply it to all dates that need to be displayed.

Solution 1

Utilize the DateTimeFormatter class, part of the Date-Time API, to format dates and times according to the pattern you want to use. The DateTimeFormatter class includes an ofPattern() method, which accepts a String pattern argument to designate the desired pattern. Each of the temporal date-time classes includes a format() method, which accepts a DateTimeFormatter and returns the String-based format of the target date-time object. In the following lines of code, the DateTimeFormatter is demonstrated:

```
DateTimeFormatter dateFormatter = DateTimeFormatter.ofPattern("MMMM dd yyyy");

LocalDateTime now = LocalDateTime.now();
String output = now.format(dateFormatter);
System.out.println(output);

DateTimeFormatter dateFormatter2 = DateTimeFormatter.ofPattern("MM/dd/YY HH:mm:ss");
String output2 = now.format(dateFormatter2);
System.out.println(output2);

DateTimeFormatter dateFormatter3 = DateTimeFormatter.ofPattern("hh 'o''clock' a, zzzz");
ZonedDateTime zdt = ZonedDateTime.now();
String output3 = zdt.format(dateFormatter3);
System.out.println(output3);
```

Here is the result:

```
December 28 2013
12/28/13 10:44:06
10 o'clock AM, Central Standard Time
```

Solution 2

Use the java.util.Calendar class to obtain the date that you require and then format that date using the java.text.SimpleDateFormat class. The following example demonstrates the use of the SimpleDateFormat class:

```
// Create new calendar
Calendar cal = Calendar.getInstance();

// Create instance of SimpleDateFormat class using pattern
SimpleDateFormat dateFormatter1 = new SimpleDateFormat("MMMMM dd yyyy");
String result = null;
```

```
result = dateFormatter1.format(cal.getTime());
System.out.println(result);

dateFormatter1.applyPattern("MM/dd/YY hh:mm:ss");
result = dateFormatter1.format(cal.getTime());
System.out.println(result);

dateFormatter1.applyPattern("hh 'o''clock' a, zzzz");
result = dateFormatter1.format(cal.getTime());
System.out.println(result);
```

Running this example would yield the following result:

```
June 22 2011
06/22/11 06:24:41
06 o'clock AM, Central Daylight Time
```

As you can see from the results, the `DateTimeFormatter` and `SimpleDateFormat` classes make it easy to convert a date into just about any format.

How It Works

Date formatting is a common concern when it comes to any program. People like to see their dates in a certain format for different situations. The Java language contains a couple of handy utilities for proper formatting of date-time data. Specifically, the newer API includes the `DateTimeFormatter` class, and previous editions of Java SE include the `SimpleDateFormat` class, each of which can come in handy for performing formatting processes.

The `DateTimeFormatter` class is a final class that has the primary purpose of printing and formatting date-time objects. To obtain a `DateTimeFormatter` that can be applied to objects, call the `DateTimeFormatter.ofPattern()` method, passing the String-based pattern that represents the desired output. Table 4-8 lists the different pattern characters that can be used within a String-based pattern. The resulting `DateTimeFormatter` can then be applied to any temporal date-time object by calling the object's `format()` method and passing the `DateTimeFormatter` as an argument. The result will be the date-time object formatted according to the specified template pattern.

Table 4-8. *Pattern Characters*

Character	Description
G	Era
y	Year
Y	Week year
M	Month in year
w	Week in year
W	Week in month
D	Day in year
d	Day in month

(*continued*)

Table 4-8. (*continued*)

Character	Description
F	Day of week in month
E	Name of day in week
u	Number of day in week
a	AM/PM
H	Hour in day (0–23)
k	Hour in day (1–24)
K	Hour in AM/PM (0–11)
h	Hour in AM/PM (1–12)
m	Minute in hour
s	Second in minute
S	Millisecond
z	General time zone
Z	RFC 822 time zone
X	ISO 8601 time zone

The SimpleDateFormat class was created in previous editions of Java, so you don't have to perform manual translations for a given date.

■ **Note**   Different date formats are used within different locales, and the SimpleDateFormat class facilitates locale-specific formatting.

To use the class, an instance must be instantiated either by passing a String-based pattern as an argument to the constructor or by passing no argument to the constructor at all. The String-based pattern provides a template that should be applied to the given date and then a String representing the date in the given pattern style is returned. A pattern consists of a number of different characters strung together. Table 4-8 shows the different characters that can be used within a pattern.

Any of the pattern characters can be placed together in a String and then passed to the SimpleDateFormat class. If the class is instantiated without passing a pattern, the pattern can be applied later using the class's applyPattern() method. The applyPattern() method also comes in handy when you want to change the pattern of an instantiated SimpleDateFormat object, as seen in the solution to this recipe. The following excerpts of code demonstrate the application of a pattern:

```
SimpleDateFormat dateFormatter1 = new SimpleDateFormat("MMMMM dd yyyy");
dateFormatter1.applyPattern("MM/dd/YY hh:mm:ss");
```

Once a pattern has been applied to a SimpleDateFormat object, a long value representing time can be passed to the SimpleDateFormat object's format() method. The format() method will return the given date\time formatted using the pattern that was applied. The String-based result can then be used however your application requires.

4-18. Writing Readable Numeric Literals

Problem

Some of the numeric literals in your application are rather long and you want to make it easier to tell how large a number is at a glance.

Solution

Use underscores in place of commas or decimals in larger numbers in order to make them more readable. The following code shows some examples of making your numeric literals more readable by using underscores in place of commas:

```
int million = 1_000_000;
int billion = 1_000_000_000;
float ten_pct = 1_0f;
double exp = 1_234_56.78_9e2;
```

▓ **Note**   Decimal point values will automatically default to a double value, unless a trailing "f" is used to indicate that the value is a float.

How It Works

Sometimes working with large numbers can become cumbersome and difficult to read. Since the release of Java 7, underscores can now be used with numeric literals in order to make code a bit easier to read. The underscores can appear anywhere between digits in a numeric literal. This allows for the use of underscores in place of commas or spaces to separate the digits and make them easier to read.

▓ **Note**   Underscores cannot be placed at the beginning or end of a number, adjacent to a decimal point or floating-point literal, prior to an *F* or *L* suffix, or in positions where a String of digits is expected.

4-19. Declaring Binary Literals

Problem

You are working on an application that requires the declaration of binary numbers.

Solution

Make use of binary literals to make your code readable. The following code segment demonstrates the use of binary literals:

```
int bin1 = 0b1100;
short bin2 = 0B010101;
short bin3 = (short) 0b1001100110011001;
System.out.println(bin1);
System.out.println(bin2);
System.out.println(bin3);
```

This will result in the following output:

```
12
21
-26215
```

How It Works

Binary literals became part of the Java language with the release of Java 7. The types byte, short, int, and long can be expressed using the binary number system. This feature can help to make binary numbers easier to recognize in code. In order to use the binary format, simply prefix the number with 0b or 0B.

Summary

Numbers and dates play an integral role in most applications. The Java language provides a bevy of classes that can be used to work with different kinds of numbers, and format them to fit most situations. This chapter reviewed some techniques that can be used for rounding and formatting numbers, as well as generating random values. A Date and Time package was introduced with the release of Java 8, bringing a refreshing, easy to use API for obtaining and working with dates. This chapter covered the basics of the new Date and Time package, and much more is covered online: http://docs.oracle.com/javase/tutorial/datetime/.

CHAPTER 5

Object-Oriented Java

Programming languages have changed a great deal since the first days of application development. Back in the day, procedural languages were state of the art; as a matter of fact, there are still thousands of COBOL and other procedural applications in use today. As time went on, coding became more efficient, and reuse, encapsulation, abstraction, and other object-oriented characteristics became fundamental keys to application development. As languages evolved, they began to incorporate the idea of using objects within programs. The Lisp language introduced some object-oriented techniques as early as the 1970s, but true object-oriented programming did not take off in full blast until the 1990s.

Object-oriented programs consist of many different pieces of code that all work together in unison. Rather than write a program that contains a long list of statements and commands, an object-oriented philosophy is to break functionality into separate organized objects. Each of the objects contains functionality that pertains to it, and as the objects are pieced together they can be used to develop sophisticated solutions. Programming techniques such as using methods to encapsulate functionality and reusing the functionality of another class began to catch on as people noticed that object orientation equated to productivity.

In this chapter, we touch upon some of the key object-oriented features of the Java language. From the basic recipes covering access modifiers, to the advanced recipes that deal with inner classes, this chapter contains recipes that will help you understand Java's object-oriented methodologies.

5-1. Controlling Access to Members of a Class

Problem

You want to create members of a class that are not accessible from any other class.

Solution

Create `private` instance members rather than making them available to other classes (`public` or `protected`). For instance, suppose you are creating an application that will be used to manage a team of players for a sport. You create a class named `Player` that will be used to represent a player on the team. You do not want the fields for that class to be accessible from any other class. The following code demonstrates the declaration of some instance members, making them accessible only from within the class in which they were defined.

```
private String firstName = null;
private String lastName = null;
private String position = null;
private int status = -1;
```

© Josh Juneau 2017
J. Juneau, *Java 9 Recipes*, DOI 10.1007/978-1-4842-1976-8_5

How It Works

To designate a class member as private, prefix its declaration or signature using the private keyword. The private access modifier is used to hide members of a class so that outside classes cannot access them. Any members of a class that are marked as private will be available only to other members of the same class. Any outside class will not be able to access fields or methods designated as private, and an Integrated Development Envionment (IDE) that uses code completion will not be able to see them.

As mentioned in the solution to this recipe, there are three different access modifiers that can be used when declaring members of a class. Those modifiers are public, protected, and private. Members that are declared as public are available for any other class. Those that are declared as protected are available for any other class within the same package. It is best to declare public or protected only those class members that need to be directly accessed from another class. Hiding members of a class using the private access modifier helps to enforce better object orientation.

5-2. Making Private Fields Accessible to Other Classes

Problem

You would like to create private instance members so that outside classes cannot access them directly. However, you would also like to make those private members accessible in a controlled manner.

Solution

Encapsulate the private fields by making getters and setters to access them. The following code demonstrates the declaration of a private field, followed by accessor (getter) and mutator (setter) methods that can be used to obtain or set the value of that field from an outside class:

```
private String firstName = null;
/**
 * @return the firstName
 */
public String getFirstName() {
 return firstName;
}

/**
 * @param firstName the firstName to set
 */
public void setFirstName(String firstName) {
    this.firstName = firstName;
}
```

The getFirstName() method can be used by an outside class to obtain the value of the firstName field. Likewise, the setFirstName(String firstName) method can be used by an outside class to set the value of the firstName field.

How It Works

Oftentimes when fields are marked as private within a class, they still need to be made accessible to outside classes for the purpose of setting or retrieving their value. Why not just work with the fields directly and make them public then? It is not good programming practice to work directly with fields of other classes because by using accessors (getters) and mutators (setters), access can be granted in a controlled fashion. By not coding directly against members of another class, you also help to decouple the code, which helps to ensure that if an object changes, others that depend upon it are not adversely affected. As you can see from the example in the solution to this recipe, hiding fields and working with public methods to access those fields is fairly easy. Simply create two methods; one is used to obtain the value of the private field, the "getter" or accessor method. And the other is used to set the value of the private field, the "setter" or mutator method. In the solution to this recipe, the getter is used to return the unaltered value that is contained within the private field. Similarly, the setter is used to set the value of the private field by accepting an argument that is of the same data type as the private field and then setting the value of the private field to the value of the argument.

The class that is using the getters or setters for access to the fields does not know any details behind the methods. For instance, a getter or setter method could contain more functionality, if required. Furthermore, the details of these methods can be changed without altering any code that accesses them.

■ **Note**   Using getters and setters does not completely decouple code. In fact, many people argue that using getters and setters is not a good programming practice. Objects that use the accessor methods still need to know the type of the instance field they are working against. That being said, getters and setters are a standard technique for providing external access to private instance fields of an object. To make the use of accessor methods in a more object-oriented manner, declare them within interfaces and code against the interface rather than the object itself. For more information regarding interfaces, refer to Recipe 5-6.

5-3. Creating a Class with a Single Instance

Problem

You would like to create a class for which only one instance can exist in the entire application, so that all application users interact with the same instance of that class.

Solution 1

Create the class using the Singleton pattern. A class implementing the Singleton pattern allows for only one instance of the class and provides a single point of access to the instance. Suppose that you wanted to create a Statistics class that would be used for calculating the statistics for each team and player within an organized sport. It does not make sense to have multiple instances of this class within the application, so you want to create the Statistics class as a Singleton in order to prevent multiple instances from being generated. The following class represents the Singleton pattern:

```
package org.java9recipes.chapter5.recipe5_03;

import java.util.ArrayList;
import java.util.List;
import java.io.Serializable;

public class Statistics implements Serializable {

// Definition for the class instance
private static volatile Statistics instance = new Statistics();
```

```
private List teams = new ArrayList();

/**
 * Constructor has been made private so that outside classes do not have
 * access to instantiate more instances of Statistics.
 */
private Statistics(){
}

/**
 * Accessor for the statistics class.  Only allows for one instance of the
 * class to be created.
 * @return
 */
public static Statistics getInstance(){

    return instance;
}

/**
 * @return the teams
 */
public List getTeams() {
    return teams;
}

/**
 * @param teams the teams to set
 */
public void setTeams(List teams) {
    this.teams = teams;
}
protected Object readResolve(){
        return instance;
    }
}
```

If another class attempts to create an instance of this class, it will use the getInstance() accessor method to obtain the Singleton instance. It is important to note that the solution code demonstrates eager instantiation, which means that the instance will be instantiated when the Singleton is loaded. For lazy instantiation, which will be instantiated upon the first request, you must take care to synchronize the getInstance() method to make it thread-safe. The following code demonstrates an example of lazy instantiation:

```
public static Statistics getInstance(){
    synchronized(Statistics.class){
        if (instance == null){
            instance = new Statistics();
        }
    }
    return instance;
}
```

Solution 2

First, create an enum and declare a single element named INSTANCE within it. Next, declare other fields within the enum that you can use to store the values that are required for use by your application. The following enum represents a Singleton that will provide the same abilities as solution 1:

```java
import java.util.ArrayList;
import java.util.List;

public enum StatisticsSingleton {
    INSTANCE;

    private List teams = new ArrayList();

    /**
     * @return the teams
     */
    public List getTeams() {
        return teams;
    }

    /**
     * @param teams the teams to set
     */
    public void setTeams(List teams) {
        this.teams = teams;
    }
}
```

▓ **Note**   There is a test class within the recipe5_03 package that you can use to work with the enum Singleton solution.

How It Works

The Singleton pattern is used to create classes that cannot be instantiated by any other class. This can be useful when you only want one instance of a class to be used for the entire application. The Singleton pattern can be applied to a class by following three steps. First, make the constructor of the class private so that no outside class can instantiate it. Next, define a private static volatile field that will represent an instance of the class. The volatile keyword guarantees each thread uses the same instance. Create an instance of the class and assign it to the field. In the solution to this recipe, the class name is Statistics, and the field definition is as follows:

```java
private static volatile Statistics instance = new Statistics();
```

Lastly, implement an accessor method called getInstance() that simply returns the instance field. The following code demonstrates such an accessor method:

```java
public static Statistics getInstance(){
    return instance;
}
```

To use the Singleton from another class, call the Singleton's getInstance() method. This will return an instance of the class. The following code shows an example of another class obtaining an instance to the Statistics Singleton that was defined in solution 1 to this recipe.

```
Statistics statistics = Statistics.getInstance();
List teams = statistics.getTeams();
```

Any class that calls the getInstance() method of the class will obtain the same instance. Therefore, the fields contained within the Singleton have the same value for every call to getInstance() within the entire application.

What happens if the Singleton is serialized and then deserialized? This situation may cause another instance of the object to be returned upon deserialization. To prevent this issue from occurring, be sure to implement the readResolve() method, as demonstrated in solution 1. This method is called when the object is deserialized, and simply returning the instance ensures that another instance is not generated.

Solution 2 demonstrates a different way to create a Singleton, which is to use a Java enum rather than a class. Using this approach can be beneficial because an enum provides serialization, prohibits multiple instantiation, and allows you to work with code more concisely. In order to implement the enum Singleton, create an enum and declare an INSTANCE element. This is a static constant that will return an instance of the enum to classes that reference it. You can then add elements to the enum that can be used by other classes within the application to store values.

As with any programming solution, there is more than one way to do things. Some believe that the standard Singleton pattern demonstrated in solution 1 is not the most desirable solution. Others do not like the enum solution for different reasons. Both of them will work, although you may find that one works better than the other in certain circumstances.

5-4. Generating Instances of a Class

Problem

In one of your applications, you would like to provide the ability to generate instances of an object on the fly. Each instance of the object should be ready to use, and the object creator should not need to know about the details of the object creation.

Solution

Make use of the factory method pattern to instantiate instances of the class while abstracting the creation process from the object creator. Creating a factory will enable new instances of a class to be returned upon invocation. The following class represents a simple factory that returns a new instance of a Player subclass each time its createPlayer(String) method is called. The subclass of Player that is returned depends upon what String value is passed to the createPlayer method.

```java
public class PlayerFactory {

    public static Player createPlayer(String playerType){
        Player returnType;
        switch(playerType){
        case "GOALIE":
            returnType = new Goalie();
            break;
        case "LEFT":
            returnType = new LeftWing();
```

```
                break;
            case "RIGHT":
                returnType = new RightWing();
                break;
            case "CENTER":
                returnType = new Center();
                break;
            case "DEFENSE":
                returnType = new Defense();
                break;
            default:
                returnType = new AllPlayer();
            }
            return returnType;
        }
}
```

If a class wants to use the factory, it simply calls the static createPlayer method, passing a String value representing a new instance of Player. The following code represents one of the Player subclasses; the others could be very similar:

```
public class Goalie extends Player implements PlayerType {

    private int totalSaves;

    public Goalie(){
        this.setPosition("GOALIE");
    }

    /**
     * @return the totalSaves
     */
    public int getTotalSaves() {
        return totalSaves;
    }

    /**
     * @param totalSaves the totalSaves to set
     */
    public void setTotalSaves(int totalSaves) {
        this.totalSaves = totalSaves;
    }
}
```

Each of the other Player subclasses is very similar to the Goalie class. The most important code to note is the factory method, createPlayer, which can be used to create new instances of the Player class.

■ **Note**   To take this example one step further, you can limit the methods that can be accessed. You do this by returning objects of type PlayerType, and only declaring the accessible methods within that interface.

How It Works

Factories are used to generate objects. They are generally used to abstract the actual creation of an object from its creators. This can come in very handy when the creator does not need to know about the actual implementation details of generating the new object. The factory pattern can also be useful when controlled access to the creation of an object is required. In order to implement a factory, create a class that contains at least one method that is used for returning a newly created object.

In the solution to this recipe, the PlayerFactory class contains a method named createPlayer(String) that returns a newly created Player object. This method doesn't do anything special behind the scenes; it simply instantiates a new Player instance depending upon the String value that is passed to the method. Another object that has access to the PlayerFactory class can use createPlayer to return new Player objects without knowing how the object is created. While this does not hide much in the case of the createPlayer method, the PlayerFactory abstracts the details of which class is being instantiated so that the developer only has to worry about obtaining a new Player object.

The factory pattern is an effective way to control how objects are created and makes it easier to create objects of a certain type. Imagine if a constructor for an object took more than just a handful of arguments; creating new objects that require more than just a couple of arguments can become a hassle. Generating a factory to create those objects so that you do not have to hard-code all the arguments with each instantiation can make you much more productive!

5-5. Creating Reusable Objects

Problem

You would like to generate an object that could be used to represent something within your application. Furthermore, you would like to be able to reuse the object to represent multiple instances. For instance, suppose that you are creating an application that will be used for generating statistics and league information for different sports teams. In this case, you would like to create an object that could be used to represent a team.

Solution

Create a JavaBean that can be used to represent the object that you want to create. JavaBean objects provide the capability for object fields to be declared as private, and they also allow the attributes to be read and updated so that an object can be passed around and used within an application. This recipe demonstrates the creation of a JavaBean named Team. The Team object contains a few different fields that can contain information:

```java
public class Team implements TeamType {

    private List<Player> players;
    private String name = null;
    private String city = null;

    /**
     * @return the players
     */
    public List<Player> getPlayers() {
        return players;
    }
```

```java
/**
 * @param players the players to set
 */
public void setPlayers(List<Player> players) {
    this.players = players;
}

/**
 * @return the name
 */
public String getName() {
    return name;
}

/**
 * @param name the name to set
 */
public void setName(String name) {
    this.name = name;
}

/**
 * @return the city
 */
public String getCity() {
    return city;
}

/**
 * @param city the city to set
 */
public void setCity(String city) {
    this.city = city;
}

}
```

As you can see, the object in this solution contains three fields, and each of those fields is declared as private. However, each field has two accessor methods—getters and setters—that allow the fields to be indirectly accessible.

How It Works

The JavaBean is an object that is used to hold information so that it can be passed around and used within an application. One of the most important aspects of a JavaBean is that its fields are declared as private. This prohibits other classes from accessing the fields directly. Instead, each field should be encapsulated by methods defined to make them accessible to other classes. These methods must adhere to the following naming conventions:

- Methods used for accessing the field data should be named using a prefix of get, followed by the field name.

- Methods used for setting the field data should be named using a prefix of set, followed by the field name.

For instance, in the solution to this recipe, the Team object contains a field with the names of players. In order to access that field, a method should be declared that is named getPlayers. That method should return the data that is contained within the players field. Likewise, to populate the players field, a method should be declared that is named setPlayers. That method should accept an argument that is of the same type as the players field, and it should set the value of the players field equal to the argument. This can be seen in the following code:

```java
public List<Player> getPlayers() {
    return players;
}

void setPlayers(List<Player> players) {
    this.players = players;
}
```

JavaBeans can be used to populate lists of data, written to a database record, or for a myriad of other functions. Using JavaBeans makes code easier to read and maintain. It also helps to increase the likelihood of future code enhancements because very little code implementation is required. Another benefit of using JavaBeans is that most major IDEs will autocomplete the encapsulation of the fields for you.

5-6. Defining an Interface for a Class

Problem

You would like to create a set of method signatures and fields that can be used as a common template to expose the methods and fields that a class implements.

Solution

Generate a Java interface to declare each of the fields and methods that a class must implement. Such an interface can then be implemented by a class, and used to represent an object type. The following code is an interface that is used to declare the methods that must be implemented by the Team object:

```java
public interface TeamType {

    void setPlayers(List<Player> players);
    void setName(String name);
    void setCity(String city);
    String getFullName();
}
```

All the methods in the interface are implicitly abstract. That is, only a method signature is provided. It is also possible to include static final field declarations in an interface.

How It Works

A Java interface is a construct that is used to define the structures, be it fields or methods that a class must implement. In most cases, interfaces do not include any method implementations; rather, they only include method signatures. Interfaces can include variables that are implicitly static and final.

■ **Note**   As of Java SE 8, it is possible for interfaces to contain method implementations. Such methods are known as *default methods.* See Recipe 5-7 for more details.

In the solution to this recipe, the interface does not include any constant field declarations. However, it includes four method signatures. All the method signatures have no access modifier specified because all declarations within an interface are implicitly `public`. Interfaces are used to expose a set of functionality; therefore, all methods exposed within an interface must be implicitly `public`. Any class that implements an interface must provide the implementation for any method signatures declared in the interface, with the exception of default methods and abstract classes (see Recipes 5-7 and 5-13 for more details), in which case an interface may leave the implementation for one of its subclasses.

While the Java language does not allow multiple inheritance, a Java class can implement multiple interfaces, allowing for a controlled form of multiple inheritance. Abstract classes can also implement interfaces. The following code demonstrates a class implementing an interface: the Team object declaration implements the TeamType interface.

```java
public class Team implements TeamType {

    private List<Player> players;
    private String name;
    private String city;

    /**
     * @return the players
     */
    public List<Player> getPlayers() {
        return players;
    }

    /**
     * @param players the players to set
     */
    public void setPlayers(List<Player> players) {
        this.players = players;
    }

    /**
     * @return the name
     */
    public String getName() {
        return name;
    }

    /**
     * @param name the name to set
     */
    public void setName(String name) {
        this.name = name;
    }
```

```java
    /**
     * @return the city
     */
    public String getCity() {
        return city;
    }

    /**
     * @param city the city to set
     */
    public void setCity(String city) {
        this.city = city;
    }

public String getFullName() {
        return this.name + " - " + this.city;
    }

}
```

Interfaces can be used to declare a type for an object. Any object that is declared to have an interface type must adhere to all the implementations declared in the interface, unless a default implementation exists. For instance, the following field declaration defines an object that contains all the properties that are declared within the TeamType interface:

```java
TeamType team;
```

Interfaces can also extend other interfaces (thus the same type of theory that is provided by multiple inheritance). However, because no method implementation is present in an interface, it is much safer to implement multiple interfaces in a Java class than it is to extend multiple classes in C++.

Interfaces are some of the single most important constructs of the Java language. They provide the interfaces between the user and the class implementations. Although it is possible to create entire applications without using interfaces, they help to promote object orientation and hide method implementations from other classes.

5-7. Modifying Interfaces Without Breaking Existing Code

Problem

You've got a utility class that implements an interface, and many different classes within the utility library implement that interface. Suppose that you want to add a new method to the utility class and make it available for use for other classes via its interface. However, if you change the interface, it will likely break some existing classes that already implement that interface.

Solution

Add the new method, along with its implementation, to the utility class interface as a default method. By doing so, each class that implements the interface will automatically gain use of the new method, and will not be forced to implement it since a default implementation exists. The following class interface contains a default method, which can be used by any class that implements the interface.

```java
public interface TeamType {

    List<Player> getPlayers();

    void setPlayers(List<Player> players);

    void setName(String name);

    void setCity(String city);

    String getFullName();

    default void listPlayers() {
        getPlayers().stream().forEach((player) -> {
            System.out.println(player.getFirstName() + " " + player.getLastName());
        });
    }

}
```

The interface TeamType contains a default method named listPlayers(). This method does not need to be implemented by any classes that implement TeamType since there is a default implementation contained within the interface.

How It Works

In previous releases of Java, interfaces could only contain method signatures and constant variables. It was not possible to define a method implementation within an interface. This works well in most cases, as interfaces are a construct that is meant to enforce type safety and abstract implementation details. However, in some circumstances, it is beneficial to allow interfaces to contain a default method implementation. For instance, if there are many classes that implement an existing interface, then lots of code can be broken if that interface were to be changed. This would create a situation where backward compatibility would not be possible. In such a case, it would make sense to place a default method implementation into an interface, rather than forcing all classes to implement a new method that is placed within the interface. This is the reason why default methods became a necessity, and were included in the Java 8 release.

To create a default method (a.k.a. "defender method") within an interface, use the keyword default within the method signature, and include a method implementation. An interface can contain zero or more default methods. In the solution to this recipe, the listPlayers() method is a default method within the TeamType interface, and any class implementing TeamType will automatically inherit the default implementation. Theoretically, any classes that implement TeamType would be completely unaffected by the addition of the listPlayers() default method. This enables one to alter an interface without breaking backward compatibility, which can be of great value.

▓ **Note** As of Java 9, it is possible to create a private method within an interface. The private method can only be used by default methods within the same interface. Therefore, if you have some code that repeats throughout two or more default methods, then that repeatable code can be encapsulated within the private method.

5-8. Constructing Instances of the Same Class with Different Values

Problem

Your application requires the ability to construct instances of the same object, but each object instance needs to contain different values, thereby creating different types of the same object.

Solution

Make use of the builder pattern in order to build different types of the same object using a step-by-step procedure. For instance, suppose that you are interested in creating the different teams for a sports league. Each of the teams must contain the same attributes, but the values for those attributes vary by team. So you create many objects of the same type, but each of the objects is unique. The following code demonstrates the builder pattern, which can be used to create the required teams.

First, you need to define a set of attributes that each team needs to contain. To do this, a Java interface should be created, containing the different attributes that need to be applied to each team object. The following is an example of such an interface:

```java
public interface TeamType {

    public void setPlayers(List<Player> players);
    public void setName(String name);
    public void setCity(String city);
    public String getFullName();

}
```

Next, define a class to represent a team. This class needs to implement the TeamType interface that was just created so that it will adhere to the format that is required to build a team:

```java
public class Team implements TeamType {

    private List<Player> players;
    private String name = null;
    private String city = null;
    private int wins = 0;
    private int losses = 0;
    private int ties = 0;

    /**
     * @return the players
     */
    public List<Player> getPlayers() {
        return players;
    }

    /**
     * @param players the players to set
     */
```

```java
    public void setPlayers(List<Player> players) {
        this.players = players;
    }

    /**
     * @return the name
     */
    public String getName() {
        return name;
    }

    /**
     * @param name the name to set
     */
    public void setName(String name) {
        this.name = name;
    }

    /**
     * @return the city
     */
    public String getCity() {
        return city;
    }

    /**
     * @param city the city to set
     */
    public void setCity(String city) {
        this.city = city;
    }

    public String getFullName(){
        return this.name + " - " + this.city;
    }

}
```

Now that the Team class has been defined, a builder needs to be created. The purpose of the builder object is to allow for a step-by-step creation of a team object. To abstract the details of building an object, a builder class interface should be created. The interface should define any of the methods that would be used to build the object as well as a method that will return a fully built object. In this case, the interface will define each of the methods needed to build a new Team object, and then the builder implementation will implement this interface.

```java
public interface TeamBuilder {
    public void buildPlayerList();
    public void buildNewTeam(String teamName);
    public void designateTeamCity(String city);
    public Team getTeam();

}
```

The following code demonstrates a builder class implementation. Although the following code would not create a custom player list, it contains all the features required to implement the builder pattern. The details of creating a more customized player list can be worked out later, probably by allowing the user to create players via a keyboard entry. Furthermore, the TeamBuilder interface could be used to implement teams for different sports. The following class is named HockeyTeamBuilder, but a similar class implementing TeamBuilder could be named FootballTeamBuilder, and so forth.

```java
public class HockeyTeamBuilder implements TeamBuilder {

    private Team team;

    public HockeyTeamBuilder(){
        this.team = new Team();
    }

    @Override
    public void buildPlayerList() {
        List players = new ArrayList();
        for(int x = 0; x <= 10; x++){
            players.add(PlayerFactory.getPlayer());
        }
        team.setPlayers(players);
    }

    @Override
    public void buildNewTeam(String teamName) {
        team.setName(teamName);
    }

    @Override
    public void designateTeamCity(String city){
        team.setCity(city);
    }

    public Team getTeam(){
        return this.team;
    }

}
```

Last, use the builder by calling upon the methods defined in its interface to create teams. The following code demonstrates how this builder could be used to create one team. You can use the Roster class within the sources for this recipe to test this code:

```java
public Team createTeam(String teamName, String city){
    TeamBuilder builder = new HockeyTeamBuilder();
    builder.buildNewTeam(teamName);
    builder.designateTeamCity(city);
    builder.buildPlayerList();
    return builder.getTeam();
}
```

114

CHAPTER 5 ▓ OBJECT-ORIENTED JAVA

Although this demonstration of the builder pattern is relatively short, it demonstrates how to hide implementation details of an object, thereby making objects easier to build. You do not need to know what the methods within the builder actually do; you only need to call upon them.

How It Works

The builder pattern provides a way to generate new instances of an object in a procedural fashion. It abstracts away the details of object creation, so the creator does not need to do any specific work in order to generate new instances. By breaking the work down into a series of steps, the builder pattern allows objects to implement its builder methods in different ways. Because the object creator only has access to the builder methods, it makes creation of different object types much easier.

There are a few classes and interfaces that are necessary for using the builder pattern. First, you need to define a class and its different attributes. As the solution to this recipe demonstrates, the class may follow the JavaBean pattern (see Recipe 5-5 for more details). By creating a JavaBean, you will be able to populate the object by using its setters and getters. Next, you should create an interface that can be used for accessing the setters of the object that you created. Each of the setter methods should be defined in the interface, and then the object itself should implement that interface. As seen in the solution, the Team object contains the following setters, and each of them is defined in the TeamType interface:

```
public void setPlayers(List<Player> players);
public void setName(String name);
public void setCity(String city);
```

In real life, a team will probably contain more attributes. For instance, you'd probably want to set up a mascot and a home stadium name and address. The code in this example can be thought of as abbreviated because it demonstrates the creation of a generic "team object" rather than show you all the code for creating a team that is true to life. Because the Team class implements these setters that are defined within the TeamType interface, the interface methods can be called upon to interact with the actual methods of the Team class.

After the object and its interface have been coded, the actual builder needs to be created. The builder consists of an interface and its implementation class. To start, you must define the methods that you want to have other classes call upon when building your object. For instance, in the solution to this recipe, the methods buildNewTeam(), designateTeamCity(), and buildPlayerList() are defined within the builder interface named TeamBuilder. When a class wants to build one of these objects later, it will only need to call upon these defined methods in order to do it. Next, define a builder class implementation. The implementation class will implement the methods defined within the builder interface, hiding all the details of those implementations from the object creator. In the solution to this recipe, the builder class, HockeyTeamBuilder, implements the TeamBuilder interface. When a class wants to create a new Team object then it simply instantiates a new builder class.

```
TeamBuilder builder = new HockeyTeamBuilder();
```

To populate the newly created class object, the builder methods are called upon it.

```
builder.buildNewTeam(teamName);
builder.designateTeamCity(city);
builder.buildPlayerList();
```

Using this technique provides a step-by-step creation for an object. The implementation details for building that object are hidden from the object creator. It would be easy enough for a different builder implementation to use the same TeamBuilder interface for building team objects for different types.

For instance, a builder implementation could be written for generating team objects for soccer, and another one could be defined for generating team objects for baseball. Each of the team object implementations would be different. However, both of them could implement the same interface—TeamBuilder—and the creator could simply call on the builder methods without caring about the details.

5-9. Interacting with a Class via Interfaces

Problem

You have created a class that implements an interface or class type. You would like to interact with the methods of that class by calling upon methods declared within the interface rather than working directly with the class.

Solution

Declare a field of the same type as an interface. You can then assign classes that implement the interface to the field you had declared and call upon the methods declared in the interface to perform work. In the following example, a field is declared to be of type TeamType. Using the same classes from Recipe 5-8, you can see that the class Team implements the TeamType interface. The field that is created in the following example holds a reference to a new Team object.

Because the Team class implements the TeamType interface, the methods that are exposed in the interface can be used:

```
TeamType team = new Team();
team.setName("Juneau Royals");
team.setCity("Chicago");
System.out.println(team.getFullName());
```

The resulting output:

```
Juneau Royals - Chicago
```

How It Works

Interfaces are useful for many reasons. Two of the most important use cases for interfaces are conformity and abstraction. Interfaces define a model, and any class that implements the interface must conform to that model. Therefore, if there is a constant defined within the interface, it will automatically be available for use in the class. If there is a method defined within the interface, then the class must implement that method, unless a default implementation has been defined (see Recipe 5-7). Interfaces provide a nice way to allow classes to conform to a standard.

Interfaces hide unnecessary information from any class that does not need to see it. Any method that is defined within the interface is made public and accessible to any class. As demonstrated in the solution to this recipe, an object was created and declared to be the type of an interface. The interface in the example, TeamType, only includes a small subset of methods that are available within the Team object. Therefore, the only methods that are accessible to any class working against an object that have been declared to be of TeamType are the ones that are defined within the interface. The class using this interface type does not have access to any of the other methods or constants, nor does it need to. Interfaces are a great way for hiding logic that does not need to be used by other classes. Another great side effect: A class that implements an interface can be changed and recompiled without affecting code that works against the interface. However, if an interface is changed, there could be an effect on any classes that implement it. Therefore, if the getFullName() method implementation changes, any class that is coded against the TeamType interface will not be affected because the interface is unchanged. The implementation will change behind the scenes, and any class working against the interface will just begin to use the new implementation without needing to know.

■ **Note**   In some cases, alterations of existing classes can cause code to break. This is more often the case when working with libraries. For instance, suppose a class implements an interface that is updated with a new method signature. All classes that implement that interface must now be updated to include an implementation of the new method, which is sometimes impossible within library classes in order to maintain backward compatibility. This is the main reason for the inclusion of default methods in Java 8; see Recipe 5-7 for more details.

Lastly, interfaces help to promote security. They hide implementation details of methods that are declared in an interface from any class that may call upon that method using the interface. As mentioned in the previous paragraph, if a class is calling the getFullName() method against the TeamType interface, it does not need to know the implementation details of that method as long as the result is returned as expected.

The older Enterprise JavaBean (EJB) model used interfaces for interacting with methods that performed database work. This model worked very well for hiding the details and logic that were not essential for use from other classes. Other frameworks use similar models, exposing functionality through Java interfaces. Interface use has proven to be a smart way to code software because it promotes reusability, flexibility, and security.

5-10. Making a Class Cloneable

Problem

You would like to enable a class to be cloned or copied by another class.

Solution

Implement the Cloneable interface within the class that you want to clone; then call that object's clone method to make a copy of it. The following code demonstrates how to make the Team class cloneable:

```
public class Team implements TeamType, Cloneable, Serializable {

    private String name;
    private String city;

    /**
     * @return the name
     */
    public String getName() {
        return name;
    }
```

```java
/**
 * @param name the name to set
 */
public void setName(String name) {
    this.name = name;
}

/**
 * @return the city
 */
public String getCity() {
    return city;
}

/**
 * @param city the city to set
 */
public void setCity(String city) {
    this.city = city;
}

public String getFullName() {
    return this.name + " - " + this.city;
}

/**
 * Overrides Object's clone method to create a deep copy
 *
 * @return
 */
@Override
public Team clone() {

    Team obj = null;
    try {
        ByteArrayOutputStream baos = new ByteArrayOutputStream();
        ObjectOutputStream oos = new ObjectOutputStream(baos);
        oos.writeObject(this);
        oos.close();

        ByteArrayInputStream bais = new ByteArrayInputStream(baos.toByteArray());
        ObjectInputStream ois = new ObjectInputStream(bais);
        obj = (Team) ois.readObject();
        ois.close();
    } catch (IOException e) {
        e.printStackTrace();
    } catch (ClassNotFoundException cnfe) {
        cnfe.printStackTrace();
    }
    return obj;
}
```

```java
/**
 * Overrides Object's clone method to create a shallow copy
 *
 * @return
 */
public Team shallowCopyClone() {

    try {
        return (Team) super.clone();
    } catch (CloneNotSupportedException ex) {
        return null;
    }
}

@Override
public boolean equals(Object obj) {

    if (this == obj) {
        return true;
    }
    if (obj instanceof Team) {
        Team other = (Team) obj;
        return other.getName().equals(this.getName())
                && other.getCity().equals(this.getCity());
    } else {
        return false;
    }

}
}
```

To make a deep copy of a Team object, the clone() method needs to be called against that object. To make a shallow copy of the object, the shallowCopyClone() method must be called. The following code demonstrates these techniques:

```java
Team team1 = new Team();
Team team2 = new Team();

team1.setCity("Boston");
team1.setName("Bandits");

team2.setCity("Chicago");
team2.setName("Wildcats");

Team team3 = team1;
Team team4 = team2.clone();

Team team5 = team1.shallowCopyClone();

System.out.println("Team 3:");
System.out.println(team3.getCity());
System.out.println(team3.getName());
```

```
System.out.println("Team 4:");
System.out.println(team4.getCity());
System.out.println(team4.getName());

// Teams move to different cities
team1.setCity("St. Louis");
team2.setCity("Orlando");

System.out.println("Team 3:");
System.out.println(team3.getCity());
System.out.println(team3.getName());

System.out.println("Team 4:");
System.out.println(team4.getCity());
System.out.println(team4.getName());

System.out.println("Team 5:");
System.out.println(team5.getCity());
System.out.println(team5.getName());

if (team1 == team3){
    System.out.println("team1 and team3 are equal");
} else {
    System.out.println("team1 and team3 are NOT equal");
}

if (team1 == team5){
    System.out.println("team1 and team5 are equal");
} else {
    System.out.println("team1 and team5 are NOT equal");
}
```

This code demonstrates how to make a clone of an object. The resulting output would be as follows.

```
Team 3:
Boston
Bandits
Team 4:
Chicago
Wildcats
Team 3:
St. Louis
Bandits
Team 4:
Chicago
Wildcats
Team 5:
Boston
Bandits
team1 and team3 are equal
team1 and team5 are NOT equal
```

How It Works

There are two different strategies that can be used to copy an object: shallow and deep copies. A *shallow copy* can be made that would copy the object without any of its contents or data. Rather, all the variables are passed by reference into the copied object. After a shallow copy of an object has been created, the objects within both the original object and its copy refer to the same data and memory. Thus, modifying the original object's contents will also modify the copied object. By default, calling the super.clone() method against an object performs a shallow copy. The shallowCopyClone() method in the solution to this recipe demonstrates this technique.

The second type of copy that can be made is known as a *deep copy*, which copies the object including all the contents. Therefore, each object refers to a different space in memory, and modifying one object will not affect the other. In the solution to this recipe, the difference between a deep and a shallow copy is demonstrated. First, team1 and team2 are created. Next, they are populated with some values. The team3 object is then set equal to the team1 object, and the team4 object is made a clone of the team2 object. When the values are changed within the team1 object, they are also changed in the team3 object because both object's contents refer to the same space in memory. This is an example of a shallow copy of an object. When the values are changed within the team2 object, they remain unchanged in the team4 object because each object has its own variables that refer to different spaces in memory. This is an example of a deep copy.

In order to make an exact copy of an object (deep copy), you must serialize the object so that it can be written to disk. The base Object class implements the clone() method. By default, the Object class's clone() method is protected. In order to make an object cloneable, it must implement the Cloneable interface and override the default clone() method. You can make a deep copy of an object by serializing it through a series of steps, such as writing the object to an output stream and then reading it back via an input stream. The steps shown in the clone() method of the solution to this recipe do just that. The object is written to a ByteArrayOutputStream and then read using a ByteArrayInputStream. Once that has occurred, the object has been serialized, which creates the deep copy. The clone() method in the solution to this recipe has been overridden so that it creates a deep copy.

Once these steps have been followed and an object implements Cloneable as well as overrides the default object clone() method, it is possible to clone the object. In order to make a deep copy of an object, simply call that object's overridden clone() method as seen in the solution. If one were to simply return Object from the clone() method, then there would need to be a typecast, as follows:

```
Team team4 = (Team) team2.clone();
```

Cloning objects is not very difficult, but a good understanding of the differences that can vary with object copies is important.

5-11. Comparing Objects

Problem

Your application requires the capability to compare two or more objects to see whether they are the same.

Solution 1

To determine whether the two object references point to the same object, make use of the == and != operators. The following solution demonstrates the comparison of two object references to determine whether they refer to the same object.

```
// Compare if two objects contain the same values
Team team1 = new Team();
Team team2 = new Team();

team1.setName("Jokers");
team1.setCity("Crazyville");

team2.setName("Jokers");
team2.setCity("Crazyville");

if (team1 == team2){
    System.out.println("These object references refer to the same object.");
} else {
    System.out.println("These object references do NOT refer to the same object.");
}

// Compare two objects to see if they refer to the same object
Team team3 = team1;
Team team4 = team1;

if (team3 == team4){
    System.out.println("These object references refer to the same object.");
} else {
    System.out.println("These object references do NOT refer to the same object.");
}
```

The results of running the code:

```
These object references do NOT refer to the same object.
These object references refer to the same object.
```

Solution 2

To determine whether the two objects contain the same values, use the equals() method. The object being compared must implement equals() and hashCode() in order for this solution to work properly. Following is the code for the Team class that overrides these two methods:

```
public class Team implements TeamType, Cloneable {

    private List<Player> players;
    private String name;
    private String city;
    // Used by the hashCode method for performance reasons
    private volatile int cachedHashCode = 0;

    /**
     * @return the players
     */
    public List<Player> getPlayers() {
        return players;
    }
```

```java
/**
 * @param players the players to set
 */
public void setPlayers(List<Player> players) {
    this.players = players;
}

/**
 * @return the name
 */
public String getName() {
    return name;
}

/**
 * @param name the name to set
 */
public void setName(String name) {
    this.name = name;
}

/**
 * @return the city
 */
public String getCity() {
    return city;
}

/**
 * @param city the city to set
 */
public void setCity(String city) {
    this.city = city;
}

public String getFullName() {
    return this.name + " - " + this.city;
}

/**
 * Overrides Object's clone method
 *
 * @return
 */
public Object clone() {

    try {
        return super.clone();
    } catch (CloneNotSupportedException ex) {
        return null;
    }
}
```

```java
    @Override
    public boolean equals(Object obj) {

        if (this == obj) {
            return true;
        }
        if (obj instanceof Team) {
            Team other = (Team) obj;
            return other.getName().equals(this.getName())
&& other.getCity().equals(this.getCity())
&& other.getPlayers().equals(this.getPlayers());
        } else {
            return false;
        }

    }

@Override
    public int hashCode() {
        int hashCode = cachedHashCode;
        if (hashCode == 0) {
            String concatStrings = name + city;
            if (players.size() > 0) {
                for (Player player : players) {
                    concatStrings = concatStrings
                            + player.getFirstName()
                            + player.getLastName()
                            + player.getPosition()
                            + String.valueOf(player.getStatus());

                }
            }
            hashCode = concatStrings.hashCode();
        }
        return hashCode;
    }
}
```

The following solution demonstrates the comparison of two objects that contain the same values.

```java
// Compare if two objects contain the same values
Team team1 = new Team();
Team team2 = new Team();

// Build Player List
Player newPlayer = new Player("Josh", "Juneau");
playerList.add(0, newPlayer);
newPlayer = new Player("Jonathan", "Gennick");
playerList.add(1, newPlayer);
newPlayer = new Player("Joe", "Blow");
playerList.add(1, newPlayer);
```

```
newPlayer = new Player("John", "Smith");
playerList.add(1, newPlayer);
 newPlayer = new Player("Paul", "Bunyan");
playerList.add(1, newPlayer);

team1.setName("Jokers");
team1.setCity("Crazyville");
team1.setPlayers(playerList);

team2.setName("Jokers");
team2.setCity("Crazyville");
team2.setPlayers(playerList);

if (team1.equals(team2)){
    System.out.println("These object references contain the same values.");
} else {
    System.out.println("These object references do NOT contain the same values.");
}
```

The results of running this code:

```
These object references do NOT refer to the same object.
These object references contain the same values.
These object references refer to the same object.
```

How It Works

The comparison operator (==) can be used to determine the equality of two objects. This equality does not pertain to the object values, but rather to the object references. Often an application is more concerned with the values of objects; in such cases, the equals() method is the preferred choice because it compares the values contained within the objects rather than the object references.

The comparison operator takes a look at the object reference and determines whether it points to the same object as the object reference that it is being compared against. If the two objects are equal, a Boolean true result will be returned; otherwise, a Boolean false result will be returned. In solution 1, the first comparison between the team1 object reference and the team2 object reference returns a false value because those two objects are separate in memory, even though they contain the same values. The second comparison in solution 1 between the team3 object reference and the team4 object reference returns a true value because both of those references refer to the team1 object.

The equals() method can be used to test whether two objects contain the same values. In order to use the equals() method for comparison, the object that is being compared should override the Object class equals()and hashCode() methods. The equals() method should implement a comparison against the values contained within the object that would yield a true comparison result. The following code is an example of an overridden equals() method that has been placed into the Team object:

```
@Override
public boolean equals(Object obj) {

    if (this == obj) {
        return true;
    }
    if (obj instanceof Team) {
```

```
        Team other = (Team) obj;
        return other.getName().equals(this.getName())
&& other.getCity().equals(this.getCity())
&& other.getPlayers().equals(this.getPlayers());
    } else {
        return false;
    }

}
```

As you can see, the overridden equals() method first checks to see whether the object that is passed as an argument is referencing the same object as the one that it is being compared against. If so, a true result is returned. If both objects are not referencing the same object in memory, the equals() method checks to see whether the fields are equal. In this case, any two Team objects that contain the same values within the name and city fields would be considered equal. Once the equals() method has been overridden, the comparison of the two objects can be performed, as demonstrated in solution 2 to this recipe.

The hashCode() method returns an int value that must consistently return the same integer. There are many ways in which to calculate the hashCode of an object. Perform a web search on the topic and you will find various techniques. One of the most basic ways to implement the hashCode() method is to concatenate all the object's variables into String format and then return the resulting String's hashCode(). It is a good idea to cache the value of the hashCode for later use because the initial calculation may take some time. The hashCode() method in solution 2 demonstrates this tactic.

Comparing Java objects can become confusing, considering that there are multiple ways to do it. If the comparison that you want to perform is against the object identity, use the comparison (==) operator. However, if you want to compare the values within the objects, or the state of the objects, then the equals() method is the way to go.

5-12. Extending the Functionality of a Class

Problem

One of your applications contains a class that you would like to use as a base for another class. You want your new class to contain the same functionality of this base class, but also include additional functionality.

Solution

Extend the functionality of the base class by using the extends keyword followed by the name of the class that you would like to extend. The following example shows two classes. The first class, named HockeyStick, represents a hockey stick object. It will be extended by the second class named WoodenStick. By doing so, the WoodenStick class will inherit all the properties and functionality contained within HockeyStick, with the exception of private variables and those that have the default access level. The WoodenStick class becomes a subclass of HockeyStick. First, let's take a look at the HockeyStick class, which contains the basic properties of a standard hockey stick:

```
public class HockeyStick {

    private int length;
    private boolean curved;
    private String material;
```

```java
    public HockeyStick(int length, boolean curved, String material){
        this.length = length;
        this.curved = curved;
        this.material = material;
    }

    /**
     * @return the length
     */
    public int getLength() {
        return length;
    }

    /**
     * @param length the length to set
     */
    public void setLength(int length) {
        this.length = length;
    }

    /**
     * @return the curved
     */
    public boolean isCurved() {
        return curved;
    }

    /**
     * @param curved the curved to set
     */
    public void setCurved(boolean curved) {
        this.curved = curved;
    }

    /**
     * @return the material
     */
    public String getMaterial() {
        return material;
    }

    /**
     * @param material the material to set
     */
    public void setMaterial(String material) {
        this.material = material;
    }

}
```

Next, look at the subclass of HockeyStick: a class named WoodenStick.

```java
public class WoodenStick extends HockeyStick {

    private static final String material = "WOOD";
    private int lie;
    private int flex;

    public WoodenStick(int length, boolean isCurved){
        super(length, isCurved, material);
    }

    public WoodenStick(int length, boolean isCurved, int lie, int flex){
        super(length, isCurved, material);
        this.lie = lie;
        this.flex = flex;
    }

    /**
     * @return the lie
     */
    public int getLie() {
        return lie;
    }

    /**
     * @param lie the lie to set
     */
    public void setLie(int lie) {
        this.lie = lie;
    }

    /**
     * @return the flex
     */
    public int getFlex() {
        return flex;
    }

    /**
     * @param flex the flex to set
     */
    public void setFlex(int flex) {
        this.flex = flex;
    }
}
```

▒ **Note**   In this example, we assume that there may be more than one type of HockeyStick. In this case, we extend HockeyStick to create a WoodenStick, but we may also extend HockeyStick to create other types of HockeyStick, such as AluminumStick or GraphiteStick.

How It Works

Object inheritance is a fundamental technique in any object-oriented language. Inheriting from a base class adds value because it allows code to become reusable in multiple places. This helps to make code management much easier. If a change is made in the base class, it will automatically be inherited in the child. On the other hand, if you had duplicate functionality scattered throughout your application, one minor change could mean that you would have to change code in many places. Object inheritance also makes it easy to designate a base class to one or more subclasses so that each class can contain similar fields and functionality.

The Java language allows a class to extend only one other class. This differs in concept from other languages such as C++, which contain multiple inheritance. Although some look at single class inheritance as a hindrance to the language, it was designed that way to add safety and ease of use to the language. When a subclass contains multiple superclasses, confusion can ensue.

5-13. Defining a Template for Classes to Extend

Problem

You would like to define a template that can be used to generate objects containing similar functionality.

Solution

Define an abstract class that contains fields and functionality that can be used in other classes. The abstract class can also include unimplemented methods, known as *abstract methods*, which will need to be implemented by a subclass of the abstract class. The following example demonstrates the concept of an abstract class. The abstract class in the example represents a team schedule, and it includes some basic field declarations and functionality that every team's schedule will need to use. The Schedule class is then extended by the TeamSchedule class, which will be used to implement specific functionality for each team. First, let's take a look at the abstract Schedule class:

```java
public abstract class Schedule {

    public String scheduleYear;
    public String teamName;

    public List<Team> teams;

    public Map<Team, LocalDate> gameMap;

    public Schedule(){}
```

```java
    public Schedule(String teamName){
        this.teamName = teamName;
    }

    abstract void calculateDaysPlayed(int month);

}
```

Next, the TeamSchedule extends the functionality of the abstract class.

```java
public class TeamSchedule extends Schedule {

    public TeamSchedule(String teamName) {
        super(teamName);
    }

    @Override
    void calculateDaysPlayed(int month) {
        int totalGamesPlayedInMonth = 0;
        for (Map.Entry<Team, LocalDate> entry : gameMap.entrySet()) {
            if (entry.getKey().equals(teamName)
                    && entry.getValue().getMonth().equals(month)) {
                totalGamesPlayedInMonth++;
            }
        }
        System.out.println("Games played in specified month: " + totalGamesPlayedInMonth);
    }

}
```

As you can see, the TeamSchedule class can use all the fields and methods that are contained within the abstract Schedule class. It also implements the abstract method that is contained within the Schedule class.

How It Works

Abstract classes are labeled as such, and they contain field declarations and methods that can be used within subclasses. What makes them different from a regular class is that they can contain abstract methods, which are method declarations with no implementation. The solution to this recipe contains an abstract method named calculateDaysPlayed(). Abstract classes may or may not contain abstract methods. They can contain fields and fully implemented methods as well. Abstract classes cannot be instantiated; other classes can only extend them. When a class extends an abstract class, it gains all the fields and functionality of the abstract class. However, any abstract methods that are declared within the abstract class must be implemented by the subclass.

You may wonder why the abstract class wouldn't just contain the implementation of the method so that it was available for all its subclasses to use. If you think about the concept, it makes perfect sense. One type of object may perform a task differently from another. Using an abstract method forces the class that is extending the abstract class to implement it, but it allows the ability to customize how it is implemented.

5-14. Increasing Class Encapsulation

Problem

One of your classes requires the use of another class's functionality. However, no other class requires the use of that same functionality. Rather than creating a separate class that includes this additional functionality, you'd like to generate an implementation that can only be used by the class that needs it, while placing the code in a logical location.

Solution

Create an *inner class* within the class that requires its functionality.

```java
import java.util.ArrayList;
import java.util.List;

/**
 * Inner class example. This example demonstrates how a team object could be
 * built using an inner class object.
 *
 * @author juneau
 */
public class TeamInner {

    private Player player;
    private List<Player> playerList;
    private int size = 4;

    /**
     * Inner class representing a Player object
     */
    class Player {

        private String firstName = null;
        private String lastName = null;
        private String position = null;
        private int status = -1;

        public Player() {
        }

        public Player(String position, int status) {
            this.position = position;
            this.status = status;
        }

        protected String playerStatus() {
            String returnValue = null;
```

```java
        switch (getStatus()) {
            case 0:
                returnValue = "ACTIVE";
                break;
            case 1:
                returnValue = "INACTIVE";
                break;
            case 2:
                returnValue = "INJURY";
                break;
            default:
                returnValue = "ON_BENCH";
                break;
        }

        return returnValue;
    }

    public String playerString() {
        return getFirstName() + " " + getLastName() + " - " + getPosition();
    }

    /**
     * @return the firstName
     */
    public String getFirstName() {
        return firstName;
    }

    /**
     * @param firstName the firstName to set
     */
    public void setFirstName(String firstName) {
        this.firstName = firstName;
    }

    /**
     * @return the lastName
     */
    public String getLastName() {
        return lastName;
    }

    /**
     * @param lastName the lastName to set
     */
    public void setLastName(String lastName) {
        this.lastName = lastName;
    }
```

```java
    /**
     * @return the position
     */
    public String getPosition() {
        return position;
    }

    /**
     * @param position the position to set
     */
    public void setPosition(String position) {
        this.position = position;
    }

    /**
     * @return the status
     */
    public int getStatus() {
        return status;
    }

    /**
     * @param status the status to set
     */
    public void setStatus(int status) {
        this.status = status;
    }

    @Override
    public String toString(){
        return this.firstName + " " + this.lastName + " - "+
                this.position + ": " + this.playerStatus();
    }
}

/**
 * Inner class that constructs the Player objects and adds them to an array
 * that was declared in the outer class;
 */
public TeamInner() {

    final int ACTIVE = 0;

    // In reality, this would probably read records from a database using
    // a loop...but for this example we will manually enter the player data.
    playerList = new ArrayList();
    playerList.add(constructPlayer("Josh", "Juneau", "Right Wing", ACTIVE));
    playerList.add(constructPlayer("Joe", "Blow", "Left Wing", ACTIVE));
    playerList.add(constructPlayer("John", "Smith", "Center", ACTIVE));
    playerList.add(constructPlayer("Bob","Coder", "Defense", ACTIVE));
    playerList.add(constructPlayer("Jonathan", "Gennick", "Goalie", ACTIVE));
}
```

133

```java
    public Player constructPlayer(String first, String last, String position, int status){
            Player player = new Player();
            player.firstName = first;
            player.lastName = last;
            player.position = position;
            player.status = status;
            return player;
    }

    public List<Player> getPlayerList() {
        return this.playerList;
    }

    public static void main(String[] args) {
TeamInner inner = new TeamInner();
        System.out.println("Team Roster");
        System.out.println("===========");
for(Player player:inner.getPlayerList()){
            System.out.println(player.playerString());
        }
    }
}
```

The result of running this code is a listing of the players on the team.

```
Team Roster
===========
Josh Juneau - Right Wing
Joe Blow - Left Wing
John Smith - Center
Bob Coder - Defense
Jonathan Gennick - Goalie
```

How It Works

Sometimes it is important to encapsulate functionality within a single class. Other times it does not make sense to include a separate class for functionality that is only used within one other class. Imagine that you are developing a GUI and you need to use a class to support functionality for one button. If there is no reusable code within that button class, it does not make sense to create a separate class and expose that functionality for other classes to use. Instead, it makes sense to encapsulate that class inside of the class that requires the functionality. This philosophy is one use case for inner classes (also known as *nested classes*).

An inner class is a class that is contained within another class. The inner class can be made public, private, or protected just like any other class. It can contain the same functionality as a normal class; the only difference is that the inner class is contained within an enclosing class, otherwise referred to as an *outer class*. The solution to this recipe demonstrates this technique. The class TeamInner contains one inner class named Player. The Player class is a JavaBean class that represents a Player object. As you can see, the

Player object has the capability to inherit functionality from its containing class, including its private fields. This is because inner classes contain an implicit reference to the outer class. It can also be accessed by the containing TeamInner class, as demonstrated within the constructPlayer() method:

```java
public Player constructPlayer(String first, String last, String position, int status){
        Player player = new Player();
        player.firstName = first;
        player.lastName = last;
        player.position = position;
        player.status = status;
        return player;
    }
```

Outer classes can instantiate an inner class as many times as needed. In the example, the constructPlayer() method could be called any number of times, instantiating a new instance of the inner class. However, when the outer class is instantiated, no instances of the inner class are instantiated. Similarly, when the outer class is no longer in use, all of the inner class instances are destroyed as well.

Inner classes can reference outer class methods by referring to the outer class and to the method(s) that it wants to call. The following line of code demonstrates such a reference using the same objects that are represented in the solution to this recipe. Suppose that the Player class needed to obtain the player list from the outer class; you would write something similar to the following:

```java
TeamInner.this.getPlayerList();
```

Although not very often used, classes other than the outside class can obtain access to a public inner class by using the following syntax:

```java
TeamInner outerClass = new TeamInner();
outerClass.player = outerClass.new Player();
```

Static inner classes are a bit different, in that they cannot directly reference any instance variables or methods of its enclosing class. The following is an example of a static inner class.

```java
public class StaticInnerExample {

    static String hello = "Hello";

    public static void sayHello(){
        System.out.println(hello);
    }

    static class InnerExample {
        String goodBye = "Good Bye";

        public void sayGoodBye(){
            System.out.println(this.goodBye);
        }
    }
}
```

```java
    public static void main (String[] args){
        StaticInnerExample.sayHello();
        StaticInnerExample.InnerExample inner =
                new StaticInnerExample.InnerExample();
        inner.sayGoodBye();
    }
}
```

Inner classes help to provide encapsulation of logic. Furthermore, they allow inheritance of `private` fields, which is not possible using a standard class.

Summary

Java is an object-oriented language. To harness the capabilities of the language, one must learn how to become proficient with object orientation. This chapter covered basics such as class creation and access modifiers. It also covered encapsulation, interfaces, and recipes to help developers take advantage of the power of object orientation.

CHAPTER 6

■ ■ ■

Lambda Expressions

There are very few means by which a new feature in an existing language can have a significant impact on the ecosystem. Lambda expressions for the Java language are one such significant new feature that has had an effect on many facets of the ecosystem. Simply defined, *lambda expressions* are a convenient way to create anonymous functions. They provide an easy way to create a single method interface using an expression or series of statements. Lambda expressions are built upon functional interfaces, which are interfaces that contain a single abstract method. They can be applied in many different contexts, ranging from simple anonymous functions to sorting and filtering Collections. Moreover, lambda expressions can be assigned to variables and then passed into other objects.

In this chapter, you will learn how to create lambda expressions, and you'll see many examples of how they can be applied in common scenarios. You'll also learn how to generate the building blocks for lambda expressions, so that you can construct applications to facilitate the use of them. The chapter will delve into the java.util.function package, which contains a bevy of useful functional interfaces that lambdas can implement. Lastly, you will see how to simplify certain types of lambda expressions into method references for a more concise approach.

After reading this chapter, you too will be able to see the impact that lambda expressions have had on the Java language. They modernize the language by allowing developers to be more productive, and opening new possibilities in many areas. Lambda expressions turned the page on Java, bringing the language into a new light, with the likes of other languages that have had similar constructs for some time. Those languages helped to pave the way for lambda expressions in the Java language, and there is no doubt that lambda expressions will continue to pave the way for many elegant solutions.

6-1. Writing a Simple Lambda Expression

Problem

You want to encapsulate a piece of functionality that prints out a simple message.

Solution

Write a lambda expression that accepts a single parameter that contains the message you want to print, and implement the printing functionality within the lambda. In the following example, a functional interface, HelloType, is implemented via a lambda expression and assigned to the variable helloLambda. Lastly, the lambda is invoked, printing the message.

```java
public class HelloLambda {

    /**
     * Functional Interface
     */
    public interface HelloType {
        /**
         * Function that will be implemented within the lambda
         * @param text
         */
        void hello(String text);
    }

    public static void main(String[] args){
        // Create the lambda, passing a parameter named "text" to the
        // hello() method, returning the String.  The lambda is assigned
        // to the helloLambda variable.
        HelloType helloLambda =
                (String text) -> {System.out.println("Hello " + text);};

        // Invoke the method call
        helloLambda.hello("Lambda");
    }
}
```

Results:

```
Hello Lambda
```

How It Works

A lambda expression is an anonymous block of code that encapsulates an expression or a series of statements and returns a result. Lambda expressions are also known as *closures* in some other languages. They can accept zero or more parameters, any of which can be passed with or without type specification since the type can be automatically derived from the context.

The syntax of a lambda expression includes an argument list, a new character to the language known as the "arrow token" (->), and a body. The following model represents the structure of a lambda expression:

```
(argument list) -> { body }
```

The argument list for a lambda expression can include zero or more arguments. If there are no arguments, then an empty set of parentheses can be used. If there is only one argument, then no parentheses are required. Each argument on the list can include an optional type specification. If the type of the argument is left off, then the type is derived from the current context.

In the solution for this recipe, curly braces surround the body of a block, which contains more than a single expression. The curly braces are not necessary if the body consists of a single expression. The curly braces in the solution could have been left off, but they've been included for ease of readability. The body is simply evaluated and then returned. If the body of the lambda is an expression and not a statement, a return is implicit. On the contrary, if the body includes more than one statement, a return must be specified, and it marks return of control back to the caller.

The following code demonstrates a lambda expression that does not contain any arguments:

```
StringReturn msg = () ->  "This is a test";
```

The StringReturn interface, which is in use by the lambda, is also known as a functional interface.

```
/**
 * Functional interface returning a String
 */
 interface StringReturn {
    String returnMessage();
}
```

Let's take a look at how this lambda expression works. In the previous listing, an object of type StringReturn is returned from the lambda expression. The empty set of parentheses denotes that there are no arguments being passed to the expression. The return is implicit, and the String "This is a test" is returned from the lambda expression to the invoker. The expression in the example is assigned to a variable identified by msg. Assume that the functional interface, StringReturn, contains an abstract method identified as returnMessage(), as seen in the code. In this case, the msg.returnMessage() method can be invoked to return the String.

The body of a lambda expression can contain any Java construct that an ordinary method may contain. For instance, suppose a String were passed as an argument to a lambda expression, and you wanted to return some value that is dependent upon the String argument. The following lambda expression body contains a block of code, which returns an int, based upon the String value of the argument passed into the expression.

```
ActionCode code = (codestr) -> {
    switch(codestr){
        case "ACTIVE": return 0;
        case "INACTIVE": return 1;
        default:
            return -1;
    }
};
```

In this example, the ActionCode functional interface is used to infer the return type of the lambda expression. For clarification, let's see what the interface looks like.

```
interface ActionCode{
    int returnCode(String codestr);
}
```

The code implies that the lambda expression implements the returnCode method, which is defined within the ActionCode interface. This method accepts a String argument (codestr), which is passed to the lambda expression, returning an int. Therefore, from this example you can see that a lambda can encapsulate the functionality of a method body.

While it is possible for code written in the Java language to move forward without the use of lambda expressions, they are an important addition that greatly improves overall maintainability, readability, and developer productivity. Lambda expressions are an evolutionary change to the Java language, as they are another step toward modernization of the language, and help keep it in sync with other languages.

■ **Note**　A lambda expression can contain any statement that an ordinary Java method contains. However, the `continue` and `break` keywords are not legal within the body of a lambda expression.

6-2. Enabling the Use of Lambda Expressions

Problem

You are interested in authoring code that enables the use of lambda expressions.

Solution 1

Write custom functional interfaces that can be implemented via lambda expressions. All lambda expressions implement a functional interface, a.k.a. an interface with a single abstract method declaration. The following lines of code demonstrate a functional interface that contains a single method declaration.

```
@FunctionalInterface
interface ReverseType {
    String reverse(String text);
}
```

The functional interface contains a single abstract method declaration, identified as `String reverse(String text)`. The following code, which contains a lambda expression, demonstrates how to implement ReverseType.

```
ReverseType newText = (testText) -> {
    String tempStr = "";
    for (String part : testText.split(" ")) {
        tempStr += new StringBuilder(part).reverse().toString() + " ";
    }
    return tempStr;
};
```

The following code could be used to invoke the lambda expression:

```
System.out.println(newText.reverse("HELLO WORLD"));
```

Result:

```
OLLEH DLROW
```

Solution 2

Use a functional interface that is contained within the `java.util.function` package to implement a lambda expression to suit the needs of the application. The following example uses the Function<T,R> interface to perform the same task as the one demonstrated in solution 1. This example accepts a String argument and returns a String result.

```
Function<String,String> newText2 = (testText) -> {
    String tempStr = "";
    for (String part : testText.split(" ")) {
        tempStr += new StringBuilder(part).reverse().toString() + " ";
    }
    return tempStr;
};
```

This lambda expression is assigned to the variable newText2, which is of type Function<String,String>. Therefore, a String is passed as an argument, and a String is to be returned from the lambda expression. The functional interface of Function<T,R> contains an abstract method declaration of apply(). To invoke this lambda expression, use the following syntax:

```
System.out.println(newText2.apply("WORLD"));
```

Result:

```
DLROW
```

How It Works

A basic building block of a lambda expression is the functional interface. A *functional interface* is a standard Java interface that contains a single abstract method declaration and provides a target type for lambda expressions and method references. A functional interface may contain default method implementations as well, but only one abstract declaration. The abstract method is then implicitly implemented by the lambda expression. As a result, the lambda expression can be assigned to a variable of the same type as the functional interface. The method can be called upon from the assigned variable at a later time, thus invoking the lambda expression. Following this pattern, lambda expressions are method implementations that can be invoked by name. They can also be passed as arguments to other methods (see Recipe 6-9).

■ **Note**   The functional interface in solution 1 contains the @FunctionalInterface annotation. This can be placed on a functional interface to catch compiler-level errors, but it has no effect on the interface itself.

At this point you may be wondering if you will be required to develop a functional interface for each situation that may be suitable for use with a lambda expression. This is not the case, as there are many functional interfaces already available for use. Some examples include java.lang.Runnable, javafx.event.EventHandler, and java.util.Comparator. See some of the other recipes in this chapter for examples using lambda expressions that implement these interfaces. However, there are also many more functional interfaces that are less specific, enabling them to be tailored to suit the needs of a particular requirement. The java.util.function package contains a number of functional interfaces that can be useful when implementing lambda expressions. The functional interfaces contained within the package are utilized throughout the JDK, and they can also be utilized in developer applications. Table 6-1 lists the functional interfaces that are contained within the java.util.function package, along with a description of each. Note that a Predicate test that returns a Boolean value.

Table 6-1. *Functional Interfaces Contained in* `java.util.function`

Interface	Implementation Description
`BiConsumer<T,U>`	Function operation that accepts two input arguments and returns no result.
`BiFunction<T,U,R>`	Function that accepts two arguments and produces a result.
`BinaryOperator<T>`	Function operation upon two operands of the same type, producing a result of the same type as the operands.
`BiPredicate<T,U>`	Predicate of two arguments. Returns a Boolean value.
`BooleanSupplier`	Supplier of Boolean-valued results.
`Consumer<T>`	Function operation that accepts a single input argument and returns no result.
`DoubleBinaryOperator`	Function operation upon two `double`-valued operands and producing a `double`-valued result.
`DoubleConsumer`	Function operation that accepts a single `double`-valued argument and returns no result.
`DoubleFunction<R>`	Function that accepts a `double`-valued argument and produces a result.
`DoublePredicate`	Predicate of one `double`-valued argument.
`DoubleSupplier`	Supplier of `double`-valued results.
`DoubleToIntFunction`	Function that accepts a `double`-valued argument and produces an `int`-valued result.
`DoubleToLongFunction`	Function that accepts a `double`-valued argument and produces a `long`-valued result.
`DoubleUnaryOperator`	Function operation on a single `double`-valued operand that produces a `double`-valued result.
`Function<T,R>`	Function that accepts one argument and produces a result.
`IntBinaryOperator`	Function operation upon two `int`-valued operands and producing an `int`-valued result.
`IntConsumer`	Function operation that accepts a single `int`-valued argument and returns no result.
`IntFunction<R>`	Function that accepts an `int`-valued argument and produces a result.
`IntPredicate`	Predicate of one `int`-valued argument.
`IntSupplier`	Supplier of `int`-valued results.
`IntToDoubleFunction`	Function that accepts an `int`-valued argument and produces a `double`-valued result.
`IntToLongFunction`	Function that accepts an `int`-valued argument and produces a `long`-valued result.
`IntUnaryOperator`	Function operation on a single `int`-valued operand that produces an `int`-valued result.
`LongBinaryOperator`	Function operation upon two `long`-valued operands and producing a `long`-valued result.
`LongConsumer`	Function operation that accepts a single `long`-valued argument and returns no result.

(continued)

Table 6-1. (*continued*)

Interface	Implementation Description
LongFunction<R>	Function that accepts a long-valued argument and produces a result.
LongPredicate	Predicate of one long-valued argument.
LongSupplier	Supplier of long-valued results.
LongToDoubleFunction	Function that accepts a long-valued argument and produces a double-valued result.
LongToIntFunction	Function that accepts a long-valued argument and produces an int-valued result.
LongUnaryOperator	Function operation on a single long-valued operand that produces a long-valued result.
ObjDoubleConsumer<T>	Function operation that accepts an object-valued and a double-valued argument and returns no result.
ObjIntConsumer<T>	Function operation that accepts an object-valued and an int-valued argument and returns no result.
ObjLongConsumer<T>	Function operation that accepts an object-valued and a long-valued argument and returns no result.
Predicate<T>	Predicate of one argument.
Supplier<T>	Supplier of results.
ToDoubleBiFunction<T,U>	Function that accepts two arguments and produces a double-valued result.
ToDoubleFunction<T>	Function that produces a double-valued result.
ToIntBiFunction<T,U>	Function that accepts two arguments and produces an int-valued result.
ToIntFunction<T>	Function that produces an int-valued result.
ToLongBiFunction<T,U>	Function that accepts two arguments and produces a long-valued result.
ToLongFunction<T>	Function that produces a long-valued result.
UnaryOperator<T>	Function operation on a single operand that produces a result of the same type as its operand.

Utilizing functional interfaces contained within the java.util.function package can greatly reduce the amount of code you need to write. Not only are the functional interfaces geared toward tasks that are performed a high percentage of the time, but they are also written using generics, allowing them to be applied in many different contexts. Solution 2 demonstrates such an example, whereby the Function<T,R> interface is used to implement a lambda expression that accepts a String argument and returns a String result.

6-3. Invoking Existing Methods by Name

Problem

You are developing a lambda expression that merely invokes a method that already exists in the object being passed to the lambda. Rather than write out the entire ceremony to invoke the method, you'd like to utilize a minimal amount of code.

Solution

Use a method reference, rather than writing a lambda expression, to call an existing method. In the following scenario, the Player object contains a static method named compareByGoals(), which takes two Player objects and compares the number of goals each contains. It then returns an integer representing the outcome. For all intents and purposes, the compareByGoals() method is the same as a Comparator.

```
public class Player {

    private String firstName = null;
    private String lastName = null;
    private String position = null;
    private int status = -1;
    private int goals;

    public Player(){

    }

    public Player(String position, int status){
        this.position = position;
        this.status = status;
    }

    public String findPlayerStatus(int status){
        String returnValue = null;

        switch(status){
                case 0:
                        returnValue = "ACTIVE";
                case 1:
                        returnValue = "INACTIVE";
                case 2:
                        returnValue = "INJURY";
                default:
                        returnValue = "ON_BENCH";
        }

        return returnValue;
    }

    public String playerString(){
        return getFirstName() + " " + getLastName() + " - " + getPosition();
    }

    // ** getters and setters removed for brevity **

    /**
     * Returns a positive integer if Player A has more goals than Player B
     * Returns a negative integer if Player A has fewer goals than Player B
     * Returns a zero if both Player A and Player B have the same number of goals
```

```
    */
    public static int compareByGoal(Player a, Player b){
        int eval;
        if(a.getGoals() > b.getGoals()){
            eval = 1;
        } else if (a.getGoals() < b.getGoals()){
            eval = -1;
        } else {
            eval = 0;
        }
        return eval;
    }

}
```

The Player.compareByGoal() method could be used to sort an array of Player objects. To do so, pass an array of Player objects (Player[]) to the Arrays.sort() method as the first argument, and pass a method reference Player::compareByGoal as the second argument. The result will be a sorted list (in ascending order) of Player objects by number of goals. The following line of code shows how to accomplish this task.

```
Arrays.sort(teamArray, Player::compareByGoal);
```

How It Works

Consider that your lambda expression is going to invoke a single method by name, perhaps returning a result. If a lambda expression fits this scenario, it is a prime candidate for use with a method reference. A method reference is a simplified form of a lambda expression, which specifies the class name or instance name, followed by the method to be called in the following format:

```
<class or instance name>::<methodName>
```

The double colon (::) operator specifies a method reference. Since a method reference is a simplified lambda method, it must implement a functional interface, and the abstract method within the interface must have the same argument list and return type as the method being referenced. Any arguments are subsequently derived from the context of the method reference. For instance, consider the same scenario as the solution, whereby you wanted to sort an array of Player objects by calling upon the Player.compareByGoal() method to perform goal comparisons. The following code could be written to enable this functionality via a lambda expression:

```
Arrays.sort(teamArray, (p1, p2) -> Player.compareByGoal(p1,p2));
```

In this code, the array is passed as the first argument to Arrays.sort(), and the second argument is a lambda expression that passes two Player objects to the Player.compareByGoal() method. The lambda expression uses the functional interface Comparator<Player>.compare, which utilizes the (Player, Player) parameter list. The compareByGoal() method contains that same parameter list. Likewise, the return type of compareByGoal() matches the return type within the functional interface. Therefore, the parameter list does not need to be specified in the listing; it can be inferred from the context of the method reference Player::compareByGoal instead.

There are four different types of method references, and Table 6-2 lists each of them.

Table 6-2. *Method Reference Types*

Type	Description
Static Reference	Uses a static method of an object.
Instance Reference	Uses an instance method of an object.
Arbitrary Object Method	Used on an arbitrary object of a particular type, rather than a particular object.
Constructor Reference	Used to generate a new object by invoking a constructor with the new keyword.

In the solution, the static method reference type is demonstrated since compareByGoal() is a static method within the Player class. It is possible to invoke a method of an object instance using an instance reference. Consider the following class, which contains a nonstatic method for comparing goals within Player objects.

```
public class PlayerUtility {

    public int compareByGoal(Player a, Player b){
        int eval;
        if(a.getGoals() > b.getGoals()){
            eval = 1;
        } else if (a.getGoals() < b.getGoals()){
            eval = -1;
        } else {
            eval = 0;
        }
        return eval;
    }
}
```

This class can be instantiated, and the new instance can be used to reference the compareByGoals() method, similarly to the technique that was used in the solution to this recipe.

```
Player[] teamArray2 = team.toArray(new Player[team.size()]);
PlayerUtility utility = new PlayerUtility();
Arrays.sort(teamArray2, utility::compareByGoal);
```

Suppose that your application contained a list of an arbitrary type, and you wanted to apply a method to each of the objects in that list. Method references can be used in this scenario, given the object contains methods that are candidates for use via reference. In the following example, the Arrays.sort() method is applied to a list of int values, and a method reference is used to apply the Integer compare() method to the elements within the list. Thus, the resulting list will be sorted, and the method reference automatically passes the int arguments and returns the int comparison.

```
Integer[] ints = {3,5,7,8,51,33,1};
Arrays.sort(ints, Integer::compare);
```

The last type of method reference can be utilized for referencing the constructor of an object. This type of method reference can be especially useful when creating new objects via a factory. Let's take a look at an example. Suppose that the Player object contained the following constructor:

```java
public Player(String position, int status, String first, String last){
    this.position = position;
    this.status = status;
    this.firstName = first;
    this.lastName = last;
}
```

You are interested in generating Player objects on the fly, using a factory pattern. The following code demonstrates an example of a functional interface containing a single abstract method named createPlayer(), which accepts the same argument list as the constructor for the Player object.

```java
public interface PlayerFactory {
    Player createPlayer(String position,
                        int status,
                        String firstName,
                        String lastName);
}
```

The factory can now be created from a lambda expression, and then called upon to create new objects. The following lines of code demonstrate:

```java
PlayerFactory player1 = Player::new;
Player newPlayer = player1.createPlayer("CENTER", 0, "Constructor", "Referenceson");
```

Method references were perhaps one of the most significant new features introduced in Java 8, although lambda expressions have more use cases. They provide an easy-to-read, simplified technique for generating lambda expressions, and they'll work in most cases where a lambda is merely invoking a single method by name.

6-4. Sorting with Fewer Lines of Code

Problem

Your application contains a list of Player objects for a hockey team. You would like to sort that list of Players by those who scored the most goals, and you would like to do so using terse, yet easy-to-follow code.

■ **Note**   The solutions in this recipe utilize Collections and sorting. To learn more about Collections, refer to Chapter 7.

Solution 1

Create a Comparator using an accessor method contained within the Player object for the field by which you want to sort. In this case, you want to sort by number of goals, so the Comparator should be based upon the value returned from getGoals(). The following line of code shows how to create such a Comparator using the Comparator interface and a method reference.

```
Comparator<Player> byGoals = Comparator.comparing(Player::getGoals);
```

Next, utilize a mixture of lambda expressions and streams (See Chapter 7 for full details on streams), along with the forEach() method, to apply the specified sort on the list of Player objects. In the following line of code, a stream is obtained from the list, which allows you to apply functional-style operations on the elements.

```
team.stream().sorted(byGoals)
             .map(p -> p.getFirstName() + " " + p.getLastName() + " - "
                    + p.getGoals())
             .forEach(element -> System.out.println(element));
```

Assuming that the List referenced by team is loaded with Player objects, the previous line of code will first sort that list by the Player goals, and then print out information on each object.

Results from the sort:

```
== Sort by Number of Goals ==
Jonathan Gennick - 1
Josh Juneau - 5
Steve Adams - 7
Duke Java - 15
Bob Smith - 18
```

Solution 2

Utilize the Collections.sort() method, passing the list to sort along with a lambda expression that performs the comparisons on the list elements. The following code demonstrates how to accomplish this task using the Collections.sort() technique.

```
Collections.sort(team, (p1, p2)
        -> p1.getLastName().compareTo(p2.getLastName()));
team.stream().forEach((p) -> {
    System.out.println(p.getLastName());
});
```

Result:

```
== Sort by Last Name ==
Adams
Gennick
Java
Juneau
Smith
```

▨ **Note**   This solution could be further simplified if the `Player` class included a comparison method. If this were the case, a method reference could be used, rather than implementing a lambda expression. For more information regarding method references, see Recipe 6-4.

How It Works

Java 8 introduced some new features that greatly increase developer productivity for sorting collections. Three such features are demonstrated in the solution to this recipe: lambda expressions, method references, and streams. We will look into streams in more detail within other recipes in this book, but we also briefly describe them here to enable the understanding of this recipe. Streams can be applied to collections of data, and they allow enhanced functional-style operations to be applied to the elements within the collections. Streams do not store any data; rather, they enable more functionality on the collections from which they are obtained.

In solution 1, a `Comparator` is generated, by which the `Player` objects will be evaluated for the number of goals scored (`getGoals`). A stream is then generated from a `List<Player>` that is referenced as team. The stream provides the `sorted()` function, which accepts a `Comparator` by which to perform a sort on a stream of data. The `Comparator` that was initially generated is passed to the `sorted()` function, and then the `map()` function is called upon the result. The `map()` function provides the ability to apply an expression to each element within the stream. Therefore, within the map, this solution utilizes a lambda expression to create a String that contains each `Player` object's `firstName`, `lastName`, and `goals` fields. Lastly, since the `List<Player>` is an iterable, it contains the `forEach()` method. The `forEach()` method enables an expression or group of statements to be applied to each element within the list. In this case, each element in the list is printed to the command line. As such, since the `map()` function was applied to the stream, each element in the list is subsequently printed per the algorithm applied within the `map()`. Therefore, the result is that the players' first and last names along with the number of goals each has scored will be printed at the command line.

Solution 2 uses a different technique to accomplish a similar task. In the second solution, the `Collections.sort()` method is invoked on the list. The first argument to `Collections.sort()` is the list itself, and the second argument is the comparison implementation in the form of a lambda expression. The lambda expression in this case has two parameters passed to it, both `Player` objects, and it compares the `lastName` of the first player to the `lastName` of the second player. Therefore, the sort will be performed on the `lastName` field of the `Player` object, in ascending order. To finish off solution 2, the sorted list is printed out. To do this a stream is generated from the sorted list, and the `forEach()` method is then invoked on the stream of data, printing out each player's `lastName`.

No doubt, the lambda expression greatly reduces the amount of code required to sort collections of data. It also makes it easy to understand the logic behind the sort, as readability is much easier than trying to follow looping implementations of the past. For more examples on using lambdas with collections of data, see Chapter 7.

6-5. Filtering a Collection of Data

Problem

You have a list of data to which you'd like to apply some filtering so that you can extract objects meeting the specified criteria.

Solution

Create a stream from the list of data and apply a filter, passing the desired predicate, or otherwise known as conditional expression. Finally, add each of the objects matching the specified filter criteria to a new list. In the following example, a list of Player objects is being filtered to capture only those players who have scored ten or more goals.

```
team.stream().filter(
    p -> p.getGoals() >= 10
    && p.getStatus() == 0)
    .forEach(element -> gteTenGoals.add(element));
System.out.println("Number of Players Matching Criteria: " + gteTenGoals.size());
```

How It Works

The solution to this recipe makes use of a data stream since it contains an easy-to-use filter function. The collection of data, team, generates a stream, and then the filter function is called upon it, accepting a predicate by which to filter the data within the collection. The predicate is written in the form of a lambda expression that contains two such filtering criteria. The lambda expression passes a Player object as an argument, and then filters the data based upon the number of goals being greater than or equal to ten and an active status.

Once the data has been filtered, the forEach() method is used to add each of the elements that meet the filtering criteria to a list. This is also done using a lambda expression. The element to be added to the list is passed to the lambda expression as an argument, and it is subsequently added to the list within the body of the expression.

Lambda expressions are very well suited for working within stream functions. Not only do they enable easier development of business logic, but they also make collections filtering easier to read and maintain.

■ **Note**   There are updated filtering options available in Java 9, including the takeWhile and dropWhile constructs, which were covered in Chapter 2. Please see Recipe 2-5 for details.

6-6. Implementing Runnable

Problem

You would like to create a runnable piece of code in a terse manner.

Solution

Utilize a lambda expression to implement the java.util.Runnable interface. The java.util.Runnable interface is a perfect match for lambda expressions since it contains only a single abstract method, run(). In this solution, we will compare the legacy technique, creating a new Runnable, and the new technique using a lambda expression.

The following lines of code demonstrate how to implement a new Runnable piece of code using the legacy technique.

```
Runnable oldRunnable = new Runnable() {
    @Override
    public void run() {
        int x = 5 * 3;
        System.out.println("The variable using the old way equals: " + x);
    }
};
```

Now take a look at how this can be written using a lambda expression instead.

```
Runnable lambdaRunnable = () -> {
    int x = 5 * 3;
    System.out.println("The variable using the lambda equals: " + x);
};

// Calling the runnables

oldRunnable.run();
lambdaRunnable.run();
```

As you can see, the legacy procedure for implementing a Runnable takes a few more lines of code than implementing Runnable with a lambda expression. The lambda expression also makes the Runnable implementation easier to read and maintain.

How It Works

Since java.util.Runnable is a functional interface, the boilerplate of implementing the run() method can be abstracted away using a lambda expression. The general format for implementing a Runnable with a lambda expression is as follows:

```
Runnable assignment = () -> {expression or statements};
```

A Runnable can be implemented by using a zero-argument lambda expression containing an expression or a series of statements within the lambda body. The key is that the implementation takes zero arguments and returns nothing.

6-7. Replacing Anonymous Inner Classes

Problem

Portions of your code contain anonymous inner classes, which are sometimes difficult to follow. You would like to replace anonymous inner classes with code that is easier to read and maintain.

Solution

Replace the anonymous inner classes with lambda expressions. By doing so, development time will be much faster as there will be fewer lines of boilerplate code required. A typical JavaFX or Java Swing application utilizes anonymous inner classes to add functionality to application constructs. For instance, anonymous classes are a great way to add an action to a button. The problem is that inner classes can be difficult to follow, and they contain lots of boilerplate code.

151

The following lines of code demonstrate a typical anonymous inner class implementation for a button action implementation. Let's look at these lines of code before taking a look at how you can achieve the same solution using a lambda expression.

```
Button btn = new Button();
btn.setText("Enter Player");
btn.setOnAction(new EventHandler<ActionEvent>() {
@Override public void handle(ActionEvent e) {
createPlayer(firstName.getText(),
            lastName.getText(),
            Integer.valueOf(goals.getText()),
            listView.getSelectionModel().getSelectedItem().toString(),
            0);
    message.setText("Player Successfully Added");
    System.out.println("Player added.");
    System.out.println("== Current Player List==");
    for (Player p : team) {
        System.out.println(p.getFirstName() + " " + p.getLastName());
    }
}
});
```

The same event handler can be implemented using a lambda expression, resulting in an easier-to-read implementation that can be achieved in fewer lines of code.

```
Button btn = new Button();
btn.setText("Enter Player");
btn.setOnAction(e -> {
    createPlayer(firstName.getText(),
                lastName.getText(),
                Integer.valueOf(goals.getText()),
                listView.getSelectionModel().getSelectedItem().toString(),
                0);
    message.setText("Player Successfully Added");
    System.out.println("Player added.");
    System.out.println("== Current Player List==");
    for (Player p : team) {
        System.out.println(p.getFirstName() + " " + p.getLastName());
    }
});
```

How It Works

A great use case for lambda expressions is that they are very well suited for taking the place of many anonymous class implementations. Most anonymous inner classes implement a functional interface, which makes them perfect candidates for replacement via lambda expressions. In the solution, the anonymous inner class for supporting a JavaFX button action has been redesigned to work within the context of a lambda expression. Since the EventHandler must implement one abstract method, handle(), it becomes a good fit for a lambda implementation.

In the solution, the EventHandler lambda expression accepts an argument, whose type is derived from the context of the expression. In this case, since the expression is implementing an EventHandler, the derived type for the argument is ActionEvent. The body of the lambda expression contains several lines of code and returns nothing to the caller, as the handle() method contains a void return type.

Although the lambda expression solution does not save more than a couple lines of code, it does help increase readability and maintainability. Although anonymous inner classes are an acceptable solution, code that is riddled with such constructs can be cumbersome to work with. Replacing anonymous inner classes with lambda expressions helps to maintain succinct code that is easy to follow.

6-8. Accessing Class Variables from a Lambda Expression

Problem

The class you are writing contains instance variables, and you would like to make them available for use via a lambda expression within the class.

Solution

Make use of instance variables that are contained in enclosing classes, as needed, from within lambda expressions. In the following class, the lambda expression contained within the VariableAccessInner. InnerClass.lambdaInMethod() method can access all enclosing class instance variables. Thus, it is able to print out the VariableAccessInner CLASSA variable, if needed.

```
public class VariableAccessInner {

    public String CLASSA = "Class-level A";

    class InnerClass {

        public String CLASSA = "Class-level B";

        void lambdaInMethod(String passedIn) {
            String METHODA = "Method-level A";

            Consumer<String> l1 = x -> {
                System.out.println(x);
                System.out.println("CLASSA Value: " + CLASSA);
                System.out.println("METHODA Value: " + METHODA);
            };

            l1.accept(CLASSA);
            l1.accept(passedIn);

        }
    }
}
```

Now, let's execute lambdaInMethod using the following code:

```
VariableAccessInner vai = new VariableAccessInner();
VariableAccessInner.InnerClass inner = vai.new InnerClass();
inner.lambdaInMethod("Hello");
```

Result:

```
Class-level B
CLASSA Value: Class-level B
METHODA Value: Method-level A
Hello
CLASSA Value: Class-level B
METHODA Value: Method-level A
```

■ **Note**   The CLASSA variable is overridden by a variable using the same identifier within the InnerClass class. Therefore, the CLASSA instance variable that belongs to VariableAccessInner is not printed from within the lambda expression.

How It Works

Lambda expressions have access to the variables located within the enclosing class. Thus, a lambda expression contained within a method of a class can access any instance variables of the enclosing class. There is no additional scope added to a lambda expression, so it can access fields, methods, and local variables of the enclosing scope. In the solution, the lambda expression contained within the lambdaInMethod() method can access all of the fields that are declared within either class. This is because both the inner class and its outer class enclose the lambda. One thing to note is that if an inner class contains an instance variable of the same name as a variable that has been declared in the outer class, then the lambda will use the variable of its enclosing class. Therefore, in the solution, the InnerClass CLASSA field is accessed from within the lambda expression, rather than the outer class reference.

Local variables that are referenced from within a lambda expression must be either final or effectively final. Therefore, if a lambda expression attempts to access a variable that has been changed within the context of an enclosing method, an error will occur. For instance, suppose that the method in the solution were changed to the following:

```
void lambdaInMethod(String passedIn) {
    String METHODA = "Method-level A";
    passedIn = "test";
    Consumer<String> l1 = x -> {
        System.out.println(x);
        System.out.println("CLASSA Value: " + CLASSA);
        System.out.println("METHODA Value: " + METHODA);
        System.out.println(passedIn);
    };

    l1.accept(CLASSA);
    l1.accept(passedIn);

}
```

Note that the String that is passed into lambdaInMethod() is assigned a new value just before the lambda expression is invoked. Therefore, the passedIn variable is no longer effectively final, and lambda expressions cannot introduce a new level of scope. Consequently, the lambda expression does not have access to the passedIn variable from within the context of the expression.

6-9. Passing Lambda Expressions to Methods

Problem

A lambda expression has been created to encapsulate some functionality. You would like to take that functionality and pass it into a method as an argument, so that the method implementation can take advantage of the expression.

Solution

Create portable functions using lambda expressions by implementing a functional interface and then assigning the lambda expression to a variable of the same type as the interface. The variable can be passed to other objects as an argument.

The following class, PassingLambdaFunctions, contains a calculate() method, which will be used to perform calculations of any type given an array of values. Note that the calculate() method accepts a Function<List<Double>,Double> and an array of Double values as arguments.

```
public class PassingLambdaFunctions {
    /**
     * Calculates a value based upon the calculation function that is passed
     * in.
     * @param f1
     * @param args
     * @param x
     * @param y
     * @param z
     * @return
     */
    public Double calculate(Function<List<Double>, Double> f1,
                            Double [] args){
        Double returnVal;
        List<Double> varList = new ArrayList();
        int idx = 0;
        while (idx < args.length){
            varList.add(args[idx]);
            idx++;
        }
        returnVal=f1.apply(varList);

        return returnVal;
    }
}
```

To make use of the calculate method, a lambda expression that implements
Function<List<Double>,Double> must be passed as the first argument to the calculate() method, along
with an array of Double arguments that contains the value to be used within the calculation. In the following
class, a function for calculating volume is generated using a lambda expression, and it is assigned to variable
identified as volumeCalc of type Function<List<Double>,Double>. Another lambda expression is used to
create a function for calculating area, and it is assigned to a variable of the same type, identified as areaCalc.
In separate calls, these variables are then passed to the PassingLambdaFunctions.calculate() method,
along with an array of values, resulting in the calculated answer.

```java
public class MainClass {
    public static void main(String[] args){

        double x = 16.0;
        double y = 30.0;
        double z = 4.0;

        // Create volume calculation function using a lambda.  The calculator
        // checks to ensure that the array contains the three necessary elements
        // for the calculation.
        Function<List<Double>, Double> volumeCalc = list -> {
            if(list.size() == 3){
                return list.get(0) * list.get(1) * list.get(2);
            } else {
                return Double.valueOf("-1");
            }
        };
        Double[] argList = new Double[3];
        argList[0] = x;
        argList[1] = y;
        argList[2] = z;

        // Create area calculation function using a lambda.  This particular
        // calculator checks to ensure that the array only contains two elements.
        Function<List<Double>, Double> areaCalc = list -> {
            if(list.size() == 2){
                return list.get(0) * list.get(1);
            } else {
                return Double.valueOf("-1");
            }
        };
        Double[] argList2 = new Double[2];
        argList2[0] = x;
        argList2[1] = y;

        PassingLambdaFunctions p1 = new PassingLambdaFunctions();

        // Pass the lambda expressions to the calculate() method, along with the
        // argument lists.
        System.out.println("The volume is: " + p1.calculate(volumeCalc, argList));
        System.out.println("The area is: " + p1.calculate(areaCalc, argList2));
    }
}
```

Result:

```
The volume is: 1920.0
The area is: 480.0
```

How It Works

Lambda expressions can be assigned to variables of the same type as the functional interface being implemented. Such expressions can contain a single-line expression or a multistatement body. Since the lambda expression can accept arguments, there are use cases for assigning such expressions to variables and then passing those variables into other objects to modify functionality. This pattern is useful for creating solutions that may contain more than one implementation. The solution to this recipe demonstrates this concept.

In the solution, a class named PassingLambdaFunctions contains a single method identified as calculate(). The calculate() method is to be used for performing calculations on Double values that are passed into it as arguments. However, the calculate() method contains no calculation functionality at all. Rather, the calculation functionality is passed into it as an argument of type Function<List<Double>,Double> via a lambda expression. This type is actually one of the standard functional interfaces contained within the java.util.function package (see Recipe 6-2), and the interface can be implemented by lambda expressions and then invoked at a later time by calling its solo apply() method. Looking at the code in the calculate() method, the arguments contained within the Double[] are first added to a list. Next, lambda expression's apply() method is invoked, passing the new list of values, and returning a result into returnVal. Finally, returnVal is returned to the method invoker.

```
returnVal=f1.apply(varList);
return returnVal;
```

To implement the calculation functionality within the solution, lambda expressions are created in a separate class named MainClass. Each expression accepts a list of arguments and then performs a calculation on the values in the list, returning a result. For instance, the first lambda generated in the MainClass calculates volume by multiplying together all of the values contained in the argument list and returns the result. This functionality is then assigned to a variable of type Function<List<Double>,Double>, and then it is passed into the PassingLambdaFunctions.calculate() method later on.

Any type of functionality can be implemented within a lambda expression and then passed around to different objects for use. This is an excellent way to promote code reuse and high maintainability.

Summary

It is not very often that a new construct added to a language can have as large of an impact as lambda expressions to Java. For years, developers have been utilizing such constructs as anonymous inner classes to add subtle functionality to applications. With the addition of lambda expressions, that subtle functionality can be developed with easy-to-read code, rather than redundant and difficult-to-read boilerplate code. Moreover, many languages today make it possible to pass functional pieces of code around, dynamically altering the functionality of existing code. Such solutions are now available in the Java language, allowing developers to make use of more modern programming techniques.

Lambda expressions brought new life to the Java language with their introduction in Java 8, providing capabilities that were not available to Java developers in the past. Developers of desktop, mobile, and enterprise applications alike are now able to take advantage of the lambda expression to create more robust and sophisticated solutions. Lambda expressions are a revolutionary change to the language, and they have a significant impact on development across the platform.

CHAPTER 7

Data Sources and Collections

Almost all applications perform tasks against user data. Sometimes data is obtained from a user, tasks are performed against the data, and the result is returned immediately. More often, data is obtained, and then it is stored within the application for later use, and eventually tasks are performed against it. Applications make use of data structures to store data that can be utilized throughout the lifetime of an application instance. The Java language contains a number of data structures that are known as Collection types, and they can be utilized for this purpose. These data structures implement the java.util.Collection interface, which provides a variety of methods that are useful for adding, removing, and performing tasks against the data that is used with the collection.

Java 8 changed the game when it comes to data structures and Collection types. The concepts of pipelines and streams were introduced, enabling easy iteration and operations against data contained within Collection types. In prior releases of Java, the developer had to tell the compiler how to iterate over data within a Collection. Oftentimes in the past, developers utilized a loop to perform iterative tasks on data structures. Java 8 enabled developers to begin utilizing streams for iterative tasks on Collection types. When using streams and pipeline of operations on collections, the developer specifies what type of operation to perform, and the JDK decides how to do it. This reduces the burden on a developer by reducing boilerplate code, and providing an easy-to-use algorithm for working with collections.

This chapter introduces some of the data structures that can be utilized within a Java application for the storage of user data. It discusses some of the data structures in detail, and introduces operations that can be performed on the data. The concepts of pipelines and streams are introduced in this chapter, and it provides recipes that demonstrate their usage. Java 8 forces developers to think differently about the way that they write collection code, enabling the development of smarter and more productive solutions.

7-1. Defining a Fixed Set of Related Constants

Problem

You need a type that can represent a fixed set of related constants.

Solution

Use an enum type. The following example defines an enum type, called FieldType, to represent various form fields you might find on the GUI of an application:

```
// See BasicFieldType.java
public enum FieldType { PASSWORD, EMAIL_ADDRESS, PHONE_NUMBER, SOCIAL_SECURITY_NUMBER }
```

This is the simplest form of an enum type, which will often suffice when all that is needed is a related set of named constants. In the following code, a `field` variable of type `FieldType` is declared and initialized to the `FieldType.EMAIL_ADDRESS` enum constant. Next, the code prints the results from calling various methods that are defined for all enum types:

```
FieldType field = FieldType.EMAIL_ADDRESS;

System.out.println("field.name(): " + field.name());
System.out.println("field.ordinal(): " + field.ordinal());
System.out.println("field.toString(): " + field.toString());

System.out.println("field.isEqual(EMAIL_ADDRESS): " +
                   field.equals(FieldType.EMAIL_ADDRESS));
System.out.println("field.isEqual(\"EMAIL_ADDRESS\"'): " + field.equals("EMAIL_ADDRESS"));

System.out.println("field == EMAIL_ADDRESS: " + (field == FieldType.EMAIL_ADDRESS));
// Won't compile - illustrates type safety of enum
// System.out.println("field == \"EMAIL_ADDRESS\": " + (field == "EMAIL_ADDRESS"));

System.out.println("field.compareTo(EMAIL_ADDRESS): " +
                   field.compareTo(FieldType.EMAIL_ADDRESS));
System.out.println("field.compareTo(PASSWORD): " + field.compareTo(FieldType.PASSWORD));

System.out.println("field.valueOf(\"EMAIL_ADDRESS\"): " + field.valueOf("EMAIL_ADDRESS"));

try {
    System.out.print("field.valueOf(\"email_address\"): ");
    System.out.println(FieldType.valueOf("email_address"));
} catch (IllegalArgumentException e) {
    System.out.println(e.toString());
}

System.out.println("FieldType.values(): " + Arrays.toString(FieldType.values()));
```

Running this code will result in the following output:

```
field.name(): EMAIL_ADDRESS
field.ordinal(): 1
field.toString(): EMAIL_ADDRESS
field.isEqual(EMAIL_ADDRESS): true
field.isEqual("EMAIL_ADDRESS"'): false
field == EMAIL_ADDRESS: true
field.compareTo(EMAIL_ADDRESS): 0
field.compareTo(PASSWORD): 1
field.valueOf("EMAIL_ADDRESS"): EMAIL_ADDRESS
field.valueOf("email_address"): java.lang.IllegalArgumentException: No enum constant org.
java9recipes.chapter4.BasicEnumExample.FieldType.email_address
FieldType.values(): [PASSWORD, EMAIL_ADDRESS, PHONE_NUMBER, SSN]
```

How It Works

A common pattern for representing a fixed set of related constants is to define each constant as an `int`, `String`, or some other data type. Often, these constants are defined in a class or interface whose sole purpose is to encapsulate constants. In any case, constants are sometimes defined with the `static` and `final` modifiers, as follows:

```
// Input field constants
public static final int PASSWORD = 0;
public static final int EMAIL_ADDRESS = 1;
public static final int PHONE_NUMBER = 2;
public static final int SOCIAL_SECURITY_NUMBER = 3;
```

There are multiple problems with this pattern, the primary issue being the lack of type safety. By defining these constants as ints, it is possible to assign an invalid value to a variable that is supposed to be allowed to hold only one of the constant values:

```
int inputField = PHONE_NUMBER;  // OK
inputField = 4;  // Bad - no input field constant with value 4; compiles without error
```

As you can see, there will be no compiler error or warning produced to inform you of this invalid value assignment. Chances are, you will discover this at runtime, when your application tries to use `inputField`, and an incorrect value is assigned to it. In contrast, Java enum types provide compile-time type safety. That is, if one attempts to assign a value of the wrong type to an enum variable, it will result in a compiler error. In the solution this recipe, the `FieldType.EMAIL_ADDRESS` enum constant was assigned to the `field` variable. Attempting to assign a value that isn't of type `FieldType` naturally results in a compiler error:

```
FieldType field = FieldType.EMAIL_ADDRESS;  // OK
field = "EMAIL_ADDRESS"; // Wrong type - compiler error
```

An enum is simply a special type of class. Under the covers, Java implements an enum type as a subclass of the abstract and final `java.lang.Enum` class. Thus, an enum type cannot be instantiated directly (outside of the enum type) or extended. The constants defined by an enum type are actually instances of the enum type. The `java.lang.Enum` class defines a number of `final` methods that all enum types inherit. In addition, all enum types have two implicitly declared `static` methods: `values()` and `valueOf(String)`. The solution code demonstrates these `static` methods and some of the more often used instance methods.

Most of these methods are fairly self-explanatory, but you should keep the following details in mind:

- Each enum constant has an ordinal value representing its relative position in the enum declaration. The first constant in the declaration is assigned an ordinal value of zero. The ordinal() method can be used to retrieve an enum constant's ordinal value; however, it is not recommended that applications be written to depend on this value for maintainability reasons.

- The name() method and the default implementation of the toString() method both return a String representation of the enum constant (toString() actually calls name()). It is common for toString() to be overridden to provide a more user-friendly String representation of the enum constant. For this reason, and for maintainability reasons, it is recommended that toString() be used in preference to name().

- When testing for equality, note that both the equals() method and == perform reference comparison. They can be used interchangeably. However, it is recommended that == be used to take advantage of compile-time type safety. This is illustrated in the solution code. Performing equals() comparison with a String parameter, for example, may allow the error to go unnoticed; it will compile, but it will always return false. Conversely, attempting to compare an enum with a String using the == comparison would result in an error at compile time. When you have the choice of catching errors sooner (at compile time) rather than later (at runtime), choose the former.

- The implicitly declared static methods values() and valueOf(String) do not appear in the Java documentation or the source code for the java.lang.Enum class. However, the Java Language Specification does detail their required implementations. To summarize these methods, values() returns an array containing the constants of the enum, in the order they are declared. The valueOf(String) method returns the enum constant whose name exactly matches (including case) the value of the String argument, or throws an IllegalArgumentException if there is no enum constant with the specified name.

Refer to the online Java documentation for further details on java.lang.Enum and each of its methods (https://docs.oracle.com/javase/9/docs/api/java/lang/Enum.html). As the next recipe demonstrates, enum types, as full-fledged Java classes, can be used to build more intelligent constants.

7-2. Designing Intelligent Constants

Problem

You need a type that can represent a fixed set of related constants, and you would like to build some state and behavior (logic) around your constants in an object-oriented fashion.

Solution

Use an enum type and take advantage of type safety and the fact that enum types are full-fledged Java classes. An enum type can have state and behavior just like any other class, and the enum constants, themselves being instances of the enum type, inherit this state and behavior. This is best illustrated by an example. Let's expand on the example from the previous recipe. Imagine that you need to process and validate all the fields from an HTML form that has been submitted. Each form field has a unique set of rules for validating its content, based on the field type. For each form field, you have the field's "name" and the value that was entered into that form field. The FieldType enum can be expanded to handle this very easily:

```java
// See FieldType.java
public enum FieldType {

    PASSWORD(FieldType.passwordFieldName) {

        // A password must contain one or more digits, one or more lowercase letters, one or
        // more uppercase letters, and be a minimum of 6 characters in length.
        //
```

```java
        @Override
        public boolean validate(String fieldValue) {
            return Pattern.matches("((?=.*\\d)(?=.*[a-z])(?=.*[A-Z]).{6,})",
                                    fieldValue);
        }
    },

    EMAIL_ADDRESS(FieldType.emailFieldName) {

        // An email address begins with a combination of alphanumeric characters, periods,
        // and hyphens, followed by a mandatory ampersand ('@') character, followed by
        // a combination of alphanumeric characters (hyphens allowed), followed by a
        // one or more periods (to separate domains and subdomains), and ending in 2-4
        // alphabetic characters representing the domain.
        //
        @Override
        public boolean validate(String fieldValue) {
            return Pattern.matches("^[\\w\\.-]+@([\\w\\-]+\\.)+[A-Z|a-z]{2,4}$",
                                    fieldValue);
        }
    },

    PHONE_NUMBER(FieldType.phoneFieldName) {

        // A phone number must contain a minium of 7 digits. Three optional digits
        // representing the area code may appear in front of the main 7 digits. The area
        // code may, optionally, be surrounded by parenthesis. If an area code is included,
        // the number may optionally be prefixed by a '1' for long distance numbers.
        // Optional hypens my appear after the country code ('1'), the area code, and the
        // first 3 digits of the 7 digit number.
        //
        @Override
        public boolean validate(String fieldValue) {
            return Pattern.matches("^1?[- ]?\\(?(\\d{3})\\)?[- ]?(\\d{3})[- ]?(\\d{4})$",
                                    fieldValue);
        }
    },

    SOCIAL_SECURITY_NUMBER(FieldType.ssnFieldName) {

        // A social security number must contain 9 digits with optional hyphens after the
        // third and fifth digits.
        //
        @Override
        public boolean validate(String fieldValue) {
            return Pattern.matches("^\\d{3}[- ]?\\d{2}[- ]?\\d{4}$",
                                    fieldValue);
        }
    };  // End of enum constants definition
```

163

```java
// Instance members
//
private String fieldName;

// Define static constants to increase type safety
static final String passwordFieldName = "password";
static final String emailFieldName = "email";
static final String phoneFieldName = "phone";
static final String ssnFieldName = "ssn";

private FieldType(String fieldName) {
    this.fieldName = fieldName;
}

public String getFieldName() {
    return this.fieldName;
}

abstract boolean validate(String fieldValue);

// Static class members
//
private static final Map<String, FieldType> nameToFieldTypeMap = new HashMap<>();

static {
    for (FieldType field : FieldType.values()) {
        nameToFieldTypeMap.put(field.getFieldName(), field);
    }
}

public static FieldType lookup(String fieldName) {
    return nameToFieldTypeMap.get(fieldName.toLowerCase());
}

private static void printValid(FieldType field, String fieldValue, boolean valid) {
    System.out.println(field.getFieldName() +
                    "(\"" + fieldValue + "\") valid: " + valid);
}

public static void main(String... args) {

    String fieldName = FieldType.passwordFieldName;
    String fieldValue = "1Cxy9";  // invalid - must be at least 6 characters
    FieldType field = lookup(fieldName);
    printValid(field, fieldValue, field.validate(fieldValue));

    fieldName = FieldType.phoneFieldName;
    fieldValue = "1-800-555-1234";  // valid
    field = lookup(fieldName);
    printValid(field, fieldValue, field.validate(fieldValue));
```

```
        fieldName = FieldType.emailFieldName;
        fieldValue = "john@doe";   // invalid - missing .<tld>
        field = lookup(fieldName);
        printValid(field, fieldValue, field.validate(fieldValue));

        fieldName = FieldType.ssnFieldName;
        fieldValue = "111-11-1111";   // valid
        field = lookup(fieldName);
        printValid(field, fieldValue, field.validate(fieldValue));
    }
}
```

Running the preceding code results in the following output:

```
password("1Cxy9") valid: false
phone("1-800-555-1234") valid: true
email("john@doe") valid: false
ssn("111-11-1111") valid: true
```

How It Works

Notice that the enhanced `FieldType` enum now defines a `fieldName` instance variable and a constructor with a `fieldName` `String` argument for initializing the instance variable. Each enum constant (again, each constant being an instance of `FieldType`) must be instantiated with a `fieldName`. `FieldType` also defines an `abstract` `validate(String)` method that each enum constant must implement to perform the field validation. Here, each `FieldType`'s `validate()` method applies a regular expression match against the field value and returns the `Boolean` result of the match. Imagine the following form input fields corresponding to our `FieldType` instances:

```
<input type="password" name="password" value=""/>
<input type="tel" name="phone" value=""/>
<input type="email" name="email" value=""/>
<input type="text" name="ssn" value=""/>
```

The value of the input field's name attribute will be used to identify the `FieldType`; you used this same name when you instantiated each `FieldType` enum constant. When a form is submitted, you have access to each input field's name and the value that was entered into the field. You need to be able to map the field's name to a `FieldType` and call the `validate()` method with the input value. The class variable, `nameToFieldTypeMap`, is declared and initialized for this purpose. For each `FieldType` enum constant, `nameToFieldTypeMap` stores an entry with the field name as the key, and the `FieldType` as the value. The `lookup(String)` class method uses this map to look up the `FieldType` from the field name. The code to validate an e-mail input field with an input value of john@doe.com is quite concise:

```
// <input type="email" name="email" value="john@doe.com"/>
String fieldName = FieldType.emailFieldName;
String fieldValue = "john@doe.com";
boolean valid = FieldType.lookup(fieldName).validate(fieldValue);
```

The `main()` method shows an example validation for each of the `FieldTypes`. The `printValid()` method prints the field name, field value, and the field's validation result.

This recipe has demonstrated that there is a lot more potential in the enum type than just the ability to define a set of named constants. Enum types have all the power of a normal class, plus additional features that allow you to create well-encapsulated and intelligent constants.

7-3. Executing Code Based on a Specified Value

Problem

You want to execute different blocks of code based on the value of a singular expression.

Solution

Consider using a switch statement if your variable or expression result is one of the allowed switch types and you want to test for equality against a type-compatible constant. These examples show various ways to use the switch statement, including a new feature that became available in Java 7: the ability to switch on Strings. First, let's play some Rock-Paper-Scissors! The RockPaperScissors class shows two different switch statements: one using an int as the switch expression type, and the other using an enum type.

```java
// See RockPaperScissors.java
public class RockPaperScissors {

    enum Hand { ROCK, PAPER, SCISSORS, INVALID };

    private static void getHand(int handVal) {
        Hand hand;
        try {
            hand = Hand.values()[handVal - 1];
        }
        catch (ArrayIndexOutOfBoundsException ex) {
            hand = Hand.INVALID;
        }
        switch (hand) {
            case ROCK:
                System.out.println("Rock");
                break;
            case PAPER:
                System.out.println("Paper");
                break;
            case SCISSORS:
                System.out.println("Scissors");
                break;
            default:
                System.out.println("Invalid");
        }
    }

    private static void playHands(int yourHand, int myHand) {

        // Rock = 1
        // Paper = 2
        // Scissors = 3
```

```java
        // Hand combinations:
        // 1,1; 2,2; 3,3 => Draw
        // 1,2 => sum = 3 => Paper
        // 1,3 => sum = 4 => Rock
        // 2,3 => sum = 5 => Scissors
        //
        switch ((yourHand == myHand) ? 0 : (yourHand + myHand)) {
            case 0:
                System.out.println("Draw!");
                break;
            case 3:
                System.out.print("Paper beats Rock. ");
                printWinner(yourHand, 2);
                break;
            case 4:
                System.out.print("Rock beats Scissors. ");
                printWinner(yourHand, 1);
                break;
            case 5:
                System.out.print("Scissors beats Paper. ");
                printWinner(yourHand, 3);
                break;
            default:
                System.out.print("You cheated! ");
                printWinner(yourHand, myHand);
        }
    }

    private static void printWinner(int yourHand, int winningHand) {
        if (yourHand == winningHand) {
            System.out.println("You win!");
        }
        else {
            System.out.println("I win!");
        }
    }

    public static void main(String[] args) {

        Scanner input = new Scanner(System.in);
        System.out.println("Let's Play Rock, Paper, Scissors");
        System.out.println("  Enter 1 (Rock)");
        System.out.println("  Enter 2 (Paper)");
        System.out.println("  Enter 3 (Scissors)");
        System.out.print("> ");

        int playerHand = input.hasNextInt() ? input.nextInt() : -99;
        int computerHand = (int)(3*Math.random()) + 1;
```

```
            System.out.print("Your hand: (" + playerHand + ") ");
            getHand(playerHand);
            System.out.print("My hand: (" + computerHand + ") ");
            getHand(computerHand);
            playHands(playerHand, computerHand);
    }
}
```

When the RockPaperScissors class is executed, an interactive game begins, allowing users to type input at the keyboard. The users can type the number corresponding to the entry they'd like to choose, and the computer utilizes random number calculations to try to beat the users' choices.

Java 7 added the capability to switch on Strings. The SwitchTypeChecker class demonstrates the use of a String as the switch expression type. The isValidSwitchType() method takes a Class object and determines whether the corresponding type is a valid type that can be used in a switch expression. So, SwitchTypeChecker is using a switch statement to simultaneously demonstrate switching on Strings and to show the valid types for use in a switch expression:

```
// See SwitchTypeChecker.java
public class SwitchTypeChecker {

    public static Class varTypeClass(Object o) { return o.getClass(); };
    public static Class varTypeClass(Enum e) { return e.getClass().getSuperclass(); };
    public static Class varTypeClass(char c) { return char.class; };
    public static Class varTypeClass(byte b) { return byte.class; };
    public static Class varTypeClass(short s) { return short.class; };
    public static Class varTypeClass(int i) { return int.class; };
    public static Class varTypeClass(long l) { return long.class; };
    public static Class varTypeClass(float f) { return float.class; };
    public static Class varTypeClass(double d) { return double.class; };
    public static Class varTypeClass(boolean d) { return boolean.class; };

    public void isValidSwitchType(Class typeClass) {
        String switchType = typeClass.getSimpleName();
        boolean valid = true;
        switch (switchType) {
            case "char":
            case "byte":
            case "short":
            case "int":
                System.out.print("Primitive type " + switchType);
                break;
            case "Character":
            case "Byte":
            case "Short":
            case "Integer":
                System.out.print("Boxed primitive type " + switchType);
                break;
            case "String":
            case "Enum":
                System.out.print(switchType);
                break;
```

```
        default:  // invalid switch type
            System.out.print(switchType);
            valid = false;
    }
    System.out.println(" is " + (valid ? "" : "not ") + "a valid switch type.");
}

public static void main(String[] args) {
    SwitchTypeChecker check = new SwitchTypeChecker();
    check.isValidSwitchType(varTypeClass('7'));
    check.isValidSwitchType(varTypeClass(7));
    check.isValidSwitchType(varTypeClass(777.7d));
    check.isValidSwitchType(varTypeClass((short)7));
    check.isValidSwitchType(varTypeClass(new Integer(7)));
    check.isValidSwitchType(varTypeClass("Java 8 Rocks!"));
    check.isValidSwitchType(varTypeClass(new Long(7)));
    check.isValidSwitchType(varTypeClass(true));
    check.isValidSwitchType(varTypeClass(java.nio.file.AccessMode.READ));
}
}
```

Here is the result of executing SwitchTypeChecker:

```
Primitive type char is a valid switch type.
Primitive type int is a valid switch type.
double is not a valid switch type.
Primitive type short is a valid switch type.
Boxed primitive type Integer is a valid switch type.
String is a valid switch type.
Long is not a valid switch type.
boolean is not a valid switch type.
Enum is a valid switch type.
```

How It Works

The switch statement is a control-flow statement that allows you to execute different blocks of code based on the value of a switch expression. It is similar to the if-then-else statement, except that the switch statement can have only a single test expression, and the expression type is restricted to one of several different types. When a switch statement executes, it evaluates the expression against constants contained in the switch statement's case labels. These case labels are branch points in the code. If the value of the expression equals the value of a case label constant, control is transferred to the section of code that corresponds to the matching case label. All code statements from that point on are then executed until either the end of the switch statement is reached or a break statement is reached. The break statement causes the switch statement to terminate, with control being transferred to the statement following the switch statement. Optionally, the switch statement can contain a default label, which provides a branch point for the case when there is no case label constant that equates to the switch expression value.

The SwitchTypeChecker isValidSwitchType() method demonstrates the use of a String as the switch test expression. If you study closely the isValidSwitchType() method, you will see that it is testing whether a Class object represents a type that corresponds to one of the valid switch expression types. The method also demonstrates how case labels can be grouped to implement a logical OR conditional test. If a case label does not have any associated code to execute, and no break statement, the flow of execution falls through to the next closest case label containing executable statements, thus allowing common code to be executed if the result of the switch expression matches any one of the grouped case constants.

The RockPaperScissors class implements a command-line Rock-Paper-Scissors game, where you are playing against the computer. There are two methods in this class that demonstrate the switch statement. The getHand() method shows the use of an enum variable in the switch expression. The playHands() method simply intends to show that the switch expression, although often just a variable, can be any expression whose result is of one of the allowed switch types. In this case, the expression is using a ternary operator that returns an int value.

7-4. Working with Fix-Sized Arrays

Problem

You need a simple data structure that can store a fixed (and possibly large) amount of same-typed data and provide for fast sequential access.

Solution

Consider using an array. While Java provides more sophisticated and flexible Collection types, the array type can be useful data structure for many applications. The following example demonstrates the simplicity of working with arrays. The GradeAnalyzer class provides a means for calculating various grade-related statistics, such as the mean (average) grade, minimum grade, and maximum grade.

```java
// See GradeAnalyzer.java
public class GradeAnalyzer {

    // The internal grades array
    private int[] _grades;

    public void setGrades(int[] grades) {
        this._grades = grades;
    }

    // Return cloned grades so the caller cannot modify our internal grades
    public int[] getGrades() {
        return _grades != null ? _grades.clone() : null;
    }

    public int meanGrade() {
        int mean = 0;
        if (_grades != null&& _grades.length > 0) {
            int sum = 0;
            for (int i = 0; i < _grades.length; i++) {
                sum += _grades[i];
            }
            mean = sum / _grades.length;
        }
        return mean;
    }
```

```java
    public int minGrade() {
        int min = 0;
        for (int index = 0; index < _grades.length; index++) {
            if (_grades[index] < min) {
                min = _grades[index];
            }
        }
        return min;
    }

    public int maxGrade() {
        int max = 0;
        for (int index = 0; index < _grades.length; index++) {
            if (_grades[index] > max) {
                max = _grades[index];
            }
        }
        return max;
    }

    static int[] initGrades1() {
        int[] grades = new int[5];
        grades[0] = 77;
        grades[1] = 48;
        grades[2] = 69;
        grades[3] = 92;
        grades[4] = 87;
        return grades;
}

    static int[] initGrades2() {
        int[] grades = { 57, 88, 67, 95, 99, 74, 81 };
        return grades;
}

    static int[] initGrades3() {
        return new int[]{ 100, 70, 55, 89, 97, 98, 82 };
    }

    public static void main(String... args) {

        GradeAnalyzer ga = new GradeAnalyzer();
        ga.setGrades(initGrades1());
        System.out.println("Grades 1:");
        System.out.println("Mean of all grades is " + ga.meanGrade());
        System.out.println("Min grade is " + ga.minGrade());
        System.out.println("Max grade is " + ga.maxGrade());
        ga.setGrades(initGrades2());
        System.out.println("Grades 2:");
        System.out.println("Mean of all grades is " + ga.meanGrade());
        System.out.println("Min grade is " + ga.minGrade());
```

```
        System.out.println("Max grade is " + ga.maxGrade());
        ga.setGrades(initGrades3());
        System.out.println("Grades 3:");
        System.out.println("Mean of all grades is " + ga.meanGrade());
        System.out.println("Min grade is " + ga.minGrade());
        System.out.println("Max grade is " + ga.maxGrade());

        Object testArray = ga.getGrades();
        Class testClass = testArray.getClass();
        System.out.println("isArray: " + testClass.isArray());
        System.out.println("getClass: " + testClass.getName());
        System.out.println("getSuperclass: " + testClass.getSuperclass().getName());
        System.out.println("getComponentType: " + testClass.getComponentType());
        System.out.println("Arrays.toString: " + Arrays.toString((int[])testArray));

    }
}
```

Running this code will result in the following output:

```
Grades 1:
Mean of all grades is 74
Min grade is 48
Max grade is 92
Grades 2:
Mean of all grades is 80
Min grade is 57
Max grade is 99
Grades 3:
Mean of all grades is 84
Min grade is 55
Max grade is 100
isArray: true
getClass: [I
getSuperclass: class java.lang.Object
getComponentType: int
Arrays.toString: [55, 70, 82, 89, 97, 98, 100]
```

How It Works

The Java array type works a bit differently than Java's ArrayList (part of the Java Collections Framework). Java arrays hold a fixed amount of data. That is, when an array is created, you must specify how much data it can hold. Once an array has been created, you cannot insert or remove array items or otherwise change the size of the array. However, if you have a fixed amount (and especially a very large amount) of data that you just need to work on while iterating over it sequentially, an array may be a good choice.

The first thing you need to know about the Java array type is that it is an Object type. All arrays, regardless of the type of data they contain, have Object as their superclass. The elements of an array may be of any type, as long as all elements are of the same type—either primitive or object reference. Regardless of the array type, the memory for an array is always allocated out of the heap space for the application. The heap is the area of memory used by the JVM for dynamic memory allocation.

■ **Note**   It is possible to create an array of Objects (Object[]) that can hold references to objects of different types; however, this is not recommended, as it requires you to check the type of elements and perform explicit type casting when retrieving elements from the array.

There are two steps to completely defining an array object in Java: array variable declaration, which specifies the array element type, and array creation, which allocates the memory for the array. Once an array is declared and the memory is allocated, it can be initialized. There are multiple ways to initialize an array, which are shown in the solution to this recipe. If you know in advance what data you need to store in the array, you can combine array declaration, creation, and initialization in one step using a shortcut syntax you will see demonstrated in the solution.

Let's walk through the GradeAnalyzer class and examine the various ways to declare, create, initialize, and access arrays. First, notice that the class has one instance variable to hold the grades to be analyzed:

```
private int[] _grades;
```

Like all other uninitialized Object reference instance variables, the _grades array instance variable is automatically initialized to null. Before you can start analyzing grades, you have to set the _grades instance variable to reference the grades data you want to analyze. This is done using the setGrades(int[]) method. Once GradeAnalyzer has a collection of grades to analyze, the meanGrade(), minGrade(), and maxGrade() methods can be called upon to compute their respective statistics. Together, these three methods demonstrate how to iterate over the elements of an array, how to access elements of an array, and how to determine the number of elements an array can hold. To determine the number of elements an array can hold, simply access the implicitly defined, final instance variable, length, which is available for all arrays:

```
_grades.length
```

To iterate over the elements of an array, simply use a for loop, whose index variable goes through all possible indices of the array. Array indices start at 0, so the last array index is always (_grades.length - 1). While iterating over the array, you can access the array element at the current index by using the name of the array variable followed by the current index enclosed in brackets (often called an array subscript):

```
// From the meanGrade() method:
for (int i = 0; i < _grades.length; i++) {
    sum += _grades[i];
}
```

Alternatively, the enhanced for loop, also known as the foreach loop, could be used to iterate over the array (see Recipe 7-7 for more discussion of the foreach loop):

```
for (int grade : _grades) {
    sum += grade;
}
```

Notice that to determine the min and max grade, the grades are first sorted in their natural (ascending) order using the utility sort method from the java.util.Arrays class. After sorting, the min grade is the simply the first element (at index 0) of the array, and the max grade is the last element (at index length -1) of the array.

The three static class methods in the solution, initGrades1(), initGrades2(), and initGrades3(), demonstrate three different ways of creating and initializing the array data you will use to "seed" the GradeAnalyzer. The initGrades1() method declares and creates an array (using new) that can hold five grades, then manually sets the value at each element index to an integer grade value. The initGrades2() method combines array creation and initialization in one line using the special array initializer syntax:

```
int[] grades = { 57, 88, 67, 95, 99, 74, 81 };
```

This syntax creates an array with a length of 7 and initializes the elements from index 0 through index 6 with the integer values shown. Note that this syntax can be used only in an array declaration, so the following is not allowed:

```
int[] grades;
grades = { 57, 88, 67, 95, 99, 74, 81 }; // won't compile
```

The initGrades3() method looks very similar to initGrades2(), but is slightly different. This code creates and returns an anonymous (unnamed) array:

```
return new int[]{ 100, 70, 55, 89, 97, 98, 82 };
```

With this syntax, you use the new keyword with the array element type, but the size of the array is not explicitly specified. Similar to the array initializer syntax shown in the initGrades2() method, the array size is implied by the number of elements given within the initializer brackets. So, again, this code is creating and returning an array with a length of 7.

After computing the grade statistics for the three sets of grades data, the remainder of the GradeAnalyzer main() method demonstrates various methods that can be used to determine array type information and to convert an array to a printable String. You see that the code first assigns the array returned from a call to the getGrades() instance method to an Object variable called testArray:

```
Object testArray = ga.getGrades();
```

You can make this assignment because, as stated previously, an array is an Object. You can also see this by the result from the call to testArray.getSuperclass(). The call to testArray.getClass().getName() is also interesting; it returns "I." The left bracket means "I am an array type", and the "I" means "with a component type of integer." This is also backed up by the result from the call to testArray.getComponentType(). Finally, you call the Arrays.toString(int[]) method, which returns a nicely formatted String representation of the array and its contents. Notice that because testArray is an Object reference, it must be cast to an int array for the Arrays.toString(int[]) method. (See the Java documentation for the java.util.Arrays class for other useful utility methods that can be used with arrays.)

As you have seen, arrays are simple and easy to work with. There will be times when this simplicity works to your advantage. Recipe 7-6 shows an alternative to the array type that provides for easy insertion and removal of elements: the ArrayList collection class.

7-5. Safely Enabling Types or Methods to Operate on Objects of Various Types

Problem

Your application makes use of many different object types, and there are containers within your class that are available for holding each of these different types. You are interested in ensuring your application remains bug-free, yet you would like to dynamically change the type of object a particular container may hold. In other words, you would like to define a generic container, but have the ability to specify its type each time a new instance of the container is instantiated.

Solution

Make use of generic types to decouple the type from the container. Generics are a way to abstract over object types, not explicitly declaring what the type of an object or container should be. You'll likely first encounter generic types when using the interfaces and classes that are part of the Java Collections Framework (http://download.oracle.com/javase/tutorial/collections/). The Collections Framework makes heavy use of Java generics. All collection types are parameterized to allow you to specify, at the time of instantiation, the type of elements the collection can hold. The following example code demonstrates how to use generics in a couple of different scenarios. The comments in the code indicate where the generics are utilized.

```java
public class MainClass {

    static List<Player> team;

    private static void loadTeam() {
        System.out.println("Loading team...");

        // Use of the diamond operator
        team = new ArrayList<>();
        Player player1 = new Player("Josh", "Juneau", 5);
        Player player2 = new Player("Duke", "Java", 15);
        Player player3 = new Player("Jonathan", "Gennick", 1);
        Player player4 = new Player("Bob", "Smith", 18);
        Player player5 = new Player("Steve", "Adams", 7);

        team.add(player1);
        team.add(player2);
        team.add(player3);
        team.add(player4);
        team.add(player5);

    }

    public static void main(String[] args) {
        loadTeam();

        // Create a list without specifying a type
        List objectList = new ArrayList();
        Object obj1 = "none";
        objectList.add(obj1);

        // Create a List that can be of type that is any superclass of Player
        List<? super Player> myTeam = objectList;
        for (Object p : myTeam) {
            System.out.println("Printing the objects...");
            System.out.println(p.toString());
        }
```

```
        // Create a Map of String keys and String values
        Map<String, String> strMap = new HashMap<>();
        strMap.put("first", "Josh");
        strMap.put("last", "Juneau");
        System.out.println(strMap.values());
    }
}
```

■ **Note**   When we talk generally about a ***collection*** or a ***collection type***, you can read this as those types that make up the Java Collections Framework. This includes all the classes and interfaces that descend from the `Collection` and `Map` interfaces. Collection types generally refer to types that descend from the `Collection` interface.

How It Works

The solution code demonstrates some basic use cases for generics. The examples in the GenericsDemo.java file, contained within the recipe sources, go into more detail to demonstrate the use of generics with Java collections versus showing you how to create generic types. Unless you are developing a library API, you probably won't be creating your own generic types. However, if you understand how generics are used with the Collection interfaces and classes, you will have the knowledge you need to create your own generic types.

The first thing to understand and remember about Java generics is that they are strictly a compile-time feature that aids the developer in creating more type-safe code. All the type information that you specify when you parameterize a generic type gets "erased" by the compiler when the code is compiled down to byte code. You'll see this described as ***type erasure***. Let's look at an example of a generic `Collection` type: the `List`. `List` is an interface defined as follows:

```
public interface List<E> extends Collection<E> { ... };
```

Now that is a strange syntax, especially because there is no object or type identified as E. As it turns out, the E is known as a type parameter, which is a placeholder to indicate to the compiler that a type will be assigned to the object at runtime. Type parameters are typically upper cased letters that are used to indicate the type of parameter being defined. There are a variety of different type parameters to note, but keep in mind that these are only applicable when defining a generic type. In most cases, generic types are only defined when developing a library or API:

- E – Element
- K – Key
- N- Number
- T – Type
- V – Value
- S, U, V, and so on—second, third, and fourth types

To specify the element type for a List (or any Collection type), simply include the type name in angle brackets when declaring and instantiating objects. When you do this, you are specifying a "parameterized type." The following code declares List of Integers. A variable, aList, of the parameterized type List<Integer> is declared and then initialized with the reference obtained from the instantiation of the parameterized type, LinkedList<Integer> (also called a "concrete parameterized type"):

```
List<Integer> aList = new LinkedList<Integer>();
```

Now that you've parameterized these types to restrict the element type to Integers, the List add(E e) method becomes:

```
boolean add(Integer e);
```

If you try to add anything other than an Integer to aList, the compiler will generate an error:

```
aList.add(new Integer(121));
aList.add(42);   // 42 is the same as new Integer(42), due to autoboxing.
aList.add("Java");  // won't compile, wrong type
```

It's important to note that it's the reference type that is checked at compile time, so the following will also result in a compiler error:

```
Number aNum = new Integer("7");
aList.add(aNum);  // won't compile, wrong type
```

This is a compile error because aNum could reference any Number object. If the compiler were to allow this, you could end up with a set that contains Doubles, Floats, and so on, which would violate the Integer parameter constraint that was specified when you created aList. Of course, a simple type cast could get you around the compiler error, but this would surely cause unintended consequences when casting between incompatible Number objects. Generics were designed to reduce the amount of explicit type casting you have to do in your code, so if you find yourself using explicit type casting when using methods of parameterized types, this is a clue of potentially dangerous code.

```
aList.add((Integer)aNum);  // compiles, but don't do this.
```

Other things to watch out for when using generic types are compiler warnings. They may indicate that you're doing something that is not recommended and it usually indicates that your code has a potential runtime error looming. An example can help to illustrate this. The following code will compile but produce two compiler warnings:

```
List rawList = new LinkedList();
aList = rawList;
```

First, you're creating rawList, which is a *raw type*, a generic type that isn't parameterized. When generics were introduced into the language, the language designers decided that in order to maintain compatibility with pregenerics code, they would need to allow the use of raw types. However, the use of raw types is strongly discouraged for newer (post–Java 5) code, so compilers will generate a raw type warning if you use them. Next, rawList is assigned to aList, which was created using parameterized types. Again, this is allowed by the compiler (due to generics type erasure and backward compatibility), but an unchecked conversion warning is generated for the assignment to flag potential runtime type incompatibility. Imagine if rawList contained Strings. Later, if you tried to retrieve Integer elements from aList, you would get a runtime error.

Regarding type compatibility, it doesn't apply to generic type parameters. For example, the following is not a valid assignment:

```
List<Number> bList = new LinkedList<Integer>();  // won't compile; incompatible types
```

Although Integers are Numbers (Integer is a subtype of Number), and LinkedList is a subtype of List, LinkedList<Integer> is not a subtype of List<Number>. Fortunately, this won't slip by you if you accidentally write code like this; the compiler will generate an "incompatible types" warning.

So you may be wondering whether there is a way to achieve a variant subtyping relationship similar to what we tried to do in the previous line of code. The answer is yes, by using a feature of generics called the **wildcard**. A wildcard is denoted by use of a question mark (?) within the type parameter angle brackets. Wildcards are used to declare parameterized types that are either bounded or unbounded. The following is an example declaration of a bounded parameterized type:

```
List<? extends Number> cList;
```

When a wildcard is used with the extends keyword, an upper bound is established for the type parameter. In this example, ? extends Number means any type that is either a Number or a subtype of a Number. Therefore, the following would be valid assignments because both Integer and Double are subtypes of Number:

```
cList = new LinkedList<Number>();
cList = new LinkedList<Integer>();
cList = new LinkedList<Double>();
```

So, cList can hold a reference to any List instance that has an element type that is compatible with Number. In fact, cList could even reference a raw type. Obviously, this makes it a challenge for the compiler to enforce type safety if it were to allow elements to be added to cList. Therefore, the compiler does not allow elements (other than a null) to be added to a collection type that is parameterized with ? extends. The following would result in a compiler error:

```
cList.add(new Integer(5));  // add() not allowed; cList could be LinkedList<Double>
```

However, you are allowed to get an element from the list without any problem:

```
Number cNum = cList.get(0);
```

The only restriction here is that the reference you get from the list has to be treated like a Number. Remember, cList could be pointing to a list of Integers, a list of Doubles, or list of any other subtype of Number.

A wildcard can also be used with the super keyword. In this case, a lower bound is established for the type parameter:

```
List<? super Integer> dList;
```

In this example, ? super Integer means any type that is either an Integer or any supertype of Integer. Therefore, the following would be valid assignments because Number and Object are the only supertypes of Integer:

```
dList = new LinkedList<Integer>();
dList = new LinkedList<Number>();
dList = new LinkedList<Object>();
```

So, you see that Integer is the lower bound. This lower bound now places a restriction on retrieving elements from the list. Because dList can hold a reference to any one of the previous parameterized types, the compiler would not be able to enforce type safety if an assumption were made about the type of the element being retrieved. Therefore, the compiler must not allow calls to get() on a collection type that is parameterized with ? super, and the following would result in a compiler error:

```
Integer n = dList.get(0);  // get() not allowed; dList.get(0) could be a Number or Object
```

However, now you can add elements to the list, but the lower bound, Integer, still applies. Only Integers can be added because Integer is compatible with Number and Object:

```
dList.add(new Integer(5));  // OK
Number dNum = new Double(7);
dList.add(dNum);  // won't compile; dList could be LinkedList<Integer>
```

You will see the use of the wildcard with both extends and super throughout the collection types. Most often, you will see them used in method parameter types, such as the addAll() method, which is defined for all Collections. Sometimes you will see the collection types using the wildcard (?) alone as a type parameter, which is called an *unbounded wildcard*. The Collection removeAll() method is such an example. In most cases, this usage is self-explanatory. You probably won't be (probably shouldn't be) defining your own parameterized types using an unbounded wildcard. If you try to do this, you will soon learn there isn't much you can do with it. If you understand concrete parameterized types, wildcard parameterized types, and the concept of bounded and unbounded types, as described in this recipe, you have most of what you need to work with the generic collection types, and create your own generic types if you so chose.

Now that we've talked a lot about parameterizing types, we're going to tell you to forget about some of it. When Java 7 was released, a new feature called the *diamond* (sometimes seen referred to as the *diamond operator*, although it is not considered to be an operator in Java) was introduced. The diamond allows the compiler to infer the type argument(s) from the context of the parameterized type usage. A simple example of the diamond usage follows:

```
List<Integer> eList = new ArrayList<>();
```

Notice there is no type argument specified between the angle brackets when instantiating the ArrayList. The compiler can easily infer the type to be Integer, based on the context of the assignment or initializer. Integer is the only type that would work in this context. In fact, the Java compiler (and most compliant IDEs) will actually warn you if you do not use a diamond where it is possible to use it. Another more complex example shows the benefit even better:

```
Map<Integer, List<String>> aMap = new HashMap<>();  // Nice!
```

The diamond can similarly be used in return statements, as well as in method arguments:

```
// diamond in method return
public static List<String> getEmptyList() {
    return new ArrayList<>();
}

// diamond in method argument
List<List<String>> gList = new ArrayList<>();
gList.set(0, new ArrayList<>(Arrays.asList("a", "b")));
```

179

Note that using the diamond as shown here is not the same as using a raw type. The following is not equivalent to the declaration of aMap that uses the diamond; it will result in an "unchecked conversion" warning, and possibly a raw type warning, from the compiler:

```
Map<Integer, List<String>> bMap = new HashMap();    // compiler warnings; avoid raw types
```

The discussion around why this is different than the diamond example is beyond the scope of this recipe. If you remember to avoid the use of raw types, you shouldn't need to worry about this. Use the diamond whenever possible to save yourself some typing, as well as to make your code more robust, readable, and concise.

7-6. Working with Dynamic Arrays

Problem

You need a flexible data structure that can store a variable amount of data and that allows for easy insertion and deletion of data.

Solution

Consider using an ArrayList. The following example code is the StockScreener class, which allows you to screen a list of stocks or a single stock based on a specific screen parameter (P/E, Yield, and Beta) and screen value. The class makes use of an ArrayList for containing stock Strings. An example screen might be "Tell me which of the stocks in this list has a P/E (price-to-earnings ratio) of 15 or less." Don't worry if you're not familiar with these stock market terms. Whatever you do, don't use this class to make your stock investment decisions!

```java
// See StockScreener.java
public class StockScreener {

    enum Screen { PE, YIELD, BETA };

    public static boolean screen(String stock, Screen screen, double threshold) {
        double screenVal = 0;
        boolean pass = false;
        switch (screen) {
            case PE:
                screenVal = Math.random() * 25;
                pass = screenVal <= threshold;
                break;
            case YIELD:
                screenVal = Math.random() * 10;
                pass = screenVal >= threshold;
                break;
            case BETA:
                screenVal = Math.random() * 2;
                pass = screenVal <= threshold;
                break;
        }
        System.out.println(stock + ": " + screen.toString() + " = " + screenVal);
```

```
        return pass;
    }

    /**
     * Parse through stock listing to determine if each stock passes the screen tests.  If
     * a particular element does not pass the screen, then remove it.
     */
    public static void screen(List<String> stocks, Screen screen, double threshold) {
        Iterator<String> iter = stocks.iterator();
        while (iter.hasNext()) {
            String stock = iter.next();
            if (!screen(stock, screen, threshold)) {
                iter.remove();
            }
        }
    }

    public static void main(String[] args) {

        List<String> stocks = new ArrayList<>();
        stocks.add("ORCL");
        stocks.add("AAPL");
        stocks.add("GOOG");
        stocks.add("IBM");
        stocks.add("MCD");
        System.out.println("Screening stocks: " + stocks);

        if (stocks.contains("GOOG") &&
            !screen("GOOG", Screen.BETA, 1.1)) {
            stocks.remove("GOOG");
        }
        System.out.println("First screen: " + stocks);

        StockScreener.screen(stocks, Screen.YIELD, 3.5);
        System.out.println("Second screen: " + stocks);
        StockScreener.screen(stocks, Screen.PE, 22);
        System.out.println("Third screen: " + stocks);

        System.out.println("Buy List: " + stocks);
    }
}
```

The output from running this code will vary because it is randomly assigning a stock's screen result value. Here is one sample of output from running the class:

```
Screening stocks: [ORCL, AAPL, GOOG, IBM, MCD]
GOOG: BETA = 1.9545048754918146
First screen: [ORCL, AAPL, IBM, MCD]
ORCL: YIELD = 5.54002319921808
AAPL: YIELD = 5.282200818124754
IBM: YIELD = 3.189521157557543
```

```
MCD: YIELD = 3.978628208965815
Second screen: [ORCL, AAPL, MCD]
ORCL: PE = 3.5561302619951993
AAPL: PE = 13.578302484429233
MCD: PE = 23.504349376296886
Third screen: [ORCL, AAPL]
Buy List: [ORCL, AAPL]
```

How It Works

The ArrayList is one of the most often used classes in the Java Collections Framework. The ArrayList class implements the List interface, which, in turn, implements the Collection interface. The Collection interface defines the set of common operations for all Collection types, and the List interface defines the set of operations that are specific to the list-oriented Collection types. The Collections Framework makes heavy use of Java generics. If you are new to generics, it is recommended that you read Recipe 7-5, which gives a brief summary of generics and their use with collections.

The StockScreener main() method starts by declaring a List of stocks, and specifying with the generic type parameter, that the stocks list elements will be of type String. Notice that the actual list type is an ArrayList that is created using the diamond, which is discussed in Recipe 7-5. The stocks list will hold a variable number of stocks, represented by their stock market symbol (a String):

```
List<String> stocks = new ArrayList<>();
```

Now that you've specified that the stocks list can only hold Strings, all the List methods, in turn, get parameterized to only allow Strings. So, next, the code makes several calls to the ArrayList's add(String) method to add the stocks to the list. After that, a screen is run on GOOG (Google) based on its Beta (a measure of stock risk); if it does not pass the screen, the List remove(String) method is called to remove the stock from the stock list. Two more screens are then run on the entire stock list to get a list of stocks that have a P/E of 22.0 or less, and a Yield of 3.5% or more. The screen() method used for these screens takes a parameter of type List<String>. It has to iterate over the list, run the screen for each stock in the list, and remove those stocks that do not pass the screen. Note that in order to safely remove an element from a Collection while iterating over it, you must use iterate using the Collection's Iterator, which can be obtained by calling its iterator() method. Here, we are showing the use of a while loop to iterate over the stocks list (a for loop could similarly be used). As long as you're not to the end of the list (iter.hasNext()), you can get the next stock from the list (iter.next()), run the screen, and remove the element from the list (iter.remove()) if the screen didn't pass.

▓ **Note** You may find that calling the list's remove() method while iterating the list seems to work. The problem is that it's not guaranteed to work and will produce unexpected results. At some point, the code will also throw a ConcurrentModificationException, regardless of whether you have multiple threads accessing the same list. Remember to always remove elements through the iterator when iterating over any Collection.

The ArrayList is a very useful data structure that should normally be used in place of the array type. It provides much more flexibility than a simple array, in that elements can be added and removed dynamically with ease. While it is true that ArrayList uses an array internally, you benefit from optimized add() and remove() operations that are implemented for you. Also, ArrayList implements many other very useful methods. Refer to the online Java documentation for further details (https://docs.oracle.com/javase/9/docs/api/java/util/ArrayList.html).

7-7. Making Your Objects Iterable

Problem

You have created a custom collection–based class that wraps (instead of extends) the underlying collection type. Without exposing the internal implementation details of your class, you would like objects of your class to become iterable, especially with the use of a foreach statement.

Solution

Have your class extend the Interable<T> interface, where T is the element type of the collection to be iterated. Implement the iterator() method to return the Iterator<T> object from this collection. The example for this recipe is the StockPortfolio class. Internally, StockPortfolio manages a collection of Stock objects. We would like users of our class to be able to treat StockPortfolio objects as iterable objects using a foreach statement. The StockPortfolio class follows:

```
// See StockPortfolio.java and Stock.java
public class StockPortfolio implements Iterable<Stock> {

    Map<String, Stock> portfolio = new HashMap<>();

    public void add(Stock stock) {
        portfolio.put(stock.getSymbol(), stock);
    }

    public void add(List<Stock> stocks) {
        for (Stock s : stocks) {
            portfolio.put(s.getSymbol(), s);
        }
    }

    @Override
    public Iterator<Stock> iterator() {
        return portfolio.values().iterator();
    }

    public static void main(String[] args) {

        StockPortfolio myPortfolio = new StockPortfolio();
        myPortfolio.add(new Stock("ORCL", "Oracle", 500.0));
        myPortfolio.add(new Stock("AAPL", "Apple", 200.0));
        myPortfolio.add(new Stock("GOOG", "Google", 100.0));
        myPortfolio.add(new Stock("IBM", "IBM", 50.0));
        myPortfolio.add(new Stock("MCD", "McDonalds", 300.0));

        // foreach loop (uses Iterator returned from iterator() method)
        System.out.println("====Print using legacy for-each loop====");
        for (Stock stock : myPortfolio) {
            System.out.println(stock);
        }
```

```
        System.out.println("====Print using Java 8 foreach implementation====");
        myPortfolio.forEach(s->System.out.println(s));
    }
}
```

The following code is that of the Stock class:

```java
public class Stock {
    private String symbol;
    private String name;
    private double shares;
    public Stock(String symbol, String name, double shares) {
        this.symbol = symbol;
        this.name = name;
        this.shares = shares;
    }
    public String getSymbol() {
        return symbol;
    }
    public String getName() {
        return name;
    }
    public double getShares() {
        return shares;
    }
    public String toString() {
        return shares + " shares of " + symbol + " (" + name + ")";
    }
}
```

The main() method creates a StockPortfolio and then calls the add() method to add a number of stocks to the portfolio. Both variations of the foreach loop (legacy and forEach implementation) are then used to loop over and print all the stocks in the portfolio. Running the StockPortfolio class results in the following output:

```
50.0 shares of IBM (IBM)
300.0 shares of MCD (McDonalds)
100.0 shares of GOOG (Google)
200.0 shares of AAPL (Apple)
500.0 shares of ORCL (Oracle)
```

■ **Note**   The order of the lines in the output may be different when you run the StockPortfolio class in your environment because the underlying implementation uses a HashMap. A HashMap does not guarantee the order of the elements stored in the map, and this extends to its iterators. If you wanted the iterator to return elements sorted by the stock symbol, you could use one of the sorted collections, such as TreeMap or TreeSet, instead of HashMap. Another option is to utilize a stream on the collection. See Recipe 7-10 for more about streams.

How It Works

The Iterable interface was introduced in Java 5 to support the enhanced for loop (also known as the foreach loop) which was introduced at the same time. Along with these enhancements to the language, all Collection classes were retrofitted to implement the Iterable interface, thus allowing Collection classes to be iterable using the foreach loop. The Iterable interface is a generic type defined as follows:

```
public interface Iterable<T> {
    Iterator<T> iterator();
}
```

Any class that implements Iterable<T> must implement the iterator() method to return an Iterator<T> object. Typically, the Iterator returned is the default iterator of the underlying collection; however, it may also return an instance of a custom Iterator. In the StockPortfolio class, a Map is used to represent the stock portfolio. The key for each map entry is the stock symbol, and the value associated with each key is a Stock object. Maps in Java are not iterable; that is, they are not Collection classes. Therefore, they do not implement Iterable. However, both the keys and the values of a map are Collections, and therefore are Iterables. We want our implementation of the Iterable iterator() method to return an Iterator over the values (Stock references) of the portfolio map; therefore, our Iterable implementation is parameterized by the Stock type:

```
public class StockPortfolio implements Iterable<Stock>
```

The Map values() method returns the Collection of map values; in this case, a Collection of Stocks. The iterator() method implementation can then simply return the Iterator for this Collection:

```
@Override
public Iterator<Stock> iterator() {
    return portfolio.values().iterator();
}
```

With this implementation of Iterable<Stock>, either the legacy a foreach loop, or the forEach implementation can be used to iterate a StockPortfolio instance and print each Stock:

```
myPortfolio.forEach(s->System.out.println(s));
```

The forEach method was new to the Iterable interface with the release of Java 8. The method performs the specified action for each element within the Iterable until all elements have been processed, or the specified action throws an exception. In this solution, the specified action is a lambda expression (see Chapter 6), which prints the value of each element within the myPortfolio Iterable.

You will notice that StockPortfolio also contains the add(List<Stock>) method, which allows the portfolio to be populated from a List. This method also uses a foreach loop to iterate through the input List. Again, this is possible because Lists are Iterables. (Note that this method is never called in the code; it exists only for illustration purposes.)

■ **Note** There's one issue with our implementation of StockPortfolio. We have gone to great lengths to not expose the internal implementation details of our class (the portfolio map). This allows us to change the implementation without affecting the StockPortfolio client code. However, when we implemented Iterable, we effectively exported the underlying portfolio map through the iterator() method. As was demonstrated in Recipe 7-5, an Iterator allows the underlying collection to be modified by calling its remove() method. Unfortunately, Java does not provide an UnmodifiableIterator class that could be used to wrap an Iterator and prevent modification of the underlying Collection. However, it would be simple to implement such a class that forwards the hasNext() and next() calls to the wrapped Iterator, but leaves the remove() method unimplemented (per the Iterator Java documentation, UnsupportedOperationException should be thrown). Alternatively, your iterator() method could return the Iterator from an unmodifiable Collection obtained through a call to the Collections. unmodifiableCollection() class method. You are encouraged to explore these two options. To give you a start, one possible implementation of UnmodifiableIterator has been provided in the source code download (see UnmodifiableIterator.java).

As you have seen in this recipe, the `Iterable` interface allows you to create iterable objects that are compatible with a `foreach` implementation. This is very useful when you want to design a custom collection-based class that encapsulates implementation details. Just keep in mind that in order to enforce the encapsulation and prevent modification of your underlying collection, you should implement one of the solutions mentioned in the preceding note.

7-8. Iterating Over Collections

Problem

Your application contains Collection types, and you want to iterate over the elements within them.

Solution

Generate a stream on any type that extends or implements `java.util.Collection`, and then perform the desired task(s) on each element of the collection. In the following code, an `ArrayList` loaded with `Stock` objects is used to demonstrate the concept of streams.

```java
public class StreamExample {
    static List<Stock> myStocks = new ArrayList();

    private static void createStocks(){
        myStocks.add(new Stock("ORCL", "Oracle", 500.0));
        myStocks.add(new Stock("AAPL", "Apple", 200.0));
        myStocks.add(new Stock("GOOG", "Google", 100.0));
        myStocks.add(new Stock("IBM", "IBM", 50.0));
        myStocks.add(new Stock("MCD", "McDonalds", 300.0));
    }
```

```
public static void main(String[] args){
    createStocks();
    // Iterate over each element and print the stock names
    myStocks.stream()
            .forEach(s->System.out.println(s.getName()));

    boolean allGt = myStocks.stream()
            .allMatch(s->s.getShares() > 100.0);
    System.out.println("All Stocks Greater Than 100.0 Shares? " + allGt);

    // Print out all stocks that have more than 100 shares
    System.out.println("== We have more than 100 shares of the following:");
    myStocks.stream()
            .filter(s -> s.getShares() > 100.0)
            .forEach(s->System.out.println(s.getName()));

    System.out.println("== The following stocks are sorted by shares:");
    Comparator<Stock> byShares = Comparator.comparing(Stock::getShares);
    Stream<Stock> sortedByShares = myStocks.stream()
            .sorted(byShares);
    sortedByShares.forEach(s -> System.out.println("Stock: " + s.getName() + " - Shares:
" + s.getShares()));

    // May or may not return a value
    Optional<Stock> maybe = myStocks.stream()
            .findFirst();
    System.out.println("First Stock: " + maybe.get().getName());

    List newStocks = new ArrayList();
    Optional<Stock> maybeNot = newStocks.stream()
            .findFirst();
    Consumer<Stock> myConsumer = (s) ->
    {
      System.out.println("First Stock (Optional): " + s.getName());
    };
    maybeNot.ifPresent(myConsumer);

    if(maybeNot.isPresent()){
        System.out.println(maybeNot.get().getName());
    }

    newStocks.add(new Stock("MCD", "McDonalds", 300.0));
    Optional<Stock> maybeNow = newStocks.stream()
            .findFirst();
    maybeNow.ifPresent(myConsumer);
}

}
```

The results of executing this code demonstrate the concept of using streams. External iteration (for loops) is no longer a requirement for iterating over a collection of data.

How It Works

Prior to Java 8, iterating over a Collection required some kind of looping block. This is known as external iteration, a.k.a. programmatic looping in sequential order. In most cases, a for loop was used to work through each element within a Collection, processing each element according to an application's requirements. While a for loop is a reasonable solution for performing iteration, it is both a nonintuitive and verbose strategy. Since the release of Java 8, the boilerplate of iterating over Collections was removed, along with the requirement to spell out how the iteration is to be completed. The compiler already knows how to iterate over a Collection, so why tell the compiler exactly how to do it? Why not simply tell the compiler: "I would like to iterate over this Collection, and perform this task on each element"? The concept of streams enables this hands-off approach to iteration.

Let the compiler take care of the nonintuitive looping, and simply hand the task off to the compiler and tell it what action to perform on each element. This concept is known as internal iteration. With internal iteration, your application determines what needs to be iterated, and the JDK decides how to perform the iteration. Internal iteration not only alleviates the requirement to program the looping logic, but it also has other advantages. One such advantage is that internal iteration is not limited to sequential iteration over elements. Therefore, the JDK decides how to iterate, choosing the best algorithm for the task at hand. Internal iteration also can more easily take advantage of parallel computing. This concept involves subdividing tasks into smaller problems, solving each in a simultaneous manner, and then combining the results.

A stream is a sequence of object references that can be generated on all Collection types. The Stream API makes it possible to perform a sequence of aggregate operations upon those object references and either return a result or apply the changes to the objects inline. This is also known as a ***pipeline***. The pseudocode for generation and use of a stream is as follows:

```
Collection -> (Stream) -> (Zero or More Intermediate Operations) -> (Terminal Operation)
```

Let's put this pseudocode into a real example. In the solution, a list of Stock objects is used for demonstrating stream iteration. Let's suppose you want to print out each stock that contains a number of shares that is over a designated threshold (100 shares in this example). You can use the following code to perform this task:

```
myStocks.stream()
            .filter(s -> s.getShares() > 100.0)
            .forEach(s->System.out.println(s.getName()));
```

In the previous example, an ***intermediate*** operation known as a filter() is used to apply a limitation on the elements, thereby filtering out all of the elements that do not match the supplied predicate. The predicate is written in the form of a lambda expression; it performs the test on each element and returns a Boolean result. The ***terminal*** operation in the example uses forEach() to print each of the matching elements. A terminal operation is the last operation in a pipeline, and it produces a nonstream result such as a primitive, collection, or no value at all. In the example case, no result is returned.

To generate a stream on a Collection type, call the stream() method, which will return a Stream type. In most cases, the Stream type is not the desired result, so the Stream API makes it possible to invoke zero or more intermediate operations upon a stream, forming a pipeline of operations. For example, in the solution the list of Stock objects is sorted by the number of shares using the following code. Note that Comparator byShares is applied to each object in the stream and a Stream<Stock> is returned as a result:

```
Stream<Stock> sortedByShares = myStocks.stream()
            .sorted(byShares);
```

In the previous example, a single intermediate operation, sorted(), is performed on the stream. As mentioned previously, there could be more than one intermediate operation chained to this pipeline, thereby performing the next operation upon those objects that meet the criteria of the previous operation. Each of the intermediate operations returns a Stream. Each pipeline can contain a terminal operation, thereby applying the terminal operation to each of the resulting stream objects. As mentioned previously, a terminal operation may or may not return a result. In the previous example, no terminal operation is applied.

■ **Note**   The online documentation for Stream (https://docs.oracle.com/javase/9/docs/api/java/util/stream/Stream.html) lists all of the intermediate and terminal operations available upon a stream.

Streams have been a revolutionary change for the Java programming language. They change the way in which a developer thinks about a program, making the developer more productive and the code more efficient. While legacy iteration techniques such as the for loop are still considered valid procedures, streams are the preferred technique for iteration when you're using Java 8 or beyond.

7-9. Iterating Over a Map

Problem

You are using one of the Map classes, such as HashMap or TreeMap, and you need to iterate over the keys, values, or both. You also want to remove elements from the map while you are iterating over it.

Solution

There are multiple ways to iterate over a Map. The method you choose should depend on which portions of the map you need to access and whether you need to remove elements from the map while iterating. The StockPortfolio1 class is a continuation of the StockPorfolio class shown in the previous recipe. It adds three methods, summary(), alertList(), and remove(List<String>), that demonstrate alternative methods for iterating over the portfolio map:

```java
// See StockPortfolio1.java
Map<String, Stock> portfolio = new HashMap<>();
...
public void summary() {
    System.out.println("==Legacy technique for traversing Map.Entry==");
    for (Map.Entry<String, Stock> entry : portfolio.entrySet()) {
        System.out.println("Stock = " + entry.getKey() + ", Shares = " + entry.getValue().
getShares());
    }

    System.out.println("==Utilization of new foreach and lambda combination==");
    portfolio.forEach((k,v)->System.out.println("Stock = " + k + ", Shares = " +
v.getShares()));
}
```

```java
/**
 * Utilize for loop to traverse Map keys and apply filter to obtain desired
 * stocks
 * @return
 */
public List<Stock> alertListLegacy() {
    System.out.println("==Legacy technique for filtering and collecting==");
    List<Stock> alertList = new ArrayList<>();
    for (Stock stock : portfolio.values()) {
        if (!StockScreener.screen(stock.getSymbol(), StockScreener.Screen.PE, 20)) {
            alertList.add(stock);
        }
    }

    return alertList;
}

/**
 * Utilize stream and filters to obtain desired stocks
 * @return
 */
public List<Stock> alertList(){
    return
    portfolio.values().stream()
            .filter(s->!StockScreener.screen(s.getSymbol(), StockScreener.Screen.PE, 20))
            .collect(Collectors.toList());

}

public void remove(List<String> sellList) {
    Iterator<String> keyIter = portfolio.keySet().iterator();
    while (keyIter.hasNext()) {
        if (sellList.contains(keyIter.next())) {
            keyIter.remove();
        }
    }
}
```

How It Works

A Map is an object that contains a collection of key/value pairs. Maps can be beneficial when you need to store an index (key) and associate it with a particular value. A Map must not contain any duplicate keys, and each key maps to exactly one value. The source code for the solution (StockPortfolio1.java) demonstrates how to add and remove entries from a Map. It also contains the source that is listed in the solution to this recipe, demonstrating how to iterate over Map entries using legacy techniques, as well as newer syntax that takes advantage of lambda expressions and streams.

The summary() method uses a foreach loop implementation to iterate over the portfolio map's Entry set. To iterate using the legacy code, the Map entrySet() method returns a Set of Map.Entry objects. Within the loop, you then have access to the key and value for the current Map.Entry by calling the respective methods, key() and value(), on that entry. Use this method of iterating when you need to access both the map keys and values while iterating, and you don't need to remove elements from the map. Taking a look at the newer syntax, you can see that the same iteration can be performed in a single line of code. The newer syntax utilizes the forEach() method, which was added to the Map interface in Java 8. It applies a lambda expression to each entry within the list. The lambda expression takes both the key and value as arguments, and then prints them out.

The alertListLegacy() method uses a foreach loop implementation to iterate over just the values of the portfolio map. The Map values() method returns a Collection of the map values; in this case, a Collection of Stocks. Use this method of iterating when you only need access to the map values and you don't need to remove elements from the list. Similarly, if you only need access to the map keys (again, without the need to remove elements), you can iterate using the keySet() method:

```
for (String symbol : portfolio.keySet()) {
    ...
}
```

If you also need to also access the map value while iterating using the key set, avoid the following, as it is very inefficient. Instead, use the method of iteration shown in the summary() method.

```
for (String symbol : portfolio.keySet()) {
    Stock stock = portfolio.get(symbol);
    ...
}
```

Taking a look at the alertList() method in the solution, you can see that the same iteration can be performed with much less work using a combination of streams, filters, and collectors. See Recipe 7-8 for more details regarding streams and the Stream API. In alertList(), a stream is generated, and then a filter, in the form of a lambda expression, is applied to that stream. Finally, a collector is applied to the filter, creating a List<Stock> to return.

The remove(List<String>) method takes a list of stock symbols representing the stocks to be removed from the portfolio. This method iterates over the portfolio map keys using the keySet() iterator, removing the current map entry if it is one of the stocks specified for removal. Notice that the map element is removed through the iterator's remove() method. This is possible because the key set is backed by the map, so changes made through the key set's iterator are reflected in the map. You could also iterate over the portfolio map using its values() iterator:

```
Iterator<Stock> valueIter = portfolio.values().iterator();
while (valueIter.hasNext()) {
    if (sellList.contains(valueIter.next().getSymbol())) {
        valueIter.remove();
    }
}
```

As with the key set, the values collection is backed by the map, so calling remove() through the values iterator will result in removal of the current entry from the portfolio map.

In summary, if you need to remove elements from a map while iterating over the map, iterate using one of the map's collection iterators and remove map elements through the iterator, as shown in the remove(List<String>) method. This is the only safe way to remove map elements during iteration. Otherwise, if you don't need to remove map elements, you can make use of a foreach loop and one of the methods of iteration shown in the solution to this recipe.

7-10. Executing Streams in Parallel

Problem

You want to iterate over a Collection in parallel to distribute the work over multiple CPUs.

Solution

Utilize a stream construct on the Collection, and invoke parallelStream() as the first intermediate operation in order to take advantage of multiple CPU processing. The following class demonstrates multiple uses of the parallelStream() operation:

```
public class StockPortfolio2 {
    static List<Stock> myStocks = new ArrayList();

    private static void createStocks(){
        myStocks.add(new Stock("ORCL", "Oracle", 500.0));
        myStocks.add(new Stock("AAPL", "Apple", 200.0));
        myStocks.add(new Stock("GOOG", "Google", 100.0));
        myStocks.add(new Stock("IBM", "IBM", 50.0));
        myStocks.add(new Stock("MCD", "McDonalds", 300.0));
    }

    public static void main(String[] args){
        createStocks();
        // Iterate over each element and print the stock names
        myStocks.stream()
                .forEach(s->System.out.println(s.getName()));

        boolean allGt = myStocks.parallelStream()
                .allMatch(s->s.getShares() > 100.0);
        System.out.println("All Stocks Greater Than 100.0 Shares? " + allGt);

        // Print out all stocks that have more than 100 shares
        System.out.println("== We have more than 100 shares of the following:");
        myStocks.parallelStream()
                .filter(s -> s.getShares() > 100.0)
                .forEach(s->System.out.println(s.getName()));

        System.out.println("== The following stocks are sorted by shares:");
        Comparator<Stock> byShares = Comparator.comparing(Stock::getShares);
        Stream<Stock> sortedByShares = myStocks.parallelStream()
                .sorted(byShares);
        sortedByShares.forEach(s -> System.out.println("Stock: " + s.getName() + " - Shares:
 " + s.getShares()));

        // May or may not return a value
        Optional<Stock> maybe = myStocks.parallelStream()
                .findFirst();
        System.out.println("First Stock: " + maybe.get().getName());
```

```java
List newStocks = new ArrayList();
Optional<Stock> maybeNot = newStocks.parallelStream()
        .findFirst();
Consumer<Stock> myConsumer = (s) ->
{
  System.out.println("First Stock (Optional): " + s.getName());
};
maybeNot.ifPresent(myConsumer);

if(maybeNot.isPresent()){
    System.out.println(maybeNot.get().getName());
}

newStocks.add(new Stock("MCD", "McDonalds", 300.0));
Optional<Stock> maybeNow = newStocks.stream()
        .findFirst();
maybeNow.ifPresent(myConsumer);

    }

}
```

How It Works

By default, operations are executed in serial stream. However, you can specify that the Java runtime split the operations between multiple subtasks, thus taking advantage of multiple CPUs for performance. When operations are executed in this manner, they are executed in "parallel." Streams can be partitioned into multiple substreams by the Java runtime by invoking the parallelStream() intermediate operation. When this operation is invoked, aggregate operations can process the multiple substreams and then the results will be combined in the end. You can also execute a stream in parallel by invoking the operation BaseStream. parallel.

Summary

This chapter looked at various data structures and how to work with them. First, you took a look at Enums and learned how to utilize them effectively. Next, we covered the basics of Arrays and ArrayList, and learned how to iterate over elements within these structures. The chapter also covered Java generics, which allow you to decouple object types from container types, providing for more type-safe and efficient code. Lastly, this chapter covered the Streams API, which is one of the most important updates introduced with the release of Java 8, for working with collections.

■ ■ ■

CHAPTER 8

Input and Output

Oftentimes in applications, there is a requirement to obtain and manipulate the I/O terminals. In today's operating systems, that usually means file access and network connectivity. In previous releases, Java was slow to adopt a good file and network framework in order to maintain universal compatibility. Standing true to its roots of write once, read everywhere, a lot of the original file I/O and network connectivity needed to be simple and universal. Since the release of Java 7, developers have been taking advantage of much better I/O APIs.

The file and network I/O has evolved over the years into a much better framework for handling files, network scalability, and ease of use. As of the network input output version 2 API (NIO.2), Java has the capability of monitoring folders, accessing OS-dependent methods, and creating scalable asynchronous network sockets. This is in addition to the already robust library for handling input and output streams, and serializing (and deserializing) object information.

In this chapter, we cover recipes that demonstrate different input and output processes. You learn about serialization of files, sending files over the network, file manipulation, and much more. After reading the recipes in this chapter, you will be armed with the capability to develop applications containing sophisticated input and output tasks.

STREAMS AND THE DECORATOR PATTERN

I/O streams are the foundation of most of the Java I/O and include a plethora of ready-made streams for just about any occasion, but they are very confusing to use if some context is not provided. A stream (like a river) represents an inflow/outflow of data. Think about it this way. When you type, you create a stream of characters that the system receives (input stream). When the system produces sounds, it sends them to the speaker (output stream). The system could be receiving keystrokes and sending sound all day long, and thus the streams can be either processing data or waiting for more data.

When a stream doesn't receive any data, it waits (nothing else to do, right?). As soon as data comes in, the stream starts processing this data. The stream then stops and waits for the next data item to come. This keeps going until this proverbial river becomes dry (the stream is closed).

Like a river, streams can be connected to each other (this is the decorator pattern). For the content of this chapter, there are mainly two input streams that you care about. One of them is the file input stream, and the other is the network socket input stream. These two streams are a source of data for your I/O programs. There are also their corresponding output streams: file output stream and the network socket output streams (how creative, isn't it?). Like a plumber, you can hook them together and create something new. For example, you could weld together a file input stream to a network output stream to send the contents of the file through a network socket. Or you could do the opposite and connect a network input stream (data coming in) to a file output stream (data being written to disk). In I/O parlance, the input streams are called *sources*, while the output streams are called *sinks*.

There are other input and output streams that can be glued together. For example, there is a BufferedInputStream, which allows you to read the data in chunks (it's more efficient than reading it byte by byte), and DataOutputStream allows you to write Java primitives to an output stream (instead of just writing bytes). One of the most useful streams is the ObjectInputStream and ObjectOutputStream pair, which will allow you to serialize/deserialize object (see Recipe 8-1).

The decorator pattern allows you to keep plucking streams together to get many different effects. The beauty of this design is that you can actually create a stream that will take any input and produce any output, and then can be thrown together with every other stream.

8-1. Serializing Java Objects

Problem

You need to serialize a class (save the contents of the class) so that you can restore it at a later time.

Solution

Java implements a built-in serialization mechanism. You access that mechanism via the ObjectOutputStream class. In the following example, the method saveSettings() uses an ObjectOutputStream to serialize the settings object in preparation for writing the object to disk:

```
public class Ch_8_1_SerializeExample {
    public static void main(String[] args) {
        Ch_8_1_SerializeExample example = new Ch_8_1_SerializeExample();
        example.start();
    }

    private void start() {
        ProgramSettings settings = new ProgramSettings(new Point(10,10),
                                            new Dimension(300,200),    Color.blue,
                                            "The title of the application" );
        saveSettings(settings,"settings.bin");
        ProgramSettings loadedSettings = loadSettings("settings.bin");
        if(loadedSettings != null)
            System.out.println("Are settings are equal? :"+loadedSettings.equals(settings));

    }

    private void saveSettings(ProgramSettings settings, String filename) {
        try {
            FileOutputStream fos = new FileOutputStream(filename);
            try (ObjectOutputStream oos = new ObjectOutputStream(fos)) {
                oos.writeObject(settings);
            }
```

```
        } catch (IOException e) {
            e.printStackTrace();
        }
    }

    private ProgramSettings loadSettings(String filename) {
        try {
            FileInputStream fis = new FileInputStream(filename);
            ObjectInputStream ois = new ObjectInputStream(fis);
            return (ProgramSettings) ois.readObject();
        } catch (IOException | ClassNotFoundException e) {
            e.printStackTrace();
        }
        return null;
    }
}
```

How It Works

Java supports *serialization*, which is the capability of taking an object and creating a byte representation that can be used to restore the object at a later time. By using an internal serialization mechanism, most of the setup to serialize objects is taken care of. Java will transform the properties of an object into a byte stream, which can then be saved to a file or transmitted over the wire.

■ **Note** The original Java Serialization framework uses reflection to serialize the objects, so it might be an issue if serializing/deserializing heavily. There are plenty of open source frameworks that offer different trade-offs depending on your need (speed versus size versus ease of use). See `https://github.com/eishay/jvm-serializers/wiki/`.

For a class to be serializable, it needs to implement the Serializable interface, which is a *Marker interface*: it doesn't have any methods, but instead tells the serialization mechanism that you have allowed your class to be serialized. While not evident from the onset, serialization exposes all the internal workings of your class (including protected and private members), so if you want to keep secret the authorization code for a nuclear launch, you might want to make any class that contains such information nonserializable.

It is also necessary that all properties (a.k.a. members, variables, or fields) of the class are serializable (and/or transient, which we will get to in a minute). All primitives—int, long, double, and float (plus their wrapper classes)—and the String class, are serializable by design. Other Java classes are serializable on a case-by-case basis. For example, you can't serialize any Swing components (like JButton or JSpinner), and you can't serialize File objects, but you can serialize the Color class (awt.color, to be more precise).

As a design principle you don't want to serialize your main classes, but instead you want to create classes that contain only the properties that you want to serialize. It will save a lot of headache in debugging because serialization becomes very pervasive. If you mark a major class as serializable (implements Serializable), and this class contains many other properties, you need to declare those classes as serializable as well. If your Java class inherits from another class, the parent class should also be serializable. In the case where the parent class is not serializable, the parent's properties will not be serialized.

If you want to mark a property as nonserializable, you may mark it as *transient*. Transient properties tell the Java compiler that you are not interested in saving/loading the property value, so it will be ignored. Some properties are good candidates for being transient, like cached calculations, or a date formatter that you always instantiate to the same value.

By the virtue of the Serialization framework, static properties are not serializable; neither are static classes. The reason is that a static class cannot be instantiated, although a public static inner class can be instantiated. Therefore, if you save and then load the static class at the same time, you will have loaded another copy of the static class, throwing the JVM for a loop.

The Java serialization mechanism works behind the scenes to convert and traverse every object within the class that is marked as `Serializable`. If an application contains objects within objects, and even perhaps contains cross-referenced objects, the Serialization framework will resolve those objects, and store only one copy of any object. Each property then gets translated to a `byte[]` representation. The format of the byte array includes the actual class name (for example: `com.somewhere.over.the.rainbow.preferences.UserPreferences`), followed by the encoding of the properties (which in turn may encode another object class, with its properties, etc., etc., *ad infinitum*).

For the curious, if you look at the file generated (even in a text editor), you can see the class name as almost the first part of the file.

■ **Note**   Serialization is very brittle. By default, the Serialization framework generates a *Stream Unique Identifier (SUID)* that captures information about what fields are presented in the class, what kind they are (public/protected), and what is transient, among other things. Even a perceived slight modification of the class (for example, changing an `int` to a `long` property) will generate a new SUID. A class that has been saved with a prior SUID cannot be deserialized on the new SUID. This is done to protect the serialization/deserialization mechanism, while also protecting the designers.

You can actually tell the Java class to use a specific SUID. This will allow you to serialize classes, modify them, and then deserialize the original classes while implementing some backward compatibility. The danger you run into is that the deserialization must be backward-compatible. Renaming or removing fields will generate an exception as the class is being deserialized. If you are specifying your own serial Serializable on your Serializable class, be sure to have some unit tests for backward compatibility every time you change the class. In general, the changes that can be made on a class to keep it backward-compatible are found here: `http://docs.oracle.com/javase/9/docs/platform/serialization/spec/serial-arch.html`.

Due to the nature of serialization, don't expect constructors to be called when an object is deserialized. If you have initialization code in constructors that is required for your object to function properly, you may need to refactor the code out of the constructor to allow proper execution after construction. The reason is that in the deserialization process, the deserialized objects are "restored" internally (not created) and do not invoke constructors.

8-2. Serializing Java Objects More Efficiently

Problem

You want to serialize a class, but want to make the output more efficient, or smaller in size, than the product generated via the built-in serialization method.

Solution

By making the object implement the Externalizable interface, you instruct the Java Virtual Machine to use a custom serialization/deserialization mechanism, as provided by the readExternal/writeExternal methods in the following example.

```java
public class ExternalizableProgramSettings implements Externalizable {
    private Point locationOnScreen;
    private Dimension frameSize;
    private Color defaultFontColor;
    private String title;

    // Empty constructor, required for Externalizable implementors
    public ExternalizableProgramSettings() {

    }

    @Override
    public void writeExternal(ObjectOutput out) throws IOException {
        out.writeInt(locationOnScreen.x);
        out.writeInt(locationOnScreen.y);
        out.writeInt(frameSize.width);
        out.writeInt(frameSize.height);
        out.writeInt(defaultFontColor.getRGB());
        out.writeUTF(title);
    }

    @Override
    public void readExternal(ObjectInput in) throws IOException, ClassNotFoundException {
        locationOnScreen = new Point(in.readInt(), in.readInt());
        frameSize = new Dimension(in.readInt(), in.readInt());
        defaultFontColor = new Color(in.readInt());
        title = in.readUTF();
    }
// getters and setters omitted for brevity
}
```

How It Works

The Java Serialization framework provides the ability for you to specify the implementation for serializing an object. As such, it requires implementing the Externalizable interface in lieu of the Serializable interface. The Externalizable interface contains two methods: writeExternal(ObjectOutput out) and readExternal(ObjectInput in). By implementing these methods, you are telling the framework how to encode/decode your object.

The `writeExternal()` method will pass in as a parameter an `ObjectOutput` object. This object will then let you write your own encoding for the serialization. The `ObjectOutput` contains the methods listed in Table 8-1.

Table 8-1. *ObjectOutput Methods*

ObjectOutput	ObjectInput	Description
writeBoolean (boolean v)	booleanreadBoolean ()	Read/writes the Boolean primitive.
writeByte(int v)	intreadByte()	Read/writes a byte. Note: Java doesn't have a byte primitive, so an `int` is used as a parameter, but only the least-significant byte will be written.
writeShort(int v)	intreadShort()	Read/writes two bytes. Note: Only the two least-significant bytes will be written.
writeChar(int v)	intreadChar()	Read/writes two bytes as a char (reverse order than `writeShort`).
writeInt (int v)	intreadInt()	Read/writes an integer.
writeLong (long v)	intreadLong()	Read/writes a long.
writeDouble (double v)	double readDouble	Read/writes a double.

One reason you may choose to implement the `Externalizable` interface instead of the `Serializable` interface is because Java's default serialization is very inefficient. Because the Java Serialization framework needs to ensure that every object (and dependent object) is serialized, it will write even objects that have default values or that might be empty and/or null. Implementing the `Externalizable` interface also provides for finer-grained control on how your class is being serialized. In our example, the `Serializable` version created a setting of 439 bytes, compared with the `Externalizable` version of only 103 bytes!

▓ **Note**   Classes that implement the `Externalizable` interface must contain an empty (no-arg) constructor.

8-3. Serializing Java Objects as XML

Problem

Although you love the Serialization framework, you want to create something that is at least cross-language-compatible (or human readable). You would like to save and load your objects using XML.

Solution

In this example, the `XMLEncoder` object is used to encode the `Settings` object, which contains program settings information and writes it to the `settings.xml` file. The `XMLDecoder` takes the `settings.xml` file and reads it as a stream, decoding the `Settings` object. A `FileSystem` is used to gain access to the machine's file system; FileOutputStream is used to write a file to the system; and FileInputStream is used to obtain input bytes from a file within the file system. In this example, these three file objects are used to create new XML files, as well as read them for processing.

```
//Encoding
FileSystem fileSystem = FileSystems.getDefault();
try (FileOutputStream fos = new FileOutputStream("settings.xml"); XMLEncoder encoder =
        new XMLEncoder(fos)) {
    encoder.setExceptionListener((Exception e) -> {
        System.out.println("Exception! :"+e.toString());
    });
    encoder.writeObject(settings);
}

// Decoding
try (FileInputStream fis = new FileInputStream("settings.xml"); XMLDecoder decoder =
        new XMLDecoder(fis)) {
    ProgramSettings decodedSettings = (ProgramSettings) decoder.readObject();
    System.out.println("Is same? "+settings.equals(decodedSettings));
}

Path file= fileSystem.getPath("settings.xml");
List<String> xmlLines = Files.readAllLines(file, Charset.defaultCharset());
xmlLines.stream().forEach((line) -> {
    System.out.println(line);
});
```

How It Works

XMLEncoder and XMLDecoder, like the Serialization framework, use reflection to determine which fields are to be written, but instead of writing the fields as binary, they are written as XML. Objects that are to be encoded do not need to be serializable, but they do need to follow the Java Beans specification.

Java Bean is the name of any object that conforms to the following contract:

- The object contains a public empty (no-arg) constructor.

- The object contains public getters and setters for each protected/private property
  that takes the name of get{Property}() and set{Property}().

The XMLEncoder and XMLDecoder will encode/decode only the properties of the Bean that have public accessors (get{property}, set{property}), so any properties that are private and do not have accessors will not be encoded/decoded.

▓ **Tip**   It is a good idea to register an Exception Listener when encoding/decoding.

The XmlEncoder creates a new instance of the class that being serialized (remember that they need to be Java Beans, so they must have an empty no-arg constructor), and then figures out which properties are accessible (via get{property}, set{property}). And if a property of the newly instantiated class contains the same value as the property of the original class (i.e., has the same default value), the XmlEncoder doesn't write that property. In other words, if the default value of a property hasn't changed, the XmlEncoder will not write it out. This provides the flexibility of changing what a "default" value is between versions. For example, if the default value of a property is 2 when an object is encoded, and later decoded after the default property changed from 2 to 4, the decoded object will contain the new default property of 4 (which might not be correct).

The XMLEncoder also keeps track of references. If an object appears more than once when being persisted in the object graph (for example, an object is inside a Map from the main class, but is also as the DefaultValue property), then the XMLEncoder will only encode it once, and link up a reference by putting a link in the xml. The XMLEncoder/XMLDecoder is much more forgiving than the Serialization framework. When decoding, if a property type is changed, or if it was deleted/added/moved/renamed, the decoding will decode "as much as it can" while skipping the properties that it couldn't decode.

The recommendation is to not persist your main classes (even though the XMLEncoder is more forgiving), but to create special objects that are simple, hold the basic information, and do not perform many tasks by themselves.

8-4. Creating a Socket Connection and Sending Serializable Objects Across the Wire

Problem

You need to open a network connection, and send/receive objects from it.

Solution

Use Java's New Input Output API version 2 (NIO.2) to send and receive objects. The following solution utilizes the NIO.2 features of nonblocking sockets (by using Future tasks):

```
public class Ch_8_4_AsyncChannel {
    private AsynchronousSocketChannel clientWorker;

    InetSocketAddress hostAddress;

    public Ch_8_4_AsyncChannel() {
    }

    private void start() throws IOException, ExecutionException, TimeoutException,
InterruptedException {
        hostAddress = new InetSocketAddress(InetAddress.getByName("127.0.0.1"), 2583);

        Thread serverThread = new Thread(() -> {
            serverStart();
        });

        serverThread.start();

        Thread clientThread = new Thread(() -> {
            clientStart();
        });
        clientThread.start();

    }
```

```java
    private void clientStart() {
        try {
            try (AsynchronousSocketChannel clientSocketChannel = AsynchronousSocketChannel.
            open()) {
                Future<Void> connectFuture = clientSocketChannel.connect(hostAddress);
                connectFuture.get();             // Wait until connection is done.
                OutputStream os = Channels.newOutputStream(clientSocketChannel);
                try (ObjectOutputStream oos = new ObjectOutputStream(os)) {
                    for (int i = 0; i < 5; i++) {
                        oos.writeObject("Look at me " + i);
                        Thread.sleep(1000);
                    }
                    oos.writeObject("EOF");
                }
            }
        } catch (IOException | InterruptedException | ExecutionException e) {
            e.printStackTrace();
        }

    }

    private void serverStart() {
        try {
            AsynchronousServerSocketChannel serverSocketChannel =
            AsynchronousServerSocketChannel.open().bind(hostAddress);
            Future<AsynchronousSocketChannel> serverFuture  = serverSocketChannel.accept();
            final AsynchronousSocketChannel clientSocket = serverFuture.get();
            System.out.println("Connected!");
            if ((clientSocket != null) && (clientSocket.isOpen())) {
                try (InputStream connectionInputStream = Channels.
                newInputStream(clientSocket)) {
                    ObjectInputStream ois = null;
                    ois = new ObjectInputStream(connectionInputStream);
                    while (true) {
                        Object object = ois.readObject();
                        if (object.equals("EOF")) {
                            clientSocket.close();
                            break;
                        }
                        System.out.println("Received :" + object);
                    }
                    ois.close();
                }
            }

        } catch (IOException | InterruptedException | ExecutionException |
ClassNotFoundException e) {
            e.printStackTrace();
        }

    }
```

```
    public static void main(String[] args) throws IOException, ExecutionException,
TimeoutException, InterruptedException {
        Ch_8_4_AsyncChannel example = new Ch_8_4_AsyncChannel();
        example.start();
    }
}
```

How It Works

At its basic level, sockets require a type, IP address, and port. While sockets literature has consumed whole books, the main idea is pretty straightforward. Like the post office, socket communication relies on addresses. These addresses are used to deliver data. In this example, we picked the loopback (the same computer where the program is running) address (127.0.0.1), and chose a random port number (2583).

The advantage of the new NIO.2 is that it is asynchronous in nature. By using asynchronous calls, you can scale your application without creating thousands of threads for each connection. In our example, we take the asynchronous calls and wait for a connection, effectively making it single-threaded for the sake of the example, but don't let that stop you for enhancing this example with more asynchronous calls. (Check the recipes on the multithreaded section of this book.)

For a client to connect, it requires a socket channel. The NIO.2 API allows creation of asynchronous socket channels. Once a socket channel is created, it will need an address to connect to. The socketChannel.connect() operation does not block; instead it returns a Future object (this is a different from traditional NIO, where calling socketChannel.connect() will block until a connection is established). The Future object allows a Java program to continue what it is doing and simply query the status of the submitted task. To take the analogy further, instead of waiting at the front door for your mail to arrive, you go do other stuff, and "check" periodically to see whether the mail has arrived. Future objects have methods like isDone() and isCancelled() that let you know if the task is done or cancelled. It also has the get() method, which allows you to actually wait for the task to finish. In our example, we use the Future.get() to wait for the client connection to be established.

Once the connection is established, we use Channels.newOutputStream() to create an output stream to send information. Using the decorator pattern, we decorate the outputStream with our ObjectOutputStream to finally send objects through the socket.

The server code is a little more elaborate. Server socket connections allow more than one connection to occur, thus they are used to monitor or receive connections instead of initiating a connection. For this reason, the server is usually waiting for a connection asynchronously.

The server begins by establishing the address it listens to (127.0.0.1:2583) and accepting connections. The call to serverSocketChannel.accept() returns another Future object that will give you the flexibility of how to deal with incoming connections. In our example, the server connection simply calls Future.get(), which will block (stop the execution of the program) until a connection is accepted.

After the server acquires a socket channel, it creates an inputStream by calling Channels.newInputStream(socket) and then wrapping that input stream with an ObjectInputStream. The server then proceeds to loop and read each object coming from the ObjectInputStream. If the object received's toString() method equals EOF, the server stops looping and the connection is closed.

■ **Note** Using an ObjectOutputStream and ObjectInputStream to send and receive a lot of objects can lead to memory leaks. ObjectOutputStream keeps a copy of the sent object for efficiency. If you were to send the same object again, ObjectOutputStream and ObjectInputStream will not send the same object again, but instead send a previously sent Object ID. This behavior or just sending the Object ID instead of the whole object raises two issues.

The first issue is that objects that are changed in place (mutable) will not get the change reflected in the receiving client when sent through the wire. The reason is that because the object was sent once, the ObjectOutputStream believes that the object is already transmitted and will only send the ID, negating any changes to the object that have happened since it was sent. To avoid this, don't make changes to objects that were sent down the wire. This rule also applies to subobjects from the object graph.

The second issue is that because ObjectOutputStream maintains a list of sent objects and their Object IDs, if you send a lot of objects the dictionary of sent objects to keys grows indefinitely, causing memory starvation on a long-running program. To alleviate this issue, you can call ObjectOutputStream.reset(), which will clear the dictionary of sent objects. Alternatively, you can invoke ObjectOutputStream.writeUnshared() to not cache the object in the ObjectOutputStream dictionary.

8-5. Obtaining the Java Execution Path

Problem

You want to get the path where the Java program is running.

Solution

Invoke the System class's getProperty method. For example:

```
String  path = System.getProperty("user.dir");
```

How It Works

When a Java program starts, the JDK updates the user.dir system property to record where the JDK was invoked. The solution example passes the property name "user.dir" to the getProperty method, which returns the value.

8-6. Copying a File

Problem

You need to copy a file from one folder to another.

Solution

From the default FileSystem, you create the "to" and "from" paths where the files/folders exist and then use the Files.copy static method to copy files between the created paths:

```
FileSystem fileSystem = FileSystems.getDefault();
Path sourcePath = fileSystem.getPath("file.log");
Path targetPath = fileSystem.getPath("file2.log");
System.out.println("Copy from "+sourcePath.toAbsolutePath().toString()+
" to "+targetPath.toAbsolutePath().toString());
try {
    Files.copy(sourcePath, targetPath, StandardCopyOption.REPLACE_EXISTING);
} catch (IOException e) {
    e.printStackTrace();
}
```

How It Works

In the new NIO.2 libraries, Java works with an abstraction level that allows for more direct manipulation of file attributes belonging to the underlying operating system.

FileSystem.getDefaults() gets the usable abstract system that you can do file operations on. For example, running this example in Windows will get you a WindowsFileSystem; if you were running this example in Linux, a LinuxFileSystem object would be returned; on OS X, a MacOSXFileSystem is returned. AllFileSystems supports basic operations; in addition, each concrete FileSystem provides access to the unique features offered for that operating system.

After getting the default FileSystem object, you can query for file objects. In the NIO.2 file, folders and links are all called *paths*. Once you get a path, you can perform operations with it. In this example, Files.copy is called with the source and destination paths. The last parameter refers to the different copy options. The different copy options are file system dependent so make sure that the one that you choose is compatible with the operating system you intend to run the application in.

8-7. Moving a File

Problem

You need to move a file from one file system location to another.

Solution

As in Recipe 8-6, you use the default FileSystem to create the "to" and "from" paths, and invoke the Files.move() static method:

```
FileSystem fileSystem = FileSystems.getDefault();
Path sourcePath = fileSystem.getPath("file.log");
Path targetPath = fileSystem.getPath("file2.log");
System.out.println("Copy from "+sourcePath.toAbsolutePath().toString()+
                    " to "+targetPath.toAbsolutePath().toString());
```

```
try {
    Files.move(sourcePath, targetPath);
} catch (IOException e) {
    e.printStackTrace();
}
```

How It Works

In the same manner as copying a file, create the path of source and destination. After having the source and destination paths, `Files.move` will take care of moving the file from one location to another for you. Other methods provided by the `Files` object are the following:

- `Delete (path)`: Deletes a file (or a folder, if it's empty).

- `Exists (path)`: Checks whether a file/folder exists.

- `isDirectory (path)`: Checks whether the path created points to a directory.

- `isExecutable (path)`: Checks whether the file is an executable.

- `isHidden (path)`: Checks whether the file is visible or hidden in the operating system.

8-8. Creating a Directory

Problem

You need to create a directory from your Java application.

Solution 1

By using the default `FileSystem`, you instantiate a path pointing to the new directory; then invoke the `Files.createDirectory()` static method, which creates the directory specified in the path.

```
FileSystem fileSystem = FileSystems.getDefault();
Path directory= fileSystem.getPath("./newDirectory");
try {
    Files.createDirectory(directory);
} catch (IOException e) {
    e.printStackTrace();
}
```

Solution 2

If using a *nix operating system, you can specify the folder attributes by invoking the `PosixFilePermission()` method, which lets you set access at the owner, group, and world levels. For example:

```
FileSystem fileSystem = FileSystems.getDefault();
Path directory= fileSystem.getPath("./newDirectoryWPermissions");
try {
    Set<PosixFilePermission> perms = PosixFilePermissions.fromString("rwxr-x---");
```

```
        FileAttribute<Set<PosixFilePermission>> attr =
            PosixFilePermissions.asFileAttribute(perms);
        Files.createDirectory(directory, attr);

} catch (IOException e) {
    e.printStackTrace();
}
```

How It Works

The `Files.createDirectory()` method takes a path as a parameter and then creates the directory, as demonstrated in solution 1. By default, the directory created will inherit the default permissions. If you wanted to specify specific permissions in Linux, you can use the `PosixAttributes` as an extra parameter in the `createDirectory()` method. Solution 2 demonstrates the ability to pass a `Set` of `PosixFilePermissions` to set up the permissions on the newly created directory.

8-9. Iterating Over Files in a Directory

Problem

You need to scan files from a directory. There are possibly subdirectories with more files. You want to include those in your scan.

Solution

Using the NIO.2, create a `FileVisitor` object and perform a desired implementation within its `visitFile` method. Next, obtain the default `FileSystem` object and grab a reference to the `Path` that you'd like to scan via the `getPath()` method. Lastly, invoke the `Files.walkFileTree()` method, passing the `Path` and the `FileVisitor` that you created. The following code demonstrates how to perform these tasks.

```
FileVisitor<Path> myFileVisitor = new SimpleFileVisitor<Path>() {
    @Override
    public FileVisitResult visitFile(Path file, BasicFileAttributes attrs)
                        throws IOException {
        System.out.println("Visited File: "+file.toString());
        return FileVisitResult.CONTINUE;
    }
};

FileSystem fileSystem = FileSystems.getDefault();
Path directory= fileSystem.getPath(".");
try {
    Files.walkFileTree(directory, myFileVisitor);
} catch (IOException e) {
    e.printStackTrace();
}
```

How It Works

Before NIO.2, trying to traverse a directory tree involved recursion, and depending on the implementation, it could be very brittle. The calls to get files within a folder were synchronous and required the scanning of the whole directory before returning; generating what would appear to be an unresponsive method call to an application user. With NIO.2, one can specify which folder to start traversing on, and the NIO.2 calls will handle the recursion details. The only item that you provide to the NIO.2 API is a class that tells it what to do when a file/folder is found (`SimpleFileVisitor` implementation). NIO.2 uses a `Visitor` pattern, so it isn't required to prescan the entire folder, but instead processes files as they are being iterated over.

The implementation of the `SimpleFileVisitor` class as an anonymous inner class includes overriding the `visitFile(Path file, BasicFileAttributesattrs()` method. When you override this method, you can specify the tasks to perform when a file is encountered.

The `visitFile` method returns a `FileVisitReturn` enum. This enum then tells the `FileVisitor` which action to take:

- `CONTINUE`: Continues with the traversing of the directory tree.

- `TERMINATE`: Stops the traversing.

- `SKIP_SUBTREE`: Stops going deeper from the current tree level (useful only if this enum is returned on the `preVisitDirectory()` method).

- `SKIP_SIBLINGS`: Skips the other directories at the same tree level as the current.

The `SimpleFileVisitor` class, aside from the `visitFile()` method, also contains the following:

- `preVisitDirectory`: Called before entering a directory to be traversed.

- `postVisitDirectory`: Called after finished traversing a directory.

- `visitFile`: Called as it visits the file, as in the example code.

- `visitFileFailed`: Called if the file cannot be visited; for example, on an I/O error.

8-10. Querying (and Setting) File Metadata

Problem

You need to get information about a particular file, such as file size, whether it is a directory, and so on. Also, you might want to mark a file as *archived* in the Windows operating system or grant specific POSIX file permissions in the *nix operating system (refer to Recipe 8-8).

Solution

Using Java NIO.2 you can obtain any file information by simply invoking methods on the `java.nio.file.Files` utility class, passing the path for which you'd like to obtain the metadata. You can obtain attribute information by calling the `Files.getFileAttributeView()` method, passing the specific implementation for the attribute view that you would like to use. The following code demonstrates these techniques for obtaining metadata.

```
Path path = FileSystems.getDefault().getPath("./file2.log");
try {
    // General file attributes, supported by all Java systems
    System.out.println("File Size:"+Files.size(path));
```

```
    System.out.println("Is Directory:"+Files.isDirectory(path));
    System.out.println("Is Regular File:"+Files.isRegularFile(path));
    System.out.println("Is Symbolic Link:"+Files.isSymbolicLink(path));
    System.out.println("Is Hidden:"+Files.isHidden(path));
    System.out.println("Last Modified Time:"+Files.getLastModifiedTime(path));
    System.out.println("Owner:"+Files.getOwner(path));

    // Specific attribute views.
    DosFileAttributeView view = Files.getFileAttributeView(path,
        DosFileAttributeView.class);
    System.out.println("DOS File Attributes\n");
    System.out.println("-----------------------------------\n");
    System.out.println("Archive  :"+view.readAttributes().isArchive());
    System.out.println("Hidden   :"+view.readAttributes().isHidden());
    System.out.println("Read-only:"+view.readAttributes().isReadOnly());
    System.out.println("System   :"+view.readAttributes().isSystem());

    view.setArchive(false);

} catch (IOException e) {
    e.printStackTrace();
}
```

How It Works

Java NIO.2 allows much more flexibility in getting and setting file attributes than older I/O techniques.
NIO.2 abstracts the different operating system attributes into both a "Common" set of attributes and an "OS
Specific" set of attributes. The standard attributes are the following:

- isDirectory: True if it's a directory.

- isRegularFile: Returns false if the file isn't considered a regular file, the file doesn't
  exist, or it can't be determined whether it's a regular file.

- isSymbolicLink: True if the link is symbolic (most prevalent in Unix systems).

- isHidden: True if the file is considered to be hidden in the operating system.

- LastModifiedTime: The time the file was last updated.

- Owner: The file's owner per the operating system.

   Also, NIO.2 allows entering the specific attributes of the underlying operating system. To do so,
you first need to get a view that represents the operating system's file attributes (in this example, it is a
DosFileAttributeView). Once you get the view, you can query and change the OS-specific attributes.

▓ **Note**   The AttributeView will only work for the operating system that is intended (you cannot use the
DosFileAttributeView in a *nix machine).

8-11. Monitoring a Directory for Content Changes

Problem

You need to keep track when a directory's content has changed (for example, a file was added, changed, or deleted) and act upon those changes.

Solution

By using a WatchService, you can subscribe to be notified about events occurring within a folder. In the following example, we subscribe for ENTRY_CREATE, ENTRY_MODIFY, and ENTRY_DELETE events:

```
try {
    System.out.println("Watch Event, press q<Enter> to exit");
    FileSystem fileSystem = FileSystems.getDefault();
    WatchService service = fileSystem.newWatchService();
    Path path = fileSystem.getPath(".");
    System.out.println("Watching :"+path.toAbsolutePath());
    path.register(service, StandardWatchEventKinds.ENTRY_CREATE, StandardWatchEventKinds.
ENTRY_DELETE, StandardWatchEventKinds.ENTRY_MODIFY);
    boolean shouldContinue = true;
    while(shouldContinue) {
        WatchKey key = service.poll(250, TimeUnit.MILLISECONDS);

        // Code to stop the program
        while (System.in.available() > 0) {
            int readChar = System.in.read();
            if ((readChar == 'q') || (readChar == 'Q')) {
                shouldContinue = false;
                break;
            }
        }
        if (key == null) continue;
        key.pollEvents().stream()
                .filter((event) -> !(event.kind() == StandardWatchEventKinds.OVERFLOW))
                .map((event) -> (WatchEvent<Path>)event).forEach((ev) -> {
            Path filename = ev.context();
            System.out.println("Event detected :"+filename.toString()+" "+ev.kind());
        });
        boolean valid = key.reset();
        if (!valid) {
            break;
        }
    }
} catch (IOException | InterruptedException e) {
    e.printStackTrace();
}
```

How It Works

NIO.2 includes a built-in polling mechanism to monitor for changes in the FileSystem. Using a poll mechanism allows you to wait for events and poll for updates at a specified interval. Once an event occurs, you can process and consume it. A consumed event tells the NIO.2 framework that you are ready to handle a new event.

To start monitoring a folder, create a WatchService that you can use to poll for changes. After the WatchService has been created, register the WatchService with a path. A path symbolizes a folder in the file system. When the WatchService is registered with the path, you define the kinds of events you want to monitor (see Table 8-2).

Table 8-2. *Types of watchEvents*

WatchEvent	Description
OVERFLOW	An event that has overflown (ignore)
ENTRY_CREATE	A directory or file was created
ENTRY_DELETE	A directory or file has been deleted
ENTRY_MODIFY	A directory or file has been modified

After registering the WatchService with the path, you can then "poll" the WatchService for event occurrences. By calling the watchService.poll() method, you will wait for a file/folder event to occur on that path. Using the watchService.poll(int timeout, Timeunit timeUnit) will wait until the specified timeout is reached before continuing. If the watchService receives an event, or if the allowed time has passed, then it will continue execution. If there were no events and the timeout was reached, the WatchKey object returned by the watchService.poll(int timeout) will be null; otherwise, the WatchKey object returned will contain the relevant information for the event that has occurred.

Because many events can occur at the same time (say, for example, moving an entire folder or pasting a bunch of files into a folder), the WatchKey might contain more than one event. You can use the WatchKey to obtain all the events that are associated with that key by calling the watchKey.pollEvents() method.

The watchKey.pollEvents() call will return a list of watchEvents that can be iterated over. Each watchEvent contains information on the actual file or folder to which the event refers (for example, an entire subfolder could have been moved or deleted), and the event type (add, edit, delete). Only those events that were registered on the WatchService will be processed. The event types you can register are listed in Table 8-2.

Once an event has been processed, it is important to call the EventKey.reset(). The reset will return a Boolean value determining whether the WatchKey is still valid. A WatchKey becomes invalid if it is cancelled or if its originating WatchService is closed. If the eventKey returns false, you should break from the watch loop.

8-12. Reading Property Files

Problem

You want to establish some configurational settings for your application, and you want to have the ability to modify the settings manually or programmatically. Moreover, you wish to enable some of the confiugations to be changed on the fly without the need to recompile and redeploy.

Solution

Create a properties file to store the application configurations. Using the Properties object, load properties stored within the properties file for application processing. Properties can also be updated and modified within the properties file. The following example demonstrates how to read a properties file named properties.conf, load the values for application use, and finally set a property and write it to the file.

```java
File file = new File("properties.conf");
Properties properties = null;
try {
    if (!file.exists()) {
        file.createNewFile();
    }
    properties = new Properties();

    properties.load(new FileInputStream("properties.conf"));
} catch (IOException e) {
    e.printStackTrace();
}
boolean shouldWakeUp = false;
int startCounter = 100;
String shouldWakeUpProperty = properties.getProperty("ShouldWakeup");
shouldWakeUp = (shouldWakeUpProperty == null) ? false : Boolean.parseBoolean(shouldWakeUp
Property.trim());

String startCounterProperty = properties.getProperty("StartCounter");
try {
    startCounter = Integer.parseInt(startCounterProperty);
} catch (Exception e) {
    System.out.println("Couldn't read startCounter, defaulting to " + startCounter);
}
String dateFormatStringProperty = properties.getProperty("DateFormatString", "MMM dd yy");

System.out.println("Should Wake up? " + shouldWakeUp);
System.out.println("Start Counter: " + startCounter);
System.out.println("Date Format String:" + dateFormatStringProperty);

//setting property
properties.setProperty("StartCounter", "250");
try {
properties.store(new FileOutputStream("properties.conf"), "Properties Description");
} catch (IOException e) {
    e.printStackTrace();
}
properties.list(System.out);
```

How It Works

The Java `Properties` class helps you manage program properties. It allows you to manage the properties either via external modification (someone editing a property file) or internally by using the `Properties.store()` method.

The `Properties` object can be instantiated either without a file or with a preloaded file. The files that the `Properties` object read are in the form of [name]=[value] and are textually represented. If you need to store values in other formats, you need to write to and read from a String.

If you are expecting the files to be modified outside the program (the user directly opens a text editor and changes the values), be sure to sanitize the inputs; like trimming the values for extra spaces and ignoring case if need be.

To query the different properties programmatically, you call the getProperty(String) method, passing the String-based name of the property whose value you want to retrieve. The method will return null if the property is not found. Alternatively, you can invoke the getProperty (String,String) method, on which if the property is not found in the `Properties` object, it will return the second parameter as its value. It is a good practice to specify default values in case the file doesn't have an entry for a particular key.

Upon looking at a generated property file, you will notice that the first two lines indicate the description of the file and the date when it was modified. These two lines start with #, which in Java property files is the equivalent of a comment. The `Properties` object will skip any line starting with # when processing the file.

■ **Note**　If you allow users to modify your configuration files directly, it is important to have validation in place when retrieving properties from the `Properties` object. One of the most common issues encountered in the value of properties is leading and/or trailing spaces. If specifying a Boolean or integer property, be sure that they can be parsed from a String. At a minimum, catch an exception when trying to parse to survive an unconventional value (and log the offending value).

8-13. Uncompressing Files

Problem

Your application has the requirement to decompress and extract files from a compressed `.zip` file.

Solution

Using the `Java.util.zip` package, you can open a `.zip` file and iterate through its entries. While traversing the entries, directories can be created for directory entries. Similarly, when a file entry is encountered, write the decompressed file to the file `.unzipped`. The following lines of code demonstrate how to perform the decompress and file iteration technique, as described.

```java
ZipFile file = null;
try {
    file = new ZipFile("file.zip");
    FileSystem fileSystem = FileSystems.getDefault();
    Enumeration<? extends ZipEntry> entries = file.entries();
    String uncompressedDirectory = "uncompressed/";
    Files.createDirectory(fileSystem.getPath(uncompressedDirectory));
```

```
    while (entries.hasMoreElements()) {
        ZipEntry entry = entries.nextElement();
        if (entry.isDirectory()) {
            System.out.println("Creating Directory:" + uncompressedDirectory + entry.getName());
            Files.createDirectories(fileSystem.getPath(uncompressedDirectory +
                                    entry.getName()));
        } else {
            InputStream is = file.getInputStream(entry);
            System.out.println("File :" + entry.getName());
            BufferedInputStream bis = new BufferedInputStream(is);

            String uncompressedFileName = uncompressedDirectory + entry.getName();
            Path uncompressedFilePath = fileSystem.getPath(uncompressedFileName);
            Files.createFile(uncompressedFilePath);
            try (FileOutputStream fileOutput = new FileOutputStream(uncompressedFileName)) {
                while (bis.available() > 0) {
                    fileOutput.write(bis.read());
                }
            }
            System.out.println("Written :" + entry.getName());
        }
    }
} catch (IOException e) {
    e.printStackTrace();
}
```

How It Works

To work with the contents of a .Zip archive, create a ZipFile object. A ZipFile object can be instantiated, passing the name of a .zip archive to the constructor. After creating the object, you gain access to the specified .zip file information. Each ZipFile object will contain a collection of entries that represent the directories and files contained within the archive, and by iterating through the entries you can obtain information on each of the compressed files. Each ZipEntry instance will have the compressed and uncompressed size, the name, and the input stream of the uncompressed bytes.

The uncompressed bytes can be read into a byte buffer by generating an InputStream, and later (in our case) written to a file. Using the FileStream, it is possible to determine how many bytes can be read without blocking the process. Once the determined number of bytes has been read, then those bytes are written to the output file. This process continues until the total number of bytes has been read.

■ **Note** Reading the entire file into memory may not be a good idea if the file is extremely large. If you need to work with a large file, it's best to first write it in an uncompressed format to disk (as in the example) and then open it and load it in chunks. If the file that you are working on is not large (you can limit the size by checking the getSize() method), you can probably load it in memory.

8-14. Managing Operating System Processes

Problem

You would like the ability to identify and control native operating system processes from your Java application.

Solution

Utilize the Process API, enhanced in Java 9, to obtain information regarding individual operating system processes or destroy them. In this example, we will call upon the ProcessHandle.info() method to retrieve information about an operating system process. In particular, we will take a look at the current JVM process that is running, and we'll start another process from it. Lastly, we'll interrogate the new process.

```java
import java.lang.ProcessBuilder;
import java.lang.Process;
import java.time.Instant;
import java.time.Duration;
import java.time.temporal.ChronoUnit;

public class Recipe08_14 {

  public static void printProcessDetails(ProcessHandle currentProcess){
    //Get the instance of process info
    ProcessHandle.Info currentProcessInfo = currentProcess.info();
    if ( currentProcessInfo.command().orElse("").equals("")){
      return;
    }
    //Get the process id
    System.out.println("Process id: " + currentProcess.getPid());
    //Get the command pathname of the process
    System.out.println("Command: " + currentProcessInfo.command().orElse(""));
    //Get the arguments of the process
    String[] arguments = currentProcessInfo.arguments().orElse(new String[]{});
    if ( arguments.length != 0){
      System.out.print("Arguments: ");
      for(String arg : arguments){
        System.out.print(arg + " ");
      }
      System.out.println();
    }
    //Get the start time of the process
    System.out.println("Started at: " + currentProcessInfo.startInstant().orElse(Instant.
    now()).toString());
    //Get the time the process ran for
    System.out.println("Ran for: " + currentProcessInfo.totalCpuDuration().orElse(Duration.
    ofMillis(0)).toMillis() + "ms");
    //Get the owner of the process
    System.out.println("Owner: " + currentProcessInfo.user().orElse(""));
  }
```

```
public static void main(String[] args){
  ProcessHandle current = ProcessHandle.current();
  ProcessHandle.Info currentInfo = current.info();
  System.out.println("Command Line Process: " + currentInfo.commandLine());
  System.out.println("Process User: " + currentInfo.user());
  System.out.println("Process Start Time: " + currentInfo.startInstant());
  System.out.println("PID: " + current.getPid());

  ProcessBuilder pb = new ProcessBuilder("ls");
  try {
  Process process = pb.start();
  System.out.println(process);
  process.children()
  .forEach((p) ->{
    System.out.println(p);
  });
      ProcessHandle pHandle = process.toHandle();
    System.out.println("Parent of Process: " + pHandle.parent());
  } catch (java.io.IOException e){
    System.out.println(e);
  }

  }
}
```

Results:

```
Command Line Process: Optional[/Library/Java/JavaVirtualMachines/jdk1.9.0.jdk/Contents/Home/
bin/java Recipe0814]
Process User: Optional[Juneau]
Process Start Time: Optional[2016-02-20T06:14:56.064Z]
PID: 10892
java.lang.ProcessImpl@7c30a502
Parent of Process: Optional.empty
```

How It Works

The process API has been enhanced in Java 9 to provide the ability to obtain valuable information about operating system processes. The ProcessHandle interface has been added to the API, providing an info() method that can be used to interrogate a specified process and retrieve more information. A number of other useful utility methods have been added to obtain information about a specified process.

The ProcessHandle.Info object, an informational snapshot of the current process, is returned from calling upon the ProcessHandle info() method. ProcessHandle.Info can be utilized to return the executable command of a process, the process start time, and several other useful features. Table 8-3 shows the different methods available to ProcessHandle.Info.

Table 8-3. ProcessHandle.Info

Method	Description
arguments()	Returns array of Strings of the process arguments.
command()	Returns executable pathname of process.
commandLine()	Returns command line of the process.
startInstant()	Returns the start time of the process.
totalCpuDuration()	Returns the total accumulated CPU time of the process.
user()	Returns the user under which the process is running.

The ProcessHandle interface can be utilized to return information, such as the process children, PID (Process ID), parent, and so forth. It can also be used to determine a number of useful bits of information, such as if the process is still alive. Table 8-4 shows the different methods of ProcessHandle.

Table 8-4. ProcessHandle

Method	Return	Description
allProcesses()	static Stream<ProcessHandle>	Returns snapshot of all processes that are visible the current process.
children()	Stream<ProcessHandle>	Returns a snapshot of direct children of the current process.
compareTo()	int	Compares one ProcessHandle to another, and returns order.
current()	static ProcessHandle	Returns a ProcessHandle for the current process.
descendents()	Stream<ProcessHandle>	Returns a snapshot of the current process descendents.
destroy()	boolean	Requests the termination of the current process.
destroyForcibly()	boolean	Requests the forced termination of current process.
equals(Object)	boolean	Compares the current process to another object, returning true if the object is not null, and represents the same system process.
getPid()	long	Returns the native process ID of the current process.
hashCode()	int	Returns a hash code value for the current ProcessHandle.
info()	ProcessHandle.info	Returns a snapshot of information for the current process.

(continued)

Table 8-4. (*continued*)

Method	Return	Description
isAlive()	boolean	Tests whether the current process is active.
of(long pid)	static Optional<ProcessHandle>	Returns an Optional<ProcessHandle> for an existing process.
onExit()	CompletableFuture<ProcessHandle>	Returns a CompleteableFuture<ProcessHandle> for the current process.
parent()	Optional<ProcessHandle>	Returns Optional<ProcessHandle> for the parent process of the current process.
supportsNormalTermination()	boolean	Returns true if the implementation of the current process contains a destroy() method that supports normal process termination.

To utilize the API, call upon the ProcessHandle.info() method to retrieve a ProcessHandle.info object. The object can then be used to execute commands, or retrieve information about the process. If utilized together with the Process and ProcessBuilder classes, the API can be used to spawn, monitor, and terminate operating system processes.

Summary

This chapter demonstrated several examples for working with file and network I/O in Java. You learned how to serialize files so that they could be stored to disk, and also how to manipulate a host's file system with the Java APIs. The chapter also covered how to read and write property files, and perform file compression. Lastly, the chapter touched upon the new features of the Process API that have been added in Java 9.

CHAPTER 9

▪▪▪

Exceptions and Logging

Exceptions are a way of describing exceptional circumstances within a program. They are an indicator that something unexpected (exceptional) has occurred. For that reason, exceptions are efficient at interrupting the current flow of the program and signaling that there is something that requires attention. As such, programs that utilize exceptions judiciously benefit from a better control flow and become more robust and informative for the user. Even so, using exceptions indiscriminately can cause performance degradation.

Within Java, exceptions can be *thrown* or *caught*. Throwing an exception involves indicating to the code that an exception has been encountered, using the throw keyword to signal the JVM to find any code capable of handling this exceptional circumstance within the current stack. Catching an exception involves telling the compiler which exceptions can be handled, and which part of the code should be monitored for these exceptions to occur. This is denoted within the try/catch Java block (described in Recipe 9-1)

All exceptions inherit from Throwable, as shown in Figure 9-1. Classes that are inherited from Throwable can be defined in the catch clause of a try/catch statement. The Error classes are primarily used by the JVM to denote serious and/or fatal errors. According to the Java documentation, applications are not expected to catch Error exceptions since they are considered fatal (think of a computer being on fire). The bulk of exceptions within a Java program will be inherited from the Exception class.

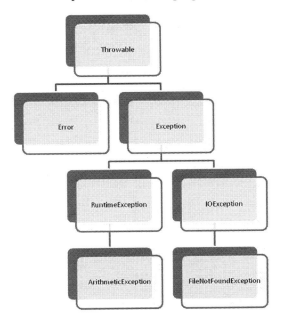

Figure 9-1. *Part of the exception class hierarchy in Java*

J. Juneau, *Java 9 Recipes*, DOI 10.1007/978-1-4842-1976-8_9

Within the JVM there are two types of exceptions: checked and unchecked. Checked exceptions are enforced by methods. In the method signature, you can specify the kind of exceptions a method can throw. This requires any caller of the method to create a try/catch block, which handles the exceptions that were declared within the method signature. Unchecked exceptions do not require such a stringent convention, and are free to be thrown anywhere without enforcing the implementation of a try/catch block. Even so, unchecked exceptions (as described in Recipe 9-6) are usually discouraged because they can lead to threads unraveling (if nothing catches the exception) and poor visibility of problems. Exception classes that inherit from RuntimeException are considered to be unchecked exceptions, whereas exception classes that inherit directly from Exception are considered to be checked exceptions.

Be aware that the act of throwing exceptions is expensive (compared with other language construct alternatives), and as such throwing exceptions makes a poor substitute for control flow. For example, you shouldn't throw an exception to indicate an expected result of a method call (say a method like isUsernameValid (String username). It is a better practice to call the method and return a boolean with the result than try to throw an InvalidUsernameException to indicate failure.

While exceptions play an essential role in solid software development, logging of exceptions can be just as important. Logging within an application helps the developer to understand what events are occurring without the need for debugging the code. This is especially true in production environments where there isn't the opportunity for live debugging. In that sense, logging collects clues on what is occurring (most likely what went wrong) and helps you troubleshoot production problems. Many developers choose to utilize a structured logging framework to provide more robust logging for an application. A solid logging framework with a sound methodology will save many late nights at work wondering, "what happened?"

Logging for Java is very mature. There are many open source projects that are widely accepted as the *de facto* standard for logging. In the recipes in this chapter, you will use Java's Logging framework and the Simple Logging Façade for Java (SLF4J). Both of these projects together create a good-enough solution for most logging needs. For the recipes involving SLF4J and Log4j, download SLF4J (http://www.slf4j.org/) and put it in your project's dependency path. This chapter will also touch upon the lower-level JVM logging that has been added with the release of Java 9.

9-1. Catching Exceptions

Problem

You want to gracefully handle any exceptions generated from your code.

Solution

Use the built-in try/catch language construct to catch exceptions. Do so by wrapping any blocks of code that may throw an exception within a try/catch block. In the following example, a method is used to generate a Boolean value to indicate whether a specified String is greater than five characters long. If the String that's passed as an argument is null, a NullPointerException is thrown by the length() method and caught within the catch block.

```
private void start() {
    System.out.println("Is th String 1234 longer than 5 chars?:"+
        isStringShorterThanFiveCharacters("1234"));
    System.out.println("Is th String 12345 longer than 5 chars?:"+
        isStringShorterThanFiveCharacters("12345"));
    System.out.println("Is th String 123456 longer than 5 chars?:"+
        isStringShorterThanFiveCharacters("123456"));
```

```
System.out.println("Is th String null longer than 5 chars?:"+
        isStringShorterThanFiveCharacters(null));

}

private boolean isStringShorterThanFiveCharacters(String aString) {
    try {
        return aString.length() > 5;
    } catch (NullPointerException e) {
        System.out.println("An Exception Occurred: " + e);
        return false;
    }
}
```

How It Works

The try keyword specifies that the enclosed code segment have the potential to raise an exception. The catch clause is placed at the end of the try clause. Each catch clause specifies which exception is being caught. If a catch clause is not provided for a checked exception, the compiler will generate an error. Two possible solutions are to add a catch clause or to include the exception in the throws clause of the enclosing method. Any checked exceptions that are thrown but not caught will propagate up the call stack. If this method doesn't catch the exception, the thread that executed the code terminates. If the thread terminating is the only thread in the program, it terminates the execution of the program.

If a try clause needs to catch more than one exception, more than one exception can be specified, separated by a bar character. For instance, the following try/catch block could be used for catching both a NumberFormatException and a NullPointerException.

```
try {
  // code here
} catch (NumberFormatException|NullPointerException ex) {
  // logging

}
```

For more information regarding catching multiple exceptions, see Recipe 9-4.

▨ **Note**   Be careful when throwing an exception. If the thrown exception is not caught, it will propagate up the call stack; and if there isn't any catch clause capable of handling the exception, it will cause the running thread to terminate (also known as *unraveling*). If your program has only one main thread, an uncaught exception will terminate your program.

9-2. Guaranteeing a Block of Code Is Executed

Problem

You want to write code that executes when control leaves a code segment, even if control leaves due to an error being thrown or the segment ending abnormally. For example, you have acquired a lock and want to be sure that you are releasing it correctly. You want to release the lock in the event of an error and also in the event of no error.

Solution

Use a try/catch/finally block to properly release locks and other resources that you acquire in a code segment. Place the code that you want to have executed regardless of exceptions into the finally clause. In the example, the finally keyword specifies a code block that will always execute, regardless of whether an exception was thrown in the try block. Within the finally block, the lock is released by calling lock.unlock():

```
private void callFunctionThatHoldsLock() {
    myLock.lock();
    try {
        int number = random.nextInt(5);
        int result = 100 / number;
        System.out.println("A result is " + result);
        FileOutputStream file = new FileOutputStream("file.out");
        file.write(result);
        file.close();
    } catch (FileNotFoundException e) {
        e.printStackTrace();
    } catch (IOException e) {
        e.printStackTrace();
    } catch (Exception e) {
        e.printStackTrace();
    } finally {
        myLock.unlock();
    }
}
```

How It Works

Code that is placed within the finally clause of a try/catch/finally block will always be executed. In this example, by acquiring the lock at the beginning of the function and then releasing it in the finally block, you guarantee that the lock will be released at the end of the function regardless of whether an exception (checked or unchecked) is thrown. In all, acquired locks should always be released in a finally block. In the example, suppose that the mylock.unlock() function call were not in the finally block (but at the end of the try block); if an exception were to happen in this case, the call to mylock.unlock() would not happen because code execution would be interrupted in the location where the exception happened. In that case, the lock would be forever acquired and never released.

■ **Caution**   If you need to return a value on a method, be very careful of returning values in the finally block. A return statement in the finally block will always execute, regardless of any other return statements that might have happened within the try block.

9-3. Throwing Exceptions

Problem

You want to abort the execution of the current code path by throwing an exception if a certain situation occurs within your application.

Solution

Use the throw keyword to throw a specified exception when the situation occurs. Using the throw keyword, you can signal the current thread to look for try/catch blocks (at the current level and up the stack), which can process the thrown exception. In the following example, the callSomeMethodThatMightThrow throws a NullPointerException if the parameter passed in is null.

```
private void start() {
    try {
        callSomeMethodThatMightThrow(null);
    } catch (IllegalArgumentException e) {
        System.out.println("There was an illegal argument exception!");
    }

}

private void callSomeFunctionThatMightThrow(Object o) {
    if (o == null) throw new NullPointerException("The object is null");

}
```

In this code example, the method callSomeMethodThatMightThrow checks to ensure that a valid argument was passed to it. If the argument is null, it then throws a NullPointerException, signaling that the caller of this method invoked it with the wrong parameters.

How It Works

The throw keyword allows you to explicitly generate an exceptional condition. When the current thread throws an exception, it doesn't execute anything beyond the throw statement and instead transfers control to the catch clause (if there are any) or terminates the thread.

▓ **Note**   When throwing an exception, be sure that you intend to do so. If an exception is not caught as it propagates up the stack, it will terminate the thread that is executing (also known as unraveling). If your program has only one main thread, an uncaught exception will terminate your program.

9-4. Catching Multiple Exceptions

Problem

A block of code in your application has the possibility of throwing multiple exceptions. You want to catch each of the exceptions that may occur within a try block.

Solution 1

More than one catch clause can be specified in situations where multiple exceptions may be encountered within the same block. Each catch clause can specify a different exception to handle, so that each exception can be handled in a different manner. In the following code, two catch clauses are used to handle an IOException and a ClassNotFoundException.

```
try {
    Class<?> stringClass = Class.forName("java.lang.String");
    FileInputStream in = new FileInputStream("myFile.log") ; // Can throw IOException
    in.read();

} catch (IOException e) {
    System.out.println("There was an exception "+e);
} catch (ClassNotFoundException e) {
    System.out.println("There was an exception "+e);
}
```

Solution 2

If your application has the tendency to throw multiple exceptions within a single block, then a vertical bar operator (|) can be utilized for handling each of the exceptions in the same manner. In the following example, the catch clause specifies multiple exception types separated with a vertical bar (|) to handle each of the exceptions in the same manner.

```
        try {
            Class<?> stringClass = Class.forName("java.lang.String");
            FileInputStream in = new FileInputStream("myFile.log") ;
// Can throw IOException
            in.read();

        } catch (IOException | ClassNotFoundException e) {
            System.out.println("An exception of type "+e.getClass()+" was thrown! "+e);
        }
```

How It Works

There are a couple of different ways to handle situations where multiple exceptions may be thrown. You can specify separate catch clauses to handle each of the exceptions in a different way. To handle each of the exceptions in the same manner, you can utilize a single catch clause and specify each exception separated with a vertical bar operator.

■ **Note** If you're catching an exception in multiple catch blocks (Solution 1), make sure that the catch blocks are defined from the most specific to the most general. Failure to follow this convention will prevent an exception from being handled by the more specific blocks. This is most important when there are catch (Exception e) blocks, which catch almost all exceptions.

Having a catch (Exception e) block—called a catch-all or *Pokémon* exception handler (gotta catch them all)—is usually poor practice because such a block will catch every exception type and treat them all the same. This becomes a problem because the block can catch other exceptions that may occur deeper within the call stack that you may not have intended the block to catch (an OutOfMemoryException). It is a best practice to specify each possible exception, rather than specifying a catch-all exception handler to catch all exceptions.

9-5. Catching the Uncaught Exceptions

Problem

You want to know when a thread is being terminated due to an uncaught exception such as a
NullPointerException.

Solution 1

When creating a Java thread, sometimes you need to ensure that any exception is caught and handled
properly to help determine the reason for the thread termination. To that effect, Java allows you to register
an ExceptionHandler() either per thread or globally. The following code demonstrates an example of
registering an exception handler on a per-thread basis.

```java
private void start() {
    Thread.setDefaultUncaughtExceptionHandler((Thread t, Throwable e) -> {
        System.out.println("Woa! there was an exception thrown somewhere! "+t.getName()+": "+e);
    });

    final Random random = new Random();
    for (int j = 0; j < 10; j++) {
        int divisor = random.nextInt(4);
        System.out.println("200 / " + divisor + " Is " + (200 / divisor));
    }
}
```

The for loop in this thread will execute properly until an exception is encountered, at which time the
DefaultUncaughtExceptionHandler will be invoked. UncaughtExceptionHandler is a functional interface,
so it is possible to utilize a lambda expression to implement the exception handler.

Solution 2

It is possible to register an UncaughtExceptionHandler on a specific thread. After doing so, any exception
that occurs within the thread and that has not been caught will be handled by the uncaughtException()
method of the UncaughtExceptionHandler(). For example:

```java
private void startForCurrentThread() {
    Thread.currentThread().setUncaughtExceptionHandler((Thread t, Throwable e) -> {
        System.out.println("In this thread "+t.getName()+" an exception was thrown "+e);
    });

    Thread someThread = new Thread(() -> {
        System.out.println(200/0);
    });
    someThread.setName("Some Unlucky Thread");
    someThread.start();

    System.out.println("In the main thread "+ (200/0));
}
```

In the previous code, an UncaughtExceptionHandler is registered on the currentThread. Just like Solution 1, UncaughtExceptionHandler is a functional interface, so it is possible to utilize a lambda expression to implement the exception handler.

How It Works

The Thread.defaultUncaughtExceptionHandler() will be invoked for each unchecked exception that has not been caught. When the UncaughtExceptionHandler() handles an exception, it means that there was no try/catch block in place to catch the exception. As such, the exception bubbled all the way up the thread stack. This is the last code executed on that thread before it terminates. When an exception is caught on either the thread's or the default's UncaughtExceptionHandler(), the thread will terminate. The UncaughtExceptionHandler() can be used to log information on the exception to help pinpoint the reason of the exception.

In the second solution, the UncaughtExceptionHandler() is set up specifically for the current thread. When the thread throws an exception that is not caught, it will bubble up to the UncaughtExceptionHandler() of the thread. If this is not present, it will bubble up to the defaultUncaughtExceptionHandler(). Again, in either situation, the thread originating the exception will terminate.

■ **Tip** When dealing with multiple threads, it is always good practice to explicitly name the threads. It makes life easier to know exactly which thread caused the exception, rather than having to trace down an unknown thread named like Thread-## (the default naming pattern of unnamed threads).

9-6. Managing Resources with try/catch Blocks

Problem

In the event of an exception, you need to ensure that any resources used within a try/catch block are released.

Solution

Make use of the Automatic Resource Management (ARM) feature, which can be specified with a try-with-resources statement. When using a try-with-resources statement, any resources that are specified within the try clause are automatically released when the block terminates. In the following code, the FileOutputStream, BufferedOutputStream, and DataOutputStream resources are automatically handled by the try-with-resources block.

```
try (
        FileOutputStream fos = new FileOutputStream("out.log");
        BufferedOutputStream bos = new BufferedOutputStream(fos);
        DataOutputStream dos = new DataOutputStream(bos)
) {
    dos.writeUTF("This is being written");
} catch (Exception e) {
    System.out.println("Some bad exception happened ");
}
```

How It Works

In most cases, you want to cleanly close/dispose of resources that are acquired within a `try`/`catch` block after the block execution is complete. If a program does not close/dispose of its resources or does so improperly, the resources could be acquired indefinitely, causing issues such as memory leaks to occur. Most resources are limited (file handles or database connections), and as such will cause performance degradation (and more exceptions to be thrown). To avoid these situations, Java provides a means of automatically releasing resources when an exception occurs within a `try`/`catch` block. By declaring a `try-with-resources` block, the resource on which the `try` block was checked will be closed if there is an exception thrown within the block. Most of the resources that are built into Java will work properly within a `try-with-resources` statement (for a full list, see implementers of the `java.lang.AutoCloseable` interface). Also, third-party implementers can create resources that will work with the `try-with-resources` statements by implementing the `AutoCloseable` interface.

The syntax for the `try-with-resources` statement involves the `try` keyword, followed by an opening parenthesis and then followed by all the resource declarations that you want to have released in the event of an exception or when the block completes, and ending with a closing parenthesis. Note that if you try to declare a resource/variable that doesn't implement the `AutoCloseable` interface, you will receive a compiler error. After the closing parenthesis, the syntax of the `try`/`catch` block is the same as a normal block.

The main advantage of the `try-with-resources` feature is that it allows a cleaner release of resources. Usually when acquiring a resource, there are a lot of interdependencies (creating file handlers, which are wrapped in output streams, which are wrapped in buffered streams). Properly closing and disposing of these resources in exceptional conditions requires checking the status of each dependent resource and carefully disposing of it, and doing so requires that you write a lot of code. By contrast, the `try-with-resources` construct allows the JVM to take care of proper disposal of resources, even in exceptional conditions.

▓ **Note**   A `try-with-resources` block will always close the defined resources, even if no exceptions were thrown.

9-7. Creating an Exception Class

Problem

You want to create a new type of exception that can be used to indicate a particular event.

Solution 1

Create a class that extends `java.lang.RuntimeException` to create an exception class that can be thrown at any time. In the following code, a class identified by `IllegalChatServerException` extends `RuntimeException` and accepts a String as an argument to the constructor. The exception is then thrown when a specified event occurs within the code.

```java
class IllegalChatServerException extends RuntimeException {
    IllegalChatServerException(String message) {
        super(message);
    }
}

private void disconnectChatServer(Object chatServer) {
    if (chatServer == null) throw new IllegalChatServerException("Chat server is empty");
}
```

Solution 2

Create a class that extends `java.lang.Exception` to generate a checked exception class. A checked exception is required to be caught or rethrown up the stack. In the following example, a class identified as `ConnectionUnavailableException` extends `java.lang.Exception` and accepts a String as an argument to the constructor. The checked exception is then thrown by a method in the code.

```java
class ConnectionUnavailableException extends Exception {
    ConnectionUnavailableException(String message) {
        super(message);
    }
}

private void sendChat(String chatMessage) throws ConnectionUnavailableException {
    if (chatServer == null)
            throw new ConnectionUnavailableException("Can't find the chat server");
}
```

How It Works

Sometimes there is a requirement to create a custom exception, especially in situations when you're creating an API. The usual recommendation is to use one of the available `Exception` classes provided by the JDK. For example, use `IOException` for I/O-related issues or the `IllegalArgumentException` for illegal parameters. If there isn't a JDK exception that fits cleanly, you can always extend `java.lang.Exception` or `java.lang.RuntimeException` and implement its own family of exceptions.

Depending on the base class, creating an `Exception` class is fairly straightforward. Extending `RuntimeException` allows you the ability to throw the resulting exception any time without requiring it to be caught up the stack. This is advantageous in that `RuntimeException` is a more lax contract to work with, but throwing such an exception can lead to thread termination if the exception is not caught. Extending `Exception` instead allows you to clearly force any code that throws the exception to be able to handle it within a `catch` clause. The checked exception is then forced by contract to implement a `catch` handler, potentially avoiding a thread termination.

In practice, we discourage extending `RuntimeException` because it can lead to poor exception handling. Our rule of thumb is that if it's possible to recover from an exception, you should create the associated exception class by extending `Exception`. If a developer cannot reasonably be expected to recover from the exception (say a `NullPointerException`), then extend `RuntimeException`.

9-8. Rethrowing the Caught Exception

Problem

Your application contains a multicatch exception, and you want to rethrow an exception that was previously caught.

Solution

Throw the exception from a `catch` block, and it will rethrow it on the same type as it was caught. In the following example, exceptions are caught within a block of code and rethrown to the method's caller.

```java
private void doSomeWork() throws IOException, InterruptedException {
    LinkedBlockingQueue<String> queue = new LinkedBlockingQueue<>();
```

```
        try {
            FileOutputStream fos = new FileOutputStream("out.log");
            DataOutputStream dos = new DataOutputStream(fos);
            while (!queue.isEmpty()) {
                dos.writeUTF(queue.take());
            }
        } catch (InterruptedException | IOException e ) {
            e.printStackTrace();
throw e;
        }

    }
```

How It Works

It is possible to simply throw the exception that has been previously caught, and the JVM will bubble the exception to the appropriate type. As is the case of throwing a checked exception; it must also be defined in the method declaration. In the example to this solution, the doSomeWork() method throws an IOException and an InterruptedException, which causes the calling code to perform a try-catch to handle the thrown exception appropriately.

9-9. Logging Events Within Your Application

Problem

You want to log events, debug messages, error conditions, and other events within your application.

Solution

Utilize SLF4J within your application, along with the Java Logging API, to implement a logging solution. The following example first creates a logger object with the name of recipeLogger. In this example, the SLF4J API is used to log an informational message, a warning message, and an error message:

```
private void loadLoggingConfiguration() {
    FileInputStream ins = null;
    try {
        ins = new FileInputStream(new File("logging.properties"));
        LogManager.getLogManager().readConfiguration(ins);
    } catch (IOException e) {
        e.printStackTrace();
    }
}
private void start() {
    loadLoggingConfiguration();
    Logger logger = LoggerFactory.getLogger("recipeLogger");
    logger.info("Logging for the first Time!");
    logger.warn("A warning to be had");
    logger.error("This is an error!");
}
```

How It Works

In the example, `loadLogConfiguration()` function opens a stream to the `logging.properties` file and passes it to `java.util.logging.LogManager()`. Doing so configures the `java.util.logging` framework to use the settings specified in the `logging.properties` file. Then, within the start method of the solution, the code acquires a `logger` object named `recipeLogger`. The example proceeds to log messages to through `recipeLogger`. More information on the actual logging parameters can be found in Recipe 9-10.

SLF4J provides a common API using a simple facade pattern that abstracts the underlying logging implementation. SLF4J can be used with most of the common logging frameworks, such as the Java Logging API (`java.util.logging`), Log4j, Jakarta Commons Logging, and others. In practice, SLF4J provides the flexibility to choose (and swap) logging frameworks and allows projects that use SLF4J to quickly become integrated into an application's selected logging framework.

To use SLF4J in an application, download the SLF4J binaries located at `http://www.slf4j.org/`. Once they're downloaded, extract the contents and add `slf4j-api-x.x.x.jar` to the project. This is the main `.jar` file that contains the SLF4J API (on which a program can call to log information). After adding the `slf4j-api-x.x.x.jar` file to the project, find `slf4j-jdk14-x.x.x.jar` and add that to the project. This second file indicates that SLF4J will use the `java.util.logging` classes to log information.

The way SLF4J works is that at runtime SLF4J scans the class path and picks the first `.jar` that implements the SLF4J API. In the example case, the `slf4j-jdk14-x.x.x.jar` is found and loaded. This `.jar` represents the native Java Logging Framework (known as `jdk.1.4` logging). If, for example, you wanted to use another logging framework, replace `slf4j-jdk14-x.x.x.jar` with the corresponding SLF4J implementation for the desired logger. For example, to use Apache's Log4j logging framework, include `slf4j-log4j12-x.x.x.jar`.

■ **Note**   The `java.util.logging` framework is configured by the properties log file.

Once SLF4J is configured, you can log information in your application by calling the SLF4J logging methods. The methods log information depending on the logging level. The logging level can then be used to filter which messages are actually logged. The ability to filter messages by log level is useful because there may be a lot of informational or debugging information being logged. If there is the need to troubleshoot an application, the logging level can be changed, and more information can be made visible in the logs without changing any code. The ability to filter messages through their level is referred to as *setting the log level*. Each logging framework reference contains its own configuration file that sets the log level (among other things, such as the logging file name and logging-file configurations). In the example case, because SLF4J is using the `java.util.logging` framework to log, you would need to configure the `java.util.logging` properties for the desired logging. See Table 9-1.

Table 9-1. *Logging Levels*

Logging Level	Recommendation
Trace	Least important of the logging events
Debug	Use for extra information that helps with debugging
Info	Use for everyday logging messages
Warn	Use for recoverable issues, or where the suspicions of a wrong setting/nonstandard behavior happens
Error	Use for exceptions, actual errors, and things that you really need to know
Fatal	Most important

■ **Note**   When setting the log level, loggers will log at that level and below. Therefore, if a logging configuration sets the log level to info, messages at the Info, Warn, Error, and Fatal levels will be logged.

9-10. Rotating and Purging Logs

Problem

You have started to log information, but the information logged continues growing out of control. You would like to keep only the last 250KB worth of log entries within your log files.

Solution

Use SLF4J with java.util.logging to configure rolling logs. In this example, a logger named recipeLogger is used to log many messages. The output will produce rolled log files with the most recent logged information in the important Log0.log file.

```
loadLoggingConfiguration();

Logger logger = LoggerFactory.getLogger("recipeLogger");
logger.info("Logging for the first Time!");
logger.warn("A warning to be had");
logger.error("This is an error!");

Logger rollingLogger = LoggerFactory.getLogger("rollingLogger");
for (int i =0;i < 5000;i++) {
    rollingLogger.info("Logging for an event with :"+i);
}
```

logging.properties file

```
handlers = java.util.logging.FileHandler

recipeLogger.level=INFO

.level=ALL

java.util.logging.FileHandler.formatter=java.util.logging.SimpleFormatter
java.util.logging.FileHandler.pattern=ImportantApplication%d.log
java.util.logging.FileHandler.limit=50000
java.util.logging.FileHandler.count=4
```

How It Works

To control the size of log files, configure the java.util.logging framework and specify rolling log files. Choosing the rolling log files option causes the latest information to be kept in ImportantApplication0.log. Progressively older information will be in ImportantApplication1.log, ImportantApplication2.log, and so forth. When ImportantApplication0.log fills to the limit you specify (50,000 bytes in this example), its name will be rotated to ImportantApplicationLog1.log, and the other files will have their names similarly rotated downward. The number of log files to maintain is determined by the java.util.logging. FileHandler.count property, which is set to 4 in this recipe's example.

The logging.properties file begins by defining the handlers that the java.util.logging framework will use. Handlers are objects that take care of logging messages. FileHandler is specified in the recipe, which logs messages to files. Other possible handlers are the ConsoleHandler (logs to the system.output device), SocketHandler (logs to a socket), and MemoryHandler (keeps logs in a circular buffer in memory). There is also the possibility of specifying your own handler implementation by creating a class that extends the Handler abstract class.

Next, the logging levels are defined. Within a logging framework there is the concept of separate logger objects. A logger can carry different configurations (for example, different logging levels) and can be identified in the log file. The example configures the recipeLogger's level to info, whereas the root logger's level is ALL (root loggers in the java.util.logging framework are denoted by not having any prefix before the property).

The next section of the logging.properties file defines the FileHandler configuration. The formatter indicates how the log information will be written to disk. The simpleFormatter writes the information as plain text, with a line indicating the date and time, a line with the logging level, and the message to be logged. The other default choice for the formatter is XMLFormatter, which will create XML markup containing the date, time, logger name, level, thread, and message information for each log event. You can create custom formatters by extending the Formatter abstract class.

Following the formatter, the fileHandler pattern is defined. This specifies the file name and location of the log files (the %d is replaced by the rolling log number [0 ~ 4]). The Limit property defines how many bytes the log can have before rolling over (50,000 bytes ~ 50kb). The count defines the maximum index of log files to keep (in this recipe's case, it's 4).

■ **Note**   Logging can be expensive; if you are logging a lot of information, your Java program will start consuming memory (as the java.util.logging framework will try to keep all the information that needs to be written to disk in memory until it can be flushed). If the java.util.logging framework cannot write the log file as fast as log entries are created, you will run into OutOfMemory errors. The best approach is to log only the necessary information, and, if needed, check to see Logger.isDebugEnabled() before writing out debugging log messages. The logging level can be changed from the logging configuration file.

9-11. Logging Exceptions

From the previous recipes you learned how to catch exceptions and how to log information. This recipe will put these two recipes together.

Problem

You want to record exceptions in your log file.

Solution

Configure your application to use SLF4J. Utilize try/catch blocks to log exceptions within the error log. In the following example, an SLF4J Logger is used to log messages from within an exception handler.

```
static Logger rootLogger = LoggerFactory.getLogger("");
private void start() {
    loadLoggingConfiguration();
    Thread.setDefaultUncaughtExceptionHandler((Thread t, Throwable e) -> {
        rootLogger.error("Error in thread "+t+" caused by ",e);
    });

    int c = 20/0;
}
private void loadLoggingConfiguration() {
    FileInputStream ins = null;
    try {
        ins = new FileInputStream(new File("logging.properties"));
        LogManager.getLogManager().readConfiguration(ins);
    } catch (IOException e) {
        e.printStackTrace();
    }
}
```

How It Works

The example demonstrates how to use an UncaughtExceptionHandler in conjunction with SLF4J to log exceptions to a logging file. When logging an exception, it is good to include the stack trace showing where the exception was thrown. In the example, a thread contains an UncaughtExceptionHandler, which utilizes a lambda expression containing a logger. The logger is used to write any caught exceptions to a log file.

■ **Note**   If an exception is thrown repeatedly, the JVM tends to stop populating the stack trace in the Exception object. This is done for performance reasons because retrieving the same stack trace becomes expensive. If this happens, you will see an exception with no stack trace being logged. When that happens, check the log's previous entries and see whether the same exception was thrown. If the same exception has been thrown previously, the full stack trace will be present on the first logged instance of the exception.

9-12. Logging with the Unified JVM Logger

Problem

You wish to perform logging of JVM processes and you want to have fine-grained control over the logging.

Solution

Utilize the unified JVM logger utility that was added as part of Java 9. In the following solution, the JVM logger utility is configured to perform logging and direct to a file on the operating system.

To initiate the logging, open the command prompt or terminal, and execute the following statement:

```
java -Xlog:all:file=test.txt:time,level
```

The statement will configure the JVM to log all tags to a file named test.txt. The decorations that will be logged are time and level. The next example demonstrates how to log tags using 'gc' using 'trace' level to stdout using the 'uptime' decoration.

```
java –Xlog:gc=trace:uptime
```

How It Works

Logging for the JVM has been enhanced with the release of Java 9 to allow a single unified system offering fine-grained control. In the past, logging a JVM system-level component could become a time consuming task since it was difficult to pinpoint the root causes of many issues. The updated logging facility provides the following features:

- Common command-line options for logging various JVM processes

- Tag categorization

- Differentiation between logging levels

- Ability to log to a file

- File rotation capability

- Dynamic configuration

To configure the JVM logging, execute the java.exe with the –Xlog flag, appending options to the flag separated by a colon [:]. If you wish to perform logging for a single run of the JVM, include the –Xlog flag when invoking the Java application.

There are several options available for the –Xlog flag that indicate "what" to log, and "where" to log in the following format:

```
-Xlog[:option=<what:level>:<output>:<decorators>:<output-options>]
```

Note that in the format, you can specify –Xlog without any options to indicate that all tags should be logged, and all logging levels will go to stdout. In the solution, we saw that to configure logging of all tags, you may also specify the "all" option. Omitting the <what> portion will default to tag-set "all" with a level of "info." Ommitting the <level> will default to "info." The available decorators are listed in Table 9-2, and omitting them altogether defaults to "uptime," "level," "tags."

Table 9-2. Xlog Decorators

Decorator	Description
Time	Current time and date (ISO-8601)
Uptime	Amount of time surpassed since the start of the JVM (seconds and milliseconds)
Timemillis	System.currentTimeMillis() output
Uptimemillis	Milliseconds surpassed since the start of the JVM
Timenanos	System.nanoTime() output
Uptimenanos	Nanoseconds surpassed since the start of the JVM
Pid	Process identifier
Tid	Thread identifier
Level	Associated log message level
Tags	Associated log message tag

Three types of output are supported: stdout, stderr, and text file. Output can be configured to rotate files, limit file size, and so on by specifying output options. The possible output options include:

- filecount=<file count>
- filesize=<file size in kb>
- parameter=value

The logging API can be controlled at runtime via the jcmd diagnostic commands utility. All of the options available at the command line are also available via the utility.

■ **Note** Help on the JVM logging utility is available using the –Xlog:help switch. This switch will print usage syntax and available tags, levels, decorators, and examples.

Summary

In this section, we took a look at one of the most important phases in application development, exception handling. The sections discussed how to handle single and multiple exceptions, and also how to log those exceptions. There are many mature logging APIs available for the JVM, and we covered SLF4J in this chapter. Lastly, we took a look at the Unified JVM logging process that was introduced in Java 9.

CHAPTER 10

Concurrency

Concurrency is one of the toughest topics to handle in modern computer programming; understanding concurrency requires the capacity of thinking abstractly, and debugging concurrent problems is like trying to pilot an airplane by dead reckoning. Even so, with modern releases of Java, it has become easier (and more accessible) to write bug-free concurrent code.

Concurrency is the ability of a program to execute different (or the same) instructions at the same time. A program that is said to be concurrent has the ability to be split up and run on multiple CPUs. By making concurrent programs, you take advantage of today's multicore CPUs. You can even see benefit on single-core CPUs that are I/O intensive.

In this chapter, we present the most common need for concurrency tasks—from running a background task to splitting a computation into work units. Throughout the chapter, you will find the most up-to-date recipes for accomplishing concurrency in Java.

10-1. Starting a Background Task

Problem

You have a task that needs to run outside of your main thread.

Solution

Create a class implementation that includes the task that needs to be run in a different thread. Implement a Runnable interface in the task implementation class and start a new Thread. In the following example, a counter is used to simulate activity, as a separate task is run in the background.

Note: The code in this example could be refactored to utilize method references (see Chapter 6), rather than creating an inner class for the new Thread implementation. However for clarity, the anonymous inner class has been shown.

```
private void someMethod()  {
     Thread backgroundThread = new Thread(new Runnable() {
         public void run() {
             doSomethingInBackground();
         }
     },"Background Thread");
```

© Josh Juneau 2017
J. Juneau, *Java 9 Recipes*, DOI 10.1007/978-1-4842-1976-8_10

```
        System.out.println("Start");
        backgroundThread.start();
        for (int i= 0;i < 10;i++) {
            System.out.println(Thread.currentThread().getName()+": is counting "+i);
        }

        System.out.println("Done");
    }

    private void doSomethingInBackground() {
        System.out.println(Thread.currentThread().getName()+
          ": is Running in the background");
    }
```

If the code is executed more than once, the output should be different from time to time. The background thread will execute separately, so its message is printed at a different time across each run.

The same code for creating the background thread can be written as follows if you're using lambda expressions:

```
Thread backgroundThread = new Thread(this::doSomethingInBackground, "Background Thread");
```

How It Works

The Thread class allows executing code in a new thread (path of execution), distinct from the current thread. The Thread constructor requires as a parameter a class that implements the Runnable interface. The Runnable interface requires the implementation of only one method: public void run(). Hence, it is a functional interface, which facilitates the use of lambda expressions. When the Thread.start() method is invoked, it will in turn create the new thread and invoke the run() method of the Runnable.

Within the JVM are two types of threads: User and Daemon. User threads keep executing until their run() method completes, whereas Daemon threads can be terminated if the application needs to exit. An application exits if there are only Daemon threads running in the JVM. When you start to create multithreaded applications, you must be aware of these differences and understand when to use each type of thread.

Usually, Daemon threads will have a Runnable interface that doesn't complete; for example a while (true) loop. This allows these threads to periodically check or perform a certain condition throughout the life of the program, and be discarded when the program is finished executing. In contrast, User threads, while alive, will execute and prevent the program from terminating. If you happen to have a program that is not closing and/or exiting when expected, you might want to check the threads that are actively running.

To set a thread as a Daemon thread, use thread.setDaemon(true) before calling the thread.start() method. By default, Thread instances are created as User thread types.

■ **Note** This recipe shows the simplest way to create and execute a new thread. The new thread created is a User thread, which means that the application will not exit until both the main thread and the background thread are done executing.

10-2. Updating (and Iterating) a Map
Problem

You need to update a Map object from multiple threads, and you want to make sure that the update doesn't break the contents of the Map object and that the Map object is always in a consistent state. You also want to traverse (look at) the content of the Map object while other threads are updating the Map object.

Solution

Use a ConcurrentMap to update Map entries. The following example creates 1,000 threads. Each thread then tries to modify the Map at the same time. The main thread waits for a second, and then proceeds to iterate through the Map (even when the other threads are still modifying the Map):

```
Set<Thread> updateThreads = new HashSet<>();

private void startProcess() {
    ConcurrentMap<Integer,String> concurrentMap = new ConcurrentHashMap<>();
    for (int i =0;i < 1000;i++) {
        startUpdateThread(i, concurrentMap);
    }
    try {
        Thread.sleep(1000);
    } catch (InterruptedException e) {
        e.printStackTrace();
    }
    concurrentMap.entrySet().stream().forEach((entry) -> {
        System.out.println("Key :"+entry.getKey()+" Value:"+entry.getValue());
    });

    updateThreads.stream().forEach((thread) -> {
        thread.interrupt();
    });
}

Random random = new Random();
private void startUpdateThread(int i, final ConcurrentMap<Integer, String> concurrentMap) {
    Thread thread = new Thread(() -> {
        while (!Thread.interrupted()) {
            int randomInt = random.nextInt(20);
            concurrentMap.put(randomInt, UUID.randomUUID().toString());
        }
    });
    thread.setName("Update Thread "+i);
    updateThreads.add(thread);
    thread.start();
}
```

How It Works

For performing work on a hash table in a concurrent manner, ConcurrentHashMap allows multiple threads to modify the hash table concurrently and safely. ConcurrentHashMap is a hash table supporting full concurrency for retrievals, and adjustable expected concurrency for updates. In the example, 1,000 threads make modifications to the Map over a short period of time. The ConcurrentHashMap iterator, as well as streams that are generated on a ConcurrentHashMap, allows safe iteration over its contents. When using the ConcurrentMap's iterator, you do not have to worry about locking the contents of the ConcurrentMap while iterating over it (and it doesn't throw ConcurrentModificationExceptions).

For a complete list of the newly added methods, refer to the online documentation at http://docs. oracle.com/javase/9/docs/api/java/util/concurrent/ConcurrentHashMap.html.

■ **Note**   ConcurrentMap iterators, while thread-safe, don't guarantee that you will see entries added/updated after the iterator was created.

10-3. Inserting a Key into a Map Only If the Key Is Not Already Present

Problem

A Map within your application is continuously being updated, and you need to put a key/value pair into it if the key does not already exist. Therefore, you need to check for the key's presence, and you need assurance that some other thread doesn't insert the same key in the meantime.

Solution

Using the ConcurrentMap.putIfAbsent() method, you can determine whether the map was modified atomically. For example, the following code uses the method to check and insert in a single step, thus avoiding the concurrency problem:

```
private void start() {
    ConcurrentMap<Integer, String> concurrentMap = new ConcurrentHashMap<>();
    for (int i = 0; i < 100; i++) {
        startUpdateThread(i, concurrentMap);
    }

    try {
        Thread.sleep(1000);
    } catch (InterruptedException e) {
        e.printStackTrace();
    }

    concurrentMap.entrySet().stream().forEach((entry) -> {
        System.out.println("Key :" + entry.getKey() + " Value:" + entry.getValue());
    });

}

Random random = new Random();

private void startUpdateThread(final int i, final ConcurrentMap<Integer, String>
concurrentMap) {
    Thread thread = new Thread(() -> {
        int randomInt = random.nextInt(20);
        String previousEntry = concurrentMap.putIfAbsent(randomInt, "Thread # " + i + " has
        made it!");
        if (previousEntry != null) {
            System.out.println("Thread # " + i + " tried to update it but guess what, we're
            too late!");
```

```
        } else {
            System.out.println("Thread # " + i + " has made it!");
        }
    });
    thread.start();
}
```

When running the program, some of the entries will be successfully inserted, while others will not because the key has already been inserted by another thread. Note that in the example, startUpdateThread() accepts a final int i argument. Marking a method argument as final ensures that the method cannot change the value of the variable i. If the value of i changes inside the method, it is not a visible change from outside of the method.

How It Works

Updating a Map concurrently is difficult because it involves two operations: a *check-then-act* type of operation. First, the Map has to be checked to see whether an entry already exists in it. If the entry doesn't exist, you can put the key and the value into the Map. On the other hand, if the key exists, the value for the key is retrieved. To do so, we use the ConcurrentMap's putIfAbsent atomic operation. This ensures that either the key was present so the value is not overwritten, or the key was not present and so the value is set. For the JDK implementations of ConcurrentMap, the putIfAbsent() method will return null if there was no value for the key or return the current value if the key has a value. By asserting that the putIfAbsent() method returns null, you are assured that the operation was successful and that a new entry in the map has been created.

There are cases when putIfAbsent() might not be efficient to execute. For example, if the result is a large database query, executing the database query all the time and then invoking putIfAbsent() will not be efficient. In this kind of scenario, you could first call the map's containsKey() method to ensure that the key is not present. If it's not present, then call the putIfAbsent() with the expensive database query. There might be a chance that the putIfAbsent() didn't put the entry, but this type of check reduces the number of potentially expensive value creation.

See the following code snippet:

```
keyPresent = concurrentMap.containsKey(randomInt);
        if (!keyPresent) {
            concurrentMap.putIfAbsent(randomInt, "Thread # " + i + " has made it!");
        }
```

In this code, the first operation is to check whether the key is already in the map. If it is, it doesn't execute the putIfAbsent() operation. If the key is not present, we can proceed to execute the putIfAbsent() operation.

If you are accessing the values of the map from different threads, you should make sure that the values are thread-safe. This is most evident when using collections as values because they then could be accessed from different threads. Ensuring that the main map is thread-safe will prevent concurrent modifications to the map. However, once you gain access to the values of the map, you must exercise good concurrency practices around the values of the map.

■ **Note**   ConcurrentMaps do not allow null keys, which is different from its non–thread-safe cousin HashMap (which does allow null keys).

243

10-4. Iterating Through a Changing Collection

Problem

You need to iterate over each element in a collection. However, other threads are constantly updating the collection.

Solution 1

By using CopyOnWriteArrayList, you can safely iterate through the collection without worrying about concurrency. In the following solution, the startUpdatingThread() method creates a new thread, which actively changes the list passed to it. While startUpdatingThread() modifies the list, it is concurrently iterated using the stream forEach() function.

```java
private void copyOnWriteSolution() {
    CopyOnWriteArrayList<String> list = new CopyOnWriteArrayList<String>();
    startUpdatingThread(list);
    list.stream().forEach((element) -> {
        System.out.println("Element :" + element);
    });
    stopUpdatingThread();

}
```

Solution 2

Using a synchronizedList() allows us to atomically change the collection. Also, a synchronizedList() provides a way to synchronize safely on the list while iterating through it (which is done in the stream). For example:

```java
private void synchronizedListSolution() {
    final List<String> list = Collections.synchronizedList(new ArrayList<String>());
    startUpdatingThread(list);
    synchronized (list) {
        list.stream().forEach((element) -> {
            System.out.println("Element :" + element);
        });
    }
    stopUpdatingThread();
}
```

How It Works

Java comes with many concurrent collection options. Which collection to use depends on how the read operations compare with the write operations within the context of your application. If writing occurs far and in-between compared with reads, using a copyOnWriteArrayList instance is most efficient because it doesn't *block* (stop) other threads from reading the list and is thread-safe to iterate over (no ConcurrentModificationException is thrown when iterating through it). If there are the same number of writes and reads, using a SynchronizedList is the preferred choice.

In solution 1, the CopyOnWriteArrayList is being updated while you traverse the list. Because the recipe uses the CopyOnWriteArrayList instance, there is no need to worry of thread safety when iterating through the collection (as is being done in this recipe by using the stream). It is good to note that the CopyOnWriteArrayList offers a snapshot in time when iterating through it. If another thread modifies the list as you're iterating through it, changes are that the modified list will not be visible when iterating.

■ **Note**   Locking properly depends on the type of collection being used. Any collections returned as a result of using Collections.synchronized can be locked via the collection itself (synchronized (collectionInstance)). However, some more efficient (newer) concurrent collections such as the ConcurrentMap cannot be used in this fashion because their internal implementations don't lock in the object itself.

Solution 2 creates a synchronized list, which is created by using the Collections helper class. The Collection.synchronizedList() method wraps a List object (it can be ArrayList, LinkedList, or another List implementation) into a list that synchronizes the access to the list operations. Each time that you need to iterate over a list (either by using the stream, a for loop, or an iterator) you must be aware of the concurrency implications for that list's iterator. The CopyOnWriteArrayList is safe to iterate over (as specified in the Javadoc), but the synchronizedList iterator must be synchronized manually (also specified in the Collections.synchronizedlist.list iterator Javadoc). In the solution, the list can safely be iterated while inside the synchronized(list) block. When synchronizing on the list, no read/ updates/other iterations can occur until the synchronized(list) block is completed.

10-5. Coordinating Different Collections

Problem

You need to modify different but related collections at the same time and you want to ensure that no other threads can see these modifications until they have been completed.

Solution 1

By synchronizing on the principal collection, you can guarantee that collection can be updated at the same time. In the following example, the fulfillOrder method needs to check the inventory of the order to be fulfilled, and if there is enough inventory to fulfill the order, it needs to add the order to the customerOrders list. The fulfillOrder() method synchronizes on the inventoryMap map and modifies both the inventoryMap and the customerOrders list before finishing the synchronized block.

```
private boolean fulfillOrder(String itemOrdered, int quantityOrdered, String
customerName) {
    synchronized (inventoryMap) {
        int currentInventory  = 0;
        if (inventoryMap != null) {
            currentInventory = inventoryMap.get(itemOrdered);
        }
        if (currentInventory < quantityOrdered) {
            System.out.println("Couldn't fulfill order for "+customerName+" not enough
            "+itemOrdered+" ("+quantityOrdered+")");
```

```
                    return false; // sorry, we sold out
                }
                inventoryMap.put(itemOrdered,currentInventory - quantityOrdered);
                CustomerOrder order = new CustomerOrder(itemOrdered, quantityOrdered,
                customerName);
                customerOrders.add(order);
                System.out.println("Order fulfilled for "+customerName+" of "+itemOrdered+"
                ("+quantityOrdered+")");
                return true;
            }
    }

    private void checkInventoryLevels() {
        synchronized (inventoryMap) {
            System.out.println("------------------------------------");
            inventoryMap.entrySet().stream().forEach((inventoryEntry) -> {
                System.out.println("Inventory Level :"+inventoryEntry.getKey()+"
                "+inventoryEntry.getValue());
            });
            System.out.println("------------------------------------");
        }
    }

    private void displayOrders() {
        synchronized (inventoryMap) {
            customerOrders.stream().forEach((order) -> {
                System.out.println(order.getQuantityOrdered()+" "+order.getItemOrdered()+"
                for "+order.getCustomerName());
            });
        }
    }
```

Solution 2

Using a reentrant lock, you can prevent multiple threads from accessing the same critical area of the code. In this solution, the inventoryLock is acquired by calling inventoryLock.lock(). Any other thread that tries to acquire the inventoryLock lock will have to wait until the inventoryLock lock is released. At the end of the fulfillOrder() method (in the finally block), the inventoryLock is released by calling the inventoryLock.unlock() method:

```
Lock inventoryLock = new ReentrantLock();
private boolean fulfillOrder(String itemOrdered, int quantityOrdered, String customerName) {
    try {
        inventoryLock.lock();
        int currentInventory = inventoryMap.get(itemOrdered);
        if (currentInventory < quantityOrdered) {
            System.out.println("Couldn't fulfill order for " + customerName +
                " not enough " + itemOrdered + " (" + quantityOrdered + ")");
            return false; // sorry, we sold out
        }
        inventoryMap.put(itemOrdered, currentInventory - quantityOrdered);
```

```
            CustomerOrder order = new CustomerOrder(itemOrdered, quantityOrdered,
            customerName);
            customerOrders.add(order);
            System.out.println("Order fulfilled for " + customerName + " of " +
                    itemOrdered + " (" + quantityOrdered + ")");
            return true;
        } finally {
            inventoryLock.unlock();
        }
    }

    private void checkInventoryLevels() {
        try {
            inventoryLock.lock();
            System.out.println("-----------------------------------");
            inventoryMap.entrySet().stream().forEach((inventoryEntry) -> {
                System.out.println("Inventory Level :" + inventoryEntry.getKey() + " " +
                    inventoryEntry.getValue());
            });
            System.out.println("-----------------------------------");
        } finally {
            inventoryLock.unlock();
        }
    }

    private void displayOrders() {
        try {
            inventoryLock.lock();
            customerOrders.stream().forEach((order) -> {
                System.out.println(order.getQuantityOrdered() + " " +
                  order.getItemOrdered() + " for " + order.getCustomerName());
            });
        } finally {
            inventoryLock.unlock();
        }
    }
```

How It Works

If you have different structures that are required to be modified at the same time, you need to make sure that these structures are updated atomically. An *atomic* operation refers to a set of instructions that can be executed as a whole or none at all. An atomic operation is visible to the rest of the program only when it is complete.

In solution 1 (atomically modifying both the inventoryMap map and the customerOrders list), you pick a "principal" collection on which you will lock (the inventoryMap). By locking on the principal collection, you guarantee that if another thread tries to lock on the same principal collection, it will have to wait until the current executing thread releases the lock on the collection.

■ **Note**   Notice that even though `displayOrders` doesn't use the `inventoryMap`, you still synchronize on it (in solution 1). Because the `inventoryMap` is the `main` collection, even operations done on secondary collections will still need to be protected by the `main` collection synchronization.

Solution 2 is more explicit, offering an independent lock that is used to coordinate the atomic operations instead of picking a principal collection. *Locking* refers to the ability of the JVM to restrict certain code paths to be executed by only one thread. Threads try to obtain the lock (locks are provided, for example, by a `ReentrantLock` instance, as shown in the example), and the lock can be given to only one thread at a time. If other threads were trying to acquire the same lock, they will be suspended (`WAIT`) until the lock becomes available. The lock becomes available when the thread that currently holds the lock releases it. When a lock is released, it can then be acquired by one (and only one) of the threads that were waiting for that lock.

Locks by default are not "fair." In other words, the order of the threads that requested the lock is not kept; this allows for very fast locking/unlocking implementation in the JVM, and in most situations, it is generally okay to use unfair locks. On a very highly contended lock, if there is a requirement to evenly distribute the lock (make it fair), you do so by setting the `setFair` property on the lock.

In solution 2, calling the `inventoryLock.lock()` method, will either acquire the lock and continue, or will suspend execution (`WAIT`) until the lock can be acquired. Once the lock is acquired, no other thread will be able to execute within the locked block. At the end of the block, the lock is released by calling `inventoryLock.unlock()`.

It is common practice when working with `Lock` objects (`ReentrantLock`, `ReadLock`, and `WriteLock`) to surround the use of these `Lock` objects by a `try`/`finally` clause. After opening the `try` block, the first instruction would be a call to the `lock.lock()` method. This guarantees that the first instruction executed is the acquisition of the lock. The release of the lock (by calling `lock.unlock()`) is done in the matching `finally` block. In the event of a `RuntimeException` occurring while you have acquired the lock, unlocking within the `finally` clause assures that one doesn't "keep" the lock and prevent other threads from acquiring it.

The use of the `ReentrantLock` object offers additional features that the `synchronized` statement doesn't offer. As an example, the `ReentrantLock` has the `tryLock()` function, which attempts to get the lock only if no other threads have it (the method doesn't make the invoking thread wait). If another thread holds the lock, the method returns `false` but continues executing. It is better to use the `synchronized` keyword for synchronization and use `ReentrantLock` only when its features are needed. For more information on the other methods provided by `ReentrantLock`, visit `https://docs.oracle.com/javase/9/docs/api/java/util/concurrent/locks/ReentrantLock.html`.

■ **Tip**   While this is only a recipe book and proper threading techniques span their own volumes, it is important to raise awareness of deadlocks. *Deadlocks* occur when two locks are involved (and are acquired in reverse order within another thread). The simplest way to avoid a deadlock is to avoid letting the lock "escape." This means that the lock, when acquired, should not execute code calling on other methods that could possibly acquire a different lock. If that's not possible, release the lock before calling such a method.

Care should be taken in that any operation that refers to one or both collections needs to be protected by the same lock. Operations that depend on the result of one collection to query the second collection need to be executed atomically; they need to be done as a unit in which neither collection can change until the operation is completed.

10-6. Splitting Work into Separate Threads

Problem

You have work that can be split into separate threads and want to maximize the use of available CPU resources.

Solution

Use a ThreadpoolExecutor instance, which allows us to break the tasks into discrete units. In the following example, a BlockingQueue is created, which includes a Runnable object. It then is passed to the ThreadPoolExecutor instance. The ThreadPoolExecutor is then initialized and started by calling the prestartAllCoreThreads() method. Next, perform an orderly shutdown in which all previously submitted tasks are executed by calling the shutdown() method, followed by the awaitTermination() method:

```java
private void start() throws InterruptedException {
    BlockingQueue<Runnable> queue = new LinkedBlockingQueue<>();
    for (int i =0;i < 10;i++) {
        final int localI = i;
        queue.add((Runnable) () -> {
            doExpensiveOperation(localI);
        });
    }
    ThreadPoolExecutor executor = new ThreadPoolExecutor(10,10,1000,
            TimeUnit.MILLISECONDS, queue);
    executor.prestartAllCoreThreads();
    executor.shutdown();
    executor.awaitTermination(100000,TimeUnit.SECONDS);

    System.out.println("Look ma! all operations were completed");
}
```

How It Works

A ThreadPoolExecutor consists of two components: the Queue of tasks to be executed, and the Executor, which tells how to execute the tasks. The Queue is filled with Runnable objects, on which the method run() contains the code to be executed.

The Queue used by a ThreadPoolExecutor is an implementer of the BlockingQueue interface. The BlockingQueue interface denotes a queue in which the consumers of the queue will wait (be suspended) if there are no elements within the Queue. This is necessary for the ThreadPoolExecutor to work efficiently.

The first step is to fill the Queue with the tasks that need to be executed in parallel. This is done by calling the Queue's add() method and passing to it a class that implements the Runnable interface. Once that's done, the executor is initialized.

The ThreadPoolExecutor constructor has many parameter options; the one used in the solution is the simplest. Table 10-1 has a description of each parameter.

Table 10-1. *ThreadPoolExecutor's Parameters*

Parameter	Description
CorePoolSize	The minimum number of threads that are created as tasks are submitted
MaximumPoolSize	The maximum number of threads that the Executor would create
KeepAliveTime	The time that the waiting threads will wait for work before being disposed (as long as the number of live threads is still more than the CorePoolSize)
TimeUnit	The unit on which the KeepAliveTime is expressed (that is, TimeUnit.SECONDS, TimeUnit.MILLISECONDS)
WorkQueue	The Blocking queue that contains the tasks to be processed by the Executor

After the ThreadPoolExecutor is initialized, you call the prestartAllCoreThreads(). This method "warms up" the ThreadPoolExecutor by creating the number of threads specified in the CorePoolSize and actively starts consuming tasks from the Queue if it is not empty.

Call the shutdown() method of the ThreadPoolExecutor to wait for all the tasks to be completed. By calling this method, the ThreadPoolExecutor is instructed to accept no new events from the queue (previously submitted events will finish processing). This is the first step in the orderly termination of a ThreadPoolExecutor. Call the awaitTermination() method to wait for all the tasks in the ThreadPoolExecutor to be done. This method will force the main thread to wait until all the Runnables in the ThreadPoolExecutor's queue have completed executing. After all the Runnables have executed, the main thread will wake up and continue.

▓ **Note**　A ThreadPoolExecutor needs to be configured correctly to maximize CPU usage. The most efficient number of threads for an executor depends on the types of tasks that are submitted. If the tasks are CPU-intensive, having an executor with the current number of cores would be ideal. If the tasks are I/O-intensive, the executor should have more threads than the current number of cores of threads. The more I/O-bound, the higher the number of threads.

10-7. Coordinating Threads

Problem

Your application requires that two or more threads be coordinated to work in unison.

Solution 1

With wait/notify for thread synchronization, threads can be coordinated. In this solution, the main thread waits for the objectToSync object until the database-loading thread is finished executing. Once the database-loading thread is finished, it notifies the objectToSync that whoever is waiting on it can continue executing. The same process occurs when loading the orders into our system. The main thread waits on objectToSync until the orders-loading thread notifies objectToSync to continue by calling the objectToSync.notify() method. After ensuring that both the inventory and the orders are loaded, the main thread executes the processOrder() method to process all orders.

```java
private final Object objectToSync = new Object();

private void start() {
    loadItems();

    Thread inventoryThread = new Thread(() -> {
        System.out.println("Loading Inventory from Database...");
        loadInventory();
        synchronized (objectToSync) {
            objectToSync.notify();
        }
    });

    synchronized (objectToSync) {
        inventoryThread.start();
        try {
            objectToSync.wait();
        } catch (InterruptedException e) {
            e.printStackTrace();
        }
    }

    Thread ordersThread = new Thread(() -> {

        System.out.println("Loading Orders from XML Web service...");
        loadOrders();
        synchronized (objectToSync) {
            objectToSync.notify();
        }

    });

    synchronized (objectToSync) {
        ordersThread.start();
        try {
            objectToSync.wait();
        } catch (InterruptedException e) {
            e.printStackTrace();
        }
    }
    processOrders();
}
```

Solution 2

You can control when the main thread continues using a CountDownLatch object. In the following code, a CountDownLatch with an initial value of 2 is created; then the two threads for loading the inventory and loading the order information are created and started. As each of the two threads finish executing, they call the CountDownLatch's countDown() method, which decrements the latch's value by one. The main thread waits until the CountDownLatch reaches 0, at which point it resumes execution.

```
CountDownLatch latch = new CountDownLatch(2);

private void start() {
    loadItems();

    Thread inventoryThread = new Thread(() -> {
        System.out.println("Loading Inventory from Database...");
        loadInventory();
        latch.countDown();
    });

    inventoryThread.start();

    Thread ordersThread = new Thread(() -> {
        System.out.println("Loading Orders from XML Web service...");
        loadOrders();
        latch.countDown();
    });

    ordersThread.start();

    try {
        latch.await();
    } catch (InterruptedException e) {
        e.printStackTrace();
    }

    processOrders();

}
```

Solution 3

By using Thread.join(), you can wait for a thread to finish executing. The following example has a thread for loading the inventory and another thread for loading the orders. Once each thread is started, a call to inventoryThread.join() will make the main thread wait for the inventoryThread to finish executing before continuing.

```
private void start() {
    loadItems();

    Thread inventoryThread = new Thread(() -> {
        System.out.println("Loading Inventory from Database...");
        loadInventory();
    });

    inventoryThread.start();
    try {
        inventoryThread.join();
    } catch (InterruptedException e) {
        e.printStackTrace();
    }
```

```
    Thread ordersThread = new Thread(() -> {
        System.out.println("Loading Orders from XML Web service...");
        loadOrders();
    });

    ordersThread.start();
    try {
        ordersThread.join();
    } catch (InterruptedException e) {
        e.printStackTrace();
    }
    processOrders();
}
```

How It Works

There are many ways of coordinating threads in Java, and these coordination efforts rely on the notion of making a thread wait. When a thread waits, it suspends execution (it doesn't continue to the next instruction and is removed from the JVM's thread scheduler). If a thread is waiting, it can then be awakened by notifying it. Within the Java's concurrency lingo, the word *notify* implies that a thread will resume execution (the JVM will add the thread to the thread scheduler). So in the natural course of thread coordination, the most common sequence of events is a main thread waiting, and a secondary thread then notifying the main thread to continue (or wake up). Even so, there is the possibility of a waiting thread being interrupted by some other event. When a thread is interrupted, it doesn't continue to the next instruction, but instead throws an InterruptedException, which is a way of signaling that even though the thread was waiting for something to happen, some other event happened that requires the thread's attention. This is better illustrated by the following example:

```
BlockingQueue queue = new LinkedBlockingQueue();
while (true) {
    synchronized (this) {
        Object itemToProcess = queue.take();
        processItem (itemToProcess);
    }
}
```

If you look at the previous code, the thread that executes this code would never terminate because it loops forever and waits for an item to be processed. If there are no items in the Queue, the main thread waits until there is something added to the Queue from another thread. You couldn't graciously shut down the previous code (especially if the thread running the loop is not a Daemon thread).

```
BlockingQueue queue = new LinkedBlockingQueue();
while (true) {
    synchronized (this) {
        Object itemToProcess = null;
        try {
            itemToProcess = queue.take();
        } catch (InterruptedException e) {
            return;
        }
        processItem (itemToProcess);
    }
}
```

The new code now has the ability of "escaping" the infinite loop. From another thread, you can call `thread.interrupt()`, which throws the `InterruptedException` that is then caught by the main thread's catch clause. The infinite loop can be exited within this clause.

`InterruptedExceptions` are a way of sending extra information to waiting (or sleeping) threads so that they may handle a different scenario (for example, an orderly program shutdown). For this reason, every operation that changes the state of the thread to sleep/wait will have to be surrounded by a try/catch block that can catch the `InterruptedException`. This is one of the cases in which the exception (`InterruptedException`) is not really an error but more of a way of signaling between threads that something has occurred that requires attention.

Solution 1 demonstrates the most common (oldest) form of coordination. The solution requires making a thread wait and suspending execution until the thread gets notified (or awakened) by another thread.

For solution 1 to work, the originating thread needs to acquire a lock. This lock will then be the "phone number" on which another thread can notify the originating thread to wake up. After the originating thread acquires the lock (phone number), it proceeds to wait. As soon as the `wait()` method is called, the lock is released, allowing other threads to acquire the same lock. The secondary thread then proceeds to acquire the lock (the phone number) and then notifies (which, in fact, would be like dialing a wake-up call) the originating thread. After the notification, the originating thread resumes execution.

In the solution 1 code, the lock is a dummy object identified as `objectToSync`. In practice, the object on which locks are waiting and notifying could be any valid instance object in Java; for example, we could have used the `this` reference to make the main thread wait (and within the threads we could have used the `Recipe 10_7_1.this` variable reference to notify the main thread to continue).

The main advantage of using this technique is the explicitness of controlling on whom to wait and when to notify (and the ability to notify all threads that are waiting on the same object; see the following tip).

■ **Tip** Multiple threads can wait on the same lock (same phone number to be awakened). When a secondary thread calls notify, it will wake up one of the "waiting" threads (there is no fairness about which is awakened). Sometimes you will need to notify all the threads; you can call the `notifyAll()` method instead of calling the `notify()` method. This is mostly used when preparing many threads to take some work, but the work is not yet finished setting up.

Solution 2 uses a more modern approach to notification, as it involves a `CountDownLatch`. When setting up, specify how many "counts" the latch will have. The main thread will then wait (stop execution) by calling the `CountDownLatch`'s `await()` method until the latch counts down to 0. When the latch reaches 0, the main thread will wake up and continue execution. As the worker thread completes, call the `latch.countdown()` method, which will decrement the latch's current count value. If the latch's current value reaches 0, the main thread that was waiting on the `CountDownLatch` will wake up and continue execution.

The main advantage of using `CountDownLatches` is that it is possible to spawn multiple tasks at the same time and just wait for all of them to complete. (In the solution example, we didn't need to wait until one or the other threads were completed before continuing; they all were started, and when the latch was 0, the main thread continued.)

Solution 3 instead offers a solution in which we have access to the thread we want to wait on. For the main thread, it's just a matter of calling the secondary thread's `join()` method. Then the main thread will wait (stop executing) until the secondary thread completes.

The advantage of this method is that it doesn't require the secondary threads to know any synchronization mechanism. As long as the secondary thread terminates execution, the main thread can wait on them.

10-8. Creating Thread-Safe Objects

Problem

You need to create an object that is thread-safe because it will be accessed from multiple threads.

Solution 1

Use synchronized getters and setters and protect critical regions that change state. In the following example, an object is created with getters and setters that are synchronized for each internal variable. The critical regions are protected by using the synchronized(this) lock:

```java
class CustomerOrder {
    private String itemOrdered;
    private int quantityOrdered;
    private String customerName;

    public CustomerOrder() {

    }

    public double calculateOrderTotal (double price) {
        synchronized (this) {
            return getQuantityOrdered()*price;
        }
    }

    public synchronized String getItemOrdered() {
        return itemOrdered;
    }

    public synchronized int getQuantityOrdered() {
        return quantityOrdered;
    }

    public synchronized String getCustomerName() {
        return customerName;
    }

    public synchronized void setItemOrdered(String itemOrdered) {
        this.itemOrdered = itemOrdered;
    }

    public synchronized void setQuantityOrdered(int quantityOrdered) {
        this.quantityOrdered = quantityOrdered;
    }

    public synchronized void setCustomerName(String customerName) {
        this.customerName = customerName;
    }
}
```

Solution 2

Create an immutable object (an object that, once created, doesn't change its internal state). In the following code, the internal variables of the object are declared final and are assigned at construction. By doing so, it is guaranteed that the object is immutable:

```
class ImmutableCustomerOrder {
    final private String itemOrdered;
    final private int quantityOrdered;
    final private String customerName;

    ImmutableCustomerOrder(String itemOrdered, int quantityOrdered, String customerName) {
        this.itemOrdered = itemOrdered;
        this.quantityOrdered = quantityOrdered;
        this.customerName = customerName;
    }

    public String getItemOrdered() {
        return itemOrdered;
    }

    public int getQuantityOrdered() {
        return quantityOrdered;
    }

    public String getCustomerName() {
        return customerName;
    }

    public double calculateOrderTotal (double price) {
        return getQuantityOrdered()*price;
    }
}
```

How It Works

Solution 1 relies on the principle that a lock protects any change done to the object. Using the synchronized keyword is a shortcut to writing the expression synchronized (this). By synchronizing your getters and setters (and any other operation that alters the internal state of your object), you guarantee that the object is consistent. Also, it is important that any operations that should occur as a unit (say something that modifies two collections at the same time, as listed in Recipe 10-5) are done within a method of the object and are protected by using the synchronized keyword.

For instance, if an object offers a getSize() method as well as getItemNumber(int index), it would be unsafe to write the following object.getItemNumber (object.getSize()-1). Even though it looks that the statement is concise, another thread can alter the contents of the object between getting the size and getting the item number. Instead, it is safer to create a object.getLastElement() method, which atomically figures out the size and the last element.

Solution 2 relies on the property of immutable objects. Immutable objects cannot change their internal state, and objects that cannot change their internal state (are *immutable*) are by definition thread-safe. If you need to modify the immutable object due to an event, instead of explicitly changing its property, create a new object with the changed properties. This new object then takes the place of the old object, and on future requests for the object, the new immutable object is returned. This is by far the easiest (albeit verbose) method for creating thread-safe code.

10-9. Implementing Thread-Safe Counters

Problem

You need a counter that is thread-safe so that it can be incremented from within different execution threads.

Solution

By using the inherently thread-safe `Atomic` objects, it is possible to create a counter that guarantees thread safety and has an optimized synchronization strategy. In the following code, an `Order` object is created, and it requires a unique order ID that is generated using the `AtomicLong incrementAndGet()` method:

```
AtomicLong orderIdGenerator = new AtomicLong(0);

        for (int i =0;i < 10;i++) {
            Thread orderCreationThread = new Thread(() -> {
                for (int i1 = 0; i1 < 10; i1++) {
                    createOrder(Thread.currentThread().getName());
                }
            });
            orderCreationThread.setName("Order Creation Thread "+i);
            orderCreationThread.start();
        }

//////////////////////////////////////////////////////
    private void createOrder(String name) {
        long orderId = orderIdGenerator.incrementAndGet();
        Order order = new Order(name, orderId);
        orders.add(order);
    }
```

How It Works

`AtomicLong` (and its cousin `AtomicInteger`) are built to be used safely in concurrent environments. They have methods to atomically increment (and get) the changed value. Even if hundreds of threads call the `AtomicLong increment()` method, the returned value will always be unique.

If you need to make decisions and update the variables, always use the atomic operations that are offered by `AtomicLong`; for example, `compareAndSet`. If not, your code will not be thread-safe (as any check-then-act operation needs to be atomic) unless you externally protect the atomic reference by using your own locks (see Recipe 10-7).

The following code illustrates several code safety issues to be aware of. First, changing a long value may be done in two memory write operations (as allowed by the Java Memory Model), and thus two threads could end up overlapping those two operations in what might on the surface appear to be thread-safe code. The result would be a completely unexpected (and likely wrong) long value:

```
long counter = 0;

public long incrementCounter() {
  return counter++;
}
```

This code also suffers from *unsafe publication*, which refers to the fact that a variable might be cached locally (in the CPU's internal cache) and might not be committed to main memory. If another thread (executing in another CPU) happens to be reading the variable from main memory, that other thread may miss the changes made by the first thread. The changed value may be cached by the first thread's CPU, and not yet committed to main memory where the second thread can see it. For safe publication, you must use the volatile Java modifier (see http://download.oracle.com/javase/tutorial/essential/concurrency/atomic.html).

A final issue with the preceding code is that it is not atomic. Even though it looks like there is only one operation to increment the counter, in reality there are two operations that occur at the machine-language level (a retrieve of the variable and then an increment). There could be two or more threads that obtain the same value as they both retrieve the variable but haven't incremented it yet. Then all the threads increment the counter to the same number.

10-10. Breaking Down Tasks into Discrete Units of Work

Problem

You have an algorithm that benefits from using a *divide-and-conquer strategy*, which refers to the ability of breaking down a unit of work into two separate subunits and then piecing together the results from these subunits. The subunits can then be broken down into more subunits of work until reaching a point where the work is small enough to just be executed. By breaking down the unit of work into subunits, you can take advantage of the multicore nature of today's processors with minimum pain.

Solution

The new Fork/Join framework makes applying the divide-and-conquer strategy straightforward. The following example creates a representation of the Game of Life. The code uses the Fork/Join framework to speed up the calculation for each iteration when advancing from one generation to the next:

//

```
        ForkJoinPool pool = new ForkJoinPool();
        long i = 0;

        while (shouldRun) {
            i++;
            final boolean[][] newBoard = new boolean[lifeBoard.length][lifeBoard[0].length];
            long startTime = System.nanoTime();
```

```
        GameOfLifeAdvancer advancer = new GameOfLifeAdvancer(lifeBoard, 0,0, lifeBoard.
        length-1, lifeBoard[0].length-1,newBoard);
        pool.invoke(advancer);
        long endTime = System.nanoTime();
        if (i % 100 == 0 ) {
            System.out.println("Taking "+(endTime-startTime)/1000 + "ms");
        }
        SwingUtilities.invokeAndWait(() -> {
            model.setBoard(newBoard);
            lifeTable.repaint();
        });
        lifeBoard = newBoard;
    }
/////////////////////////////////////////////////////////////////

    class GameOfLifeAdvancer extends RecursiveAction{

        private boolean[][] originalBoard;
        private boolean[][] destinationBoard;
        private int startRow;
        private int endRow;
        private int endCol;
        private int startCol;

        GameOfLifeAdvancer(boolean[][] originalBoard, int startRow, int startCol, int
        endRow, int endCol, boolean [][] destinationBoard) {
            this.originalBoard = originalBoard;
            this.destinationBoard = destinationBoard;
            this.startRow = startRow;
            this.endRow = endRow;
            this.endCol = endCol;
            this.startCol = startCol;
        }

        private void computeDirectly() {
            for (int row = startRow; row <= endRow;row++) {
                for (int col = startCol; col <= endCol; col++) {
                    int numberOfNeighbors = getNumberOfNeighbors (row, col);
                    if (originalBoard[row][col]) {
                        destinationBoard[row][col] = true;
                        if (numberOfNeighbors < 2) destinationBoard[row][col] = false;
                        if (numberOfNeighbors > 3) destinationBoard[row][col] = false;
                    } else {
                        destinationBoard[row][col] = false;
                        if (numberOfNeighbors == 3) destinationBoard[row][col] = true;
                    }
                }
            }
        }
```

```java
        private int getNumberOfNeighbors(int row, int col) {
            int neighborCount = 0;
            for (int leftIndex = -1; leftIndex < 2; leftIndex++) {
                for (int topIndex = -1; topIndex < 2; topIndex++) {
                    if ((leftIndex == 0) && (topIndex == 0)) continue; // skip own
                    int neighbourRowIndex = row + leftIndex;
                    int neighbourColIndex = col + topIndex;
                    if (neighbourRowIndex<0) neighbourRowIndex =
                    originalBoard.length + neighbourRowIndex;
                    if (neighbourColIndex<0) neighbourColIndex =
                    originalBoard[0].length + neighbourColIndex ;
                    boolean neighbour = originalBoard[neighbourRowIndex % originalBoard.
                    length][neighbourColIndex % originalBoard[0].length];
                    if (neighbour) neighborCount++;
                }
            }
            return neighborCount;
        }

        @Override
        protected void compute() {
            if (getArea() < 20) {
                computeDirectly();
                return;
            }
            int halfRows = (endRow - startRow) / 2;
            int halfCols = (endCol - startCol) / 2;
            if (halfRows > halfCols) {
                // split the rows
                invokeAll(new GameOfLifeAdvancer(originalBoard, startRow, startCol,
                startRow+halfRows, endCol,destinationBoard),
                        new GameOfLifeAdvancer(originalBoard, startRow+halfRows+1,
                        startCol, endRow, endCol,destinationBoard));
            } else {
                invokeAll(new GameOfLifeAdvancer(originalBoard, startRow, startCol, endRow,
                startCol+ halfCols,destinationBoard),
                        new GameOfLifeAdvancer(originalBoard, startRow,
                        startCol+halfCols+1, endRow, endCol,destinationBoard));
            }
        }

        private int getArea() { return (endRow - startRow) * (endCol - startCol);  }

    }
```

How It Works

The Fork/Join framework can be used for breaking down tasks into discrete units of work. The first part of the solution creates a ForkJoinPool object. The default constructor provides reasonable defaults (such as creating as many threads as there are CPU cores) and sets up an entry point to submit divide-and-conquer work. While the ForkJoinPool inherits from ExecutorService, it is best suited to handle tasks that extend from RecursiveAction. The ForkJoinPool object has the invoke(RecursiveAction) method, which will take a RecursiveAction object and apply the divide-and-conquer strategy.

The second part of the solution creates the GameOfLifeAdvancer class, which extends the RecursiveAction class. By extending the RecursiveAction class, the work can be split. The GameOfLifeAdvancer class advances the Game of Life board to the next generation. The constructor takes a two-dimensional Boolean array (which represents a Game of Life board), a start row/column, an end row/column, and a destination two-dimensional Boolean array, on which the result of advancing the Game of Life for one generation is collected.

The GameOfLifeAdvancer is required to implement the compute() method. In this method, determine how much work there is to be completed. If the work is small enough, the work is completed directly (achieved by calling the computeDirectly() method and returning). If the work is not small enough, the method splits the work by creating two GameOfLifeAdvancer instances that process only half of the current GameOfLifeAdvancer work. This is done by either splitting the number of rows to be processed into two chunks or by splitting the number of columns into two chunks. The two GameOfLifeAdvancer instances are then passed to the ForkJoin pool by calling the invokeAll() method of the RecursiveAction class. The invokeAll() method takes the two instances of GameOfLifeAdvancer (it can take as many as needed) and waits until they both are finished executing (that is, the meaning of the –all postfix in the invokeAll() method name; it waits for all of the tasks submitted to be completed before returning control).

In this way, the GameOfLifeAdvancer instance is broken down into new GameOfLifeAdvancer instances that each processes only part of the Game of Life board. Each instance waits for all the subordinate parts to be completed before returning control to the caller. The resulting division of work can take advantage of the multiple CPUs available in the typical system today.

■ **Tip** The ForkJoinPool is generally more efficient than an ExecutorService because it implements a work-stealing policy. Each thread has a Queue of work to complete; if the Queue of any thread is empty, the thread will "steal" work from another thread queue, making a more efficient use of CPU processing power.

10-11. Updating a Common Value Across Multiple Threads

Problem

Your application needs to safely maintain a single summed value across multiple threads.

Solution

Utilize a DoubleAdder or LongAdder to contain the value that is being summed across multiple threads in order to ensure safe handling. In the following example, two threads are adding values to a DoubleAdder at the same time, and in the end the value is summed and displayed.

```
DoubleAdder da = new DoubleAdder();

private void start() {

        Thread thread1 = new Thread(() -> {
            for (int i1 = 0; i1 < 10; i1++) {
                da.add(i1);
                System.out.println("Adding " + i1);
            }
        });
```

```
        Thread thread2 = new Thread(() -> {
            for (int i1 = 0; i1 < 10; i1++) {
                da.add(i1);
                System.out.println("Adding " + i1);
            }
        });

        thread1.start();
        thread2.start();

        try {
            System.out.println("Sleep while summing....");
            Thread.sleep(10000);
        } catch (InterruptedException e) {
            e.printStackTrace();
        }

        System.out.println("The sum is: " + da.doubleValue());

    }
}
```

Results:

```
Adding 0
Adding 1
Adding 2
Adding 3
Adding 4
Adding 5
Adding 6
Adding 7
Adding 0
Adding 8
Adding 9
Adding 1
Adding 2
Adding 3
Adding 4
Adding 5
Adding 6
Adding 7
Adding 8
Adding 9
The sum is: 90.0
```

How It Works

Prior to the release of Java 8, it was important to utilize atomic numbers when working with values across multiple threads. Atomic variables prevent thread interference without causing obstruction in the way that synchronized access may cause in some cases. Java 8 introduced a new line of atomic variables that provide for faster throughput than standard atomic variables. The java.util.concurrent.atomic.DoubleAdder and java.util.concurrent.atomic.LongAdder classes are preferable to AtomicDouble and AtomicLong in most cases when the values may be accessed and updated across multiple threads. Both DoubleAdder and LongAdder extend Number, and they are useful when summing values across threads, especially under high contention.

In the solution, a DoubleAdder is used to sum numbers across two different threads. Using the add() method, various numbers are "added" to the DoubleAdder value. After the threads have had ample time to perform their work, the doubleValue() method is called upon to return the sum of all values as a double.

Both the DoubleAdder and LongAdder classes contain similar methods, although the LongAdder does contain a couple of additional helper methods for incrementing and decrementing the value of the adder. Table 10-2 shows the methods that are contained within each of the classes.

***Table 10-2.** DoubleAdder and LongAdder Methods*

Method	Description
add()	Adds the given value.
decrement()	(LongAdder only.) Equivalent to add(-1).
doubleValue()	Returns the sum() as a double value (after performing widening primitive conversion on LongAdder).
floatValue()	Returns the sum() as a float value after performing a widening primitive conversion.
increment()	(LongAdder only.) Equivalent to add(1).
intValue()	Returns the sum() as an int value after performing a narrowing conversion.
longValue()	Returns the sum() as a long value (after performing narrowing conversion on DoubleAdder).
reset()	Resets the variable's values to zero.
sum()	Returns the current summed value.
sumThenReset()	Returns the current summed value and then resets the variable's values to zero.
toString()	Returns the String representation of the summed value.

■ **Tip**   In the same family as DoubleAdder and LongAdder are the DoubleAccumulator and LongAccumulator classes. These classes allow one or more variables that are being maintained across threads to be updated using a supplied function. Both of these classes accept an accumulator function as the first argument and an identity as the second argument. When updates are applied across the thread, the set of variables used to perform the calculations may grow dynamically to reduce contention. For more information regarding these classes, which are new to Java 8, refer to the online documentation: http://docs.oracle.com/javase/9/docs/api/java/util/concurrent/atomic/package-summary.html.

10-12. Executing Multiple Tasks Asynchronously

Problem

Your application requires multiple tasks to be performed at the same time in an asynchronous manner, such that none of the tasks block one another.

Solution

Utilize CompletableFuture objects to represent the state of each task that is currently being performed. Each CompletableFuture object will run on a designated or application-determined background thread, issuing a callback to the original calling method once completed.

In the following solution, two long-running tasks are invoked by a calling method, and they each utilize the CompletableFuture to report status once the task has been completed.

```java
public class Recipe10_12 {

    public static void main(String[] args) {
        try {
            CompletableFuture tasks = performWork()
                    .thenApply(work -> {
                        String newTask = work + " Second task complete!";
                        System.out.println(newTask);
                        return newTask;
                    }).thenApply(finalTask -> finalTask + " Final Task Complete!");

            CompletableFuture future = performSecondWork("Java 9 is Great! ");
            while(!tasks.isDone()){
                System.out.println(future.get());
            }
            System.out.println(tasks.get());

        } catch (ExecutionException | InterruptedException ex) {

        }
    }

    /**
     * Returns a CompleableFuture object.
     * @return
     */
    public static CompletableFuture performWork() {
        CompletableFuture resultingWork = CompletableFuture.supplyAsync(
                () -> {
                    String taskMessage = "First task complete!";
                    try {
                        Thread.sleep(1000);
                    } catch (InterruptedException ex) {
                        System.out.println(ex);
                    }
```

```
                System.out.println(taskMessage);
                return taskMessage;
            });
        return resultingWork;

    }

    /**
     * Accepts a String and returns a CompletableFuture.
     * @param message
     * @return
     */
    public static CompletableFuture performSecondWork(String message) {
        CompletableFuture resultingWork = CompletableFuture.supplyAsync(
                () -> {
                    String taskMessage = message + " Another task complete!";
                    try {
                        Thread.sleep(1000);
                    } catch (InterruptedException ex) {
                        System.out.println(ex);
                    }

                    return taskMessage;
                });
        return resultingWork;

    }
}
```

Results:

```
First task complete!
First task complete! Second task complete!
Java 9 is Great! Another task complete!
First task complete! Second task complete! Final Task Complete!
```

How It Works

CompletableFuture<T> was added in Java 8 to build out support for asynchronous tasks.
CompletableFuture<T> is an extension of Future<T>, which adds many methods to promote asynchronous,
event-driven programming models, and also allows for values to be set at any time. The latter functionality
means that a CompletableFuture can be created prior to when it is required, in the case that an application
will need to use it in the future.

There are a couple of options for creating a CompletableFuture object, either manually or via the
utilization of factory methods. Manual creation of a CompleteableFuture will can be done without binding
to any thread, and such a tactic can be useful in cases such as when an application requires a placeholder for
an event that will occur in the future. The following code demonstrates how to create a CompletableFuture
manually:

```
final <CompletableFutureString> completableFuture = new CompletableFuture<>();
```

One would utilize a factory to generate a CompletableFuture to return an object that is geared toward a specific task or outcome. There are a number of different factory methods to call upon to return such an object. Some of the factory methods accept arguments, and others do not. For instance, the CompletableFuture.runAsync(Runnable) method returns a CompletableFuture that first executes the provided Runnable, and then asynchronously completes by a task running in the ForkJoinPool. commonPool(). Another variation of the runAsync() method accepts both a Runnable and an Executor, which first executes the provided Runnable, then asynchronously completes by a task within the given Executor.

The CompletableFuture object also contains a number of methods that are much like that of the standard Future object. For instance, the isDone(), cancel(), and isCompletedExceptionally() methods each return boolean to indicate a status on the object. It is also possible to stack asynchronous tasks with a CompletableFuture by calling upon the thenApply() method, which accepts lambda expressions and method references. The solution to this recipe demonstrates how to utilize the thenApply() method to invoke an asynchronous task from another. First, a CompletableFuture object named performWork() is executed, then a lambda is executed creating a concatenated String based upon the String that was generated within performWork(). Once the second task has completed, another task is invoked to append more text to the String. The future.get() method is then called within a loop in order to see the String being transformed by the application over time. Lastly, the outcome of the fully completed task is printed.

Java 9 added some enhancements to the CompletableFuture. There is now better support for delays and timeouts by maintaining a thread for triggering and canceling actions. It also maintains better support for subclassing and some utility methods.

Summary

It is important to understand the fundamentals of concurrency when developing applications. There is nothing worse than testing an application successfully, and then having it fail with a deadlock once it is released into production. This chapter started with the basics, demonstrating how to spawn a background task. It then went on to cover various techniques for handing concurrency, from creating threads to using the Fork/Join framework to divide work into discrete tasks. Lastly, the chapter closed out with coverage of the CompletableFuture and some of the new additions to the class in Java 9.

CHAPTER 11

■ ■ ■

Debugging and Unit Testing

Debugging is a big part of software development. To effectively debug, you must be able to "think" like a computer and dive into the code, deconstructing every step that lead to the logic error that you're working to resolve. In the beginning of computer programming, there weren't a lot of tools to help in debugging. Mostly, debugging involved taking a look at your code and spotting inconsistencies; then resubmitting the code to be compiled again. Today, every IDE offers the ability of using breakpoints and inspecting memory variables, making it much easier to debug. Outside the IDE there are other tools that help in daily debugging, building, and testing of your project; and these tools ensure that your code is being continually tested for errors that may be introduced when programming. In this chapter, you explore the different tools that will help aid in debugging, analyzing, and testing Java software.

This chapter covers some debugging and unit testing basics. You will learn how to perform unit testing from the command line or terminal using Apache Ant, along with JUnit. You will also learn how to make use of the NetBeans Profiler, among other tools, for profiling and monitoring your applications.

11-1. Understanding Exceptions

Problem

You caught and logged an exception, and you need to determine its cause.

Solution

Analyze the output from the exception's `printStackTrace()` method:

```java
public class Recipe11_1 {
    public static void main (String[] args) {
        Recipe11_1 recipe = new Recipe11_1();
        recipe.startProcess();
    }

    private void startProcess() {
        try {
            int a = 5/0;
        } catch (Exception e) {
            e.printStackTrace();
        }

    }
}
```

© Josh Juneau 2017
J. Juneau, *Java 9 Recipes*, DOI 10.1007/978-1-4842-1976-8_11

Result:

```
java.lang.ArithmeticException: / by zero
    at org.java8recipes.chapter11.recipe11_01.Recipe11_1.start(Recipe11_1.java:18)
    at org.java8recipes.chapter11.recipe11_01.Recipe11_1.main(Recipe11_1.java:13)
```

How It Works

In programming lingo, a *stack* refers to the list of functions that were called to get to a point in your program, usually starting from the immediate (System.out.println()) to the more general (public static void main). Every program keeps track of which code was executed in order to reach a specific part of the code. Stack trace's output refers to the stack that was in memory when an error occurred. Exceptions thrown in Java keep track of where they occurred and which code path was executed when the exception was thrown. Stack trace shows from the most specific place where the exception occurred (the line where the exception occurred) to the top-level invoker of the offending code (and everything in between). This information then allows you to pinpoint which method calls were performed, and may help shed some light on why the exception was thrown.

In this example, the divide-by-zero exception occurred on line 18 of Recipe11_1.java and was caused by a call from the main() method (at line 13). Sometimes, when looking at the stack trace's output, you will see methods that don't belong to the project. This happens naturally as sometimes method calls are generated in other parts of a working system. It is, for example, very common to see Abstract Window Toolkit (AWT) methods in Swing applications when an exception is raised (due to the nature of the EventQueue). If you look at the more specific function calls (earliest), you will eventually run with the project's own code and can then try to determine why the exception was thrown.

■ **Note**   The Stack trace output will contain line number information if the program is compiled with "Debug" info. By default, most IDEs will include this information when running in a Debug configuration. Oftentimes, the IDE will also make the line number of the error(s) easily accessible by generating a direct link that will take you to the offending line of code. If using the command line, use the –g option to compile and generate debugging information.

11-2. Locking Down Behavior of Your Classes

Problem

You need to lock down the behavior of your class and want to create unit tests that will be used to verify the specific behavior in your application.

Solution

Use JUnit to create unit tests that verify behavior in your classes. To use this solution, you need to include the JUnit dependencies in your class path. JUnit can be downloaded from http://www.junit.org, or you can simply add the Maven dependency to your project. If you choose to download it then you will need to load both junit.jar and hamcrest.jar. At the time of this writing, the Maven dependency was as follows, please change version accordingly:

```
<dependency>
  <groupId>junit</groupId>
  <artifactId>junit</artifactId>
  <version>4.12</version>
  <scope>test</scope>
</dependency>
```

When JUnit becomes part of your project, you will be able to include the org.junit and junit. framework namespaces. In this example two unit tests are created for the MathAdder class. The MathAdder class contains two methods: addNumber (int, int) and substractNumber (int,int). These two methods return the addition (or subtraction) of their passed parameters (a simple class). The unit tests (marked by the @Test annotation) verify that the MathAdder class does, in fact, add and/or subtract two numbers.

```java
package org.java8recipes.chapter11;

import junit.framework.Assert;
import org.junit.Test;

public class Recipe11_2_MathAdderTest {

    @Test
    public void testAddBehavior() {
        Recipe_11_2_MathAdder adder = new Recipe_11_2_MathAdder();
        for (int i =0;i < 100;i++) {
            for (int j =0;j < 100;j++) {
                Assert.assertEquals(i+j,adder.addNumbers(i,j));

            }
        }
    }

    @Test
    public void testSubstractBehavior() {
        Recipe_11_2_MathAdder adder = new Recipe_11_2_MathAdder();
        for (int i =0;i < 100;i++) {
            for (int j =0;j < 100;j++) {
                Assert.assertEquals(i-j,adder.substractNumber(i,j));

            }
        }
    }
}
```

To execute this test, use your IDE to run the test class. For example, in NetBeans, you must refactor the test class by right-clicking it and moving it into the "Test Packages" module within the NetBeans project. Once you've moved the test class into the desired package within "Test Packages," right-click and run the file to perform the tests.

■ **Note**   At the time of this writing, the JUnit 5 library was in active development. It is the next generation of JUnit and includes many new pieces of functionality that take advantage of newer JVM language constructs, such as lambdas. This recipe focuses on JUnit 4, since it is a mature test suite. For more information on JUnit 5, please refer to the following website: `http://junit.org/junit5/`

How It Works

Unit tests are useful for testing your code to ensure that expected behaviors occur within your classes. Including unit tests in your project makes it less likely to break functionality when adding or refactoring code. When you create unit tests, you are specifying how an object should behave (what is referred to as its *contract*). The unit tests ensure that the expected behavior occurs (they do this by verifying the result of a method and using the different JUnit.Assert methods).

The first step to writing a unit test is to create a new class that describes the behavior you want to verify. One of the general unit–test naming conventions is to create a class with the same name as the class being tested with the postfix of Test; in this recipe's example, the main class is called Recipe11_2_MathAdder, while the testing class is called Recipe11_2_MathAdderTest.

The unit test class (MathAdderTest) will contain methods that check and verify the behavior of the class. To do so, method names are annotated. *Annotations* are forms of metadata, and a developer can "annotate" specified portions of code, thereby adding information to the annotated code. This extra information is not used by the program, but by the compiler/builder (or external tools) to guide the compilation, building, and/ or testing of the code. For unit-testing purposes, you annotate the methods that are part of the unit test by specifying **@Test** before each method name. Within each method, you use Assert.assertEquals (or any of the other Assert static methods) to verify behavior.

The Assert.assertEquals method instructs the unit-testing framework to verify that the expected value of the method call from the class that you are testing is the same as the actual value returned by its method call. In the recipe example, Assert.assertEquals verifies that the MathAdder is correctly adding the two integers. While the scope of this class is trivial, it shows the bare minimum requirements to have a fully functional unit test.

If the Assert call succeeds, it gets reported in the unit test framework as a "passed" test; if the Assert call fails, then the unit test framework will stop and display a message showing where the unit test failed. Most modern IDEs have the capability of running unit test classes by simply right-clicking the name and selecting Run/Debug (and that's the intended way of running the Chapter_11_2_MathAdderTest recipe).

While it is true that IDEs can run unit tests while developing, they are created with the intention of being run automatically (usually triggered by a scheduled build or by a version control system's check-in), which is what the Recipe 11-3 talks about.

11-3. Scripting Your Unit Tests

Problem

You want to automatically run your unit tests, rather than manually invoke them.

Solution

Use and configure JUnit and Ant. To do so, follow these steps:

1. Download Apache Ant (located at `http://ant.apache.org/`).

2. Uncompress Apache Ant into a folder (for example, `c:\ant` for Windows systems or `/Development` for OS X).

3. Make sure that Apache Ant can be executed from the command line or terminal. In Windows, this means adding the `apache-ant/bin` folder to the path as follows:

    a. Go to Control Panel ➤ System.

    b. Click Advanced system settings.

    c. Click Environment Variables.

    d. In the System Variables list, double-click the variable name `PATH`.

    e. At the end of the String, add `;C:\apache-ant-1.8.2\bin` (or the folder that you uncompressed Apache Ant into).

    f. Click OK (on each of the popup boxes that were opened before) to accept the changes.

■ **Note**   Apache Ant comes preinstalled on OS X, so you do not have to install or configure it. To verify this, open a terminal window and type `ant -version` to see which version is installed on the system.

Make sure that the `JAVA_HOME` environment variable is defined. In Windows, this means adding a new environment variable called `JAVA_HOME`. For example:

Go to Control Panel ➤ System.

4. Click Advanced system settings.

5. Click Environment Variables. In the System Variables list, check to see whether there is variable named `JAVA_HOME` and that the value points to your JDK distribution. If `JAVA_HOME` is not present, click New. Set the variable name to `JAVA_HOME` and set the variable value to `C:\Program Files\Java\jdk1.9.0` or the root of your JDK 9 installation.

On OS X, environment variables are set up within the `.bash` profile file, which resides within the user home directory. To add `JAVA_HOME`, add a line such as the following to the `.bash_profile`:

`export JAVA_HOME=/Library/Java/JavaVirtualMachines/jdk1.9.0.jdk/Contents/Home`

Test that you can reach Ant, and that Ant can find your JDK installation. To test that the changes took effect, do the following:

6. Open a command window or terminal.

7. Type **ant**.

If you receive the message "Ant is not recognized as an internal or external command," redo the first steps of setting up the PATH variable (the first set of instructions). If you receive the message "unable to locate tools.jar," you need to create and/or update the JAVA_HOME path for your installation (the second set of instructions).

The message "Buildfile: build.xml does not exist!" means that your setup is ready to be built using Ant. Congratulations!

▪ **Note**   When changing environment variables in Microsoft Windows or OS X, it is necessary to close previous command-line or terminal windows and reopen them because changes are only applied to new command windows.

Create build.xml at the root of your project and put the following bare-bones Ant script as the contents of the build.xml file. This particular build.xml file contains information that Ant will use to compile and test this recipe.

```xml
<project default="test" name="Chapter11Project" basedir=".">
<property name="src" location="src"/>
<property name="build" location="build/"/>
<property name="src.tests" location="src/"/>
<property name="reports.tests" location="report/" />

<path id="build.path">
<fileset dir="dep">
<include name="**/*.jar" />
</fileset>
<pathelement path="build" />
</path>

<target name="build">
<mkdir dir="${build}" />
<javac srcdir="${src}" destdir="${build}">
<classpath refid="build.path" />
</javac>
</target>

<target name="test" depends="build">
<mkdir dir="${reports.tests}" />
<junit fork="yes" printsummary="yes" haltonfailure="yes">
<classpath refid="build.path" />
<formatter type="plain"/>

<batchtest fork="yes" todir="${reports.tests}">
<fileset dir="${src.tests}">
<include name="**/*Test*.java"/>
</fileset>
</batchtest>
</junit>
</target>
</project>
```

■ **Note**   To execute this recipe, open a command-line window or terminal, navigate to the Chapter 11 folder, type ant, and press Enter.

How It Works

Apache Ant (or simply Ant) is a program that allows you to script your project's build and unit testing. By configuring Ant, you can build, test, and deploy your application using the command line. (In turn, it can be scheduled to be run automatically by the operating system.) Ant can automatically run unit tests and report on the result of these tests. These results can then be analyzed after each run to pinpoint changes in behavior.

Due to Ant's complexity, it has a large learning curve, but it allows for a lot of flexibility on compiling, building, and weaving code. By using Ant, it is possible to achieve the utmost configuration on how your project is built.

■ **Note**   Visit http://ant.apache.org/manual/index.html for a more in-depth tutorial of Ant.

The build.xml file contains instructions on how to compile your project, which class path to use, and what unit tests to run. Each build.xml contains a <project> tag that encapsulates the steps to build the project. Within each <project> there are targets, which are "steps" in the build process. A <target> can depend on other targets, allowing you to establish dependencies in your project (in this recipe's example, the target "test" depends on the target "build," meaning that to run the test target, Ant will first run the build target).

Each target contains tasks. These tasks are extensible, and there is a core set of tasks that you can use out of the box. The <javac>task will compile a set of Java files specified within the src attribute and write the output to the dest attribute. As part of the <javac> task, you can specify which class path to use. In this example, the class path is specified by referring to a previously defined path, known as build.path. Ant provides ample support for creating class paths. In this recipe, the class path is defined as any file that has the .jar extension located in the dep folder.

The other task in the build target is <junit>. This task will find a unit test specified in its task and run it. The unit tests are defined within the <batchtest> property. By using the <fileset> property, it is possible to tell JUnit to find any file that has the word Test in its name and ends with the .java extension. Once JUnit runs each test, it will write out a summary to the console and write a report on the results of the unit tests to the reports.tests folder.

■ **Note**   You can define variables in a build.xml file by using the <property> tag. Once a property is defined, it can be accessed as part of another task using the ${propertyName} syntax. This allows you to quickly change a build script in response to structural changes (for example, switching target/source folders around).

11-4. Finding Bugs Early

Problem

You want to ensure that you are able to find the maximum number of bugs at design time.

Solution

Use FindBugs to scan your software for issues. Use an Ant build file that includes FindBugs for reporting purposes.

The following is the new build.xml file that adds FindBugs reporting:

```xml
<project default="test" name="Chapter11Project" basedir=".">

<property name="src" location="src"/>
<property name="build" location="build/"/>
<property name="reports.tests" location="report/" />
<property name="classpath" location="dep/" />

<!-- Findbugs Static Analyzer Info -->
<property name="findbugs.dir" value="dep/findbugs" />
<property name="findbugs.report" value="findbugs" />

<path id="findbugs.lib" >
<fileset dir="${findbugs.dir}" includes="*.jar"/>
</path>
<taskdef name="findbugs" classpathref="findbugs.lib" classname="edu.umd.cs.findbugs.anttask.
FindBugsTask"/>

<path id="build.path">
<fileset dir="dep">
<include name="**/*.jar" />
</fileset>
</path>

<target name="clean">
<delete dir="${build}" />
<delete dir="${reports.tests}" />
<delete dir="${coverage.dir}" />
<delete dir="${instrumented}" />
<mkdir dir="${build}" />
<mkdir dir="${reports.tests}" />
<mkdir dir="${coverage.dir}" />

</target>

<target name="build">
<javac srcdir="${src}" destdir="${build}" debug="${debug}">
<classpath refid="build.path" />
</javac>
</target>

<target name="test" depends="clean,build">
<junit fork="yes" printsummary="yes" haltonfailure="yes">
<classpath refid="build.path" />
<formatter type="plain"/>
```

```
<batchtest fork="yes" todir="${reports.tests}">
<fileset dir="${build}">
<include name="**/*Test*.class"/>
</fileset>
</batchtest>
<jvmarg value="-XX:-UseSplitVerifier" />
</junit>

</target>

<target name="findbugs" depends="clean">
<antcall target="build">
<param name="debug" value="true" />
</antcall>

<mkdir dir="${findbugs.report}" />
<findbugs home="${findbugs.dir}"
                output="html"
                outputFile="${findbugs.report}/index.html"
                reportLevel="low"
>
<class location="${build}/" />
<auxClasspath refid="build.path" />
<sourcePath path="${src}" />
</findbugs>
</target>
</project>
```

To run this recipe, download FindBugs (`http://findbugs.sourceforge.net/downloads.html`). Uncompress into a folder in your computer, then copy the contents of the `./lib/` folder into your project's `/dep/findbugs` folder (create the `/dep/findbugs` folder if necessary). Make sure that `/dep/findbugs/findbugs.jar` and `/dep/findbugs/findbugs-ant.jar` are present.

How It Works

FindBugs is a *Static Code Analyzer (SCA)*. It will parse your program's compiled file and spot commonly found errors in coding (not syntax errors, but certain types of logic errors). As an example, one of the errors that `FindBugs` will spot is comparing two Strings using `==` instead of `String.equals()`. The analysis is then written as HTML (or text) that can be viewed with a browser. Catching errors from `FindBugs` is easy, and adding it as part of your continuous integration process is extremely beneficial.

At the beginning of `build.xml`, you define the `FindBugs` tasks. This section specifies where the `.jar` files are that define the new task (`dep\findbugs`), and also determines where to put the report when done.

The `build.xml` also has a new target project called "findbugs." The findbugs target compiles the source files with debug information (having debug information helps on the `FindBugs` report as it will include the line number when reporting errors), and then proceeds to analyze the byte-code for errors. In the findbugs task, you specify the location of the compiled `.class` files (this is the `<class>` property), the location of the dependencies for your project (`<auxClasspath>` property), and the location of the source code (`<sourcePath>` property).

Within the findbugs target, there is an `<antcall>` task. The `<antcall>` task simply runs the target specified within the `<antcall>` task. Just before the `<antcall>` task, you assign the debug `<property>` to true. This in turn gets passed to the `<javac>` task as debug=`"${debug}"`. When the debug `<property>` is set to true, the `<javac>` task will include debug information into the compilation of the Java source files.

Having debug information in the compiled files will help generate a more readable FindBugs report, as it will include line numbers for where issues are found. The trick of assigning properties from within an Ant target is used throughout build.xml files to selectively enable certain behavior when going through specific build targets. If you were to build the regular build target, the results of the build would not contain debug information. If instead, you were to build the findbugs target because the findbugs target replaces the debug <property> to true, the result of the build would have debug information.

■ **Tip**   To invoke Ant to run the default "target" (as specified in the build.xml), just type ant. To specify another .xml file (instead of build.xml), type ant -f nameofotherfile.xml. To change the default target to run, type the name of the target at the end (for example, **ant clean**). To run this example, type ant -f findbugsbuild.xml findbugs. This will ask Ant to use the findbugsbuild.xml file and to run the findbugs target.

11-5. Monitoring Garbage Collection in Your Application

Problem

You notice that your application seems to be slowing down and suspect that there are garbage collections happening.

Solution 1

Add -Xloggc:gc.log-XX:+PrintGCDetails-XX:+PrintGCTimeStamps as parameters when starting your Java program. These parameters allow you to log garbage collection information to the gc.log file, including the time garbage collections occur, along with the details (if it was a minor or major garbage collection and how long it took).

Ant target that executes Recipe 11_5 with garbage logging on.

```
<target name="Recipe11_5" depends="build">
<java classname="org.java9recipes.chapter11.Recipe11_5" fork="true">
    <classpath refid="build.path" />
    <jvmarg value="-Xloggc:gc.log" />
    <jvmarg value="-XX:+PrintGCDetails" />
    <jvmarg value="-XX:+PrintGCTimeStamps" />
</java>
</target>
```

   In this build.xml file, the Java task is being used to add the arguments for garbage collection logging to the compiler before launching the application. To run this example throughout Ant, type **ant Recipe11_5**.

Solution 2

Analyze your program's memory consumption and more by using the NetBeans "Profiler" tool. To run the profiler, select the file or project that you want to perform the profiling against and choose the Profile Project or Profile File command from within the NetBeans Profile menu. You can also right-click the project or file to access the contextual menu Profile option.

The Profiler dialog (Figure 11-1) will open, allowing you to select and configure options. In this solution, simply select the Run button to perform the profiling with the default settings.

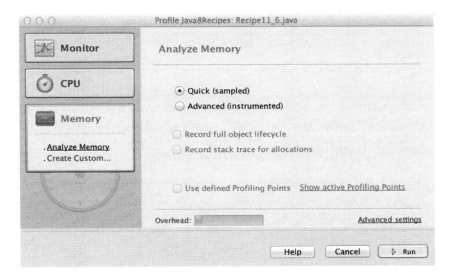

Figure 11-1. *NetBeans Profiler*

Once the profiler begins, it will run until you stop it using the Stop button on the Controls panel. The generated output should resemble something like that shown in Figure 11-2.

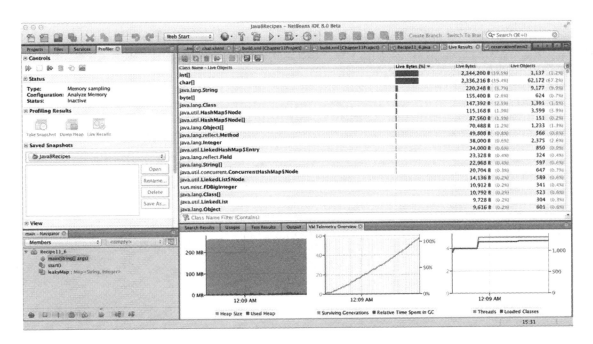

Figure 11-2. *NetBeans Profiler results*

How It Works

Adding the flag to log garbage collection in solution 1 will cause your Java application to write minor and major garbage collections information into a log file. This allows you to "reconstruct" in time what happened to the application and to spot probable memory leaks (or at least other memory-related issues). This is the preferred troubleshooting method for production systems, as it is usually lightweight and can be analyzed after the garbage collection has occurred.

Solution 2 instead involves using an open source tool that comes installed with NetBeans IDE. This tool allows you to profile code while it is running. It is a great tool to understanding *in situ* what's occurring within your application, as you can see real-time CPU consumption, garbage collections, threads created, and classes loaded.

This recipe barely scratches the surface of the NetBeans Profiler. See the online documentation at https://profiler.netbeans.org/ for more information.

▪ **Note**   Before you can use the NetBeans Profiler, you must calibrate the target JVM. To do so, open the Manage Calibration Data dialog within NetBeans and select the JVM that you want to calibrate. You can find the Manage Calibration Data option by opening the Profile menu, then choosing Advanced Commands.

11-6. Obtaining a Thread Dump

Problem

Your program seems to "hang" without doing anything, and you suspect that there might be a deadlock.

Solution

Use JStack to get a thread dump, and then analyze the thread dump for deadlocks. The following JStack is a thread dump from the class org.java9recipes.chapter11.recipe11_06.Recipe 11_6, which creates a deadlock. The code of Recipe11_6.java is as follows:

```
public class Recipe11_6 {
    Lock firstLock = new ReentrantLock();
    Lock secondLock = new ReentrantLock();

    public static void main (String[] args) {
        Recipe11_6 recipe = new Recipe11_6();
        recipe.start();
    }

    private void start() {
        firstLock.lock();
        Thread secondThread = new Thread(() -> {
            secondLock.lock();
            firstLock.lock();
        });
```

```
        secondThread.start();
        try {
            Thread.sleep(250);
        } catch (InterruptedException e) {
            e.printStackTrace();
        }
        secondLock.lock();

        secondLock.unlock();
        firstLock.unlock();

    }

}
```

Execute the code from the command line or IDE, and then inspect the process ID using an operating system utility such as the Task Manager. As can be seen from the following command, the example code is running under process ID of 19705:

jstack -l 19705

```
Full thread dump Java HotSpot(TM) 64-Bit Server VM (25.66-b17 mixed mode):

"Attach Listener" #11 daemon prio=9 os_prio=31 tid=0x00007f95c5818000 nid=0x380b waiting on
condition [0x0000000000000000]
   java.lang.Thread.State: RUNNABLE

   Locked ownable synchronizers:
      - None


"Thread-0" #10 prio=5 os_prio=31 tid=0x00007f95c41ba000 nid=0x5503 waiting on condition
[0x000000012afba000]
   java.lang.Thread.State: WAITING (parking)
        at sun.misc.Unsafe.park(Native Method)
        - parking to wait for  <0x000000076ab76698> (a java.util.concurrent.locks.
        ReentrantLock$NonfairSync)
        at java.util.concurrent.locks.LockSupport.park(LockSupport.java:175)
        at java.util.concurrent.locks.AbstractQueuedSynchronizer.parkAndCheckInterrupt
        (AbstractQueuedSynchronizer.java:836)
        at java.util.concurrent.locks.AbstractQueuedSynchronizer.acquireQueued(AbstractQueue
        dSynchronizer.java:870)
        at java.util.concurrent.locks.AbstractQueuedSynchronizer.acquire(AbstractQueuedSync
        hronizer.java:1199)
        at java.util.concurrent.locks.ReentrantLock$NonfairSync.lock(ReentrantLock.java:209)
        at java.util.concurrent.locks.ReentrantLock.lock(ReentrantLock.java:285)
        at org.java9recipes.chapter11.recipe11_06.Recipe11_6.lambda$start$0(Recipe11_6.
        java:25)
        at org.java9recipes.chapter11.recipe11_06.Recipe11_6$$Lambda$1/1418481495.
        run(Unknown Source)
        at java.lang.Thread.run(Thread.java:745)
```

```
    Locked ownable synchronizers:
        - <0x000000076ab766c8> (a java.util.concurrent.locks.ReentrantLock$NonfairSync)

"Service Thread" #9 daemon prio=9 os_prio=31 tid=0x00007f95c4051000 nid=0x5103 runnable
[0x0000000000000000]
    java.lang.Thread.State: RUNNABLE

    Locked ownable synchronizers:
        - None

"C1 CompilerThread3" #8 daemon prio=9 os_prio=31 tid=0x00007f95c4031800 nid=0x4f03 waiting
on condition [0x0000000000000000]
    java.lang.Thread.State: RUNNABLE

    Locked ownable synchronizers:
        - None

"C2 CompilerThread2" #7 daemon prio=9 os_prio=31 tid=0x00007f95c4031000 nid=0x4d03 waiting
on condition [0x0000000000000000]
    java.lang.Thread.State: RUNNABLE

    Locked ownable synchronizers:
        - None

"C2 CompilerThread1" #6 daemon prio=9 os_prio=31 tid=0x00007f95c4030000 nid=0x4b03 waiting
on condition [0x0000000000000000]
    java.lang.Thread.State: RUNNABLE

    Locked ownable synchronizers:
        - None

"C2 CompilerThread0" #5 daemon prio=9 os_prio=31 tid=0x00007f95c402e800 nid=0x4903 waiting
on condition [0x0000000000000000]
    java.lang.Thread.State: RUNNABLE

    Locked ownable synchronizers:
        - None

"Signal Dispatcher" #4 daemon prio=9 os_prio=31 tid=0x00007f95c401a000 nid=0x3c17 runnable
[0x0000000000000000]
    java.lang.Thread.State: RUNNABLE

    Locked ownable synchronizers:
        - None

"Finalizer" #3 daemon prio=8 os_prio=31 tid=0x00007f95c283a800 nid=0x3503 in Object.wait()
[0x0000000128e91000]
    java.lang.Thread.State: WAITING (on object monitor)
        at java.lang.Object.wait(Native Method)
        - waiting on <0x000000076ab070b8> (a java.lang.ref.ReferenceQueue$Lock)
        at java.lang.ref.ReferenceQueue.remove(ReferenceQueue.java:143)
```

```
        - locked <0x000000076ab070b8> (a java.lang.ref.ReferenceQueue$Lock)
        at java.lang.ref.ReferenceQueue.remove(ReferenceQueue.java:164)
        at java.lang.ref.Finalizer$FinalizerThread.run(Finalizer.java:209)

    Locked ownable synchronizers:
        - None

"Reference Handler" #2 daemon prio=10 os_prio=31 tid=0x00007f95c4003800 nid=0x3303 in
Object.wait() [0x0000000128d8e000]
    java.lang.Thread.State: WAITING (on object monitor)
        at java.lang.Object.wait(Native Method)
        - waiting on <0x000000076ab06af8> (a java.lang.ref.Reference$Lock)
        at java.lang.Object.wait(Object.java:502)
        at java.lang.ref.Reference$ReferenceHandler.run(Reference.java:157)
        - locked <0x000000076ab06af8> (a java.lang.ref.Reference$Lock)

    Locked ownable synchronizers:
        - None

"main" #1 prio=5 os_prio=31 tid=0x00007f95c280d800 nid=0x1303 waiting on condition
[0x000000010d286000]
    java.lang.Thread.State: WAITING (parking)
        at sun.misc.Unsafe.park(Native Method)
        - parking to wait for  <0x000000076ab766c8> (a java.util.concurrent.locks.
        ReentrantLock$NonfairSync)
        at java.util.concurrent.locks.LockSupport.park(LockSupport.java:175)
        at java.util.concurrent.locks.AbstractQueuedSynchronizer.parkAndCheckInterrupt(Abstr
        actQueuedSynchronizer.java:836)
        at java.util.concurrent.locks.AbstractQueuedSynchronizer.acquireQueued(AbstractQueue
        dSynchronizer.java:870)
        at java.util.concurrent.locks.AbstractQueuedSynchronizer.acquire(AbstractQueuedSync
        hronizer.java:1199)
        at java.util.concurrent.locks.ReentrantLock$NonfairSync.lock(ReentrantLock.java:209)
        at java.util.concurrent.locks.ReentrantLock.lock(ReentrantLock.java:285)
        at org.java9recipes.chapter11.recipe11_06.Recipe11_6.start(Recipe11_6.java:34)
        at org.java9recipes.chapter11.recipe11_06.Recipe11_6.main(Recipe11_6.java:18)

    Locked ownable synchronizers:
        - <0x000000076ab76698> (a java.util.concurrent.locks.ReentrantLock$NonfairSync)

"VM Thread" os_prio=31 tid=0x00007f95c3830800 nid=0x3103 runnable

"GC task thread#0 (ParallelGC)" os_prio=31 tid=0x00007f95c3005000 nid=0x2103 runnable

"GC task thread#1 (ParallelGC)" os_prio=31 tid=0x00007f95c3005800 nid=0x2303 runnable

"GC task thread#2 (ParallelGC)" os_prio=31 tid=0x00007f95c3006000 nid=0x2503 runnable

"GC task thread#3 (ParallelGC)" os_prio=31 tid=0x00007f95c4000000 nid=0x2703 runnable

"GC task thread#4 (ParallelGC)" os_prio=31 tid=0x00007f95c4001000 nid=0x2903 runnable
```

```
"GC task thread#5 (ParallelGC)" os_prio=31 tid=0x00007f95c3007000 nid=0x2b03 runnable

"GC task thread#6 (ParallelGC)" os_prio=31 tid=0x00007f95c3007800 nid=0x2d03 runnable

"GC task thread#7 (ParallelGC)" os_prio=31 tid=0x00007f95c3807000 nid=0x2f03 runnable

"VM Periodic Task Thread" os_prio=31 tid=0x00007f95c401b000 nid=0x5303 waiting on condition

JNI global references: 308

Found one Java-level deadlock:
=============================
"Thread-0":
  waiting for ownable synchronizer 0x000000076ab76698, (a java.util.concurrent.locks.
  ReentrantLock$NonfairSync),
  which is held by "main"
"main":
  waiting for ownable synchronizer 0x000000076ab766c8, (a java.util.concurrent.locks.
  ReentrantLock$NonfairSync),
  which is held by "Thread-0"

Java stack information for the preceding threads:
===================================================
"Thread-0":
        at sun.misc.Unsafe.park(Native Method)
        - parking to wait for  <0x000000076ab76698> (a java.util.concurrent.locks.
        ReentrantLock$NonfairSync)
        at java.util.concurrent.locks.LockSupport.park(LockSupport.java:175)
        at java.util.concurrent.locks.AbstractQueuedSynchronizer.parkAndCheckInterrupt(Abstr
        actQueuedSynchronizer.java:836)
        at java.util.concurrent.locks.AbstractQueuedSynchronizer.acquireQueued(AbstractQueue
        dSynchronizer.java:870)
        at java.util.concurrent.locks.AbstractQueuedSynchronizer.acquire(AbstractQueuedSync
        hronizer.java:1199)
        at java.util.concurrent.locks.ReentrantLock$NonfairSync.lock(ReentrantLock.java:209)
        at java.util.concurrent.locks.ReentrantLock.lock(ReentrantLock.java:285)
        at org.java9recipes.chapter11.recipe11_06.Recipe11_6.lambda$start$0(Recipe11_6.
        java:25)
        at org.java9recipes.chapter11.recipe11_06.Recipe11_6$$Lambda$1/1418481495.
        run(Unknown Source)
        at java.lang.Thread.run(Thread.java:745)
"main":
        at sun.misc.Unsafe.park(Native Method)
        - parking to wait for  <0x000000076ab766c8> (a java.util.concurrent.locks.
        ReentrantLock$NonfairSync)
        at java.util.concurrent.locks.LockSupport.park(LockSupport.java:175)
        at java.util.concurrent.locks.AbstractQueuedSynchronizer.parkAndCheckInterrupt(Abstr
        actQueuedSynchronizer.java:836)
        at java.util.concurrent.locks.AbstractQueuedSynchronizer.acquireQueued(AbstractQueue
        dSynchronizer.java:870)
```

```
    at java.util.concurrent.locks.AbstractQueuedSynchronizer.acquire(AbstractQueuedSync
hronizer.java:1199)
    at java.util.concurrent.locks.ReentrantLock$NonfairSync.lock(ReentrantLock.java:209)
    at java.util.concurrent.locks.ReentrantLock.lock(ReentrantLock.java:285)
    at org.java9recipes.chapter11.recipe11_06.Recipe11_6.start(Recipe11_6.java:34)
    at org.java9recipes.chapter11.recipe11_06.Recipe11_6.main(Recipe11_6.java:18)
```

Found 1 deadlock.

For this recipe to function properly on Windows, you must have as part of your PATH environment variable the JDK's bin folder (For example C:\Program Files\java\jdk1.9.0\bin). If you have this path, you can run the tools such as JStack and JPS. JStack comes preinstalled on OS X, so you should be able to run it out of the box.

The JStack command uses as an argument –l (a dash and the letter L), which specifies a Long listing (it does extra work to get more information about the threads running). The JStack also needs to know the PID of the target VM. A quick way to list all running JVMs is to type **JPS** and press Enter. This will list the running VMs and their PIDs. Figure 11-3 shows a screenshot of a JStack finding a deadlock in Recipe 11-6 from an OS X machine.

■ **Note**   For the purposes of this example, j.u.c.l represents java.util.concurrent.locks, and aqs represents AbstractQueuedSynchronizer.

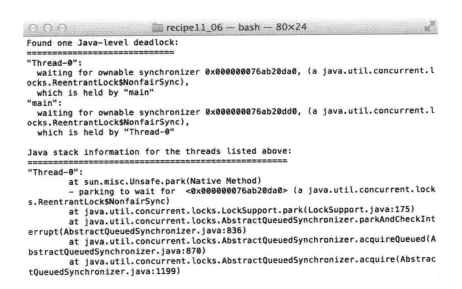

Figure 11-3. *JStack results*

How It Works

JStack allows you to see all the stack traces that the current running threads have. JStack will also try to find *deadlocks* (circular dependencies of locks) that might be stalling your system. JStack will not find other problems such as *livelock* (when a thread is always spinning, such as with something like `while(true)`), or *starvation* (when a thread cannot execute because it is too low of a priority or there are too many threads competing for resources), but it will help you understand what each of the threads in your program is doing.

Deadlocks happen because one thread is waiting for a resource that another thread has, and the second thread is waiting for a resource that the first thread has. In this situation, neither thread can continue because both are waiting for each other to release the resource that each one owns. Deadlocks don't only happen between two threads, but can also involve a "String" of threads so that Thread A is waiting for Thread B is waiting for Thread C is waiting for Thread D is waiting for the original Thread A. It is important to understand the dump to find the culprit resource.

In this recipe's example, `Thread-0` wants to acquire the lock named 0x000000076ab76698; it's described in the thread dump as "waiting for ownable synchronizer." `Thread-0` cannot acquire the lock because it is held by the main thread. The main thread, on the other hand, wants to acquire the lock 0x000000076ab766c8 (notice that they are different; the first lock ends in 98, while the second ends in c8), which is held by `Thread-0`. This is a textbook definition of a deadlock on which each thread is forever waiting for each other to release the lock the other thread has.

Aside from deadlock, looking at thread dumps gives you an idea about what your program is doing in realtime. Especially in multithreaded systems, using thread dumps will help clarify where a thread is sleeping or what condition it is waiting for.

▓ **Note**   JStack is usually lightweight enough to be run in a live system, so if you need to troubleshoot live problems, you can safely use JStack.

Summary

In this chapter, we took a look at some of the most overlooked, yet most important pieces of software development. Debugging, unit testing, and evaluation of application performance are key tasks that must be performed in order to ensure that solid software is delivered. There are a number of useful utilities for achieving these tasks, and this chapter briefly looked at a number of them.

CHAPTER 12

■ ■ ■

Unicode, Internationalization, and Currency Codes

The Java platform provides a rich set of internationalization features to help you create applications that can be used across the world. The platform provides the means to localize your applications, format dates and numbers in a variety of culturally appropriate formats, and display characters used in dozens of writing systems.

This chapter describes only some of the most frequent and common tasks that programmers must perform when developing internationalized applications. Because new features have been added to the Java language with regard to its abstraction of languages and regions, this chapter describes some of the new ways you might use the Locale class. Other new features will be transparent to the developer, such as the update to adhere to newer Unicode standards, but the updates provide compliance so that JDK 9 will remain relevant for years to come. Java 9 includes support for Unicode 7.0, which adds 3000 characters, and over 20 scripts.

■ **Note**   The source code for this chapter's examples is available in the org.java9recipes.chapter12 package.

12-1. Converting Unicode Characters to Digits

Problem

You want to convert a Unicode digit character to its respective integer value. For example, you have a String containing the Thai digit for the value 8 and you want to generate an integer with that value.

Solution

The java.lang.Character class has several static methods to convert characters to integer digit values:

- public static intdigit(char ch, int radix)
- public static intdigit(intch, int radix)

© Josh Juneau 2017
J. Juneau, *Java 9 Recipes*, DOI 10.1007/978-1-4842-1976-8_12

The following code snippet iterates through the entire range of Unicode code points from 0x0000 through 0x10FFFF. For each code point that is also a digit, it displays the character and its digit value 0 through 9. You can find this example in the org.java9recipes.chapter12.recipe12_1.Recipe12_1 class.

```
int x = 0;
for (int c=0; c <= 0x10FFFF; c++) {
    if (Character.isDigit(c)) {
        ++x;
        System.out.printf("Codepoint: 0x%04X\tCharacter: %c\tDigit: %d\tName: %s\n", c, c,
            Character.digit(c, 10), Character.getName(c));
    }
}
System.out.printf("Total digits: %d\n", x);
```

Some of the output follows:

```
Codepoint: 0x0030    Character: 0    Digit: 0    Name: DIGIT ZERO
Codepoint: 0x0031    Character: 1    Digit: 1    Name: DIGIT ONE
Codepoint: 0x0032    Character: 2    Digit: 2    Name: DIGIT TWO
Codepoint: 0x0033    Character: 3    Digit: 3    Name: DIGIT THREE
Codepoint: 0x0034    Character: 4    Digit: 4    Name: DIGIT FOUR
Codepoint: 0x0035    Character: 5    Digit: 5    Name: DIGIT FIVE
Codepoint: 0x0036    Character: 6    Digit: 6    Name: DIGIT SIX
Codepoint: 0x0037    Character: 7    Digit: 7    Name: DIGIT SEVEN
Codepoint: 0x0038    Character: 8    Digit: 8    Name: DIGIT EIGHT
Codepoint: 0x0039    Character: 9    Digit: 9    Name: DIGIT NINE
Codepoint: 0x0660    Character: ٠    Digit: 0    Name: ARABIC-INDIC DIGIT ZERO
Codepoint: 0x0661    Character: ١    Digit: 1    Name: ARABIC-INDIC DIGIT ONE
Codepoint: 0x0662    Character: ٢    Digit: 2    Name: ARABIC-INDIC DIGIT TWO
Codepoint: 0x0663    Character: ٣    Digit: 3    Name: ARABIC-INDIC DIGIT THREE
Codepoint: 0x0664    Character: ٤    Digit: 4    Name: ARABIC-INDIC DIGIT FOUR
Codepoint: 0x0665    Character: ٥    Digit: 5    Name: ARABIC-INDIC DIGIT FIVE
Codepoint: 0x0666    Character: ٦    Digit: 6    Name: ARABIC-INDIC DIGIT SIX
Codepoint: 0x0667    Character: ٧    Digit: 7    Name: ARABIC-INDIC DIGIT SEVEN
Codepoint: 0x0668    Character: ٨    Digit: 8    Name: ARABIC-INDIC DIGIT EIGHT
Codepoint: 0x0669    Character: ٩    Digit: 9    Name: ARABIC-INDIC DIGIT NINE
...
Codepoint: 0x0E50    Character: ๐    Digit: 0    Name: THAI DIGIT ZERO
Codepoint: 0x0E51    Character: ๑    Digit: 1    Name: THAI DIGIT ONE
Codepoint: 0x0E52    Character: ๒    Digit: 2    Name: THAI DIGIT TWO
Codepoint: 0x0E53    Character: ๓    Digit: 3    Name: THAI DIGIT THREE
Codepoint: 0x0E54    Character: ๔    Digit: 4    Name: THAI DIGIT FOUR
Codepoint: 0x0E55    Character: ๕    Digit: 5    Name: THAI DIGIT FIVE
Codepoint: 0x0E56    Character: ๖    Digit: 6    Name: THAI DIGIT SIX
Codepoint: 0x0E57    Character: ๗    Digit: 7    Name: THAI DIGIT SEVEN
Codepoint: 0x0E58    Character: ๘    Digit: 8    Name: THAI DIGIT EIGHT
Codepoint: 0x0E59    Character: ๙    Digit: 9    Name: THAI DIGIT NINE
...
```

▓ **Note**   The sample code prints to the console. Your console may not print all the character glyphs shown in this example because of font or platform differences. However, the characters will be correctly converted to integers.

How It Works

The Unicode character set is large, containing more than a million unique code points with integer values ranging from 0x0000 through 0x10FFFF. Each character value has a set of properties. One of the properties is isDigit. If this property is true, the character represents a numeric digit from 0 through 9. For example, the characters with code point values 0x30 through 0x39 have the character glyphs 0, 1, 2, 3, 4, 5, 6, 7, 8, and 9. If you simply convert these code values to their corresponding integer values, you would get the hexadecimal values 0x30 through 0x39. The corresponding decimal values are 48 through 57. However, these characters also represent numeric digits. When using them in calculations, these characters represent the values 0 through 9.

When a character has the digit property, use the Character.digit() static method to convert it to its corresponding integer digit value. Note that the digit() method is overloaded to accept either char or int arguments. Additionally, the method requires a radix. Common values for the radix are 2, 10, and 16. Interestingly, although the characters a–f and A–F do not have the digit property, they can be used as digits using radix 16. For these characters, the digit() method returns the expected integer values 10 through 15.

A complete understanding of the Unicode character set and Java's implementation requires familiarity with several new terms: character, code point, char, encoding, serialization encoding, UTF-8, and UTF-16. These terms are beyond the scope of this recipe, but you can learn more about these and other Unicode concepts from the Unicode website at http://unicode.org or from the Character class Java API documentation.

12-2. Creating and Working with Locales

Problem

You want to display numbers, dates, and time in a user-friendly way that conforms to the language and cultural expectations of your customers.

Solution

The display format for numbers, dates, and time varies across the world and depends on your user's language and cultural region. Additionally, text collation rules vary by language. The java.util.Locale class represents a specific language and region of the world. By determining and using your customer's locale, you can apply that locale to a variety of format classes, which can be used to create user-visible data in expected forms. Classes that use Locale instances to modify their behavior for a particular language or region are called *locale-sensitive* classes. You can learn more about locale-sensitive classes in Chapter 4. That chapter shows you how to use Locale instances in the NumberFormat and DateFormat classes. In this recipe, however, you learn different options for creating these Locale instances.

You can create a Locale instance in any of the following ways:

- Use the Locale.Builder class to configure and build a Locale object.

- Use the static Locale.forLanguageTag() method.

- Use the Locale constructors to create an object.

- Use preconfigured static Locale objects.

The Java Locale.Builder class has setter methods that allow you to create locales that can be transformed into well-formed Best Common Practices (BCP) 47 language tags. The "How It Works" section describes the BCP 47 standard in more detail. For now, you should simply understand that a Builder creates Locale instances that comply with that standard.

The following code snippet from the org.java9recipes.chapter12.recipe12_2.Recipe12_2 class demonstrates how to create Builder and Locale instances. You use the created locales in locale-sensitive classes to produce culturally correct display formats:

```
private static final long number = 123456789L;
private static final Date now = new Date();

private void createFromBuilder() {
    System.out.printf("Creating from Builder...\n\n");
    String[][] langRegions = {{"fr", "FR"}, {"ja", "JP"}, {"en", "US"}};
    Builder builder = new Builder();
    Locale l = null;
    NumberFormat nf = null;
    DateFormat df = null;
    for (String[] lr: langRegions) {
        builder.clear();
        builder.setLanguage(lr[0]).setRegion(lr[1]);
        l = builder.build();
        nf = NumberFormat.getInstance(l);
        df = DateFormat.getDateTimeInstance(DateFormat.LONG, DateFormat.LONG, l);
        System.out.printf("Locale: %s\nNumber: %s\nDate: %s\n\n",
            l.getDisplayName(),
            nf.format(number),
            df.format(now));
    }
}
```

The previous code prints the following to the standard console:

```
Creating from Builder...

Locale: French (France)
Number: 123 456 789
Date: 14 septembre 2016 00:08:06 PDT

Locale: Japanese (Japan)
Number: 123,456,789
Date: 2016/09/14 0:08:06 PDT

Locale: English (United States)
Number: 123,456,789
Date: September 14, 2016 12:08:06 AM PDT
```

Another way to create Locale instances is by using the static Locale.forLanguageTag() method. This method allows you to use BCP 47 language tag arguments. The following code uses the forLanguageTag() method to create three locales from their corresponding language tags:

```
...
System.out.printf("Creating from BCP 47 language tags...\n\n");
String[] bcp47LangTags= {"fr-FR", "ja-JP", "en-US"};
Locale l = null;
NumberFormat nf = null;
DateFormat df = null;
for (String langTag: bcp47LangTags) {
    l = Locale.forLanguageTag(langTag);
    nf = NumberFormat.getInstance(l);
    df = DateFormat.getDateTimeInstance(DateFormat.LONG, DateFormat.LONG, l);
    System.out.printf("Locale: %s\nNumber: %s\nDate: %s\n\n",
        l.getDisplayName(),
        nf.format(number),
        df.format(now));
}
...
```

The output is similar to the results created from the Builder-generated Locale instance:

```
Creating from BCP 47 language tags...

Locale: French (France)
Number: 123 456 789
Date: 14 septembre 2016 01:07:22 PDT
...
```

You can also use constructors to create instances. The following code shows how to do this:

```
Locale l = new Locale("fr", "FR");
```

Other constructors allow you to pass fewer or more arguments. The argument parameters can include language, region, and optional variant codes.

Finally, the Locale class has many predefined static instances for some commonly used cases. Because the instances are predefined, your code needs to reference only the static instances. For example, the following example shows how to reference existing static instances representing fr-FR, ja-JP, and en-US locales:

```
Locale frenchInFrance = Locale.FRANCE;
Locale japaneseInJapan = Locale.JAPAN;
Locale englishInUS = Locale.US;
```

Refer to the locale Java API documentation for examples of other static instances.

How It Works

The Locale class gives locale-sensitive classes the context they need to perform culturally appropriate data formatting and parsing. Some of the locale-sensitive classes include the following:

- `java.text.NumberFormat`
- `java.text.DateFormat`
- `java.util.Calendar`

A Locale instance identifies a specific language and can be finely tuned to identify languages written in a particular script or spoken in a specific world region. Locale is an important and necessary element for creating anything that depends on language or regional influences.

The Java Locale class is always being enhanced to provide better support for modern BCP 47 language tags. BCP 47 defines Best Common Practices for using ISO standards for language, region, script, and variant identifiers. Although the existing Locale constructors continue to be compatible with prior versions of the Java platform, the constructors do not support the additional script tags. For example, only the more recently added Locale.Builder class and Locale.forLanguageTag() method support the newer functionality that identifies scripts. Because the Locale constructors do not enforce strict BCP 47 compliance, you should avoid the constructors in any new code. Instead, developers should use the Builder class and the forLanguageTag() method.

A Locale.Builder instance has a variety of setter methods that help you configure it to create a valid, BCP 47–compliant Locale instance:

- `public Locale.BuildersetLanguage(String language)`
- `public Locale.BuildersetRegion(String region)`
- `public Locale.BuildersetScript(String script)`

Each of these methods throws a `java.util.IllFormedLocaleException` if its argument is not a well-formed element of the BCP 47 standard. The language parameter must be a valid two- or three-letter ISO 639 language identifier. The region parameter must be a valid two-letter ISO 3166 region code or a three-digit M.49 United Nations "area" code. Finally, the script parameter must be a valid four-letter ISO 15924 script code.

The Builder lets you configure it to create a specific BCP 47–compliant locale. Once you set all the configurations, the build() method creates and returns a Locale instance. Notice that all the setters can be chained together for a single statement. The Builder pattern works by having each configuration method return a reference to the current instance, on which further configuration methods may be called.

```
Locale aLocale = new Builder().setLanguage("fr").setRegion("FR").build();
```

The BCP 47 document and the standards that comprise it can be found at the following locations:

- BCP 47 (language tags): `http://www.rfc-editor.org/rfc/bcp/bcp47.txt`
- ISO 639 (language identifiers): `http://www.loc.gov/standards/iso639-2/php/code_list.php`
- ISO 3166 (region identifiers): `http://www.iso.org/iso/country_codes/iso_3166_code_lists/country_names_and_code_elements.htm`
- ISO 15924 (script identifiers): `http://unicode.org/iso15924/`
- United Nations M.49 (area identifiers): `http://unstats.un.org/unsd/methods/m49/m49.htm`

12-3. Setting the Default Locale

Problem

You want to set the default locale for all locale-sensitive classes.

Solution

Use the Locale.setDefault() method to set a Locale instance that all locale-sensitive classes will use by default. This method is overloaded with the following two forms:

- Locale.setDefault(Locale aLocale)
- Locale.setDefault(Locale.Category c, Locale aLocale)

This example code demonstrates how to set the default locale for all locale-sensitive classes:

```
Locale.setDefault(Locale.FRANCE);
```

You can also set the default for two additional locale categories, DISPLAY and FORMAT:

```
Locale.setDefault(Locale.Category.DISPLAY, Locale.US);
Locale.setDefault(Locale.Category.FORMAT, Locale.FR);
```

You can create code that uses these specific locale categories within your application to mix locale choices for different purposes. For example, you may choose to use the DISPLAY locale for ResourceBundle text while using the FORMAT locale for date and time formats. The example code from the org.java9recipes. chapter12.recipe12_3.Recipe12_3 class demonstrates this more complex usage:

```java
public class Recipe12_3 {

    private static final Date NOW = new Date();

    public void run() {
        // Set ALL locales to fr-FR
        Locale.setDefault(Locale.FRANCE);
        demoDefaultLocaleSettings();

        // System default is still fr-FR
        // DISPLAY default is es-MX
        // FORMAT default is en-US
        Locale.setDefault(Locale.Category.DISPLAY, Locale.forLanguageTag("es-MX"));
        Locale.setDefault(Locale.Category.FORMAT, Locale.US);
        demoDefaultLocaleSettings();

        // System default is still fr-FR
        // DISPLAY default is en-US
        // FORMAT default is es-MX
        Locale.setDefault(Locale.Category.DISPLAY, Locale.US);
        Locale.setDefault(Locale.Category.FORMAT, Locale.forLanguageTag("es-MX"));
        demoDefaultLocaleSettings();

        // System default is Locale.US
        // Resets both DISPLAY and FORMAT locales to en-US as well.
        Locale.setDefault(Locale.US);
        demoDefaultLocaleSettings();
    }
```

291

```
    public void demoDefaultLocaleSettings() {
        DateFormat df =
            DateFormat.getDateTimeInstance(DateFormat.SHORT, DateFormat.SHORT);
        ResourceBundle resource =
            ResourceBundle.getBundle("SimpleResources",
                Locale.getDefault(Locale.Category.DISPLAY));
        String greeting = resource.getString("GOOD_MORNING");
        String date = df.format(NOW);
        System.out.printf("DEFAULT LOCALE: %s\n", Locale.getDefault());
        System.out.printf("DISPLAY LOCALE: %s\n", Locale.getDefault(Locale.Category.DISPLAY));
        System.out.printf("FORMAT LOCALE:  %s\n", Locale.getDefault(Locale.Category.FORMAT));
        System.out.printf("%s, %s\n\n", greeting, date );
    }

    public static void main(String[] args) {
        Recipe12_3 app = new Recipe12_3();
        app.run();
    }
}
```

This code produces the following output:

```
DEFAULT LOCALE: fr_FR
DISPLAY LOCALE: fr_FR
FORMAT LOCALE:  fr_FR
Bonjour!, 19/09/16 20:31

DEFAULT LOCALE: fr_FR
DISPLAY LOCALE: es_MX
FORMAT LOCALE:  en_US
¡Buenos días!, 9/19/16 8:31 PM

DEFAULT LOCALE: fr_FR
DISPLAY LOCALE: en_US
FORMAT LOCALE:  es_MX
Good morning!, 19/09/16 08:31 PM

DEFAULT LOCALE: en_US
DISPLAY LOCALE: en_US
FORMAT LOCALE:  en_US
Good morning!, 9/19/16 8:31 PM
```

How It Works

The Locale class allows you to set the default locale for two different categories. The categories are represented by the Locale.Category enumeration:

- Locale.Category.DISPLAY

- Locale.Category.FORMAT

Use the DISPLAY category for your application's user interface. Setting the default DISPLAY locale means that the ResourceBundle class can load user interface resources for that particular locale independently from the FORMAT locale. Setting the FORMAT default locale affects how the various Format subclasses behave. For example, a default DateFormat instance will use the FORMAT default locale to create a locale-sensitive output format. Again, these two categories are independent, so you can use different Locale instances for different needs.

In this recipe's sample code, the Locale.setDefault(Locale.FRANCE) method call sets the default system, DISPLAY, and FORMAT locales to fr-FR (French in France). This method always resets both the DISPLAY and FORMAT locales to match the system locale. When creating a new resource bundle, the ResourceBundle class uses the system locale by default. However, by providing a Locale instance argument, you tell the bundle to load resources for a specific locale. For example, even though the system locale is Locale.FRANCE, you can specify a DISPLAY default locale and use that DISPLAY locale in your ResourceBundle.getBundle() method call. For example, this code attempts to load a language bundle for es-MX even though the system locale is still Locale.FRANCE:

```
Locale.setDefault(Locale.Category.DISPLAY, Locale.forLanguageTag("es-MX"));
Locale.setDefault(Locale.Category.FORMAT, Locale.US);
DateFormat df = DateFormat.getDateTimeInstance(DateFormat.SHORT, DateFormat.SHORT);
ResourceBundle resource =
        ResourceBundle.getBundle("org.java9recipes.chapter12.resource.SimpleResources",
                Locale.getDefault(Locale.Category.DISPLAY));
String greeting = resource.getString("GOOD_MORNING");
```

In this case, it finds a GOOD_MORNING resource with the "¡Buenos días!" value because the DISPLAY default locale is an argument. The resource bundle is a file with translated property Strings for various locales. The file named SimpleResources_en.properties (English) has a GOOD_MORNING property that is written "Good morning!" Note that translations of each property in the resource bundle must exist in the locale-specific resource files in order to be displayed. The Java code does not translate these Strings. Instead, it just selects an appropriate translation of the desired property based on the selected locale.

■ **Note** Although the DateFormat and NumberFormat classes will automatically use the default FORMAT locale if you do not provide a locale argument in their creation method, the ResourceBundle.getBundle() method always uses the system locale by default. To use the DISPLAY default locale in a ResourceBundle(), you must explicitly provide it as an argument.

12-4. Matching and Filtering Locales

Problem

You would like to match against or filter a list of locales and return only those that meet the specified criteria.

Solution

Make use of the new locale matching and filtering methods that have been introduced in the java.util. Locale class in Java 8. If you're given a comma-separated list of locales in String format, you can apply a filter or "priority list" to that String to return only those locales within the String that meet the filter.

In the following example, a list of language tags is filtered using the java.util.Locale filterTag method, returning the matching tags in String format:

```
List<Locale.LanguageRange> list1 = Locale.LanguageRange.parse("ja-JP, en-US");
list1.stream().forEach((range) -> {
    System.out.println("Range:" + range.getRange());
});
ArrayList localeList = new ArrayList();
localeList.add("en-US");
localeList.add("en-JP");

List<String> tags1 = Locale.filterTags(list1, localeList);
System.out.println("The following is the filtered list of locales:");
tags1.stream().forEach((tag) -> {
    System.out.println(tag);
});
```

Results:

```
Range:ja-jp
Range:en-us
The following is the filtered list of Locales:
en-us
```

The filter() method of the Locale classes allows you to return a list of matching Locale instances. In the following example, a list of locale language tags is used to filter Locale classes out of a list of locales.

```
String localeTags = Locale.ENGLISH.toLanguageTag() + "," +
                    Locale.CANADA.toLanguageTag();
List<Locale.LanguageRange> list1 = Locale.LanguageRange.parse(localeTags);
list1.stream().forEach((range) -> {
    System.out.println("Range:" + range.getRange());
});
ArrayList<Locale> localeList = new ArrayList();
localeList.add(new Locale("en"));
localeList.add(new Locale("en-JP"));

List<Locale> tags1 = Locale.filter(list1, localeList);
System.out.println("The following is the matching list of Locales:");
tags1.stream().forEach((tag) -> {
    System.out.println(tag);
});
```

Here are the results:

```
Range:en
Range:en-ca
The following is the matching list of locales:
en
```

How It Works

Methods have been added to the `java.util.Locale` class in Java 8 that allow you to filter `Locale` instances or language tags based on a supplied priority list in `List<Locale.LanguageRange>` format. The filtering mechanism is based on RFC 4647. The following list contains a short summary of these filtering methods:

- `filter(List<Locale.LanguageRange>, Collection<Locale>)`

  `filter(List<Locale.LanguageRange>, Collection<Locale>, Locale.FilteringMode)`

  (Returns matching list of `Locale` instances)

- `filterTags(List<Locale.LanguageRange>, Collection<String>)`

  `filterTags(List<Locale.LanguageRange>, Collection<String>, Locale.FilteringMode)`

  (Returns matching list of language tags)

To work with each of the methods, a sorted priority order should be sent as the first parameter. This priority order is a list of `Locale.LanguageRange` objects, and it should be sorted in descending order, based on priority or weight. The second argument in the `filter()` methods is a collection of locales. This collection contains the locales that will be filtered. The optional third argument contains a `Locale.FilteringMode`. Table 12-1 lists the different filtering modes.

Table 12-1. *Locale.FilteringMode Values*

Mode	Description
AUTOSELECT_FILTERING	Specifies filtering mode that is based on the given priority list of languages.
EXTENDED_FILTERING	Specifies extended filtering.
IGNORE_EXTENDED_RANGES	Specifies basic filtering.
MAP_EXTENDED_RANGES	Specifies basic filtering, and if any extended languages are included in the language priority list, they are mapped to the basic language range.
REJECT_EXTENDED_RANGES	Specifies basic filtering, and if any extended languages are included in the language priority list, the list is rejected and `IllegalArgumentException` is thrown.

12-5. Searching Unicode with Regular Expressions

Problem

You want to find or match Unicode characters in a String. You want to do that using regular expression syntax.

Solution 1

The easiest way to find or match characters is to use the `String` class itself. `String` instances store Unicode character sequences and provide relatively simple operations for finding, replacing, and tokenizing characters using regular expressions.

To determine whether a String matches a regular expression, use the `matches()` method. The `matches()` method returns `true` if the entire String exactly matches the regular expression.

The following code from the org.java9recipes.chapter12.recipe12_4.Recipe12_4 class uses two different expressions with two Strings. The regular expression matches simply confirm that the Strings match a particular pattern as defined in the variables enRegEx and jaRegEx.

```
private String enText = "The fat cat sat on the mat with a brown rat.";
private String jaText = "Fight 文字化け!";

boolean found = false;
String enRegEx = "^The \\w+ cat.*";
String jaRegEx = ".*文字.*";
String jaRegExEscaped = ".*\u6587\u5B57.*";
found = enText.matches(enRegEx);
if (found) {
    System.out.printf("Matches %s.\n", enRegEx);
}
found = jaText.matches(jaRegEx);
if (found) {
    System.out.printf("Matches %s.\n", jaRegEx);
}
found = jaText.matches(jaRegExEscaped);
if (found) {
    System.out.printf("Matches %s.\n", jaRegExEscaped);
}
```

This code prints the following:

```
Matches ^The \w+ cat.*.
Matches .*文字.*.
Matches .*文字.*.
```

Use the replaceFirst() method to create a new String instance in which the first occurrence of the regular expression in the target text is replaced with the replacement text. The code demonstrates how to use this method:

```
String replaced = jaText.replaceFirst("文字化け", "mojibake");
System.out.printf("Replaced: %s\n", replaced);
```

The replacement text is shown in the output:

```
Replaced: Fight mojibake!
```

The replaceAll() method replaces all occurrences of the expression with the replacement text.

Finally, the split() method creates a String[] that contains text that is separated by the matched expression. In other words, it returns text that is delimited by the expression. Optionally, you can provide a limit argument that constrains the number of times the delimiter will be applied in the source text. The following code demonstrates the split() method splitting on space characters:

```
String[] matches = enText.split("\\s", 3);
for(String match: matches) {
    System.out.printf("Split: %s\n",match);
}
```

The code's output is as follows:

```
Split: The
Split: fat
Split: cat sat on the mat with a brown rat.
```

Solution 2

When the simple String methods aren't sufficient, you can use the more powerful java.util.regex package to work with regular expressions. Create a regular expression using the Pattern class. A Matcher works on a String instance using the pattern. All Matcher operations perform their functions using Pattern and String instances.

The following code demonstrates how to search for both ASCII and non-ASCII text in two separate Strings. See the org.java9recipes.chapter12.recipe12_4.Recipe12_4 class for the complete source code. The demoSimple() method finds text with any character followed by ".at". The demoComplex() method finds two Japanese symbols in a String:

```
public void demoSimple() {
Pattern p = Pattern.compile(".at");
    Matcher m = p.matcher(enText);
    while(m.find()) {
        System.out.printf("%s\n", m.group());
    }
}

public void demoComplex() {
    Pattern p = Pattern.compile("文字");
    Matcher m = p.matcher(jaText);
    if (m.find()) {
        System.out.println(m.group());
    }
}
```

Running these two methods on the previously defined English and Japanese text shows the following:

```
fat
cat
sat
mat
rat
文字
```

How It Works

The String methods that work with regular expressions are the following:

- `public boolean matches(String regex)`

- `public String replaceFirst(String regex, String replacement)`

- `public String replaceAll(String regex, String replacement)`

- `public String[] split(String regex, int limit)`

- `public String[] split(String regex)`

The `String` methods are limited and relatively simple wrappers around the more powerful functionality of the `java.util.regex` classes:

- `java.util.regex.Pattern`

- `java.util.regex.Matcher`

- `java.util.regex.PatternSyntaxException`

The Java regular expressions are similar to those used in the Perl language. Although there is a lot to learn about Java regular expressions, probably the most important points to understand from this recipe are these:

- Your regular expressions can definitely contain non-ASCII characters from the full range of Unicode characters.

- Because of a peculiarity of how the Java language compiler understands the backslash character, you will have to use two backslashes in your code instead of one for the predefined character class expressions.

The most convenient and readable way to use non-ASCII characters in regular expressions is to type them directly into your source files using your keyboard input methods. Operating systems and editors differ in how they allow you to enter complex text outside of ASCII. Regardless of operating system, you should save the file in the UTF-8 encoding if your editor allows. As an alternate but more difficult way to use non-ASCII regular expressions, you can encode characters using the \uXXXX notation. Using this notation, instead of directly typing the character using your keyboard, you enter \u or \U, followed by the hexadecimal representation of the Unicode code point. This recipe's code sample uses the Japanese word "文字" (pronounced *mo-ji*). As the example shows, you can use the actual characters in the regular expression or you can look up the Unicode code point values. For this particular Japanese word, the encoding will be \u6587\u5B57.

The Java language's regular expression support includes special character classes. For example, \d and \w are shortcut notations for the regular expressions `[0-9]` and `[a-zA-Z_0-9]`, respectively. However, because of the Java compiler's special handling of the backslash character, you must use an extra backslash when using predefined character classes such as \d (digits), \w (word characters), and \s (space characters). To use them in source code, for example, you enter **d**, **w**, and **s**, respectively. The sample code used the double backslash in Solution 1 to represent the \w character class:

```
String enRegEx = "^The \\w+ cat.*";
```

12-6. Overriding the Default Currency

Problem

You want to display a number value using a currency that is not associated with the default locale.

Solution

Take control of which currency is printed with a formatted currency value by explicitly setting the currency used in a `NumberFormat` instance. The following example assumes that the default locale is `Locale.JAPAN`. It changes the currency by calling the `setCurrency(Currency c)` method of its `NumberFormat` instance. This example comes from the `org.java9recipes.chapter12.recipe12_6.Recipe12_6` class.

```
BigDecimal value = new BigDecimal(12345);
System.out.printf("Default locale: %s\n", Locale.getDefault().getDisplayName());
NumberFormat nf = NumberFormat.getCurrencyInstance();
String formattedCurrency = nf.format(value);
System.out.printf("%s\n", formattedCurrency);
Currency c = Currency.getInstance(Locale.US);
nf.setCurrency(c);
formattedCurrency = nf.format(value);
System.out.printf("%s\n\n", formattedCurrency);
```

The previous code prints out the following:

```
Default locale: 日本語 (日本)
¥12,345
USD12,345
```

How It Works

You use a NumberFormat instance to format currency values. You should explicitly call the getCurrencyInstance() method to create a formatter for currencies:

```
NumberFormat nf = NumberFormat.getCurrencyInstance();
```

The previous formatter will use your default locale's preferences for formatting numbers as currency values. Also, it will use a currency symbol that is associated with the locale's region. However, one very common use case involves formatting a value for a different region's currency.

Use the setCurrency() method to explicitly set the currency in the number formatter:

```
nf.setCurrency(aCurrencyInstance); // requires a Currency instance
```

Note that the java.util.Currency class is a factory. It allows you to create currency objects in two ways:

- Currency.getInstance(Locale locale)
- Currency.getInstance(String currencyCode)

The first getInstance call uses a Locale instance to retrieve a currency object. The Java platform associates a default currency with the locale's region. In this case, the default currency currently associated with the United States is the U.S. dollar:

```
Currency c1 = Currency.getInstance(Locale.US);
```

The second getInstance call uses a valid ISO 4217 currency code. The currency code for the U.S. dollar is USD:

```
Currency c2 = Currency.getInstance("USD");
```

Once you have a currency instance, you simply have to use that instance in your formatter:

```
nf.setCurrency(c2);
```

This formatter now is configured to use the default locale's number format symbols and patterns to format the number value, but it will display the targeted currency code as part of the displayable text. This allows you to mix the default number format patterns with other currency codes.

▦ **Note**   Currencies have both symbols and codes. A currency code always refers to the three-letter ISO 4217 code. A currency symbol is often different from the code. For example, the US dollar has the code USD and the symbol $. A currency formatter will typically use a symbol when formatting a number in the default locale using the currency of that locale's region. However, when you explicitly change the currency of a formatter, the formatter doesn't always have knowledge of a localized symbol for the target currency. In that case, the format instance will often use the currency code in the displayed text.

12-7. Converting Byte Arrays to and from Strings

Problem

You need to convert characters in a byte array from a legacy character set encoding to a Unicode String.

Solution

Convert legacy character encodings from a byte array to a Unicode String using the String class. The following code snippet from the org.java9recipes.chapter12.recipe12_7.Recipe12_7 class demonstrates how to convert a legacy Shift-JIS encoded byte array to a String. Later in this same example, the code demonstrates how to convert from Unicode back to the Shift-JIS byte array.

```
byte[] legacySJIS = {(byte)0x82,(byte)0xB1,(byte)0x82,(byte)0xF1,
(byte)0x82,(byte)0xC9,(byte)0x82,(byte)0xBF,
(byte)0x82,(byte)0xCD,(byte)0x81,(byte)0x41,
(byte)0x90,(byte)0xA2,(byte)0x8A,(byte)0x45,
(byte)0x81,(byte)0x49};

// Convert a byte[] to a String
Charset cs =Charset.forName("SJIS");
String greeting = new String(legacySJIS, cs);
System.out.printf("Greeting: %s\n", greeting);
```

This code prints out the converted text, which is "Hello, world!" in Japanese:

```
Greeting: こんにちは、世界!
```

Use the getBytes() method to convert characters from a String to a byte array. Building on the previous code, convert back to the original encoding with the following code and compare the results:

```
// Convert a String to a byte[]
byte[] toSJIS = greeting.getBytes(cs);

// Confirm that the original array and newly converted array are same
Boolean same = false;
```

```
if (legacySJIS.length == toSJIS.length) {
    for (int x=0; x< legacySJIS.length; x++) {
        if(legacySJIS[x] != toSJIS[x]) break;
    }
    same = true;
}
System.out.printf("Same: %s\n", same.toString());
```

As expected, the output indicates that the round-trip conversion back to the legacy encoding was successful. The original byte array and the converted byte array contain the same bytes:

```
Same: true
```

How It Works

The Java platform provides conversion support for many legacy character set encodings. When you create a String instance from a byte array, you must provide a charset argument to the String constructor so that the platform knows how to perform the mapping from the legacy encoding to Unicode. All Java Strings use Unicode as their native encoding.

The number of bytes in the original array does not usually equal the number of characters in the result String. In this recipe's example, the original array contains 18 bytes. The 18 bytes are needed by the Shift-JIS encoding to represent the Japanese text. However, after conversion, the result String contains nine characters. There is not a 1:1 relationship between bytes and characters. In this example, each character requires two bytes in the original Shift-JIS encoding.

There are literally hundreds of different charset encodings. The number of encodings is dependent on your Java platform implementation. However, you are guaranteed support of several of the most common encodings, and your platform most likely contains many more than this minimal set:

- US-ASCII

- ISO-8859-1

- UTF-8

- UTF-16BE

- UTF-16LE

- UTF-16

When constructing a charset, you should be prepared to handle the possible exceptions that can occur when the character set is not supported:

- java.nio.charset.IllegalCharsetNameException, thrown when the charset name is illegal

- java.lang.IllegalArgumentException, thrown when the charset name is null

- java.nio.charset.UnsupportedCharsetException, thrown when your JVM doesn't support the targeted charset

12-8. Converting Character Streams and Buffers

Problem

You need to convert large blocks of Unicode character text to and from an arbitrary byte-oriented encoding. Large blocks of text may come from streams or files.

Solution 1

Use `java.io.InputStreamReader` to decode a byte stream to Unicode characters. Use `java.io.OutputStreamWriter` to encode Unicode characters to a byte stream.

The following code uses `InputStreamReader` to read and convert a potentially large block of text bytes from a file in the class path. The `org.java9recipes.chapter12.recipe12_8.StreamConversion` class provides the complete code for this example:

```java
public String readStream() throws IOException {
    InputStream is = getClass().getResourceAsStream("resource/helloworld.sjis.txt");
    StringBuilder sb = new StringBuilder();
    if (is != null) {
        try (InputStreamReader reader =
                new InputStreamReader(is, Charset.forName("SJIS"))) {
            int ch = reader.read();
            while (ch != -1) {
                sb.append((char) ch);
                ch = reader.read();
            }
        }
    }
    return sb.toString();
}
```

Similarly, you can use an `OutputStreamWriter` to write text to a byte stream. The following code writes a String to a UTF-8 encoded byte stream:

```java
public void writeStream(String text) throws IOException {
    FileOutputStream fos = new FileOutputStream("helloworld.utf8.txt");
    try (OutputStreamWriter writer
            = new OutputStreamWriter(fos, Charset.forName("UTF-8"))) {
        writer.write(text);
    }
}
```

Solution 2

Use `java.nio.charset.CharsetEncoder` and `java.nio.charset.CharsetDecoder` to convert Unicode character buffers to and from byte buffers. Retrieve an encoder or decoder from a charset instance with the `newEncoder()` or `newDecoder()` method. Then use the encoder's `encode()` method to create byte buffers. Use the decoder's `decode()` method to create character buffers. The following code from the `org.java9recipes.chapter12.recipe12_8.BufferConversion` class encodes and decodes character sets from buffers:

```
    public ByteBuffer encodeBuffer(String charsetName, CharBuffer charBuffer)
            throws CharacterCodingException {
        Charset charset = Charset.forName(charsetName);
CharsetEncoder encoder = charset.newEncoder();
        ByteBuffer targetBuffer = encoder.encode(charBuffer);
return targetBuffer;

    }
    public CharBuffer decodeBuffer(String charsetName, ByteBuffer srcBuffer)
            throws CharacterCodingException {
        Charset charset = Charset.forName(charsetName);
        CharsetDecoder decoder = charset.newDecoder();
        CharBuffer charBuffer = decoder.decode(srcBuffer);
        return charBuffer;
    }
```

How It Works

The java.io and java.nio.charset packages contain several classes that can help you perform encoding conversions on large text streams or buffers. Streams are convenient abstractions that can assist you in converting text using a variety of sources and targets. A stream can represent incoming or outgoing text in an HTTP connection or even a file.

If you use an InputStream to represent the underlying source text, you will wrap that stream in an InputStreamReader to perform conversions from a byte stream. The reader instance performs the conversion from bytes to Unicode characters.

Using an OutputStream instance to represent the target text, wrap the stream in an OutputStreamWriter. A writer will convert your Unicode text to a byte-oriented encoding in the target stream.

To effectively use either an OutputStreamWriter or an InputStreamReader, you must know the character encoding of your target or source text. When you use an OutputStreamWriter, the source text is always Unicode, and you must supply a charset argument to tell the writer how to convert to the target byte-oriented text encoding. When you use an InputStreamReader, the target encoding is always Unicode. You must supply the source text encoding as an argument so that the reader understands how to convert the text.

■ **Note** The Java platform's String represents characters in the UTF-16 encoding of Unicode. Unicode can have several encodings, including UTF-16, UTF-8, and even UTF-32. Converting to Unicode in this discussion always means converting to UTF-16. Converting to a byte-oriented encoding usually means to a legacy non–Unicode charset encoding. However, a common byte-oriented encoding is UTF-8, and it is entirely reasonable to convert Java's "native" UTF-16 Unicode characters to or from UTF-8 using the InputStreamReader or OutputStreamWriter class.

Yet another way to perform encoding conversions is to use the CharsetEncoder and CharsetDecoder classes. A CharsetEncoder will encode your Unicode CharBuffer instances to ByteBuffer instances. A CharsetDecoder will decode ByteBuffer instances into CharBuffer instances. In either case, you must provide a charset argument.

A charset represents a character set encoding defined in the Internet Signed Numbers Authority (IANA) Charset Registry. When creating a charset instance, you should use the canonical or alias names of the charset as defined by the Registry. You can find the Registry at http://www.iana.org/assignments/character-sets.

Remember that your Java implementation will not necessarily support all the IANA charset names. However, all implementations are required to support at least those shown in Recipe 12-7 of this chapter.

12-9. Setting the Search Order of Locale-Sensitive Services

Problem

You want to designate a specified search order for locale-sensitive services within the Java runtime environment.

Solution

Specify the desired order for locale-sensitive services using the java.locale.providers property. In the following example, the SPI and CLDR providers are specified within the property.

```
java.locale.providers=SPI,CLDR
```

How It Works

Setting the java.locale.providers property, since the release of Java 8, specifies the search order of locale-sensitive services. This property is read upon Java runtime startup. To set the order of services, specify the acronym(s), separated by commas. The following services are available for use:

- SPI: Locale-sensitive services represented by SPI (Service Provider Interface) providers

- JRE: Locale-sensitive services in the Java runtime environment

- CLDR: Provider based on the Unicode Consortium's CLDR project

- HOST: Provider that reflects the user's custom settings in the underlying operating system

Summary

Internationalization is a key to developing culturally responsive applications. It allows for application text to be changed in an effort to adhere to the culture and language in which the application is being used. This chapter provided some examples of how to make use of internationalization techniques to overcome the nuances of cross-culture development. The chapter also covered topics regarding Unicode conversions.

CHAPTER 13

Working with Databases

Almost any nontrivial application contains a database of some sort. Some applications use in-memory databases, while others use traditional relational database management systems (RDBMSs). Whatever the case, it is essential that every Java developer have some skills working with databases. Over the years, the Java Database Connectivity (JDBC) API has evolved quite a bit, and over the past couple of releases there have been some major advancements.

This chapter covers the basics of using JDBC for working with databases. You will learn how to perform all the standard database operations, as well as some advanced techniques for manipulating data. You'll also learn how you can create secure database applications and save time on development using some of the latest advancements in the API. In the end, you will be able to develop Java applications that work with traditional RDBMSs such as Oracle database, PostgreSQL, and MySQL.

> ■ **Note**   To follow along with the examples in this chapter, run the `create_user.sql` script to create a database user schema. Then, run the `create_database.sql` script within the database schema that you just created.
>
> The database examples in this book are tailored for use with an Apache Derby or Oracle database, but they can be altered to work with any relational database.

13-1. Connecting to a Database

Problem

You want to create a connection to a database from within a desktop Java application.

Solution 1

Use a JDBC `Connection` object to obtain the connection. Do this by creating a new connection object, and then load the driver that you need to use for your particular database vendor. Once the connection object is ready, call its `getConnection()` method. The following code demonstrates how to obtain a connection to an Oracle or Apache Derby database, depending on the specified driver.

© Josh Juneau 2017
J. Juneau, *Java 9 Recipes*, DOI 10.1007/978-1-4842-1976-8_13

```java
public Connection getConnection() throws SQLException {
    Connection conn = null;
    String jdbcUrl;
    if(driver.equals("derby")){
        jdbcUrl = "jdbc:derby://" + this.hostname + ":" +
                    this.port  + "/" + this.database;
    } else {
        jdbcUrl = "jdbc:oracle:thin:@" + this.hostname + ":" +
                    this.port  + ":" + this.database;
    }
    System.out.println(jdbcUrl);
    conn = DriverManager.getConnection(jdbcUrl, username, password);
    System.out.println("Successfully connected");
    return conn;
}
```

The method portrayed in this example returns a Connection object that is ready to be used for database access.

Solution 2

Use a DataSource to create a connection pool. The DataSource object must have been properly implemented and deployed to an application server environment. After a DataSource object has been implemented and deployed, it can be used by an application to obtain a connection to a database. The following code shows code that you can use to obtain a database connection via a DataSource object:

```java
public Connection getDSConnection() {
    Connection conn = null;
    try {
        Context ctx = new InitialContext();
        DataSource ds = (DataSource)ctx.lookup("jdbc/myOracleDS");
        conn = ds.getConnection();

    } catch (NamingException | SQLException ex) {
        ex.printStackTrace();
    }
    return conn;
}
```

Notice that the only information required in the DataSource implementation is the name of a valid DataSource object. All the information that is required to obtain a connection with the database is managed within the application server.

How It Works

There are a couple of different ways to create a connection to a database within a Java application. How you do so depends on the type of application you are writing. Utilization of the DriverManager is often used if an application will be stand-alone or if it is a desktop application. Web-based and intranet applications commonly rely on the application server to provide the connection for the application via a DataSource object.

Creating a JDBC connection involves a few steps. First, you need to determine which database driver you will need. After you've determined which driver you will need, you download the JAR file containing that driver and place it into your CLASSPATH. For this recipe, either an Oracle database or Apache Derby connection is made. Each of the database vendors will provide different JDBC drivers packaged in JAR files that have different names; consult the documentation for your particular database for more information. Once you have obtained the appropriate JAR file for your database, include it in your application CLASSPATH. Next, use a JDBC DriverManager to obtain a connection to the database. As of JDBC version 4.0, drivers that are contained within the CLASSPATH are automatically loaded into the DriverManager object. If you are using a JDBC version prior to 4.0, the driver will have to be manually loaded.

To obtain a connection to your database using the DriverManager, you need to pass a String containing the JDBC URL to it. The JDBC URL consists of the database vendor name, along with the name of the server that hosts the database, the name of the database, the database port number, and a valid database username and password that has access to the schema or database objects that you want to work with. Many times, the values used to create the JDBC URL are obtained from a Properties file so that they can be easily changed if needed. To learn more about using a Properties file to store connection values, see Recipe 13-5. The code that is used to create the Oracle database JDBC URL for Solution 1 looks like the following:

```
String jdbcUrl = "jdbc:oracle:thin:@" + this.hostname + ":" +
                 this.port  + ":" + this.database;
```

Once all the variables have been substituted into the String, it will look something like the following:

```
jdbc:oracle:thin:@hostname:1521:database
```

Similarly, the Apache Derby URL String would look like the following:

```
jdbc:derby://hostname:1521/database
```

Once the JDBC URL has been created, it can be passed to the DriverManager.getConnection() method to obtain a java.sql.Connection object. If incorrect information has been passed to the getConnection() method, a java.sql.SQLException will be thrown; otherwise, a valid Connection object will be returned.

The preferred way to obtain a database connection is to use a DataSource when running on an application server or to have access to a Java Naming and Directory Interface (JNDI) service. To work with a DataSource object, you need to have an application server deploy it to. Any compliant Java application server such as GlassFish, Oracle Weblogic, Payara, or WildFly will work. Most of the application servers contain a web interface that can be used to easily deploy a DataSource object. However, you can manually deploy a DataSource object by using code that will look like the following:

```
org.java9recipes.chapter13.recipe13_01.FakeDataSourceDriver ds =
        new org.java9recipes.chapter13.recipe13_1.FakeDataSourceDriver();
ds.setServerName("my-server");
ds.setDatabaseName("JavaRecipes");
ds.setDescription("Database connection for Java 9 Recipes");
```

This code instantiates a new DataSource driver class and then sets properties based on the database that you want to register. DataSource code such as that demonstrated here is typically used when registering a DataSource in an application server or with access to a JNDI server. Application servers usually do this work behind the scenes if you are using a web-based administration tool to deploy a DataSource. Most database vendors will supply a DataSource driver along with their JDBC drivers, so if the correct JAR resides within the application or server CLASSPATH, it should be recognized and available for use. Once a DataSource has been instantiated and configured, the next step is to register the DataSource with a JNDI naming service.

The following code demonstrates the registration of a DataSource with JNDI:

```
try {
    Context ctx = new InitialContext();
    DataSource ds =
            (DataSource) ctx.bind("java9recipesDB");
} catch (NamingException ex) {
    ex.printStackTrace();
}
```

Once the DataSource has been deployed, any application that has been deployed to the same application server will have access to it. The beauty of working with a DataSource object is that your application code doesn't need to know anything about the database; it only needs to know the name of the DataSource. Usually the name of the DataSource begins with a jdbc/ prefix, followed by an identifier. To look up the DataSource object, an InitialContext is used. The InitialContext looks at all the DataSources available within the application server and returns a valid DataSource if it is found; otherwise, it will throw a java.naming.NamingException exception. In Solution 2, you can see that the InitialContext returns an object that must be casted as a DataSource.

```
Context ctx = new InitialContext();
DataSource ds = (DataSource)ctx.lookup("jdbc/myOracleDS");
```

If the DataSource is a connection pool cache, it will send one of the available connections within the pool when an application requests it. The following line of code returns a Connection object from the DataSource:

```
conn = ds.getConnection();
```

Of course, if no valid connection can be obtained, a java.sql.SQLException is thrown. The DataSource technique is preferred over the DriverManager because database connection information is stored in only one place: the application server. Once a valid DataSource is deployed, it can be used by many applications.

After a valid connection has been obtained by your application, it can be used to work with the database. To learn more about working with the database using a Connection object, see Recipes 13-2 and 13-4.

13-2. Handling Connection and SQL Exceptions

Problem

A database activity in your application has thrown an exception. You need to handle the SQL exception so that your application does not crash.

Solution

Use a try-catch block in order to capture and handle any SQL exceptions that are thrown by your JDBC connection or SQL queries. The following code demonstrates how to implement a try-catch block in order to capture SQL exceptions:

```
try {
    // perform database tasks
} catch (java.sql.SQLException){
    // perform exception handling
}
```

How It Works

A standard try-catch block can be used to catch java.sql.Connection or java.sql.SQLException exceptions. Your code will not compile if these exceptions are not handled, and it is a good idea to handle them properly in order to prevent your application from crashing if one of these exceptions is thrown. Almost any work that is performed against a java.sql.Connection object will need to contain error handling to ensure that database exceptions are handled correctly. In fact, nested try-catch blocks are often required to handle all the possible exceptions. You need to ensure that connections are closed once work has been performed and the Connection object is no longer used. Similarly, it is a good idea to close java.sql.Statement objects for memory allocation cleanup as well.

Because Statement and Connection objects need to be closed, it is common to see try-catch-finally blocks used to ensure that all resources have been tended to as needed. It is not unlikely that you will see older JDBC code that resembles the following style:

```
try {
    // perform database tasks
} catch (java.sql.SQLException ex) {
    // perform exception handling
} finally {
    try {
        // close Connection and Statement objects
    } catch (java.sql.SQLException ex){
        // perform exception handling
    }
}
```

Newer code should be written to take advantage of the try-with-resources statement, which allows one to offload resource management to Java, rather than performing manual closes. The following code demonstrates how to use try-with-resources to open a connection, create a statement, and then close both the connection and statement when finished.

■ **Note**   The createConn object in the examples abstracts away the details of obtaining a connection to the database, which can be returned via a call to the getConnection() method.

```
try (Connection conn = createConn.getConnection();
        Statement stmt = conn.createStatement();) {
    ResultSet rs = stmt.executeQuery(qry);
    while (rs.next()) {
        // PERFORM SOME WORK
    }
} catch (SQLException e) {
    e.printStackTrace();
}
```

As seen in the previous pseudocode, nested try-catch blocks are often required in order to clean unused resources. Proper exception handling sometimes makes JDBC code rather laborious to write, but it will also ensure that an application requiring database access will not fail, causing data to be lost.

13-3. Querying a Database and Retrieving Results

Problem

A process in your application needs to query a database table for data.

Solution

Obtain a JDBC connection using one of the techniques as described in Recipe 13-1, and then use the `java.sql.Connection` object to create a `Statement` object. A `java.sql.Statement` object contains the `executeQuery()` method, which parses a String of text and uses it to query a database. Once you've executed the query, you can retrieve the results of the query into a `ResultSet` object. The following example queries a database table named RECIPES and prints the results:

```java
String qry = "select recipe_num, name, description from recipes";
try (Connection conn = createConn.getConnection();
        Statement stmt = conn.createStatement();) {
    ResultSet rs = stmt.executeQuery(qry);
    while (rs.next()) {
        String recipe = rs.getString("RECIPE_NUM");
        String name = rs.getString("NAME");
        String desc = rs.getString("DESCRIPTION");

        System.out.println(recipe + "\t" + name + "\t" + desc);
    }
} catch (SQLException e) {
    e.printStackTrace();
}
```

If you execute this code using the database script that is included with this chapter, you will receive the following results:

```
13-1    Connecting to a Database          DriverManager and DataSource Implementations
13-2    Querying a Database and Retrieving Results      Obtaining and Using Data from a DBMS
13-3    Handling SQL Exceptions Using SQLException
```

How It Works

One of the most commonly performed operations against a database is a query. Performing database queries using JDBC is quite easy, although there is a bit of boilerplate code that needs to be used each time a query is executed. First, you need to obtain a `Connection` object for the database and schema that you want to run the query against. You can do this by using one of the solutions found in Recipe 13-1. Next, you need to form a query and store it in String format. The `Connection` object is then used to create a `Statement`. Your query String will be passed to the `Statement` object's `executeQuery()` method in order to actually query the database. Here, you can see what this looks like without the use of `try-with-resources` for resource management.

```java
String qry = "select recipe_num, name, description from recipes";
Connection conn;
Statement stmt = null;
```

```
try {
    conn = createConn.getConnection()
    stmt = conn.createStatement();
    ResultSet rs = stmt.executeQuery(qry);
...
```

The same code can be more efficiently written as follows:

```
try (Connection conn = createConn.getConnection();
        Statement stmt = conn.createStatement();) {
    ResultSet rs = stmt.executeQuery(qry);
...
```

As you can see, the Statement object's executeQuery() method accepts a String and returns a ResultSet object. The ResultSet object makes it easy to work with the query results so that you can obtain the information you need in any order. If you take a look at the next line of code in the example, a while loop is created on the ResultSet object. This loop will continue to call the ResultSet object's next() method, obtaining the next row that is returned from the query with each iteration. In this case, the ResultSet object is named rs, so while rs.next() returns true, the loop will continue to be processed. Once all the returned rows have been processed, rs.next() will return a false to indicate that there are no more rows to be processed.

Within the while loop, each returned row is processed. The ResultSet object is parsed to obtain the values of the given column names with each pass. Notice that if the column is expected to return a String, you must call the ResultSet getString() method, passing the column name in String format. Similarly, if the column is expected to return an int, you'd call the ResultSet getInt() method, passing the column name in String format. The same holds true for the other data types. These methods will return the corresponding column values. In the example in the solution to this recipe, those values are stored into local variables.

```
String recipe = rs.getString("RECIPE_NUM");
String name = rs.getString("NAME");
String desc = rs.getString("DESCRIPTION");
```

Once the column value has been obtained, you can do what you want to do with the values you have stored within local variables. In this case, they are printed out using the System.out() method.

```
System.out.println(recipe + "\t" + name + "\t" + desc);
```

A java.sql.SQLException could be thrown when attempting to query a database (for instance, if the Connection object has not been properly obtained or if the database tables that you are trying to query do not exist). You must provide exception handling to handle errors in these situations. Therefore, all database-processing code should be placed within a try block. The catch block then handles a SQLException, so if one is thrown, the exception will be handled using the code within the catch block. Sounds easy enough, right? It is, but you must do it each time you perform a database query. Lots of boilerplate code.

It is always a good idea to close statements and connections if they are open. Using the try-with-resources construct is the most efficient solution to resource management. Closing resources when finished will help ensure that the system can reallocate resources as needed, and act respectfully on the database. It is important to close connections as soon as possible so that other processes can use them.

13-4. Performing CRUD Operations

Problem

You need to have the ability to perform standard database operations within your application. That is, you need the ability to create, retrieve, update, and delete (CRUD) database records.

Solution

Create a Connection object and obtain a database connection using one of the solutions provided in Recipe 13-1; then perform the CRUD operation using a java.sql.Statement object that is obtained from the java.sql.Connection object. The database table that will be used for these operations has the following format:

```
RECIPES (
    id              int not null,
    recipe_number   varchar(10) not null,
    recipe_name     varchar(100) not null,
    description     varchar(500),
    text            clob,
    constraint recipes_pk primary key (id) enable
);
```

The following code excerpts demonstrate how to perform each of the CRUD operations using JDBC:

```java
import java.sql.Connection;
import java.sql.ResultSet;
import java.sql.SQLException;
import java.sql.Statement;
import org.java9recipes.chapter13.recipe13_01.CreateConnection;

public class CrudOperations {

    static CreateConnection createConn;
    public static void main(String[] args) {

            createConn = new CreateConnection();
            performCreate();
            performRead();
            performUpdate();
            performDelete();
            System.out.println("-- Final State --");
            performRead();

    }

    private static void performCreate(){
        String sql = "INSERT INTO RECIPES VALUES(" +
                    "next value for recipes_seq, " +
                    "'13-4', " +
```

```java
                    "'Performing CRUD Operations', " +
                    "'How to perform create, read, update, delete functions', " +
                    "'Recipe Text')";

        try (Connection conn = createConn.getConnection();
                Statement stmt = conn.createStatement();) {
            // Returns row-count or 0 if not successful
            int result = stmt.executeUpdate(sql);
            if (result == 1{
                System.out.println("-- Record created --");
            } else {
                System.err.println("!! Record NOT Created !!");
            }
        } catch (SQLException e) {
            e.printStackTrace();
        }

    }

    private static void performRead(){
        String qry = "select recipe_number, recipe_name, description from recipes";

        try (Connection conn = createConn.getConnection();
                Statement stmt = conn.createStatement();) {
            ResultSet rs = stmt.executeQuery(qry);
            while (rs.next()) {
                String recipe = rs.getString("RECIPE_NUMBER");
                String name = rs.getString("RECIPE_NAME");
                String desc = rs.getString("DESCRIPTION");

                System.out.println(recipe + "\t" + name + "\t" + desc);
            }
        } catch (SQLException e) {
            e.printStackTrace();
        }

    }

    private static void performUpdate(){
        String sql = "UPDATE RECIPES " +
                    "SET RECIPE_NUMBER = '13-5' " +
                    "WHERE RECIPE_NUMBER = '13-4'";

        try (Connection conn = createConn.getConnection();
                Statement stmt = conn.createStatement();) {
            int result = stmt.executeUpdate(sql);
            if (result > 0){
                System.out.println("-- Record Updated --");
            } else {
                System.out.println("!! Record NOT Updated !!");
            }
```

```
        } catch (SQLException e) {
            e.printStackTrace();
        }

    }

    private static void performDelete(){
        String sql = "DELETE FROM RECIPES WHERE RECIPE_NUMBER = '13-5'";

        try (Connection conn = createConn.getConnection();
                Statement stmt = conn.createStatement();) {
            int result = stmt.executeUpdate(sql);
            if (result > 0){
                System.out.println("-- Record Deleted --");
            } else {
                System.out.println("!! Record NOT Deleted!!");
            }
        } catch (SQLException e) {
            e.printStackTrace();
        }
    }

}
```

Here is the result of running the code:

```
Successfully connected
-- Record created --
13-1     Connecting to a Database—DriverManager and DataSource Implementations
13-2     Querying a Database and Retrieving Results      Obtaining and Using Data from a DBMS
13-3     Handling SQL Exceptions Using SQLException
13-4     Performing CRUD Operations      How to Perform Create, Read, Update, Delete Functions
-- Record Updated --
-- Record Deleted --
-- Final State --
13-1     Connecting to a Database         DriverManager and DataSource Implementations
13-2     Querying a Database and Retrieving Results      Obtaining and Using Data from a DBMS
13-3     Handling SQL Exceptions Using SQLException
```

How It Works

The same basic code format is used for performing just about every database task. The format is as follows:

1. Obtain a connection to the database.

2. Create a statement from the connection.

3. Perform a database task with the statement.

4. Do something with the results of the database task.

5. Close the statement (and database connection if you're finished using it).

The main difference between performing a query using JDBC and using data manipulation language (DML) is that you will call different methods on the Statement object, depending on which operation you want to perform. To perform a query, you need to call the Statement executeQuery() method. In order to perform DML tasks such as insert, update, and delete, call the executeUpdate() method.

The performCreate() method in the solution to this recipe demonstrates the operation of inserting a record into a database. To insert a record in the database, construct a SQL INSERT statement in String format. To perform the insert, pass the SQL String to the Statement object's executeUpdate() method. If the INSERT is performed, an int value will be returned that specifies the number of rows that have been inserted. If the INSERT operation is not performed successfully, either a zero will be returned or a SQLException will be thrown, indicating a problem with the statement or database connection.

The performRead() method in the solution to this recipe demonstrates the operation of querying the database. To execute a query, call the Statement object's executeQuery() method, passing a SQL statement in String format. The result will be a ResultSet object, which can then be used to work with the returned data. For more information on performing queries, see Recipe 13-3.

The performUpdate() method in the solution to this recipe demonstrates the operation of updating record(s) within a database table. First, construct a SQL UPDATE statement in String format. Next, to perform the update operation pass the SQL String to the Statement object's executeUpdate() method. If the UPDATE is successfully performed, an int value will be returned, which specifies the number of records that were updated. If the UPDATE operation is not performed successfully, either a zero will be returned or a SQLException will be thrown, indicating a problem with the statement or database connection.

The last database operation that needs to be covered is the DELETE operation. The performDelete() method in the solution to this recipe demonstrates the operation of deleting record(s) from the database. First, construct a SQL DELETE statement in String format. Next, to execute the deletion, pass the SQL String to the Statement object's executeUpdate() method. If the deletion is successful, an int value specifying the number of rows deleted will be returned. Otherwise, if the deletion fails, a zero will be returned or a SQLException will be thrown, indicating a problem with the statement or database connection.

Almost every database application uses at least one of the CRUD operations at some point. This is foundational JDBC that needs to be known if you are working with databases within Java applications. Even if you will not work directly with the JDBC API, it is good to know these foundational basics.

13-5. Simplifying Connection Management

Problem

Your application requires the use of a database, and in order to work with the database, you need to open a connection for each interaction. Rather than code the logic to open a database connection every time you need to access the database, you want to use a single class to perform that task.

Solution

Write a class to handle all the connection management within your application. Doing so will allow you to call that class in order to obtain a connection, rather than setting up a new Connection object each time you need access to the database. Perform the following steps to set up a connection management environment for your JDBC application:

1. Create a class named CreateConnection.java that will encapsulate all the connection logic for your application.

2. Create a PROPERTIES file to store your connection information. Place the file somewhere on your CLASSPATH so that the CreateConnection class can load it.

3. Use the CreateConnection class to obtain your database connections.

The following code is a listing of the CreateConnection class that can be used for centralized connection management:

```java
import java.io.File;
import java.io.IOException;
import java.io.InputStream;
import java.nio.file.FileSystems;
import java.nio.file.Files;
import java.sql.Connection;
import java.sql.DriverManager;
import java.sql.SQLException;
import java.util.Properties;
import javax.naming.Context;
import javax.naming.InitialContext;
import javax.naming.NamingException;
import javax.sql.DataSource;

public class CreateConnection {

    static Properties props = new Properties();

    String hostname = null;
    String port = null;
    String database = null;
    String username = null;
    String password = null;
    String driver = null;
    String jndi = null;

    public CreateConnection() {
        // Looks for properties file in the root of the src directory in Netbeans project
        try (InputStream in = Files.newInputStream(FileSystems.getDefault().
                getPath(System.getProperty("user.dir") + File.separator + "db_props.
                properties"));) {
            props.load(in);
            in.close();
        } catch (IOException ex) {
            ex.printStackTrace();
        }
        loadProperties();
    }

    public final void loadProperties() {
        hostname = props.getProperty("host_name");
        port = props.getProperty("port_number");
        database = props.getProperty("db_name");
        username = props.getProperty("username");
        password = props.getProperty("password");
        driver = props.getProperty("driver");
        jndi = props.getProperty("jndi");
    }

}
```

```
/**
 * Demonstrates obtaining a connection via DriverManager
 *
 * @return
 * @throws SQLException
 */
public Connection getConnection() throws SQLException {
    Connection conn = null;
    String jdbcUrl;
    if (driver.equals("derby")) {
        jdbcUrl = "jdbc:derby://" + this.hostname + ":"
                + this.port + "/" + this.database;
    } else {
        jdbcUrl = "jdbc:oracle:thin:@" + this.hostname + ":"
                + this.port + ":" + this.database;
    }
    conn = DriverManager.getConnection(jdbcUrl, username, password);
    System.out.println("Successfully connected");
    return conn;
}

/**
 * Demonstrates obtaining a connection via a DataSource object
 *
 * @return
 */
public Connection getDSConnection() {
    Connection conn = null;
    try {
        Context ctx = new InitialContext();
        DataSource ds = (DataSource) ctx.lookup(this.jndi);
        conn = ds.getConnection();
    } catch (NamingException | SQLException ex) {
        ex.printStackTrace();
    }
    return conn;
}
}
```

Next, the following lines of text are an example of what should be contained in the properties file that is used for obtaining a connection to the database. For this example, the properties file is named db_props. properties:

```
host_name=your_db_server_name
db_name=your_db_name
username=db_username
password=db_username_password
port_number=db_port_number
#driver = derby or oracle
driver=db_driver
jndi=jndi_connection_String
```

Finally, use the `CreateConnection` class to obtain connections for your application. The following code demonstrates this concept:

```
CreateConnection createConn = new CreateConnection();
try(Connection conn = createConn.getConnection()) {
    performDbTask();
} catch (java.sql.SQLException ex) {
    ex.printStackTrace();
}
```

This code uses `try-with-resources` to automatically close the connection when it is finished performing the database task.

How It Works

Obtaining a connection within a database application can be code-intensive. Moreover, the process can be prone to error if you retype the code each time you need to obtain a connection. By encapsulating database connection logic within a single class, you can reuse the same connection code each time you require a connection to the database. This increases your productivity, reduces the chances of typing errors, and also enhances manageability because if you have to make a change, it can occur in one place rather than in several different locations.

Creating a strategic connection methodology is beneficial to you and others who might need to maintain your code in the future. Although data sources are the preferred technique for managing database connections when using an application server or JNDI, the solution to this recipe demonstrates the use standard JDBC `DriverManager` connections. One of the security implications of using the `DriverManager` is that you will need to store the database credentials somewhere for use by the application. It is not safe to store those credentials in plain text anywhere, and it is also not safe to embed them in application code, which might be decompiled at some point in the future. As seen in the solution, a properties file that on disk is used to store the database credentials. Assume that this properties file will be encrypted at some point before deployment to a server, and that the application will be able to handle decryption.

As seen in the solution, the code reads the database credentials, hostname, database name, and port number from the properties file. That information is then pieced together to form a JDBC URL that can be used by `DriverManager` to obtain a connection to the database. Once obtained, that connection can be used anywhere and then closed. Similarly, if using a `DataSource` that has been deployed to an application server, the properties file can be used to store the JNDI connection. That is the only piece of information that is needed to obtain a connection to the database using the `DataSource`. To the developer using the connection class, the only difference between the two types of connections is the method name that is called in order to obtain the `Connection` object.

You could develop a JDBC application so that the code used to obtain a connection needs to be hard-coded throughout. Instead, this solution enables all the code for obtaining a connection to be encapsulated by a single class so that the developer does not need to worry about it. Such a technique also allows the code to become more maintainable. For instance, if the application were originally deployed using the `DriverManager`, but then later had the ability to use a `DataSource`, very little code would need to be changed.

13-6. Guarding Against SQL Injection

Problem

Your application performs database tasks. To reduce the chances of a SQL injection attack, you need to ensure that no unfiltered Strings of text are being appended to SQL statements and executed against the database.

■ **Tip** Although prepared statements are the solution to this recipe, they can be used for more than just protecting against SQL injection. They also provide a way to centralize and better control the SQL used in an application. Instead of creating multiple, possibly different, versions of the same query, for example, you can create the query once as a prepared statement and invoke it from many different places throughout your code. Any change to the query logic need happen only at the point where you prepare the statement.

Solution

Use PreparedStatements for performing the database tasks. PreparedStatements send a precompiled SQL statement to the DBMS rather than a String. The following code demonstrates how to perform a database query and a database update using a java.sql.PreparedStatement object.

In the following code example, a PreparedStatement is used to query a database for a given record. Assume that the a String[] of recipe numbers is passed to this code as a variable.

```
private static void queryDbRecipe(String[] recipeNumbers) {
    String sql = "SELECT ID, RECIPE_NUMBER, RECIPE_NAME, DESCRIPTION "
            + "FROM RECIPES "
            + "WHERE RECIPE_NUMBER = ?";

    try (PreparedStatement pstmt = conn.prepareStatement(sql)) {
        for (String recipeNumber : recipeNumbers) {
            pstmt.setString(1, recipeNumber);
            ResultSet rs = pstmt.executeQuery();
            while (rs.next()) {
                System.out.println(rs.getString(2) + ": " + rs.getString(3)
                        + " - " + rs.getString(4));
            }
        }
    } catch (SQLException ex) {
        ex.printStackTrace();
    }

}
```

The next example demonstrates the use of a PreparedStatement for inserting a record into the database. Assume that the recipeNumber, title, description, and text Strings are passed to this code as variables.

```
String sql = "INSERT INTO RECIPES VALUES(" +
            "NEXT VALUE FOR RECIPES_SEQ, ?,?,?,?)";
try(PreparedStatement pstmt = conn.prepareStatement(sql);) {
    pstmt.setString(1, recipeNumber);
    pstmt.setString(2, title);
    pstmt.setString(3, description);
    pstmt.setString(4, text);
    pstmt.executeUpdate();
    System.out.println("Record successfully inserted.");
} catch (SQLException ex){
    ex.printStackTrace();
}
```

In this last example, a `PreparedStatement` is used to delete a record from the database. Again, assume that the recipeNumber String is passed to this code as a variable.

```
String sql = "DELETE FROM RECIPES WHERE " +
             "RECIPE_NUMBER = ?";
try(PreparedStatement pstmt = conn.prepareStatement(sql);) {
    pstmt.setString(1, recipeNumber);
    pstmt.executeUpdate();
    System.out.println("Recipe " + recipeNumber + " successfully deleted.");
} catch (SQLException ex){
    ex.printStackTrace();
}
```

As you can see, a `PreparedStatement` is very much the same as a standard JDBC statement object, but instead it sends precompiled SQL to the DBMS rather than Strings of text.

How It Works

While standard JDBC statements will get the job done, the harsh reality is that they can sometimes be insecure and cumbersome to work with. For instance, bad things can occur if a dynamic SQL statement is used to query a database, and a user-accepted String is assigned to a variable and concatenated with the intended SQL String. In most ordinary cases, the user-accepted String would be concatenated, and the SQL String would be used to query the database as expected. However, an attacker could decide to place malicious code inside of the String (a.k.a. SQL Injection), which would then be inadvertently sent to the database using a standard `Statement` object. The use of `PreparedStatements` prevents such malicious Strings from being concatenated into a SQL String and passed to the DBMS because they use a different approach. `PreparedStatements` use substitution variables rather than concatenation to make SQL Strings dynamic. They are also precompiled, which means that a valid SQL String is formed prior to the SQL being sent to the DBMS. Moreover, `PreparedStatements` can help your application perform better because if the same SQL has to be run more than one time, it has to be compiled only once. After that, the substitution variables are interchangeable, but the overall SQL can be executed by the `PreparedStatement` very quickly.

Let's take a look at how a `PreparedStatement` works in practice. If you look at the first example in the solution to this recipe, you can see that the database table RECIPES is being queried, passing a RECIPE_NUMBER and retrieving the results for the matching record. The SQL String looks like the following:

```
String sql = "SELECT ID, RECIPE_NUMBER, RECIPE_NAME, DESCRIPTION " +
             "FROM RECIPES " +
             "WHERE RECIPE_NUM = ?";
```

Everything looks standard with the SQL text except for the question mark (?) at the end of the String. Placing a question mark in a String of SQL signifies that a substitute variable will be used in place of that question mark when the SQL is executed. The next step for using a `PreparedStatement` is to declare a variable of type `PreparedStatement`. This can be seen with the following line of code:

```
PreparedStatement pstmt = null;
```

A `PreparedStatement` implements AutoCloseable, and therefore it can be utilized within the context of a `try-with-resources` block. Once a `PreparedStatement` has been declared, it can be put to use. However, use of a `PreparedStatement` might not cause an exception to be thrown. Therefore, in the event that try-with-resources is not used, a PreparedStatement should occur within a try-catch block so that any exceptions can be handled gracefully. For instance, exceptions can occur if the database connection is unavailable for some reason or if the SQL String is invalid. Rather than crashing an application due to such issues, it is best to handle the exceptions wisely within a catch block. The following try-catch block includes the code that is necessary to send the SQL String to the database and retrieve results:

```
try(PreparedStatement pstmt = conn.prepareStatement(sql);) {
    pstmt.setString(1, recipeNumber);
    ResultSet rs = pstmt.executeQuery();
    while(rs.next()){
        System.out.println(rs.getString(2) + ": " + rs.getString(3) +
                        " - " + rs.getString(4));
    }
} catch (SQLException ex) {
    ex.printStackTrace();
}
```

First, you can see that the Connection object is used to instantiate a PreparedStatement object. The SQL String is passed to the PreparedStatement object's constructor on creation. Since the PreparedStatement is instantiated within the try-with-resources construct, it will be automatically closed when it is no longer in use. Next, the PreparedStatement object is used to set values for any substitution variables that have been placed into the SQL String. As you can see, the PreparedStatement setString() method is used in the example to set the substitution variable at position 1 equal to the contents of the recipeNumber variable. The positioning of the substitution variable is associated with the placement of the question mark (?) within the SQL String. The first question mark within the String is assigned to the first position, the second one is assigned to the second position, and so forth. If there were more than one substitution variable to be assigned, there would be more than one call against the PreparedStatement, assigning each of the variables until each one has been accounted for. PreparedStatements can accept substitution variables of many different data types. For instance, if an int value were being assigned to a substitution variable, a call to the setInt(position, variable) method would be in order. See the online documentation or your IDE's code completion for a complete set of methods that can be used for assigning substitution variables using PreparedStatement objects.

Once all the variables have been assigned, the SQL String can be executed. The PreparedStatement object contains an executeQuery() method that is used to execute a SQL String that represents a query. The executeQuery() method returns a ResultSet object, which contains the results that have been fetched from the database for the particular SQL query. Next, the ResultSet can be traversed to obtain the values retrieved from the database. Again, positional assignments are used to retrieve the results by calling the ResultSet object's corresponding getter methods and passing the position of the column value that you want to obtain. The position is determined by the order in which the column names appear within the SQL String. In the example, the first position corresponds to the RECIPE_NUMBER column, the second corresponds to the RECIPE_NAME column, and so forth. If the recipeNumber String variable was equal to "13-1," the results of executing the query in the example would look something like the following:

13-1: Connecting to a Database - DriverManager and DataSource Implementations

Of course, if the substitution variable is not set correctly or if there is an issue with the SQL String, an exception will be thrown. This would cause the code that is contained within the catch block to be executed. You should also be sure to clean up after using PreparedStatements by closing the statement when you are finished using it. If you're not using a try-with-resources construct, it is a good practice to put all the cleanup code within a `finally` block to be sure that the `PreparedStatement` is closed properly even if an exception is thrown. In the example, the `finally` block looks like the following:

```
finally {
    if (pstmt != null){
        try {
            pstmt.close();
        } catch (SQLException ex) {
            ex.printStackTrace();
        }
    }
}
```

You can see that the `PreparedStatement` object that was instantiated, `pstmt`, is checked to see whether it is NULL. If not, it is closed by calling the `close()` method.

Working through the code in the solution to this recipe, you can see that similar code is used to process database INSERT, `Update`, and DELETE statements. The only difference in those cases is that the `PreparedStatement` `executeUpdate()` method is called rather than the `executeQuery()` method. The `executeUpdate()` method will return an `int` value representing the number of rows affected by the SQL statement.

The use of `PreparedStatement` objects is preferred over JDBC `Statement` objects. This is due to the fact that they are more secure and perform better. They can also make your code easier to follow and maintain.

13-7. Performing Transactions

Problem

The way in which your application is structured requires a sequential processing of tasks. One task depends on another, and each process performs a different database action. If one of the tasks along the way fails, the database processing that has already occurred needs to be reversed.

Solution

Set your `Connection` object autocommit to false and then perform the transactions you want to complete. Once you've successfully performed each of the transactions, manually commit the `Connection` object; otherwise, roll back each of the transactions that have taken place. The following code example demonstrates transaction management. If you look at the `main()` method of the `TransactionExample` class, you will see that the `Connection` object's `autoCommit()` preference has been set to false, so that database statements are grouped together to form one transaction. If all the statements within the transaction are successful, the `Connection` object is manually committed by calling the `commit()` method; otherwise, all the statements are rolled back by calling the `rollback()` method. By default, autoCommit is set to true, which automatically treats every statement as a single transaction.

```
import java.sql.Connection;
import java.sql.PreparedStatement;
import java.sql.ResultSet;
import java.sql.SQLException;
import org.java9recipes.chapter13.recipe13_01.CreateConnection;
```

```java
public class TransactionExample {
    public static Connection conn = null;

    public static void main(String[] args) {
        boolean successFlag = false;
        try {
            CreateConnection createConn = new CreateConnection();
            conn = createConn.getConnection();
            conn.setAutoCommit(false);
            queryDbRecipes();
            successFlag = insertRecord(
                    "13-6",
                    "Simplifying and Adding Security with Prepared Statements",
                    "Working with Prepared Statements",
                    "Recipe Text");

            if (successFlag == true){

                successFlag = insertRecord(
                        "13-6B",
                        "Simplifying and Adding Security with Prepared Statements",
                        "Working with Prepared Statements",
                        "Recipe Text");
            }

            // Commit Transactions
            if (successFlag == true)
                conn.commit();
            else
                conn.rollback();

            conn.setAutoCommit(true);
            queryDbRecipes();
        } catch (java.sql.SQLException ex) {
            System.out.println(ex);
        } finally {
            if (conn != null) {
                try {
                    conn.close();
                } catch (SQLException ex) {
                    ex.printStackTrace();
                }
            }
        }
    }

}
```

```java
    private static void queryDbRecipes(){
        String sql = "SELECT ID, RECIPE_NUMBER, RECIPE_NAME, DESCRIPTION " +
                        "FROM RECIPES";

        try(PreparedStatement pstmt = conn.prepareStatement(sql);) {
            ResultSet rs = pstmt.executeQuery();
            while(rs.next()){
                System.out.println(rs.getString(2) + ": " + rs.getString(3) +
                                    " - " + rs.getString(4));
            }
        } catch (SQLException ex) {
            ex.printStackTrace();
        }

    }

    private static boolean insertRecord(String recipeNumber,
                            String title,
                            String description,
                            String text){
        String sql = "INSERT INTO RECIPES VALUES(" +
                        "NEXT VALUE FOR RECIPES_SEQ, ?,?,?,?)";
        boolean success = false;
        try(PreparedStatement pstmt = conn.prepareStatement(sql);) {
            pstmt.setString(1, recipeNumber);
            pstmt.setString(2, title);
            pstmt.setString(3, description);
            pstmt.setString(4, text);
            pstmt.executeUpdate();
            System.out.println("Record successfully inserted.");
            success = true;
        } catch (SQLException ex){
            success = false;
            ex.printStackTrace();
        }
        return success;
    }

}
```

In the end, if any of the statements fails, all transactions will be rolled back. However, if all the statements execute properly, everything will be committed.

How It Works

Transaction management can play an important role in an application. This holds true especially for applications that perform different tasks that depend on each other. In many cases, if one of the tasks performed within a transaction fails, it is preferable for the entire transaction to fail rather than having it only partially complete. For instance, imagine that you were adding database user records to your application database. Now let's say that adding a user for your application required a couple of different database tables to be modified, maybe a table for roles, and so on. What would happen if your first table was modified correctly and the second table modification failed? You would be left with a partially complete application user addition, and your user would most likely not be able to access the application as expected. In such a situation, it would be nicer to roll back all the already-completed database modifications if one of the updates failed so that the database was left in a clean state and the transaction could be attempted once again.

By default, a Connection object is set up so that autocommit is turned on. That means that each database INSERT, UPDATE, or DELETE statement is committed right away. Usually, this is the way that you will want your applications to function. However, in circumstances where you have many database statements that rely on one another, it is important to turn off autocommit so that all the statements can be committed at once. To do so, call the Connection object's setAutoCommit() method and pass a false value. As you can see in the solution to this recipe, the setAutoCommit() method is called passing a false value, the database statements are executed. Doing so will cause all the database statement changes to be temporary until the Connection object's commit() method is called. This provides you with the ability to ensure that all the statements execute properly before issuing commit(). Take a look at this transaction management code that is contained within the main() method of the TransactionExample class within the solution to this recipe:

```
boolean successFlag = false;
...
CreateConnection createConn = new CreateConnection();
conn = createConn.getConnection();
conn.setAutoCommit(false);
queryDbRecipes();
successFlag = insertRecord(
                    "13-6",
                    "Simplifying and Adding Security with Prepared Statements",
                    "Working with Prepared Statements",
                    "Recipe Text");

if (successFlag == true){

    successFlag = insertRecord(
        null,
        "Simplifying and Adding Security with Prepared Statements",
        "Working with Prepared Statements",
        "Recipe Text");
}
// Commit Transactions
if (successFlag == true)
    conn.commit();
else
    conn.rollback();

conn.setAutoCommit(true);
```

Note that the commit() method is called only if all transaction statements were processed successfully. If any of them fail, the successFlag is equal to false, which would cause the rollback() method to be called instead. In the solution to this recipe, the second call to insertRecord() attempts to insert a NULL value into the RECIPE.ID column, which is not allowed. Therefore, that insert fails and everything, including the previous insert, gets rolled back.

13-8. Creating a Scrollable ResultSet

Problem

You have queried the database and obtained some results. You want to store those results in an object that will allow you to traverse forward and backward through the results, updating values as needed.

Solution

Create a scrollable ResultSet object and then you will have the ability to read the next, first record, last, and previous record. Using a scrollable ResultSet allows the results of a query to be fetched in any direction so that the data can be retrieved as needed. The following example method demonstrates the creation of a scrollable ResultSet object:

```
private static void queryDbRecipes(){
    String sql = "SELECT ID, RECIPE_NUMBER, RECIPE_NAME, DESCRIPTION " +
                "FROM RECIPES";

    try(PreparedStatement pstmt =conn.prepareStatement(sql,
            ResultSet.TYPE_SCROLL_INSENSITIVE, ResultSet.CONCUR_READ_ONLY);
        ResultSet rs = pstmt.executeQuery()) {

        rs.first();
        System.out.println(rs.getString(2) + ": " + rs.getString(3) +
                    " - " + rs.getString(4));
        rs.next();
        System.out.println(rs.getString(2) + ": " + rs.getString(3) +
                    " - " + rs.getString(4));
        rs.previous();
        System.out.println(rs.getString(2) + ": " + rs.getString(3) +
                    " - " + rs.getString(4));
        rs.last();
        System.out.println(rs.getString(2) + ": " + rs.getString(3) +
                    " - " + rs.getString(4));
    } catch (SQLException ex) {
        ex.printStackTrace();
    }

}
```

Executing this method will result in the following output using the data that was originally loaded for this chapter:

```
Successfully connected
13-1: Connecting to a Database - DriverManager and DataSource Implementations - More to Come
13-2: Querying a Database and Retrieving Results - Obtaining and Using Data from a DBMS
13-1: Connecting to a Database - DriverManager and DataSource Implementations - More to Come
13-3: Handling SQL Exceptions - Using SQLException
```

How It Works

Ordinary ResultSet objects allow results to be fetched in a forward direction. That is, an application can process a default ResultSet object from the first record retrieved forward to the last. Sometimes an application requires more functionality when it comes to traversing a ResultSet. For instance, let's say you want to write an application that allows for someone to display the first or last record that was retrieved, or perhaps page forward or backward through results. You could not do this very easily using a standard ResultSet. However, by creating a scrollable ResultSet, you can easily move backward and forward through the results.

To create a scrollable ResultSet, you must first create an instance of a Statement or PreparedStatement that has the ability to create a scrollable ResultSet. That is, when creating the Statement, you must pass the ResultSet scroll type constant value to the Connection object's createStatement() method. Likewise, you must pass the scroll type constant value to the Connection object's prepareStatement() method when using a PreparedStatement. There are three scroll type constants that can be used. Table 13-1 displays those three constants.

Table 13-1. *ResultSet Scroll Type Constants*

Constant	Description
ResultSet.TYPE_FORWARD_ONLY	Default type, allows forward movement only.
ResultSet.TYPE_SCROLL_INSENSITIVE	Allows forward and backward movement. Not sensitive to ResultSet updates.
ResultSet.TYPE_SCROLL_SENSITIVE	Allows forward and backward movement. Sensitive to ResultSet updates.

You must also pass a ResultSet concurrency constant to advise whether the ResultSet is intended to be updatable. The default is ResultSet.CONCUR_READ_ONLY, which means that the ResultSet is not updatable. The other concurrency type is ResultSet.CONCUR_UPDATABLE, which signifies an updatable ResultSet object.

In the solution to this recipe, a PreparedStatement object is used, and the code to create a PreparedStatement object that has the ability to generate a scrollable ResultSet looks like the following line:

```
pstmt = conn.prepareStatement(sql, ResultSet.TYPE_SCROLL_INSENSITIVE,
                                    ResultSet.CONCUR_READ_ONLY);
```

Once the PreparedStatement has been created as such, a scrollable ResultSet is returned. You can traverse in several directions using a scrollable ResultSet by calling the ResultSet methods indicating the direction you want to move or the placement that you want to be. The following line of code will retrieve the first record within the ResultSet:

```
ResultSet rs = pstmt.executeQuery();
rs.first();
```

The solution to this recipe demonstrates a few different scroll directions. Specifically, you can see that the ResultSet first(), next(), last(), and previous() methods are called in order to move to different positions within the ResultSet. For a complete reference to the ResultSet object, see the online documentation that can be found at http://docs.oracle.com/javase/8/docs/api/java/sql/ResultSet.html.

Scrollable ResultSet objects have a niche in application development. They are one of those niceties that are there when you need them, but they are also something that you might not need very often.

13-9. Creating an Updatable ResultSet

Problem

An application task has queried the database and obtained results. You have stored those results into a ResultSet object, and you want to update some of those values in the ResultSet and commit them back to the database.

Solution

Make your ResultSet object updatable, and then update the rows as needed while iterating through the results. The following example method demonstrates how to make ResultSet updatable and then how to update content within that ResultSet, eventually persisting it in the database:

```
private static void queryAndUpdateDbRecipes(String recipeNumber){
       String sql = "SELECT ID, RECIPE_NUMBER, RECIPE_NAME, DESCRIPTION " +
                    "FROM RECIPES " +
                    "WHERE RECIPE_NUMBER = ?";
       ResultSet rs = null;
       try (PreparedStatement pstmt =
               conn.prepareStatement(sql, ResultSet.TYPE_SCROLL_SENSITIVE, ResultSet.
               CONCUR_UPDATABLE);){

           pstmt.setString(1, recipeNumber);
           rs = pstmt.executeQuery();
           while(rs.next()){
               String desc = rs.getString(4);
               System.out.println("Updating row" + desc);

               rs.updateString(4, desc + " -- More to come");
               rs.updateRow();
           }

       } catch (SQLException ex) {
           ex.printStackTrace();
       } finally {
           if (rs != null){
               try {
                   rs.close();
               } catch (SQLException ex) {
                   ex.printStackTrace();
               }
           }
       }
}
```

This method could be called passing a String value containing a recipe number. Suppose that the recipe number "13-1" was passed to this method; the following output would be the result:

```
Successfully connected
13-1: Connecting to a Database - DriverManager and DataSource Implementations
13-2: Querying a Database and Retrieving Results - Obtaining and Using Data from a DBMS
13-3: Handling SQL Exceptions - Using SQLException
Updating rowDriverManager and DataSource Implementations
13-1: Connecting to a Database - DriverManager and DataSource Implementations - More to come
13-2: Querying a Database and Retrieving Results - Obtaining and Using Data from a DBMS
13-3: Handling SQL Exceptions - Using SQLException
```

How It Works

Sometimes you need to update data as you are parsing it. Usually this technique involves testing the values that are being returned from the database and updating them after comparison with another value. The easiest way to do this is to make the ResultSet object updatable by passing the ResultSet.CONCUR_UPDATABLE constant to the Connection object's createStatement() or prepareStatement() method. Doing so causes the Statement or PreparedStatement to produce an updatable ResultSet.

■ **Note** Some database JDBC drivers do not support updatable ResultSets. See the documentation of your JDBC driver for more information. This code was run using Oracle's ojdbc6.jar JDBC driver on Oracle database 11.2 release.

The format for creating a Statement that will produce an updatable ResultSet is to pass the ResultSet type as the first argument and the ResultSet concurrency as the second argument. The scroll type must be TYPE_SCROLL_SENSITIVE to ensure that the ResultSet will be sensitive to any updates that are made. The following code demonstrates this technique by creating a Statement object that will produce a scrollable and updatable ResultSet object:

```
Statement stmt = conn.createStatement(ResultSet.TYPE_SCROLL_SENSITIVE,
ResultSet.CONCUR_UPDATABLE);
```

The format for creating a PreparedStatement that will produce an updatable ResultSet is to pass the SQL String as the first argument, the ResultSet type as the second argument, and the ResultSet concurrency as the third argument. The solution to this recipe demonstrates this technique using the following line of code:

```
pstmt = conn.prepareStatement(sql, ResultSet.TYPE_SCROLL_SENSITIVE,

ResultSet.CONCUR_UPDATABLE);
```

Both of the lines of code discussed in this section will produce scrollable and updatable ResultSet objects. Once you have obtained an updatable ResultSet, you can use it just like an ordinary ResultSet for fetching values that are retrieved from the database. In addition, you can call one of the ResultSet object's updateXXX() methods to update any value within the ResultSet. In the solution to this recipe, the updateString() method is called, passing the position of the value from the query as the first argument and the updated text as the second argument. In this case, the fourth element column listed in the SQL query will be updated.

```
rs.updateString(4, desc + " -- More to come");
```

Finally, to persist the values that you have changed, call the ResultSet updateRow() method, as seen in the solution to this recipe:

```
rs.updateRow();
```

Creating an updatable ResultSet is not something that you will need to do every day. In fact, you might never need to create an updatable ResultSet. However, for the cases in which such a strategy is needed, this technique can come in very handy.

13-10. Caching Data for Use When Disconnected

Problem

You want to work with data from a DBMS when you are in a disconnected state. That is, you are working on a device that is not connected to the database, and you still want to have the ability to work with a set of data as though you are connected. For instance, you are working with data on a portable device, and you are away from the office without a connection. You want to have the ability to query, insert, update, and delete data, even though there is no connection. Once a connection becomes available, you want to have your device synchronize any database changes that have been made while you were disconnected.

Solution

Use a CachedRowSet object to store the data that you want to work with while offline. This will afford your application the ability to work with data as though it were connected to a database. Once your connection is restored or you connect back to the database, synchronize the data that has been changed within the CachedRowSet with the database repository. The following example class demonstrates the use of a CachedRowSet. In this scenario, the main() method executes the example. Suppose that there were no main() method, though, and that another application on a portable device were to invoke the methods of this class. Follow the code in the example and consider the possibility of working with the results that are stored within the CachedRowSet while not connected to the database. For instance, suppose that you began some work in the office while connected to the network and are now outside of the office, where the network is spotty and you cannot maintain a constant connection to the database:

```
package org.java9recipes.chapter13.recipe13_10;

import java.sql.Connection;
import java.sql.SQLException;
import javax.sql.rowset.CachedRowSet;
import javax.sql.rowset.RowSetFactory;
import javax.sql.rowset.RowSetProvider;
import javax.sql.rowset.spi.SyncProviderException;
import org.java9recipes.chapter13.recipe13_01.CreateConnection;

public class CachedRowSetExample {

    public static Connection conn = null;
    public static CreateConnection createConn;
    public static CachedRowSet crs = null;
```

```java
public static void main(String[] args) {
    boolean successFlag = false;
    try {
        createConn = new CreateConnection();
        conn = createConn.getConnection();
        // Perform Scrollable Query
        queryWithRowSet();

        // Update the CachedRowSet
        updateData();

        // Synchronize changes
        syncWithDatabase();
    } catch (java.sql.SQLException ex) {
        System.out.println(ex);
    } finally {

        if (conn != null) {
            try {
                conn.close();
            } catch (SQLException ex) {
                ex.printStackTrace();
            }
        }
    }

}

/**
 * Call this method to synchronize the data that has been used in the
 * CachedRowSet with the database
 */
public static void syncWithDatabase() {
    try {
        crs.acceptChanges(conn);
    } catch (SyncProviderException ex) {
        // If there is a conflict while synchronizing, this exception
        // will be thrown.
        ex.printStackTrace();
    } finally {
        // Clean up resources by closing CachedRowSet
        if (crs != null) {
            try {
                crs.close();
            } catch (SQLException ex) {
                ex.printStackTrace();
            }
        }
    }
}
```

```java
public static void queryWithRowSet() {
    RowSetFactory factory;

    try {

        // Create a new RowSetFactory
        factory = RowSetProvider.newFactory();

        // Create a CachedRowSet object using the factory
        crs = factory.createCachedRowSet();

        // Alternatively populate the CachedRowSet connection settings
        // crs.setUsername(createConn.getUsername());
        // crs.setPassword(createConn.getPassword());
        // crs.setUrl(createConn.getJdbcUrl());

        // Populate a query that will obtain the data that will be used
        crs.setCommand("select id, recipe_number, recipe_name, description from recipes");
        // Set key columns
        int[] keys = {1};
        crs.setKeyColumns(keys);
        crs.execute(conn);

        // You can now work with the object contents in a disconnected state
        while (crs.next()) {
            System.out.println(crs.getString(2) + ": " + crs.getString(3)
                    + " - " + crs.getString(4));
        }

    } catch (SQLException ex) {
        ex.printStackTrace();
    }
}

public static boolean updateData() {
    boolean returnValue = false;
    try {
        // Move to the position before the first row in the result set
        crs.beforeFirst();

        // traverse result set
        while (crs.next()) {
            // If the recipe_num equals 11-2 then update
            if (crs.getString("RECIPE_NUMBER").equals("13-2")) {
                System.out.println("updating recipe 13-2");
                crs.updateString("description", "Subject to change");
                crs.updateRow();
            }

        }
        returnValue = true;
```

```
        // Move to the position before the first row in the result set
        crs.beforeFirst();

        // traverse result set to see changes
        while (crs.next()) {

                System.out.println(crs.getString(2) + ": " + crs.getString(3)
                    + " - " + crs.getString(4));

        }

    } catch (SQLException ex) {
        returnValue = false;
        ex.printStackTrace();
    }
    return returnValue;
    }
}
```

Running this example code will display output that looks similar to the following code, although the text might vary depending on the values in the database. Notice that the database record for Recipe 13-2 has a changed description after the update of the CachedRowSet.

```
Successfully connected
13-1: Connecting to a Database - DriverManager and DataSource Implementations - More to Come
13-2: Querying a Database and Retrieving Results - Subject to Change
13-3: Handling SQL Exceptions - Using SQLException
Updating Recipe 13-2
13-1: Connecting to a Database - DriverManager and DataSource Implementations - More to Come
13-2: Querying a Database and Retrieving Results - Obtaining and Using Data from a DBMS
13-3: Handling SQL Exceptions - Using SQLException
```

How It Works

It is not possible to remain connected to the Internet all the time if you are working on a mobile device and traveling. Nowadays there are devices that allow you to perform substantial work while you are on the go, even when you are not connected directly to a database. In such cases, solutions like the CachedRowSet object can come into play. The CachedRowSet is the same as a regular ResultSet object, except it does not have to maintain a connection to a database in order to remain usable. You can query the database, obtain the results, and place them into a CachedRowSet object; and then work with them while not connected to the database. If changes are made to the data at any point, those changes can be synchronized with the database at a later time.

There are a couple of ways to create a CachedRowSet. The solution to this recipe uses a RowSetFactory to instantiate a CachedRowSet. However, you can also use the CachedRowSet default constructor to create a new instance. Doing so would look like the following line of code:

```
CachedRowSet crs = new CachedRowSetImpl();
```

Once instantiated, you need to set up a connection to the database. There are also a couple of ways to do this. Properties could be set for the connection that will be used, and the solution to this recipe demonstrates this technique within comments. The following excerpt from the solution sets the connection properties using the CachedRowSet object's setUsername(), setPassword(), and setUrl() methods. Each of them accepts a String value, and in the example that String is obtained from the CreateConnection class:

```
// Alternatively populate the CachedRowSet connection settings
// crs.setUsername(createConn.getUsername());
// crs.setPassword(createConn.getPassword());
// crs.setUrl(createConn.getJdbcUrl());
```

Another way to set up the connection is to wait until the query is executed and pass a Connection object to the executeQuery() method. This is the technique that is used in the solution to this recipe. But before you can execute the query, it must be set using the setCommand() method, which accepts a String value. In this case, the String is the SQL query that you need to execute:

```
crs.setCommand("select id, recipe_number, recipe_name, description from recipes");
```

Next, if a CachedRowSet will be used for updates, the primary key values should be noted using the setKeys() method. This method accepts an int array that includes the positional indices of the key columns. These keys are used to identify unique columns. In this case, the first column listed in the query, ID, is the primary key:

```
int[] keys = {1};
crs.setKeyColumns(keys);
```

Finally, execute the query and populate the CachedRowSet using the execute() method. As mentioned previously, the execute() method optionally accepts a Connection object, which allows the CachedRowSet to obtain a database connection.

```
crs.execute(conn);
```

Once the query has been executed and the CachedRowSet has been populated, it can be used just like any other ResultSet. You can use it to fetch records forward and backward, or by specifying the absolute position of the row you'd like to retrieve. The solution to this recipe demonstrates only a couple of these fetching methods, but the most often used ones are listed in Table 13-2.

Table 13-2. *CachedRowSet Fetching Methods*

Method	Description
first()	Moves to the first row in the set.
beforeFirst()	Moves to the position before the first row in the set.
afterLast	Moves to the position after the last row in the set.
next()	Moves to the next position in the set.
last()	Moves to the last position in the set.

It is possible to insert and update rows within a CachedRowSet. To insert rows, use the moveToInsertRow() method to move to a new row position. Then populate a row by using the various methods [CachedRowSet, updateString(), updateInt(), and so on] that correspond to the data type of the column you are populating within the row. Once you have populated each of the required columns within the row, call the insertRow() method, followed by the moveToCurrentRow() method. The following lines of code demonstrate inserting a record into the RECIPES table:

```
crs.moveToInsertRow();
crs.updateInt(1, sequenceValue); // obtain current sequence values with a prior query
crs.updateString(2, "13-x");
crs.updateString(3, "This is a new recipe title");
crs.insertRow();
crs.moveToCurrentRow();
```

Updating rows is similar to using an updatable ResultSet. Simply update the values using the CachedRowSet object's methods [updateString(), updateInt(), and so on] that correspond to the data type of the column that you are updating within the row. Once you have updated the column or columns within the row, call the updateRow() method. This technique is demonstrated in the solution to this recipe.

```
crs.updateString("description", "Subject to change");
crs.updateRow();
```

To propagate any updates or inserts to the database, the acceptChanges() method must be called. This method can accept an optional Connection argument in order to connect to the database. Once called, all changes are flushed to the database. Unfortunately, because time might have elapsed since the data was last retrieved for the CachedRowSet, there could be conflicts. If such a conflict arises, a SyncProviderException will be thrown. You can catch these exceptions and handle the conflicts manually using a SyncResolver object. However, resolving conflicts is out of the scope of this recipe, so for more information, see the online documentation that can be found at http://download.oracle.com/javase/tutorial/jdbc/basics/cachedrowset.html.

CachedRowSet objects provide great flexibility for working with data, especially when you are using a device that is not always connected to the database. However, they can also be overkill in situations where you can simply use a standard ResultSet or even a scrollable ResultSet.

13-11. Joining RowSet Objects When Not Connected to the Data Source

Problem

You want to join two or more RowSets while not connected to a database. Perhaps your application is loaded on a mobile device that is not always connected to the database. In such a case, you are looking for a solution that will allow you to join the results of two or more queries.

Solution

Use a JoinRowSet to take data from two relational database tables and join them. The data from each table that will be joined should be fetched into a RowSet and then the JoinRowSet can be used to join each of those RowSet objects based on related elements contained within them. For instance, suppose that there were two related tables within a database. One of the tables stores a list of authors, and the other table contains a list of chapters that are written by those authors. The two tables can be joined using SQL by the primary and foreign key relationship.

■ **Note** A *primary key* is a unique identifier within each record of a database table, and a foreign key is a referential constraint between two tables.

However, the application will not be connected to the database to make the JOIN query, so it must be done using a JoinRowSet. The following class listing demonstrates one strategy that can be used. In this scenario, the database table BOOK_AUTHOR and is set up as follows:

```
BOOK_AUTHOR(
id          int primary key,
last        varchar(30),
first       varchar(30));

author_work(
id              int primary key,
author_id       int not null,
chapter_number  int not null,
chapter_title   varchar(100) not null,
constraint author_work_fk
foreign key(author_id) references book_author(id));

book(
id          int primary key,
title       varchar(150),
image       varchar(150),
description clob);
```

The Java code to work with this table is as follows:

```java
package org.java9recipes.chapter13.recipe13_11;

import com.sun.rowset.JoinRowSetImpl;
import java.sql.Connection;
import java.sql.SQLException;
import javax.sql.rowset.CachedRowSet;
import javax.sql.rowset.JoinRowSet;
import javax.sql.rowset.RowSetFactory;
import javax.sql.rowset.RowSetProvider;
import org.java9recipes.chapter13.recipe13_01.CreateConnection;

public class JoinRowSetExample {

    public static Connection conn = null;
    public static CreateConnection createConn;
    public static CachedRowSet bookAuthors = null;
    public static CachedRowSet authorWork = null;
    public static JoinRowSet jrs = null;
```

```java
public static void main(String[] args) {
    boolean successFlag = false;
    try {
        createConn = new CreateConnection();
        conn = createConn.getConnection();
        // Perform Scrollable Query
        queryBookAuthor();
        queryAuthorWork();

        joinRowQuery();
    } catch (java.sql.SQLException ex) {
        System.out.println(ex);
    } finally {

        if (conn != null) {
            try {
                conn.close();
            } catch (SQLException ex) {
                ex.printStackTrace();
            }
        }
        if (bookAuthors != null) {
            try {
                bookAuthors.close();
            } catch (SQLException ex) {
                ex.printStackTrace();
            }
        }
        if (authorWork != null) {
            try {
                authorWork.close();
            } catch (SQLException ex) {
                ex.printStackTrace();
            }
        }
        if (jrs != null) {
            try {
                jrs.close();
            } catch (SQLException ex) {
                ex.printStackTrace();
            }
        }
    }

}

public static void queryBookAuthor() {
    RowSetFactory factory;

    try {
        // Create a new RowSetFactory
        factory = RowSetProvider.newFactory();
```

```
            // Create a CachedRowSet object using the factory
            bookAuthors = factory.createCachedRowSet();

            // Alternatively populate the CachedRowSet connection settings
            // crs.setUsername(createConn.getUsername());
            // crs.setPassword(createConn.getPassword());
            // crs.setUrl(createConn.getJdbcUrl());

            // Populate a query that will obtain the data that will be used
            bookAuthors.setCommand("SELECT ID, LASTNAME, FIRSTNAME FROM BOOK_AUTHOR");

            bookAuthors.execute(conn);

            // You can now work with the object contents in a disconnected state
            while (bookAuthors.next()) {
                System.out.println(bookAuthors.getString(1) + ": " + bookAuthors.getString(2)
                        + ", " + bookAuthors.getString(3));
            }

        } catch (SQLException ex) {
            ex.printStackTrace();
        }
    }

    public static void queryAuthorWork() {
        RowSetFactory factory;

        try {
            // Create a new RowSetFactory
            factory = RowSetProvider.newFactory();

            // Create a CachedRowSet object using the factory
            authorWork = factory.createCachedRowSet();

            // Alternatively populate the CachedRowSet connection settings
            // crs.setUsername(createConn.getUsername());
            // crs.setPassword(createConn.getPassword());
            // crs.setUrl(createConn.getJdbcUrl());

            // Populate a query that will obtain the data that will be used
            authorWork.setCommand("SELECT AW.ID, AUTHOR_ID, B.TITLE FROM AUTHOR_WORK AW, " +
                    "BOOK B " +
                    "WHERE B.ID = AW.BOOK_ID");

            authorWork.execute(conn);

            // You can now work with the object contents in a disconnected state
            while (authorWork.next()) {
                System.out.println(authorWork.getString(1) + ": " + authorWork.getString(2)
                        + " - " + authorWork.getString(3));
            }
```

```
        } catch (SQLException ex) {
            ex.printStackTrace();
        }
    }

    public static void joinRowQuery() {
        try {
            // Create JoinRowSet
            jrs = new JoinRowSetImpl();

            // Add RowSet & Corresponding Keys
            jrs.addRowSet(bookAuthors, 1);
            jrs.addRowSet(authorWork, 2);
            // Alternatively use join-column name
            // jrs.addRowSet(authorWork, "AUTHOR_ID");

            // Traverse Results
            while(jrs.next()){
                System.out.println(jrs.getInt("ID") + ": " +
                                   jrs.getString("TITLE") + " - " +
                                   jrs.getString("FIRSTNAME") + " " +
                                   jrs.getString("LASTNAME"));
            }

        } catch (SQLException ex) {
            ex.printStackTrace();
        }

    }
}
```

Running this class will result in output that resembles the following:

```
Successfully connected
100: JUNEAU, JOSH
101: DEA, CARL
102: BEATY, MARK
103: GUIME, FREDDY
104: JOHN, OCONNER
105: TESTER, JOE
110: TESTER, JOE
111: OCONNER, JOHN
1: 100 - Java 8 Recipes
2: 100 - Java 7 Recipes
3: 100 - Java EE 7 Recipes
4: 100 - Introducing Java EE 7
5: 103 - Java 7 Recipes
6: 101 - Java 7 Recipes
7: 111 - Java 7 Recipes
8: 102 - Java 7 Recipes
9: 101 - Java FX 2.0 - Introduction by Example
111: Java 7 Recipes - JOHN OCONNER
```

```
103: Java 7 Recipes - FREDDY GUIME
102: Java 7 Recipes - MARK BEATY
101: Java FX 2.0 - Introduction by Example - CARL DEA
101: Java 7 Recipes - CARL DEA
100: Introducing Java EE 7 - JOSH JUNEAU
100: Java EE 7 Recipes - JOSH JUNEAU
100: Java 7 Recipes - JOSH JUNEAU
100: Java 8 Recipes - JOSH JUNEAU
```

How It Works

A JoinRowSet is a combination of two or more populated RowSet objects. It can be used to join two RowSet objects based on key/value relationships, just as if it were a SQL JOIN query. In order to create a JoinRowSet, you must first populate two or more RowSet objects with related data, and then they can each be added to the JoinRowSet to create the combined result.

In the solution to this recipe, the tables that are queried are named BOOK_AUTHOR, BOOK, and AUTHOR_WORK. The BOOK_AUTHOR table contains a list of author names, while the AUTHOR_WORK table contains the list of books along with the corresponding AUTHOR_ID. The BOOK table contains book specifics. Following along with the main() method, first the BOOK_AUTHOR table is queried, and its results are fetched into a CachedRowSet using the queryBookAuthor() method. For more details regarding the use of CachedRowSet objects, see Recipe 13-10.

Next, another CachedRowSet is populated with the results of querying the AUTHOR_WORK and BOOK tables, as the queryAuthorBook() method is called. At this point, there are two populated CacheRowSet objects, and they can now be combined using a JoinRowSet. In order to do so, each query must contain one or more columns that relate to the other table. In this case, the BOOK_AUTHOR.ID column relates to the AUTHOR_WORK. AUTHOR_ID column, so the RowSet objects must be joined on those column values.

The final method that is invoked within the main() is joinRowQuery(). This method is where all the JoinRowSet work takes place. First, a new JoinRowSet is created by instantiating a JoinRowSetImpl() object:

```
jrs = new JoinRowSetImpl();
```

■ **Note**   You will receive a compile-time warning when using JoinRowSetImpl because it is an internal SUN proprietary API. However, the Oracle version is OracleJoinRowSet, which is not as versatile.

Next, the two CachedRowSet objects are added to the newly created JoinRowSet by calling its addRowSet() method. The addRowSet() method accepts a couple of arguments. The first is the name of the RowSet object that you want to add to the JoinRowSet, and the second is an int value indicating the position within the CachedRowSet, which contains the key value that will be used to implement the join. In the solution to this recipe, the first call to addRowSet() passes the bookAuthors CachedRowSet, along with the number 1 because the element in the first position of the bookAuthors CachedRowSet corresponds to the BOOK_AUTHOR.ID column. The second call to addRowSet() passes the authorWork CachedRowSet, along with number 2 because the element in the second position of the authorWork CachedRowSet corresponds to the AUTHOR_WORK.AUTHOR_ID column.

```
// Add RowSet & Corresponding Keys
jrs.addRowSet(bookAuthors, 1);
jrs.addRowSet(authorWork, 2);
// Alternatively specify the join-column name
jrs.addRowSet(authorWork, "AUTHOR_ID");
```

The JoinRowSet can now be used to fetch the results of the join, just as if it were a normal RowSet. When calling the corresponding methods [getString(), getInt(), and so on] of the JoinRowSet, pass the name of the database column corresponding to the data you want to store:

```
while(jrs.next()){
System.out.println(jrs.getInt("ID") + ": " +
                jrs.getString("TITLE") + " - " +
                jrs.getString("FIRSTNAME") + " " +
                jrs.getString("LASTNAME"));
}
```

Although a JoinRowSet is not needed every day, it can be handy when performing work against two related sets of data. This holds true especially when the application is not connected to a database all the time, or if you are trying to use as few Connection objects as possible.

13-12. Filtering Data in a RowSet

Problem

Your application queries the database and returns a large number of rows. The number of rows within the cached ResultSet is too large for the user to work with at one time. You would like to limit the number of rows that are visible so that you can perform different activities with different sets of data that have been queried from the table.

Solution

Use a FilteredRowSet to query the database and store the contents. The FilteredRowSet can be configured to filter the results that are returned from the query so that the only contents visible are the rows that you want to see. In the following example, a filter class is created that will later be used to filter the results that are returned from a database query. The filter in the example is used to limit the number of rows that are visible based on an author's last name. The following class contains the implementation of the filter:

```
package org.java9recipes.chapter13.recipe13_12;

import java.sql.SQLException;
import javax.sql.RowSet;
import javax.sql.rowset.Predicate;

public class AuthorFilter implements Predicate {

  private String[] authors;
  private String colName = null;
  private int colNumber = -1;

  public AuthorFilter(String[] authors, String colName) {
    this.authors = authors;
    this.colNumber = -1;
    this.colName = colName;
  }
```

```java
  public AuthorFilter(String[] authors, int colNumber) {
    this.authors = authors;
    this.colNumber = colNumber;
    this.colName = null;
  }

  @Override
  public boolean evaluate(Object value, String colName) {

    if (colName.equalsIgnoreCase(this.colName)) {
        for (String author : this.authors) {
            if (author.equalsIgnoreCase((String)value)) {
                return true;
            }
        }
    }
    return false;
  }

  @Override
  public boolean evaluate(Object value, int colNumber) {

    if (colNumber == this.colNumber) {
        for (String author : this.authors) {
            if (author.equalsIgnoreCase((String)value)) {
                return true;
            }
        }
    }
    return false;
  }

  @Override
  public boolean evaluate(RowSet rs) {

    if (rs == null)
      return false;

    try {
      for (int i = 0; i < this.authors.length; i++) {

        String authorLast = null;

        if (this.colNumber > 0) {
          authorLast = (String)rs.getObject(this.colNumber);
        } else if (this.colName != null) {
          authorLast = (String)rs.getObject(this.colName);
        } else {
          return false;
        }
```

```
      if (authorLast.equalsIgnoreCase(authors[i])) {
        return true;
      }
    }
  } catch (SQLException e) {
    return false;
  }
  return false;
  }

}
```

The filter is used by a `FilteredRowSet` to limit the visible results from a query. As you will see, utilizing a `FilteredRowSet` provides the capability of filtering data in an object-oriented manner at the application level, rather than doing so at the SQL database level. The benefit is that you can implement a series of filters and apply them to the same result set, returning the desired result. Using such an option eliminates the requirement to perform multiple database queries returning different data sets.

The following class demonstrates how to implement a `FilteredRowSet`. The `main()` method calls a method that is appropriately named `implementFilteredRowSet()`, and it contains the code that is used to filter the results of a query on the BOOK_AUTHOR and AUTHOR_WORK tables so that only results from the authors with the last name of DEA and JUNEAU are returned:

```
package org.java9recipes.chapter13.recipe13_12;

import com.sun.rowset.FilteredRowSetImpl;
import java.sql.Connection;
import java.sql.SQLException;
import javax.sql.RowSet;
import javax.sql.rowset.FilteredRowSet;
import org.java9recipes.chapter13.recipe13_01.CreateConnection;

public class FilteredRowSetExample {

    public static Connection conn = null;
    public static CreateConnection createConn;
    public static FilteredRowSet frs = null;

    public static void main(String[] args) {
        boolean successFlag = false;
        try {
            createConn = new CreateConnection();
            conn = createConn.getConnection();
            implementFilteredRowSet();
        } catch (java.sql.SQLException ex) {
            System.out.println(ex);
        } finally {

            if (conn != null) {
                try {
                    conn.close();
```

```
                    } catch (SQLException ex) {
                        ex.printStackTrace();
                    }
                }
                if (frs != null) {
                    try {
                        frs.close();
                    } catch (SQLException ex) {
                        ex.printStackTrace();
                    }
                }
            }
        }
    }

    public static void implementFilteredRowSet() {

        String[] authorArray = {"DEA", "JUNEAU"};

        AuthorFilter authorFilter = new AuthorFilter(authorArray, 2);

        try {
            frs = new FilteredRowSetImpl();

            frs.setCommand("SELECT TITLE, LASTNAME "
                    + "FROM BOOK_AUTHOR BA, "
                    + "     AUTHOR_WORK AW, "
                    + "     BOOK B "
                    + "WHERE AW.AUTHOR_ID = BA.ID "
                    + "AND B.ID = AW.BOOK_ID");

            frs.execute(conn);

            System.out.println("Prior to adding filter:");
            viewRowSet(frs);
            System.out.println("Adding author filter:");
            frs.beforeFirst();
            frs.setFilter(authorFilter);
            viewRowSet(frs);
        } catch (SQLException e) {
            e.printStackTrace();
        }

    }

    public static void viewRowSet(RowSet rs) {
        try {
            while (rs.next()) {
                System.out.println(rs.getString(1) + " - "
                        + rs.getString(2));
            }
```

```
        } catch (SQLException ex) {
            ex.printStackTrace();
        }
    }
}
```

The results of running this code would look similar to the following lines. Notice that only the rows of data corresponding to the authors listed in the filter are returned with the FilteredRowSet.

```
Successfully connected
Prior to adding filter:
Java 7 Recipes - JUNEAU
Java 7 Recipes - BEATY
Java 7 Recipes - DEA
Java 7 Recipes - GUIME
Java 7 Recipes - OCONNER
Java EE 7 Recipes - JUNEAU
Java FX 2.0 - Introduction by Example - DEA
Adding author filter:
Java 7 Recipes - JUNEAU
Java 7 Recipes - DEA
Java EE 7 Recipes - JUNEAU
Java FX 2.0 - Introduction by Example – DEA
```

How It Works

Often, the results that are returned from a database query contain a large number of rows. As you probably know, too many rows can create issues when it comes to visually working with data. It usually helps to limit the number of rows that are returned from a query by using a WHERE clause on a SQL statement so that only relevant data is returned. However, if an application retrieves data into an in-memory RowSet and then needs to filter the data by various criteria without additional database requests, an approach other than a query needs to be used. A FilteredRowSet can be used to filter data that is displayed within a populated RowSet so that it can be more manageable to work with.

There are two parts to working with a FilteredRowSet. First, a filter needs to be created which will be used to specify how the data should be filtered. The filter class should implement the Predicate interface. There may be multiple constructors, each accepting a different set of arguments, and the filter may contain multiple evaluate() methods that each accept different arguments and contain different implementations. The constructors should accept an array of contents that can be used to filter the RowSet. They should also accept a second argument, either the column name that the filter should be used against or the position of the column that the filter should be used against. In the solution to this recipe, the filter class is named AuthorFilter, and it is used to filter data per an array of author names. Its constructors each accept an array containing the author names to filter, along with either the column name or position. Each of the evaluate() methods has the task of determining whether a given row of data matches the specified filter; in this case, the author names that have been passed in via an array. The first evaluate() method is called if a column name is passed to the filter rather than a position, and the second evaluate() method is called if a column position is passed. The final evaluate() method accepts the RowSet itself, and it does the work of going through the data and returning a Boolean to indicate whether the corresponding column name/position values match the filter data.

The second part of the FilteredRowSet implementation is the work of the FilteredRowSet. This can be seen within the implementFilteredRowSet() method of the FilteredRowSetExample class. The FilteredRowSet will actually use the filter class that you've written to determine which rows to display. You can see that the array of values that will be passed to the filter class is the first declaration within the method. The second declaration is the instantiation of the filter class AuthorFilter. Of course, the array of filter values and the column position that corresponds to the filter values is passed into the filter constructor.

```
String[] authorArray = {"DEA", "JUNEAU"};

// Creates a filter using the array of authors
AuthorFilter authorFilter = new AuthorFilter(authorArray, 2);
```

To instantiate a FilteredRowSet, create a new instance of the FilteredRowSetImpl class. After it is instantiated, simply set the SQL query that will be used to obtain the results using the setCommand() method and then execute it by calling the executeQuery() method.

```
// Instantiate a new FilteredRowSet
frs = new FilteredRowSetImpl();
// Set the query
frs.setCommand("SELECT TITLE, LASTNAME "
            + "FROM BOOK_AUTHOR BA, "
            + "     AUTHOR_WORK AW, "
            + "     BOOK B "
            + "WHERE AW.AUTHOR_ID = BA.ID "
            + "AND B.ID = AW.BOOK_ID");
// Execute the query
frs.execute(conn);
```

▩ **Note**   You will receive a compile-time warning when using FilteredRowSetImpl because it is an older internal proprietary API produced by Sun Microsystems.

Notice that the filter has not yet been applied. Actually, at this point what you have is a scrollable RowSet that is populated with all the results from the query. The example displays those results before applying the filter. To apply the filter, use the setFilter() method, passing the filter as an argument. Once that has been done, the FilteredResultSet will display only those rows that match the criteria specified by the filter.

Again, the FilteredRowSet technique has its place, especially when you are working with an application that might not always be connected to a database. It is a powerful tool to use for filtering data, working with it, and then applying different filters and working on the new results. It is similar to applying WHERE clauses to a query without querying the database.

13-13. Querying and Storing Large Objects

Problem

The application that you are developing requires the storage of Strings of text that can include an unlimited number of characters.

Solution

It is best to use a character large object (CLOB) data type to store text when the size of the Strings that need to be stored is very large. The database diagram for the RECIPE_TEXT table is as follows:

```
RECIPE_TEXT (
id              int primary key,
recipe_id       int not null,
text            clob,
constraint recipe_text_fk
foreign key (recipe_id)
references recipes(id))
```

The code in the following example demonstrates how to load a CLOB into the database and how to query it:

```java
package org.java9recipes.chapter13.recipe13_13;

import java.sql.Clob;
import java.sql.Connection;
import java.sql.PreparedStatement;
import java.sql.ResultSet;
import java.sql.SQLException;
import org.java9recipes.chapter13.recipe13_01.CreateConnection;

public class LobExamples {

    public static Connection conn = null;
    public static CreateConnection createConn;

    public static void main(String[] args) {
        boolean successFlag = false;
        try {
            createConn = new CreateConnection();
            conn = createConn.getConnection();
            loadClob();
            readClob();
        } catch (java.sql.SQLException ex) {
            System.out.println(ex);
        } finally {

            if (conn != null) {
                try {
                    conn.close();
                } catch (SQLException ex) {
                    ex.printStackTrace();
                }
            }

        }
    }
```

347

```java
    public static void loadClob() {
        Clob textClob = null;
        String sql = "INSERT INTO RECIPE_TEXT VALUES("
                        + "next value for recipe_text_seq, "
                        + "(select id from recipes where recipe_number = '13-1'), "
                        + "?)";
        try (PreparedStatement pstmt = conn.prepareStatement(sql);) {
            textClob = conn.createClob();
            textClob.setString(1, "This will be the recipe text in clob format");
            // obtain the sequence number in real world
            // set the clob value
            pstmt.setClob(1, textClob);
            pstmt.executeUpdate();

        } catch (SQLException ex) {
            ex.printStackTrace();
        }
    }

    public static void readClob() {
        String qry = "select text from recipe_text";
        Clob theClob = null;
        try(PreparedStatement pstmt = conn.prepareStatement(qry);
                ResultSet rs = pstmt.executeQuery();) {

            while (rs.next()) {
                theClob = rs.getClob(1);
                System.out.println("Clob length: " + theClob.length());
                System.out.println(theClob.toString());
            }
            System.out.println(theClob.toString());

        } catch (SQLException ex) {

            ex.printStackTrace();
        }
    }
}
```

How It Works

If your application requires the storage of String values, you need to know how large those Strings might possibly become. Most databases have an upper boundary when it comes to the storage size of VARCHAR fields. For instance, the Oracle database has an upper boundary of 2,000 characters and anything exceeding that length will be cut off. If you have large amounts of text that need to be stored, use a CLOB field in the database.

A CLOB is handled a bit differently from a String within Java code. In fact, it is actually a bit odd to work with the first couple of times you use it because you have to create a CLOB from a Connection.

▦ **Note**   In reality, CLOBs and BLOBs (binary large objects) are not stored in the Oracle table where they are defined. Instead, a large object (LOB) locator is stored in the table column. Oracle might place the CLOB in a separate file on the database server. When Java creates the Clob object, it can be used to hold data for update to a specific LOB location in the database or to retrieve the data from a specific LOB location within the database.

Let's take a look at the loadClob() method contained in the solution to this recipe. As you can see, a Clob object is created using the Connection createClob() method. Once the Clob has been created, you set its contents using the setString() method by passing the position indicating where to place the String and the String of text itself:

```
textClob = conn.createClob();
textClob.setString(1, "This will be the recipe text in clob format");
```

Once you have created and populated the Clob, you simply pass it to the database using the PreparedStatement setClob() method. In the case of this example, the PreparedStatement performs a database insert into the RECIPE_TEXT table by calling the executeUpdate() method as usual.

Querying a Clob is fairly straightforward as well. As you can see in the readClob() method that is contained within the solution to this recipe, a PreparedStatement query is set up and the results are retrieved into a ResultSet. The only difference between using a Clob and a String is that you must load the Clob into a Clob type.

▦ **Note**   Calling the Clob getString() method will pass a funny-looking String of text that denotes a Clob object. Therefore, calling the Clob object's getAsciiStream() method will return the actual data that is stored in the Clob.

Although Clobs are fairly easy to use, they take a couple of extra steps to prepare. It is best to plan your applications accordingly and try to estimate whether the database fields you are using might need to be CLOBs due to size restrictions. Proper planning will prevent you from going back and changing standard String-based code to work with Clobs later.

13-14. Invoking Stored Procedures

Problem

Some logic that is required for your application is written as a database-stored procedure. You require the ability to invoke the stored procedure from within your application.

Solution

The following block of code shows the PL/SQL that is required to create the stored procedure that will be called by Java. The functionality of this stored procedure is very minor; it simply accepts a value and assigns that value to an OUT parameter so that the program can display it:

```
create or replace procedure dummy_proc (text IN VARCHAR2,
                                        msg OUT VARCHAR2) as
begin
    -- Do something, in this case the IN parameter value is assigned to the OUT parameter
    msg :=text;
end;
```

The CallableStatement in the following code executes this stored procedure that is contained within the database, passing the necessary parameters. The results of the OUT parameter are then displayed back to the user.

```
try(CallableStatement cs = conn.prepareCall("{call DUMMY_PROC(?,?)}");) {
    cs.setString(1, "This is a test");
    cs.registerOutParameter(2, Types.VARCHAR);
    cs.executeQuery();

    System.out.println(cs.getString(2));

} catch (SQLException ex){
    ex.printStackTrace();
}
```

Running the example class for this recipe will display the following output, which is the same as the input. This is because the DUMMY_PROC procedure simply assigns the contents if the IN parameter to the OUT parameter.

```
Successfully connected
This is a test
```

How It Works

It is not uncommon for an application to use database-stored procedures for logic that can be executed directly within the database. In order to call a database-stored procedure from Java, you must create a CallableStatement object, rather than use a PreparedStatement. In the solution to this recipe, a CallableStatement invokes a stored procedure named DUMMY_PROC. The syntax for instantiating the CallableStatement is similar to that of using a PreparedStatement. Use the Connection object's prepareCall() method, passing the call to the stored procedure. The stored procedure call must be enclosed in curly braces {} or the application will throw an exception.

```
cs = conn.prepareCall("{call DUMMY_PROC(?,?)}");
```

Once the CallableStatement has been instantiated, it can be used just like a PreparedStatement for setting the values of parameters. However, if a parameter is registered within the database-stored procedure as an OUT parameter, you must call a special method, registerOutParameter(), passing the parameter position and database type of the OUT parameter that you want to register. In the solution to this recipe, the OUT parameter is in the second position and it has a VARCHAR type.

```
cs.registerOutParameter(2, Types.VARCHAR);
```

To execute the stored procedure, call the executeQuery() method on the CallableStatement. Once this has been done, you can see the value of the OUT parameter by making a call to the CallableStatement getXXX() method that corresponds to the data type:

```
System.out.println(cs.getString(2));
```

A NOTE REGARDING STORED FUNCTIONS

Calling a stored database function is essentially the same as calling a stored procedure. However, the syntax to prepareCall() is slightly modified. To call a stored function, change the call within the curly braces to entail a returned value using a ? character. For instance, suppose that a function named DUMMY_FUNC accepted one parameter and returned a value. The following code would be used to make the call and return the value:

```
cs = conn.prepareCall("{? = call DUMMY_FUNC(?)}");
cs.registerOutParameter(1, Types.VARCHAR);
cs.setString(2, "This is a test");
cs.execute();
```

A call to cs.getString(1) would then retrieve the returned value.

13-15. Obtaining Dates for Database Use

Problem

You want to convert a LocalDate properly, in order to insert it into a database record.

Solution

Utilize the static java.sql.Date.valueOf(LocalDate) method to convert a LocalDate object to a java.sql.Date object, which can be utilized by JDBC for insertion or querying of the database. In the following example, the current date is inserted into a database column of type Date.

```
private static void insertRecord(
        String title,
        String publisher) {
    String sql = "INSERT INTO PUBLICATION VALUES("
            + "NEXT VALUE FOR PUBLICATION_SEQ, ?,?,?,?)";
    LocalDate pubDate = LocalDate.now();
```

```
    try (Connection conn = createConn.getConnection();
           PreparedStatement pstmt = conn.prepareStatement(sql);) {
        pstmt.setInt(1, 100);
        pstmt.setString(2, title);
        pstmt.setDate(3,  java.sql.Date.valueOf(pubDate));
        pstmt.setString(4, publisher);
        pstmt.executeUpdate();
        System.out.println("Record successfully inserted.");
    } catch (SQLException ex) {
        ex.printStackTrace();
    }
}
```

How It Works

In Java 8, the new Date-Time API (Chapter 4) is the preferred API for working with dates and times. Therefore, when working with date values and databases, the JDBC API must convert between SQL dates and new Date-Time LocalDate objects. The solution to this recipe demonstrates that to obtain an instance of java.sql.Date from a LocalDate object, you simply invoke the static java.sql.Date.valueOf() method, passing the pertinent LocalDate object.

13-16. Closing Resources Automatically

Problem

Rather than manually opening and closing resources with each database call, you would prefer to have the application handle such boilerplate code for you.

Solution

Use the try-with-resources syntax to automatically close the resources that you open. The following block of code uses this tactic to automatically close the Connection, Statement, and ResultSet resources when it is finished using them:

```
String qry = "select recipe_number, recipename, description from recipes";

try (Connection conn = createConn.getConnection();
        Statement stmt = conn.createStatement();
        ResultSet rs = stmt.executeQuery(qry);) {

    while (rs.next()) {
        String recipe = rs.getString("RECIPE_NUMBER");
        String name = rs.getString("RECIPE_NAME");
        String desc = rs.getString("DESCRIPTION");

        System.out.println(recipe + "\t" + name + "\t" + desc);
    }
} catch (SQLException e) {
    e.printStackTrace();
}
```

The resulting output from running this code should look similar to the following:

```
Successfully connected
13-1    Connecting to a Database        DriverManager and DataSource Implementations - More to Come
13-2    Querying a Database and Retrieving Results        Subject to Change
13-3    Handling SQL Exceptions Using SQLException
```

How It Works

Handling JDBC resources has always been a pain in the neck. There is a lot of boilerplate code that is required for closing resources when they are no longer needed. Since the release of Java SE 7, this has not been the case. Java 7 introduced automatic resource management using try-with-resources. Through the use of this technique, the developer no longer needs to close each resource manually, which is a change that can cut down on many lines of code.

In order to use this technique, you must instantiate all the resources for which you want to have automatic handling enabled within a set of parentheses after a try clause. In the solution to this recipe, the resources that are declared are Connection, Statement, and ResultSet.

```
try (Connection conn = createConn.getConnection();
        Statement stmt = conn.createStatement();
        ResultSet rs = stmt.executeQuery(qry);) {
```

Once those resources are out of scope, they are automatically closed. This means there is no longer a requirement to code a finally block to ensure that resources are closed. The automatic resource handling is available not only to database work, but to any resource that complies with the new java.lang.Autocloseable API. Other operations such as file I/O adhere to the new API as well. There is a single close() method within java.lang.Autoclosable that manages the closing of the resource. Classes that implement the java.io.Closeable interface can adhere to the API.

Summary

In many applications, databases have become essential for storing important information. As such, it is important to have a good understanding of how to utilize databases for use within applications. This chapter started from the beginning, covering recipes on getting started with database access. It then covered important topics such as how to securely access and modify data, transaction management, and data access when not connected to a network. You should now have a sound understanding of some techniques for working with data for your Java solutions. Do keep in mind that there are many data access solutions, and the recipes in this chapter cover just some of the ways to tackle the beast of information management.

CHAPTER 14

■ ■ ■

JavaFX Fundamentals

The JavaFX 8 API is Java's rich client GUI toolkit for developers to build cross-platform applications. JavaFX 8 was an update from JavaFX 2.2 that's based on a scene graph paradigm (retained mode) as opposed to the traditional immediate mode style rendering. JavaFX's scene graph is a tree-like data structure that maintains vector-based graphic nodes. The goal of JavaFX is to be used across many types of devices such as mobile devices, smartphones, TVs, tablet computers, and desktops. In the early days of JavaFX, applets were used to make JavaFX available via the web, and use on mobile devices was not yet possible, but nowadays these limitations are a thing of the past and JavaFX has much more traction across devices.

Before the creation of JavaFX, the development of rich Internet applications involved the gathering of many separate libraries and APIs to achieve highly functional applications. These separate libraries include Media, UI controls, Web, 3D, and 2D APIs. Because integrating these APIs can be rather difficult, the talented engineers at Sun Microsystems (now Oracle) created a new set of JavaFX libraries that combine all the same capabilities under one roof. JavaFX is the Swiss Army Knife of GUIs. JavaFX 8 is a pure Java (language) API that allows developers to leverage existing Java libraries and tools to develop applications that can be used just about everywhere.

Depending on who you talk to, you will likely encounter different definitions of "user experience" (or in the UI world, UX). But one fact still remains: users will always demand better content and increased usability from GUI applications. In light of this fact, developers and designers often work together to craft applications to fulfill this demand. JavaFX provides a toolkit that enables both the developer and designer (in many cases, they are the same person) to create functional yet aesthetically pleasing applications. Another thing to acknowledge is that if you are developing a game, media player, or the usual enterprise application, JavaFX will not only assist in developing richer UIs but you'll also find that the APIs are extremely well designed to greatly improve developer productivity.

There are entire books written on JavaFX, and it would be impossible to cover all the capabilities of the toolkit in just a few chapters. Hopefully, the recipes in this book can steer you in the right direction by providing practical and real-world examples. I encourage you to explore other resources to gain further insight into JavaFX. I highly recommend the following books: *Pro JavaFX Platform* (Apress, 2009), *Pro JavaFX 2.0 Platform* (Apress, 2012), *Pro JavaFX 8* **(Apress, 2014)**, and *JavaFX 8: Introduction by Example* (Apress, 2014). These books go in depth to help you create professional grade applications. In this chapter you will learn the fundamentals of JavaFX to rapidly develop Rich Internet applications. It provides you with a solid foundation for working with JavaFX.

© Josh Juneau 2017
J. Juneau, *Java 9 Recipes*, DOI 10.1007/978-1-4842-1976-8_14

■ **Note** For releases of JavaFX prior to JavaFX 8, the SDK was a separate download from the standard JDK. That is, the JavaFX 1.x and 2.x SDKs had to be downloaded and installed separately. JavaFX 8 changes that requirement, as it comes as part of JDK 8. This book covers JavaFX 8 only, although many of the solutions may function properly on JavaFX 2.x. If you need to install JavaFX 2.x, refer to the online documentation (http:// docs.oracle.com/javafx/) or a book that covers JavaFX 2.x, such as *JavaFX 2.0: Introduction by Example,* which was written by Carl Dea and published by Apress. To see the online JavaFX 8 documentation, visit http://docs.oracle.com/javase/8/javase-clienttechnologies.htm.

14-1. Creating a Simple User Interface

Problem

You want to create, code, compile, and run a simple JavaFX Hello World application.

Solution 1

Develop a JavaFX Hello World application using the JavaFX project-creation wizard in the NetBeans IDE.

Creating a JavaFX Hello World Application in NetBeans

To quickly get started with creating, coding, compiling, and running a simple JavaFX Hello World application using the NetBeans IDE, follow these steps:

1. Launch NetBeans IDE.

2. From the File menu, select New Project.

3. Under Choose Project and Categories, select the JavaFX folder.

4. Under Projects, select the JavaFX Application and click Next.

■ **Note** If this is your first JavaFX project in NetBeans, the JavaFX module may automatically activate at this time.

5. Specify **HelloWorldMain** for your project name.

6. Change or accept the defaults for the Project Location and Project Folder fields.

7. Ensure that the JavaFX Platform is set to JDK 1.9. Leave the *Create a Custom Preloader* box checked, as it automatically generates the code that is required to load and run your application.

8. Make sure the *Create Application Class* option is selected. Click Finish.

9. In the NetBeans IDE on the **Projects** tab, select the newly created project. Open the **Project Properties** dialog box to verify that the **Source/Binary** format settings are JDK 9. Click **Sources** under **Categories**.

10. After closing the Java Platform Manager window, click OK to close the **Project Properties** window.

To run and test your JavaFX Hello World application, access the Run menu and select Run Main Project. You could also right-click the project directory and choose Run from the contextual menu.

Figure 14-1 shows a simple JavaFX Hello World application launched from the NetBeans IDE.

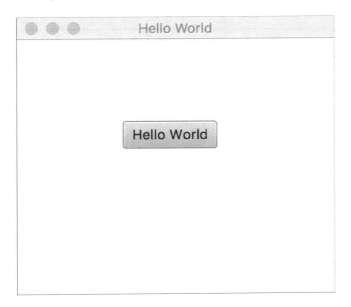

Figure 14-1. JavaFX Hello World launched from the NetBeans IDE

Solution 2

Use your favorite editor to code your JavaFX Hello World application. Once the Java file is created, you will use the command-line prompt to compile and run your JavaFX application. Following are the steps to create a JavaFX Hello World application to be compiled and run on the command-line prompt.

Creating a JavaFX Hello World Application in a Text Editor

To quickly get started:

1. Copy and paste the following code into your favorite editor and save the file as HelloWorldMain.java.

The following source code is for the JavaFX Hello World application:

```
package org.java9recipes.chapter14.recipe14_01;

import javafx.application.Application;
import javafx.scene.Scene;
import javafx.scene.control.Button;
import javafx.stage.Stage;
```

```java
import javafx.scene.Group;
public class HelloWorldMain extends Application {

    final Group root = new Group();
    /**
     * @param args the command line arguments
     */
    public static void main(String[] args) {
        Application.launch(args);
    }

    @Override
    public void start(Stage primaryStage) {
        primaryStage.setTitle("Hello World");
        Scene scene = new Scene(root, 300, 250);
        Button btn = new Button();
        btn.setLayoutX(100);
        btn.setLayoutY(80);
        btn.setText("Hello World");
        btn.setOnAction((event) -> {
                System.out.println("Hello World");
        });
        root.getChildren().add(btn);
        primaryStage.setScene(scene);
        primaryStage.show();
    }
}
```

2. After saving the file named HelloWorldMain.java, use the command-line
    prompt to navigate to the file.

3. Compile the source code file HelloWorldMain.java using the Java compiler
    javac:

    ```
    javac -d . HelloWorldMain.java
    ```

4. Run and test your JavaFX Hello World application. Assuming you are located
    in the same directory as the HelloWorldMain.java file, type the following
    command to run your JavaFX Hello World application from the command-line
    prompt:

    ```
    java org.java9recipes.chapter14.recipe14_01.HelloWorldMain
    ```

■ **Note**   This class can also be created within an existing JDK 8 or JDK 9 application. For instance, the project
that contains the sources for this book contains all of the JavaFX recipes in the org.java9recipes.chapter14
source package. This is possible since JavaFX no longer requires additional configuration; it is already part of
any JDK 8 or JDK 9 project.

How It Works

Following are descriptions of the two solutions. Both solutions require JavaFX 8 (or JavaFX 2.x along with JDK 7). Solution 1 demonstrates how to build a JavaFX application using the NetBeans IDE. Solution 2 covers the development of a simple JavaFX application via your favorite text editor, and use of the command-line or terminal to compile and execute JavaFX programs.

The NetBeans IDE makes it very easy to develop a JavaFX application via a JavaFX project. In fact, NetBeans provides a template Hello World application after following the JavaFX project-creation wizard. This is a great solution for beginning any JavaFX application, as it provides a great starting point for building more sophisticated solutions.

To create a simple JavaFX Hello World application using your favorite text editor, follow Solution 2, Steps 1 and 2. To compile and run your Hello World program on the command line, follow Solution 2, Steps 3 and 4. Once you enter the source code into your favorite editor and save the source file, compile and run the JavaFX program. Open the command-line or terminal window and navigate to the directory location of the Java file named `HelloWorldMain.java`.

Next, we review a way to compile the file using the command `javac -d . HelloWorldMain.java`. You will notice the `-d .` before the file name. This lets the Java compiler know where to put class files based on their package name. In this scenario, the `HelloWorldMain` package statement is `helloworldmain`, which will create a subdirectory under the current directory. The following commands will compile and run the JavaFX Hello World application:

```
cd \<path to project>\org\java9recipes\chapter14\recipe14_01

javac -d . HelloWorldMain.java

java helloworldmain.HelloWorldMain
```

▓ **Note** There are many ways to package and deploy JavaFX applications. To learn more, see "Learning How to Deploy and Package JavaFX Applications" at `http://docs.oracle.com/javafx/2/deployment/jfxpub-deployment.htm`. For in-depth JavaFX deployment strategies, see Oracle's "Deployment Guide" at `http://docs.oracle.com/javase/9/docs/technotes/guides/deploy/`.

In both solutions you'll notice in the source code that JavaFX applications extend the `javafx.application.Application` class. The Application class provides application lifecycle functions such as launching and stopping during runtime. This also provides a mechanism for Java applications to launch JavaFX GUI components in a thread safe manner. Keep in mind that synonymous to Java Swing's event dispatch thread (EDT), JavaFX has its own JavaFX application thread. New in JavaFX 8, it is possible for the EDT and the JavaFX application thread to be merged (see Recipe 14-18).

Taking a look at the code, in the `main()` method's entry point you launch the JavaFX application by simply passing in the command-line arguments to the `Application.launch()` method. Once the application is in a ready state, the framework internals will invoke the `start()` method to begin. When the `start()` method is invoked, a JavaFX `javafx.stage.Stage` object is available for the developer to use and manipulate.

You'll notice that some objects are oddly named, such as Stage and Scene. The designers of the API have modeled things similar to a theater or a play in which actors perform in front of an audience. With this same analogy, in order to show a play, there are basically one-to-many scenes that actors perform in. And, of course, all scenes are performed on a stage. In JavaFX the Stage is equivalent to an application window similar to Java Swing API JFrame or JDialog. You may think of a Scene object as a content pane capable

359

of holding zero-to-many Node objects. A Node is a fundamental base class for all scene graph nodes to be rendered. A scene graph is a tree data structure that maintains an internal model of all nodes or graphical objects that are part of an application. Commonly used nodes are UI controls and Shape objects. Similar to a tree data structure, a scene graph will contain children nodes by using a container class Group. You'll learn more about the Group class later when you look at the ObservableList, but for now think of them as Java Lists or Collections that are capable of holding Nodes.

Once the child nodes have been added, you set the primaryStage's (Stage) scene and call the show() method on the Stage object to show the JavaFX window.

One last thing: in this chapter most of the example applications are structured the same as this example, in which recipe code solutions will reside inside the start() method. Most of the recipes in this chapter follow the same pattern. For the sake of brevity, much of the boilerplate code is not shown. To see the full source listings of all the recipes, download the source code from the book's website.

14-2. Drawing Text

Problem

You want to draw custom text within a JavaFX application.

Solution

Create Text nodes to be placed on the JavaFX scene graph by utilizing the javafx.scene.text.Text class. As Text nodes are to be placed on the scene graph, you decide you want to create randomly positioned Text nodes rotated around their (x, y) positions scattered about the scene area.

The following code implements a JavaFX application that displays Text nodes scattered about the scene graph with random positions and colors:

```
primaryStage.setTitle("Chapter 14-2 Drawing Text");
Group root = new Group();
Scene scene = new Scene(root, 300, 250, Color.WHITE);
Random rand = new Random(System.currentTimeMillis());
for (int i = 0; i < 100; i++) {
    int x = rand.nextInt((int) scene.getWidth());
    int y = rand.nextInt((int) scene.getHeight());
    int red = rand.nextInt(255);
    int green = rand.nextInt(255);
    int blue = rand.nextInt(255);

    Text text = new Text(x, y, "Java 9 Recipes");

    int rot = rand.nextInt(360);
    text.setFill(Color.rgb(red, green, blue, .99));
    text.setRotate(rot);
    root.getChildren().add(text);
}

primaryStage.setScene(scene);
primaryStage.show();
```

Figure 14-2 shows random Text nodes scattered about the JavaFX scene graph.

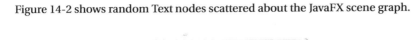

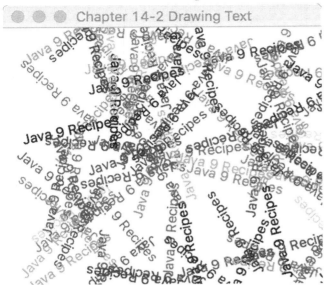

Figure 14-2. *Drawing text in random places*

How It Works

To draw text in JavaFX, you create a `javafx.scene.text.Text` node to be placed on the scene graph (`javafx.scene.Scene`). In this example you'll notice text objects with random colors and positions scattered about the Scene area.

First, you create a loop to generate random (x,y) coordinates to position Text nodes. Second, you create random color components between (0–255 RGB) to be applied to the Text nodes. Third, the rotation angle (in degrees) is a randomly generated value between (0–360 degrees) to cause the text to be slanted. The following code creates random values that will be assigned to a Text node's position, color, and rotation:

```
int x = rand.nextInt((int) scene.getWidth());
int y = rand.nextInt((int) scene.getHeight());
int red = rand.nextInt(255);
int green = rand.nextInt(255);
int blue = rand.nextInt(255);
int rot = rand.nextInt(360);
```

Once the random values are generated, they will be applied to the Text nodes, which will be drawn onto the scene graph. The following code snippet applies position (x, y), color (RGB), and rotation (angle in degrees) onto the Text node:

```
Text text = new Text(x, y, "Java 9 Recipes");
text.setFill(Color.rgb(red, green, blue, .99));
text.setRotate(rot);

root.getChildren().add(text);
```

You will begin to see the power of the scene graph API by its ease of use. Text nodes can be easily manipulated as if they were Shapes. Well, actually they are Shapes. Defined in the inheritance hierarchy, Text nodes extend from the javafx.scene.shape.Shape class and are therefore capable of doing interesting things such as being filled with colors or rotated about an angle. Although the text is colorized, this still tends to be somewhat boring. However, in the next recipe you will learn how to change a text's font.

14-3. Changing Text Fonts

Problem

You want to change text fonts and add special effects to the Text nodes.

Solution 1

Create a JavaFX application that uses the following classes to set the text font and apply embedded effects to Text nodes:

```
javafx.scene.text.Font
javafx.scene.effect.DropShadow
javafx.scene.effect.Reflection
```

The code that follows sets the font and applies effects to Text nodes. It uses the Serif, SanSerif, Dialog, and Monospaced fonts along with the drop shadow and reflection effects:

```
primaryStage.setTitle("Chapter 14-3 Changing Text Fonts");
Group root = new Group();
Scene scene = new Scene(root, 330, 250, Color.WHITE);

// Serif with drop shadow
Text java9recipes2 = new Text(50, 50, "Java 9 Recipes");
Font serif = Font.font("Serif", 30);
java9recipes2.setFont(serif);
java9recipes2.setFill(Color.RED);
DropShadow dropShadow = new DropShadow();
dropShadow.setOffsetX(2.0f);
dropShadow.setOffsetY(2.0f);
dropShadow.setColor(Color.rgb(50, 50, 50, .588));
java9recipes2.setEffect(dropShadow);
root.getChildren().add(java9recipes2);

// SanSerif
Text java9recipes3 = new Text(50, 100, "Java 8 Recipes");
Font sanSerif = Font.font("SanSerif", 30);
java9recipes3.setFont(sanSerif);
java9recipes3.setFill(Color.BLUE);
root.getChildren().add(java9recipes3);

// Dialog
Text java9recipes4 = new Text(50, 150, "Java 8 Recipes");
Font dialogFont = Font.font("Dialog", 30);
```

```
java9recipes4.setFont(dialogFont);
java9recipes4.setFill(Color.rgb(0, 255, 0));
root.getChildren().add(java9recipes4);

// Monospaced
Text java9recipes5 = new Text(50, 200, "Java 8 Recipes");
Font monoFont = Font.font("Monospaced", 30);
java9recipes5.setFont(monoFont);
java9recipes5.setFill(Color.BLACK);
root.getChildren().add(java9recipes5);

Reflection refl = new Reflection();
refl.setFraction(0.8f);
java9recipes5.setEffect(refl);

primaryStage.setScene(scene);
primaryStage.show();
```

Figure 14-3 shows the JavaFX application with various font styles and effects (drop shadow and reflection) applied to the Text nodes.

Figure 14-3. *Changing text fonts*

Solution 2

Make use of the new TextFlow node to assist in stringing rich text together. Use an FXML file to construct an object graph, and then apply Cascading Style Sheet (CSS) styles to the nodes of the graph within the FXML. This solution provides a better path for those who are more comfortable working in a markup language than in Java code. It also demonstrates how to use a style sheet to declare the styles for your application.

First, let's take a look at the FXML that's used to construct the layout. The following lines of markup construct a scene graph that contains a Pane enclosing a TextFlow. The TextFlow contains a series of Text nodes, each of which has different styles applied. The following listing contains the sources for textfonts.fxml.

```xml
<?xml version="1.0" encoding="UTF-8"?>

<?import java.net.*?>
<?import javafx.geometry.*?>
<?import javafx.scene.*?>
<?import javafx.scene.control.*?>
<?import javafx.scene.layout.*?>
<?import javafx.scene.text.*?>

<Scene width="200" height="75" fill="white" xmlns:fx="http://javafx.com/fxml">
    <stylesheets>
        <URL value="@textfonts.css"/>
    </stylesheets>
    <Pane fx:id="pane">

        <TextFlow styleClass="mainmessage">
            <Text styleClass="span1">Hello </Text>
            <Text text=" "/>
            <Text styleClass="span2, large">Java</Text>
            <Text styleClass="span3, slant">FX</Text>
            <Text text=" "/>
            <Text styleClass="cool">8</Text>

        </TextFlow>
    </Pane>
</Scene>
```

Within the FXML, a CSS named textfonts.css is imported. The following listing contains the styles, which reside in textfonts.css.

```css
.mainmessage {
    -fx-font-family: "Helvetica";
    -fx-font-size: 30px;
}

.span1 {
    -fx-color: "red";
}

.span2 {
    -fx-font-family: "Serif";
    -fx-font-size: 30px;
    -fx-color: "red";
}

.span3 {
    -fx-font-family: "Serif";
    -fx-font-size: 30px;
```

```
    -fx-fill: "orange";
    -fx-font-style: italic;
}

.cool {
    -fx-effect: dropshadow(gaussian, gray, 8, 0.5, 8, 8);
}
```

Lastly, a standard JavaFX application class is used to instantiate the example. The following sources are taken from ChangingTextFontsSolution2.java, and they demonstrate how to load the FXML and construct the stage.

```
@Override
public void start(Stage stage) throws Exception {
    stage.setTitle("Chapter 14-3 Changing Text Fonts Using TextFlow and FXML");
    stage.setScene((Scene) FXMLLoader.load(getClass().getResource("textfonts.fxml")));
    stage.show();
}
```

The resulting application will render a scene that resembles the result shown in Figure 14-4.

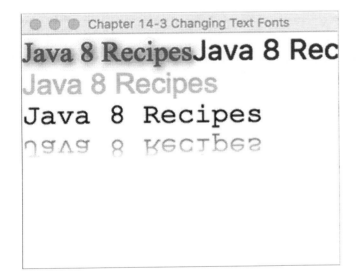

Figure 14-4. *TextFlow and FXML*

How It Works

Solution 1 demonstrates how to apply fonts to text using standard Java code. Vector-based graphics allow you to scale shapes and apply effects without issues of pixilation (jaggies). JavaFX nodes use vector-based graphics. In each Text node, you can create and set the font to be rendered onto the scene graph. Here is the code to create and set the font on a Text node:

```
Text java9recipes2 = new Text(50, 50, "Java 9 Recipes");
Font serif = Font.font("Serif", 30);
Java9recipes2.setFont(serif);
```

In solution 1, the drop shadow is a real effect (DropShadow) object and is actually applied to a single Text node instance. The DropShadow object is set to be positioned based on an x and y offset in relation to the Text node. You also can set the color of the shadow; here we set it to gray with a .588 opacity. Following is an example of setting a Text node's effect property with a drop shadow effect (DropShadow):

```
DropShadow dropShadow = new DropShadow();
dropShadow.setOffsetX(2.0f);
dropShadow.setOffsetY(2.0f);
dropShadow.setColor(Color.rgb(50, 50, 50, .588));
java9recipes2.setEffect(dropShadow);
```

Although this recipe is about setting text fonts, it also applied effects to Text nodes. Another effect has been added (just kicking it up a notch). While creating the last Text node using the monospaced font, the popular reflection effect is applied. The code following code is set so that .8 or 80% of the reflection is shown. The reflection values range from zero (0%) to one (100%). The following code snippet implements a reflection of 80% with a float value of 0.8f:

```
Reflection refl = new Reflection();
refl.setFraction(0.8f);
java9recipes5.setEffect(refl);
```

Solution 2 demonstrates how to construct a user interface using FXML, CSS, and Java. While this recipe focuses on text and fonts, it is important to note that FXML solutions clearly follow a model-view-controller standard, separating UI code from business logic. It is also important to note that if the UI in this example were to contain buttons or other nodes that contained actions, a controller class would need to be created as well to embody the action logic.

In the second example, an FXML file contains the structured layout for the user interface, which consists of a Scene, Pane, TextFlow, and a series of Text nodes. The scene contains a `<stylesheets>` element, which is used to specify which style sheets to apply to the elements within the XML. The Pane node is used as a base for the layout, and it contains each of the other nodes within the UI. The TextFlow node was introduced in JavaFX 8, and it is a special layout that is designed to lay out rich text. The TextFlow can lay many different Text nodes into a single flow.

As you can see from the FXML, each of the Text nodes within the TextFlow have different styles associated with them, based on those styles that have been defined within the attached style sheet. The properties for styles in JavaFX style sheets are preceded by –fx-, and property names and values are separated by a colon and terminated by a semicolon (;). For the most part, JavaFX style properties align nicely with standard CSS properties. For a complete summary, refer to the documentation at http://docs.oracle.com/javafx/2/css_tutorial/jfxpub-css_tutorial.htm.

The TextFlow uses the text and font of each node that is embedded within, as well as its own width and text alignment, to determine the placement of the text. Nodes other than Text can also be embedded within a TextFlow. When adding Text nodes to a TextFlow, you can set word wrap by specifying a maximum width of the TextFlow via the setMaxWidth() method. It is also possible to include a \n at the end of any Strings within a Text node to initiate a line break. The following code performs the same solution as 1, but uses TextFlow to lay out the Text nodes, rather than adding each to the scene graph separately.

```
primaryStage.setTitle("Chapter 14-3 Changing Text Fonts");
Group root = new Group();
Scene scene = new Scene(root, 330, 250, Color.WHITE);

// Serif with drop shadow
Text java9recipes2 = new Text(50, 50, "Java 9 Recipes");
Font serif = Font.font("Serif", 30);
```

```
java9recipes2.setFont(serif);
java9recipes2.setFill(Color.RED);
DropShadow dropShadow = new DropShadow();
dropShadow.setOffsetX(2.0f);
dropShadow.setOffsetY(2.0f);
dropShadow.setColor(Color.rgb(50, 50, 50, .588));
java9recipes2.setEffect(dropShadow);

// SanSerif
Text java9recipes3 = new Text(50, 100, "Java 8 Recipes\n");
Font sanSerif = Font.font("SanSerif", 30);
java9recipes3.setFont(sanSerif);
java9recipes3.setFill(Color.BLUE);

// Dialog
Text java9recipes4 = new Text(50, 150, "Java 8 Recipes\n");
Font dialogFont = Font.font("Dialog", 30);
java9recipes4.setFont(dialogFont);
java9recipes4.setFill(Color.rgb(0, 255, 0));

// Monospaced
Text java9recipes5 = new Text(50, 200, "Java 8 Recipes");
Font monoFont = Font.font("Monospaced", 30);
java9recipes5.setFont(monoFont);
java9recipes5.setFill(Color.BLACK);

Reflection refl = new Reflection();
refl.setFraction(0.8f);
java9recipes5.setEffect(refl);
TextFlow flow = new TextFlow(java9recipes2, java9recipes3, java9recipes4, java9recipes5);

root.getChildren().add(flow);
```

There were a lot of concepts introduced within this recipe. You will learn more about FXML in a later recipe, or for more information you can see the online documentation at http://docs.oracle.com/javafx/2/get_started/fxml:tutorial.htm. You an learn more about the TextFlow layout reading the documentation at http://docs.oracle.com/javase/8/javafx/api/javafx/scene/text/TextFlow.html.

14-4. Creating Shapes

Problem

You want to create shapes to be placed on the scene graph.

Solution

Use JavaFX's Arc, Circle, CubicCurve, Ellipse, Line, Path, Polygon, Polyline, QuadCurve, Rectangle, SVGPath, and Text classes in the javafx.scene.shape.* package. The following code draws various complex shapes. The first complex shape involves a cubic curve drawn in the shape of a sine wave. The next

shape, called the ice cream cone, uses the path class that contains path elements (javafx.scene.shape.
PathElement). The third shape is a Quadratic Bézier curve (QuadCurve) and it forms a smile. The final shape is
a delectable donut. You can create this donut shape by subtracting two ellipses (one smaller and one larger):

```
@Override
public void start(Stage primaryStage) {
    primaryStage.setTitle("Chapter 14-4 Creating Shapes");
    Group root = new Group();
    Scene scene = new Scene(root, 306, 550, Color.WHITE);

    // CubicCurve
    CubicCurve cubicCurve = new CubicCurve();
    cubicCurve.setStartX(50);
    cubicCurve.setStartY(75); // start pt (x1,y1)
    cubicCurve.setControlX1(80);
    cubicCurve.setControlY1(-25);// control pt1
    cubicCurve.setControlX2(110);
    cubicCurve.setControlY2(175);  // control pt2
    cubicCurve.setEndX(140);
    cubicCurve.setEndY(75);
    cubicCurve.setStrokeType(StrokeType.CENTERED);
    cubicCurve.setStrokeWidth(1);
    cubicCurve.setStroke(Color.BLACK);
    cubicCurve.setStrokeWidth(3);
    cubicCurve.setFill(Color.WHITE);

    root.getChildren().add(cubicCurve);

    // Ice cream
    Path path = new Path();

    MoveTo moveTo = new MoveTo();
    moveTo.setX(50);
    moveTo.setY(150);

    QuadCurveTo quadCurveTo = new QuadCurveTo();
    quadCurveTo.setX(150);
    quadCurveTo.setY(150);
    quadCurveTo.setControlX(100);
    quadCurveTo.setControlY(50);

    LineTo lineTo1 = new LineTo();
    lineTo1.setX(50);
    lineTo1.setY(150);

    LineTo lineTo2 = new LineTo();
    lineTo2.setX(100);
    lineTo2.setY(275);

    LineTo lineTo3 = new LineTo();
    lineTo3.setX(150);
    lineTo3.setY(150);
```

```
path.getElements().add(moveTo);
path.getElements().add(quadCurveTo);
path.getElements().add(lineTo1);
path.getElements().add(lineTo2);
path.getElements().add(lineTo3);
path.setTranslateY(30);
path.setStrokeWidth(3);
path.setStroke(Color.BLACK);

root.getChildren().add(path);

// QuadCurve create a smile
QuadCurve quad = new QuadCurve();
quad.setStartX(50);
quad.setStartY(50);
quad.setEndX(150);
quad.setEndY(50);
quad.setControlX(125);
quad.setControlY(150);
quad.setTranslateY(path.getBoundsInParent().getMaxY());
quad.setStrokeWidth(3);
quad.setStroke(Color.BLACK);
quad.setFill(Color.WHITE);

root.getChildren().add(quad);

// outer donut
Ellipse bigCircle = new Ellipse(100, 100, 50, 75/2);
//bigCircle.setTranslateY(quad.getBoundsInParent().getMaxY());
bigCircle.setStrokeWidth(3);
bigCircle.setStroke(Color.BLACK);
bigCircle.setFill(Color.WHITE);

// donut hole
Ellipse smallCircle = new Ellipse(100, 100, 35/2, 25/2);

// make a donut
Shape donut = Path.subtract(bigCircle, smallCircle);
donut.setStrokeWidth(1);
donut.setStroke(Color.BLACK);
// orange glaze
donut.setFill(Color.rgb(255, 200, 0));

// add drop shadow
DropShadow dropShadow = new DropShadow();
dropShadow.setOffsetX(2.0f);
dropShadow.setOffsetY(2.0f);
dropShadow.setColor(Color.rgb(50, 50, 50, .588));

donut.setEffect(dropShadow);
```

369

```
// move slightly down for spacing
donut.setTranslateY(quad.getBoundsInParent().getMinY() + 10);

root.getChildren().add(donut);

primaryStage.setScene(scene);
primaryStage.show();
}
```

Figure 14-5 displays the sine wave, ice cream cone, smile, and donut shapes created using JavaFX.

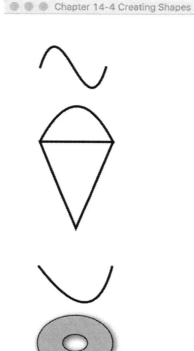

Figure 14-5. *Creating shapes*

How It Works

In this solution, you generated some basic 2D shapes. The first shape is a javafx.scene.shape.CubicCurve class, which allows you to construct a cubic curve (a "squiggly line") effect. To create a cubic curve, simply look for the appropriate constructor to be instantiated. The following code snippet is used to create a javafx.scene.shape.CubicCurve instance:

```
CubicCurve cubicCurve = new CubicCurve();
cubicCurve.setStartX(50);
cubicCurve.setStartY(75); // start pt (x1,y1)
```

```
cubicCurve.setControlX1(80);
cubicCurve.setControlY1(-25);// control pt1
cubicCurve.setControlX2(110);
cubicCurve.setControlY2(175);  // control pt2
cubicCurve.setEndX(140);
cubicCurve.setEndY(75);
cubicCurve.setStrokeType(StrokeType.CENTERED);
cubicCurve.setStrokeWidth(1);
cubicCurve.setStroke(Color.BLACK);
cubicCurve.setStrokeWidth(3);
cubicCurve.setFill(Color.WHITE);
```

You begin by instantiating a CubicCurve() instance. Next, the curve's attributes are specified in any order by utilizing the object's setter methods and passing a single value to each. Once you're finished specifying values on the CubicCurve() object, you can add it to the scene graph using the following notation:

```
root.getChildren().add(cubicCurve);
```

The ice cream cone shape is created using the javafx.scene.shape.Path class. As each path element is created and added to the Path object, each element is ***not*** considered a graph node (javafx.scene.Node). This means they do not extend from the javafx.scene.shape.Shape class and cannot be a child node in a scene graph to be displayed. When looking at the Javadoc (see http://docs.oracle.com/javase/8/javafx/api/javafx/scene/shape/Path.html), you will notice that a Path class extends from the Shape class that extends from the (javafx.scene.Node) class, and therefore a Path is a graph node, but Path elements do not extend from the Shape class. Path elements actually extend from the javafx.scene.shape.PathElement class, which is only used in the context of a Path object. So you won't be able to instantiate a LineTo class to be put in the scene graph. Just remember that the classes with To as a suffix are path elements, not real Shape nodes. For example, the MoveTo and LineTo object instances are Path elements added to a Path object, not shapes that can be added to the scene. The following are Path elements added to a Path object to draw an ice cream cone:

```
// Ice cream
Path path = new Path();

MoveTo moveTo = new MoveTo();
moveTo.setX(50);
moveTo.setY(150);

...// Additional Path Elements created.
LineTo lineTo1 = new LineTo();
lineTo1.setX(50);
lineTo1.setY(150);

...// Additional Path Elements created.

path.getElements().add(moveTo);
path.getElements().add(quadCurveTo);
path.getElements().add(lineTo1);
```

Rendering the QuadCurve (smile) object, you instantiate a new QuadCurve object and set each of the attributes accordingly. Again, each of the attributes accepts a single value.

Last is the tasty donut shape with a drop shadow effect, which is actually created by two circular ellipses. By subtracting the smaller ellipse (donut hole) from the larger ellipse area, a newly derived shape is created and returned using the `Path.subtract()` method. Following is the code snippet that creates the donut shape using the `Path.subtract()` method:

```
// outer donut
Ellipse bigCircle = ...//Outer shape area

// donut hole
Ellipse smallCircle = ...// Inner shape area

// make a donut
Shape donut = Path.subtract(bigCircle, smallCircle);
```

Next, a drop shadow effect is added to the donut. This time instead of drawing the shape twice, similar to a prior recipe, you draw it once and use the `setEffect()` method to apply a `DropShadow` object instance to the donut Shape object. Similar to the prior technique, you set the offset of the shadow by calling `setOffsetX()` and `setOffsetY()`.

■ **Note**   In previous releases, builder objects could be used to create shapes a bit more easily. However, the builder classes were removed from JavaFX 8+ due to performance and bloating issues. If you're maintaining code that utilizes builder classes, it is recommended that you to migrate away from them and make use of the standard objects, as demonstrated in this recipe.

14-5. Assigning Colors to Objects

Problem

You want to fill your shapes with simple colors and gradient colors.

Solution

In JavaFX, all shapes can be filled with simple colors and gradient colors. The following are the main classes used to fill shape nodes:

```
javafx.scene.paint.Color
javafx.scene.paint.LinearGradient
javafx.scene.paint.Stop
javafx.scene.paint.RadialGradient
```

The following code uses the preceding classes to add radial and linear gradient colors as well as transparent (alpha channel level) colors to shapes. This recipe uses an ellipse, a rectangle, and a rounded rectangle. A solid black line (as depicted in Figure 14-5) also appears in the recipe to demonstrate the transparency of the shape's color.

```java
public void start(Stage primaryStage) {
    primaryStage.setTitle("Chapter 14-5 Assigning Colors To Objects");
    Group root = new Group();
    Scene scene = new Scene(root, 350, 300, Color.WHITE);

    Ellipse ellipse = new Ellipse(100, 50 + 70/2, 50, 70/2);
    RadialGradient gradient1 = new RadialGradient(0,
                                    .1,    // focus angle
                                    80,    // focus distance
                                    45,    // centerX
                                    120,   // centerY
                                    false, // proportional
                                    CycleMethod.NO_CYCLE,
                                    new Stop(0, Color.RED), new Stop(1, Color.
                                    BLACK));

    ellipse.setFill(gradient1);
    root.getChildren().add(ellipse);

    // Create line
    Line blackLine = new Line();
    blackLine.setStartX(170);
    blackLine.setStartY(30);
    blackLine.setEndX(20);
    blackLine.setEndY(140);
    blackLine.setFill(Color.BLACK);
    blackLine.setStrokeWidth(10.0f);
    blackLine.setTranslateY(ellipse.prefHeight(-1) + ellipse.getLayoutY() + 10);

    root.getChildren().add(blackLine);

    // Create rectangle
    Rectangle rectangle = new Rectangle();
    rectangle.setX(50);
    rectangle.setY(50);
    rectangle.setWidth(100);
    rectangle.setHeight(70);
    rectangle.setTranslateY(ellipse.prefHeight(-1) + ellipse.getLayoutY() + 10);

    // Create linear gradient
    LinearGradient linearGrad = new LinearGradient(
            50,    //startX
            50,    //startY
            50,    //endX
            50 + rectangle.prefHeight(-1) + 25,    //endY
            false, //proportional
            CycleMethod.NO_CYCLE,
            new Stop(0.1f, Color.rgb(255, 200, 0, .784)),
            new Stop(1.0f, Color.rgb(0, 0, 0, .784)));

    rectangle.setFill(linearGrad);
    root.getChildren().add(rectangle);
```

```
// Create rectangle with rounded corners
Rectangle roundRect = new Rectangle();
roundRect.setX(50);
roundRect.setY(50);
roundRect.setWidth(100);
roundRect.setHeight(70);
roundRect.setArcWidth(20);
roundRect.setArcHeight(20);
roundRect.setTranslateY(ellipse.prefHeight(-1) +
                ellipse.getLayoutY() +
                10 +
                roundRect.prefHeight(-1) +
                roundRect.getLayoutY() + 10);

LinearGradient cycleGrad = new LinearGradient(50,
                                50,
                                70,
                                70,
                                false,
                                CycleMethod.REFLECT,
                                new Stop(0f, Color.rgb(0, 255, 0, .784)),
                                new Stop(1.0f, Color.rgb(0, 0, 0, .784)));

roundRect.setFill(cycleGrad);
root.getChildren().add(roundRect);

primaryStage.setScene(scene);
primaryStage.show();
}
```

Figure 14-6 displays the various types of colorized fills that can be applied to shapes.

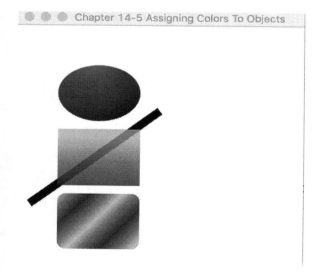

Figure 14-6. *Color shapes*

How It Works

Figure 14-5 shows shapes displayed from top to bottom starting with an ellipse, rectangle, and a rounded rectangle having colored gradient fills. When drawing the eclipse shape, you will be using a radial gradient that appears as if it were a 3D spherical object. Next, a rectangle filled with a yellow semitransparent linear gradient is created. A thick black line shape was drawn behind the yellow rectangle to demonstrate the rectangle's semitransparent color. Lastly, a rounded rectangle filled with a green-and-black reflective linear gradient resembling 3D tubes in a diagonal direction is generated.

The amazing thing about colors with gradients is that they can often make shapes appear three-dimensional. Gradient paint allows you to interpolate between two or more colors, which gives the shape depth. JavaFX provides two types of gradients: a radial (RadialGradient) and a linear (LinearGradient) gradient. A radial gradient (RadialGradient) is applied to the ellipse shape in the example.

Table 14-1 is taken from the JavaFX 8 Javadoc definitions found for the RadialGradient class (http://docs.oracle.com/javase/8/javafx/api/javafx/scene/paint/RadialGradient.html).

Table 14-1. *RadialGradient Properties*

Property	Data Type	Description
focusAngle	double	Angle in degrees from the center of the gradient to the focus point to which the first color is mapped
focusDistance	double	Distance from the center of the gradient to the focus point to which the first color is mapped
centerX	double	X coordinate of the center point of the gradient's circle
centerY	double	Y coordinate of the center point of the gradient's circle
Radius	double	Radius of the circle defining the extents of the color gradient
Proportional	boolean	Coordinates and sizes are proportional to the shape that this gradient fills
cycleMethod	CycleMethod	Cycle method applied to the gradient
opaque stops	boolean List<Stop>	Whether the paint is completely opaque Gradient's color specification

In this recipe, the focus angle is set to zero, the distance is set to .1, the center X and Y are set to (80,45), the radius is set to 120 pixels, the proportional is set to false, the cycle method is set to the no cycle (CycleMethod.NO_CYCLE), and the two color stop values are set to red (Color.RED) and black (Color.BLACK). These settings create a radial gradient by starting with the color red at a center position of (80, 45) (upper left of the ellipse) and then interpolating it to the color black with a distance of 120 pixels (radius).

Next, a rectangle having a yellow semitransparent linear gradient is created. A linear gradient (LinearGradient) paint is used for the yellow rectangle.

Table 14-2 is taken from the JavaFX 8 Javadoc definitions found for the LinearGradient class (see http://docs.oracle.com/javase/8/javafx/api/javafx/scene/paint/LinearGradient.html).

Table 14-2. LinearGradient Properties

Property	Data Type	Description
startX	double	X coordinate of the gradient axis start point
startY	double	Y coordinate of the gradient axis start point
endX	double	X coordinate of the gradient axis end point
endY	double	Y coordinate of the gradient axis end point
proportional	boolean	Whether the coordinates are proportional to the shape that this gradient fills
cycleMethod opaque	CycleMethod boolean	Cycle method applied to the gradient Whether this paint is completely opaque
stops	List<Stop>	Gradient's color specification

To create a linear gradient paint, you specify the `startX`, `startY`, `endX`, and `endY` for the start\end points. The start and end point coordinates denote where the gradient pattern starts and stops.

To create the second shape (yellow rectangle), set the start X and Y to (50, 50), the end X and Y to (50, 75), the proportional to false, the cycle method to no cycle (`CycleMethod.NO_CYCLE`), and the two color stop values to yellow (`Color.YELLOW`) and black (`Color.BLACK`), with an alpha transparency of .784. These settings provide a linear gradient for the rectangle from top to bottom, with a starting point of (50, 50) (top left of the rectangle). It then interpolates to the color black (bottom left of the rectangle).

Finally, you'll notice a rounded rectangle with a repeating pattern of a gradient using green and black in a diagonal direction. This is a simple linear gradient paint that is the same as the linear gradient paint (`LinearGradient`), except that the start X, Y and the end X, Y are set in a diagonal position, and the cycle method is set to reflect (`CycleMethod.REFLECT`). When specifying the cycle method to reflect (`CycleMethod.REFLECT`), the gradient pattern will repeat or cycle between the colors. The following code snippet implements the rounded rectangle having a cycle method of reflect (`CycleMethod.REFLECT`):

```
LinearGradient cycleGrad = new LinearGradient(50,
                                  50,
                                  70,
                                  70,
                                  false,
                                  CycleMethod.REFLECT,
                                  new Stop(0f, Color.rgb(0, 255, 0, .784)),
                                  new Stop(1.0f, Color.rgb(0, 0, 0, .784)));
```

14-6. Creating Menus

Problem

You want to create standard menus in your JavaFX applications.

Solution

Employ JavaFX's menu controls to provide standardized menu capabilities such as check box menus, radio menus, submenus, and separators. The following are the main classes used to create menus.

```
javafx.scene.control.MenuBar
javafx.scene.control.Menu
javafx.scene.control.MenuItem
```

The following code calls into play all the menu capabilities listed previously. The example code simulates a building security application containing menu options to turn on cameras, sound an alarm, and select contingency plans.

```java
public void start(Stage primaryStage) {
    primaryStage.setTitle("Chapter 14-6 Creating Menus");
    Group root = new Group();
    Scene scene = new Scene(root, 300, 250, Color.WHITE);

    MenuBar menuBar = new MenuBar();

    // File menu - new, save, exit
    Menu menu = new Menu("File");
    menu.getItems().add(new MenuItem("New"));
    menu.getItems().add(new MenuItem("Save"));
    menu.getItems().add(new SeparatorMenuItem());
    menu.getItems().add(new MenuItem("Exit"));

    menuBar.getMenus().add(menu);

    // Cameras menu - camera 1, camera 2
    Menu tools = new Menu("Cameras");
    CheckMenuItem item1 = new CheckMenuItem();
    item1.setText("Show Camera 1");
    item1.setSelected(true);
    tools.getItems().add(item1);

    CheckMenuItem item2 = new CheckMenuItem();
    item2.setText("Show Camera 2");
    item2.setSelected(true);
    tools.getItems().add(item2);

    menuBar.getMenus().add(tools);

    // Alarm
    Menu alarm = new Menu("Alarm");
    ToggleGroup tGroup = new ToggleGroup();

    RadioMenuItem soundAlarmItem = new RadioMenuItem();
    soundAlarmItem.setToggleGroup(tGroup);
    soundAlarmItem.setText("Sound Alarm");

    RadioMenuItem stopAlarmItem = new RadioMenuItem();
    stopAlarmItem.setToggleGroup(tGroup);
    stopAlarmItem.setText("Alarm Off");
    stopAlarmItem.setSelected(true);
```

```
alarm.getItems().add(soundAlarmItem);
alarm.getItems().add(stopAlarmItem);

Menu contingencyPlans = new Menu("Contingent Plans");
contingencyPlans.getItems().add(new CheckMenuItem("Self Destruct in T minus 50"));
contingencyPlans.getItems().add(new CheckMenuItem("Turn off the coffee machine "));
contingencyPlans.getItems().add(new CheckMenuItem("Run for your lives! "));

alarm.getItems().add(contingencyPlans);
menuBar.getMenus().add(alarm);

menuBar.prefWidthProperty().bind(primaryStage.widthProperty());

root.getChildren().add(menuBar);
primaryStage.setScene(scene);
primaryStage.show();
}
```

Figure 14-7 shows a simulated building security application containing checked, and submenu items.

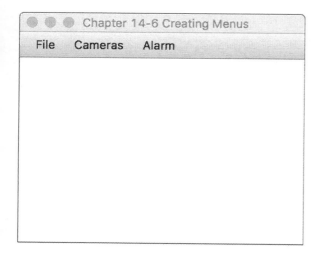

Figure 14-7. *Creating menus*

How It Works

Menus provide standard ways to allow users to select options from windowed platform applications. Menus should also have hot keys or keyboard equivalents. Users will often want to use the keyboard instead of the mouse to navigate the menu. This recipe parallels Recipe 14-8, and you'll notice lots of similarities.

To create a menu, first create an instance of a MenuBar that will contain one-to-many menu (MenuItem) objects. Creating a menu bar:

```
MenuBar menuBar = new MenuBar();
```

Secondly, create menu (Menu) objects that contain one-to-many menu item (MenuItem) objects and other Menu objects making submenus. To create a menu:

```
Menu menu = new Menu("File");
```

Third, create menu items to be added to Menu objects, such as menu (MenuItem), check (CheckMenuItem), and radio menu items (RadioMenuItem). Menu items can have icons in them. We don't showcase this in the recipe, but we encourage you to explore the various constructors for all menu items (MenuItem). When creating a radio menu item (RadioMenuItem), you should be aware of the ToggleGroup class. The ToggleGroup class is also used on regular radio buttons (RadioButtons) to allow only one selected option at any one time. The following code creates radio menu items (RadioMenuItems) to be added to a Menu object:

```
// Alarm
Menu alarm = new Menu("Alarm");
ToggleGroup tGroup = new ToggleGroup();

RadioMenuItem soundAlarmItem = new RadioMenuItem();
soundAlarmItem.setToggleGroup(tGroup);
soundAlarmItem.setText("Sound Alarm");

RadioMenuItem stopAlarmItem = new RadioMenuItem();
stopAlarmItem.setToggleGroup(tGroup);
stopAlarmItem.setText("Alarm Off");
stopAlarmItem.setSelected(true);

alarm.getItems().add(soundAlarmItem);
alarm.getItems().add(stopAlarmItem);
```

At times you may want to separate menu items with a visual line separator. To create a visual separator, create an instance of a SeparatorMenuItem class to be added to a menu via the getItems() method. The method getItems() returns an observable list of MenuItem objects (ObservableList<MenuItem>). As you will see in Recipe 14-10, you can be notified when items in a collection are altered. The following code line adds a visual line separator (SeparatorMenuItem) to the menu:

```
menu.getItems().add(new SeparatorMenuItem());
```

Other menu items used are the check menu item (CheckMenuItem) and the radio menu item (RadioMenuItem), and they are similar to their counterparts in JavaFX UI controls check box (CheckBox) and radio button (RadioButton), respectively.

Prior to adding the menu bar to the scene, you will notice the bound property between the preferred width of the menu bar and the width of the Stage object via the bind() method. When binding these properties you will see the menu bar's width stretch when the user resizes the screen. You will see how binding works in Recipe 14-9. This code snippet shows the binding between the menu bar's width property and the stage's width property.

```
menuBar.prefWidthProperty().bind(primaryStage.widthProperty());
root.getChildren().add(menuBar);
```

14-7. Adding Components to a Layout

Problem

You want to add UI components to a layout similar to a grid type layout for easy placement.

Solution

Use JavaFX's *javafx.scene.layout.GridPane* class. This source code implements a simple UI form containing first and last name field controls and using the grid pane layout node (*javafx.scene.layout.GridPane*):

```
GridPane gridpane = new GridPane();
gridpane.setPadding(new Insets(5));
gridpane.setHgap(5);
gridpane.setVgap(5);

Label fNameLbl = new Label("First Name");
TextField fNameFld = new TextField();
Label lNameLbl = new Label("First Name");
TextField lNameFld = new TextField();
Button saveButt = new Button("Save");

// First name label
GridPane.setHalignment(fNameLbl, HPos.RIGHT);
gridpane.add(fNameLbl, 0, 0);

// Last name label
GridPane.setHalignment(lNameLbl, HPos.RIGHT);
gridpane.add(lNameLbl, 0, 1);

// First name field
GridPane.setHalignment(fNameFld, HPos.LEFT);
gridpane.add(fNameFld, 1, 0);

// Last name field
GridPane.setHalignment(lNameFld, HPos.LEFT);
gridpane.add(lNameFld, 1, 1);

// Save button
GridPane.setHalignment(saveButt, HPos.RIGHT);
gridpane.add(saveButt, 1, 2);

root.getChildren().add(gridpane);
```

Figure 14-8 depicts a small form containing UI controls laid out using a grid pane layout node.

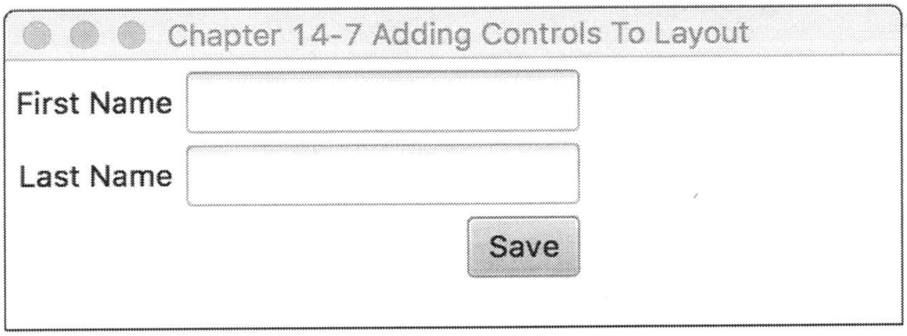

Figure 14-8. *Adding controls to a layout*

How It Works

One of the greatest challenges in building user interfaces is how controls can be placed onto the display area. When developing GUI applications, it is ideal for an application to allow the users to move and adjust the size of their viewable area while maintaining a pleasant user experience. Similar to Java Swing, JavaFX layout has stock layouts that provide the most common ways to display UI controls on the scene graph. This recipe demonstrates the GridPane class.

Recall Recipe 14-4, in which you implemented a custom layout to display components in a grid-like manner. You may notice similarities, but we left a lot of implementation features out, such as adjusting min/max sizes, padding, and vertical alignments. Amazingly, the JavaFX team has created a robust grid-like layout called the GridPane.

First you create an instance of a GridPane. Next, you set the padding by using an instance of an Inset object. After setting the padding, you simply set the horizontal and vertical gap. The following code snippet instantiates a grid pane (GridPane) with padding, horizontal, and vertical gaps set to 5 (pixels):

```
GridPane gridpane = new GridPane();
gridpane.setPadding(new Insets(5));
gridpane.setHgap(5);
gridpane.setVgap(5);
```

The padding is the top, right, bottom, and left spacing around the region's content in pixels. When obtaining the preferred size, the padding will be included in the calculation. Setting the horizontal and vertical gaps relate to the spacing between UI controls within the cells.

Next, simply place each UI control into its respective cell location. All cells are zero relative. Following is a code snippet that adds a Save button UI control into a grid pane layout node (GridPane) at cell (1, 2):

```
gridpane.add(saveButt, 1, 2);
```

The layout also allows you to horizontally or vertically align controls in the cell. The following code statement right-aligns the Save button:

```
GridPane.setHalignment(saveButt, HPos.RIGHT);
```

14-8. Generating Borders

Problem

You want to create and customize borders around an image.

Solution

Create an application to dynamically customize border regions using JavaFX's CSS styling API.

The following code creates an application that has a CSS editor text area and a border view region surrounding an image. By default, the editor's text area will contain JavaFX styling selectors that create a dashed blue line surrounding the image. You will have the opportunity to modify styling selector values in the CSS Editor by clicking the Bling! button to apply border settings.

```
primaryStage.setTitle("Chapter 14-8 Generating Borders");
Group root = new Group();
Scene scene = new Scene(root, 600, 330, Color.WHITE);

// create a grid pane
GridPane gridpane = new GridPane();
gridpane.setPadding(new Insets(5));
gridpane.setHgap(10);
gridpane.setVgap(10);

// label CSS Editor
Label cssEditorLbl = new Label("CSS Editor");
GridPane.setHalignment(cssEditorLbl, HPos.CENTER);
gridpane.add(cssEditorLbl, 0, 0);

// label Border View
Label borderLbl = new Label("Border View");
GridPane.setHalignment(borderLbl, HPos.CENTER);
gridpane.add(borderLbl, 1, 0);

// Text area for CSS editor
final TextArea cssEditorFld = new TextArea();
cssEditorFld.setPrefRowCount(10);
cssEditorFld.setPrefColumnCount(100);
cssEditorFld.setWrapText(true);
cssEditorFld.setPrefWidth(150);
GridPane.setHalignment(cssEditorFld, HPos.CENTER);
gridpane.add(cssEditorFld, 0, 1);

String cssDefault = "-fx-border-color: blue;\n"
        + "-fx-border-insets: 5;\n"
        + "-fx-border-width: 3;\n"
        + "-fx-border-style: dashed;\n";

cssEditorFld.setText(cssDefault);
```

```
// Border decorate the picture
final ImageView imv = new ImageView();
final Image image2 = new Image(GeneratingBorders.class.getResourceAsStream("smoke_glass_
buttons1.png"));
imv.setImage(image2);

final HBox pictureRegion = new HBox();
pictureRegion.setStyle(cssDefault);
pictureRegion.getChildren().add(imv);
gridpane.add(pictureRegion, 1, 1);

Button apply = new Button("Bling!");
GridPane.setHalignment(apply, HPos.RIGHT);
gridpane.add(apply, 0, 2);

apply.setOnAction((e) -> {
    pictureRegion.setStyle(cssEditorFld.getText());
});

root.getChildren().add(gridpane);
primaryStage.setScene(scene);
primaryStage.show();
```

Figure 14-9 illustrates the border customizer application.

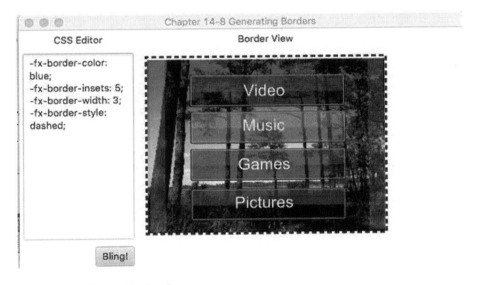

Figure 14-9. *Generating borders*

383

How It Works

JavaFX is capable of styling JavaFX nodes similar to CSS in the world of web development (also demonstrated in Recipe 14-3). This powerful API can alter a node's background color, font, border, and many other attributes, essentially allowing the developer or designer to skin GUI controls using CSS.

This solution to this recipe allows users to enter JavaFX CSS styles in the left text area and, by clicking the Bling! button on the UI, apply the style around the image shown to the right. Based on the type of node, there are limitations to what styles can be set. To see a full listing of all style selectors, refer to the JavaFX CSS Reference Guide: http://docs.oracle.com/javase/8/javafx/api/javafx/scene/doc-files/cssref.html.

In the first step of applying JavaFX CSS styles, you must determine which type of node you want to style. When setting attributes on various node types, you will discover that certain nodes have limitations. In this recipe, the intent was to put a border around the ImageView object. Because ImageView is not extending from Region, it doesn't contain border style properties. So, to resolve this, simply create an HBox layout to contain the imageView and apply the JavaFX CSS against the HBox. The following code applies JavaFX CSS border styles to a horizontal box region (HBox) using the setStyle() method:

```
String cssDefault = "-fx-border-color: blue;\n"
        + "-fx-border-insets: 5;\n"
        + "-fx-border-width: 3;\n"
  + "-fx-border-style: dashed;\n";
final ImageView imv = new ImageView();
...//
final HBox pictureRegion = new HBox();
pictureRegion.setStyle(cssDefault);
pictureRegion.getChildren().add(imv);
```

14-9. Binding Expressions

Problem

You want to synchronize changes between two values.

Solution

Use the javafx.beans.binding.* and javafx.beans.property.* packages to bind variables. There is more than one scenario to consider when binding values or properties. This recipe demonstrates the following three binding strategies:

- Bidirectional binding on a Java Bean

- High-level binding using the Fluent API

- Low-level binding using javafx.beans.binding.* binding objects

The following code is a console application implementing these three strategies. The console application will output property values based on various binding scenarios. The first scenario is a bidirectional binding between a String property variable and a String property owned by a domain object (Contact), such as the firstName property. The next scenario is a high-level binding using a fluent interface API to calculate the area of rectangle. The last scenario is using a low-level binding strategy to calculate the volume of a sphere. The difference between the high- and low-level binding is that the high level uses methods such as multiply() and subtract() instead of the operators * and -. When using low-level binding, you use a derived `NumberBinding` class such as a `DoubleBinding` class. With a `DoubleBinding` class you override its `computeValue()` method so that you can use the familiar operators such as * and - to formulate complex math equations:

```java
package org.java9recipes.chapter14.recipe14_09;

import javafx.beans.binding.DoubleBinding;
import javafx.beans.binding.NumberBinding;
import javafx.beans.property.DoubleProperty;
import javafx.beans.property.IntegerProperty;
import javafx.beans.property.SimpleDoubleProperty;
import javafx.beans.property.SimpleIntegerProperty;
import javafx.beans.property.SimpleStringProperty;
import javafx.beans.property.StringProperty;

/**
 * Recipe 14-9: Binding Expressions
 * @author cdea
 * Update:  J. Juneau
 */
public class BindingExpressions {

    /**
     * @param args the command line arguments
     */
    public static void main(String[] args) {
        System.out.println("Chapter 14-9 Binding Expressions\n");

        System.out.println("Binding a Contact bean [Bi-directional binding]");
        Contact contact = new Contact("John", "Doe");
        StringProperty fname = new SimpleStringProperty();
        fname.bindBidirectional(contact.firstNameProperty());
        StringProperty lname = new SimpleStringProperty();
        lname.bindBidirectional(contact.lastNameProperty());

        System.out.println("Current - StringProperty values    : " + fname.getValue() + " "
        + lname.getValue());
        System.out.println("Current - Contact values           : " + contact.getFirstName()
        + " " + contact.getLastName());

        System.out.println("Modifying StringProperty values");
        fname.setValue("Jane");
        lname.setValue("Deer");

        System.out.println("After - StringProperty values    : " + fname.getValue() + " " +
        lname.getValue());
        System.out.println("After - Contact values           : " + contact.getFirstName() + "
        " + contact.getLastName());

        System.out.println();
        System.out.println("A Area of a Rectangle [High level Fluent API]");
```

```java
        // Area = width * height
        final IntegerProperty width = new SimpleIntegerProperty(10);
        final IntegerProperty height = new SimpleIntegerProperty(10);

        NumberBinding area = width.multiply(height);

        System.out.println("Current - Width and Height    : " + width.get() + " " + height.
        get());
        System.out.println("Current - Area of the Rectangle: " + area.getValue());
        System.out.println("Modifying width and height");

        width.set(100);
        height.set(700);

        System.out.println("After - Width and Height    : " + width.get() + " " + height.
        get());
        System.out.println("After - Area of the Rectangle: " + area.getValue());

        System.out.println();
        System.out.println("A Volume of a Sphere [low level API]");

        // volume = 4/3 * pi r^3
        final DoubleProperty radius = new SimpleDoubleProperty(2);

        DoubleBinding volumeOfSphere = new DoubleBinding() {
            {
                super.bind(radius);
            }

            @Override
            protected double computeValue() {
                return (4 / 3 * Math.PI * Math.pow(radius.get(), 3));
            }
        };

        System.out.println("Current - radius for Sphere: " + radius.get());
        System.out.println("Current - volume for Sphere: " + volumeOfSphere.get());
        System.out.println("Modifying DoubleProperty radius");

        radius.set(50);
        System.out.println("After - radius for Sphere: " + radius.get());
        System.out.println("After - volume for Sphere: " + volumeOfSphere.get());

    }
}

class Contact {

    private SimpleStringProperty firstName = new SimpleStringProperty();
    private SimpleStringProperty lastName = new SimpleStringProperty();
```

```java
    public Contact(String fn, String ln) {
        firstName.setValue(fn);
        lastName.setValue(ln);
    }

    public final String getFirstName() {
        return firstName.getValue();
    }

    public StringProperty firstNameProperty() {
        return firstName;
    }

    public final void setFirstName(String firstName) {
        this.firstName.setValue(firstName);
    }

    public final String getLastName() {
        return lastName.getValue();
    }

    public StringProperty lastNameProperty() {
        return lastName;
    }

    public final void setLastName(String lastName) {
        this.lastName.setValue(lastName);
    }
}
```

The following output demonstrates the three binding scenarios:

```
Binding a Contact bean [Bi-directional binding]
Current - StringProperty values    : John Doe
Current - Contact values           : John Doe
Modifying StringProperty values
After - StringProperty values    : Jane Deer
After - Contact values           : Jane Deer

A Area of a Rectangle [High level Fluent API]
Current - Width and Height     : 10 10
Current - Area of the Rectangle: 100
Modifying width and height
After - Width and Height     : 100 700
After - Area of the Rectangle: 70000

A Volume of a Sphere [low level API]
Current - radius for Sphere: 2.0
Current - volume for Sphere: 25.132741228718345
Modifying DoubleProperty radius
After - radius for Sphere: 50.0
After - volume for Sphere: 392699.0816987241
```

How It Works

Binding implies that at least two values are being synchronized. This means when a dependent variable changes, the other variable changes. JavaFX provides many binding options that enable developers to synchronize properties in domain objects and GUI controls. This recipe demonstrates the three common binding scenarios.

One of the easiest ways to bind variables is using a ***bidirectional bind***. This scenario is often used when domain objects contain data that will be bound to a GUI form. This recipe creates a simple contact (Contact) object containing a first name and last name. Notice the instance variables using the SimpleStringProperty class. Many of these classes, which end in Property, are javafx.beans.Observable classes that can all be bound. In order for these properties to be bound, they must be the same data type. In the preceding example, you create the first name and last name variables of type SimpleStringProperty outside the created Contact domain object. Once they have been created, you bind them bidirectionally to allow changes to update on either end. So if you change the domain object, the other bound properties are updated. And when the outside variables are modified, the domain object's properties are updated. The following demonstrates bidirectional binding against String properties on a domain object (Contact):

```
Contact contact = new Contact("John", "Doe");
StringProperty fname = new SimpleStringProperty();
fname.bindBidirectional(contact.firstNameProperty());
StringProperty lname = new SimpleStringProperty();
lname.bindBidirectional(contact.lastNameProperty());
```

Next up is how to bind numbers. Binding numbers is simple when using the Fluent API. This high-level mechanism allows developers to bind variables to compute values using simple arithmetic. Basically, a formula is "bound" to change its result based on changes to the variables it's bound to. Look at the Javadoc (http://docs.oracle.com/javase/8/javafx/api/javafx/beans/binding/Bindings.html) for details on all the available methods and number types. In this example, you simply create a formula for an area of a rectangle. The area (NumberBinding) is the binding, and its dependencies are the width and height (IntegerProperty) properties. When binding using the fluent interface API, you'll notice the multiply() method. According to the Javadoc, all property classes inherit from the NumberExpressionBase class, which contains the number-based fluent interface APIs. The following code snippet uses the fluent interface API:

```
// Area = width * height
final IntegerProperty width = new SimpleIntegerProperty(10);
final IntegerProperty height = new SimpleIntegerProperty(10);
NumberBinding area = width.multiply(height);
```

The last scenario on binding numbers is considered more of a low-level approach. This allows developers to use primitives and more complex math operations. Here, you use a DoubleBinding class to solve the volume of a sphere given the radius. You begin by implementing the computeValue() method to perform the calculation of the volume. Shown is the low-level binding scenario to compute the volume of a sphere by overriding the computeValue() method:

```
final DoubleProperty radius = new SimpleDoubleProperty(2);

DoubleBinding volumeOfSphere = new DoubleBinding() {
        {
            super.bind(radius);
        }
```

```
    @Override
    protected double computeValue() {
            return (4 / 3 * Math.PI * Math.pow(radius.get(), 3));
    }
};
```

14-10. Creating and Working with Observable Lists

Problem

You want to create a GUI application containing two list view controls that allow users to pass items between the two lists.

Solution

You can take advantage of JavaFX's `javafx.collections.ObservableList` and `javafx.scene.control.ListView` classes to provide a model-view-controller (MVC) mechanism that updates the UI's list view control whenever the backend list is manipulated.

The following code creates a GUI application containing two lists that allow users to send items contained in one list to the other. Here you will create a contrived application to pick candidates to be considered heroes. The user picks potential candidates from the list on the left to be moved into the list on the right to be considered heroes. This demonstrates UI list controls' (`ListView`) ability to be synchronized with backend store lists (`ObservableList`).

```
public void start(Stage primaryStage) {
    primaryStage.setTitle("Chapter 14-10 Creating and Working with ObservableLists");
    Group root = new Group();
    Scene scene = new Scene(root, 400, 250, Color.WHITE);

    // create a grid pane
    GridPane gridpane = new GridPane();
    gridpane.setPadding(new Insets(5));
    gridpane.setHgap(10);
    gridpane.setVgap(10);

    // candidates label
    Label candidatesLbl = new Label("Candidates");
    GridPane.setHalignment(candidatesLbl, HPos.CENTER);
    gridpane.add(candidatesLbl, 0, 0);

    Label heroesLbl = new Label("Heroes");
    gridpane.add(heroesLbl, 2, 0);
    GridPane.setHalignment(heroesLbl, HPos.CENTER);

    // candidates
    final ObservableList<String> candidates = FXCollections.observableArrayList("Super man",
            "Spider man",
            "Wolverine",
            "Police",
            "Fire Rescue",
            "Soldiers",
```

```
                "Dad & Mom",
                "Doctor",
                "Politician",
                "Pastor",
                "Teacher");
        final ListView<String> candidatesListView = new ListView<>(candidates);
        candidatesListView.setPrefWidth(150);
        candidatesListView.setPrefHeight(150);

        gridpane.add(candidatesListView, 0, 1);

        // heros
        final ObservableList<String> heroes = FXCollections.observableArrayList();
        final ListView<String> heroListView = new ListView<>(heroes);
        heroListView.setPrefWidth(150);
        heroListView.setPrefHeight(150);

        gridpane.add(heroListView, 2, 1);

        // select heroes
        Button sendRightButton = new Button(">");
        sendRightButton.setOnAction((e) -> {
                String potential = candidatesListView.getSelectionModel().getSelectedItem();
                if (potential != null) {
                    candidatesListView.getSelectionModel().clearSelection();
                    candidates.remove(potential);
                    heroes.add(potential);
                }
        });

        // deselect heroes
        Button sendLeftButton = new Button("<");
        sendLeftButton.setOnAction((e) -> {
                String notHero = heroListView.getSelectionModel().getSelectedItem();
                if (notHero != null) {
                    heroListView.getSelectionModel().clearSelection();
                    heroes.remove(notHero);
                    candidates.add(notHero);
                }
        });

        VBox vbox = new VBox(5);
        vbox.getChildren().addAll(sendRightButton,sendLeftButton);

        gridpane.add(vbox, 1, 1);
        GridPane.setConstraints(vbox, 1, 1, 1, 2,HPos.CENTER, VPos.CENTER);

        root.getChildren().add(gridpane);
        primaryStage.setScene(scene);
        primaryStage.show();
}
```

Figure 14-10 depicts the hero selection application.

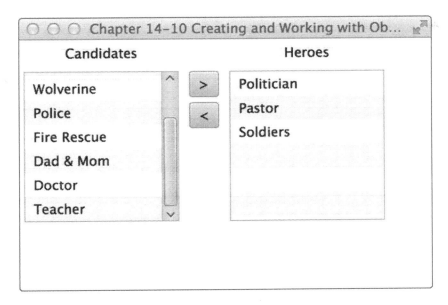

Figure 14-10. *ListViews and ObservableLists*

How It Works

When dealing with Java collections you'll notice there are so many useful container classes that represent all kinds of data structures. One commonly used collection is the `java.util.ArrayList` class. When building applications with domain objects that contain an `ArrayList`, developers can easily manipulate objects inside the collection. But, in the past (back in the day), when using Java Swing components combined with collections was a challenge, especially updating the GUI to reflect changes in the domain object. How do you resolve this issue? Well, JavaFX's `ObservableList` to the rescue!

Speaking of rescue, this recipe demonstrates a GUI application to allow users to choose their favorite heroes. This is quite similar to application screens that manage user roles by adding or removing items from list box components. In JavaFX, use a `ListView` control to hold String objects. Before creating an instance of a `ListView`, the `ObservableList` containing the candidates is created. In the example, you'll notice the use of a factory class called `FXCollections`, in which you can pass in common collection types to be wrapped and returned to the caller as an `ObservableList`. This recipe passes in an array of Strings instead of an `ArrayList`, so hopefully you get the idea about how to use the `FXCollections` class. Be sure to use it wisely: "With great power, there must also come great responsibility." This code line calls the `FXCollections` class to return an observable list (`ObservableList`):

```
ObservableList<String> candidates = FXCollections.observableArrayList(...);
```

After creating an ObservableList, a ListView class is instantiated using a constructor that receives the observable list. Shown here is code to create and populate a ListView object:

```
ListView<String> candidatesListView = new ListView<String>(candidates);
```

In the last item of business, the code will manipulate the ObservableLists as if they were java.util. ArrayLists. Once manipulated, the ListView will be notified and automatically updated to reflect the changes of the ObservableList. The following code snippet implements the event handler and action event when the user presses the send right button:

```
// select heroes
Button sendRightButton = new Button(">");
sendRightButton.setOnAction((e) -> {
        String potential = candidatesListView.getSelectionModel().getSelectedItem();
        if (potential != null) {
            candidatesListView.getSelectionModel().clearSelection();
            candidates.remove(potential);
            heroes.add(potential);
        }
});
```

When setting an action, you implement an EventHandler via a lambda expression to listen for a button press event. When a button press event arrives, the code will determine which item in the ListView was selected. Once the item was determined, you clear the selection, remove the item, and add the item to the hero's ObservableList.

14-11. Generating a Background Process

Problem

You want to create a GUI application that simulates a long-running process using background processing while displaying the progress to the users.

Solution

Create an application typical of a dialog box that shows the progress indicators while copying files in the background. The following are the main classes used in this recipe:

- javafx.scene.control.ProgressBar

- javafx.scene.control.ProgressIndicator

- javafx.concurrent.Task classes

The following source code is an application that simulates a file copy dialog box displaying progress indicators and performing background processes:

```
package org.java9recipes.chapter14.recipe14_11;

import java.util.Random;
import javafx.application.Application;
import javafx.beans.value.ChangeListener;
import javafx.beans.value.ObservableValue;
import javafx.concurrent.Task;
import javafx.geometry.Pos;
import javafx.scene.Group;
import javafx.scene.Scene;
```

```java
import javafx.scene.control.Button;
import javafx.scene.control.Label;
import javafx.scene.control.ProgressBar;
import javafx.scene.control.ProgressIndicator;
import javafx.scene.control.TextArea;
import javafx.scene.layout.BorderPane;
import javafx.scene.layout.HBox;
import javafx.scene.paint.Color;
import javafx.stage.Stage;

public class BackgroundProcesses extends Application {

    static Task copyWorker;
    final int numFiles = 30;

    /**
     * @param args the command line arguments
     */
    public static void main(String[] args) {
        Application.launch(args);
    }

    @Override
    public void start(Stage primaryStage) {
        primaryStage.setTitle("Chapter 14-11 Background Processes");
        Group root = new Group();
        Scene scene = new Scene(root, 330, 120, Color.WHITE);

        BorderPane mainPane = new BorderPane();
        mainPane.layoutXProperty().bind(scene.widthProperty().subtract(mainPane.
        widthProperty()).divide(2));
        root.getChildren().add(mainPane);

        final Label label = new Label("Files Transfer:");
        final ProgressBar progressBar = new ProgressBar(0);
        final ProgressIndicator progressIndicator = new ProgressIndicator(0);

        final HBox hb = new HBox();
        hb.setSpacing(5);
        hb.setAlignment(Pos.CENTER);
        hb.getChildren().addAll(label, progressBar, progressIndicator);
        mainPane.setTop(hb);

        final Button startButton = new Button("Start");
        final Button cancelButton = new Button("Cancel");
        final TextArea textArea = new TextArea();
        textArea.setEditable(false);
        textArea.setPrefSize(200, 70);
        final HBox hb2 = new HBox();
        hb2.setSpacing(5);
        hb2.setAlignment(Pos.CENTER);
```

```java
        hb2.getChildren().addAll(startButton, cancelButton, textArea);
        mainPane.setBottom(hb2);

        // wire up start button
        startButton.setOnAction((e) -> {
            startButton.setDisable(true);
            progressBar.setProgress(0);
            progressIndicator.setProgress(0);
            textArea.setText("");
            cancelButton.setDisable(false);
            copyWorker = createWorker(numFiles);

            // wire up progress bar
            progressBar.progressProperty().unbind();
            progressBar.progressProperty().bind(copyWorker.progressProperty());
            progressIndicator.progressProperty().unbind();
            progressIndicator.progressProperty().bind(copyWorker.progressProperty());

            // append to text area box
            copyWorker.messageProperty().addListener(new ChangeListener<String>() {

                public void changed(ObservableValue<? extends String> observable, String
                oldValue, String newValue) {
                    textArea.appendText(newValue + "\n");
                }
            });

            new Thread(copyWorker).start();
        });

        // cancel button will kill worker and reset.
        cancelButton.setOnAction((e) -> {
            startButton.setDisable(false);
            cancelButton.setDisable(true);
            copyWorker.cancel(true);

            // reset
            progressBar.progressProperty().unbind();
            progressBar.setProgress(0);
            progressIndicator.progressProperty().unbind();
            progressIndicator.setProgress(0);
            textArea.appendText("File transfer was cancelled.");
        });

        primaryStage.setScene(scene);
        primaryStage.show();
    }

    public Task createWorker(final int numFiles) {
        return new Task() {
```

```
        @Override
        protected Object call() throws Exception {
            for (int i = 0; i < numFiles; i++) {
                long elapsedTime = System.currentTimeMillis();
                copyFile("some file", "some dest file");
                elapsedTime = System.currentTimeMillis() - elapsedTime;
                String status = elapsedTime + " milliseconds";

                // queue up status
                updateMessage(status);
                updateProgress(i + 1, numFiles);
            }
            return true;
        }
    };
}

public void copyFile(String src, String dest) throws InterruptedException {
    // simulate a long time
    Random rnd = new Random(System.currentTimeMillis());
    long millis = rnd.nextInt(1000);
    Thread.sleep(millis);
}
}
```

Figure 14-11 shows the Background Processes application, which simulates a file copy window.

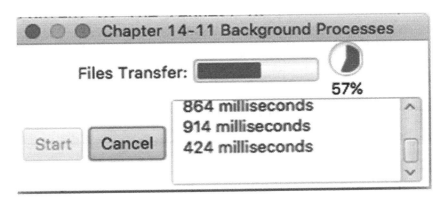

Figure 14-11. *Background processes*

How It Works

One of the main pitfalls of GUI development is knowing when and how to delegate work (Threads). You are constantly reminded of thread safety, especially when it comes to blocking the GUI thread. When using the Java Swing API, the SwingWorker object must be implemented to defer non-GUI work off of the EDT. Similar patterns and principles still apply in the world of JavaFX.

395

You begin by creating not one but two progress controls to show the user the work being done. One is a progress bar and the other is a progress indicator. The progress indicator shows a percentage below the indicator icon. The following code snippet shows the initial creation of progress controls:

```
final ProgressBar progressBar = new ProgressBar(0);
final ProgressIndicator progressIndicator = new ProgressIndicator(0);
```

Next, you create a worker thread via the createWorker() method. The createWorker() convenience method will instantiate and return a javafx.concurrent.Task object, which is similar to the Java Swing's SwingWorker class. Unlike the SwingWorker class, the Task object is greatly simplified and easier to use. If you compare the last recipe you will notice that none of the GUI controls is passed into the Task. The clever JavaFX team has created observable properties that allow you to bind against. This fosters a more event-driven approach to handling work (tasks). When creating an instance of a Task object you implement the call() method to perform work in the background. During the work being done, you may wish to queue up intermediate results such as progress or text info. For this, you can call the updateProgress() and updateMessage() methods. These methods will update information in a threadsafe manner so that the observer of the progress properties will be able to update the GUI safely without blocking the GUI thread. The following code snippet demonstrates the ability to queue up messages and progress:

```
// queue up status
updateMessage(status);
updateProgress(i + 1, numFiles);
```

After creating a worker Task, you unbind any old tasks bound to the progress controls. Once the progress controls are unbound, you then bind the progress controls to the newly created Task object called copyWorker. Shown here is the code used to rebind a new Task object to the progress UI controls:

```
// wire up progress bar
progressBar.progressProperty().unbind();
progressBar.progressProperty().bind(copyWorker.progressProperty());
progressIndicator.progressProperty().unbind();
progressIndicator.progressProperty().bind(copyWorker.progressProperty());
```

Next, implement a ChangeListener to append the queued results into the TextArea control. Another remarkable thing about JavaFX properties is that you can attach many listeners similar to Java Swing components. Finally, the worker and controls are all wired up to spawn a thread to go off in the background. The following code line shows how to launch a Task worker object:

```
new Thread(copyWorker).start();
```

Lastly, the Cancel button will simply call the Task object's cancel() method to kill the process. Once the task is cancelled the progress controls are reset. Once a worker Task is cancelled it cannot be reused. When pressed, the Start button recreates a new Task. If you want a more robust solution, you should look at the javafx.concurrent.Service class. The following code line will cancel a Task worker object:

```
copyWorker.cancel(true);
```

14-12. Associating Keyboard Sequences with Applications

Problem

You want to create keyboard shortcuts for menu options.

Solution

Create an application that will use JavaFX's key combination APIs. The main classes you will be using are shown here:

- javafx.scene.input.KeyCode

- javafx.scene.input.KeyCodeCombination

- javafx.scene.input.KeyCombination

The following source code listing is an application that displays the available keyboard shortcuts that are bound to the menu items. When the user performs a keyboard shortcut, the application will display the key combination on the screen:

```
public void start(Stage primaryStage) {
    primaryStage.setTitle("Chapter 14-12 Associating Keyboard Sequences");
    Group root = new Group();
    Scene scene = new Scene(root, 530, 300, Color.WHITE);

    final StringProperty statusProperty = new SimpleStringProperty();

    InnerShadow iShadow = new InnerShadow();
    iShadow.setOffsetX(3.5f);
    iShadow.setOffsetY(3.5f);

    final Text status = new Text();
    status.setEffect(iShadow);
    status.setX(100);
    status.setY(50);
    status.setFill(Color.LIME);
    status.setFont(Font.font(null, FontWeight.BOLD, 35));
    status.setTranslateY(50);

    status.textProperty().bind(statusProperty);
    statusProperty.set("Keyboard Shortcuts \nCtrl-N, \nCtrl-S, \nCtrl-X");
    root.getChildren().add(status);

    MenuBar menuBar = new MenuBar();
    menuBar.prefWidthProperty().bind(primaryStage.widthProperty());
    root.getChildren().add(menuBar);

    Menu menu = new Menu("File");
    menuBar.getMenus().add(menu);
```

```
MenuItem newItem = new MenuItem();
newItem.setText("New");
newItem.setAccelerator(new KeyCodeCombination(KeyCode.N, KeyCombination.CONTROL_DOWN));
newItem.setOnAction((e) -> {
    statusProperty.set("Ctrl-N");
});
menu.getItems().add(newItem);

MenuItem saveItem = new MenuItem();
saveItem.setText("Save");
saveItem.setAccelerator(new KeyCodeCombination(KeyCode.S, KeyCombination.CONTROL_DOWN));
saveItem.setOnAction((e) -> {
    statusProperty.set("Ctrl-S");
});
menu.getItems().add(saveItem);

menu.getItems().add(new SeparatorMenuItem());

MenuItem exitItem = new MenuItem();
exitItem.setText("Exit");
exitItem.setAccelerator(new KeyCodeCombination(KeyCode.X, KeyCombination.CONTROL_DOWN));
exitItem.setOnAction((e) -> {
    statusProperty.set("Ctrl-X");
});
menu.getItems().add(exitItem);

primaryStage.setScene(scene);
primaryStage.show();
}
```

Figure 14-12 displays an application that demonstrates keyboard shortcuts.

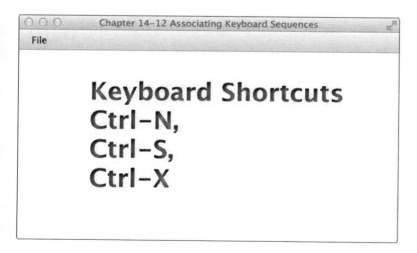

Figure 14-12. *Keyboard sequences/shortcuts*

How It Works

The solution to this recipe demonstrates how to create key combination or keyboard shortcuts using the javafx.scene.input.KeyCodeCombination and javafx.scene.input.KeyCombination classes. Seeing that the previous recipe was a tad boring, we decided to make things a little more interesting here. This recipe displays Text nodes onto the scene graph when the user performs the key combinations. When displaying the Text nodes, we applied an inner shadow effect. The following code snippet creates a Text node with an inner shadow effect:

```
InnerShadow iShadow = new InnerShadow();
iShadow.setOffsetX(3.5f);
iShadow.setOffsetY(3.5f);

final Text status = new Text();
status.setEffect(iShadow);
status.setX(100);
status.setY(50);
status.setFill(Color.LIME);
status.setFont(Font.font(null, FontWeight.BOLD, 35));
status.setTranslateY(50);
```

To create a keyboard shortcut, you simply call a menu or button control's setAccelerator() method. In this recipe, the key combination are set using the MenuItem node's setAccelerator() method. The following code line specifies the key combinations for a Ctrl-N:

```
MenuItem newItem = new MenuItem();
newItem.setText("New");
newItem.setAccelerator(new KeyCodeCombination(KeyCode.N, KeyCombination.CONTROL_DOWN));
newItem.setOnAction((e) -> {
    statusProperty.set("Ctrl-N");
});
```

As you can see from the code, when the accelerator (key combination) is pressed in the example, the onAction ActionEvent is triggered. It sets the statusProperty value to Ctrl-N via a lambda expression.

14-13. Creating and Working with Tables

Problem

You want to display items in a UI table control similar to Java Swing's JTable component.

Solution

Create an application using JavaFX's javafx.scene.control.TableView class. The TableView control provides the equivalent functionality to Swing's JTable component.

To exercise the TableView control you will be creating an application that will display bosses and employees. On the left you will implement a ListView control containing bosses, and employees (subordinates) will be displayed in a TableView control on the right.

Shown here is the source code of a simple domain (Person) class to represent a boss or an employee to be displayed in a ListView or TableView control:

```java
package org.java9recipes.chapter15.recipe15_14;

import javafx.beans.property.SimpleStringProperty;
import javafx.beans.property.StringProperty;
import javafx.collections.FXCollections;
import javafx.collections.ObservableList;

public class Person {

    private StringProperty aliasName;
    private StringProperty firstName;
    private StringProperty lastName;
    private ObservableList<Person> employees = FXCollections.observableArrayList();

    public final void setAliasName(String value) {
        aliasNameProperty().set(value);
    }

    public final String getAliasName() {
        return aliasNameProperty().get();
    }

    public StringProperty aliasNameProperty() {
        if (aliasName == null) {
            aliasName = new SimpleStringProperty();
        }
        return aliasName;
    }

    public final void setFirstName(String value) {
        firstNameProperty().set(value);
    }

    public final String getFirstName() {
        return firstNameProperty().get();
    }

    public StringProperty firstNameProperty() {
        if (firstName == null) {
            firstName = new SimpleStringProperty();
        }
        return firstName;
    }

    public final void setLastName(String value) {
        lastNameProperty().set(value);
    }
```

```java
    public final String getLastName() {
        return lastNameProperty().get();
    }

    public StringProperty lastNameProperty() {
        if (lastName == null) {
            lastName = new SimpleStringProperty();
        }
        return lastName;
    }

    public ObservableList<Person> employeesProperty() {
        return employees;
    }

    public Person(String alias, String firstName, String lastName) {
        setAliasName(alias);
        setFirstName(firstName);
        setLastName(lastName);
    }

}
```

The following is the main application code. It displays a list view component on the left containing bosses and a table view control on the right containing employees:

```java
public void start(Stage primaryStage) {
    primaryStage.setTitle("Chapter 14-13 Working with Tables");
    Group root = new Group();
    Scene scene = new Scene(root, 500, 250, Color.WHITE);

    // create a grid pane
    GridPane gridpane = new GridPane();
    gridpane.setPadding(new Insets(5));
    gridpane.setHgap(10);
    gridpane.setVgap(10);

    // candidates label
    Label candidatesLbl = new Label("Boss");
    GridPane.setHalignment(candidatesLbl, HPos.CENTER);
    gridpane.add(candidatesLbl, 0, 0);

    // List of leaders
    ObservableList<Person> leaders = getPeople();
    final ListView<Person> leaderListView = new ListView<>(leaders);
    leaderListView.setPrefWidth(150);
    leaderListView.setPrefHeight(150);

    // display first and last name with tooltip using alias
    leaderListView.setCellFactory((ListView<Person> param) -> {
        final Label leadLbl = new Label();
```

```
        final Tooltip tooltip = new Tooltip();
        final ListCell<Person> cell = new ListCell<Person>() {
            @Override
            public void updateItem(Person item, boolean empty) {
                super.updateItem(item, empty);
                if (item != null) {
                    leadLbl.setText(item.getAliasName());
                    setText(item.getFirstName() + " " + item.getLastName());
                    tooltip.setText(item.getAliasName());
                    setTooltip(tooltip);
                }
            }
        }; // ListCell
        return cell;
    }); // setCellFactory

    gridpane.add(leaderListView, 0, 1);

    Label emplLbl = new Label("Employees");
    gridpane.add(emplLbl, 2, 0);
    GridPane.setHalignment(emplLbl, HPos.CENTER);

    final TableView<Person> employeeTableView = new TableView<>();
    employeeTableView.setPrefWidth(300);

    final ObservableList<Person> teamMembers = FXCollections.observableArrayList();
    employeeTableView.setItems(teamMembers);

    TableColumn<Person, String> aliasNameCol = new TableColumn<>("Alias");
    aliasNameCol.setEditable(true);
    aliasNameCol.setCellValueFactory(new PropertyValueFactory("aliasName"));

    aliasNameCol.setPrefWidth(employeeTableView.getPrefWidth() / 3);

    TableColumn<Person, String> firstNameCol = new TableColumn<>("First Name");
    firstNameCol.setCellValueFactory(new PropertyValueFactory("firstName"));
    firstNameCol.setPrefWidth(employeeTableView.getPrefWidth() / 3);

    TableColumn<Person, String> lastNameCol = new TableColumn<>("Last Name");
    lastNameCol.setCellValueFactory(new PropertyValueFactory("lastName"));
    lastNameCol.setPrefWidth(employeeTableView.getPrefWidth() / 3);

    employeeTableView.getColumns().setAll(aliasNameCol, firstNameCol, lastNameCol);
    gridpane.add(employeeTableView, 2, 1);

    // selection listening
    leaderListView.getSelectionModel().selectedItemProperty().addListener(
            (ObservableValue<? extends Person> observable, Person oldValue, Person
            newValue) -> {
```

```
        if (observable != null && observable.getValue() != null) {
            teamMembers.clear();
            teamMembers.addAll(observable.getValue().employeesProperty());
        }
    });

    root.getChildren().add(gridpane);

    primaryStage.setScene(scene);
    primaryStage.show();
}
```

The following code shows the getPeople() method contained in the WorkingWithTables main application class. This method populates the UI TableView control shown previously:

```
private ObservableList<Person> getPeople() {
    ObservableList<Person> people = FXCollections.<Person>observableArrayList();
    Person docX = new Person("Professor X", "Charles", "Xavier");
    docX.employeesProperty().add(new Person("Wolverine", "James", "Howlett"));
    docX.employeesProperty().add(new Person("Cyclops", "Scott", "Summers"));
    docX.employeesProperty().add(new Person("Storm", "Ororo", "Munroe"));

    Person magneto = new Person("Magneto", "Max", "Eisenhardt");
    magneto.employeesProperty().add(new Person("Juggernaut", "Cain", "Marko"));
    magneto.employeesProperty().add(new Person("Mystique", "Raven", "Darkhölme"));
    magneto.employeesProperty().add(new Person("Sabretooth", "Victor", "Creed"));

    Person biker = new Person("Mountain Biker", "Jonathan", "Gennick");
    biker.employeesProperty().add(new Person("JavaJuneau", "Joshua", "Juneau"));
    biker.employeesProperty().add(new Person("Freddy", "Freddy", "Guime"));
    biker.employeesProperty().add(new Person("Mark", "Mark", "Beaty"));
    biker.employeesProperty().add(new Person("John", "John", "O'Conner"));
    biker.employeesProperty().add(new Person("D-Man", "Carl", "Dea"));

    people.add(docX);
    people.add(magneto);
    people.add(biker);

    return people;
}
```

Figure 14-13 displays the application that demonstrates JavaFX's TableView control.

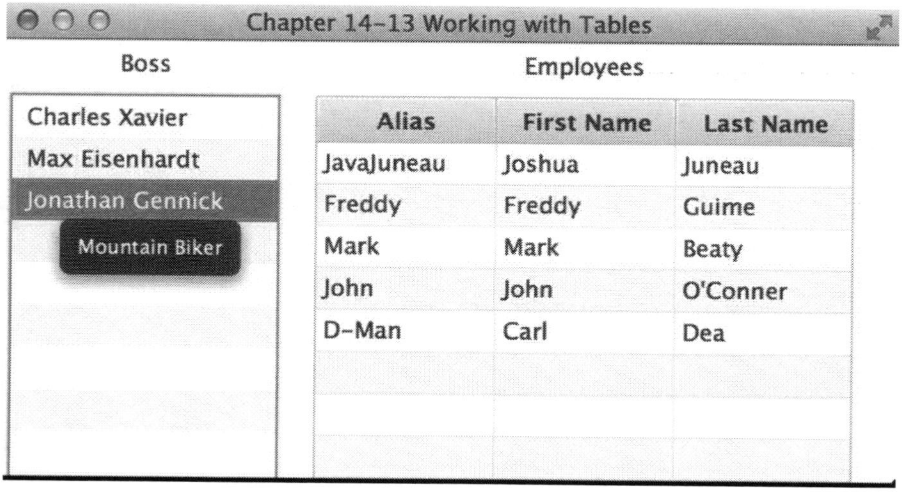

Figure 14-13. *Working with tables*

How It Works

Just for fun we created a simple GUI to display employees and their bosses. You notice in Figure 14-13 on the left is a list of people (the bosses). When users select a boss, their employees will be shown to in the TableView area to the right. You'll also notice the tooltip when you hover over the selected boss.

Before considering the TableView control, it's important that you understand the ListView that is responsible for updating the TableView. In model-view fashion, an ObservableList is created that contains all the bosses for the ListView control's constructor. This code calls the bosses *leaders*. The following code creates a ListView control:

```
// List of leaders
ObservableList<Person> leaders = getPeople();
final ListView<Person> leaderListView = new ListView<Person>(leaders);
```

Next, create a cell factory to properly display the person's name in the ListView control. Because each item is a Person object, the ListView does not know how to render each row in the ListView control. You simply create a javafx.util.Callback generic type object by specifying the ListView<Person> and a ListCell<Person> data types. If you're using a trusty IDE such as NetBeans, it will pregenerate things such as the implementing method call(). Next is the variable cell of type ListCell<Person> (within the call() method), in which you create a lambda expression. The lambda expression contains an implementation for an updateItem() method. To implement the updateItem() method, obtain the person information and update the Label control (leadLbl). Lastly, you set the tooltip to the associated text.

You then create a TableView control to display the employee base on the selected boss from the ListView. When creating a TableView, first create the column headers. Use the following code to create a table column:

```
TableColumn<String> firstNameCol = new TableColumn<String>("First Name");
firstNameCol.setProperty("firstName");
```

Once you have created a column, you'll notice the setProperty() method, which is responsible for calling the person Bean's property. When the list of employees is put into the TableView, it will know how to pull the properties to be placed in each cell in the table.

Last is the implementation of the selection listener on the ListViewer in JavaFX, called a selection item property (selectionItemProperty). Create and add a ChangeListener to listen to selection events. When a user selects a boss, the TableView is cleared and populated with the boss's employees. Actually it is the magic of the ObservableList that notifies the TableView of changes. To populate the TableView via the teamMembers (ObservableList) variable, use this code:

```
teamMembers.clear();
teamMembers.addAll(observable.getValue().employeesProperty());
```

14-14. Organizing the UI with Split Views

Problem

You want to split up a GUI screen by using split divider controls.

Solution

Use JavaFX's split pane control. The javafx.scene.control.SplitPane class is a UI control that enables you to divide a screen into frame-like regions. The split control allows users to move the divider between any two split regions with the mouse.

Shown here is the code used to create the GUI application that utilizes the javafx.scene.control. SplitPane class. That class divides the screen into three windowed regions. The three windowed regions are a left column, an upper right region, and a lower right region. In addition, Text nodes are added to the three regions.

```
public void start(Stage primaryStage) {
    primaryStage.setTitle("Chapter 14-4 Organizing UI with Split Views");
    Group root = new Group();
    Scene scene = new Scene(root, 350, 250, Color.WHITE);

    // Left and right split pane
    SplitPane splitPane = new SplitPane();
    splitPane.prefWidthProperty().bind(scene.widthProperty());
    splitPane.prefHeightProperty().bind(scene.heightProperty());

    //List<Node> items = splitPane.getItems();
    VBox leftArea = new VBox(10);

    for (int i = 0; i < 5; i++) {
        HBox rowBox = new HBox(20);
        final Text leftText = new Text();
        leftText.setText("Left " + i);
        leftText.setTranslateX(20);
        leftText.setFill(Color.BLUE);
        leftText.setFont(Font.font(null, FontWeight.BOLD, 20));

        rowBox.getChildren().add(leftText);
        leftArea.getChildren().add(rowBox);
    }
    leftArea.setAlignment(Pos.CENTER);
```

```java
// Upper and lower split pane
SplitPane splitPane2 = new SplitPane();
splitPane2.setOrientation(Orientation.VERTICAL);
splitPane2.prefWidthProperty().bind(scene.widthProperty());
splitPane2.prefHeightProperty().bind(scene.heightProperty());

HBox centerArea = new HBox();

InnerShadow iShadow = new InnerShadow();
iShadow.setOffsetX(3.5f);
iShadow.setOffsetY(3.5f);

final Text upperRight = new Text();
upperRight.setText("Upper Right");
upperRight.setX(100);
upperRight.setY(50);
upperRight.setEffect(iShadow);
upperRight.setFill(Color.LIME);
upperRight.setFont(Font.font(null, FontWeight.BOLD, 35));
upperRight.setTranslateY(50);
centerArea.getChildren().add(upperRight);

HBox rightArea = new HBox();

final Text lowerRight = new Text();
lowerRight.setText("Lower Right");
lowerRight.setX(100);
lowerRight.setY(50);
lowerRight.setEffect(iShadow);
lowerRight.setFill(Color.RED);
lowerRight.setFont(Font.font(null, FontWeight.BOLD, 35));
lowerRight.setTranslateY(50);
rightArea.getChildren().add(lowerRight);

splitPane2.getItems().add(centerArea);
splitPane2.getItems().add(rightArea);

// add left area
splitPane.getItems().add(leftArea);

// add right area
splitPane.getItems().add(splitPane2);

// evenly position divider
ObservableList<SplitPane.Divider> dividers = splitPane.getDividers();
for (int i = 0; i < dividers.size(); i++) {
    dividers.get(i).setPosition((i + 1.0) / 3);
}
```

```
HBox hbox = new HBox();
hbox.getChildren().add(splitPane);
root.getChildren().add(hbox);

primaryStage.setScene(scene);
primaryStage.show();
}
```

Figure 14-14 depicts the application using split pane controls.

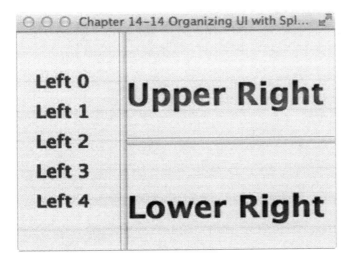

Figure 14-14. *Split views*

How It Works

If you've ever seen a simple Rich Site Summary (RSS) reader or the Javadocs, you'll notice that the screen is divided into sections with dividers. This recipe creates three areas: the left, upper right, and lower right.

You begin by creating a SplitPane that divides the left from the right area of the scene. Then you bind its width and height properties to the scene so the areas will take up the available space as the user resizes the stage. Next, you create a VBox layout control representing the left area. In the VBox (leftArea), you loop to generate a series of Text nodes. Next, generate the right side of the split pane. The following code snippet allows the split pane control (SplitPane) to divide horizontally:

```
SplitPane splitPane = new SplitPane();
splitPane.prefWidthProperty().bind(scene.widthProperty());
splitPane.prefHeightProperty().bind(scene.heightProperty());
```

Now you create the SplitPane to divide the area vertically, which will form the upper right and lower right regions. Shown here is the code used to split a window region vertically:

```
// Upper and lower split pane
SplitPane splitPane2 = new SplitPane();
splitPane2.setOrientation(Orientation.VERTICAL);
```

At last you assemble the split panes and adjust the dividers to be positioned so that the screen real estate is divided evenly. The following code assembles the split panes and iterates through the list of dividers to update their positions:

```
splitPane.getItems().add(splitPane2);

// evenly position divider
ObservableList<SplitPane.Divider> dividers = splitPane.getDividers();
for (int i = 0; i < dividers.size(); i++) {
    dividers.get(i).setPosition((i + 1.0) / 3);
}

HBox hbox = new HBox();
hbox.getChildren().add(splitPane);
root.getChildren().add(hbox);
```

14-15. Adding Tabs to the UI

Problem

You want to create a GUI application with tabs.

Solution

Use JavaFX's tab and tab pane control. The tab (javafx.scene.control.Tab) and tab pane control (javafx. scene.control.TabPane) classes allow you to place graph nodes in individual tabs.

The following code example creates a simple application having menu options that allow users to choose a tab orientation. The available tab orientations are top, bottom, left, and right.

```
public void start(Stage primaryStage) {
    primaryStage.setTitle("Chapter 14-15 Adding Tabs to a UI");
    Group root = new Group();
    Scene scene = new Scene(root, 400, 250, Color.WHITE);

    TabPane tabPane = new TabPane();

    MenuBar menuBar = new MenuBar();

    EventHandler<ActionEvent> action = changeTabPlacement(tabPane);

    Menu menu = new Menu("Tab Side");
    MenuItem left = new MenuItem("Left");

    left.setOnAction(action);
    menu.getItems().add(left);

    MenuItem right = new MenuItem("Right");
    right.setOnAction(action);
    menu.getItems().add(right);
```

```java
        MenuItem top = new MenuItem("Top");
        top.setOnAction(action);
        menu.getItems().add(top);

        MenuItem bottom = new MenuItem("Bottom");
        bottom.setOnAction(action);
        menu.getItems().add(bottom);

        menuBar.getMenus().add(menu);

        BorderPane borderPane = new BorderPane();

        // generate 10 tabs
        for (int i = 0; i < 10; i++) {
            Tab tab = new Tab();
            tab.setText("Tab" + i);
            HBox hbox = new HBox();
            hbox.getChildren().add(new Label("Tab" + i));
            hbox.setAlignment(Pos.CENTER);
            tab.setContent(hbox);
            tabPane.getTabs().add(tab);
        }

        // add tab pane
        borderPane.setCenter(tabPane);

        // bind to take available space
        borderPane.prefHeightProperty().bind(scene.heightProperty());
        borderPane.prefWidthProperty().bind(scene.widthProperty());

        // add menu bar
        borderPane.setTop(menuBar);

        // add border Pane
        root.getChildren().add(borderPane);

        primaryStage.setScene(scene);
        primaryStage.show();
    }

    private EventHandler<ActionEvent> changeTabPlacement(final TabPane tabPane) {
        return (ActionEvent event) -> {
            MenuItem mItem = (MenuItem) event.getSource();
            String side = mItem.getText();
            if ("left".equalsIgnoreCase(side)) {
                tabPane.setSide(Side.LEFT);
            } else if ("right".equalsIgnoreCase(side)) {
                tabPane.setSide(Side.RIGHT);
            } else if ("top".equalsIgnoreCase(side)) {
                tabPane.setSide(Side.TOP);
```

```
    } else if ("bottom".equalsIgnoreCase(side)) {
        tabPane.setSide(Side.BOTTOM);
    }
};
}
```

Figure 14-15 displays the tabs application, which allows users to change the tab orientation.

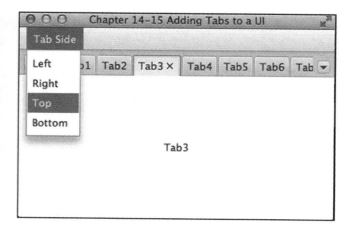

Figure 14-15. *TabPane*

How It Works

When you use the TabPane control, you may already know the orientation in which you want your tabs to appear. This application allows you to set the orientation by the left, right, top, and bottom menu options.

If you're familiar with the Swing API, you may notice that the JavaFX TabPane is very similar to the Swing JTabbedPanel. Instead of adding JPanels, you simply add javafx.scene.control.Tab instances. The following code snippet adds Tab controls to a TabPane control:

```
TabPane tabPane = new TabPane();
Tab tab = new Tab();
tab.setText("Tab" + i);
tabPane.getTabs().add(tab);
```

When you're changing the orientation the TabPane control, use the setSide() method. The following code sets the orientation of the TabPane control:

```
tabPane.setSide(Side.BOTTOM);
```

In this recipe, a Menu is used to change the orientation of the TabPane control. Different orientations were assigned to the different MenuItem nodes of the Menu, and an EventHandler identified as changeTabPlacement is used to change the orientation when the different MenuItem is selected. The EventHandler simply inspects the text of the MenuItem to determine which orientation should be applied to the TabPane.

14-16. Developing a Dialog Box

Problem

You want to create an application that contains a dialog box containing some text fields for user entry.

Solution

Use JavaFX's stage (javafx.stage.Stage) and scene (javafx.scene.Scene) APIs to create a dialog box.

The following source code listing is an application that simulates a change password dialog box. The application contains menu options to pop up the dialog box. In addition to using the menu options, users can set the dialog box's modal state (modality).

```java
public class DevelopingADialog extends Application {

    static Stage LOGIN_DIALOG;
    static int dx = 1;
    static int dy = 1;

    /**
     * @param args the command line arguments
     */
    public static void main(String[] args) {
        Application.launch(args);
    }

    private static Stage createLoginDialog(Stage parent, boolean modal) {
        if (LOGIN_DIALOG != null) {
            LOGIN_DIALOG.close();
        }
        return new MyDialog(parent, modal, "Welcome to JavaFX!");
    }

    @Override
    public void start(final Stage primaryStage) {
        primaryStage.setTitle("Chapter 14-16 Developing a Dialog");
        Group root = new Group();
        Scene scene = new Scene(root, 433, 312, Color.WHITE);

        MenuBar menuBar = new MenuBar();
        menuBar.prefWidthProperty().bind(primaryStage.widthProperty());

        Menu menu = new Menu("Home");

        // add change password menu itme
        MenuItem newItem = new MenuItem("Change Password", null);
        newItem.setOnAction((ActionEvent event) -> {
            if (LOGIN_DIALOG == null) {
                LOGIN_DIALOG = createLoginDialog(primaryStage, true);
            }
```

```java
        LOGIN_DIALOG.sizeToScene();
        LOGIN_DIALOG.show();
    });

    menu.getItems().add(newItem);

    // add separator
    menu.getItems().add(new SeparatorMenuItem());

    // add non modal menu item
    ToggleGroup modalGroup = new ToggleGroup();
    RadioMenuItem nonModalItem = new RadioMenuItem();
    nonModalItem.setToggleGroup(modalGroup);
    nonModalItem.setText("Non Modal");
    nonModalItem.setSelected(true);

    nonModalItem.setOnAction((ActionEvent event) -> {
        LOGIN_DIALOG = createLoginDialog(primaryStage, false);
    });

    menu.getItems().add(nonModalItem);

    // add modal selection
    RadioMenuItem modalItem = new RadioMenuItem();
    modalItem.setToggleGroup(modalGroup);
    modalItem.setText("Modal");
    modalItem.setSelected(true);

    modalItem.setOnAction((ActionEvent event) -> {
        LOGIN_DIALOG = createLoginDialog(primaryStage, true);
    });
    menu.getItems().add(modalItem);

    // add separator
    menu.getItems().add(new SeparatorMenuItem());

    // add exit
    MenuItem exitItem = new MenuItem("Exit", null);
    exitItem.setMnemonicParsing(true);
    exitItem.setAccelerator(new KeyCodeCombination(KeyCode.X, KeyCombination.CONTROL_
DOWN));
    exitItem.setOnAction((ActionEvent event) -> {
        Platform.exit();
    });
    menu.getItems().add(exitItem);

    // add menu
    menuBar.getMenus().add(menu);

    // menu bar to window
    root.getChildren().add(menuBar);
```

```java
        primaryStage.setScene(scene);
        primaryStage.show();

        addBouncyBall(scene);
    }

    private void addBouncyBall(final Scene scene) {

        final Circle ball = new Circle(100, 100, 20);
        RadialGradient gradient1 = new RadialGradient(0,
                .1,
                100,
                100,
                20,
                false,
                CycleMethod.NO_CYCLE,
                new Stop(0, Color.RED),
                new Stop(1, Color.BLACK));

        ball.setFill(gradient1);

        final Group root = (Group) scene.getRoot();
        root.getChildren().add(ball);

        Timeline tl = new Timeline();
        tl.setCycleCount(Animation.INDEFINITE);
        KeyFrame moveBall = new KeyFrame(Duration.seconds(.0200), (ActionEvent event) -> {
            double xMin = ball.getBoundsInParent().getMinX();
            double yMin = ball.getBoundsInParent().getMinY();
            double xMax = ball.getBoundsInParent().getMaxX();
            double yMax = ball.getBoundsInParent().getMaxY();

            // Collision - boundaries
            if (xMin < 0 || xMax > scene.getWidth()) {
                dx = dx * -1;
            }
            if (yMin < 0 || yMax > scene.getHeight()) {
                dy = dy * -1;
            }

            ball.setTranslateX(ball.getTranslateX() + dx);
            ball.setTranslateY(ball.getTranslateY() + dy);
        });

        tl.getKeyFrames().add(moveBall);
        tl.play();
    }
}
```

413

```java
class MyDialog extends Stage {

    public MyDialog(Stage owner, boolean modality, String title) {
        super();
        initOwner(owner);
        Modality m = modality ? Modality.APPLICATION_MODAL : Modality.NONE;
        initModality(m);
        setOpacity(.90);
        setTitle(title);
        Group root = new Group();
        Scene scene = new Scene(root, 250, 150, Color.WHITE);
        setScene(scene);

        GridPane gridpane = new GridPane();
        gridpane.setPadding(new Insets(5));
        gridpane.setHgap(5);
        gridpane.setVgap(5);

        Label mainLabel = new Label("Enter User Name & Password");
        gridpane.add(mainLabel, 1, 0, 2, 1);

        Label userNameLbl = new Label("User Name: ");
        gridpane.add(userNameLbl, 0, 1);

        Label passwordLbl = new Label("Password: ");
        gridpane.add(passwordLbl, 0, 2);

        // username text field
        final TextField userNameFld = new TextField("Admin");
        gridpane.add(userNameFld, 1, 1);

        // password field
        final PasswordField passwordFld = new PasswordField();
        passwordFld.setText("drowssap");
        gridpane.add(passwordFld, 1, 2);

        Button login = new Button("Change");
        login.setOnAction((ActionEvent event) -> {
            close();
        });
        gridpane.add(login, 1, 3);
        GridPane.setHalignment(login, HPos.RIGHT);
        root.getChildren().add(gridpane);
    }
}
```

Figure 14-16 depicts the change password dialog box application with the nonmodal option enabled.

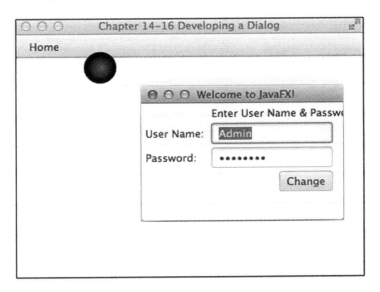

Figure 14-16. *Developing a dialog box*

How It Works

To create dialogs, JavaFX uses another instance of a `javafx.stage.Stage` class to be displayed to the user. Similar to extending from a JDialog class in Swing, you simply extend from a Stage class. You have the opportunity to pass in the owning window in the constructor, which then calls the `initOwner()` method. The modal state of the dialog box can be set using the `initModality()` method. The following class extends from the Stage class, having a constructor initializing the owning stage and modal state:

```
class MyDialog extends Stage {

    public MyDialog(Stage owner, boolean modality, String title) {
        super();
        initOwner(owner);
        Modality m = modality ? Modality.APPLICATION_MODAL : Modality.NONE;
initModality(m);

        ...// The rest of the class
```

The rest of the code creates a scene (Scene) similar to the main application's start() method. Because login forms are pretty boring, we decided to create an animation of a bouncing ball while the user is busy changing the password in the dialog box. (You will see more about creating animation in future recipes.)

When the menu item for Change Password is selected, the createLoginDialog method checks to see if there is already an instance of MyDialog instantiated. If so, it closes that instance and generates a new one. The newly created dialog is then displayed. Similarly, the RadioMenuItem controls call the createLoginDialog method, passing different Boolean values to indicate whether the instantiated MyDialog instance should be set to modal or not. As mentioned earlier, the bouncy ball has no bearing on the dialog; it's just added for effect.

415

14-17. Printing with JavaFX

Problem

You want to provide the ability to print a designated node in your application scene graph.

Solution

Utilize the JavaFX Print API to print designated nodes, and to construct sophisticated print dialogs. In this solution, a JavaFX application for drawing is generated. The drawing application allows you to print the canvas via a Print button. When the Print button is invoked, a dialog is opened that provides printing options such as printer and layout selection.

The following code is used to construct the application stage, including all buttons and drawing features. This first class does not contain any of the printing logic...you'll see that next...and these sources are being shown to make it easy to follow along with the example.

```java
public class PrintingWithJavaFX extends Application {

    static Stage PRINT_DIALOG;

    /**
     * @param args the command line arguments
     */
    public static void main(String[] args) {
        Application.launch(PrintingWithJavaFX.class, args);
    }

    private static Stage createPrintDialog(Stage parent, boolean modal, Canvas node) {
        if (PRINT_DIALOG != null) {
            PRINT_DIALOG.close();
        }
        // Copy canvas
        WritableImage wim = new WritableImage(300, 300);
        node.snapshot(null, wim);
        ImageView iv = new ImageView();
        iv.setImage(wim);
        return new PrintDialog(parent, modal, "Printing Menu", iv);
    }

    @Override
    public void start(Stage primaryStage) {

        StackPane root = new StackPane();
        Canvas canvas = new Canvas(300, 300);
        final GraphicsContext graphicsContext = canvas.getGraphicsContext2D();

        final Button printButton = new Button("Print");
        final BooleanProperty printingProperty = new SimpleBooleanProperty(false);
        printButton.setOnAction(actionEvent-> {
            printingProperty.set(true);
```

```
    if (PRINT_DIALOG == null) {
        PRINT_DIALOG = createPrintDialog(primaryStage, true, canvas);
    }
    PRINT_DIALOG.sizeToScene();
    PRINT_DIALOG.show();
});
printButton.setTranslateX(3);

final Button resetButton = new Button("Reset");
resetButton.setOnAction(actionEvent-> {
    graphicsContext.clearRect(1, 1,
            graphicsContext.getCanvas().getWidth()-2,
            graphicsContext.getCanvas().getHeight()-2);
});
resetButton.setTranslateX(10);

// Set up the pen color chooser
ChoiceBox colorChooser = new ChoiceBox(FXCollections.observableArrayList(
    "Black", "Blue", "Red", "Green", "Brown", "Orange")
);
// Select the first option by default
colorChooser.getSelectionModel().selectFirst();

colorChooser.getSelectionModel().selectedIndexProperty().addListener(
        (ChangeListener)(ov, old, newval) -> {
                Number idx = (Number)newval;
                Color newColor;
                switch(idx.intValue()){
                    case 0: newColor = Color.BLACK;
                            break;
                    case 1: newColor = Color.BLUE;
                            break;
                    case 2: newColor = Color.RED;
                            break;
                    case 3: newColor = Color.GREEN;
                            break;
                    case 4: newColor = Color.BROWN;
                            break;
                    case 5: newColor = Color.ORANGE;
                            break;
                    default: newColor = Color.BLACK;
                            break;
                }
                graphicsContext.setStroke(newColor);

        });
colorChooser.setTranslateX(5);

ChoiceBox sizeChooser = new ChoiceBox(FXCollections.observableArrayList(
    "1", "2", "3", "4", "5")
);
```

```java
        // Select the first option by default
        sizeChooser.getSelectionModel().selectFirst();

        sizeChooser.getSelectionModel().selectedIndexProperty().addListener(
                (ChangeListener)(ov, old, newval) -> {
                        Number idx = (Number)newval;

                        switch(idx.intValue()){
                            case 0: graphicsContext.setLineWidth(1);
                                    break;
                            case 1: graphicsContext.setLineWidth(2);
                                    break;
                            case 2: graphicsContext.setLineWidth(3);
                                    break;
                            case 3: graphicsContext.setLineWidth(4);
                                    break;
                            case 4: graphicsContext.setLineWidth(5);
                                    break;
                            default: graphicsContext.setLineWidth(1);
                                    break;
                        }
                });
        sizeChooser.setTranslateX(5);

        canvas.addEventHandler(MouseEvent.MOUSE_PRESSED, (MouseEvent event) -> {
            graphicsContext.beginPath();
            graphicsContext.moveTo(event.getX(), event.getY());
            graphicsContext.stroke();
        });

        canvas.addEventHandler(MouseEvent.MOUSE_DRAGGED, (MouseEvent event) -> {
            graphicsContext.lineTo(event.getX(), event.getY());
            graphicsContext.stroke();
        });

        canvas.addEventHandler(MouseEvent.MOUSE_RELEASED, (MouseEvent event) -> {
        });

        HBox buttonBox = new HBox();
        buttonBox.getChildren().addAll(printButton, colorChooser, sizeChooser, resetButton);

        initDraw(graphicsContext, canvas.getLayoutX(), canvas.getLayoutY());

        BorderPane container = new BorderPane();
        container.setTop(buttonBox);

        container.setCenter(canvas);

        root.getChildren().add(container);
        Scene scene = new Scene(root, 400, 400);
        primaryStage.setTitle("Recipe 14-17:  Printing from JavaFX");
```

```
        primaryStage.setScene(scene);
        primaryStage.show();
    }

    private void initDraw(GraphicsContext gc, double x, double y){
        double canvasWidth = gc.getCanvas().getWidth();
        double canvasHeight = gc.getCanvas().getHeight();

        gc.fill();
        gc.strokeRect(
                x,                   //x of the upper left corner
                y,                   //y of the upper left corner
                canvasWidth,         //width of the rectangle
                canvasHeight);       //height of the rectangle

        //gc.setFill(Color.RED);
        //gc.setStroke(Color.BLUE);
        //gc.setLineWidth(1);

    }

}
```

Next, you will take a look at the sources to create the `PrintDialog` class, which contains all of the application's printing logic. When use press the Print button, the dialog opens. It contains a handful of nodes that use the JavaFX Print API.

```
class PrintDialog extends Stage {

    public PrintDialog(Stage owner, boolean modality, String title, Node printNode) {
        super();
        initOwner(owner);
        Modality m = modality ? Modality.APPLICATION_MODAL : Modality.NONE;
        initModality(m);
        setOpacity(.90);
        setTitle(title);
        Group root = new Group();
        Scene scene = new Scene(root, 450, 150, Color.WHITE);
        setScene(scene);

        GridPane gridpane = new GridPane();
        gridpane.setPadding(new Insets(5));
        gridpane.setHgap(5);
        gridpane.setVgap(5);

        Label printerLabel = new Label("Printer: ");
        gridpane.add(printerLabel, 0, 1);

        Label layoutLabel = new Label("Layout: ");
        gridpane.add(layoutLabel, 0, 2);
```

```
        final Printer selectedPrinter = Printer.getDefaultPrinter();
        // printer pick list
        ChoiceBox printerChooser = new ChoiceBox(FXCollections.observableArrayList(
            Printer.getAllPrinters())
        );
        // Select the first option by default
        printerChooser.getSelectionModel().selectFirst();

        gridpane.add(printerChooser, 1, 1);

        ChoiceBox layoutChooser = new ChoiceBox(FXCollections.observableArrayList(
            "Portait", "Landscape")
        );
        layoutChooser.getSelectionModel().selectFirst();

        layoutChooser.getSelectionModel().selectedIndexProperty().addListener(
                (ChangeListener)(ov, old, newval) -> {
                        Number idx = (Number)newval;
                        switch(idx.intValue()){
                            case 0: selectedPrinter.createPageLayout(Paper.A0,
                                        PageOrientation.PORTRAIT, Printer.MarginType.EQUAL);
                                    break;
                            case 1: selectedPrinter.createPageLayout(Paper.A0,
                                        PageOrientation.LANDSCAPE, Printer.MarginType.EQUAL);
                                    break;

                            default: selectedPrinter.createPageLayout(Paper.A0,
                                         PageOrientation.PORTRAIT, Printer.MarginType.EQUAL);
                                    break;
                        }
                });
        gridpane.add(layoutChooser,1,2);
        Button printButton = new Button("Print");
        printButton.setOnAction((ActionEvent event) -> {
            print(printNode, selectedPrinter);
        });
        gridpane.add(printButton, 0, 3);

        GridPane.setHalignment(printButton, HPos.RIGHT);
        root.getChildren().add(gridpane);
    }

    public void print(final Node node, Printer printer) {

        PrinterJob job = PrinterJob.createPrinterJob();
        job.setPrinter(printer);
        if (job != null) {
            boolean success = job.printPage(node);
```

```
        if (success) {
            job.endJob();
        }
    }
  }
}
```

Figure 14-17 shows the application. The area within the canvas (drawing area) is printed using the dialog (see Figure 14-18).

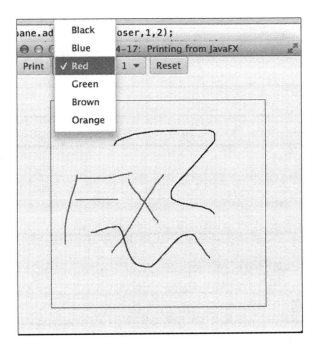

Figure 14-17. JavaFX drawing application with print functionality

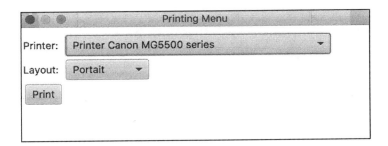

Figure 14-18. Printing the menu by utilizing the JavaFX Print API

How It Works

In releases of JavaFX prior to JavaFX 8, there was no standard API for printing portions of an application stage. In JavaFX 8, a Print API has been added to standardize the way in which printing features are handled. The API also makes it easy to enable applications with printing functionality using very little code. The API is quite large, as it contains a number of classes, but it is very straightforward and easy to use.

To enable print functionality for a specified node, start by working with the javafx.print.PrinterJob class, as it contains all of the functionality for generating a very simple printing task. To send a node to the default system printer, simply invoke PrintJob.createPrinterJob() to return a PrinterJob object. Once the object has been returned, check to ensure that it is not null, and then call its printPage() method, passing the node to be printed. The excerpt of the solution that contains this functionality is shown in the following lines of code:

```
public void print(final Node node, Printer printer) {

    PrinterJob job = PrinterJob.createPrinterJob()
    job.setPrinter(printer);
    if (job != null) {
        boolean success = job.printPage(node);
        if (success) {
            job.endJob();
        }
    }
}
```

While use of the PrinterJob is all that is required to send a node to the printer, the API allows for much more customization. Table 14-3 lists the different classes available in the API, along with a brief description of what they do.

Table 14-3. *JavaFX Print API*

Class Name	Description
JobSettings	Encapsulates settings for a print job
PageLayout	Encapsulates layout settings
PrintRange	Used to select the range or constrain print pages
Paper	Encapsulates the paper sizes for printers
PaperSource	Input tray used for Paper
Printer	Represents the destination for a print job
PrinterAttributes	Encapsulates the attributes for a printer
PrinterJob	Used to invoke a JavaFX scene graph print
PrintResolution	Represents supported device resolution

In the example, a Print dialog is generated that allows users to select where to send the print job. It also provides the controls to select the desired print layout (portrait or landscape). The Printer.getDefaultPrinter() method can be invoked to return the default printer for the host machine. In the example, a ChoiceBox is used to display all of the printers that are available on the host by calling the Printer.getAllPrinters() method. The selected printer is then set on the PrinterJob within the print method, which sends the desired node to that printer.

The printer layout is chosen via another ChoiceBox, and the selected printer's options are updated when a layout selection is made. The following line of code demonstrates how to set the layout to PageOrientation.PORTRAIT for a selected print:

```
selectedPrinter.createPageLayout(Paper.AO, PageOrientation.PORTRAIT, Printer.MarginType.
EQUAL);
```

Any Node can be sent to a PrinterJob, but it is important to send a copy of the Node that you want to print, as the print task may modify that Node.

The Print API is large, but it is easy to understand. This recipe just scratches the surface on what is possible with the API. We recommend that you read through the Javadoc for more details, once you are ready to develop your own printer processes. However, this recipe should provide a basic understanding of how to get started. See the following link for the Javadoc: http://docs.oracle.com/javase/8/javafx/api/javafx/print/package-summary.html.

14-18. Embedding Swing Content in JavaFX

Problem

You want to embed some simple Java Swing content into a JavaFX application.

Solution

Create a JavaFX application and embed the Swing content into it using the SwingNode class. In the following example, a simple JavaFX application is used to toggle between a Swing-based user entry form and a JavaFX-based form. A JavaFX button within the application can be used to determine which of the forms should be displayed when the user clicks it.

First, let's take a look at the code for the Swing form that is embedded into the JavaFX application. The code resides in a class entitled SwingForm.java.

```
import java.awt.GridLayout;
import javax.swing.JLabel;
import javax.swing.JPanel;
import javax.swing.JTextField;
public class SwingForm extends JPanel {

    JLabel formTitle, first, last, buttonLbl;
    protected JTextField firstField, lastField;

    public SwingForm(){

    JPanel innerPanel = new JPanel();

    GridLayout gl = new GridLayout(3,2);
    innerPanel.setLayout(gl);

    first = new JLabel("First Name:");
    innerPanel.add(first);
    firstField = new JTextField(10);
    innerPanel.add(firstField);
```

```java
    last = new JLabel("Last Name:");
    innerPanel.add(last);
    lastField = new JTextField(10);
    innerPanel.add(lastField);

    JButton button = new JButton("Submit");
    button.addActionListener((event) -> {
        Platform.runLater(()-> {
            UserEntryForm.fxLabel.setText("Message from Swing form...");
        });
    });
    buttonLbl = new JLabel("Click Me:");
    innerPanel.add(buttonLbl);
    innerPanel.add(button);
    add(innerPanel);

    }
}
```

Next, let's look at the JavaFX code that is used to create the graphical user interface, including the toggle button and the JavaFX form. Note that the Swing form is embedded using the SwingNode object.

```java
public class UserEntryForm extends Application {

    private static ToggleButton fxbutton;
    private static GridPane grid;
    public static Label fxLabel;

    @Override
    public void start(Stage stage) {
        final SwingNode swingNode = new SwingNode();
        createSwingContent(swingNode);
        BorderPane pane = new BorderPane();
        Image fxButtonIcon = new Image(
                getClass().getResourceAsStream("images/duke1.gif"));
        String buttonText = "Use Swing Form";
        fxbutton = new ToggleButton(buttonText, new ImageView(fxButtonIcon));
        fxbutton.setTooltip(
                new Tooltip("This button chooses between the Swing and FX form"));
        fxbutton.setStyle("-fx-font: 22 arial; -fx-base: #cce6ff;");
        fxbutton.setAlignment(Pos.CENTER);
        fxbutton.setOnAction((event)->{
            ToggleButton toggle = (ToggleButton) event.getSource();
            if(!toggle.isSelected()){
                swingNode.setDisable(true);
                swingNode.setVisible(false);
                grid.setDisable(false);
                grid.setVisible(true);
                fxbutton.setText("Use Swing Form");
            } else {
                swingNode.setDisable(false);
                swingNode.setVisible(true);
```

```
                    grid.setDisable(true);
                    grid.setVisible(false);
                    fxbutton.setText("Use JavaFX Form");
                }
        });
        // Disable SwingNode by default
        swingNode.setVisible(false);
        Text appTitle = new Text("Swing/FX Form Demo");
        appTitle.setFont(Font.font("Tahoma", FontWeight.NORMAL, 20));

        pane.setTop(appTitle);
        HBox formPanel = new HBox();
        formPanel.setSpacing(10);
        fxLabel = new Label("Message from JavaFX form...");

        formPanel.getChildren().addAll(fxFormContent(), swingNode);

        pane.setCenter(formPanel);
        VBox vbox = new VBox();
        vbox.getChildren().addAll(fxbutton, fxLabel);

        pane.setBottom(vbox);

        Scene scene = new Scene(pane, 700, 500);
        stage.setScene(scene);
        stage.setTitle("Swing Form Embedded In JavaFX");
        stage.show();
}

private void createSwingContent(final SwingNode swingNode) {
        SwingUtilities.invokeLater(() -> {
            swingNode.setContent(new SwingForm());
        });
}

private GridPane fxFormContent() {
        grid = new GridPane();
        grid.setAlignment(Pos.CENTER);
        grid.setHgap(10);
        grid.setVgap(10);
        grid.setPadding(new Insets(25, 25, 25, 25));

        Text scenetitle = new Text("Enter User");
        scenetitle.setFont(Font.font("Tahoma", FontWeight.NORMAL, 20));
        grid.add(scenetitle, 0, 0, 2, 1);

        Label first = new Label("First Name:");
        grid.add(first, 0, 1);

        TextField firstField = new TextField();
        grid.add(firstField, 1, 1);
```

```
        Label last = new Label("Last Name:");
        grid.add(last, 0, 2);

        TextField lastField = new TextField();
        grid.add(lastField, 1, 2);

        Button messageButton = new Button("Click");
        messageButton.setOnAction((event) ->{
            fxLabel.setText("Message from JavaFX Form...");
        });
        grid.add(messageButton, 0,3);

        return grid;

    }

    /**
     * @param args the command line arguments
     */
    public static void main(String[] args) {
        launch(args);
    }

}
```

Upon invocation, the application looks like the one shown in Figure 14-19.

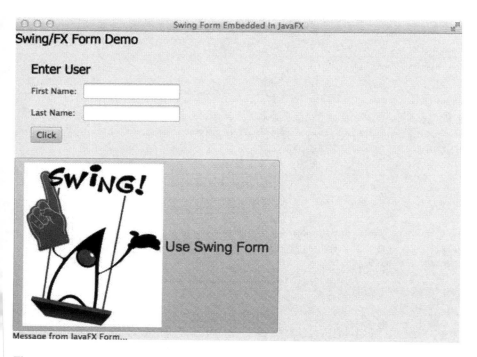

Figure 14-19. *Using SwingNode to embed a Swing form*

How It Works

There are a great number of applications that have been written using the Java Swing framework. Sometimes it makes sense to make use of those applications from within a JavaFX application, or embed portions of those Swing applications where it makes sense. The javafx.embed.swing.SwingNode class makes it possible to embed a JComponent instance into a JavaFX application with little effort, by passing the JComponent to the SwingNode setContent() method. The content is repainted automatically and all events are forwarded to the JComponent instance without user intervention.

In the example to this recipe, a simple Java Swing form is embedded by instantiating a new SwingNode object and passing to it an instance of the class SwingForm. The Swing content should run on the EDT, so any Swing access should be made on the EDT. That said, a new thread is created using SwingUtilities. invokeLater, and a lambda expression encapsulates the Runnable that is used to set the Swing content.

It is possible to interact with JavaFX content from within Swing code as well. To do so, you must run the JavaFX code within the JavaFX application thread by making a call to the javafx.application.Platform class and invoking the runLater() method, passing a Runnable. For instance, in the example code, the button in the Swing form can call back to the JavaFX label to change the text using the following code. Note that the JavaFX label is a public field, so it is accessible directly from within the Swing class.

```
JButton button = new JButton("Submit");
    button.addActionListener((event) -> {
        Platform.runLater(()-> {
            UserEntryForm.fxLabel.setText("Message from Swing form...");
        });
    });
```

■ **Note** By default, the JavaFX application thread and the Swing EDT are separated. The EDT does not run the GUI code for a Swing application. However, in JavaFX, the platform GUI thread runs the application code. There is an experimental setting that enables single threading mode, which allows the JavaFX platform GUI thread to become the EDT when using Swing and JavaFX together. To enable the experimental setting, execute your code with the following option: Djavafx.embed.singleThread=true

---

By utilizing the new features of JavaFX 8, you can generate a JavaFX application that contains embedded Swing code that can communicate directly with the JavaFX code.

Summary

JavaFX is the successor to the Java Swing API. It enables developers to produce sophisticated and powerful user interfaces for the next generation of applications. This chapter provided you with a basic understanding of JavaFX, along with some of the most widely used JavaFX APIs. Over the course of the next few chapters, you'll learn more about JavaFX, such as how to construct 3D objects and WebViews.

CHAPTER 15

■ ■ ■

Graphics with JavaFX

Have you ever heard someone say, "When two worlds collide"? This expression is used when a person from a different background or culture is put in a situation where they are at odds and must face very difficult decisions. When we build a GUI application requiring animations, we are often in a collision course between business and gaming worlds.

In the ever-changing world of rich client applications, you probably have noticed an increase of animations such as pulsing buttons, transitions, moving backgrounds, and so on. When GUI applications use animations, they can provide visual cues to the users to let them know what to do next. With JavaFX, you can have the best of both worlds.

Figure 15-1 illustrates a simple drawing coming alive.

Figure 15-1. *Graphics with JavaFX*

In this chapter you will create images, animations, and Look and Feels. Fasten your seatbelts; you'll discover solutions to integrate cool game-like interfaces into your everyday applications.

■ **Note**   Refer to Chapter 14 if you are new to JavaFX. Among other things, it will help you create an environment in which you can be productive using JavaFX.

J. Juneau, *Java 9 Recipes*, DOI l0.1007/978-1-4842-1976-8_15

15-1. Creating Images

Problem

There are photos in your file directory that you would like to quickly browse through and showcase within a graphical user interface.

Solution

Create a simple JavaFX image viewer application. The main Java classes used in this recipe are:

- `javafx.scene.image.Image`
- `javafx.scene.image.ImageView`
- `EventHandler<DragEvent>` classes

The following source code is an implementation of an image viewer application:

```java
package org.java9recipes.chapter15.recipe15_01;

import java.io.File;
import java.util.ArrayList;
import java.util.List;
import javafx.application.Application;
import javafx.scene.Group;
import javafx.scene.Scene;
import javafx.scene.image.Image;
import javafx.scene.image.ImageView;
import javafx.scene.input.DragEvent;
import javafx.scene.input.Dragboard;
import javafx.scene.input.MouseEvent;
import javafx.scene.input.TransferMode;
import javafx.scene.layout.HBox;
import javafx.scene.paint.Color;
import javafx.scene.shape.Arc;
import javafx.scene.shape.ArcType;
import javafx.scene.shape.Rectangle;
import javafx.stage.Stage;

/**
 * Recipe 15-1: Creating Images
 *
 * @author cdea
 * Update: J Juneau
 */
public class CreatingImages extends Application {

    private final List<String> imageFiles = new ArrayList<>();
    private int currentIndex = -1;
    private final String filePrefix = "file:";
```

```java
public enum ButtonMove {

    NEXT, PREV
};

/**
 * @param args the command line arguments
 */
public static void main(String[] args) {
    Application.launch(args);
}

@Override
public void start(Stage primaryStage) {
    primaryStage.setTitle("Chapter 15-1 Creating a Image");
    Group root = new Group();
    Scene scene = new Scene(root, 551, 400, Color.BLACK);

    // image view
    final ImageView currentImageView = new ImageView();

    // maintain aspect ratio
    currentImageView.setPreserveRatio(true);

    // resize based on the scene
    currentImageView.fitWidthProperty().bind(scene.widthProperty());

    final HBox pictureRegion = new HBox();
    pictureRegion.getChildren().add(currentImageView);
    root.getChildren().add(pictureRegion);

    // Dragging over surface
    scene.setOnDragOver((DragEvent event) -> {
        Dragboard db = event.getDragboard();
        if (db.hasFiles()) {
            event.acceptTransferModes(TransferMode.COPY);
        } else {
            event.consume();
        }
    });

    // Dropping over surface
    scene.setOnDragDropped((DragEvent event) -> {
        Dragboard db = event.getDragboard();
        boolean success = false;
        if (db.hasFiles()) {
            success = true;
            String filePath = null;
            for (File file : db.getFiles()) {
                filePath = file.getAbsolutePath();
                System.out.println(filePath);
```

```
                currentIndex += 1;
                imageFiles.add(currentIndex, filePath);
            }
            filePath = filePrefix + filePath;
            // set new image as the image to show.
            Image imageimage = new Image(filePath);
            currentImageView.setImage(imageimage);

        }
        event.setDropCompleted(success);
        event.consume();

    });

    // create slide controls
    Group buttonGroup = new Group();

    // rounded rect
    Rectangle buttonArea = new Rectangle();
    buttonArea.setArcWidth(15);
    buttonArea.setArcHeight(20);
    buttonArea.setFill(new Color(0, 0, 0, .55));
    buttonArea.setX(0);
    buttonArea.setY(0);
    buttonArea.setWidth(60);
    buttonArea.setHeight(30);
    buttonArea.setStroke(Color.rgb(255, 255, 255, .70));

    buttonGroup.getChildren().add(buttonArea);
    // left control
    Arc leftButton = new Arc();
    leftButton.setType(ArcType.ROUND);
    leftButton.setCenterX(12);
    leftButton.setCenterY(16);
    leftButton.setRadiusX(15);
    leftButton.setRadiusY(15);
    leftButton.setStartAngle(-30);
    leftButton.setLength(60);
    leftButton.setFill(new Color(1, 1, 1, .90));

    leftButton.addEventHandler(MouseEvent.MOUSE_PRESSED, (MouseEvent me) -> {
        int indx = gotoImageIndex(ButtonMove.PREV);
        if (indx > -1) {
            String namePict = imageFiles.get(indx);
            namePict = filePrefix + namePict;
            final Image image = new Image(namePict);
            currentImageView.setImage(image);
        }
    });
    buttonGroup.getChildren().add(leftButton);
```

```
        // right control
        Arc rightButton = new Arc();
        rightButton.setType(ArcType.ROUND);
        rightButton.setCenterX(12);
        rightButton.setCenterY(16);
        rightButton.setRadiusX(15);
        rightButton.setRadiusY(15);
        rightButton.setStartAngle(180 - 30);
        rightButton.setLength(60);
        rightButton.setFill(new Color(1, 1, 1, .90));
        rightButton.setTranslateX(40);
        buttonGroup.getChildren().add(rightButton);

        rightButton.addEventHandler(MouseEvent.MOUSE_PRESSED, (MouseEvent me) -> {
            int indx = gotoImageIndex(ButtonMove.NEXT);
            if (indx > -1) {
                String namePict = imageFiles.get(indx);
                namePict = filePrefix + namePict;
                final Image image = new Image(namePict);
                currentImageView.setImage(image);
            }
        });

        // move button group when scene is resized

        buttonGroup.translateXProperty().bind(scene.widthProperty().subtract
        (buttonArea.getWidth() + 6));

        buttonGroup.translateYProperty().bind(scene.heightProperty().subtract
        (buttonArea.getHeight() + 6));
        root.getChildren().add(buttonGroup);

        primaryStage.setScene(scene);
        primaryStage.show();
    }
    /**
     * Returns the next index in the list of files to go to next.
     *
     * @param direction PREV and NEXT to move backward or forward in the list of
     * pictures.
     * @return int the index to the previous or next picture to be shown.
     */
    public int gotoImageIndex(ButtonMove direction) {
        int size = imageFiles.size();
        if (size == 0) {
            currentIndex = -1;
        } else if (direction == ButtonMove.NEXT && size > 1 && currentIndex < size - 1) {
            currentIndex += 1;
        } else if (direction == ButtonMove.PREV && size > 1 && currentIndex > 0) {
            currentIndex -= 1;
        }

        return currentIndex;
    }
```

Figure 15-2 depicts the drag-and-drop operation that gives the user visual feedback with a thumbnail-sized image over the surface. In the figure, I'm dragging the image onto the application window.

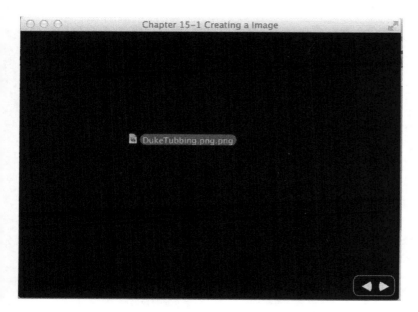

Figure 15-2. *Drag-and-drop in progress*

Figure 15-3 shows that the drop operation has succesfully loaded the image.

Figure 15-3. *Drop operation completed*

How It Works

This recipe is a simple application that allows you to view images having file formats such as .jpg, .png, and .gif. Loading an image requires using the mouse to drag and drop a file onto the window area. The application also allows you to resize the window, which automatically causes the image to scale while maintaining its aspect ratio. After a few images are successfully loaded, you will be able to page through each image conveniently by clicking the left and right button controls, as shown in Figure 15-3.

Before the code walk-through, let's discuss the application's variables. Table 15-1 describes instance variables for this sleek image viewer application.

Table 15-1. *The* CreatingImages *Instance Variables*

Variable	Data Type	Example	Description
imageFiles	List<String>	/User/pictures/fun.jpg	A list of Strings, each containing an image's absolute file path
currentIndex	int	0	A zero relative index number into the imageFiles list; -1 means no images to view
NEXT	enum	-	User clicks the right arrow button
PREV	enum	-	User clicks the left arrow button

When you're dragging an image into the application, the imageFiles variable will cache the absolute file path as a String instead of as the actual image file in order to save memory space. If a user drags the same image file into the display area, the list will contain duplicate Strings representing the image file. As an image is being displayed, the currentIndex variable contains the index into the imageFiles list. The imageFiles list points to the String representing the current image file. As the user clicks the buttons to display the previous and next image, the currentIndex will decrement or increment, respectively. Next, let's walk through the code detailing the steps for loading and displaying an image. Later, you will learn the steps for paging through each image with the next and previous buttons.

Begin by instantiating an instance of the javafx.scene.image.ImageView class. The ImageView class is a graph node (Node) used to display an already loaded javafx.scene.image.Image object. Using the ImageView node will enable you to create special effects on the image to be displayed without manipulating the physical image. To avoid performance degradation when rendering many effects, you can use numerous ImageView objects that reference a single Image object. Many types of effects include blurring, fading, and transforming an image.

One of the requirements is preserving the displayed image's aspect ratio as the user resizes the window. Here, you will simply call the setPreserveRatio() method with a value of true to preserve the image's aspect ratio. Remember that because the user resizes the window, you want to bind the width of the ImageView to the Scene's width to allow the image to be scaled. After setting up the ImageView, you will want to pass it to an HBox instance (pictureRegion) to be put into the scene. The following code creates the ImageView instance, preserves the aspect ratio, and scales the image:

```
// image view
final ImageView currentImageView = new ImageView();

// maintain aspect ratio
currentImageView.setPreserveRatio(true);

// resize based on the scene
currentImageView.fitWidthProperty().bind(scene.widthProperty());
```

Next, let's cover JavaFX's native drag-and-drop support, which provides many options for users, such as dragging visual objects from an application to be dropped into another application. In this scenario, the user will be dragging an image file from the host windowing operating system to the image viewer application. In this scenario, EventHandler objects must be generated to listen to DragEvents. To fulfill this requirement, you'll set up a scene's drag-over and drag-dropped event handler methods.

To set up the drag-over attribute, call the scene's setOnDragOver() method with the appropriate generic EventHandler<DragEvent> type. In the example, a lambda expression is used to implement the event handler. Implement the handle() method via the lambda expression to listen for the drag-over event (DragEvent). In the event handler, notice the event (DragEvent) object's invocation to the getDragboard() method. The call to getDragboard() will return the drag source (Dragboard), better known as the *clipboard*. Once the Dragboard object is obtained, it is possible to determine and validate what is being dragged over the surface. In this scenario, you need to determine whether the Dragboard object contains any files. If it does, you call the event object's acceptTransferModes() by passing in the constant TransferMode.COPY to provide visual feedback to the user of the application (refer to Figure 15-2). Otherwise, it should consume the event by calling the event.consume() method. The following code demonstrates setting up a scene's OnDragOver attribute:

```
// Dragging over surface
scene.setOnDragOver((DragEvent event) -> {
    Dragboard db = event.getDragboard();
    if (db.hasFiles()) {
        event.acceptTransferModes(TransferMode.COPY);
    } else {
        event.consume();
    }
});
```

Once the drag-over event handler attribute is set, you create a drag-dropped event handler attribute so it can finalize the operation. Listening to a drag-dropped event is similar to listening to a drag-over event in which the handle() method will be implemented via a lambda expression. Once again, you obtain the Dragboard object from the event to determine whether the clipboard contains any files. If it does, the list of files is iterated and the file names are added to the imageFiles list. This code demonstrates setting up a scene's OnDragDropped attribute:

```
// Dropping over surface
scene.setOnDragDropped((DragEvent event) -> {
    Dragboard db = event.getDragboard();
    boolean success = false;
    if (db.hasFiles()) {
        success = true;
        String filePath = null;
        for (File file : db.getFiles()) {
            filePath = file.getAbsolutePath();
            System.out.println(filePath);
            currentIndex += 1;
            imageFiles.add(currentIndex, filePath);
        }
```

```
        filePath = filePrefix + filePath;
        // set new image as the image to show.
        Image imageimage = new Image(filePath);
        currentImageView.setImage(imageimage);

    }
    event.setDropCompleted(success);
    event.consume();

});
```

As the last file is determined, the current image is displayed. The following code demonstrates loading an image to be displayed:

```
// set new image as the image to show.
Image imageimage = new Image(filePath);
currentImageView.setImage(imageimage);
```

For the last requirements relating to the image viewer application, simple controls are generated that allow the users to view the next or previous image. I emphasize "simple" controls because JavaFX contains two other methods for creating custom controls. One way, Cascading Style Sheets (CSS) styling, is discussed later, in Recipe 15-5. To explore the other alternative, refer to the Javadoc on the Skin and Skinnable APIs.

The simple buttons in this example are created using Java FX's javafx.scene.shape.Arc to build the left and right arrows on top of a small transparent rounded rectangle called javafx.scene.shape.Rectangle. Next, an EventHandler that listens to mouse-pressed events is added via a lambda expression, and it will load and display the appropriate image based on the enums ButtonMove.PREV and ButtonMove.NEXT.

When instantiating a generic class with a type variable between the < and > symbols, the same type variable will be defined in the handle()'s signature. When implementing the event handler logic, you determine which button was pressed and then return the index into the imageFiles list of the next image to display. When loading an image using the Image class, it is possible to load images from the file system or from a URL. The following code instantiates an EventHandler<MouseEvent> lambda expression to display the previous image in the imageFiles list:

```
leftButton.addEventHandler(MouseEvent.MOUSE_PRESSED, (MouseEvent me) -> {
    int indx = gotoImageIndex(ButtonMove.PREV);
    if (indx > -1) {
        String namePict = imageFiles.get(indx);
        namePict = filePrefix + namePict;
        final Image image = new Image(namePict);
        currentImageView.setImage(image);
    }
});
```

The right button's (rightButton) event handler is identical. The only thing different is that it must determine whether the previous or next button was pressed via the ButtonMove enum. This information is passed to the gotoImageIndex() method to determine whether an image is available in that direction.

To finish the image viewer application, you bind the rectangular button's control to the scene's width and height, which repositions the control as the user resizes the window. Here, you bind the translateXProperty() to the scene's width property by subtracting the buttonArea's width (Fluent API). In the example, you also bind the translateYProperty() based on the scene's height property. Once your buttons control is bound, your user will experience user interface goodness. The following code uses the Fluent API to bind the button control's properties to the scene's properties:

437

```
// move button group when scene is resized
buttonGroup.translateXProperty().bind(scene.widthProperty().subtract(buttonArea.getWidth()
    + 6));

buttonGroup.translateYProperty().bind(scene.heightProperty().subtract
(buttonArea.getHeight()
    + 6));
root.getChildren().add(buttonGroup);
```

15-2. Generating an Animation

Problem

You want to generate an animation. For example, you want to create a news ticker and photo viewer application with the following requirements:

- It will have a news ticker control that scrolls to the left.

- It will fade out the current picture and fade in the next picture as the user clicks the button controls.

- It will fade in and out button controls when the cursor moves in and out of the scene area, respectively.

- The news ticker will pause when the mouse hovers over the text, and will start again once the mouse moves away from the text.

Solution

Create animated effects by accessing JavaFX's animation APIs (javafx.animation.*).To create the aforementioned news ticker, you need the following classes:

- javafx.animation.TranslateTransition

- javafx.util.Duration

- javafx.event.EventHandler<ActionEvent>

- javafx.scene.shape.Rectangle

To fade out the current picture and fade in next picture, you need the following classes:

- javafx.animation.SequentialTransition

- javafx.animation.FadeTransition

- javafx.event.EventHandler<ActionEvent>

- javafx.scene.image.Image

- javafx.scene.image.ImageView

- javafx.util.Duration

To fade in and out button controls when the cursor moves into and out of the scene area, respectively, you need the following classes:

- `javafx.animation.FadeTransition`
- `javafx.util.Duration`

Shown here is the code used to create a news ticker control:

```
// create ticker area
final Group tickerArea = new Group();
final Rectangle tickerRect = new Rectangle();
tickerRect.setArcWidth(15);
tickerRect.setArcHeight(20);
tickerRect.setFill(new Color(0, 0, 0, .55));
tickerRect.setX(0);
tickerRect.setY(0);
tickerRect.setWidth(scene.getWidth() - 6);
tickerRect.setHeight(30);
tickerRect.setStroke(Color.rgb(255, 255, 255, .70));

Rectangle clipRegion = new Rectangle();
clipRegion.setArcWidth(15);
clipRegion.setArcHeight(20);
clipRegion.setX(0);
clipRegion.setY(0);
clipRegion.setWidth(scene.getWidth() - 6);
clipRegion.setHeight(30);
clipRegion.setStroke(Color.rgb(255, 255, 255, .70));

tickerArea.setClip(clipRegion);

// Resize the ticker area when the window is resized
tickerArea.setTranslateX(6);
tickerArea.translateYProperty().bind(scene.heightProperty().subtract(
    tickerRect.getHeight() + 6));
tickerRect.widthProperty().bind(scene.widthProperty().subtract(
    buttonRect.getWidth() + 16));
clipRegion.widthProperty().bind(scene.widthProperty().subtract(
    buttonRect.getWidth() + 16));
tickerArea.getChildren().add(tickerRect);

root.getChildren().add(tickerArea);

// add news text
Text news = new Text();
news.setText("JavaFX 8 News Ticker... | New Features: Swing Node, Event Dispatch Thread and
JavaFX Application Thread Merge,  " +
        "New Look and Feel - Modena, Rich Text Support, Printing, Tree Table Control,
        Much More!");
news.setTranslateY(18);
news.setFill(Color.WHITE);
tickerArea.getChildren().add(news);
```

```
final TranslateTransition ticker = new TranslateTransition();
ticker.setNode(news);
int newsLength = news.getText().length();

// Calculated guess based upon length of text
ticker.setDuration(Duration.millis((newsLength * 4/300) * 15000));
ticker.setFromX(scene.widthProperty().doubleValue());
ticker.setToX(-scene.widthProperty().doubleValue() - (newsLength * 5));
ticker.setFromY(19);
ticker.setInterpolator(Interpolator.LINEAR);
ticker.setCycleCount(1);

// when ticker has finished reset and replay ticker animation
ticker.setOnFinished((ActionEvent ae) -> {
    ticker.stop();
    ticker.setFromX(scene.getWidth());
    ticker.setDuration(new Duration((newsLength * 4/300) * 15000));
    ticker.playFromStart();
});

// stop ticker if hovered over
tickerArea.setOnMouseEntered((MouseEvent me) -> {
    ticker.pause();
});

// restart ticker if mouse leaves the ticker
tickerArea.setOnMouseExited((MouseEvent me) -> {
    ticker.play();
});

ticker.play();
```

The following is the code used to fade out the current picture and fade in the next picture:

```
// previous button
Arc prevButton = // create arc ...

prevButton.addEventHandler(MouseEvent.MOUSE_PRESSED, (MouseEvent me) -> {
    int indx = gotoImageIndex(PREV);
    if (indx > -1) {
        String namePict = imagesFiles.get(indx);
        final Image nextImage = new Image(namePict);
        SequentialTransition seqTransition = transitionByFading
        (nextImage, currentImageView);
        seqTransition.play();
    }
});

buttonGroup.getChildren().add(prevButton);
```

```
    // next button
    Arc nextButton = //... create arc

    buttonGroup.getChildren().add(nextButton);

    nextButton.addEventHandler(MouseEvent.MOUSE_PRESSED, (MouseEvent me) -> {
        int indx = gotoImageIndex(NEXT);
        if (indx > -1) {
            String namePict = imagesFiles.get(indx);
            final Image nextImage = new Image(namePict);
            SequentialTransition seqTransition = transitionByFading
            (nextImage, currentImageView);
            seqTransition.play();

        }
    });

//... the rest of the start(Stage primaryStage) method

public int gotoImageIndex(int direction) {
    int size = imagesFiles.size();
    if (size == 0) {
        currentIndexImageFile = -1;
    } else if (direction == NEXT && size > 1 && currentIndexImageFile < size - 1) {
        currentIndexImageFile += 1;
    } else if (direction == PREV && size > 1 && currentIndexImageFile > 0) {
        currentIndexImageFile -= 1;
    }

    return currentIndexImageFile;
}

public SequentialTransition transitionByFading(final Image nextImage, final ImageView
imageView) {
    FadeTransition fadeOut = new FadeTransition(Duration.millis(500), imageView);
    fadeOut.setFromValue(1.0);
    fadeOut.setToValue(0.0);
    fadeOut.setOnFinished((ActionEvent ae) -> {
        imageView.setImage(nextImage);
    });
    FadeTransition fadeIn = new FadeTransition(Duration.millis(500), imageView);
    fadeIn.setFromValue(0.0);
    fadeIn.setToValue(1.0);
    SequentialTransition seqTransition = new SequentialTransition();
    seqTransition.getChildren().addAll(fadeOut, fadeIn);
    return seqTransition;
}
```

The following code is used to fade in and out the button controls when the cursor moves into and out of the scene area, respectively:

```
// Fade in button controls
scene.setOnMouseEntered((MouseEvent me) -> {
    FadeTransition fadeButtons = new FadeTransition(Duration.millis(500), buttonGroup);
    fadeButtons.setFromValue(0.0);
    fadeButtons.setToValue(1.0);
    fadeButtons.play();
});

// Fade out button controls
scene.setOnMouseExited((MouseEvent me) -> {
    FadeTransition fadeButtons = new FadeTransition(Duration.millis(500), buttonGroup);
    fadeButtons.setFromValue(1);
    fadeButtons.setToValue(0);
    fadeButtons.play();
});
```

Figure 15-4 shows the photo viewer application with a ticker control in the bottom region of the screen.

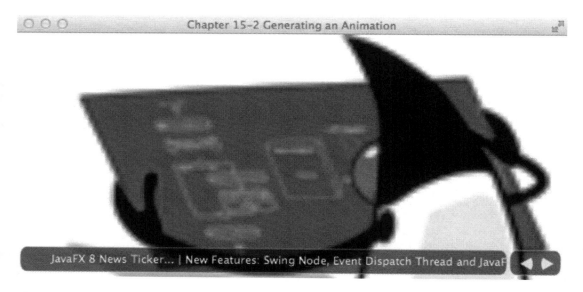

Figure 15-4. *Photo viewer with a news ticker*

How It Works

This recipe takes the photo viewer application from Recipe 15-1 and adds a news ticker and some nice photo-changing animation to it. The main animation effects focus on translating and fading. First, a news ticker control is created, and it scrolls Text nodes to the left by using a translation transition (javafx.animation.TranslateTransition). Next, another fading effect is applied so that slow transitions will occur when the user clicks the previous and next buttons to transition to the next image. To perform this effect, a compound transition (javafx.animation.SequentialTransition) is used, consisting of multiple animations. Finally, to create the effect of the button controls fading in and out based on where the mouse is located, you use a fade transition (javafx.animation.FadeTransition).

Before I begin to discuss the steps to fulfill the requirements, I want to mention the basics of JavaFX animation. The JavaFX animation API allows you to assemble timed events that can interpolate over a node's attribute values to produce animated effects. Each timed event is called a keyframe (KeyFrame), and it is responsible for interpolating over a node's property over a period of time (javafx.util.Duration). Knowing that a keyframe's job is to operate on a node's property value, you have to create an instance of a KeyValue class that will reference the desired node property. The idea of interpolation is simply the distributing of values between a start and end value. An example is to move a rectangle by its current x position (zero) to 100 pixels in 1,000 milliseconds; in other words, move the rectangle 100 pixels to the right during one second. Shown here is a keyframe and key value to interpolate a rectangle's x property for 1,000 milliseconds:

```
final Rectangle rectangle = new Rectangle(0, 0, 50, 50);
KeyValue keyValue = new KeyValue(rectangle.xProperty(), 100);
KeyFrame keyFrame = new KeyFrame(Duration.millis(1000), keyValue);
```

When creating many keyframes that are assembled consecutively, you need to create a timeline. Because timeline is a subclass of javafx.animation.Animation, there are standard attributes, such as its cycle count and autoreverse, that you can set. The *cycle count* is the number of times you want the timeline to play the animation. If you want the cycle count to play the animation indefinitely, use the value Timeline.INDEFINITE. The autoreverse is the capability for the animation to play the timeline backward. By default, the cycle count is set to 1, and the autoreverse is set to false. When adding keyframes you simply add them using the getKeyFrames().add() method on the TimeLine object. The following code snippet demonstrates a timeline playing indefinitely with autoreverse set to true:

```
Timeline timeline = new Timeline();
timeline.setCycleCount(Timeline.INDEFINITE);
timeline.setAutoReverse(true);
timeline.getKeyFrames().add(keyFrame);
timeline.play();
```

With this knowledge of timelines you can animate any graph node in JavaFX. Although you can create timelines in a low-level way, it can become very cumbersome. You are probably wondering whether there are easier ways to express common animations. Good news! JavaFX has transitions (Transition), which are convenience classes that perform common animated effects. Some of the common animation effects you can create with transitions include:

- javafx.animation.FadeTransition

- javafx.animation.PathTransition

- javafx.animation.ScaleTransition

- javafx.animation.TranslateTransition

To see more transitions, see javafx.animation in the Javadoc. Because Transition objects are also subclasses of the javafx.animation.Animation class, you can set the cycle count and autoreverse attributes. This recipe focuses on two transition effects: translate transition (TranslateTransition) and fade transition (FadeTransition).

The first requirement in the problem statement is to create a news ticker. In a news ticker control, Text nodes scroll from right to left inside a rectangular region. When the text scrolls to the left edge of the rectangular region you will want the text to be clipped to create a view port that only shows pixels inside of the rectangle. To do this, you first create a Group to hold all the components that comprise a ticker control.

Next you create a white rounded rectangle filled with 55% opacity. After creating the visual region, you create a similar rectangle that represents the clipped region using the setClip(someRectangle) method on the Group object. Figure 15-5 shows a rounded rectangular area that serves as the clipped region.

Figure 15-5. *Setting the clipped region on the Group object*

Once the ticker control is created, you bind the translate Y based on the scene's height property minus the ticker control's height. You also bind the ticker control's width property based on the width of scene minus the button control's width. By binding these properties, the ticker control can change its size and position whenever a user resizes the application window. This makes the ticker control appear to float at the bottom of the window. The following code binds the ticker control's translate Y, width, and clip region's width property:

```
tickerArea.translateYProperty().bind(scene.heightProperty().subtract(tickerRect.getHeight() + 6));
tickerRect.widthProperty().bind(scene.widthProperty().subtract(buttonRect.getWidth() + 16));
clipRegion.widthProperty().bind(scene.widthProperty().subtract(buttonRect.getWidth() + 16));
tickerArea.getChildren().add(tickerRect);
```

Now that the ticker control is complete, you'll create some news to feed into it. In the example, a Text node with text that represents a news feed is used. To add a newly created Text node to the ticker control, you call its getChildren().add() method. The following code adds a Text node to the ticker control:

```
final Group tickerArea = new Group();
final Rectangle tickerRect = //...
Text news = new Text();
news.setText("JavaFX 8 News Ticker... | New Features: Swing Node, Event Dispatch Thread and
JavaFX Application Thread Merge,  " +
        "New Look and Feel - Modena, Rich Text Support, Printing, Tree Table Control, Much
More!");
news.setTranslateY(18);
news.setFill(Color.WHITE);
tickerArea.getChildren().add(news);
```

Next you have to scroll the Text node from right to left using JavaFX's TranslateTransition API. The first step is to set the target node to perform the TranslateTransition. Then you set the duration, which is the total amount of time the TranslateTransition will spend animating. A TranslateTransition simplifies the creation of an animation by exposing convenience methods that operate on a Node's translate X and Y properties. The convenience methods are prepended with from and to. For instance, in the scenario in which you use translate X on a Text node, there are the methods fromX() and toX(). The fromX() is the starting value and the toX() is the end value that will be interpolated. In the example, you base these calculations on the length of the text in the Text node. Therefore, if you are reading from a remote source, such as an RSS feed, the text length difference should not break the ticker. Next, you set the TranslateTransition to a linear transition (Interpolator.LINEAR) to interpolate evenly between the start and end values. To see more interpolator types or to see how to create custom interpolators, see the Javadoc on javafx.animation.Interpolators. Finally, in the example the cycle count is set to 1, which will animate the ticker once based on the specified duration. The following code snippet details creating a TranslateTransition that animates a Text node from right to left:

```
final TranslateTransition ticker = new TranslateTransition();
ticker.setNode(news);
int newsLength = news.getText().length();
ticker.setDuration(Duration.millis((newsLength * 4/300) * 15000));
ticker.setFromX(scene.widthProperty().doubleValue());
ticker.setToX(-scene.widthProperty().doubleValue() - (newsLength * 5));
ticker.setFromY(19);
ticker.setInterpolator(Interpolator.LINEAR);
ticker.setCycleCount(1);
```

When the ticker's news has scrolled completely off of the ticker area to the far left of the scene, you will want to stop and replay the news feed from the start (the far right). To do this, you create an instance of an EventHandler<ActionEvent> object via a lambda expression, to be set on the ticker (TranslateTransition) object using the setOnFinished() method. Here is how you replay the TranslateTransition animation:

```
// when window resizes width wise the ticker will know how far to move
// when ticker has finished reset and replay ticker animation
ticker.setOnFinished((ActionEvent ae) -> {
    ticker.stop();
    ticker.setFromX(scene.getWidth());
    ticker.setDuration(new Duration((newsLength * 4/300) * 15000));
    ticker.playFromStart();
});
```

Once the animation is defined, you simply invoke the play() method to get it started. The following code snippet shows how to play a TranslateTransition:

```
ticker.play();
```

To pause and start the ticker when the mouse hovers over and leaves the text, you need to implement similar event handlers:

```
// stop ticker if hovered over
tickerArea.setOnMouseEntered((MouseEvent me) -> {
    ticker.pause();
});
```

```
// restart ticker if mouse leaves the ticker
tickerArea.setOnMouseExited((MouseEvent me) -> {
    ticker.play();
});
```

Now that you have a better understanding of animated transitions, what about a transition that can trigger any number of transitions? JavaFX has two transitions that provide this behavior. The two transitions can invoke individual dependent transitions sequentially or in parallel. In this recipe, you'll use a sequential transition (SequentialTransition) to contain two FadeTransitions in order to fade out the current image displayed and to fade in the next image. When creating the previous and next button's event handlers, you first determine the next image to be displayed by calling the gotoImageIndex() method. Once the next image to be displayed is determined, you call the transitionByFading() method, which returns an instance of a SequentialTransition. When calling the transitionByFading() method, you'll notice that two FadeTransitions are created. The first transition will change the opacity level from 1.0 to 0.0 to fade out the current image, and the second transition will interpolate the opacity level from 0.0 to 1.0, fading in the next image, which then becomes the current image. At last the two FadeTransitions are added to the SequentialTransition and returned to the caller. The following code creates two FadeTransitions and adds them to a SequentialTransition:

```
FadeTransition fadeOut = new FadeTransition(Duration.millis(500), imageView);
fadeOut.setFromValue(1.0);
fadeOut.setToValue(0.0);
fadeOut.setOnFinished((ActionEvent ae) -> {
    imageView.setImage(nextImage);
});
FadeTransition fadeIn = new FadeTransition(Duration.millis(500), imageView);
fadeIn.setFromValue(0.0);
fadeIn.setToValue(1.0);
SequentialTransition seqTransition = new SequentialTransition();
seqTransition.getChildren().addAll(fadeOut, fadeIn);
return seqTransition;
```

For the last requirements relating to fading in and out, use the button controls. Use the FadeTransition to create a ghostly animated effect. For starters, you create an EventHandler (more specifically, an EventHandler<MouseEvent> via a lambda expression). It is easy to add mouse events to the scene; all you have to do is override the handle() method where the inbound parameter is a MouseEvent type (the same as its formal type parameter). Inside of the lambda, you create an instance of a FadeTransition object by using the constructor that takes the duration and node as parameters. Next, you'll notice the setFromValue() and setToValue() methods that are called to interpolate values between 1.0 and 0.0 for the opacity level, causing the fade in effect to occur. The following code adds an EventHandler to create the fade in effect when the mouse cursor is positioned inside of the scene:

```
// Fade in button controls
scene.setOnMouseEntered((MouseEvent me) -> {
    FadeTransition fadeButtons = new FadeTransition(Duration.millis(500), buttonGroup);
    fadeButtons.setFromValue(0.0);
    fadeButtons.setToValue(1.0);
    fadeButtons.play();
});
```

Last but not least, the fade out EventHandler is basically the same as the fade in, except that the opacity From and To values are from 1.0 to 0.0, which make the buttons vanish mysteriously when the mouse pointer moves off the scene area.

15-3. Animating Shapes Along a Path

Problem

You want to create a way to animate shapes along a path.

Solution

Create an application that allows users to draw the path for a shape to follow. The main Java classes used in this recipe are these:

- `javafx.animation.PathTransition`
- `javafx.scene.input.MouseEvent`
- `javafx.event.EventHandler`
- `javafx.geometry.Point2D`
- `javafx.scene.shape.LineTo`
- `javafx.scene.shape.MoveTo`
- `javafx.scene.shape.Path`

The following code demonstrates drawing a path for a shape to follow:

```
package org.java9recipes.chapter15.recipe15_03;

import javafx.animation.PathTransition;
import javafx.application.Application;
import javafx.event.ActionEvent;
import javafx.event.EventHandler;
import javafx.geometry.Point2D;
import javafx.scene.Group;
import javafx.scene.Scene;
import javafx.scene.input.MouseEvent;
import javafx.scene.paint.Color;
import javafx.scene.paint.CycleMethod;
import javafx.scene.paint.RadialGradient;
import javafx.scene.paint.Stop;
import javafx.scene.shape.Circle;
import javafx.scene.shape.LineTo;
import javafx.scene.shape.MoveTo;
import javafx.scene.shape.Path;
import javafx.stage.Stage;
import javafx.util.Duration;

/**
 * Recipe 15-3: Working with the Scene Graph
 * @author cdea
 * Update: J Juneau
 */
public class WorkingWithTheSceneGraph extends Application {

    Path onePath = new Path();
    Point2D anchorPt;
    /**
     * @param args the command line arguments
     */
```

```java
public static void main(String[] args) {
    Application.launch(args);
}

@Override
public void start(Stage primaryStage) {
    primaryStage.setTitle("Chapter 15-3 Working with the Scene Graph");

    final Group root = new Group();
    // add path
    root.getChildren().add(onePath);

    final Scene scene = new Scene(root, 300, 250);
    scene.setFill(Color.WHITE);

    RadialGradient gradient1 = new RadialGradient(0,
            .1,
            100,
            100,
            20,
            false,
            CycleMethod.NO_CYCLE,
            new Stop(0, Color.RED),
            new Stop(1, Color.BLACK));

    // create a sphere
    final Circle sphere = new Circle();
    sphere.setCenterX(100);
    sphere.setCenterY(100);
    sphere.setRadius(20);
    sphere.setFill(gradient1);

    // add sphere
    root.getChildren().add(sphere);

    // animate sphere by following the path.
    final PathTransition pathTransition = new PathTransition();
    pathTransition.setDuration(Duration.millis(4000));
    pathTransition.setCycleCount(1);
    pathTransition.setNode(sphere);
    pathTransition.setPath(onePath);
    pathTransition.setOrientation(PathTransition.OrientationType.ORTHOGONAL_TO_TANGENT);

    // once finished clear path
    pathTransition.onFinishedProperty().set((EventHandler<ActionEvent>)
    (ActionEvent event) -> {
        onePath.getElements().clear();
    });
```

```
    // starting initial path
    scene.onMousePressedProperty().set((EventHandler<MouseEvent>)
    (MouseEvent event) -> {
        onePath.getElements().clear();
        // start point in path
        anchorPt = new Point2D(event.getX(), event.getY());
        onePath.setStrokeWidth(3);
        onePath.setStroke(Color.BLACK);
        onePath.getElements().add(new MoveTo(anchorPt.getX(), anchorPt.getY()));
    });

    // dragging creates lineTos added to the path
    scene.onMouseDraggedProperty().set((EventHandler<MouseEvent>)
    (MouseEvent event) -> {
        onePath.getElements().add(new LineTo(event.getX(), event.getY()));
    });

    // end the path when mouse released event
    scene.onMouseReleasedProperty().set((EventHandler<MouseEvent>)
    (MouseEvent event) -> {
        onePath.setStrokeWidth(0);
        if (onePath.getElements().size() > 1) {
            pathTransition.stop();
            pathTransition.playFromStart();
        }
    });

    primaryStage.setScene(scene);
    primaryStage.show();
    }
}
```

Figure 15-6 shows the drawn path the circle will follow. When the user performs a mouse release, the drawn path will disappear and the red ball will follow the path drawn earlier.

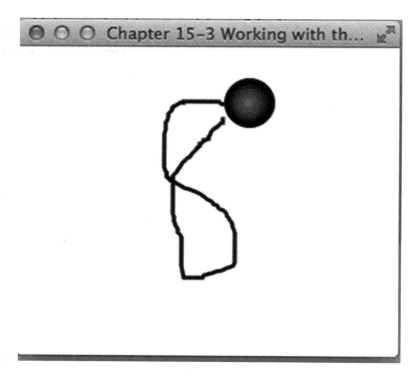

Figure 15-6. Path transition

How It Works

In this recipe, you create a simple application enabling objects to follow a drawn path on the scene graph. To make things simple, the example uses one shape (Circle) that performs a path transition (javafx.animation.PathTransition). The application user will draw a path on the scene surface by pressing the mouse button like a drawing program. Once satisfied with the path drawn, the user releases the mouse press, which triggers the red ball to follow the path, similar to objects moving through pipes inside a building.

You first create two instance variables to maintain the coordinates that make up the path. To hold the path being drawn, create an instance of a javafx.scene.shape.Path object. The path instance should be added to the scene graph before the start of the application. Shown here is the process of adding the instance variable onePath to the scene graph:

```
// add path
root.getChildren().add(onePath);
```

Next, you create an instance variable anchorPt (javafx.geometry.Point2D) that will hold the path's starting point. Later, you will see how these variables are updated based on mouse events. Shown here are the instance variables that maintain the currently drawn path:

```
Path onePath = new Path();
Point2D anchorPt;
```

First, let's create a shape that will be animated. In this scenario, you'll create a cool-looking red ball. To create a spherical-looking ball, create a gradient color RadialGradient that's used to paint or fill a circle shape. (Refer to Recipe 15-6 for how to fill shapes with a gradient paint.) Once you have created the red spherical ball, you need to create the PathTransition object to perform the path-following animation. After instantiating a PathTransition() object, simply set the duration to four seconds and the cycle count to one. The cycle count is the number of times the animation cycle will occur. Next, you set the node to reference the red ball (sphere). Then, you set the path() method to the instance variable onePath, which contains all the coordinates and lines that make up a drawn path. After setting the path for the sphere to animate, you should specify how the shape will follow the path, such as perpendicular to a tangent point on the path. The following code creates an instance of a path transition:

```
// animate sphere by following the path.
final PathTransition pathTransition = new PathTransition();
pathTransition.setDuration(Duration.millis(4000));
pathTransition.setCycleCount(1);
pathTransition.setNode(sphere);
pathTransition.setPath(onePath);
pathTransition.setOrientation(PathTransition.OrientationType.ORTHOGONAL_TO_TANGENT);
```

After you've created the path transition, you'll want it to clean up when the animation is completed. To reset or clean up the path variable when the animation is finished, create and add an event handler to listen to the onFinished property event on the path transition object.

The following code snippet adds an event handler to clear the current path information:

```
// once finished clear path
pathTransition.onFinishedProperty().set((EventHandler<ActionEvent>)
(ActionEvent event) -> {
        onePath.getElements().clear();
});
```

With the shape and transition all set up, the application needs to respond to mouse events that will update the instance variable mentioned earlier. To do so, listen to mouse events occurring on the Scene object. Here, you will once again rely on creating event handlers to be set on the scene's onMouseXXXProperty methods, where the XXX denotes the actual mouse event name such as pressed, dragged, and released.

When a user draws a path, he or she will perform a mouse-press event to begin the start of the path. To listen to a mouse-press event, create an event handler with a formal type parameter of MouseEvent. In the example, a lambda expression is used. As a mouse-press event occurs, clear the instance variable onePath of any prior drawn path information. Next, simply set the stroke width and color of the path so the users can see the path being drawn. Finally, add the starting point to the path using an instance of a MoveTo object. Shown here is the handler code that responds when the user performs a mouse press:

```
    // starting initial path
  scene.onMousePressedProperty().set((EventHandler<MouseEvent>)
(MouseEvent event) -> {
      onePath.getElements().clear();
      // start point in path
      anchorPt = new Point2D(event.getX(), event.getY());
      onePath.setStrokeWidth(3);
      onePath.setStroke(Color.BLACK);
      onePath.getElements().add(new MoveTo(anchorPt.getX(), anchorPt.getY()));
    });
```

Once the mouse-press event handler is in place, you create another handler for mouse-drag events. Again, look for the scene's onMouseXXXProperty() methods that correspond to the proper mouse event that you care about. In this case, the onMouseDraggedProperty() will be set. Inside the lambda expression, obtain mouse coordinates that will be converted to LineTo objects to be added to the path (Path). These LineTo objects are instances of path element (javafx.scene.shape.PathElement), as discussed in Recipe 15-5. The following code is an event handler responsible for mouse-drag events:

```
// dragging creates lineTos added to the path
scene.onMouseDraggedProperty().set((EventHandler<MouseEvent>)
(MouseEvent event) -> {
        onePath.getElements().add(new LineTo(event.getX(), event.getY()));
});
```

Finally, create an event handler to listen to a mouse-release event. When a user releases the mouse, the path's stroke is set to zero to appear as if it has removed. Then you reset the path transition by stopping it and playing it from the start. The following code is an event handler responsible for a mouse-release event:

```
// end the path when mouse released event
        scene.onMouseReleasedProperty().set((EventHandler<MouseEvent>)
 (MouseEvent event) -> {
            onePath.setStrokeWidth(0);
            if (onePath.getElements().size() > 1) {
                pathTransition.stop();
                pathTransition.playFromStart();
            }
});
```

15-4. Manipulating Layout via Grids

Problem

You want to create a nice-looking form-based user interface using a grid type layout.

Solution

Create a simple using the JavaFX's javafx.scene.layout.GridPane. In this solution, a form designer application will be created to demonstrate the GridPane. The application will have the following features:

- It will toggle the display of the grid layout's grid lines for debugging.
- It will adjust the top padding of the GridPane.
- It will adjust the left padding of the GridPane.
- It will adjust the horizontal gap between cells in the GridPane.
- It will adjust the vertical gap between cells in the GridPane.
- It will align controls within cells horizontally.
- It will align controls within cells vertically.

The following code is the main launching point for the form designer application:

```java
public class ManipulatingLayoutViaGrids extends Application {

    /**
     * @param args the command line arguments
     */
    public static void main(String[] args) {
        Application.launch(args);
    }

    @Override
    public void start(Stage primaryStage) {
        primaryStage.setTitle("Chapter 15-4 Manipulating Layout via Grids ");
        Group root = new Group();
        Scene scene = new Scene(root, 640, 480, Color.WHITE);

        // Left and right split pane
        SplitPane splitPane = new SplitPane();
        splitPane.prefWidthProperty().bind(scene.widthProperty());
        splitPane.prefHeightProperty().bind(scene.heightProperty());

        // Form on the right
        GridPane rightGridPane = new MyForm();

        GridPane leftGridPane = new GridPaneControlPanel(rightGridPane);

        VBox leftArea = new VBox(10);
        leftArea.getChildren().add(leftGridPane);
        HBox hbox = new HBox();
        hbox.getChildren().add(splitPane);
        root.getChildren().add(hbox);
        splitPane.getItems().addAll(leftArea, rightGridPane);

        primaryStage.setScene(scene);

        primaryStage.show();
    }

}
```

When the form designer application is launched, the target form to be manipulated is shown on the right side of the window's split pane. The following code is a simple grid-like form class that extends from GridPane. It will be manipulated by the form designer application:

```java
/**
 * MyForm is a form to be manipulated by the user.
 * @author cdea
 */
public class MyForm extends GridPane{
    public MyForm() {
```

```java
        setPadding(new Insets(5));
        setHgap(5);
        setVgap(5);

        Label fNameLbl = new Label("First Name");
        TextField fNameFld = new TextField();
        Label lNameLbl = new Label("Last Name");
        TextField lNameFld = new TextField();
        Label ageLbl = new Label("Age");
        TextField ageFld = new TextField();

        Button saveButt = new Button("Save");

        // First name label
        GridPane.setHalignment(fNameLbl, HPos.RIGHT);
        add(fNameLbl, 0, 0);

        // Last name label
        GridPane.setHalignment(lNameLbl, HPos.RIGHT);
        add(lNameLbl, 0, 1);

        // Age label
        GridPane.setHalignment(ageLbl, HPos.RIGHT);
        add(ageLbl, 0, 2);

        // First name field
        GridPane.setHalignment(fNameFld, HPos.LEFT);
        add(fNameFld, 1, 0);

        // Last name field
        GridPane.setHalignment(lNameFld, HPos.LEFT);
        add(lNameFld, 1, 1);

        // Age Field
        GridPane.setHalignment(ageFld, HPos.RIGHT);
        add(ageFld, 1, 2);

        // Save button
        GridPane.setHalignment(saveButt, HPos.RIGHT);
        add(saveButt, 1, 3);

    }
}
```

When the application is launched, the grid property control panel is shown on the left side of the window's split pane. The property control panel allows the users to manipulate the target form's grid pane attributes dynamically. The following code represents the grid property control panel that will manipulate a target grid pane's properties:

```java
/**
 * GridPaneControlPanel represents the left area of the split pane
 * allowing the user to manipulate the GridPane on the right.
```

```java
 *
 * Manipulating Layout Via Grids
 * @author cdea
 */
public class GridPaneControlPanel extends GridPane{
    public GridPaneControlPanel(final GridPane targetGridPane) {
        super();

        setPadding(new Insets(5));
        setHgap(5);
        setVgap(5);

        // Setting Grid lines
        Label gridLinesLbl = new Label("Grid Lines");
        final ToggleButton gridLinesToggle = new ToggleButton("Off");
        gridLinesToggle.selectedProperty().addListener((ObservableValue<? extends Boolean> ov,
        Boolean oldValue, Boolean newVal) -> {
            targetGridPane.setGridLinesVisible(newVal);
            gridLinesToggle.setText(newVal ? "On" : "Off");
        });

        // toggle grid lines label
        GridPane.setHalignment(gridLinesLbl, HPos.RIGHT);
        add(gridLinesLbl, 0, 0);

        // toggle grid lines
        GridPane.setHalignment(gridLinesToggle, HPos.LEFT);
        add(gridLinesToggle, 1, 0);

        // Setting padding [top]
        Label gridPaddingLbl = new Label("Top Padding");

        final Slider gridPaddingSlider = new Slider();
        gridPaddingSlider.setMin(0);
        gridPaddingSlider.setMax(100);
        gridPaddingSlider.setValue(5);
        gridPaddingSlider.setShowTickLabels(true);
        gridPaddingSlider.setShowTickMarks(true);
        gridPaddingSlider.setMinorTickCount(1);
        gridPaddingSlider.setBlockIncrement(5);

        gridPaddingSlider.valueProperty().addListener((ObservableValue<? extends Number> ov,
        Number oldVal, Number newVal) -> {
            double top1 = targetGridPane.getInsets().getTop();
            double right1 = targetGridPane.getInsets().getRight();
            double bottom1 = targetGridPane.getInsets().getBottom();
            double left1 = targetGridPane.getInsets().getLeft();
            Insets newInsets = new Insets((double) newVal, right1, bottom1, left1);
            targetGridPane.setPadding(newInsets);
        });
```

```java
// padding adjustment label
GridPane.setHalignment(gridPaddingLbl, HPos.RIGHT);
add(gridPaddingLbl, 0, 1);

// padding adjustment slider
GridPane.setHalignment(gridPaddingSlider, HPos.LEFT);
add(gridPaddingSlider, 1, 1);

// Setting padding [top]
Label gridPaddingLeftLbl = new Label("Left Padding");

final Slider gridPaddingLeftSlider = new Slider();
gridPaddingLeftSlider.setMin(0);
gridPaddingLeftSlider.setMax(100);
gridPaddingLeftSlider.setValue(5);
gridPaddingLeftSlider.setShowTickLabels(true);
gridPaddingLeftSlider.setShowTickMarks(true);
gridPaddingLeftSlider.setMinorTickCount(1);
gridPaddingLeftSlider.setBlockIncrement(5);

gridPaddingLeftSlider.valueProperty().addListener((ObservableValue<? extends Number>
ov, Number oldVal, Number newVal) -> {
    double top1 = targetGridPane.getInsets().getTop();
    double right1 = targetGridPane.getInsets().getRight();
    double bottom1 = targetGridPane.getInsets().getBottom();
    double left1 = targetGridPane.getInsets().getLeft();
    Insets newInsets = new Insets(top1, right1, bottom1, (double) newVal);
    targetGridPane.setPadding(newInsets);
});

// padding adjustment label
GridPane.setHalignment(gridPaddingLeftLbl, HPos.RIGHT);
add(gridPaddingLeftLbl, 0, 2);

// padding adjustment slider
GridPane.setHalignment(gridPaddingLeftSlider, HPos.LEFT);
add(gridPaddingLeftSlider, 1, 2);

// Horizontal gap
Label gridHGapLbl = new Label("Horizontal Gap");

final Slider gridHGapSlider = new Slider();
gridHGapSlider.setMin(0);
gridHGapSlider.setMax(100);
gridHGapSlider.setValue(5);
gridHGapSlider.setShowTickLabels(true);
gridHGapSlider.setShowTickMarks(true);
gridHGapSlider.setMinorTickCount(1);
gridHGapSlider.setBlockIncrement(5);
```

```java
gridHGapSlider.valueProperty().addListener((ObservableValue<? extends Number> ov,
Number oldVal, Number newVal) -> {
    targetGridPane.setHgap((double) newVal);
});

// hgap label
GridPane.setHalignment(gridHGapLbl, HPos.RIGHT);
add(gridHGapLbl, 0, 3);

// hgap slider
GridPane.setHalignment(gridHGapSlider, HPos.LEFT);
add(gridHGapSlider, 1, 3);

// Vertical gap
Label gridVGapLbl = new Label("Vertical Gap");

final Slider gridVGapSlider = new Slider();
gridVGapSlider.setMin(0);
gridVGapSlider.setMax(100);
gridVGapSlider.setValue(5);
gridVGapSlider.setShowTickLabels(true);
gridVGapSlider.setShowTickMarks(true);
gridVGapSlider.setMinorTickCount(1);
gridVGapSlider.setBlockIncrement(5);

gridVGapSlider.valueProperty().addListener((ObservableValue<? extends Number> ov,
Number oldVal, Number newVal) -> {
    targetGridPane.setVgap((double) newVal);
});

// vgap label
GridPane.setHalignment(gridVGapLbl, HPos.RIGHT);
add(gridVGapLbl, 0, 4);

// vgap slider
GridPane.setHalignment(gridVGapSlider, HPos.LEFT);
add(gridVGapSlider, 1, 4);

// Cell Column
Label cellCol = new Label("Cell Column");
final TextField cellColFld = new TextField("0");

// cell Column label
GridPane.setHalignment(cellCol, HPos.RIGHT);
add(cellCol, 0, 5);

// cell Column field
GridPane.setHalignment(cellColFld, HPos.LEFT);
add(cellColFld, 1, 5);
```

```java
// Cell Row
Label cellRowLbl = new Label("Cell Row");
final TextField cellRowFld = new TextField("0");

// cell Row label
GridPane.setHalignment(cellRowLbl, HPos.RIGHT);
add(cellRowLbl, 0, 6);

// cell Row field
GridPane.setHalignment(cellRowFld, HPos.LEFT);
add(cellRowFld, 1, 6);

// Horizontal Alignment
Label hAlignLbl = new Label("Horiz. Align");
final ChoiceBox hAlignFld = new ChoiceBox(FXCollections.observableArrayList(
    "CENTER", "LEFT", "RIGHT")
);
hAlignFld.getSelectionModel().select("LEFT");

// cell Row label
GridPane.setHalignment(hAlignLbl, HPos.RIGHT);
add(hAlignLbl, 0, 7);

// cell Row field
GridPane.setHalignment(hAlignFld, HPos.LEFT);
add(hAlignFld, 1, 7);

// Vertical Alignment
Label vAlignLbl = new Label("Vert. Align");
final ChoiceBox vAlignFld = new ChoiceBox(FXCollections.observableArrayList(
    "BASELINE", "BOTTOM", "CENTER", "TOP")
);
vAlignFld.getSelectionModel().select("TOP");
// cell Row label
GridPane.setHalignment(vAlignLbl, HPos.RIGHT);
add(vAlignLbl, 0, 8);

// cell Row field
GridPane.setHalignment(vAlignFld, HPos.LEFT);
add(vAlignFld, 1, 8);

// Vertical Alignment
Label cellApplyLbl = new Label("Cell Constraint");
final Button cellApplyButton = new Button("Apply");
cellApplyButton.setOnAction((ActionEvent event) -> {
    for (Node child:targetGridPane.getChildren()) {

        int targetColIndx = 0;
        int targetRowIndx = 0;
        try {
            targetColIndx = Integer.parseInt(cellColFld.getText());
```

```
                targetRowIndx = Integer.parseInt(cellRowFld.getText());
            } catch (NumberFormatException e) {

            }
            System.out.println("child = " + child.getClass().getSimpleName());
            int col = GridPane.getColumnIndex(child);
            int row = GridPane.getRowIndex(child);
            if (col == targetColIndx && row == targetRowIndx) {
                GridPane.setHalignment(child, HPos.valueOf(hAlignFld.getSelectionModel().
                getSelectedItem().toString()));
                GridPane.setValignment(child, VPos.valueOf(vAlignFld.getSelectionModel().
                getSelectedItem().toString()));
            }
        }
    });

    // cell Row label
    GridPane.setHalignment(cellApplyLbl, HPos.RIGHT);
    add(cellApplyLbl, 0, 9);

    // cell Row field
    GridPane.setHalignment(cellApplyButton, HPos.LEFT);
    add(cellApplyButton, 1, 9);

    }
}
```

Figure 15-7 shows an application with the GridPane property control panel on the left and the target form on the right.

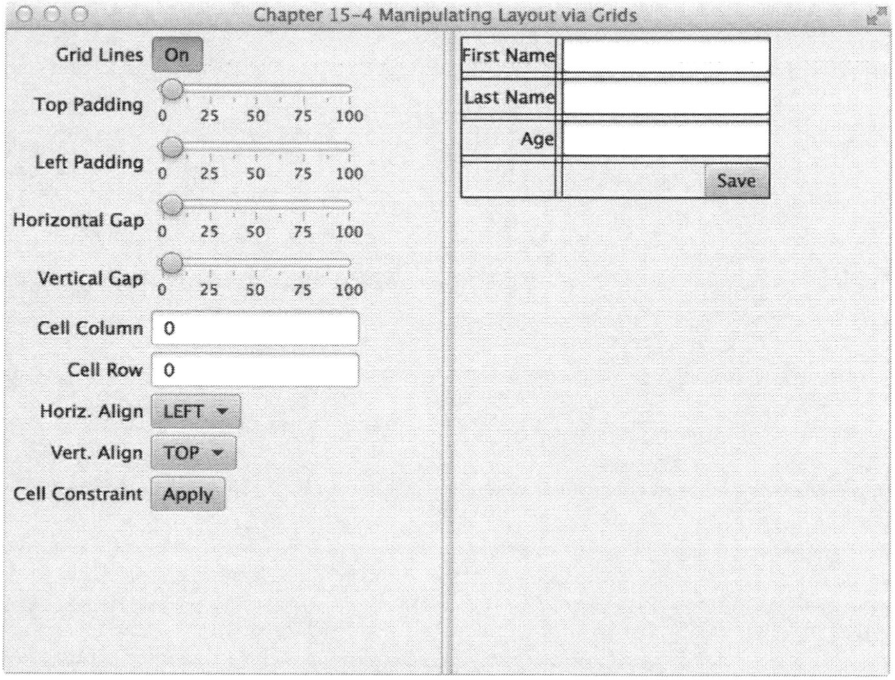

Figure 15-7. Manipulating layout via grids

How It Works

The form designer application allows the users to adjust properties using the GridPane property control panel to the left. While adjusting properties from the left control panel, the target form on the right side will be manipulated dynamically. When creating such an application, you will be binding controls to various properties onto the target form (GridPane). This designer application is basically broken into three classes: ManipulatingLayoutViaGrids, MyForm, and GridPaneControlPanel. The ManipulatingLayoutViaGrids class is the main application to be launched. MyForm is the target form that will be manipulated, and GridPaneControlPanel is the grid property control panel that has UI controls bound to the targets form's grid pane properties.

Begin by creating the main launching point for the application (ManipulatingLayoutViaGrids). This class is responsible for creating a split pane (SplitPane) that sets up the target form to the right and instantiates a GridPaneControlPanel to be displayed to the left. To instantiate a GridPaneControlPanel you must pass in the target form you want to manipulate into the constructor. I will discuss this further, but suffice it to say that the GridPaneControlPanel constructor will wire its controls to properties on the target form.

Next, you create a dummy form named MyForm. This is your target form that the property control panel will manipulate. Here, notice that the MyForm extends GridPane. In the MyForm's constructor, you create and add controls to be put into the form (GridPane).

To learn more about the GridPane, refer to Recipe 15-8. The following code is a target form to be manipulated by the form designer application:

```
/**
 * MyForm is a form to be manipulated by the user.
 * @author cdea
 */
public class MyForm extends GridPane{
    public MyForm() {

        setPadding(new Insets(5));
        setHgap(5);
        setVgap(5);

        Label fNameLbl = new Label("First Name");
        TextField fNameFld = new TextField();
        Label lNameLbl = new Label("Last Name");
        TextField lNameFld = new TextField();
        Label ageLbl = new Label("Age");
        TextField ageFld = new TextField();

        Button saveButt = new Button("Save");

        // First name label
        GridPane.setHalignment(fNameLbl, HPos.RIGHT);
        add(fNameLbl, 0, 0);
    //... The rest of the form code
```

To manipulate the target form you need to create a grid property control panel (GridPaneControlPanel). This class is responsible for binding the target form's grid pane properties to UI controls that allow users to adjust values using the keyboard and mouse. As you learned in Chapter 14, in Recipe 14-9, you can bind values with JavaFX properties. But instead of binding values directly, you can also be notified when a property has changed.

Another feature that you can add to properties is the change listener. JavaFX javafx.beans.value. ChangeListeners are similar to Java swing's property change support (java.beans.PropertyChangeListener). Similarly, when a bean's property value has changed, you will want to be notified. Change listeners are designed to intercept the change by making the old and new value available to the developer. The example starts this process by creating a JavaFXchange listener for the toggle button to turn gridlines on or off. When a user interacts with the toggle button, the change listener will simply update the target's grid pane's gridlinesVisible property. Because a toggle button's (ToggleButton) selected property is a Boolean value, you instantiate a ChangeListener class with its formal type parameter as Boolean. You'll also notice the lambda expression change listener implementation, where its inbound parameters will match the generic formal type parameter specified when instantiating a ChangeListener<Boolean>. When a property change event occurs, the change listener will invoke setGridLinesVisible() on the target grid pane with the new value and update the toggle button's text. The following code snippet shows a ChangeListener<Boolean> added to a ToggleButton:

```
gridLinesToggle.selectedProperty().addListener(
        (ObservableValue<? extends Boolean> ov,
                Boolean oldValue, Boolean newVal) -> {
    targetGridPane.setGridLinesVisible(newVal);
    gridLinesToggle.setText(newVal ? "On" : "Off");
});
```

Next, you apply a change listener to a slider control that allows the user to adjust the target grid pane's top padding. To create a change listener for a slider, you instantiate a ChangeListener<Number>. Again, you'll use a lambda expression with a signature the same as its formal type parameter Number. When a change occurs, the slider's value is used to create an Insets object, which becomes the new padding for the target grid pane. Shown here is the change listener for the top padding and slider control:

```
gridPaddingSlider.valueProperty().addListener((
        ObservableValue<? extends Number> ov, Number oldVal, Number newVal) -> {
    double top1 = targetGridPane.getInsets().getTop();
    double right1 = targetGridPane.getInsets().getRight();
    double bottom1 = targetGridPane.getInsets().getBottom();
    double left1 = targetGridPane.getInsets().getLeft();
    Insets newInsets = new Insets((double) newVal, right1, bottom1, left1);
    targetGridPane.setPadding(newInsets);
});
```

Because the implementation of the other slider controls that handle left padding, horizontal gap, and vertical gap are virtually identical to the top padding slider control mentioned previously, you can fast-forward to cell constraints controls.

The last bits of grid control panel properties that you want to manipulate are the target grid pane's cell constraints. For brevity, the example only allows the user to set a component's alignment inside of a cell of a GridPane. To see more properties to modify, refer to the Javadoc on javafx.scene.layout.GridPane. Figure 15-8 depicts the cell constraint settings for individual cells. An example is to left-justify the label Age on the target grid pane. Because cells are zero-relative, you will enter 0 in the Cell Column field and 2 into the Cell Row field. Next, you select the drop-down box Horiz. Align to LEFT. Once you're satisfied with the settings, click Apply. Figure 15-9 shows the Age label control left-aligned horizontally. To implement this change, create a lambda expression that implements EventHandler<ActionEvent> for the apply button's onAction attribute. Inside of the lambda expression, you iterate the node children owned by the target grid pane to determine whether it is the specified cell. Once the specified cell and child node is determined, the alignment is applied. The following code shows an EventHandler that applies a cell constraint when the apply button is pressed:

```
cellApplyButton.setOnAction((ActionEvent event) -> {
    for (Node child:targetGridPane.getChildren()) {

        int targetColIndx = 0;
        int targetRowIndx = 0;
        try {
            targetColIndx = Integer.parseInt(cellColFld.getText());
            targetRowIndx = Integer.parseInt(cellRowFld.getText());
        } catch (NumberFormatException e) {

        }
        System.out.println("child = " + child.getClass().getSimpleName());
        int col = GridPane.getColumnIndex(child);
        int row = GridPane.getRowIndex(child);
        if (col == targetColIndx && row == targetRowIndx) {
            GridPane.setHalignment(child, HPos.valueOf(hAlignFld.getSelectionModel().
            getSelectedItem().toString()));
```

```
            GridPane.setValignment(child, VPos.valueOf(vAlignFld.getSelectionModel().
            getSelectedItem().toString()));
        }
    }
});
```

Figure 15-8 depicts the cell constraint grid control panel section that left-aligns the control at cell column 0 and cell row 2.

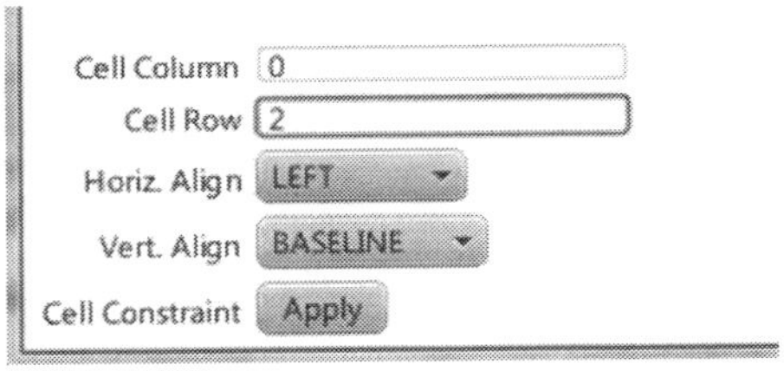

Figure 15-8. *Cell constraints*

Figure 15-9 depicts the target grid pane with the grid lines turned on and the Age label left-aligned horizontally at cell column 0 and cell row 2.

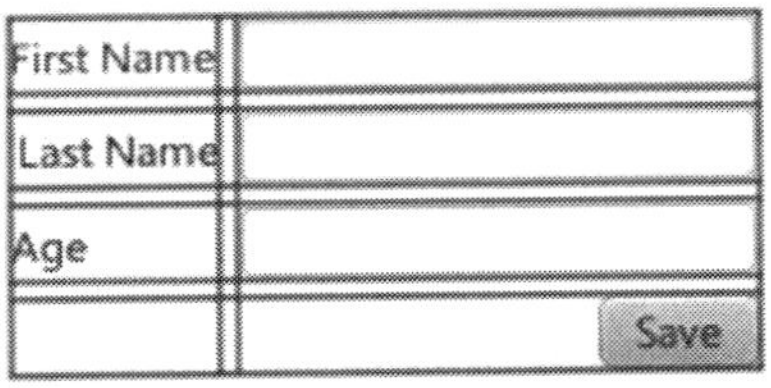

Figure 15-9. *Target grid pane*

15-5. Enhancing the Interface with CSS

Problem

You want to change the Look and Feel of the GUI interface.

Solution

Apply JavaFX's CSS styling to graph nodes. The following code demonstrates using CSS styling on graph nodes. The code creates five themes: Modena, Caspian, Control Style 1, Control Style 2, and Sky. Each theme is defined using CSS and affects the Look and Feel of a dialog box. Following the code, you can see the two different renditions of the dialog box:

```
package org.java9recipes.chapter15.recipe15_05;

import javafx.application.Application;
import javafx.collections.FXCollections;
```

463

```java
import javafx.collections.ObservableList;
import javafx.event.ActionEvent;
import javafx.event.EventHandler;
import javafx.scene.Group;
import javafx.scene.Scene;
import javafx.scene.control.Menu;
import javafx.scene.control.MenuBar;
import javafx.scene.control.MenuItem;
import javafx.scene.control.SplitPane;
import javafx.scene.layout.GridPane;
import javafx.scene.layout.HBox;
import javafx.scene.layout.VBox;
import javafx.scene.paint.Color;
import javafx.stage.Stage;

/**
 * Recipe 15-5:  Enhancing with CSS
 * @author cdea
 * Update: J Juneau
 */
public class EnhancingWithCss extends Application {

    /**
     * @param args the command line arguments
     */
    public static void main(String[] args) {
        Application.launch(args);
    }

    @Override
    public void start(Stage primaryStage) {

            primaryStage.setTitle("Chapter 15-5 Enhancing with CSS ");
            Group root = new Group();
            final Scene scene = new Scene(root, 640, 480, Color.BLACK);
            MenuBar menuBar = new MenuBar();
            Menu menu = new Menu("Look and Feel");

            //  Modena Look and Feel
            MenuItem modenaLnf = new MenuItem("Modena");
            modenaLnf.setOnAction(enableCss(STYLESHEET_MODENA,scene));
            menu.getItems().add(modenaLnf);

            // Old default, Caspian Look and Feel
            MenuItem caspianLnf = new MenuItem("Caspian");
            caspianLnf.setOnAction(enableCss(STYLESHEET_CASPIAN, scene));

            menu.getItems().add(caspianLnf);
```

```
        menu.getItems().add(createMenuItem("Control Style 1", "controlStyle1.css", scene));
        menu.getItems().add(createMenuItem("Control Style 2", "controlStyle2.css", scene));
        menu.getItems().add(createMenuItem("Sky", "sky.css", scene));

        menuBar.getMenus().add(menu);
        // stretch menu
        menuBar.prefWidthProperty().bind(primaryStage.widthProperty());

        // Left and right split pane
        SplitPane splitPane = new SplitPane();
        splitPane.prefWidthProperty().bind(scene.widthProperty());
        splitPane.prefHeightProperty().bind(scene.heightProperty());

        // Form on the right
        GridPane rightGridPane = new MyForm();

        GridPane leftGridPane = new GridPaneControlPanel(rightGridPane);
        VBox leftArea = new VBox(10);
        leftArea.getChildren().add(leftGridPane);

        HBox hbox = new HBox();
        hbox.getChildren().add(splitPane);
        VBox vbox = new VBox();
        vbox.getChildren().add(menuBar);
        vbox.getChildren().add(hbox);
        root.getChildren().add(vbox);
        splitPane.getItems().addAll(leftArea, rightGridPane);

        primaryStage.setScene(scene);

        primaryStage.show();

    }

    protected final MenuItem createMenuItem(String label, String css, final Scene scene){
        MenuItem menuItem = new MenuItem(label);
        ObservableList<String> cssStyle = loadSkin(css);
        menuItem.setOnAction(skinForm(cssStyle, scene));
        return menuItem;
    }

    protected final ObservableList<String> loadSkin(String cssFileName) {
        ObservableList<String> cssStyle = FXCollections.observableArrayList();
        cssStyle.addAll(getClass().getResource(cssFileName).toExternalForm());
        return cssStyle;
    }
```

```
protected final EventHandler<ActionEvent> skinForm
    (final ObservableList<String> cssStyle, final Scene scene) {
    return (ActionEvent event) -> {
        scene.getStylesheets().clear();
        scene.getStylesheets().addAll(cssStyle);
    };
}

protected final EventHandler<ActionEvent> enableCss(String style, final Scene scene){
    return (ActionEvent event) -> {

        scene.getStylesheets().clear();
        setUserAgentStylesheet(style);
    };
}

}
```

Figure 15-10 depicts the standard JavaFX Modena Look and Feel (theme).

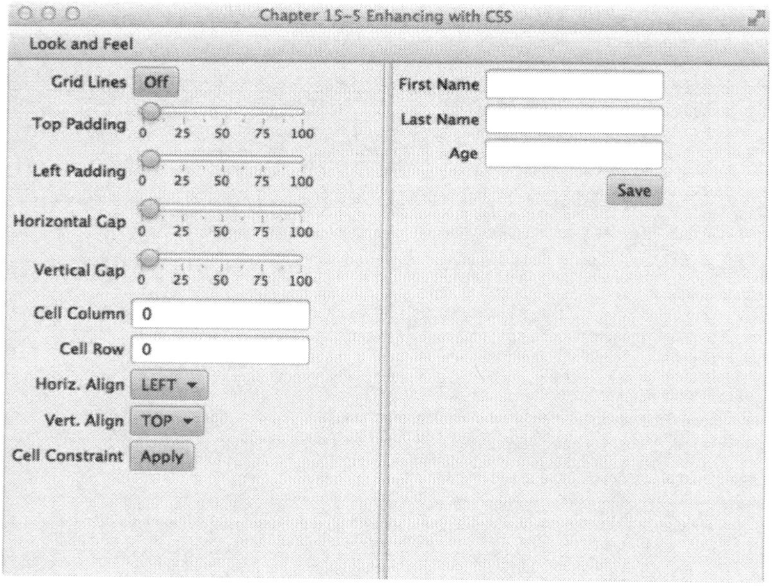

Figure 15-10. *Modena Look and Feel*

Figure 15-11 depicts the Control Style 1 Look and Feel (theme).

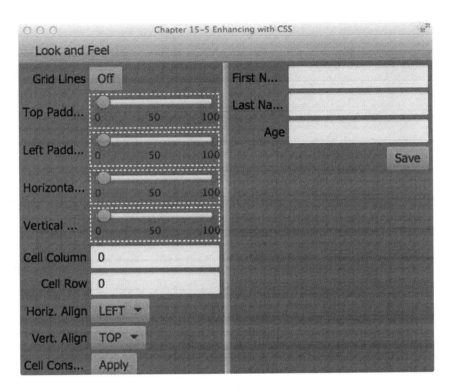

Figure 15-11. *Control Style 1 Look and Feel*

How It Works

JavaFX has the capability to apply CSS styles to the scene graph and its nodes just like browsers apply CSS styles to elements in an HTML document object model (DOM). In this recipe, you will be skinning a user interface using JavaFX styling attributes. You basically use the recipe's UI to apply the various Look and Feels. To showcase the available skins, a menu selection allows the users to choose the Look and Feel to apply to the UI.

Before discussing the CSS styling properties, take a look at how you load the CSS styles to be applied to a JavaFX application. The application in the example uses menu items to allow the user to choose the preferred Look and Feel. When creating a menu item, you'll create a convenience method to build a menu item that loads the specified CSS and an EventHandler action, via a lambda expression, to apply the chosen CSS style to the current UI. The Modena Look and Feel is loaded by default. Different Look and Feels can be applied by passing their respective style sheets to the setUserAgentStylesheet() method. For instance, to load the Caspian Look and Feel, you simply pass the constant STYLESHEET_CASPIAN to the setUserAgentStylesheet() method. The following code shows how to create these menu items:

```
MenuItem caspianLnf = new MenuItem("Caspian");
caspianLnf.setOnAction(skinForm(caspian, scene));
```

467

Shown next is the code for adding a menu item containing the Sky Look and Feel CSS style, which is ready to be applied to the current UI.

```
// Modena Look and Feel
MenuItem modenaLnf = new MenuItem("Modena");
modenaLnf.setOnAction(enableCss(STYLESHEET_MODENA,scene));
menu.getItems().add(modenaLnf);
```

The setOnAction() method calls a method named enableCss(), which takes a style sheet and the current scene. The code for enableCss() is as follows:

```
protected final EventHandler<ActionEvent> enableCss(String style, final Scene scene){
        return (ActionEvent event) -> {

            scene.getStylesheets().clear();
            setUserAgentStylesheet(style);
        };
    }
```

For each of the other CSS styles, which are not part of the default JavaFX distribution, the menu item creation is a bit different. This is an example of the code that utilizes the convenience method that was previously discussed.

```
menu.getItems().add(createMenuItem("Control Style 1", "controlStyle1.css", scene));
```

Calling the createMenuItem() method will also call another convenience method to load the CSS file called loadSkin(). It will also set the menu item's onAction attribute with an appropriate EventHandler by calling the skinForm() method. To recap, the loadSkin is responsible for loading the CSS file, and the skinForm() method's job is to apply the skin onto the UI application. Shown here are the convenience methods to build menu items that apply CSS styles to a UI application:

```
    protected final MenuItem createMenuItem(String label, String css, final Scene scene){
        MenuItem menuItem = new MenuItem(label);
        ObservableList<String> cssStyle = loadSkin(css);
        menuItem.setOnAction(skinForm(cssStyle, scene));
        return menuItem;
    }

    protected final ObservableList<String> loadSkin(String cssFileName) {
        ObservableList<String> cssStyle = FXCollections.observableArrayList();
        cssStyle.addAll(getClass().getResource(cssFileName).toExternalForm());
        return cssStyle;
    }

    protected final EventHandler<ActionEvent> skinForm
    (final ObservableList<String> cssStyle, final Scene scene) {
    return (ActionEvent event) -> {
        scene.getStylesheets().clear();
        scene.getStylesheets().addAll(cssStyle);
    };
}
```

■ **Note** To run this recipe, make sure the CSS files are located in the compiled classes area. Resource files can be loaded easily when placed in the same directory (package) as the compiled class file that is loading them. The CSS files are colocated with this code example file. In NetBeans, you can select Clean and Build Project or you can copy files to your classes' build area.

Now that you know how to load CSS styles, let's talk about the JavaFX CSS selectors and styling properties. Like CSS style sheets, there are selectors or style classes associated with Node objects in the scene graph. All scene graph nodes have a method called setStyle() that applies styling properties that could potentially change the node's background color, border, stroke, and so on. Because all graph nodes extend from the Node class, derived classes will be able to inherit the same styling properties. Knowing the inheritance hierarchy of node types is very important because the type of node will determine the types of styling properties you can affect. For instance, a Rectangle extends from Shape, which extends from Node. The inheritance does not include -fx-border-style, which is the part of node that extends from Region. Based on the type of node, there are limitations to what styles you are able to set. To see a full list of all the style selectors, refer to the JavaFX CSS Reference Guide:

http://docs.oracle.com/javase/8/javafx/api/javafx/scene/doc-files/cssref.html

All JavaFX styling properties are prefixed with -fx-. For example, all Nodes have the styling property to affect opacity, and that attribute is -fx-opacity. Following are selectors that style the JavaFX javafx.scene.control.Labels and javafx.scene.control.Buttons:

```
.label {
    -fx-text-fill: rgba(17, 145, 213);
    -fx-border-color: rgba(255, 255, 255, .80);
    -fx-border-radius: 8;
    -fx-padding: 6 6 6 6;
    -fx-font: bold italic 20pt "LucidaBrightDemiBold";

}
.button{
    -fx-text-fill: rgba(17, 145, 213);
    -fx-border-color: rgba(255, 255, 255, .80);
    -fx-border-radius: 8;
    -fx-padding: 6 6 6 6;
    -fx-font: bold italic 20pt "LucidaBrightDemiBold";

}
```

Summary

In this chapter, we covered a variety of topics that deal with JavaFX graphics. We learned how to create images by developing an application that allows one to drag and drop images onto a stage, thereby creating a copy of the image. We then covered recipes; which enable animation of text and also of shapes. Lastly, we learned how to utilize grids and/or CSS to lay out application components.

■ ■ ■

CHAPTER 16

Media with JavaFX

JavaFX provides a media-rich API capable of playing audio and video. The Media API allows developers to incorporate audio and video into their Rich Client Applications. One of the main benefits of the Media API is its cross-platform abilities when distributing media content via the web. With a range of devices (tablets, music players, TVs, and so on) that need to play multimedia content, the need for a cross-platform API is essential.

Imagine a not-so-distant future where your TV or wall is capable of interacting with you in ways that you've never dreamed possible. For instance, while viewing a movie you could select items or clothing used in the movie to be immediately purchased, all from the comfort of your home. With this future in mind, developers seek to enhance the interactive qualities of their media-based applications.

In this chapter you will learn how to play audio and video in an interactive way. Find your seats for Act III of JavaFX as audio and video take center stage—as depicted in Figure 16-1.

Figure 16-1. *Audio and video*

16-1. Playing Audio

Problem

You want to code an application that will allow you to listen to music and become entertained with a graphical visualization.

© Josh Juneau 2017
J. Juneau, *Java 9 Recipes*, DOI 10.1007/978-1-4842-1976-8_16

Solution

Create an MP3 player by utilizing the following classes:

- `javafx.scene.media.Media`
- `javafx.scene.media.MediaPlayer`
- `javafx.scene.media.AudioSpectrumListener`

The following source code is an implementation of a simple MP3 player:

```java
package org.java9recipes.chapter16.recipe16_01;

import java.io.File;
import java.util.Random;
import javafx.application.Application;
import javafx.application.Platform;
import javafx.geometry.Point2D;
import javafx.scene.Group;
import javafx.scene.Node;
import javafx.scene.Scene;
import javafx.scene.input.DragEvent;
import javafx.scene.input.Dragboard;
import javafx.scene.input.MouseEvent;
import javafx.scene.input.TransferMode;
import javafx.scene.media.AudioSpectrumListener;
import javafx.scene.media.Media;
import javafx.scene.media.MediaPlayer;
import javafx.scene.paint.Color;
import javafx.scene.shape.Arc;
import javafx.scene.shape.ArcType;
import javafx.scene.shape.Circle;
import javafx.scene.shape.Line;
import javafx.scene.shape.Rectangle;
import javafx.scene.text.Text;
import javafx.stage.Stage;
import javafx.stage.StageStyle;

public class PlayingAudio extends Application {

    private MediaPlayer mediaPlayer;
    private Point2D anchorPt;
    private Point2D previousLocation;

    /**
     * @param args the command line arguments
     */
    public static void main(String[] args) {
        Application.launch(args);
    }
```

```java
@Override
public void start(final Stage primaryStage) {
    primaryStage.setTitle("Chapter 16-1 Playing Audio");
    primaryStage.centerOnScreen();
    primaryStage.initStyle(StageStyle.TRANSPARENT);

    Group root = new Group();
    Scene scene = new Scene(root, 551, 270, Color.rgb(0, 0, 0, 0));

    // application area
    Rectangle applicationArea = new Rectangle();
    applicationArea.setArcWidth(20);
    applicationArea.setArcHeight(20);
    applicationArea.setFill(Color.rgb(0, 0, 0, .80));
    applicationArea.setX(0);
    applicationArea.setY(0);
    applicationArea.setStrokeWidth(2);
    applicationArea.setStroke(Color.rgb(255, 255, 255, .70));

    root.getChildren().add(applicationArea);
    applicationArea.widthProperty().bind(scene.widthProperty());
    applicationArea.heightProperty().bind(scene.heightProperty());

    final Group phaseNodes = new Group();
    root.getChildren().add(phaseNodes);

    // starting initial anchor point
    scene.setOnMousePressed((MouseEvent event) -> {
        anchorPt = new Point2D(event.getScreenX(), event.getScreenY());
    });

    // dragging the entire stage
    scene.setOnMouseDragged((MouseEvent event) -> {
        if (anchorPt != null && previousLocation != null) {
            primaryStage.setX(previousLocation.getX() + event.getScreenX() - anchorPt.
            getX());
            primaryStage.setY(previousLocation.getY() + event.getScreenY() - anchorPt.
            getY());
        }
    });

    // set the current location
    scene.setOnMouseReleased((MouseEvent event) -> {
        previousLocation = new Point2D(primaryStage.getX(), primaryStage.getY());
    });

    // Dragging over surface
    scene.setOnDragOver((DragEvent event) -> {
        Dragboard db = event.getDragboard();
        if (db.hasFiles()) {
            event.acceptTransferModes(TransferMode.COPY);
        } else {
```

```
            event.consume();
        }
    });

    // Dropping over surface
    scene.setOnDragDropped((DragEvent event) -> {
        Dragboard db = event.getDragboard();
        boolean success = false;
        if (db.hasFiles()) {
            success = true;
            String filePath = null;
            for (File file : db.getFiles()) {
                filePath = file.getAbsolutePath();
                System.out.println(filePath);
            }
            // play file
            Media media = new Media(new File(filePath).toURI().toString());

            if (mediaPlayer != null) {
                mediaPlayer.stop();
            }

            mediaPlayer = new MediaPlayer(media);

            // Maintained Inner Class for Tutorial, could be changed to lambda
            mediaPlayer.setAudioSpectrumListener(new AudioSpectrumListener() {
                @Override
                public void spectrumDataUpdate(double timestamp, double duration,
                float[] magnitudes, float[] phases) {
                    phaseNodes.getChildren().clear();
                    int i = 0;
                    int x = 10;
                    int y = 150;
                    final Random rand = new Random(System.currentTimeMillis());
                    for (float phase : phases) {
                        int red = rand.nextInt(255);
                        int green = rand.nextInt(255);
                        int blue = rand.nextInt(255);

                        Circle circle = new Circle(10);
                        circle.setCenterX(x + i);
                        circle.setCenterY(y + (phase * 100));
                        circle.setFill(Color.rgb(red, green, blue, .70));
                        phaseNodes.getChildren().add(circle);
                        i += 5;
                    }
                }
            });

            mediaPlayer.setOnReady(mediaPlayer::play);
        }
```

```
        event.setDropCompleted(success);
        event.consume();
});

// create slide controls
final Group buttonGroup = new Group();

// rounded rect
Rectangle buttonArea = new Rectangle();
buttonArea.setArcWidth(15);
buttonArea.setArcHeight(20);
buttonArea.setFill(new Color(0, 0, 0, .55));
buttonArea.setX(0);
buttonArea.setY(0);
buttonArea.setWidth(60);
buttonArea.setHeight(30);
buttonArea.setStroke(Color.rgb(255, 255, 255, .70));

buttonGroup.getChildren().add(buttonArea);
// stop audio control
Rectangle stopButton = new Rectangle();
stopButton.setArcWidth(5);
stopButton.setArcHeight(5);
stopButton.setFill(Color.rgb(255, 255, 255, .80));
stopButton.setX(0);
stopButton.setY(0);
stopButton.setWidth(10);
stopButton.setHeight(10);
stopButton.setTranslateX(15);
stopButton.setTranslateY(10);
stopButton.setStroke(Color.rgb(255, 255, 255, .70));

stopButton.setOnMousePressed((MouseEvent me) -> {
    if (mediaPlayer != null) {
        mediaPlayer.stop();
    }
});
buttonGroup.getChildren().add(stopButton);

// play control
final Arc playButton = new Arc();
playButton.setType(ArcType.ROUND);
playButton.setCenterX(12);
playButton.setCenterY(16);
playButton.setRadiusX(15);
playButton.setRadiusY(15);
playButton.setStartAngle(180 - 30);
playButton.setLength(60);
playButton.setFill(new Color(1, 1, 1, .90));
playButton.setTranslateX(40);

playButton.setOnMousePressed((MouseEvent me) -> {
    mediaPlayer.play();
});
```

```java
// pause control
final Group pause = new Group();
final Circle pauseButton = new Circle();
pauseButton.setCenterX(12);
pauseButton.setCenterY(16);
pauseButton.setRadius(10);
pauseButton.setStroke(new Color(1, 1, 1, .90));
pauseButton.setTranslateX(30);

final Line firstLine = new Line();
firstLine.setStartX(6);
firstLine.setStartY(16 - 10);
firstLine.setEndX(6);
firstLine.setEndY(16 - 2);
firstLine.setStrokeWidth(3);
firstLine.setTranslateX(34);
firstLine.setTranslateY(6);
firstLine.setStroke(new Color(1, 1, 1, .90));

final Line secondLine = new Line();
secondLine.setStartX(6);
secondLine.setStartY(16 - 10);
secondLine.setEndX(6);
secondLine.setEndY(16 - 2);
secondLine.setStrokeWidth(3);
secondLine.setTranslateX(38);
secondLine.setTranslateY(6);
secondLine.setStroke(new Color(1, 1, 1, .90));

pause.getChildren().addAll(pauseButton, firstLine, secondLine);

pause.setOnMousePressed((MouseEvent me) -> {
    if (mediaPlayer != null) {
        buttonGroup.getChildren().remove(pause);
        buttonGroup.getChildren().add(playButton);
        mediaPlayer.pause();
    }
});

playButton.setOnMousePressed((MouseEvent me) -> {
    if (mediaPlayer != null) {
        buttonGroup.getChildren().remove(playButton);
        buttonGroup.getChildren().add(pause);
        mediaPlayer.play();
    }
});

buttonGroup.getChildren().add(pause);
// move button group when scene is resized

buttonGroup.translateXProperty().bind(scene.widthProperty().subtract(buttonArea.
getWidth() + 6));
```

```
buttonGroup.translateYProperty().bind(scene.heightProperty().subtract(buttonArea.
getHeight() + 6));
root.getChildren().add(buttonGroup);

// close button
final Group closeApp = new Group();
Circle closeButton = new Circle();
closeButton.setCenterX(5);
closeButton.setCenterY(0);
closeButton.setRadius(7);
closeButton.setFill(Color.rgb(255, 255, 255, .80));

Node closeXmark = new Text(2, 4, "X");
closeApp.translateXProperty().bind(scene.widthProperty().subtract(15));
closeApp.setTranslateY(10);
closeApp.getChildren().addAll(closeButton, closeXmark);
closeApp.setOnMouseClicked((MouseEvent event) -> {
    Platform.exit();
});

root.getChildren().add(closeApp);

primaryStage.setScene(scene);
primaryStage.show();
previousLocation = new Point2D(primaryStage.getX(), primaryStage.getY());

    }
}
```

Figure 16-2 shows a JavaFX MP3 player with visualizations.

Figure 16-2. *JavaFX MP3 player*

How It Works

Before you get started, I'll discuss the instructions on how to operate the MP3 player application that is created. The users will be able to drag and drop an audio file into the application area to be played. Located on the lower right of the application are buttons to stop, pause, and resume play of audio media. (The button controls are shown in Figure 16-2.) As the music is playing, the user will also notice randomly colored balls bouncing around to the music. Once the users are done listening to the music, they can quit the application by clicking the white rounded close button located in the upper right corner.

It is similar to Recipe 15-1, in which you learned how to use the drag-and-drop desktop metaphor to load files into a JavaFX application. Instead of image files, however, the user is accessing audio files. JavaFX currently supports the following audio file formats: `.mp3`, `.wav`, and `.aiff`.

Following the same look and feel, you will use the same style as Recipe 15-1. In this recipe, you modify the button controls to resemble buttons, similar to many media player applications. When the pause button is pressed, it will pause the audio media from playing and toggle to the play button control, thus allowing the users to resume. As an added bonus, the MP3 player will appear as an irregular shaped, semitransparent window without borders that can also be dragged around the desktop using the mouse. Now that you know how the music player will operate, let's walk through the code.

First, you need to create instance variables that will maintain state information for the lifetime of the application. Table 16-1 describes all the instance variables used in this music player application. The first variable is a reference to a media player (`MediaPlayer`) object that will be created in conjunction with a `Media` object containing an audio file. Next, you create an `anchorPt` variable used to save the starting coordinate of a mouse press when the users begin to drag the window across the screen. When calculating the upper left bounds of the application window during a mouse-dragged operation, the `previousLocation` variable will contain the previous window's screen X and Y coordinates.

Table 16-1 lists the MP3 player application's instance variables.

Table 16-1. *MP3 Player Application Instance Variables*

Variable	Data Type	Example	Description
mediaPlayer	MediaPlayer	N/A	A media player control that plays audio and video
anchorPt	Point2D	100,100	A coordinate where the user begins to drag the window
previousLocation	Point2D	0,0	The upper left corner of the stage's previous coordinate; assists in dragging the window

In previous chapters relating to GUIs, you saw that GUI applications normally contain a title bar and windowed borders surrounding the scene. Here, I wanted to raise the bar a little by showing you how to create irregularly shaped semitransparent windows, thus making things look more hip or modern. As you begin to create the media player, you'll notice in the `start()` method that you prepare the `Stage` object by initializing the style using `StageStyle.TRANSPARENT`. After you initialize the style to `StageStyle.TRANSPARENT`, the window will be undecorated, with the entire window area's opaque value set to zero (invisible). The following code shows you how to create a transparent window without a title bar or windowed borders:

```
primaryStage.initStyle(StageStyle.TRANSPARENT);
```

With the invisible stage, you create a rounded rectangular region that will be the application's surface or main content area. Next, notice the width and height of the rectangle bound to the scene object in case the window is resized. Because the window isn't going to be resized, the bind isn't necessary (it will be needed, however, in Recipe 16-2, when you provide the ability to enlarge a video screen to take on a full-screen mode).

After creating a black, semitransparent, rounded rectangular area (`applicationArea`), you'll be creating a simple `Group` object to hold all the randomly colored `Circle` nodes that will show off graphical visualizations while the audio is being played. Later, you will see how the `phaseNodes` (Group) variable is updated based on sound information using an `AudioSpectrumListener`.

Next, you add `EventHandler<MouseEvent>` instances to the `Scene` object (the example uses lambda expressions) to monitor mouse events as the user drags the window around the screen. The first event in this scenario is a mouse press, which will save the cursor's current (X, Y) coordinates to the variable `anchorPt`. The following code is adding an `EventHandler` to the mouse-press property of the `Scene`:

```
// starting initial anchor point
scene.setOnMousePressed((MouseEvent event) -> {
    anchorPt = new Point2D(event.getScreenX(), event.getScreenY());
});
```

After implementing the mouse-press event handler, you can create an `EventHandler` to the Scene's mouse-drag property. The mouse–drag event handler will update and position the application window (Stage) dynamically, based on the previous window's location (upper left corner) along with the `anchorPt` variable. Shown here is an event handler responsible for the mouse-drag event on the Scene object:

```
// dragging the entire stage
scene.setOnMouseDragged((MouseEvent event) -> {
    if (anchorPt != null && previousLocation != null) {
        primaryStage.setX(previousLocation.getX() + event.getScreenX() - anchorPt.getX());
        primaryStage.setY(previousLocation.getY() + event.getScreenY() - anchorPt.getY());
    }
});
```

You will want to handle the mouse-release event to perform actions. Once the mouse is released, the event handler will update the `previousLocation` variable for subsequent mouse-drag events to move the application window about the screen. The following code snippet updates the `previousLocation` variable:

```
// set the current location
scene.setOnMouseReleased((MouseEvent event) -> {
    previousLocation = new Point2D(primaryStage.getX(), primaryStage.getY());
});
```

Next, you will be implementing the drag-and-drop scenario to load the audio file from the file system (using the File Manager). When handling a drag-and-drop scenario, it is similar to Recipe 15-1, in which you created an `EventHandler` to handle `DragEvents`. Instead of loading image files, you'll be loading audio files from the host file system. For brevity, I simply mention the code lines of the drag-and-dropped event handler. Once the audio file is available, you will create a `Media` object by passing in the file as a URI. The following code snippet is how to create a `Media` object:

```
Media media = new Media(new File(filePath).toURI().toString());
```

Once you have created a `Media` object you will have to create an instance of a `MediaPlayer` in order to play the sound file. Both the `Media` and `MediaPlayer` objects are immutable, which is why new instances of each will be created every time the user drags a file into the application. Next, you will check the instance variable `mediaPlayer` for a previous instance to make sure it is stopped before creating a new `MediaPlayer` instance. The following code checks for a prior media player to be stopped:

```
if (mediaPlayer != null) {
    mediaPlayer.stop();
}
```

So, here is where you create a MediaPlayer instance. A MediaPlayer object is responsible for controlling the playing of media objects. Notice that a MediaPlayer will treat sound or video media the same in terms of playing, pausing, and stopping media. When creating a media player, you specify the media and audioSpectrumListener attribute methods. Setting the autoPlay attribute to true will play the audio media immediately after it has been loaded. The last thing to specify on the MediaPlayer instance is an AudioSpectrumListener. So, what exactly is this type of listener, you say? Well, according to the Javadoc, it is an observer receiving periodic updates of the audio spectrum. In layman's terms, it is the audio media's sound data such as volume, tempo, and so on. To create an instance of an AudioSpectrumListener, you create an inner class that overrides the method spectrumDataUpdate(). You could have also used a lambda expression here; the example uses the inner class to provide better insight into the functionality. Table 16-2 lists all the inbound parameters for the audio spectrum listener's method. For more details, refer to the Javadoc at http://docs.oracle.com/javase/8/javafx/api/javafx/scene/media/AudioSpectrumListener.html.

Table 16-2. The AudioSpectrumListener's Method spectrumDataUpdate() Inbound Parameters

Variable	Data Type	Example	Description
timestamp	double	2.4261	When the event occurred, in seconds
duration	Double	0.1	The duration of time (in seconds) the spectrum was computed
magnitudes	float[]	-50.474335	An array of float values representing each band's spectrum magnitude in decibels (nonpositive float value)
phases	float[]	1.2217305	An array of float values representing each band's phase

In the example, randomly colored circle nodes are created, positioned, and placed on the scene based on the variable phases (array of floats). To draw each colored circle, the circle's center X is incremented by five pixels and the circle's center Y is added with each phase value multiplied by 100. Shown here is the code snippet that plots each randomly colored circle:

```
circle.setCenterX(x + i);
circle.setCenterY(y + (phase * 100));
... // setting the circle
i+=5;
```

Here is an inner class implementation of an AudioSpectrumListener:

```
new AudioSpectrumListener() {
    @Override
    public void spectrumDataUpdate(double timestamp, double duration, float[] magnitudes,
    float[] phases) {

        phaseNodes.getChildren().clear();
        int i = 0;
        int x = 10;
        int y = 150;
        final Random rand = new Random(System.currentTimeMillis());
        for(float phase:phases) {
        int red = rand.nextInt(255);
        int green = rand.nextInt(255);
        int blue = rand.nextInt(255);
```

```
        Circle circle = new Circle(10);
        circle.setCenterX(x + i);
        circle.setCenterY(y + (phase * 100));
        circle.setFill(Color.rgb(red, green, blue, .70));
        phaseNodes.getChildren().add(circle);
        i+=5;
    }

    }
};
```

Once the media player is created, you create a `java.lang.Runnable` to be set to the onReady attribute to be invoked when the media is in a ready state. Once the ready event is realized, the run() method will call the media player object's play() method to begin the audio. With the dragged-drop sequence completed, you notify the drag-and-drop system by invoking the event's setDropCompleted() method with a value of true. The following code snippet demonstrates how to implement a Runnable to begin the media player as soon as the media player is in a ready state using a method reference:

```
mediaPlayer.setOnReady(mediaPlayer::play);
```

Finally, create buttons with JavaFX shapes to represent the stop, play, pause, and close buttons. When creating shapes or custom nodes, you can add event handlers to nodes in order to respond to mouse clicks. Although there are advanced ways to build custom controls in JavaFX, this example uses custom-built button icons from simple rectangles, arcs, circles, and lines. To see more advanced ways to create custom controls, refer to the Javadoc on the Skinnable API or to Recipe 16-5. To attach event handlers for a mouse press, simply call the setOnMousePress() method by passing in an EventHandler<MouseEvent> instance. The following code demonstrates adding an EventHandler to respond to mouse press on the stopButton node:

```
stopButton.setOnMousePressed((MouseEvent me) -> {
    if (mediaPlayer != null) {
        mediaPlayer.stop();
    }
});
```

Because all the buttons use the same code snippet, only the method calls that each button will perform on the media player are listed. The last button, Close, isn't related to the media player, but it provides a way to exit the MP3 player application. The following actions are responsible for stopping, pausing, playing, and exiting the MP3 player application:

```
Stop - mediaPlayer.stop();
Pause - mediaPlayer.pause();
Play - mediaPlayer.play();
Close - Platform.exit();
```

16-2. Playing Video

Problem

You want to create an application to view a video file complete with controls to play, pause, stop, and seek.

Solution

Create a video media player application by utilizing the following classes:

- javafx.scene.media.Media
- javafx.scene.media.MediaPlayer
- javafx.scene.media.MediaView

The following code is an implementation of a JavaFX basic video player:

```java
public void start(final Stage primaryStage) {
    primaryStage.setTitle("Chapter 16-2 Playing Video");
    primaryStage.centerOnScreen();
    primaryStage.initStyle(StageStyle.TRANSPARENT);

    final Group root = new Group();
    final Scene scene = new Scene(root, 540, 300, Color.rgb(0, 0, 0, 0));

    // rounded rectangle with slightly transparent
    Node applicationArea = createBackground(scene);
    root.getChildren().add(applicationArea);

    // allow the user to drag window on the desktop
    attachMouseEvents(scene, primaryStage);

    // allow the user to see the progress of the video playing
    progressSlider = createSlider(scene);
    root.getChildren().add(progressSlider);

    // Dragging over surface
    scene.setOnDragOver((DragEvent event) -> {
        Dragboard db = event.getDragboard();
        if (db.hasFiles() || db.hasUrl() || db.hasString()) {
            event.acceptTransferModes(TransferMode.COPY);
            if (mediaPlayer != null) {
                mediaPlayer.stop();
            }
        } else {
            event.consume();
        }
    });

    // update slider as video is progressing (later removal)
    progressListener = (ObservableValue<? extends Duration> observable, Duration oldValue,
    Duration newValue) -> {
        progressSlider.setValue(newValue.toSeconds());
    };

    // Dropping over surface
    scene.setOnDragDropped((DragEvent event) -> {
        Dragboard db = event.getDragboard();
```

```
boolean success = false;
URI resourceUrlOrFile = null;

// dragged from web browser address line?
if (db.hasContent(DataFormat.URL)) {
    try {
        resourceUrlOrFile = new URI(db.getUrl());
    } catch (URISyntaxException ex) {
        ex.printStackTrace();
    }
} else if (db.hasFiles()) {
    // dragged from the file system
    String filePath = null;
    for (File file:db.getFiles()) {
        filePath = file.getAbsolutePath();
    }
    resourceUrlOrFile = new File(filePath).toURI();
    success = true;
}
// load media
Media media = new Media(resourceUrlOrFile.toString());

// stop previous media player and clean up
if (mediaPlayer != null) {
    mediaPlayer.stop();
    mediaPlayer.currentTimeProperty().removeListener(progressListener);
    mediaPlayer.setOnPaused(null);
    mediaPlayer.setOnPlaying(null);
    mediaPlayer.setOnReady(null);
}

// create a new media player
mediaPlayer = new MediaPlayer(media);

// as the media is playing move the slider for progress
mediaPlayer.currentTimeProperty().addListener(progressListener);

// play video when ready status
mediaPlayer.setOnReady(() -> {
    progressSlider.setValue(1);
    progressSlider.setMax(mediaPlayer.getMedia().getDuration().toMillis()/1000);
    mediaPlayer.play();
});

// Lazy init media viewer
if (mediaView == null) {
    mediaView = new MediaView();
    mediaView.setMediaPlayer(mediaPlayer);
    mediaView.setX(4);
    mediaView.setY(4);
    mediaView.setPreserveRatio(true);
```

```
            mediaView.setOpacity(.85);
            mediaView.setSmooth(true);

            mediaView.fitWidthProperty().bind(scene.widthProperty().subtract(220));
            mediaView.fitHeightProperty().bind(scene.heightProperty().subtract(30));

            // make media view as the second node on the scene.
            root.getChildren().add(1, mediaView);
        }

        // sometimes loading errors occur, print error when this happens
        mediaView.setOnError((MediaErrorEvent event1) -> {
            event1.getMediaError().printStackTrace();
        });

        mediaView.setMediaPlayer(mediaPlayer);

        event.setDropCompleted(success);
        event.consume();
    });

    // rectangular area holding buttons
    final Group buttonArea = createButtonArea(scene);

    // stop button will stop and rewind the media
    Node stopButton = createStopControl();

    // play button can resume or start a media
    final Node playButton = createPlayControl();

    // pause media play
    final Node pauseButton = createPauseControl();

    stopButton.setOnMousePressed((MouseEvent me) -> {
        if (mediaPlayer!= null) {
            buttonArea.getChildren().removeAll(pauseButton, playButton);
            buttonArea.getChildren().add(playButton);
            mediaPlayer.stop();
        }
    });
    // pause media and swap button with play button
    pauseButton.setOnMousePressed((MouseEvent me) -> {
        if (mediaPlayer!=null) {
            buttonArea.getChildren().removeAll(pauseButton, playButton);
            buttonArea.getChildren().add(playButton);
            mediaPlayer.pause();
            paused = true;
        }
    });
```

```
    // play media and swap button with pause button
    playButton.setOnMousePressed((MouseEvent me) -> {
        if (mediaPlayer != null) {
            buttonArea.getChildren().removeAll(pauseButton, playButton);
            buttonArea.getChildren().add(pauseButton);
            paused = false;
            mediaPlayer.play();
        }
    });

    // add stop button to button area
    buttonArea.getChildren().add(stopButton);

    // set pause button as default
    buttonArea.getChildren().add(pauseButton);

    // add buttons
    root.getChildren().add(buttonArea);

    // create a close button
    Node closeButton= createCloseButton(scene);
    root.getChildren().add(closeButton);

    primaryStage.setOnShown((WindowEvent we) -> {
        previousLocation = new Point2D(primaryStage.getX(), primaryStage.getY());
    });

    primaryStage.setScene(scene);
    primaryStage.show();

}
```

Following is the attachMouseEvents() method, which adds an EventHandler to the scene so the video player can enter full-screen mode.

```
private void attachMouseEvents(Scene scene, final Stage primaryStage) {

    // Full screen toggle
    scene.setOnMouseClicked((MouseEvent event) -> {
        if (event.getClickCount() == 2) {
            primaryStage.setFullScreen(!primaryStage.isFullScreen());
        }
    });
        ... // the rest of the EventHandlers
}
```

The following method creates a slider control with a ChangeListener to enable the users to search backward and forward through the video:

```
private Slider createSlider(Scene scene) {
    Slider slider = new Slider();
    slider.setMin(0);
```

485

```
slider.setMax(100);
slider.setValue(1);
slider.setShowTickLabels(true);
slider.setShowTickMarks(true);

slider.valueProperty().addListener((ObservableValue<? extends Number> observable,
        Number oldValue, Number newValue) -> {
    if (paused) {
        long dur = newValue.intValue() * 1000;
        mediaPlayer.seek(new Duration(dur));
    }
});

slider.translateYProperty().bind(scene.heightProperty().subtract(30));
return slider;
}
```

Figure 16-3 depicts the JavaFX basic video player with a slider control.

Figure 16-3. *JavaFX basic video player*

How It Works

To create a video player, you will model the application similar to the example in Recipe 16-1 by reusing the same application features such as drag-and-drop files, media button controls, and so on. For the sake of clarity, I took the previous recipe and moved much of the UI code into convenience functions so you will be able to focus on the Media APIs without getting lost in the UI code. The rest of the recipes in this chapter consist of adding simple features to the JavaFX basic media player created in this recipe. This being said, the code snippets in the following recipes will be brief, consisting only of the necessary code for each new desired feature.

It is important to note that the JavaFX media player supports various media formats. The supported formats are as follows:

- AIFF

- FXM, FLV

- HLS (*)

- MP3

- MP4

- WAV

For a complete summary of the supported media types, see the online documentation at `http://docs.oracle.com/javase/8/javafx/api/javafx/scene/media/package-summary.html`.

Just like the audio player created in the last recipe, the JavaFX basic video player has the same basic media controls, including stop, pause, and play. In addition to these simple controls, you've added new capabilities such as seeking and full-screen mode.

When playing a video you'll need a view area (`javafx.scene.media.MediaView`) to show it. You also create a slider control to monitor the progress of the video, which is located at the lower left portion of the application shown in Figure 16-3. The slider control allows the users to seek backward and forward through the video. One last bonus feature is enabling the video to become full screen by double-clicking the application window. To restore the window, users repeat the double-click or press Escape.

To quickly get started, let's jump into the code. After setting the stage in the `start()` method, you create a black semitransparent background by calling the `createBackground()` method (`applicationArea`). Next, the `attachMouseEvents()` method is invoked to set up the `EventHandlers` so they can enable the users to drag the application window around the desktop. Another `EventHandler` to be attached to the scene will allow the users to switch to full-screen mode. A conditional is used to check for a double-click in the application window in order to invoke full-screen mode. Once the double-click is performed, the `Stage`'s method `setFullScreen()` is invoked with a Boolean value opposite of the currently set value. Shown here is the code needed to make a window go to full-screen mode:

```
// Full screen toggle
scene.setOnMouseClicked((MouseEvent event) -> {
    if (event.getClickCount() == 2) {
        primaryStage.setFullScreen(!primaryStage.isFullScreen());
    }
});
```

As you continue the steps inside the `start()` method, a slider control is created by calling the convenience method `createSlider()`. The `createSlider()` method instantiates a `Slider` control and adds a `ChangeListener` to move the slider as the video is playing. The `ChangeListener`'s `changed()` method is invoked any time the slider's value changes. Once the `changed()` method is invoked you will have an opportunity to see the old and new values. The following code creates a `ChangeListener` to update the slider as the video is being played:

```
// update slider as video is progressing (later removal)
progressListener = (ObservableValue<? extends Duration> observable,
                Duration oldValue, Duration newValue) -> {
    progressSlider.setValue(newValue.toSeconds());
};
```

After creating the progress listener (progressListener), the drag-dropped EventHandler for the scene needs to be created. The goal is to determine whether the pause button was pressed before the user can move the slider. Once a slider.isPressed() flag is determined, you will obtain the new value to be converted to milliseconds. The dur variable is used to move the mediaPlayer to seek the position into the video as the user slides the control left or right. The ChangeListener's changed() method is invoked any time the slider's value changes. The following code is responsible for moving the seek position into the video based on the user moving the slider.

```
slider.valueProperty().addListener((ObservableValue<? extends Number> observable,
        Number oldValue, Number newValue) -> {
    if (slider.isPressed()) {
        long dur = newValue.intValue() * 1000;
        mediaPlayer.seek(new Duration(dur));
    }
});
```

Moving right along, you next implement a drag-dropped EventHandler to handle the media file being dropped into the application window area. Here the example first checks to see whether there was a previous mediaPlayer. If there was, the previous mediaPlayer object is stopped and cleanup is performed:

```
        // stop previous media player and clean up
        if (mediaPlayer != null) {
            mediaPlayer.stop();
            mediaPlayer.currentTimeProperty().removeListener(progressListener);
            mediaPlayer.setOnPaused(null);
            mediaPlayer.setOnPlaying(null);
            mediaPlayer.setOnReady(null);
        }
        ...
        // play video when ready status
        mediaPlayer.setOnReady(() -> {
            progressSlider.setValue(1);
            progressSlider.setMax(mediaPlayer.getMedia().getDuration().toMillis() / 1000);
            mediaPlayer.play();
        });// setOnReady()
```

As with the audio player, you create a Runnable instance to be run when the media player is in a ready state. You'll notice also that the progressSlider control uses values in seconds.

Once the media player object is in a ready state, a MediaView instance is created to display the media. The following code creates a MediaView object to be placed into the scene graph to display video content:

```
// Lazy init media viewer
if (mediaView == null) {
    mediaView = new MediaView();
    mediaView.setMediaPlayer(mediaPlayer);
    mediaView.setX(4);
    mediaView.setY(4);
    mediaView.setPreserveRatio(true);
    mediaView.setOpacity(.85);
    mediaView.setSmooth(true);
```

```
    mediaView.fitWidthProperty().bind(scene.widthProperty().subtract(220));
    mediaView.fitHeightProperty().bind(scene.heightProperty().subtract(30));

    // make media view as the second node on the scene.
    root.getChildren().add(1, mediaView);
}

// sometimes loading errors occur, print error when this happens
mediaView.setOnError((MediaErrorEvent event1) -> {
    event1.getMediaError().printStackTrace();
});

mediaView.setMediaPlayer(mediaPlayer);

event.setDropCompleted(success);
event.consume();
});
```

Whew! You are finally finished with the scene's drag-dropped EventHandler. Up next is pretty much the rest of the media button controls, which are similar to the code at the end of Recipe 16-1. The only difference is a single instance variable named paused of type Boolean that denotes whether the video was paused. The following code shows the pauseButton and playButton controlling the mediaPlayer object and setting the paused flag accordingly:

```
// pause media and swap button with play button
pauseButton.setOnMousePressed((MouseEvent me) -> {
    if (mediaPlayer != null) {
        buttonArea.getChildren().removeAll(pauseButton, playButton);
        buttonArea.getChildren().add(playButton);
        mediaPlayer.pause();
        paused = true;
    }
});

// play media and swap button with pause button
playButton.setOnMousePressed((MouseEvent me) -> {
    if (mediaPlayer != null) {
        buttonArea.getChildren().removeAll(pauseButton, playButton);
        buttonArea.getChildren().add(pauseButton);
        paused = false;
        mediaPlayer.play();
    }
});
```

That is how you create a video media player. In the next recipe, you learn how to listen to media events and invoke actions.

16-3. Controlling Media Actions and Events

Problem

You want the media player application to provide feedback in response to certain events, such as displaying the text "Paused" on the screen when the media player's paused event is triggered.

Solution

You can use one or more of the media event handler methods. Shown in Table 16-3 are all the possible media events that are raised to allow developers to attach EventHandlers or Runnables.

Table 16-3. *Media Events*

Class	Set On Method	On Method Property Method	Description
Media	setOnError()	onErrorProperty()	When an error occurs
MediaPlayer	setOnEndOfMedia()	onEndOfMediaProperty()	Reached the end of the media play
MediaPlayer	setOnError()	onErrorProperty()	Error occurred
MediaPlayer	setOnHalted()	onHaltedProperty()	Media status changes to HALTED
MediaPlayer	setOnMarker()	onMarkerProperty()	Marker event triggered
MediaPlayer	setOnPaused()	onPausedProperty()	Paused event occurred
MediaPlayer	setOnPlaying()	onPlayingProperty()	The media is currently playing
MediaPlayer	setOnReady()	onReadyProperty()	Media player is in a ready state
MediaPlayer	setOnRepeat()	onRepeatProperty()	Repeat property is set
MediaPlayer	setOnStalled()	onStalledProperty()	Media player is stalled
MediaPlayer	setOnStopped()	onStoppedProperty()	Media player has stopped
MediaView	setOnError()	onErrorProperty()	Error occurred in media view

The following code presents the "Paused" text the users, with the "Duration" having a decimal of milliseconds. This text is overlaid on top of the video when the user clicks the pause button (see Figure 16-4).

```
// when paused event display pause message
mediaPlayer.setOnPaused(() -> {
    pauseMessage.setText("Paused \nDuration: " +
        mediaPlayer.currentTimeProperty().getValue().toMillis());
    pauseMessage.setOpacity(.90);
});
```

Figure 16-4. *Paused event*

How It Works

Event-driven architecture (EDA) is a *prominent* architectural pattern used to model loosely coupled components and services that pass messages asynchronously. The JavaFX team designed the Media API to be event-driven, and this recipe demonstrates how to implement it in response to media events.

With event-based programming in mind, you will discover nonblocking or callback behaviors when invoking functions. In this recipe, you will implement the display of text in response to an onPaused event instead of placing your code into the pause button logic. Instead of tying code directly to a button via an EventHandler, you will be implementing code that will respond to the media player's onPaused event being triggered. When responding to media events, you will be implementing java.lang.Runnables.

You'll be happy to know that you've been using event properties and implementing Runnables all along, albeit usually in the form of lambda expressions. Hopefully you noticed this in all the recipes in this chapter. When the media player is in a ready state, the Runnable code will be invoked. Why is this correct? Well, when the media player is finished loading the media, the onReady property will be notified. That way, you can be sure you can invoke the MediaPlayer's play() method. I trust that you will get used to event style programming. The following code snippet demonstrates setting a Runnable instance into a media player object's OnReady property using a lambda expression:

```
mediaPlayer.setOnReady(() -> {
    mediaPlayer.play();
});
```

So that you can see the difference between the lambda style of programming versus the older style, here is the same code implemented without using a lambda expression:

```
mediaPlayer.setOnReady(new Runnable() {
    @Override
    public void run() {
        mediaPlayer.play();
    }
});
```

See how many lines of code you got rid of by using lambdas? You will be taking steps similar to the onReady property. Once a Paused event has been triggered, the run() method will be invoked to present to the user a message containing a Text node with the word Paused and a duration showing the time in milliseconds into the video. Once the text is displayed, you might want to write down the duration as markers (as you'll learn in Recipe 16-4). The following code snippet shows an attached Runnable instance, which is responsible for displaying a paused message and duration in milliseconds at the point at which it was paused in the video:

```
// when paused event display pause message
mediaPlayer.setOnPaused(() -> {
pauseMessage.setText("Paused \nDuration: " +
        mediaPlayer.currentTimeProperty().getValue().toMillis());
pauseMessage.setOpacity(.90);
});
```

16-4. Marking a Position in a Video

Problem

You want to provide closed caption text while playing a video in the media player application.

Solution

Begin by applying the solution in Recipe 16-3. By obtaining the marked durations (in milliseconds) from the previous recipe, you will create media marker events at points into the video. With each media marker you will associate text that will be displayed as closed captions. When a marker comes to pass, the text will be shown in the upper right side.

The following code snippet demonstrates media marker events being handled in the onDragDropped event property of the Scene object:

```
... // inside the start() method

final VBox messageArea = createClosedCaptionArea(scene);
root.getChildren().add(messageArea);

// Dropping over surface
scene.setOnDragDropped((DragEvent event) -> {
    Dragboard db = event.getDragboard();
    boolean success = false;
    URI resourceUrlOrFile = null;

    // dragged from web browser address line?
    if (db.hasContent(DataFormat.URL)) {
        try {
            resourceUrlOrFile = new URI(db.getUrl().toString());
        } catch (URISyntaxException ex) {
            ex.printStackTrace();
        }
    } else if (db.hasFiles()) {
```

```
        // dragged from the file system
        String filePath = null;
        for (File file:db.getFiles()) {
            filePath = file.getAbsolutePath();
        }
        resourceUrlOrFile = new File(filePath).toURI();
        success = true;
}
// load media
Media media = new Media(resourceUrlOrFile.toString());

// stop previous media player and clean up
if (mediaPlayer != null) {
    mediaPlayer.stop();
    mediaPlayer.currentTimeProperty().removeListener(progressListener);
    mediaPlayer.setOnPaused(null);
    mediaPlayer.setOnPlaying(null);
    mediaPlayer.setOnReady(null);
}

// create a new media player
mediaPlayer = new MediaPlayer(media);

// as the media is playing move the slider for progress
mediaPlayer.currentTimeProperty().addListener(progressListener);

// when paused event display pause message
mediaPlayer.setOnPaused(() -> {
    pauseMessage.setOpacity(.90);
});

// when playing make pause text invisible
mediaPlayer.setOnPlaying(() -> {
    pauseMessage.setOpacity(0);
});

// play video when ready status
mediaPlayer.setOnReady(() -> {
    progressSlider.setValue(1);
    progressSlider.setMax(mediaPlayer.getMedia().getDuration().toMillis()/1000);
    mediaPlayer.play();
});

// Lazy init media viewer
if (mediaView == null) {
    mediaView = new MediaView(mediaPlayer);
    mediaView.setX(4);
    mediaView.setY(4);
    mediaView.setPreserveRatio(true);
    mediaView.setOpacity(.85);
    mediaView.setSmooth(true);
```

```
        mediaView.fitWidthProperty().bind(scene.widthProperty().subtract(messageArea.
        widthProperty().add(70)));
        mediaView.fitHeightProperty().bind(scene.heightProperty().subtract(30));

        // make media view as the second node on the scene.
        root.getChildren().add(1, mediaView);
    }

    // sometimes loading errors occur
    mediaView.setOnError((MediaErrorEvent event1) -> {
        event1.getMediaError().printStackTrace();
    });

    mediaView.setMediaPlayer(mediaPlayer);

    media.getMarkers().put("First marker", Duration.millis(10000));
    media.getMarkers().put("Second marker", Duration.millis(20000));
    media.getMarkers().put("Last one...", Duration.millis(30000));

    // display closed caption
    mediaPlayer.setOnMarker((MediaMarkerEvent event1) -> {
        closedCaption.setText(event1.getMarker().getKey());
    });

    event.setDropCompleted(success);
    event.consume();
}); // end of setOnDragDropped
```

The following code shows a factory method that returns an area that will contain the closed caption to be displayed to the right of the video:

```
private VBox createClosedCaptionArea(final Scene scene) {
    // create message area
    final VBox messageArea = new VBox(3);
    messageArea.setTranslateY(30);
    messageArea.translateXProperty().bind(scene.widthProperty().subtract(152) );
    messageArea.setTranslateY(20);
    closedCaption = new Text();
    closedCaption.setStroke(Color.WHITE);
    closedCaption.setFill(Color.YELLOW);
    closedCaption.setFont(new Font(15));

    messageArea.getChildren().add(closedCaption);
    return messageArea;
}
```

Figure 16-5 depicts the video media player displaying the closed caption text.

Figure 16-5. *Closed caption text*

How It Works

The Media API has many event properties to which the developer can attach EventHandlers or Runnables instances so they can respond when the events are triggered. This recipe focused on the OnMarker event property. The Marker property is responsible for receiving marker events (MediaMarkerEvent).

Let's begin by adding markers to the Media object. It contains a method getMarkers() that returns a javafx.collections.ObservableMap<String, Duration>. With an observable map, you can add key/value pairs that represent each marker. Adding keys should be a unique identifier, and the value is an instance of Duration. For simplicity, this example uses the closed caption text as the key for each media marker. The marker durations are those written down as users press the pause button at points in the video determined in Recipe 16-3. Be advised that this is not the recommended approach to use for production-quality code. You may want to use a parallel Map instead.

After adding markers you will be setting an EventHandler into the MediaPlayer object's OnMarker property using the setOnMarker() method. Next, you implement an EventHandler via a lambda expression to handle MediaMarkerEvents that are raised. Once an event has been received, you obtain the key representing the text to be used in the closed caption. The instance variable closedCaption (javafx.scene.text.Text node) will simply be shown by calling the setText() method with the key or String associated with the marker.

That's it for media markers. That goes to show how you can coordinate special effects, animations, and so on during a video quite easily.

16-5. Synchronizing Animation and Media

Problem

You want to incorporate animated effects in your media display application, such as scrolling the text "The End" after the video is finished playing.

Solution

Simply use Recipe 16-3 together with Recipe 16-2 to achieve the desired result. Recipe 16-3 shows how to respond to media events and Recipe 16-2 demonstrates how to use the translate transition to animate text.

The following code demonstrates an attached action when the end of a media event is triggered:

```
mediaPlayer.setOnEndOfMedia(() -> {
    closedCaption.setText("");
    animateTheEnd.getNode().setOpacity(.90);
    animateTheEnd.playFromStart();
    });
```

The following method creates a `translateTransition` of a Text node containing the String "The End" that appears after an end of media event is triggered:

```
public TranslateTransition createTheEnd(Scene scene) {
Text theEnd = new Text("The End");
theEnd.setFont(new Font(40));
theEnd.setStrokeWidth(3);
theEnd.setFill(Color.WHITE);
theEnd.setStroke(Color.WHITE);
theEnd.setX(75);

TranslateTransition scrollUp = new TranslateTransition();
scrollUp.setNode(theEnd);
scrollUp.setDuration(Duration.seconds(1));
scrollUp.setInterpolator(Interpolator.EASE_IN);
scrollUp.setFromY(scene.getHeight() + 40);
scrollUp.setToY(scene.getHeight()/2);

return scrollUp;
}
```

Figure 16-6 depicts the "The End" text node scrolling along after the OnEndOfMedia event is triggered.

Figure 16-6. *Animating "The End"*

How It Works

This recipe showcases how to synchronize events to animated effects. In the code example, when the video reaches the end, an `OnEndOfMedia` property event initiates a `Runnable` instance. Once the instance is initiated, a `TranslateTransition` animation is performed by scrolling a `Text` node upward that contains the String `"The End"`.

Let's take a look at the `setOnEndOfMedia()` method associated with the `MediaPlayer` object. Just like in Recipe 16-3, you simply call the `setOnEndOfMedia()` method by passing in a lambda expression implementing `Runnable`, which contains the code that will invoke an animation. If you don't know how the animation works, refer to Recipe 16-2. Once the event occurs, you will see the text scroll upward. The following code snippet is from inside the `scene.setOnDragDropped()` method:

```
mediaPlayer.setOnEndOfMedia(() -> {
    closedCaption.setText("");
    animateTheEnd.getNode().setOpacity(.90);
    animateTheEnd.playFromStart();
    });
```

For the sake of space, I trust you know where the code block would reside. If not, refer to Recipe 16-3, in which you will notice other OnXXX properties methods. To see the entire code listing and download the source code, visit the book's website.

To animate `"The End"` you create a convenience `createTheEnd()` method to create an instance of a `Text` node and return a `TranslateTransition` object to the caller. The `TranslateTransition` that's returned does the following: it waits a second before playing the video. Next is the interpolator in which you used the `Interpolator.EASE_IN` to move the `Text` node by easing in before a full stop. Last is setting the Y property of the node to move from the bottom to the center of the viewing area.

The following code creates an animation that scrolls a node in an upward motion:

```
TranslateTransition scrollUp = new TranslateTransition();
scrollUp.setNode(theEnd);
scrollUp.setDuration(Duration.seconds(1));
scrollUp.setInterpolator(Interpolator.EASE_IN);
scrollUp.setFromY(scene.getHeight() + 40);
scrollUp.setToY(scene.getHeight()/2);
```

Summary

JavaFX has been a venue for development of media-based applications since its beginning. The JavaFX Media API enables developers to easily add media and media-based controls to any application. In previous versions of JavaFX, video and audio types were more limited. Java 8 added more support for different media types and also added the ability to implement media controls via lambda expressions.

This chapter provided a brief overview of some JavaFX Media API capabilities. However, we haven't even scratched the surface of the possibilities. For more information regarding the JavaFX Media API, see the online documentation at `http://docs.oracle.com/javase/8/javafx/api/javafx/scene/media/package-summary.html`.

CHAPTER 17

■ ■ ■

Java Web Applications with JavaServer Faces

Java development is not just on the desktop alone. Thousands of enterprise applications are written using Java Enterprise Edition (Java EE), which enables development of sophisticated, robust, and secure applications. The most mainstream and mature framework for developing Java EE applications is JavaServer Faces (JSF). JDK 9 can be used along with some Java EE application servers, such as GlassFish, to enable use of the Java 9 features. Although Java EE and JSF are far too big to cover in one chapter, this will provide you with a glimpse into the world of web development with Java 9 and Java EE.

In this chapter, I will cover the basics of the JSF framework, from developing a basic application to creating a sophisticated front end. Throughout the process, I will cover important information such as how to correctly scope your controller classes, and also how to generate a web application template. In the end, you will be able to get started developing Java web applications, or maintain existing JSF projects.

Since web application development contains a number of interconnected processes, it is recommended to utilize an integrated development environment such as NetBeans to more easily organize web projects. Throughout this chapter, I will demonstrate the solutions to the recipes utilizing NetBeans IDE 8.2. However, you can apply these same basic concepts to projects using any number of Java IDEs.

■ **Note**   This book was written using an early access release of the GlassFish 5 application server along with JDK 9. To configure the server to utilize JDK 9, modify the GlassFish `<<GlassFish-Home>>/config/asenv.conf` file and add the AS_JAVA property, pointing to an installation of JDK 9. Next, modify the `<<GlassFish-Home>>/bin/asadmin` file to make the last line as follows:

`exec "$JAVA" --add-modules java.annotations.common -jar "$AS_INSTALL_LIB/client/appserver-cli.jar" "$@"`

17-1. Creating and Configure a Web Project

Problem

You would like to create and configure a simple Java web application project that will utilize the JSF web framework.

© Josh Juneau 2017
J. Juneau, *Java 9 Recipes*, DOI 10.1007/978-1-4842-1976-8_17

Solution

There are a number of different project formats that can be used to create a web application. One of the most flexible is the Maven web application format. The Apache Maven build system makes it easy to organize a build and expand functionality of an application as time goes on since it contains a robust dependency management system. In this solution, utilize NetBeans IDE to generate a Maven Web Application project, and then configure the project for developing JSF application.

First, open NetBeans IDE and select "File," "New Project," and then from the New Project window, choose the "Maven" category, and the "Web Application" project (Figure 17-1), then click "Next."

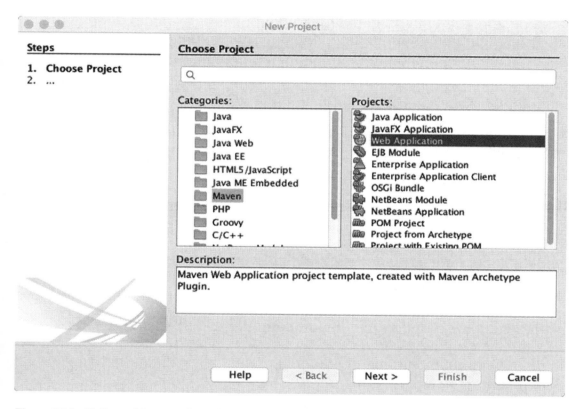

Figure 17-1. *NetBeans Maven Web Application project*

Name the application "HelloJsf," and place it into a directory on your hard disk. Change the "Package Name" to org.java9recipes, and keep all of the other defaults (Figure 17-2).

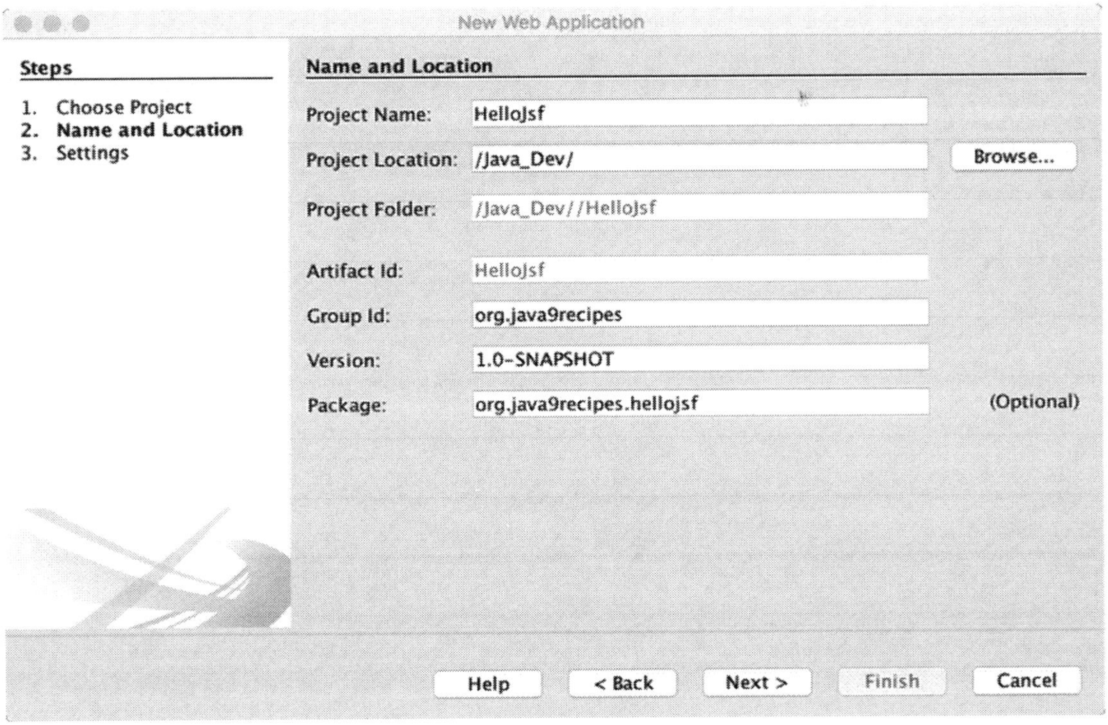

Figure 17-2. *New Java Web Application configuration*

Next, select a server to which the application will be deployed, and a Java EE version. In this case, I will utilize Payara 5 server (GlassFish will also suffice), and Java EE 7 (Figure 17-3).

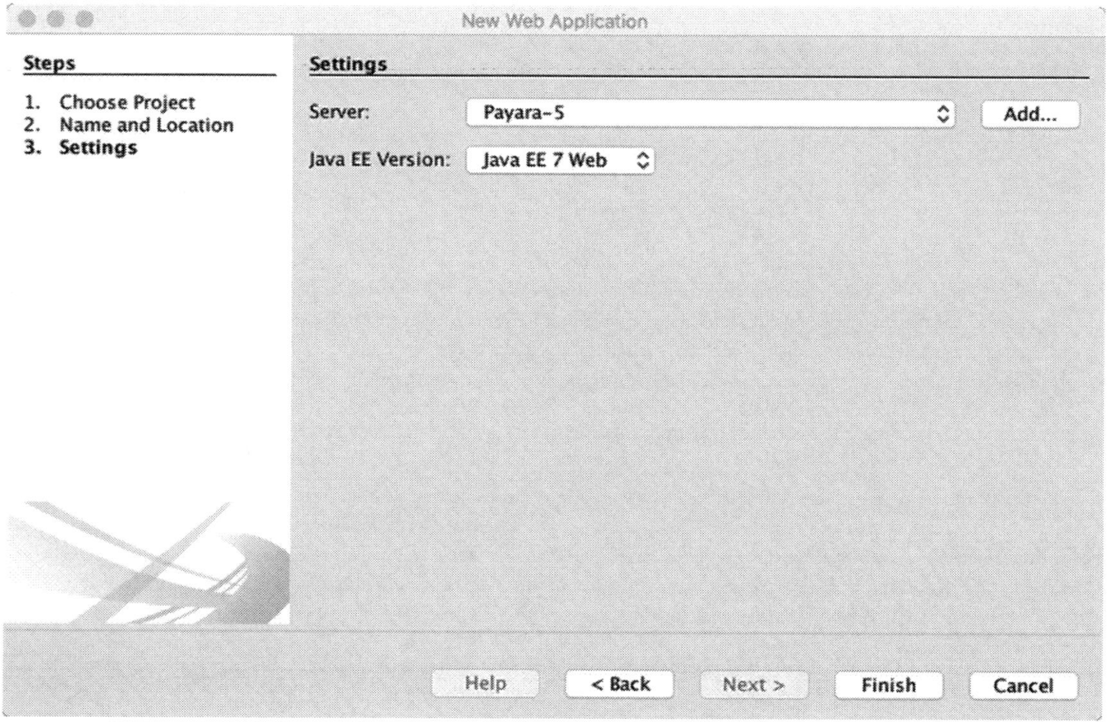

Figure 17-3. *Choose server and Java EE version*

After the project is created, right-click the project and choose "Properties" to configure it for JSF and to assign a Java Platform. In the property menu, select the "Frameworks" category, then choose "Add" and select JSF. Next, click the "Components" tab within the same window and select "PrimeFaces" (Figure 17-4).

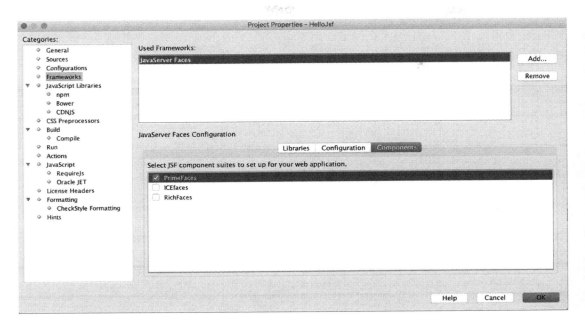

Figure 17-4. Configure project properties

Click "OK" to save the project properties, and the project is now ready to be built utilizing JSF as the framework, along with the PrimeFaces UI library.

How It Works

Development of web applications requires orchestration of a number of different files. While it is possible to develop a Java EE web application without the use of an IDE, using a development environment makes it almost a trivial task. In this recipe, the NetBeans IDE is used to configure a Maven based web application. Maven is a build system similar to Apache Ant, and it is very useful for organization of application projects. Maven is not necessarily better than Ant, but it is easier to get started using. Both Ant and Maven are build systems; however, Maven uses convention over configuration, whereby it assumes many default configurations so that one can use very easily. Ant, on the other hand, requires one to configure and write a build script before it can be used. One of the key components of Maven is that it makes dependency management very easy. It has become one of the most popular project formats, and developing a Maven project in NetBeans creates a project that is portable.

During the project creation wizard, a number of fields must be filled in, although many of the defaults can be left in place. Most importantly, set up a proper package naming convention for the application, and choose the server and Java EE version.

■ **Note** The settings that are completed when utilizing the wizard can be changed after the project has been created by going into the project properties.

Once the initial wizard has completed, a basic Maven web project will have been generated. At this point, the project can be configured to utilize web frameworks, different versions of the JDK, and so on, by changing the project properties. Right-click a NetBeans project to enter the project properties screen, and utilize the category selection to view or change properties pertaining to the selected category. In this case selecting the "Frameworks" category will allow you the ability to add a web framework, such as JSF. When a framework is added to the project, all plumbing and configuration for the framework is completed. Also at this point when choosing JSF, select the "Components" tab on the Frameworks properties and add any other JSF libraries that will be in use. In this case, add "PrimeFaces" since the application developed in this chapter will utilize the PrimeFaces component library.

Once frameworks have been configured, be sure to select the "Sources" category within the properties dialog and select the "Source/Binary Format" pertaining to the JDK version that will be used for coding the application. In this case, select 1.8, since Java 9 has not yet been certified to run on an application server at the time of this writing. Next, select the "Build"->"Compile" category within the properties dialog and ensure that the "Java Platform" select aligns with the one that has been chosen on the "Source/Binary Format" category.

Once these selections have been made, the configuration is complete. Choose "OK" in the project properties. The project will be altered to include new views (index.xhtml and welcomePrimefaces.xhtml) (Figure 17-5). The web.xml deployment descriptor will also be altered for JSF configuration. The welcome file will now point to index.xhtml, and the FacesServlet, a key component of the JSF framework, will be configured.

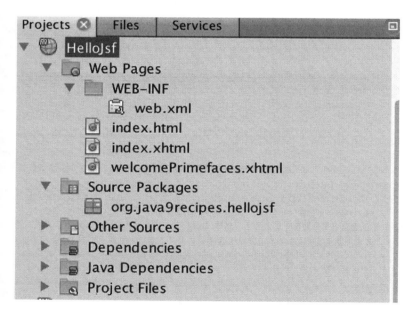

Figure 17-5. *Maven Web project fully configured for JSF*

The web.xml Configuration for a JSF Application usually looks very similar to the following:

```
<?xml version="1.0" encoding="UTF-8"?>
<web-app version="3.1" xmlns="http://xmlns.jcp.org/xml/ns/javaee" xmlns:xsi="http://www.
w3.org/2001/XMLSchema-instance" xsi:schemaLocation="http://xmlns.jcp.org/xml/ns/javaee
http://xmlns.jcp.org/xml/ns/javaee/web-app_3_1.xsd">
    <context-param>
        <param-name>javax.faces.PROJECT_STAGE</param-name>
        <param-value>Development</param-value>
    </context-param>
    <servlet>
        <servlet-name>Faces Servlet</servlet-name>
        <servlet-class>javax.faces.webapp.FacesServlet</servlet-class>
        <load-on-startup>1</load-on-startup>
    </servlet>
    <servlet-mapping>
        <servlet-name>Faces Servlet</servlet-name>
        <url-pattern>/faces/*</url-pattern>
    </servlet-mapping>
    <session-config>
        <session-timeout>
            30
        </session-timeout>
    </session-config>
    <welcome-file-list>
        <welcome-file>faces/index.xhtml</welcome-file>
    </welcome-file-list>
</web-app>
```

At this point, right-click the NetBeans project and choose "Run." This will cause the application to be compiled and deployed to the application server that was selected in the project properties or at project creation time (Figures 17-6 and 17-7).

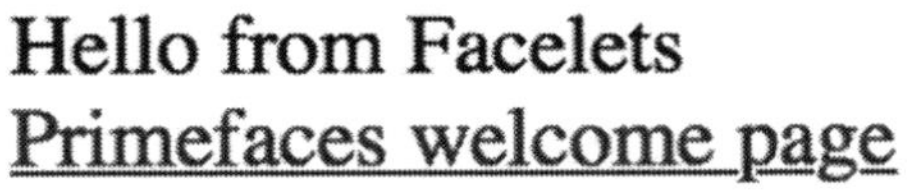

Hello from Facelets
Primefaces welcome page

Figure 17-6. *Deployed HelloJsf application*

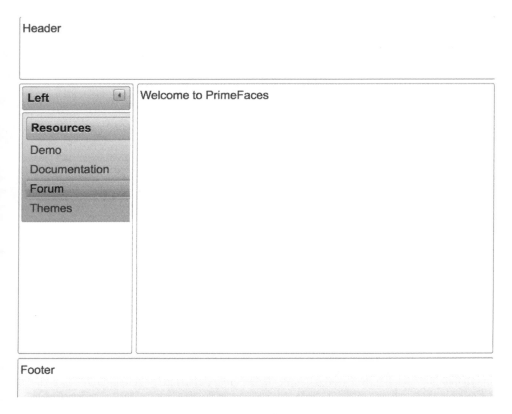

Figure 17-7. *Selecting the "Welcome to PrimeFaces" link*

That does it for the creation and configuration of a JSF project within NetBeans. In the next recipe, I will delve into the world of JSF as the HelloJsf application is modified to add some functionality.

17-2. Developing a JSF Application

Problem

You have created a Maven web project configured with JSF, and you wish to add functionality to the application.

Solution

Build the application such that it will contain an HTML form with a number of fields to populate. The form, when submitted, will invoke a controller method.

First, create a Java class that will be used as a container to hold the data that is submitted in the form. Create a new Java class in a package named `org.java9recipes.hellojsf.model`, and name it `User`. In the class, create three private fields of type `String` for now: `firstName`, `lastName`, and `email`. Next, generate accessor methods (getters and setters) for these fields by right-clicking in the file and choosing "Refactor->Encapsulate Fields" from the contextual menu. This will open the "Encapsulate Fields" dialog, in which you should select all fields for creation of accessor methods and click "Refactor" (Figure 17-8).

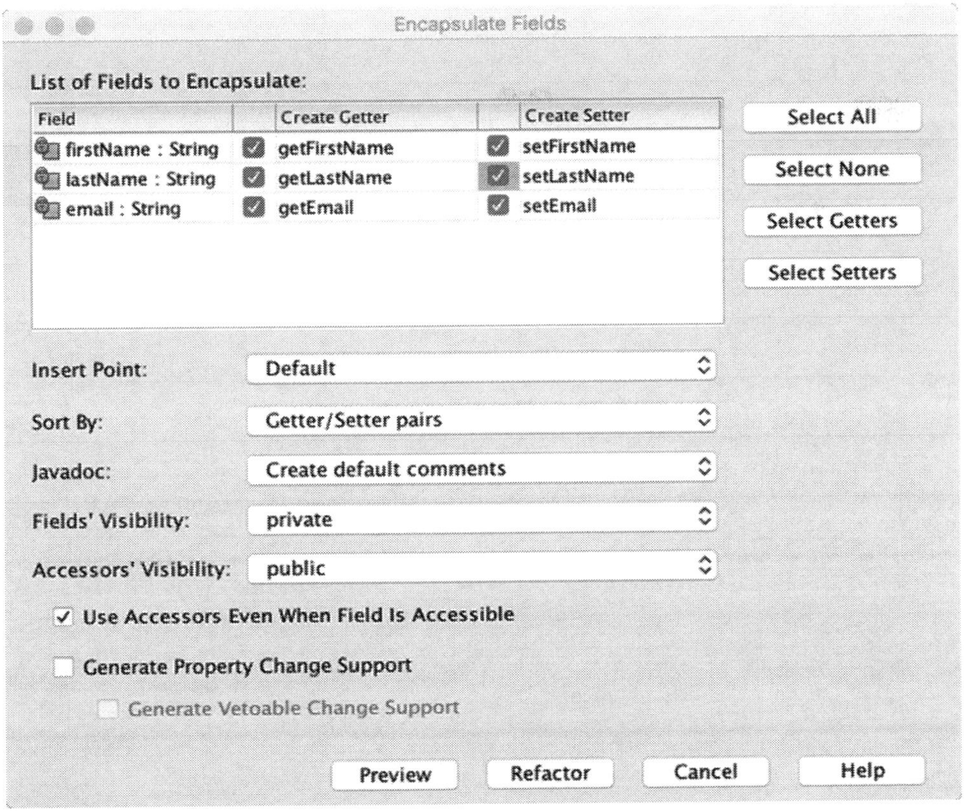

Figure 17-8. Encapsulate Fields

Next, create the Contexts and Dependency Injection (CDI) managed bean. Right-click the project's "Source Packages" node, and create a new package named org.java9recipes.hellojsf.jsf, which will be used to package all of the managed bean controller classes for the application. Next, create a new Java class in the new package named HelloJsfController and make the class implement java.io.Serializable so that it can be passivation capable. Annotate the class with @ViewScoped to indicate that this bean will be managed in the view scope (more about scopes in Recipe 17-6). Also, annotate the class with @Named, which makes the controller class injectable and also allows one to reference the class from expression language within JSF views. Next, create a private field of type User, name the field user and encapsulate fields to generate the accessor methods. Within the getUser() method that is generated, perform a check to see if the user field is null, and if so, then instantiate a new User. At this point, the class should look as follows:

```
package org.java9recipes.hellojsf.jsf;

import javax.faces.view.ViewScoped;
import javax.inject.Named;
import org.java9recipes.hellojsf.model.User;

@Named
@ViewScoped
public class HelloJsfController implements java.io.Serializable {
```

507

```
    private User user;

    public User getUser() {
        if(user == null){
            user = new User();
        }
        return user;
    }

    public void setUser(User user) {
        this.user = user;
    }

}
```

Lastly, create a public method that has a void return type and name it createUser(). This method will be invoked when someone clicks the submit button on the form. In the method, simply print a message to the screen to indicate that the user has been successfully created. To do this, obtain a handle on the current FacesContext instance, which pertains to the current session. Once obtained, add a new FacesMessage to it by passing a null as the first parameter since the message will not be assigned to any single component, and pass the message as the second parameter. Finally, set the user object to null so that a new user object can be created.

■ **Note**   FacesContext contains state information regarding a JSF request. The FacesContext is updated throughout the different phases of a JSF request processing lifecycle.

The method should look as follows once complete.

```
public void createUser(){
    FacesContext context = FacesContext.getCurrentInstance();
    context.addMessage(null, new FacesMessage("Successfully Added User: " +
                        user.getFirstName() + " " + user.getLastName()));
    user = null;
}
```

Next, it is time to create the view. In this case, open the index.xhtml view file within NetBeans IDE, and add the HTML markup and JSF components that will comprise the form.
    <?xml version='1.0' encoding='UTF-8' ?>

```
<!DOCTYPE html PUBLIC "-//W3C//DTD XHTML 1.0 Transitional//EN" "http://www.w3.org/TR/xhtml1/
DTD/xhtml1-transitional.dtd">
<html xmlns="http://www.w3.org/1999/xhtml"
    xmlns:h="http://xmlns.jcp.org/jsf/html"
    xmlns:p="http://primefaces.org/ui">
    <h:head>
        <title>Facelet Title</title>
    </h:head>
    <h:body>
        Hello from Facelets
        <br />
        <h:link outcome="welcomePrimefaces" value="Primefaces welcome page" />
```

```
        <br/>
        <h:form>
            <p:messages id="messages"/>
            <br/>
            <p:outputLabel for="firstName" value="First: "/>
            <p:inputText id="firstName" value="#{helloJsfController.user.firstName}"/>
            <br/>
            <p:outputLabel for="lastName" value="Last: " />
            <p:inputText id="lastName" value="#{helloJsfController.user.lastName}"/>
            <br/>
            <p:outputLabel for="email" value="Email: " />
            <p:inputText id="email" value="#{helloJsfController.user.email}"/>
            <br/><br/>
            <p:commandButton id="submitUser" value="Submit" ajax="false"
                             action="#{helloJsfController.createUser()}"/>

        </h:form>
    </h:body>
</html>
```

Once the view has been generated and the CDI controller has been created, the application can be built and ran by right-clicking the project and choosing "Run." The screen will look similar to that in Figure 17-9.

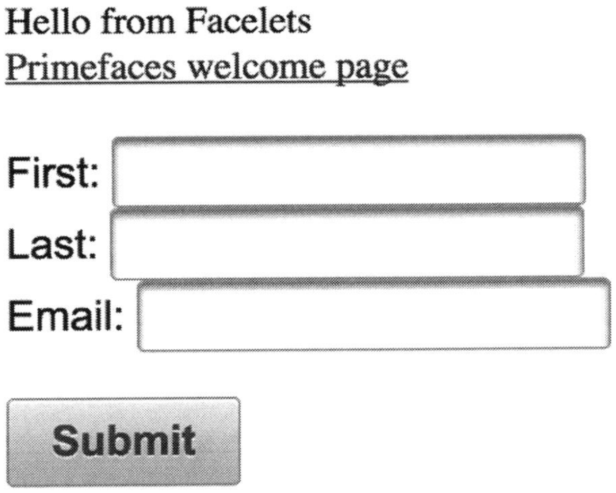

Hello from Facelets
Primefaces welcome page

First: [   ]

Last: [   ]

Email: [   ]

[**Submit**]

Figure 17-9. JSF form

How It Works

JSF was developed in 2004 by Sun Microsystems in an effort to help simplify web application development and make web applications easier to manage/support. It was an evolution of the JavaServer Pages (JSP) framework, adding a more organized development life cycle and the ability to more easily utilize modern web technologies. JSF uses XML files in the XHTML format for view construction and Java classes for application logic, allowing it to adhere to the MVC architecture. Every request in a JSF application is processed by the FacesServlet. The FacesServlet is responsible for building the component trees, processing events, determining navigation, and rendering responses. JSF has now become a mature web framework, and has many advantages over its previous renditions. There are also a large number of component and functional libraries that can be used to extend JSF applications.

The framework is very powerful, including easy integration with technologies such as Ajax and HTML5 making it effortless to develop dynamic content. JSF works well with databases, using JDBC, Enterprise Java Bean (EJB), or RESTful technology to work with the back end. JavaBeans, known as JSF **managed beans**, are used for application logic and support the dynamic content within each view. They can adhere to different life spans depending upon the scope that is used (Recipe 17-6). Views can invoke methods within the beans to perform actions such as data manipulation and form processing. Properties can also be declared within the beans and exposed within the views and evaluated utilizing a standard expression language, providing a convenient way to pass values to and from the server. JSF allows developers to customize their applications with preexisting validation and conversion tags that can be used on components with the view. It is also easy to build custom validators, as well as custom components, that can be applied to components in a view. In a nutshell, JSFs maturity makes it easy to develop just about any web application using the framework.

In this solution, a small application named HelloJsf is created. The application view contains a simple HTML form for submitting a few fields of data, a button for submitting the form to the back end, and a message component for displaying the response. The controller class named `UserController` is `ViewScoped`, meaning that the scope of objects within the class will be retained for the life of the view. Once the user navigates to another view or closes the window, the objects are destroyed. An object named User is used as a container for passing the user data around within the application, and the User is declared within the controller class and made available to the view via accessor methods.

```
private User user;

/**
 * @return the user
 */
public User getUser() {
    if(user == null){
        user = new User();
    }
    return user;
}

/**
 * @param user the user to set
 */
public void setUser(User user) {
    this.user = user;
}
```

CDI controller classes contain the business logic for the views of a JSF application. In the solution, a class named HelloJsfController manages the processing and data for the `HelloJsf` application. The code for the controller can be seen in Recipe 17-4. The controller is responsible for exposing fields and action methods to the JSF views such that data can be submitted directly into the fields and processed accordingly. The controller also facilitates communication with the end user as messages can be created to clearly indicate if processing is successful or if issues have occurred, and the messages can be made available to the views.

The view for the application is an XHTML file, `index.xhtml`, and it includes an HTML form via the JSF <h:form> tags. At the top of the view, the required namespaces are imported so that PrimeFaces and JSF HTML components can be utilized. The form is composed of a number of HTML elements and JSF components. The PrimeFaces components must be prefixed with "p" since the PrimeFaces namespace is assigned to that letter. Each of the JSF components contains a number of attributes that can be used to set values and configure the component's behavior and functionality. The message component <p:messages> is used to display messages that are made available via the FacesContext. The p:outputLabel components render to an HTML labels, and the p:inputText components are rendered to HTML input elements of type text. The value attribute of the p:inputText components contains JSF expression language, referencing the HelloJsfController User object fields. Finally, the p:commandButton component renders an HTML button (input element of type "submit") to submit the form. The action attribute of the commandButton also utilizes JSF expression language to invoke the controller action method named createUser(). The ajax="false" attribute indicates that ajax should not be used to process the form values asynchronously, but rather, the form should be submitted and refreshed.

This recipe packs a lot of information, but it demonstrates how easy it is to develop a simple JSF view with a managed controller class. In a real-life application, the data is likely stored in an RDBMS, such as Oracle or the like. The next recipe covers how to add a database and bind it to the application to store and retrieve user objects.

17-3. Developing a Model for Data

Problem

You would like to store data from a Java EE application within a relational database.

Solution

Bind the data within the application to Java objects so that the objects can be used to store and retrieve data from the database. In most cases, the Java Persistence API (JPA) is a suitable choice for working with data in the form of Java objects. In the previous recipe, a JSF application was developed to submit User objects to a CDI controller. In this recipe, the data will be bound to an entity class and then stored/retrieved from a relational data store using JPA.

For the purposes of this recipe, the Apache derby database will be utilized. First, create a database table to store the User objects. The following SQL can be used to generate the table, which includes a primary key field identified as ID.

```
CREATE TABLE HELLO_USER (
ID                  NUMERIC PRIMARY KEY,
FIRST_NAME          VARCHAR(100),
LAST_NAME           VARCHAR(50),
EMAIL               VARCHAR(150));
```

Once the database table has been created, generate a corresponding entity class. For this solution, NetBeans IDE will be used to automatically create the class. To do so, right-click the "Source Packages" node of the HelloJsf project, and creating a package named org.java9recipes.hellojsf.entity. Next, right-click the newly created package and select "New"->"Entity Classes from Database" from the contextual menu. Once the "New Entity Classes from Database" dialog appears, select or create a JDBC Data Source for your Apache Derby database. Once selected, choose the USER table from the listing of available tables and add it to the "Selected Tables" list, then choose "Next." On the dialog screens that follow, accept all defaults and click through to "Finish" and create the entity class (Figure 17-10).

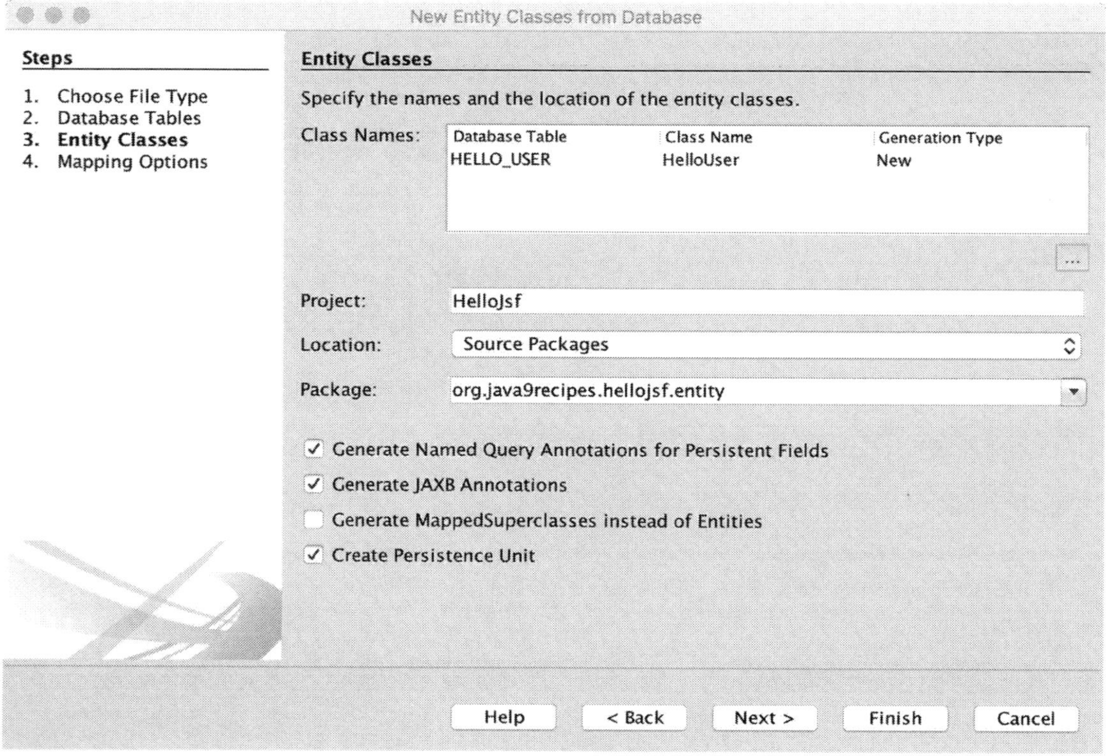

Figure 17-10. *Create entity class from database within NetBeans IDE*

Once the entity class has been created, develop an EJB or JAX-RS RESTful web service class to work with the corresponding entity. In this solution, an EJB will be developed using NetBeans IDE by first creating another new package in the project named org.java9recipes.hellojsf.session. This package will be used to hold the session beans or EJBs. Next, right-click the newly created package and select "Session Beans for Entity Classes" from the contextual menu. This will open the dialog which allows entity class(es) to be selected so that NetBeans IDE can automatically create the corresponding session beans (Figure 17-11).

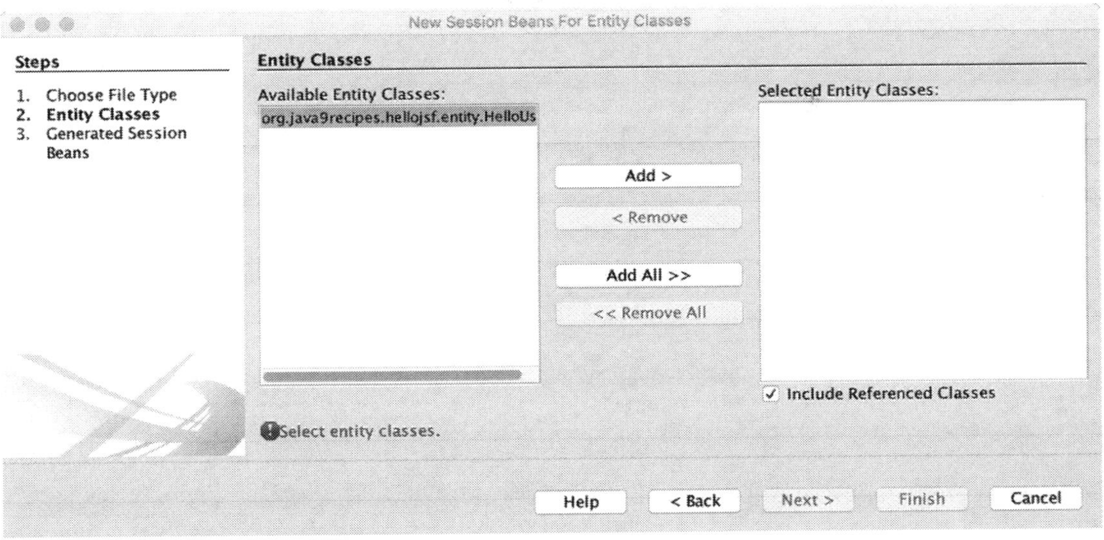

Figure 17-11. *Select entity classes to generate session beans*

Once selected, choose "Next," then finally select "Finish" to create the EJB. After doing so, NetBeans IDE will generate an abstract class entitled AbstractFacade, which will be extended by any entity class that is generated. The NetBeans IDE will also generate the session bean, HelloJsfFacade. Once these classes have been generated, the model for the application is complete and the controller will be able to successfully work with the data.

How It Works

The model for an enterprise application is one of the most important components, because data is at the heart of the enterprise. To generate a model for a Java EE application, one must have a data store, usually an RDBMS, and an object-relational mapping strategy must be coded to represent the database in a code format. In this solution, the model is comprised of three classes: entity class, an abstract class containing standard object-relational mapping methods, and an EJB that extends the abstract class.

An entity class is essentially a Plain Old Java Object (POJO) that represents a database table as a Java object. The entity class has a field declared for each of the columns of the database table, and accessor methods are defined for each of the fields. Annotations make entity classes work like magic, whereby a few easy annotations perform the task of binding the class, and subsequently the fields, to the database table and its columns. The @Entity annotation tells the compiler that this is an entity class. Table 17-1 lists some common entity class annotations.

Table 17-1. *Common Entity Class Annotations*

Annotation	Description
@Entity	Marks a class as an entity class.
@Table	Maps the entity class to a database table.
@Id	Denotes the primary key field of the entity class.
@XmlRootElement	Maps class to an XML Element.
@NamedQueries	List of @NamedQuery elements which map names to predefined queries.
@Embeddable	Denotes an embedded class.

The entity class is mapped to a named database table by annotating it with @Table, and specifying the name of the database table as an attribute. NetBeans IDE also adds a couple of more annotations to the entity class for convenience, those being @XmlRootElement, and @NamedQueries. The @XmlRootElement annotation associates an XML root element with the class, thereby making the entity class available with XML-based APIs, such as JAX-RS and JAXB. The @NamedQueries annotation provides a number of named queries for the entity (one for each field), making it easy to query the entity class by name, rather than writing JPQL each time it needs to be queried. Entity classes also always contain a primary key, which is denoted via the @Id annotation, and each column of the database table are mapped to the class fields with @ Column. Bean validation can also be added to the fields of an entity class, providing validation for any input or content that is added to the associated entity class field. Lastly, an entity class contains an equals() method to help compare objects against entities, and a toString() method. The final entity class for HelloUser should look as follows:

```
@Entity
@Table(name = "HELLO_USER")
@XmlRootElement
@NamedQueries({
    @NamedQuery(name = "HelloUser.findAll", query = "SELECT h FROM HelloUser h"),
    @NamedQuery(name = "HelloUser.findById", query = "SELECT h FROM HelloUser h
    WHERE h.id = :id"),
    @NamedQuery(name = "HelloUser.findByFirstName", query = "SELECT h FROM HelloUser h
    WHERE h.firstName = :firstName"),
    @NamedQuery(name = "HelloUser.findByLastName", query = "SELECT h FROM HelloUser h
    WHERE h.lastName = :lastName"),
    @NamedQuery(name = "HelloUser.findByEmail", query = "SELECT h FROM HelloUser h
    WHERE h.email = :email")})
public class HelloUser implements Serializable {

    private static final long serialVersionUID = 1L;
    @Id
    @Basic(optional = false)
    @NotNull
    @Column(name = "ID")
    private Integer id;
    @Size(max = 100)
    @Column(name = "FIRST_NAME")
    private String firstName;
    @Size(max = 50)
    @Column(name = "LAST_NAME")
```

```java
private String lastName;
// @Pattern(regexp="[a-z0-9!#$%&'*+/=?^_`{|}~-]+(?:\\.[a-z0-9!#$%&'*+/=?^_`{|}~-]+)*@
    (?:[a-z0-9](?:[a-z0-9-]*[a-z0-9])?\\.)+[a-z0-9](?:[a-z0-9-]*[a-z0-9])?",
    message="Invalid email")//if the field contains e-mail address consider using this
    annotation to enforce field validation
@Size(max = 150)
@Column(name = "EMAIL")
private String email;

public HelloUser() {
}

public HelloUser(Integer id) {
    this.id = id;
}

public Integer getId() {
    return id;
}

public void setId(Integer id) {
    this.id = id;
}

public String getFirstName() {
    return firstName;
}

public void setFirstName(String firstName) {
    this.firstName = firstName;
}

public String getLastName() {
    return lastName;
}

public void setLastName(String lastName) {
    this.lastName = lastName;
}

public String getEmail() {
    return email;
}

public void setEmail(String email) {
    this.email = email;
}

@Override
public int hashCode() {
    int hash = 0;
    hash += (id != null ? id.hashCode() : 0);
```

515

```
        return hash;
    }

    @Override
    public boolean equals(Object object) {
        // TODO: Warning - this method won't work in the case the id fields are not set
        if (!(object instanceof HelloUser)) {
            return false;
        }
        HelloUser other = (HelloUser) object;
        if ((this.id == null && other.id != null) || (this.id != null && !this.
        id.equals(other.id))) {
            return false;
        }
        return true;
    }

    @Override
    public String toString() {
        return "org.java9recipes.hellojsf.entity.HelloUser[ id=" + id + " ]";
    }

}
```

Once an entity class has been generated, a session bean can be generated to facilitate work with the entity class. The session bean (a.k.a. EJB) declares a PersistenceContext, which provides communication with the underlying data store. It then calls upon the PersistenceContext to perform any number of JPA tasks, such as creating, updating, or deleting records from a database via the entity class data. The NetBeans IDE generates the AbstractFacade abstract class, which is extended by all of the entity classes for the project. This class essentially contains the methods that allow for basic manipulation of the entities: create(), findAll(), edit(), and remove(), enabling the developer to automatically gain access to such methods without recoding for each entity class. This leaves the developer with a fully functional session bean without any coding. If additional queries or work against an entity needs to be created, the developer can modify the contents of the session bean, in this case HelloJsfFacade, accordingly.

An EJB must be annotated with either @Stateful or @Stateless to designate whether the class will be a stateful or stateless session bean. A stateful session bean can be bound to a single user session, allowing state to be managed throughout that user's session. Stateless is more often used such that the session bean will be shared across all of the user sessions in the application. The simple stateless session bean named HelloJsfFacade looks as follows:

```
@Stateless
public class HelloUserFacade extends AbstractFacade<HelloUser> {

    @PersistenceContext(unitName = "org.java9recipes_HelloJsf_war_1.0-SNAPSHOTPU")
    private EntityManager em;

    @Override
    protected EntityManager getEntityManager() {
        return em;
    }
```

```
public HelloUserFacade() {
    super(HelloUser.class);
}
```

}

The classes and code that has been discussed in this recipe constitute the model of an application. In summary, the model binds the application to an underlying data store, thus making it possible to create, remove, update, and delete data using Java objects, rather than working directly with the database via SQL. For more information on developing entity classes, please see the Java EE Tutorial online: https://docs. oracle.com/javaee/7/tutorial/.

17-4. Writing View Controllers

Problem

You have developed a JSF view which contains bound fields and a form, and you need to create the business logic to process the form and facilitate work with the session bean.

Solution

Create a managed bean controller class (CDI bean), which can be used to bind actions and fields to JSF views and facilitate work that needs to be performed within the EJB session bean. In this solution, the HelloJsfController class, seen in the following, is used as the CDI controller.

```
@Named
@ViewScoped
public class HelloJsfController implements java.io.Serializable {

    private User user;

    /**
     * @return the user
     */
    public User getUser() {
        if(user == null){
            user = new User();
        }
        return user;
    }

    /**
     * @param user the user to set
     */
    public void setUser(User user) {
        this.user = user;
    }

    public void createUser(){
        FacesContext context = FacesContext.getCurrentInstance();
```

```
            context.addMessage(null, new FacesMessage("Successfully Added User: " +
                            user.getFirstName() + " " + user.getLastName()));
        user = null;
    }

}
```

In the previous recipe, a data model was added to the HelloJsf application. Next, the controller class and view needs to be modified to make use of the data model. To modify the controller, simply add a new private field of type HelloUser, and generate accessor methods for it. In the getHelloUser method, check first to see if the field is null, and if so, instantiate a new instance.

```
...
private HelloUser helloUser;
...
public HelloUser getHelloUser() {
        if(helloUser == null){
            helloUser = new HelloUser();
        }
        return helloUser;
}

public void setHelloUser(HelloUser helloUser) {
        this.helloUser = helloUser;
}
...
```

Next, inject the EJB into the controller class so that a new HelloUser can be persisted. To do so, inject a new private field of type HelloUserFacade as follows:

```
@EJB
private HelloUserFacade helloUserFacade;
```

Lastly, create a new action method named createAndPersistUser(), which will generally do the same as the createUser() method. However, this new method will persist a HelloUser object into the database by calling upon the EJB.

```
public void createAndPersistUser(){
    FacesContext context = FacesContext.getCurrentInstance();
    helloUserFacade.create(helloUser);
    context.addMessage(null, new FacesMessage("Successfully Persisted User: " +
                        user.getFirstName() + " " + user.getLastName()));
    helloUser = null;
}
```

The data model has now been integrated into the controller logic. When a user clicks the button in the view, it should invoke the action method createAndPersistUser() within the controller. The fields contained within the form are processed via the controller as well since the User object was injected and exposed to the user interface.

How It Works

A JSF managed bean controller is used to facilitate work between the views and the session beans of a Java EE application. In the past, managed bean controllers used to adhere to a different set of rules, as JSF contained its own set of annotations for developing managed beans. In recent releases of Java EE, JSF-specific managed beans have been phased out, and CDI beans have taken their place, allowing for a more cohesive and universal controller class.

In the solution, the class implements java.io.Serializable since it may need to be persisted to disk in the event of the session ending abruptly. The class is annotated with @Named to make it injectable and accessible via JSF expression language. The class is also annotated with a designated CDI scope, in this case @ViewScoped, to indicate the CDI scope of the controller. There are a number of different scopes, these are covered in Recipe 17-6. ViewScoped means that the controller state will be saved for the lifetime of the view. The User object is declared within the controller as a private field, and it is made accessible as a property via the accessor methods. Lastly, the class contains a method named createUser(), which is public, and it creates a FacesMessage object and places it into the current FacesContext to display onscreen. The user object is then set to null.

The modified version of the controller class, which includes the data model, declares an instance field of type HelloUser. Accessor methods for the HelloUser field are created, and within the getter method a new instance is created if the field is null. The HelloUserFacade is injected into the controller so that it can be utilized to perform data model transactions (a.k.a.: database transactions). The createAndPersistUser() method calls upon the HelloUserFacade create() method, passing a HelloUser instance to persist the object into the database. Similarly, if one wished to edit a HelloUser object, the HelloUserFacade edit() method can be invoked. Lastly, if one wishes to remove a user, the remove() method can be invoked.

A controller class may contain any number of action methods and field declarations, however, it is important to manage the size of a controller such that the controller is not responsible for performing too much work. If a controller class contains too much functionality, for instance if it is used to back more than one view, then it can become cumbersome and difficult to maintain. To learn more about CDI scopes for controller classes, please see Recipe 17-6.

17-5. Developing Asynchronous Views

Problem

Rather than follow the old-style submit and response web application, you would like to generate a modern ui which will asynchronously submit data and post responses without refreshing the browser page or re-rendering the view to provide a better user experience.

Solution

Incorporate Asynchronous JavaScript and XML into your application to asynchronously send data to the server and render responses without refresh. There are a number of ways to create an AJAX-based view for a JSF application, and this recipe will demonstrate how to leverage the PrimeFaces AJAX API. In this solution, a new view will be created named helloAjax.xhtml (Figure 17-12), and it will generally be a copy of the original index.xhtml view which utilizes AJAX to submit the form. The view will also asynchronously update the messages component, displaying the message that has been generated by the controller class. A dataTable component is also added to helloAjax.xhtml, which is asynchronously updated to display the list of users that has been created and persisted to the database. The enhanced view looks as follows:

```xml
<?xml version='1.0' encoding='UTF-8' ?>
<!DOCTYPE html PUBLIC "-//W3C//DTD XHTML 1.0 Transitional//EN" "http://www.w3.org/TR/xhtml1/
DTD/xhtml1-transitional.dtd">
<html xmlns="http://www.w3.org/1999/xhtml"
      xmlns:h="http://xmlns.jcp.org/jsf/html"
      xmlns:f="http://xmlns.jcp.org/jsf/core"
      xmlns:p="http://primefaces.org/ui">
    <h:head>
        <title>Facelet Title</title>
    </h:head>
    <h:body>
        Hello from Facelets
        <br />
        <h:link outcome="welcomePrimefaces" value="Primefaces welcome page" />
        <br/>
        <h:form>
            <h:inputText id="firstNameType" value="#{helloJsfController.freeText}">
                <f:ajax execute="@this" event="keyup" listener="#{helloJsfController.
                displayText}"
                        render="messages"/>
            </h:inputText>
            <p:messages id="messages"/>
            <br/>
            <p:panelGrid columns="2" style="width: 100%">

                <p:outputLabel for="firstName" value="First: "/>
                <p:inputText id="firstName" value="#{helloJsfController.user.firstName}"/>

                <p:outputLabel for="lastName" value="Last: " />
                <p:inputText id="lastName" value="#{helloJsfController.user.lastName}"/>

                <p:outputLabel for="email" value="Email: " />
                <p:inputText id="email" value="#{helloJsfController.user.email}"/>
            </p:panelGrid>
            <br/>
            <p:commandButton id="submitUser" value="Submit"
                             action="#{helloJsfController.createUser()}"
                             update="messages, helloUsers"/>

            <br/>
            <p:dataTable id="helloUsers" var="user" value="#{helloJsfController.
            helloUserList}">
                <p:column headerText="First Name">
                    <h:outputText value="#{user.firstName}"/>
                </p:column>
                <p:column headerText="Last Name">
                    <h:outputText value="#{user.lastName}"/>
                </p:column>
                <p:column headerText="Email">
                    <h:outputText value="#{user.email}"/>
                </p:column>
            </p:dataTable>
```

```
        </h:form>
    </h:body>
</html>
```

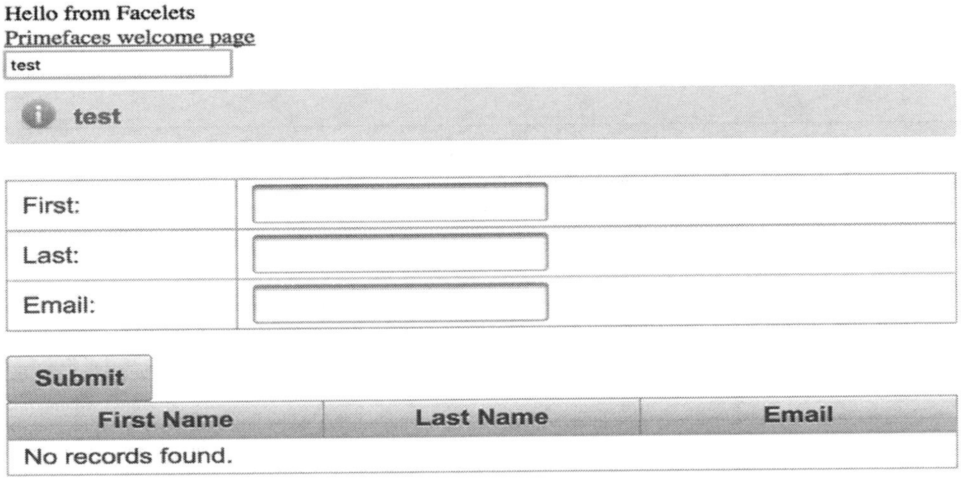

Hello from Facelets

Primefaces welcome page

test

ⓘ test

First:	
Last:	
Email:	

Submit

First Name	Last Name	Email
No records found.		

Figure 17-12. *Asychronous form*

How It Works

It is very easy to apply the principles of AJAX to a JSF view. There are a few different ways to apply AJAX functionality, but the easiest is to utilize a sophisticated user interface framework, such as PrimeFaces, which includes the built-in AJAX functionality. In fact, many of the PrimeFaces components perform AJAX submits by default, so they include an ajax attribute that can be set to false in order to operate in a synchronous manner.

In the solution to this recipe, a PrimeFaces commandButton is utilized to asynchronously send the form contents to the controller class. Once the action method is invoked, the data is persisted and a FacesMessage is generated, then the response is sent back to the view. When the view receives the response, it asynchronously updates the components that are listed in the commandButton update attribute, those being the messages component, and the helloUsers dataTable component.

It is possible to asynchronously submit the contents of a JSF component without PrimeFaces by embedding the <f:ajax/> tag between the component's opening and closing tag. The f:ajax tag makes use of an execute attribute to indicate which part of the view will be executed or submitted asynchronously, an onevent attribute to indicate which JavaScript event should invoke the asynchronous action, a listener attribute to bind an action method, amongst others. For example, the following inputText component has been made asynchronous via the use of the f:ajax tag:

```
<h:inputText id="firstNameType" value="#{helloJsfController.freeText}">
    <f:ajax execute="@this" event="keyup" listener="#{helloJsfController.displayText}"
                    render="messages"/>
</h:inputText>
```

In the example, when the keyup event occurs, the value that is typed within the inputText field is submitted to the helloJsfController.freeText property. The displayText() action method is also invoked, which places the contents of the freeText property into a FacesMessage, as seen in the following. Once the action is invoked and the request is sent back, the messages component is updated because the render attribute of f:ajax specifies its id.

```
public void displayText(AjaxBehaviorEvent evt){
    FacesContext context = FacesContext.getCurrentInstance();
    System.out.println("test: " + freeText);
    context.addMessage(null, new FacesMessage(freeText));
}
```

There are a number of different techniques that can be used to asynchronously update JSF views. There are even more asynchronous components that are available amongst the many UI libraries that are available. Although this solution demonstrates the use of PrimeFaces, as well as the f:ajax tag, small books could be written on the topic. JSF is a mature web framework, offering a plethora of tools to get the job done. Choose which works best for the situation, and enjoy the ease of working with AJAX and limiting exposure to the underlying JavaScript.

17-6. Applying the Correct Scope

Problem

You are developing a JSF application, and you want to be sure that the controllers are configured to remain in scope for the correct amount of time, depending upon functionality and requirement.

Solution

Utilize CDI scopes to apply desired scoping to controller classes. For instance, if a controller class contains logic and data that is pertinent throughout the entire session, annotate the class with the javax. enterprise.context.SessionScoped. However, if a controller class is only pertinent at the request level, annotate the class with javax.enterprise.context.RequestScoped. Apply each of the different scopes to the controller class(es) according to this logic.

How It Works

A controller class scope can change the way that an application functions entirely. The amount of time in which a controller is in scope can make a big difference across the individual views of an application. Fortunately, it is an easy task to apply different scopes to different controllers. However, programming methodology changes drastically depending upon the scope in which a controller class has been placed. CDI offers a number of scopes that can be utilized, as seen in Table 17-2.

Table 17-2. *CDI Scopes*

Scope	Duration
@ApplicationScoped	State is shared across all users' sessions within an application.
@Dependent	Object receives the same lifecycle as a client bean. (Default scope)
@ConversationScoped	Developer controls the start and end of the conversation, and state is maintained throughout the entire conversation.
@RequestScoped	State lasts for the duration of a single HTTP request.
@SessionScoped	State lasts for the duration of a user's session.
javax.faces.view.ViewScoped	State lasts as long as NavigationHandler does not cause navigation to a different viewId.

As mentioned previously, one thing to keep in mind while applying scope is a controller's chosen scope will affect the rest of the application. If a controller will be containing data that will be of use throughout a user's session, then @SessionScoped may be the best choice. Just keep in mind that all data within a @ SessionScoped bean will be retained throughout the session. Therefore, if a List is declared and populated within the bean, the content of the bean must be refreshed or altered programmatically. Such is not the case if using some scope that causes a bean to be refreshed throughout the course of a user's session. For instance, if the same bean is @RequestScoped, then the data in the List will be requeried and repopulated each time a request is made.

■ **Note** Scoping can also have a big impact on interaction with other managed beans. It is important to inject beans of the same scope

17-7. Generating and Applying a Template

Problem

You would like to apply the same visual template across all the views of an application.

Solution

Utilize a Facelets template and apply to each view. To create a template, you must first develop a new XHTML view file and then add the appropriate HTML/JSF/ XML markup to it. Content from other views will displace the ui:insert elements in the template once the template has been applied to one or more JSF views. The following source is that of a template named template.xhtml this is the template that will be applied to all views within the HelloJsf application:

```
<html xmlns="http://www.w3.org/1999/xhtml"
      xmlns:ui="http://xmlns.jcp.org/jsf/facelets"
      xmlns:h="http://xmlns.jcp.org/jsf/html"
      xmlns:p="http://primefaces.org/ui">
```

```
<h:head>
    <meta http-equiv="Content-Type" content="text/html; charset=UTF-8" />
    <h:outputStylesheet library="css" name="default.css"/>
    <h:outputStylesheet library="css" name="cssLayout.css"/>

    <title>Hello JSF</title>

</h:head>

<h:body>

    <p:growl id="growl" life="3000" />

    <p:layout fullPage="true">
        <p:layoutUnit position="north" size="65" header="#{bundle.AppName}">
            <h:form id="menuForm">
                <p:menubar>
                    <p:menuitem value="Home" outcome="/index.xhtml" icon="ui-icon-home"/>

                        <p:menuitem value="Hello Main" outcome="/helloUser.xhtml" />
                        <p:menuitem value="PrimeFaces" outcome="/welcomePrimefaces.xhtml" />
                        <p:menuitem value="Hello Ajax" outcome="/helloAjax.xhtml" />

                </p:menubar>
            </h:form>
        </p:layoutUnit>

        <p:layoutUnit position="south" size="60">
            <ui:insert name="footer"/>
        </p:layoutUnit>

        <p:layoutUnit position="center">
            <ui:insert name="content"/>
        </p:layoutUnit>

    </p:layout>

</h:body>

</html>
```

The template defines the overall structure for the application views. However, it can use a CSS style sheet to declare the formatting for each of the elements within the template. The style sheet should be contained within a resources directory in the application so that it will be accessible to the views. It is also possible to utilize JSF EL within a template. If EL is utilized, typically a session or application scoped managed bean drives the content. A JSF client view of the template would contain `<ui:composition/>` tags surrounding the view content, and `<ui:define/>` tags surrounding the named segment of markup that belongs to the corresponding `<ui:insert/>` tags within the template. The following view would be an example of a client view of the template shown previously.

```xml
<?xml version='1.0' encoding='UTF-8' ?>
<!DOCTYPE html PUBLIC "-//W3C//DTD XHTML 1.0 Transitional//EN" "http://www.w3.org/TR/xhtml1/
DTD/xhtml1-transitional.dtd">
<html xmlns="http://www.w3.org/1999/xhtml"
      xmlns:h="http://xmlns.jcp.org/jsf/html"
      xmlns:f="http://xmlns.jcp.org/jsf/core"
      xmlns:p="http://primefaces.org/ui"
      xmlns:ui="http://xmlns.jcp.org/jsf/facelets">

    <ui:composition template="layout/template.xhtml">

      <ui:define name="content">
      Hello from Facelets
      <br />
      <h:link outcome="welcomePrimefaces" value="Primefaces welcome page" />
      <br/>
      <h:form>
          <p:messages id="messages"/>
          <br/>

          <p:outputLabel for="firstName" value="First: "/>
          <p:inputText id="firstName" value="#{helloJsfController.user.firstName}"/>
          <br/>
          <p:outputLabel for="lastName" value="Last: " />
          <p:inputText id="lastName" value="#{helloJsfController.user.lastName}"/>
          <br/>
          <p:outputLabel for="email" value="Email: " />
          <p:inputText id="email" value="#{helloJsfController.user.email}"/>
          <br/>
          <p:commandButton id="submitUser" value="Submit"
                           action="#{helloJsfController.createUser()}"
                           update="messages, helloUsers"/>

          <br/>
          <p:dataTable id="helloUsers" var="user" value="#{helloJsfController.
          helloUserList}">
              <p:column headerText="First Name">
                  <h:outputText value="#{user.firstName}"/>
              </p:column>
              <p:column headerText="Last Name">
                  <h:outputText value="#{user.lastName}"/>
              </p:column>
              <p:column headerText="Email">
                  <h:outputText value="#{user.email}"/>
              </p:column>
          </p:dataTable>

      </h:form>
      </ui:define>

    </ui:composition>

</html>
```

How It Works

To create a unified application experience, the views should be coherent in that they look similar and function in a uniform manner. The idea of developing web page templates has been around for a number of years, but unfortunately many template implementations contain duplicate markup on every application page. While duplicating the same layout for every separate web page works, it creates a maintenance nightmare. What happens when there is a need to update a single link within the page header? Such a conundrum would cause a developer to visit and manually update every web page for an application if the template was duplicated on every page. The Facelets view definition language provides a robust solution for the development of view templates, and it is one of the major bonuses of working with the JSF technology.

Facelets provides the ability for a single template to be applied to one or more views within an application. This means a developer can create one view that constructs the header, footer, and other portions of the template, and then this view can be applied to any number of other views that are responsible for containing the main view content. This technique mitigates issues such as changing a single link within the page header, because now the template can be updated with the new link, and every other view within the application will automatically reflect the change.

To create a template using Facelets, create an XHTML view, declare the required namespaces, and then add HTML, JSF, and Facelets tags accordingly to design the layout you desire. The template can be thought of as an "outer shell" for a web view, in that it can contain any number of other views within it. Likewise, any number of JSF views can have the same template applied, so the overall look and feel of the application will remain constant.

Facelets tags that are responsible for controlling the view layout. To utilize these Facelets tags, you'll need to declare the XML namespace for the Facelets tag library in the <html> element within the template. Note that the XML namespace for the standard JSF tag libraries is also specified here.

```
<html xmlns="http://www.w3.org/1999/xhtml"
      xmlns:ui="http://xmlns.jcp.org/jsf/facelets"
      xmlns:h="http://xmlns.jcp.org/jsf/html">
...
```

Facelets contains a number of special tags that can be used to help control page flow and layout. Table 17-3 in the lists the Facelets tags that are useful for controlling page flow and layout. The only Facelets tag that is used within the template for this example is ui:insert. The ui:insert tag contains a name attribute, which is set to the name of the corresponding ui:define element that will be included in the view. Taking a look at the source for this example, you can see the following ui:insert tag:

```
<ui:insert name="content">Content</ui:insert>
```

Table 17-3. *Facelets Page Control and Template Tags*

Tag	Description
ui:component	Defines a template component and specifies a file name for the component
ui:composition	Defines a page composition and encapsulates all other JSF markup
ui:debug	Creates a debug component, which captures debugging information, namely, the state of the component tree and the scoped variables in the application, when the component is rendered
ui:define	Defines content that is inserted into a page by a template
ui:decorate	Decorates pieces of a page
ui:fragment	Defines a template fragment, much like ui:component, except that all content outside of tag is not disregarded
ui:include	Allows another XHTML page to be encapsulated and reused within a view
ui:insert	Inserts content into a template
ui:param	Passes parameters to an included file or template
ui:repeat	Iterates over a collection of data
ui:remove	Removes content from a page

If a view that uses the template, a.k.a. template client, it must list the template within the view <ui:composition> tag. Within the <ui:composition>, the view must specify a <ui:define> tag with the same name as the <ui:insert> name, then any content that is placed between the opening and closing <ui:define> tags will be inserted into the view in that location. However, if the template client does not contain a <ui:define> tag with the same name as the <ui:insert> tag, then the content between the opening and closing <ui:insert> tags within the template will be displayed.

Summary

Development of Java EE web applications can be a very large topic, and this chapter just touched upon a few of the many technologies that can be utilized. The JSF web framework is mature and robust, and offers many options for developing sophisticated and easy to use applications. Combined with the underlying Java EE technologies including EJB, JAX-RS, JPA, and others, Java web development is powerful and it is easy to get started.

■ ■ ■

CHAPTER 18

Nashorn and Scripting

In Java 6, the `javax.script` package was included for incorporating scripting languages with Java. It enabled developers to embed code written in scripting languages directly into Java applications. This began a new generation of polyglot applications, as developers were able to construct Java solutions containing scripts written in languages such as JavaScript and Python. The JavaScript engine that was used in Java 6 was called Rhino. It is an implementation of the JavaScript engine, developed entirely in Java. While it contains a full JavaScript implementation, it is an older engine and is no longer compliant with current JavaScript Standards.

Java 8 introduced a new JavaScript engine called Nashorn. It is based on the ECMAScript-262 Edition 5.1 language specification and supports the `javax.script` API introduced in Java 6. Besides bringing a modern JavaScript engine to the Java platform, Nashorn also contains a few new features that make developing JavaScript and Java solutions easier and more robust. The new command-line tool called `jjs` provides scripting abilities above and beyond those that were available with `jrunscript`. Nashorn also has full access to the JavaFX 8 API, allowing developers to construct JavaFX applications completely in JavaScript.

JDK 9 increases the usability of Nashorn even further by including a selected set of features from EMCAScript 6 specification at release. Over time, more features from EMCAScript 6 will likely be incorporated in updates of JDK 9 and subsequent releases of the JDK.

This chapter touches on using the Nashorn engine to construct solutions that integrate the worlds of Java and JavaScript. It does not cover all of the features available with Nashorn, but you with provides enough to get up and running.

18-1. Loading and Executing JavaScript from Java

Problem

You want to load and execute JavaScript code from within your Java application.

Solution

Execute the JavaScript using the Nashorn engine, the next-generation JavaScript engine that is part of Java 8 and is used to execute JavaScript code. The Nashorn engine can be called upon to process in-line JavaScript, or an external JavaScript file directly within Java code. Execute an external JavaScript file or in-line JavaScript code using the Java ScriptEngineManager. Once you've obtained a `ScriptEngineManager()`, you get an instance of the Nashorn engine to use for JavaScript code execution.

In the following example, a Nashorn `ScriptEngine` is used to invoke a JavaScript file that resides on the local file system.

© Josh Juneau 2017
J. Juneau, *Java 9 Recipes*, DOI 10.1007/978-1-4842-1976-8_18

```
public static void loadExternalJs(){
    ScriptEngineManager sem = new ScriptEngineManager();
    ScriptEngine nashorn = sem.getEngineByName("nashorn");
    try {
        nashorn.eval("load('src/org/java9recipes/chapter18/js/helloNashorn.js')");
    } catch (ScriptException ex) {
        Logger.getLogger(NashornInvoker.class.getName()).log(Level.SEVERE, null, ex);
    }
}
```

The code that resides in the helloNashorn.js file is as follows:

```
print("Hello Nashorn!");
```

Next, let's take a look at some in-line JavaScript. In the following example, a Nashorn ScriptEngine is obtained, and then a JavaScript function is created for obtaining the gallons of water for an in-ground pool. The function is then executed to return a result.

```
public static void loadInlineJs(){
    ScriptEngineManager sem = new ScriptEngineManager();
    ScriptEngine nashorn = sem.getEngineByName("nashorn");
    try {
        nashorn.eval("function gallons(width, length, avgDepth){var volume =
                    avgDepth * width * length;" +
                    "return volume * 7.48; }");
        nashorn.eval("print('Gallons of water in pool: '+ gallons(16,32,5))");
    } catch (ScriptException ex) {
        Logger.getLogger(NashornInvoker.class.getName()).log(Level.SEVERE, null, ex);
    }
}
```

Results:

```
run:
Hello Nashorn!
Gallons of water in pool: 19148.800000000003
```

How It Works

There are a couple of different ways to use the Nashorn engine to execute JavaScript within a Java application. For example, Nashorn can be invoked from the command-line interface (CLI) named jjs, or the ScriptEngineManager can be used. In this recipe, the example covers two such techniques for executing JavaScript with Nashorn, and each of them requires the use of the ScriptEngineManager, which has been part of the JDK since Java 6. To obtain a Nashorn engine from the ScriptEngineManager, first create a new instance of the ScriptEngineManager. Once obtained, you can obtain a particular engine by passing the String value that represents the desired engine to the getEngineByName() method. In this case, you pass the name nashorn to obtain the Nashorn engine for working with JavaScript. After obtaining the Nashorn engine, you are ready to invoke a JavaScript file or evaluate inline JavaScript code by calling on the engine's eval() method.

The first code example in this recipe demonstrates how to pass a JavaScript file to the engine for invocation. The helloNashorn.js in this case contains a single line of JavaScript that prints a message without returning any results. Perhaps the most difficult part of executing a .js file is that you must ensure that the file is contained in the class path, or that you are passing the full path to the file to the eval() method.

The second code example demonstrates how to write and evaluate inline JavaScript. First, a function identified as gallons is defined and it accepts three parameters and returns the number of gallons based on the width, length, and average depth of a pool. In a subsequent eval() call, the function is invoked, passing parameters and returning a result. The important point to note in this example is that although the JavaScript spanned multiple eval() calls, the scope is maintained so that each eval() call within the engine can see objects created within previous calls.

Since Java 6, it has been possible to work with scripting languages from within Java code. The Nashorn engine is obtained in the same manner as others, by passing a String to indicate the engine by name. The difference between this JavaScript engine and the previous rendition Rhino is that the new JavaScript engine is much faster and provides better compliance with the EMCA-normalized JavaScript specification. Since JDK 8 Update 40, some features from the updated EMCAScript 6 specification have been ported into Nashorn. Since there are a large number of new features in the updated specification, they will be added over time through various releases of the JDK. JDK 9 introduces support for a significant subset of the EMCAScript 6 features.

18-2. Executing JavaScript via the Command Line

Problem

You want to execute JavaScript via the command line for prototyping or execution purposes

Solution 1

Invoke the jjs tool, which comes as part of Java. To execute a JavaScript file, invoke the jjs tool from the command line, and then pass the fully qualified name (path included if not in CLASSPATH) of a JavaScript file to execute. For example, to execute helloNashorn.js, use the following command:

```
jjs /src/org/java9recipes/chapter18/js/helloNashorn.js
Hello Nashorn!
```

To pass arguments to a JavaScript file for processing, call the script in the same manner, but include trailing dashes --, followed by the argument(s) you want to pass. For example, the following code resides within a file named helloParameter.js:

```
#! /usr/bin/env
var parameter = $ARG[0];
print(parameter ? "Hello ${parameter}!": "Hello Nashorn!");
```

Use the following command to invoke this JavaScript file, passing the parameter Oracle:

```
jjs /src/org/java9recipes/chapter18/js/helloParameter.js - Oracle
```

Here is the result:

```
Hello Oracle!
```

The jjs tool can also be utilized as an interactive interpreter by simply executing jjs without any options. The command interpreter allows you to work in a fully interactive JavaScript environment. In the following lines of code, the jjs tool is invoked to open a command shell, and a function is declared and executed. Finally, the command shell is exited.

```
jjs
jjs> function gallon(width, length, avgDepth){return (avgDepth * width * length) * 7.48;}
function gallon(width, length, avgDepth){return (avgDepth * width * length) * 7.48;}
jjs> gallon(16,32,5)
19148.800000000003
jjs> exit()
```

Solution 2

Make use of the JSR 223 jrunscript tool to execute JavaScript. To execute a JavaScript file, invoke the jrunscript tool from the command line and pass the fully qualified name (path included if not in CLASSPATH) of a JavaScript file to execute. For example, to execute helloNashorn.js, use the following command:

```
jrunscript /src/org/java9recipes/chapter18/js/helloNashorn.js
Hello Nashorn!
```

Perhaps you want to pass JavaScript code inline, rather than executing a JavaScript file. In this case, you would invoke jrunscript with the –e flag and pass the script in-line.

```
jrunscript -e "print('Hello Nashorn')"
Hello Nashorn
```

■ **Note**   String interpolation is not available if you're using the jrunscript utility. Therefore, you must use concatenation to achieve a similar effect. To learn more about String interpolation, refer to Recipe 18-3.

Similarly to jjs, the jrunscript tool also accepts arguments to pass to a JavaScript file for processing. To pass arguments using the jrunscript tool, simply append them to the command when invoking the script, with each argument separated by spaces. For instance, to call the file helloParameter.js and pass an argument, execute the following command:

```
jrunscript src/org/java9recipes/chapter18/js/helloParameter.js Oracle
```

Also similar to jjs, the jrunscript tool can execute an interactive interpreter, allowing you to develop and prototype on the fly as seen in the following illustration.

```
nashorn> function gallon(width, length, avgDepth){return (avgDepth * width * length) * 7.48;}
function gallon(width, length, avgDepth){return (avgDepth * width * length) * 7.48;}
nashorn> gallon(16,32,5)
19148.800000000003
nashorn> ▊
```

How It Works

Since the release of Java SE 6, it has been possible to work with scripting languages from Java. In this recipe, two solutions were demonstrated for executing JavaScript via the command line or terminal. In Solution 1, you looked at the `jjs` command-line tool, which was new in Java 8. This tool can be used to invoke one or more JavaScript files, or to start an interactive Nashorn interpreter. In the example, you took a look at how to invoke a JavaScript file with and without passing arguments. You also took a look at how to invoke `jjs` as an interactive interpreter. The tool contains several useful options. To see an entire list, refer to the documentation online at http://docs.oracle.com/javase/9/docs/technotes/tools/windows/jjs.html. The `jjs` tool is the desired tool for use with Nashorn because it contains many more options than the `jrunscript` tool, which was demonstrated in Solution 2.

The `jrunscript` tool was introduced in Java 6 and it allows you to execute scripts from the command line or invoke an interactive interpreter, similar to `jjs`. The difference is that `jrunscript` also allows you to use other scripting languages by passing the –l flag, along with the scripting engine name.

```
jrunscript -l js myTest.js
```

The jrunscript tool also contains options, but it is limited in comparison to those available with jjs. To see all of the options available for jrunscript, refer to the online documentation at http://docs.oracle.com/javase/9/docs/technotes/tools/windows/jrunscript.html.

18-3. Embedding Expressions in Strings

Problem

You want to refer to expressions or values within a String when invoking JavaScript via the `jjs` utility.

Solution

When using Nashorn as a shell scripting language via the `jjs` tool, it is possible to embed expressions or values in Strings by enclosing them within dollar signs $ and curly brackets {} in a double quoted String of text. The following JavaScript resides in a file named `recipe18_3.js`, and it can be executed by the `jjs` tool as a shell script. The String interpolation works in this example because the script has been made executable by adding the shebang as the first line. Refer to Recipe 18-10 for more information on the shebang.

```
#! /usr/bin/env
function gallons(width, length, avgDepth){var volume = avgDepth * width * length;
                                    return volume * 7.48; }
print("Gallons of water in pool: ${gallons(16,32,5)}");
```

Execute the JavaScript file via `jjs` as follows:

```
jjs src/org/java9recipes/chapter18/js/recipe18_3.js
Gallons of water in pool: 19148.800000000003
```

■ **Note**   This example JavaScript file cannot be run from a ScriptEngineManager because it contains a shebang (it is an executable script).

How It Works

When you're using Nashorn's shell scripting features, you can embed expressions or values in double-quoted Strings of text by enclosing them in dollar signs and curly braces ${...}. This concept is known a String interpolation in the Unix world, and Nashorn borrows the concept to make it easy to develop shell scripts for evaluating and displaying information. String interpolation makes it possible alter the contents of a String, replacing variables and expressions with values. Using this feature, it is easy to embed the contents of a variable in-line within a String without performing manual concatenation.

In the example for this recipe, a script that is stored within a .js file contains an embedded expression, and it calls on a JavaScript function to return the calculated number of liquid gallons. This is likely the most useful technique for real-world scenarios, but it is also possible to make use of embedded expressions when using the jjs tool as an interactive interpreter.

```
jjs -scripting
jjs> "The current date is ${Date()}"
The current date is Wed Apr 30 2014 23:44:41 GMT-0500 (CDT)
```

■ **Note** If you're not using the scripting features of jjs, String interpolation will not be available. Also, double quotes must be placed around the String of text, as Strings in single quotes are not interpolated. In the example, the shebang (#! usr/bin/env) is used to make the script executable, thereby invoking the scripting features of jjs.

18-4. Passing Java Parameters

Problem

You want to pass Java parameters to JavaScript for use.

Solution

Utilize a javax.script.SimpleBindings instance to provide a String-based name for any Java field, and then pass the SimpleBindings instance to the JavaScript engine invocation. In the following example, a Java String parameter is passed to the Nashorn engine, and then it's printed via JavaScript.

```
String myJavaString = "This is a Java parameter!";
SimpleBindings simpleBindings = new SimpleBindings();
simpleBindings.put("myString", myJavaString);
ScriptEngineManager sem = new ScriptEngineManager();
ScriptEngine nashorn = sem.getEngineByName("nashorn");
nashorn.eval("print (myString)", simpleBindings);
```

Here is the result:

```
This is a Java parameter!
```

More than one Java type value can be passed in a SimpleBindings instance. In the following example, three float values are passed in a single SimpleBindings instance, and then they're passed to a JavaScript function.

```
float width = 16;
float length = 32;
float depth = 5;
SimpleBindings simpleBindings2 = new SimpleBindings();
simpleBindings2.put("globalWidth", width);
simpleBindings2.put("globalLength", length);
simpleBindings2.put("globalDepth", depth);
nashorn.eval("function gallons(width, length, avgDepth){var volume = avgDepth * width *
length; "+
            "           return volume * 7.48; }    " +
            "print(gallons(globalWidth, globalLength, globalDepth));", simpleBindings2);
```

Result:

19148.800000000003

How It Works

To pass Java field values to JavaScript, use the `javax.script.SimpleBindings` construct, which is basically a HashMap that can be used for binding and passing values to the `ScriptEngineManager`. When values are passed to the Nashorn engine in this manner, they can be accessed as global variables within the JavaScript engine.

18-5. Passing Return Values from JavaScript to Java

Problem

You want to invoke a JavaScript function and return the result to the Java class that invoked it.

Solution

Create a `ScriptEngine` for use with Nashorn and then pass the JavaScript function to it for evaluation. Next, create an Invocable from the engine and then call its `invokeFunction()` method, passing the String-based name of the JavaScript function, along with an array of the arguments to be used. In the following example, a JavaScript function named gallons is passed to the `ScriptEngine` for evaluation, and it is later invoked using this technique. It then returns a double value.

```
ScriptEngineManager manager = new ScriptEngineManager();
ScriptEngine engine = manager.getEngineByName("nashorn");

// JavaScript code in a String
String gallonsFunction = "function gallons(width, length, avgDepth){var volume = avgDepth *
width * length; "
        + " return volume * 7.48; } ";
try {
    // evaluate script
    engine.eval(gallonsFunction);
    double width = 16.0;
    double length = 32.0;
    double depth = 5.0;
```

```
    Invocable inv = (Invocable) engine;
    double returnValue = (double) inv.invokeFunction("gallons",
                            new Double[]{width,length,depth});
    System.out.println("The returned value:" + returnValue);

} catch (ScriptException | NoSuchMethodException ex) {
    Logger.getLogger(Recipe18_5.class.getName()).log(Level.SEVERE, null, ex);
}
```

Here's the result:

```
run:
The returned value:19148.800000000003
```

In the following example, a JavaScript file is invoked and returns a String value. The name of the JavaScript file is recipe18_5.js and its contents are as follows:

```
function returnName( name){
    return "Hello " + name;
}
```

Next, use the ScriptEngine to create an Invocable and call on the JavaScript function within the external JavaScript file.

```
engine.eval("load('/path-to/src/org/java9recipes/chapter18/recipe18_05/js/recipe18_5.js')");
Invocable inv2 = (Invocable) engine;
String returnValue2 = (String) inv2.invokeFunction("returnName", new String[]{"Nashorn"});
System.out.println("The returned value:" + returnValue2);
```

How It Works

One of the most useful features of embedded scripting is the ability to integrate the code invoked via a script engine along with a Java application. In order to effectively integrate script engine code and Java code, the two must be able to pass values to each other. This recipe covers the concept of returning values from JavaScript back to Java. To do so, set up a ScriptEngine and then coerce it into a javax.script.Invocable object. The Invocable object can then be used to execute script functions and methods, returning values from those invocations.

An Invocable object enables you to execute a named JavaScript function or method and return values to the caller. Invocable can also return an interface that will provide a way to invoke the member functions of the scripting object. To provide this functionality, the Invocable object contains several methods (see Table 18-1).

Before an Invocable can be generated, the JavaScript file or function must be evaluated by the ScriptEngine. The example demonstrates calling on the eval() method to evaluate an in-line JavaScript function (a String named gallonsFunction), and it shows how to evaluate an external JavaScript file. Once the eval() method has been called, the ScriptEngine can be coerced into an Invocable object, as follows:

```
Invocable inv = (Invocable) engine;
```

Invocable can then be called upon to execute functions or methods within the evaluated script code. Table 18-1 lists the methods of Invocable that can be used.

Table 18-1. *Invocable Methods*

Method	Description
getInterface(Class<T>)	Returns an implementation of an interface using the functions compiled by the interpreter.
getInterface(Object, Class<T>)	Returns an implementation of an interface using member functions of a scripting object that has been compiled in the interpreter.
invokeFunction(String, Object)	Calls on top-level procedures and functions. Returns an object.
invokeFunction(Object, String, Object)	Calls a method on a script object that was compiled during a previous execution.

In this recipe's examples, the invokeFunction method is used to call on the functions contained in the script. The first argument to invokeFunction is the String-based name of the function being called upon, and the second argument is a list of Objects that are being passed as arguments. The Invocable returns an Object from the JavaScript function call, which can be coerced into the appropriate Java type.

Sharing values between Java and ScriptEngine instances is very useful. In a real-life scenario, it may be very useful to call on an external JavaScript file, and have the ability to pass values back and forth between the Java code and the script. The underlying JavaScript file can be modified, if needed, without recompiling the application. This situation can be very useful when your application contains some business logic that needs to change from time to time. Imagine that you have a rules processor that can be used to evaluate Strings, and the rules are constantly evolving. In this case, the rule engine can be written as an external JavaScript file, enabling dynamic changes to that file.

18-6. Using Java Classes and Libraries

Problem

You want to call upon Java classes and libraries within your Nashorn solution.

Solution

Create JavaScript objects based on Java classes or libraries using the Java.type() function. Pass the fully qualified String-based name of the Java class that you want to utilize to this function and assign it to a variable. The following code represents a Java object named Employee, which will be utilized via a JavaScript file in this application.

```
package org.java9recipes.chapter18.recipe18_06;

import java.util.Date;
public class Employee {
    private int age;
    private String first;
    private String last;
    private String position;
    private Date hireDate;
```

```java
    public Employee(){

    }

    public Employee(String first,
                    String last,
                    Date hireDate){
        this.first = first;
        this.last = last;
        this.hireDate = hireDate;
    }

    /**
     * @return the first
     */
    public String getFirst() {
        return first;
    }

    /**
     * @param first the first to set
     */
    public void setFirst(String first) {
        this.first = first;
    }

    /**
     * @return the last
     */
    public String getLast() {
        return last;
    }

    /**
     * @param last the last to set
     */
    public void setLast(String last) {
        this.last = last;
    }

...
}
```

Next, let's take a look the JavaScript file that makes use of the Employee class. This JavaScript code creates a couple of Employee instances and then prints them back out. It also uses the java.util.Date class to demonstrate using standard Java classes.

```javascript
var oldDate = Java.type("java.util.Date");
var array = Java.type("java.util.ArrayList");
var emp = Java.type("org.java9recipes.chapter18.recipe18_06.Employee");
```

```
var empArray = new array();
var emp1 = new emp("Josh", "Juneau", new oldDate());
var emp2 = new emp("Joe", "Blow", new oldDate());
empArray.add(emp1);
empArray.add(emp2);
empArray.forEach(function(value, index, ar){
    print("Employee: " + value);
    print("Hire Date: " + value.hireDate);
});
```

Lastly, you execute the JavaScript file using a ScriptEngineManager:

```
ScriptEngineManager sem = new ScriptEngineManager();
ScriptEngine nashorn = sem.getEngineByName("nashorn");
try {
    nashorn.eval("load('/path-to/employeeFactory.js');");
} catch (ScriptException ex) {
    Logger.getLogger(NashornInvoker.class.getName()).log(Level.SEVERE, null, ex);
}
```

Here are the results:

```
Employee: Josh Juneau
Hire Date: Thu April 24 23:03:53 CDT 2016
Employee: Joe Blow
Hire Date: Fri April 25 12:00:00 CDT 2016
```

How It Works

It is very natural to use Java classes and libraries from within a Nashorn solution. The example in this recipe demonstrates how to use a Java class that has been generated specifically for use with a custom application, as well as how to use Java classes and libraries that are part of Java SE. In order to make such classes available to JavaScript, you must call the Java.type function from within the JavaScript and pass the String-based fully qualified name of the Java class to be used. The Java.type function returns a JavaScript reference to the Java type. In the following excerpt from the example, the java.util.Date, java.util.ArrayList, and Employee classes are made available to JavaScript using this technique.

```
var oldDate = Java.type("java.util.Date");
var array = Java.type("java.util.ArrayList");
var emp = Java.type("org.java9recipes.chapter18.recipe18_06.Employee");
```

Once the types have been made available to JavaScript, they can be invoked in a similar manner to their Java counterparts. For instance, new oldDate() is used to instantiate a new instance of java.util.Date in the example. An important difference is that you don't use getters and setters to call upon Java properties. Rather, you omit the "get" or "set" portion of the method and begin with a lowercase letter for the field name, thereby calling upon the fields directly. This makes property access from within JavaScript quite easy and much more productive and readable. An example of such access can be seen from within the forEach loop in the script. To access the employee hireDate property, simply call employee.hireDate rather than employee.getHireDate().

The ability to access Java seamlessly from within JavaScript makes it possible to create seamless Java and JavaScript integrations.

18-7. Accessing Java Arrays and Collections in Nashorn

Problem

You need to gain access to a Java array or collection from within your Nashorn solution.

Solution

Use the Java.type function to coerce Java arrays to JavaScript. Once coerced, you instantiate the arrays by calling new and then accessing the members by specifying their index by number. In the following example, a Java int array type is created within JavaScript, and then it is instantiated and used for storage.

```
jjs> var intArray = Java.type("int[]");
jjs> var intArr = new intArray(5);
jjs> intArr[0] = 0;
0
jjs> intArr[1] = 1;
1
jjs> intArr[0]
0
jjs> intArr.length
5
```

Working with collections is quite similar. To access a Java Collection type, you call upon the Java.type function, passing the String-based name of the type you want to create. Once the type reference has been obtained, it can be instantiated and accessed from JavaScript.

```
jjs> var ArrayList = Java.type("java.util.ArrayList")
jjs> var array = new ArrayList();
jjs> array.add('hi');
true
jjs> array.add('bye');
true
jjs> array
[hi, bye]
jjs> var map = Java.type("java.util.HashMap")
jjs> var jsMap = new map();
jjs> jsMap.put(0, "first");
null
jjs> jsMap.put(1, "second");
null
jjs> jsMap.get(1);
second
```

How It Works

To make use of Java arrays and collections from within JavaScript, you invoke the Java.type() function and pass the name of the Java type that you want to access, assigning it to a JavaScript variable. The JavaScript variable can then be instantiated and utilized in the same manner as the Java type would be used from within Java code. The examples in this recipe demonstrate how to access Java arrays, ArrayLists, and HashMaps from within JavaScript.

When working with a Java array type from JavaScript, the type of array must be passed to the `Java.type()` function, including an empty set of brackets. Once the type has been obtained and assigned to a JavaScript variable, it can be instantiated by including the static size of the array within brackets, just as an array would be instantiated in the Java language. Similarly, the array can be accessed by specifying indices to assign and retrieve values from the array. To go backward and pass a JavaScript array to Java, use the `Java.to()` function, passing the JavaScript array to its Java-type counterpart. In the following code, a JavaScript String array is coerced into a Java type.

```
jjs> var strArr = ["one","two","three"]
jjs> var javaStrArr = Java.type("java.lang.String[]");
jjs> var javaArray = Java.to(strArr, javaStrArr);
jjs> javaArray[1];
two
jjs> javaArray.class
class [Ljava.lang.String;
```

Collections are very similar to arrays, in that the `Java.type()` function must be used to obtain the Java type and assign it to a JavaScript variable. The variable is then instantiated and the `Collection` type is then accessed in the same manner as it would be in the Java language.

18-8. Implementing Java Interfaces

Problem

You want to make use of a Java interface from your Nashorn solution.

Solution

Create a new instance of the interface, passing a JavaScript object consisting of properties. The JavaScript object properties will implement the methods defined in the interface. In the following example, an interface used for declaring employee position types is implemented within a JavaScript file. The example demonstrates custom method implementation, as well as use of a default method. The following code is the interface, `PositionType`, which will be implemented in JavaScript.

```java
import java.math.BigDecimal;

public interface PositionType {

    public double hourlyWage(BigDecimal hours, BigDecimal wage);

    /**
     * Hourly salary calculation
     * @param wage
     * @return
     */
    public default BigDecimal yearlySalary(BigDecimal wage){
        return (wage.multiply(new BigDecimal(40))).multiply(new BigDecimal(52));
    }
}
```

Next, let's take a look at the code within the JavaScript file that implements the `PositionType` interface.

```
var somePosition = new org.java9recipes.chapter18.recipe18_08.PositionType({
    hourlyWage: function(hours, wage){
        return hours * wage;
    }
});

print(somePosition instanceof Java.type("org.java9recipes.chapter18.recipe18_08.
PositionType"));
var bigDecimal = Java.type("java.math.BigDecimal");

print(somePosition.hourlyWage(new bigDecimal(40), new bigDecimal(12.75)));
```

How It Works

Using a Java interface in JavaScript can be beneficial for creating objects that adhere to the implementation criteria. However, using interfaces in JavaScript is a bit different than using them in a Java solution. For example, interfaces cannot be instantiated in Java. This is not the case when using them in JavaScript; you must actually instantiate an object of the interface type in order to use it.

The example demonstrates the implementation of an interface, `PositionType`, which is used for defining a number of methods within an employee position. The methods are used for calculating an employee's hourly and yearly wage. To make use of the `PositionType` interface from JavaScript, the new keyword is used to instantiate an instance of that interface, assigning it to a JavaScript variable. When instantiating the interface, a JavaScript object is passed to the constructor. The object contains implementations for each of the nondefault methods within the interface by identifying the name of the method, followed by the implementation. In the example, there is only one method implemented on instantiation, and it is identified as `hourlyWage()`. If there had been more than one method implemented, the implementations would be separated by commas.

Although using Java interfaces is a bit different in JavaScript, they certainly provide a benefit. In reality, they are performing the same task within JavaScript as they are within Java. In Java, in order to implement an interface, you must create an object that implements it. You do the same thing within JavaScript, except that in order to create the implementing object, you must instantiate an instance of the interface.

18-9. Extending Java Classes

Problem

You want to extend a concrete Java class in your Nashorn JavaScript solution.

Solution

First obtain a reference to the Java class that is to be extended by calling the `Java.type()` function within your JavaScript file. Then create the subclass by calling on the `Java.extend()` function and passing the reference to the class that will be extended, along with a JavaScript object containing the implementations that will be altered.

The following code is that of the `Employee` class, which will later be extended from within a JavaScript file.

```
package org.java9recipes.chapter18.recipe18_09;

import java.math.BigDecimal;
import java.util.Date;

public class Employee {
    private int age;
    private String first;
    private String last;
    private String position;
    private Date hireDate;

    ...

    public BigDecimal grossPay(BigDecimal hours, BigDecimal rate){
        return hours.multiply(rate);
    }
}
```

Here's the JavaScript code used to extend the class and use it:

```
var Employee = Java.type("org.java9recipes.chapter18.recipe18_09.Employee");
var bigDecimal = Java.type("java.math.BigDecimal");
var Developer = Java.extend(Employee, {
    grossPay: function(hours, rate){
        var bonus = 500;
        return hours.multiply(rate).add(new bigDecimal(bonus));
    }
});

var javaDev = new Developer();
javaDev.first = "Joe";
javaDev.last = "Dynamic";
print(javaDev + "'s gross pay for the week is: " + javaDev.grossPay(new bigDecimal(60),
                                                        new bigDecimal(80)));
```

Here's the result:

```
Joe Dynamic's gross pay for the week is: 5300
```

How It Works

To extend a standard Java class from within JavaScript, you call on the Java.extend() function, passing the Java class that you'd like to extend, along with a JavaScript object containing any fields or functions that will be altered in the subclass. For the example in this recipe, a Java class entitled Employee is extended. However, the same technique can be used to extend any other Java interface, such as Runnable, Iterator, and so on.

In this example, to obtain the Employee class in JavaScript, the Java.type() function is called upon, passing the fully qualified class name. The object that is received from the call is stored in a JavaScript variable named Employee. Next, the class is extended by calling on the Java.extend() function and passing the Employee class, along with a JavaScript object. In the example, the JavaScript object that is sent to the Java.extend() function includes a different implementation of the Employee class grossPay() method. The object that is returned from the Java.extend() function is then instantiated and accessed via JavaScript.

Extending Java classes within JavaScript can be a very useful feature when you're working with a Nashorn solution. The ability to share objects from Java makes it possible to access exiting Java solutions and build on them.

18-10. Creating Executable Scripts in Unix

Problem

You want to enable your JavaScript file to become executable.

Solution

Make a JavaScript file executable by adding a shebang (#!) as the first line of the script, followed by the path to the location of the jjs executable. In the following example, a very simple JavaScript file is made executable by the inclusion of a shebang, which points to the symbolic link of the jjs tool.

```
#! /usr/bin/env jjs
print('I am an executable');
```

To execute the script, it must be given the proper permissions. Apply the chmod a+x permissions (in Unix) to make the script executable.

```
chmod a+x src/org/java9recipes/chapter18/recipe18_10/jsExecutable.js
```

The script can now be invoked as an executable, as shown in the following command:

```
Juneau$ ./src/org/java9recipes/chapter18/recipe18_10/jsExecutable.js
I am an executable
```

How It Works

To make a script executable, you simply add a shebang to the first line. The shebang is used in Unix-based operating systems to tell the program loader that the script's first line should be treated as an interpreter directive, and that the script should be passed to that interpreter for execution. In the solution to this recipe, the first line of the script tells the program loader that the script's contents should be executed using the jjs tool:

```
#! /usr/bin/env jjs
```

By invoking the jjs tool in this manner, the scripting options are automatically enabled, allowing you to utilize scripting features within the script. The following list includes extra scripting features that can be used when executing via jjs with scripting options are enabled:

- String interpolation: (See Recipe 18-3)

  ```
  var threeyr = 365 * 3;
  print("The number of days in three years is ${threeyr}");
  ```

- Shell invocations: The ability to invoke external programs
- Special environment variables are available for use ($ARG and $ENV)

The ability to develop executable scripts in JavaScript can be very powerful. Not only is the world of JavaScript available at your fingertips, but the entire Java world is available, since you can import Java classes and libraries into your scripts.

18-11. Implementing JavaFX with Nashorn

Problem

You wish to implement a Java GUI using JavaScript.

Solution 1

Develop a JavaFX application using JavaScript and store it in a JavaScript file. Invoke the file using the jjs tool, along with the -fx option. The following code is a JavaFX application that is written in JavaScript. The JavaFX application can be used for collecting car data.

```
var ArrayList = Java.type("java.util.ArrayList");
var Scene = javafx.scene.Scene;
var Button = javafx.scene.control.Button;
var TextField = javafx.scene.control.TextField;
var GridPane = javafx.scene.layout.GridPane;
var Label = javafx.scene.control.Label;
var TextArea = javafx.scene.control.TextArea;

var carList = new ArrayList();
var carCount = "There are currently no cars";
var car = {
    make:"",
    model:"",
    year:"",
    description:""
};
print(carCount);
function start(primaryStage) {

    primaryStage.title="Car Form JS Demo";

    var grid = new GridPane();
    grid.hgap = 10;
    grid.vgap = 10;

    var makeLabel = new Label("Make:");
    grid.add(makeLabel, 0, 1);

    var makeText = new TextField();
    grid.add(makeText, 1, 1);

    var modelLabel = new Label("Model:");
    grid.add(modelLabel, 0, 2);
```

```
    var modelText = new TextField();
    grid.add(modelText, 1, 2);

    var yearLabel = new Label("Year:");
    grid.add(yearLabel, 0, 3);

    var yearText = new TextField();
    grid.add(yearText, 1, 3);

    var descriptionLabel = new Label("Description:");
    grid.add(descriptionLabel, 0, 4);

    var descriptionText = new TextArea();
    grid.add(descriptionText, 1, 4);

    var button = new Button("Add Car");
    button.onAction = function(){
        print("Adding Car:" + makeText.text);
        car.make=makeText.text;
        car.model=modelText.text;
        car.year=yearText.text;
        car.description=descriptionText.text;
        carList.add(car);
        carCount = "The number of cars is: "+ carList.size();
        print(carCount);
    };
    grid.add(button, 0,5);

    primaryStage.scene = new Scene(grid, 800, 500);
    primaryStage.show();
}
```

The resulting application looks like that shown in Figure 18-1.

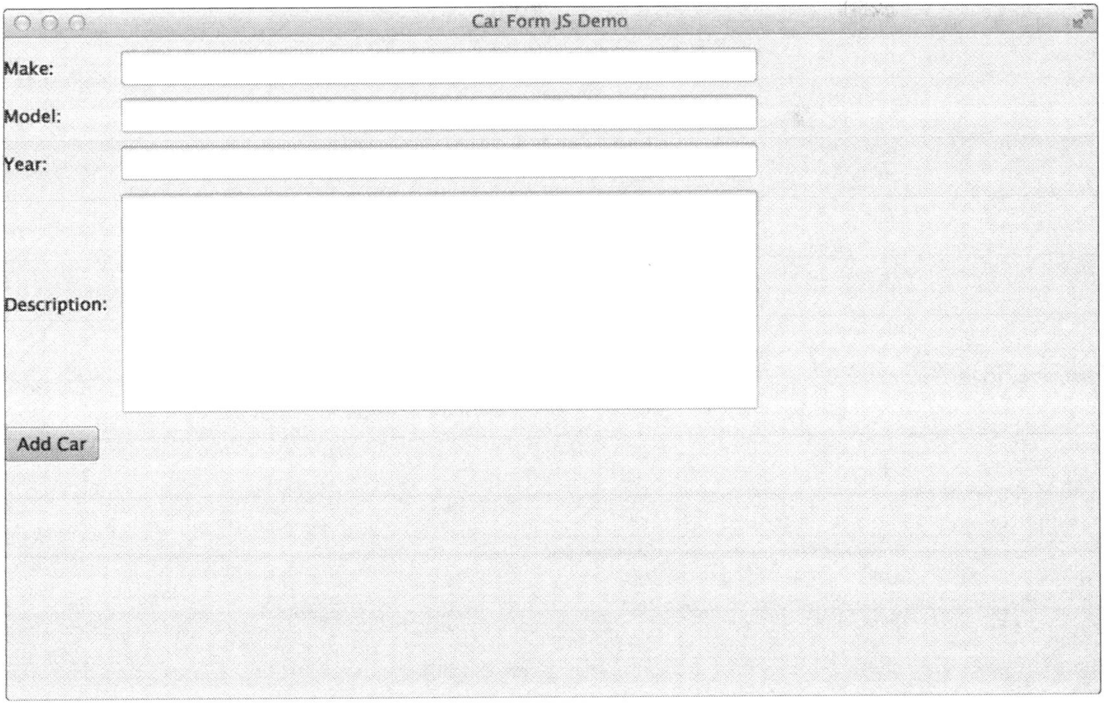

Figure 18-1. *JavaFX application written in JavaScript*

Solution 2

Write a JavaFX application using Java and embed the JavaScript application implementation using a ScriptEngine. The following Java class is called CarCollector.java and it implements javafx. application.Application. The Java class implements the start() method, which contains a ScriptEngine to embed the JavaScript code that implements the application.

```
package org.java9recipes.chapter18.recipe18_11;

import java.io.FileReader;
import javafx.application.Application;
import javafx.stage.Stage;
import javax.script.ScriptEngine;
import javax.script.ScriptEngineManager;

public class CarCollector extends Application {

    private final String SCRIPT = getClass().getResource("carCollector.js").getPath();

    public static void main(String args[]) {
        launch(args);
    }
```

```java
    @Override
    public void start(Stage stage) {
        try {
            ScriptEngine engine = new ScriptEngineManager().getEngineByName("nashorn");
            engine.put("primaryStage", stage);
            engine.eval(new FileReader(SCRIPT));
        } catch (Exception e) {
            e.printStackTrace();
        }
    }
}
```

Next, let's take a look at the JavaScript file named carCollector.js, which implements the application. Note that the code does not contain a start() function, because the application start() method is already implemented in the Java code. The JavaScript file merely contains the implementation.

```javascript
var ArrayList = Java.type("java.util.ArrayList");
var Scene = javafx.scene.Scene;
var Button = javafx.scene.control.Button;
var TextField = javafx.scene.control.TextField;
var GridPane = javafx.scene.layout.GridPane;
var Label = javafx.scene.control.Label;
var TextArea = javafx.scene.control.TextArea;

var carList = new ArrayList();
var carCount = "There are currently no cars";
var car = {
    make: "",
    model: "",
    year: "",
    description: ""
};
print(carCount);

primaryStage.title = "Car Form JS Demo";

var grid = new GridPane();
grid.hgap = 10;
grid.vgap = 10;

var makeLabel = new Label("Make:");
grid.add(makeLabel, 0, 1);

var makeText = new TextField();
grid.add(makeText, 1, 1);

var modelLabel = new Label("Model:");
grid.add(modelLabel, 0, 2);

var modelText = new TextField();
grid.add(modelText, 1, 2);
```

```
var yearLabel = new Label("Year:");
grid.add(yearLabel, 0, 3);

var yearText = new TextField();
grid.add(yearText, 1, 3);

var descriptionLabel = new Label("Description:");
grid.add(descriptionLabel, 0, 4);

var descriptionText = new TextArea();
grid.add(descriptionText, 1, 4);

var button = new Button("Add Car");
button.onAction = function() {
    print("Adding Car:" + makeText.text);
    car.make = makeText.text;
    car.model = modelText.text;
    car.year = yearText.text;
    car.description = descriptionText.text;
    carList.add(car);
    carCount = "The number of cars is: " + carList.size();
    print(carCount);
};
grid.add(button, 0, 5);

primaryStage.scene = new Scene(grid, 800, 500);
primaryStage.show();
```

How It Works

The Nashorn engine has full access to the JavaFX API. This means that it is possible to construct JavaFX applications that are written either entirely or partially in JavaScript. The two solutions to this recipe demonstrate each of these techniques. The first solution demonstrates how to develop a JavaFX application entirely of JavaScript. When you're using the technique demonstrated in Solution 1, the JavaScript implementation can be executed by using the jjs tool and specifying the -fx option, as follows:

```
jjs -fx recipe18_11.js
```

Solution 2 demonstrates how to construct a JavaFX application from Java code, embedding the implementation code written in JavaScript. To use this technique, construct a standard JavaFX application class by extending the javafx.application.Application class and overriding the start() method. Within the start() method, create a Nashorn ScriptEngine object and use it to embed a JavaScript file that contains the application implementation. Prior to calling the engine's eval() method and passing the JavaScript file, pass the JavaFX stage to the engine using the engine's put() method.

```
engine.put("primaryStage", stage);
```

Digging into the JavaScript code a bit, any of the JavaFX API classes can be imported by using the Java.type() function and passing the fully qualified class name. Assign the imported classes to JavaScript variables, which will later be used in the application construction. When written entirely in JavaScript, a start() function must be created to contain the JavaFX application stage construction. On the other hand, when you're using Java code to launch the application, there is no need to create a start() function. In the example, a GridPane layout is used to construct a form for capturing car data. The form fields are each constructed with a Label and a TextField or TextArea. The car data is stored in a JavaScript object when a button is clicked.

There are a few things to note about the JavaScript code in both implementations. The syntax is a bit different than Java code because getters and setters are not used. Also, the implementation for the button action handler is a simple JavaScript function.

Constructing JavaFX applications using JavaScript can be a fun alternative to using Java code. The syntax has the feel of using the prior JavaFX Script language, and it is a bit less verbose than Java. It is also nice to be able to change the application without having to recompile if you're using the full JavaScript implementation.

18-12. Utilizing ECMAScript6 Features

Problem

You wish to make use of some ECMAScript6 features, such as template Strings, more scoping options, and new looping constructs.

Solution

Utilize a subset of the new ECMAScript6 features in Java 9. The initial release includes a small subset of the new ECMAScript6 features, but the feature set will expand with subsequent Java 9 releases.

To make use of these new features, utilize one of the solutions described in previous recipes within this chapter, using the updated ECMAScript6 syntax. In this recipe, open up the jjs utility and type in the following examples to see the new features.

The template String feature works by allowing Strings to contain dynamic variables such that the variables can be changed, altering the text of the String. The following example demonstrates how to utilize a template String:

```
jjs> var customer = {name:"Josh"}
jjs> var message = `Hello ${customer.name}`
```

The let keyword has been added to ECMAScript, allowing for block-scoped variables:

```
let name = "Josh";
console.log("first: " + name)
if (name.length > 1){
    let name = "Duke";
    console.log(name);
}
console.log(name);
```

Output:

```
first: Josh
Duke
Josh
```

ECMAScript6 contains new looping constructs, such as for-in:

```
var names = ['Josh', 'Duke']
for (var x of names){
    console.log(x);
}
```

How It Works

There are many new features in ECMAScript 6, and some of those features are part of Nashorn in Java 9. Actually, a few of the new features made it into Java 8, Update 40, those being *let, const,* and *block scope.* The list of new features is so large, that it would be a daunting task to try and put each of them into Nashorn in a single release. Therefore, the initial release of Nashorn for Java 9 contains another subset of the new features, and more new features will be added in subsequent Java 9 releases.

The initial release of Java 9 contains the following new Nashorn ECMAScript 6 features:

- Template Strings
- let, const, and block scope
- Iterators for..of loops
- Map, Set, WeakMap, and WeakSet
- Symbols
- Binary and Octal literals

The following features are planned for future releases the Nashorn engine in Java 9:

- Arrow functions
- Enhanced object literals
- Destructuring assignment
- Default, rest, and spread parameters
- Unicode
- Subclassable built-ins
- Promises
- Proxies
- Math, Number, String, and Object APIs
- Reflection API

Summary

Nashorn enables developers to make use of modern JavaScript capabilities from within the Java ecosystem. The Nashorn engine has full access to all of the Java APIs, including JavaFX. The new jjs tool provides scripting capabilities, allowing developers to create executable scripts written entirely in JavaScript. Lastly, we covered some new features of ECMAScript6 that have been added to the Nashorn engine in Java 9.

CHAPTER 19

E-mail

E-mail notification is an integral part of today's enterprise systems. Java enables e-mail notification by offering JavaMail API. Using this API, you can send e-mail communications in response to an event (say a completed form or a finalized script). You can also use the JavaMail API to check an IMAP or POP3 mailbox.

To follow along with the recipes in this chapter, make sure that you have set up your firewall to allow e-mail communication. Most of the time, firewalls allow outbound communications to e-mail servers without an issue, but if you are running your own local SMTP (e-mail) server, you may need to configure your firewall to allow the e-mail server to operate correctly.

Note The JavaMail API is included as part of the Java EE download. If you are using Java SE, you will need to download and install the JavaMail API.

19-1. Installing JavaMail

Problem

You want to install JavaMail for use by your application in sending e-mail notifications.

Solution

Download JavaMail from Oracle's JavaMail website. Currently, the download you need is found at

`http://www.oracle.com/technetwork/java/javamail/`.

Once you download it, unzip it and add the JavaMail `.jar` files as dependencies from your project (both `mail.jar` and `lib\*.jar`).

How It Works

The JavaMail API is included in the Java EE SDK, but if you are working with the Java SE SDK, you will need to download and add the JavaMail API to your Java SE project. By downloading and adding the dependencies, you get access to the robust e-mail API that allows you to send and receive e-mails.

Note If you are not using Java SE 6 or newer, you will also need the JavaBeans Activation Framework (JAF) to use JavaMail. It is included in Java SE 6 and newer.

19-2. Sending an E-Mail

Problem

You need your application to send an e-mail.

Solution

Using the Transport() methods, you can send an e-mail to specific recipients. In this solution, an e-mail message is constructed and sent through the smtp.somewhere.com server:

```
private void start() {
    Properties properties = new Properties();
    properties.put("mail.smtp.host", "smtp.somewhere.com");
    properties.put("mail.smtp.auth", "true");

    Session session = Session.getDefaultInstance(properties, new MessageAuthenticator("user
    name","password"));

    Message message = new MimeMessage(session);
    try {
        message.setFrom(new InternetAddress("someone@somewhere.com"));
        message.setRecipient(Message.RecipientType.TO, new InternetAddress("someone@
        somewhere.com"));
        message.setSubject("Subject");
        message.setContent("This is a test message", "text/plain");
        Transport.send(message);
    } catch (MessagingException e) {
        e.printStackTrace();
    }
}

class MessageAuthenticator extends Authenticator {
    PasswordAuthentication authentication = null;

    public MessageAuthenticator(String username, String password) {
        authentication = new PasswordAuthentication(username,password);
    }

    @Override
    protected PasswordAuthentication getPasswordAuthentication() {
        return authentication;
    }
}
```

How It Works

To utilize the JavaMail API, start by creating a Properties object that works as a standard Map object (in fact, it inherits from it), in which you put the different properties that the JavaMail service might need. The hostname is set using the mail.smtp.host property, and if the host requires authentication then you must set the mail.smtp.auth property to true. After the properties object is configured, fetch a javax.mail. Session that will hold the connection information for the e-mail message.

When you're creating a session, you can specify the login information if the service requires authentication. This might be necessary when connecting to an SMTP service that is outside of your local area network. To specify the login information, you must create an Authenticator object, which will contain the getPasswordAuthentication() method. In this example, there is a new class identified as MessageAuthenticator, which extends the Authenticator class. By making the getPasswordAuthentication() method return a PasswordAuthentication object, you can specify the username/password used for the SMTP service.

The Message object represents an actual e-mail message and exposes e-mail properties such as From/To/Subject and Content. After setting these properties, you call the Transport.send() static method to send the e-mail message.

■ **Tip** If you don't need authentication information, you can call the Session. getDefaultInstance(properties, null) method, passing a null for the Authenticator parameter.

19-3. Attaching Files to an E-Mail Message

Problem

You need to attach one or more files to an e-mail message.

Solution

Creating a message that contains different parts (called a *multipart message*) is what allows you to send attachments such as files and images. You can specify the body of the e-mail message and an attachment. Messages that contain different parts are referred to as Multipurpose Internet Mail Extensions (MIME) messages. They are represented in the javax.mail API by the MimeMessage class. The following code creates such a message:

```
Message message = new MimeMessage(session);
message.setFrom(new InternetAddress(from));
message.setRecipient(Message.RecipientType.TO, new InternetAddress(to));
message.setSubject("Subject");

// Create Mime "Message" part
MimeBodyPart messageBodyPart = new MimeBodyPart();
messageBodyPart.setContent("This is a test message", "text/plain");

// Create Mime "File" part
MimeBodyPart fileBodyPart = new MimeBodyPart();
fileBodyPart.attachFile("<path-to-attachment>/attach.txt");

MimeBodyPart fileBodyPart2 = new MimeBodyPart();
fileBodyPart2.attachFile("<path-to-attachment>/attach2.txt");
```

```
// Piece the body parts together
Multipart multipart = new MimeMultipart();
multipart.addBodyPart(messageBodyPart);
multipart.addBodyPart(fileBodyPart);
//add another body part to supply another attachment
multipart.addBodyPart(fileBodyPart2);

// Set the content of the message to be the MultiPart
message.setContent(multipart);
Transport.send(message);
```

How It Works

Within the JavaMail API you can create a MIME e-mail. This type of message allows it to contain different body parts. In the example, a plain text body part is generated (which contains the text that the e-mail displays), and then two attachment body parts containing the attachments you are trying to send are created. Depending on the type of attachments, the Java API will automatically choose an appropriate encoding for the attachment body part.

After each of the body parts are created, they are combined by creating a `MultiPart` object and adding each individual part (the plain text and the attachments) to it. Once the `MultiPart` object has been assembled to contain all the parts, it is assigned as the content of the `MimeMessage` and sent (just like in Recipe 19-2).

19-4. Sending an HTML E-Mail

Problem

You want to send an e-mail that contains HTML.

Solution

You specify the content type of the e-mail as `text/html` and send a String of HTML as the message body. In the following example, an e-mail is constructed using HTML content and then it is sent.

```
MimeMessage message = new MimeMessage(session);
try {
    message.setFrom(new InternetAddress(from));
    message.setRecipient(Message.RecipientType.TO, new InternetAddress(to));
    message.setSubject("Subject Test");

    // Create Mime Content
    MimeBodyPart messageBodyPart = new MimeBodyPart();
    String html = "<H1>Important Message</H1>" +
                  "<b>This is an important message...</b>"+
                  "<br/><br/>" +
                  "<i>Be sure to code your Java today!</i>" +
                  "<H2>It is the right thing to do!</H2>";
    messageBodyPart.setContent(html, "text/html; charset=utf-8");

    MimeBodyPart fileBodyPart = new MimeBodyPart();
    fileBodyPart.attachFile("/path-to/attach.txt");
```

```
        MimeBodyPart fileBodyPart2 = new MimeBodyPart();
        fileBodyPart2.attachFile("/path-to/attach2.txt");

        Multipart multipart = new MimeMultipart();
        multipart.addBodyPart(messageBodyPart);
        multipart.addBodyPart(fileBodyPart);
        //add another body part to supply another attachment
        multipart.addBodyPart(fileBodyPart2);
        message.setContent(multipart);
        Transport.send(message);
} catch (MessagingException | IOException e) {
    e.printStackTrace();
}
```

How It Works

Sending an e-mail message that contains HTML content is basically the same as sending an e-mail with standard text—the only difference is the content type. When you're setting the content on the message body part of the e-mail, you set the content to text/html to have the content treated as HTML. There are various ways to construct the HTML content, including using links, photos, or any other valid HTML markup. In this example, a few basic HTML tags have been embedded into a String.

Although the example code may not be very useful in real-life systems, it is easy to generate dynamic HTML content for inclusion within an e-mail. At its most basic form, dynamically generated HTML can be Strings of text that are concatenated to formulate the HTML.

19-5. Sending E-Mail to a Group of Recipients

Problem

You want to send the same e-mail to multiple recipients.

Solution

Use the setRecipients() method from the JavaMail API to send e-mail to multiple recipients. The setRecipients() method allows you to specify more than one recipient at a time. For example:

```
// Main send body
    message.setFrom(new InternetAddress("someone@somewhere.com"));
    message.setRecipients(Message.RecipientType.TO, getRecipients(emails));
    message.setSubject("Subject");
    message.setContent("This is a test message", "text/plain");
    Transport.send(message);

// ------------------

    private Address[] getRecipients(List<String> emails) throws AddressException {
        Address[] addresses = new Address[emails.size()];
        for (int i =0;i < emails.size();i++) {
            addresses[i] = new InternetAddress(emails.get(i));
        }
        return addresses;
    }
```

How It Works

By using the setRecipients() method of the Message object, you can specify multiple recipients on the same message. The setRecipients() method accepts an array of Address objects. In this recipe, because you have a collection of Strings, you create the array as the size of the collection and create InternetAddress objects to fill the array. Sending e-mails using multiple e-mail addresses (as opposed to individual e-mails) is much more efficient because only one message is sent from your client to the target mail servers. Each target mail server will then deliver to all recipients that it has mailboxes for. For example, if you're sending to five different yahoo.com accounts, the yahoo.com mail server will need to receive only one copy of the message and it will deliver the message to all the yahoo.com recipients specified in the message.

▓ **Tip**   If you want to send bulk messages, you might want to specify the Recipient Type as BCC, so that the e-mail received doesn't show everyone else that is getting the e-mail. To do so, specify Message. RecipientType.BCC in the setRecipients() method.

19-6. Checking E-Mail

Problem

You need to check if a new e-mail has arrived for a specified e-mail account.

Solution

You can use javax.mail.Store to connect, query, and retrieve messages from an Internet Message Access Protocol (IMAP) e-mail account. For example, the following code connects to an IMAP account, retrieves the last five messages from that IMAP account, and marks the messages as read.

```
Session session = Session.getDefaultInstance(properties, null);
Store store = session.getStore("imaps");
    store.connect(host,username,password);
    System.out.println(store);
    Folder inbox = store.getFolder(folder);
    inbox.open(Folder.READ_WRITE);
    int messageCount = inbox.getMessageCount();
    int startMessage = messageCount - 5;
    int endMessage = messageCount;
    if (messageCount < 5) startMessage =0;
    Message messages[]  = inbox.getMessages(startMessage,endMessage);
for (Message message : messages) {
    boolean hasBeenRead = false;
    for (Flags.Flag flag :message.getFlags().getSystemFlags()) {
        if (flag == Flags.Flag.SEEN) {
            hasBeenRead = true;
            break;
        }
    }
    message.setFlag(Flags.Flag.SEEN, false);
```

```
System.out.println(message.getSubject() + " "+ (hasBeenRead? "(read)" : "") + message.
getContent());

}
inbox.close(true);
```

How It Works

A Store object allows you to access e-mail mailbox information. By creating a Store and then requesting the Inbox folder, you gain access to the messages in the main mailbox of your IMAP account. With the folder object, you can request to download the messages from the inbox. To do so, you use the getMessages (start, end) method. The inbox also provides a getMessageCount() method, which allows you to know how many e-mails are in the inbox. Keep in mind that the messages start at index 1.

Each message will have a set of flags that can then tell whether the message has been read (Flags.Flag. SEEN) or whether the message has been replied to (Flags.Flag.ANSWERED). By parsing the SEEN flag, you can then process messages that haven't been read before.

To set a message as being read (or answered), call the message.setFlag() method. This method allows you to set (or reset) e-mail flags. If you're setting message flags, you need to open the folder as READ_WRITE, which allows you to make changes to e-mail flags. You also need to call inbox.close(true) at the end of your code, which will tell the JavaMail API to flush the changes to the IMAP store.

▓ **Tip**   For IMAP over SSL, you should use session.getStore("imaps"). This creates a secure IMAP store.

19-7. Monitoring an E-Mail Account

Problem

You want to monitor when e-mails arrive to a certain account, and you want to process them depending upon their content.

Solution

Begin with the implementation from Recipe 19-6. Then add IMAP flag manipulation to create a robust e-mail monitor for your application. In the following example, the checkForMail() method is used to process mail that is being sent to a mailing list. In this scenario, users can subscribe or unsubscribe from the list by placing one of those words in the subject line. The following example checks the subject of new messages and deals with them appropriately. The example also uses message flags to delete processed messages so they need not be read twice. Messages that can't be processed are marked as read but left in the server for troubleshooting by a human.

```
private void checkForMail() {
        System.out.println("Checking for mail");
        Properties properties = new Properties();
        String username = "username";
        String password = "password";
        String folder = "Inbox";
        String host = "imap.server.com";
```

```
        try {
            Session session = Session.getDefaultInstance(properties, null);
            Store store = session.getStore("imaps");
            store.connect(host,username,password);
            Folder inbox = store.getFolder(folder);
            inbox.open(Folder.READ_WRITE);
            int messageCount = inbox.getMessageCount();
            Message messages[]  = inbox.getMessages(1,messageCount);
            for (Message message : messages) {
                boolean hasBeenRead = false;
                if (Arrays.asList(message.getFlags().getSystemFlags()).contains(Flags.Flag.
                SEEN)) {
                    continue;                        // not interested in "seen" messages
                }
                if (processMessage(message)) {
                    System.out.println("Processed :"+message.getSubject());
                    message.setFlag(Flags.Flag.DELETED, true);
                } else {
                    System.out.println("Couldn't Understand :"+message.getSubject());
                    // set it as seen, but keep it around
                    message.setFlag(Flags.Flag.SEEN, true);
                }
            }
            inbox.close(true);
        } catch (MessagingException e) {
            e.printStackTrace();
        }
    }

    private boolean processMessage(Message message) throws MessagingException {
        boolean result = false;

        String subject = message.getSubject().toLowerCase();
        if (subject.startsWith("subscribe")) {
            String emailAddress = extractAddress (message.getFrom());
            if (emailAddress != null) {
                subscribeToList(emailAddress);
                result = true;
            }

        } else if (subject.startsWith("unsubscribe")) {
            String emailAddress = extractAddress (message.getFrom());
            if (emailAddress != null) {
                unSubscribeToList(emailAddress);
                result = true;
            }
        }

        return result;
    }
```

```
private String extractAddress(Address[] addressArray) {
    if ((addressArray == null) || (addressArray.length < 1)) return null;
    if (!(addressArray[0] instanceof InternetAddress)) return null;
    InternetAddress internetAddress = (InternetAddress) addressArray[0];
    return internetAddress.getAddress();
}
```

How It Works

After connecting to the IMAP server, the example requests all messages received. The code skips over the ones that are marked as SEEN. To do so, the recipe uses the Arrays.AsList to convert the array of system message flags into an ArrayList. Once the list is created, it is a matter of querying the list to see whether it contains the Flag.SEEN enum value. If that value is present, the example skips to the next item.

When an unread message is found, the message is processed by the processMessage() method. The method subscribes or unsubscribes the sender of the message depending on the start of the subject line. (This is akin to a mailing list, where sending a message with the subject of "subscribe" adds the sender to the mailing list.)

After determining which command to execute, the code proceeds to extract the sender's e-mail from the message. To do so, the processMessage() calls the extractEmail() method. Each message contains an array of possible "From" addresses. These Address objects are generic because the Address object can represent Internet or newsgroup addresses. After checking that the Address object is indeed an InternetAddress, the code casts the Address object as an InternetAddress and calls the getAddress() method, which contains the actual e-mail address.

Once the e-mail address is extracted, the recipe calls subscribe or unsubscribe, depending on the subject line. If the message could be understood (meaning that the message was processed), the processMessage() method returns true (if it couldn't understand the message, it returns false). In the checkForMail() method, when the processMessage() method returns true, the message is flagged for deletion (by calling message.setFlag(Flags.Flag.DELETED, true); otherwise, the message is just flagged as Seen. This allows the message to still be around if it wasn't understood or deleted if it was processed. Finally, to commit the new flags on the messages (and expunge deleted messages), you need to call the inbox.close(true) method.

19-8. Summary

E-mail plays an important role in many systems that we use today. The Java language includes the JavaMail API, which enables developers to include robust e-mail functionality within their Java applications. The recipes in this chapter covered the JavaMail API from installation through advanced usage. To learn more about JavaMail, and also about mail integration with Java applications deployed to enterprise applications servers, please refer to the online documentation: http://www.oracle.com/technetwork/java/javamail/index-141777.html.

▓ ▓ ▓

CHAPTER 20

JSON and XML Processing

JSON is one of the newest, yet most widely used forms of media for sending communications between two or more machines. In expanded form, it stands for JavaScript Object Notation. In the planning stages for Java 9, there were plans to include a standard JSON processing (JSON-P) API with the release, however, the enhancement proposal did not make it int o the release. Instead, it is still very easy to work with JSON data by simply including the JSON-P library, which is currently included in Java EE. Part of the plan for an upcoming release of JSON-P is to provide direct support for Java SE.

XML APIs have always been available to the Java developer, usually supplied as third-party libraries that could be added to the runtime class path. Beginning in Java 7, the Java API for XML Processing (JAXP), Java API for XML Binding (JAXB), and the Java API for XML Web Services (JAX-WS) were included in the core runtime libraries. The most fundamental XML processing tasks that you will encounter involve only a few use cases: writing and reading XML documents, validating those documents, and using JAXB to assist in marshalling/unmarshalling Java objects.

This chapter provides recipes for performing XML and JSON-P tasks. The JSON-P recipes will require inclusion of the JSON-P API, which can be done by adding the dependencies to a maven application. In this chapter, you will learn how to create JSON, as well as write it to disk and perform parsing.

▓ **Note**   The source code for this chapter's examples is available in the `org.java9recipes.chapter20` package.

20-1. Writing an XML File

Problem

You want to create an XML document to store application data.

Solution

To write an XML document, use the `javax.xml.stream.XMLStreamWriter` class. The following code iterates over an array of `Patient` objects and writes the data to an `.xml` file. This sample code comes from the `org.java9recipes.chapter20.recipe20_1.DocWriter` example:

```
import javax.xml.stream.XMLOutputFactory;
import javax.xml.stream.XMLStreamException;
import javax.xml.stream.XMLStreamWriter;
```

```
...
public void run(String outputFile) throws FileNotFoundException, XMLStreamException,
        IOException {
    List<Patient> patients = new ArrayList<>();
    Patient p1 = new Patient();
    Patient p2 = new Patient();
    Patient p3 = new Patient();
    p1.setId(BigInteger.valueOf(1));
    p1.setName("John Smith");
    p1.setDiagnosis("Common Cold");
    p2.setId(BigInteger.valueOf(2));
    p2.setName("Jane Doe");
    p2.setDiagnosis("Broken Ankle");
    p3.setId(BigInteger.valueOf(3));
    p3.setName("Jack Brown");
    p3.setDiagnosis("Food Allergy");
    patients.add(p1);
    patients.add(p2);
    patients.add(p3);
    XMLOutputFactory factory = XMLOutputFactory.newFactory();
    try (FileOutputStream fos = new FileOutputStream(outputFile)) {
        XMLStreamWriter writer = factory.createXMLStreamWriter(fos, "UTF-8");
        writer.writeStartDocument();
        writer.writeCharacters("\n");
        writer.writeStartElement("patients");
        writer.writeCharacters("\n");
        for (Patient p : patients) {
            writer.writeCharacters("\t");
            writer.writeStartElement("patient");
            writer.writeAttribute("id", String.valueOf(p.getId()));
            writer.writeCharacters("\n\t\t");
            writer.writeStartElement("name");
            writer.writeCharacters(p.getName());
            writer.writeEndElement();
            writer.writeCharacters("\n\t\t");
            writer.writeStartElement("diagnosis");
            writer.writeCharacters(p.getDiagnosis());
            writer.writeEndElement();
            writer.writeCharacters("\n\t");
            writer.writeEndElement();
            writer.writeCharacters("\n");
        }
        writer.writeEndElement();
        writer.writeEndDocument();
        writer.close();
    }
}

}
```

The previous code writes the following file contents:

```xml
<?xml version="1.0" ?>
<patients>
    <patient id="1">
        <name>John Smith</name>
        <diagnosis>Common Cold</diagnosis>
    </patient>
    <patient id="2">
        <name>Jane Doe</name>
        <diagnosis>Broken ankle</diagnosis>
    </patient>
    <patient id="3">
        <name>Jack Brown</name>
<diagnosis>Food allergy</diagnosis>
</patient>
</patients>
```

How It Works

The Java standard library provides several ways to write XML documents. One model is the Simple API for XML (SAX). The newer, simpler, and more efficient model is the Streaming API for XML (StAX). This recipe uses StAX defined in the `javax.xml.stream` package. Writing an XML document takes five steps:

1. Create a file output stream.

2. Create an XML output factory and an XML output stream writer.

3. Wrap the file stream in the XML stream writer.

4. Use the XML stream writer's write methods to create the document and write the XML elements.

5. Close the output streams.

Create a file output stream using the `java.io.FileOutputStream` class. You can use a `try-block` to open and close this stream. Learn more about the new `try-block` syntax in Chapter 9.

The `javax.xml.stream.XMLOutputFactory` provides a static method that creates an output factory. Use the factory to create a `javax.xml.stream.XMLStreamWriter`.

Once you have the writer, wrap the file stream object in the XML writer instance. You will use the various write methods to create the XML document elements and attributes. Finally, you simply close the writer when you finish writing to the file. Some of the more useful methods of the `XMLStreamWriter` instance are these:

- `writeStartDocument()`

- `writeStartElement()`

- `writeEndElement()`

- `writeEndDocument()`

- `writeAttribute()`

After creating the file and `XMLStreamWriter`, you always should begin the document by calling the `writeStartDocumentMethod()` method. Follow this by writing individual elements using the writeStartElement() and writeEndElement() methods in combination. Of course, elements can have nested elements. You have the responsibility to call these in proper sequence to create well-formed documents. Use the writeAttribute() method to place an attribute name and value into the current element. You should call writeAttribute() immediately after calling the writeStartElement() method. Finally, signal the end of the document with the writeEndDocument() method and close the Writer instance.

One interesting point of using the XMLStreamWriter is that it does not format the document output. Unless you specifically use the writeCharacters() method to output space and newline characters, the output will stream to a single unformatted line. Of course, this doesn't invalidate the resulting XML file, but it does make it inconvenient and difficult for humans to read. Therefore, you should consider using the writeCharacters() method to output spacing and newline characters as needed to create a human readable document. You can safely ignore this method of writing additional whitespace and line breaks if you do not need a document for human readability. Regardless of the format, the XML document will be well formed because it adheres to correct XML syntax.

The command-line usage pattern for this example code is this:

```
java org.java9recipes.chapter20.recipe20_1.DocWriter <outputXmlFile>
```

Invoke this application to create a file named patients.xml in the following way:

```
java org.java9recipes.chapter20.recipe20_1.DocWriter patients.xml
```

20-2. Reading an XML File

Problem

You need to parse an XML document, retrieving known elements and attributes.

Solution 1

Use the javax.xml.stream.XMLStreamReader interface to read documents. Using this API, your code will pull XML elements using a cursor-like interface similar to that in SQL to process each element in turn. The following code snippet from org.java9recipes.DocReader demonstrates how to read the patients.xml file that was generated in the previous recipe:

```java
public void cursorReader(String xmlFile)
throws FileNotFoundException, IOException, XMLStreamException {
    XMLInputFactory factory = XMLInputFactory.newFactory();
    try (FileInputStream fis = new FileInputStream(xmlFile)) {
        XMLStreamReader reader = factory.createXMLStreamReader(fis);
        boolean inName = false;
        boolean inDiagnosis = false;
        String id = null;
        String name = null;
        String diagnosis = null;

        while (reader.hasNext()) {
            int event = reader.next();
            switch (event) {
                case XMLStreamConstants.START_ELEMENT:
                    String elementName = reader.getLocalName();
```

```
                switch (elementName) {
                    case "patient":
                        id = reader.getAttributeValue(0);
                        break;
                    case "name":
                        inName = true;
                        break;
                    case "diagnosis":
                        inDiagnosis = true;
                        break;
                    default:
                        break;
                }
                break;
            case XMLStreamConstants.END_ELEMENT:
                String elementname = reader.getLocalName();
                if (elementname.equals("patient")) {
                    System.out.printf("Patient: %s\nName: %s\nDiagnosis: %s\n\n",id, name,
                    diagnosis);
                    id = name = diagnosis = null;
                    inName = inDiagnosis = false;
                }
                break;
            case XMLStreamConstants.CHARACTERS:
                if (inName) {
                    name = reader.getText();
                    inName = false;
                } else if (inDiagnosis) {
                    diagnosis = reader.getText();
                    inDiagnosis = false;
                }
                break;
            default:
                break;
        }
    }
    reader.close();
}
}
```

Solution 2

Use the XMLEventReader to read and process events using an event-oriented interface. This API is called
an iterator-oriented API as well. The following code is much like the code in Solution 1, except that it
uses the event-oriented API instead of the cursor-oriented API. This code snippet is available from the same
org.java9recipes.chapter20.recipe20_1.DocReader class used in Solution 1:

```
public void eventReader(String xmlFile)
        throws FileNotFoundException, IOException, XMLStreamException {
    XMLInputFactory factory = XMLInputFactory.newFactory();
    XMLEventReader reader = null;
```

```java
try(FileInputStream fis = new FileInputStream(xmlFile)) {
    reader = factory.createXMLEventReader(fis);
    boolean inName = false;
    boolean inDiagnosis = false;
    String id = null;
    String name = null;
    String diagnosis = null;

    while(reader.hasNext()) {
        XMLEvent event = reader.nextEvent();
        String elementName = null;
        switch(event.getEventType()) {
            case XMLEvent.START_ELEMENT:
                StartElement startElement = event.asStartElement();
                elementName = startElement.getName().getLocalPart();
                switch(elementName) {
                    case "patient":
                        id = startElement.getAttributeByName(QName.valueOf("id")).getValue();
                        break;
                    case "name":
                        inName = true;
                        break;
                    case "diagnosis":
                        inDiagnosis = true;
                        break;
                    default:
                        break;
                }
                break;
            case XMLEvent.END_ELEMENT:
                EndElement endElement = event.asEndElement();
                elementName = endElement.getName().getLocalPart();
                if (elementName.equals("patient")) {
                    System.out.printf("Patient: %s\nName: %s\nDiagnosis: %s\n\n",id,
                    name, diagnosis);
                    id = name = diagnosis = null;
                    inName = inDiagnosis = false;
                }
                break;
            case XMLEvent.CHARACTERS:
                String value = event.asCharacters().getData();
                if (inName) {
                    name = value;
                    inName = false;
                } else if (inDiagnosis) {
                    diagnosis = value;
                    inDiagnosis = false;
                }
                break;
        }
    }
}
```

```
    if(reader != null) {
        reader.close();
    }
}
```

How It Works

Java provides several ways to read XML documents. One way is to use StAX, a streaming model. It is better than the older SAX API because it allows you to both read and write XML documents. Although StAX is not quite as powerful as a DOM API, it is an excellent and efficient API that is less taxing on memory resources.

StAX provides two methods for reading XML documents: a cursor API and an iterator API. The cursor-oriented API utilizes a cursor that can walk an XML document from start to finish, pointing to one element at a time, and always moving forward. The iterator API represents an XML document stream as a set of discrete event objects, provided in the order that they are read in the source XML. The event-oriented, iterator API is preferred over the cursor API at this time because it provides XMLEvent objects with the following benefits:

- The XMLEvent objects are immutable and can persist even though the StAX parser has moved on to subsequent events. You can pass these XMLEvent objects to other processes or store them in lists, arrays, and maps.

- You can subclass XMLEvent, creating your own specialized events as needed.

- You can modify the incoming event stream by adding or removing events, which is more flexible than the cursor API.

To use StAX to read documents, create an XML event reader on your file input stream. Check that events are still available with the hasNext() method and read each event using the nextEvent() method. The nextEvent() method will return a specific type of XMLEvent that corresponds to the start and stop elements, attributes, and value data in the XML file. Remember to close your readers and file streams when you're finished with those objects.

You can invoke the example application like this, using the patients.xml file as your <xmlFile> argument:

```
java org.java9recipes.chapter20.recipe20_2.DocReader <xmlFile>
```

20-3. Transforming XML

Problem

You want to convert an XML document to another format, for example to HTML.

Solution

Use the javax.xml.transform package to transform an XML document to another document format.

The following code demonstrates how to read a source document, apply an Extensible Stylesheet Language (XSL) transform file, and produce the transformed, new document. Use the sample code from the org.java9recipes.chapter20.recipe20_3.TransformXml class to read the patients.xml file and create a patients.html file. The following snippet shows the important pieces of this class:

```
import javax.xml.transform.TransformerConfigurationException;
import javax.xml.transform.TransformerException;
```

```
import javax.xml.transform.TransformerFactory;
import javax.xml.transform.Transformer;
import javax.xml.transform.Source;
import javax.xml.transform.stream.StreamResult;
import javax.xml.transform.stream.StreamSource;
...
public void run(String xmlFile, String xslFile, String outputFile)
        throws FileNotFoundException, TransformerConfigurationException,
        TransformerException {
    InputStream xslInputStream = new FileInputStream(xslFile);
    Source xslSource = new StreamSource(xslInputStream);
    TransformerFactory factory = TransformerFactory.newInstance();
    Transformer transformer = factory.newTransformer(xslSource);
    InputStream xmlInputStream = new FileInputStream(xmlFile);
    StreamSource in = new StreamSource(xmlInputStream);
    StreamResult out = new StreamResult(outputFile);
    transformer.transform(in, out);
    ...
}
```

How It Works

The javax.xml.transform package contains all the classes you need to transform an XML document into any other document type. The most common use case is to convert data-oriented XML documents into user-readable HTML documents.

Transforming from one document type to another requires three files:

- An XML source document

- An XSL transformation document that maps XML elements to the new document elements

- A target output file

The XML source document is, of course, your source data file. It will most often contain data-oriented content that is easy to parse programmatically. However, people don't easily read XML files, especially complex, data-rich files. Instead, people are much more comfortable reading properly rendered HTML documents.

The XSL transformation document specifies how an XML document should be transformed into a different format. An XSL file will usually contain an HTML template that specifies dynamic fields that will hold the extracted contents of a source XML file.

In this example's source code, you'll find two source documents:

- chapter20/recipe20_3/patients.xml

- chapter20/recipe20_3/patients.xsl

The patients.xml file is short and contains the following data:

```
<?xml version="1.0" encoding="UTF-8"?>
<patients>
    <patient id="1">
        <name>John Smith</name>
        <diagnosis>Common Cold</diagnosis>
    </patient>
```

```
    <patient id="2">
        <name>Jane Doe</name>
        <diagnosis>Broken ankle</diagnosis>
    </patient>
    <patient id="3">
        <name>Jack Brown</name>
        <diagnosis>Food allergy</diagnosis>
    </patient>
</patients>
```

The patients.xml file defines a root element called patients. It has three nested patient elements. The patient elements contain three pieces of data:

- Patient identifier, provided as the id attribute of the patient element

- Patient name, provided as the name subelement

- Patient diagnosis, provided as the diagnosis subelement

The transformation XSL document (patients.xsl) is quite small as well, and it simply maps the patient data to a more user-readable HTML format using XSL:

```
<?xml version="1.0" encoding="UTF-8"?>
<xsl:stylesheet xmlns:xsl="http://www.w3.org/1999/XSL/Transform" version="1.0">
<xsl:output method="html"/>
<xsl:template match="/">
<html>
<head>
    <title>Patients</title>
</head>
<body>
    <table border="1">
        <tr>
            <th>Id</th>
            <th>Name</th>
            <th>Diagnosis</th>
        </tr>
        <xsl:for-each select="patients/patient">
        <tr>
            <td>
        <xsl:value-of select="@id"/>
            </td>
            <td>
        <xsl:value-of select="name"/>
            </td>
            <td>
        <xsl:value-of select="diagnosis"/>
            </td>
            </tr>
        </xsl:for-each>
    </table>
```

```
</body>
</html>
        </xsl:template>
        </xsl:stylesheet>
```

Using this style sheet, the sample code transforms the XML into an HTML table containing all the patients and their data. Rendered in a browser, the HTML table should look like the one in Figure 20-1.

Id	Name	Diagnosis
1	John Smith	Common Cold
2	Jane Doe	Broken ankle
3	Jack Brown	Food allergy

Figure 20-1. *A common rendering of an HTML table*

The process for using this XSL file to convert the XML to an HTML file is straightforward, but every step can be enhanced with additional error checking and processing. For this example, refer to the previous code in the solution section.

The most basic transformation steps are these:

1. Read the XSL document into your Java application as a Source object.

2. Create a Transformer instance and provide your XSL Source instance for it to use during its operation.

3. Create a SourceStream that represents the source XML contents.

4. Create a StreamResult instance for your output document, which is an HTML file in this case.

5. Use the Transformer object's transform() method to perform the conversion.

6. Close all the relevant streams and file instances, as needed.

If you choose to execute the sample code, you should invoke it in the following way, using patients. xml, patients.xsl, and patients.html as arguments:

```
java org.java9recipes.chapter20.recipe20_3.TransformXml <xmlFile><xslFile><outputFile>
```

20-4. Validating XML

Problem

You want to confirm that your XML is valid—that it conforms to a known document definition or schema.

Solution

Validate that your XML conforms to a specific schema by using the `javax.xml.validation` package. The following code snippet from `org.java9recipes.chapter20.recipe20_4.ValidateXml` demonstrates how to validate against an XML schema file:

```java
import java.io.File;
import java.io.IOException;
import javax.xml.XMLConstants;
import javax.xml.transform.Source;
import javax.xml.transform.stream.StreamSource;
import javax.xml.validation.Schema;
import javax.xml.validation.SchemaFactory;
import javax.xml.validation.Validator;
import org.xml.sax.SAXException;
...
public void run(String xmlFile, String validationFile) {
    boolean valid = true;
    SchemaFactory sFactory =
            SchemaFactory.newInstance(XMLConstants.W3C_XML_SCHEMA_NS_URI);
    try {
        Schema schema = sFactory.newSchema(new File(validationFile));
        Validator validator = schema.newValidator();
        Source source = new StreamSource(new File(xmlFile));
        validator.validate(source);
    } catch (SAXException | IOException | IllegalArgumentException ex) {
        valid = false;
    }
    System.out.printf("XML file is %s.\n", valid ? "valid" : "invalid");
}
...
```

How It Works

When utilizing XML, it is important to validate it to ensure that the correct syntax is in place, and to ensure that an XML document is an instance of the specified XML schema. The validation process involves comparing the schema and the XML document to find any discrepancies. The `javax.xml.validation` package provides all the classes needed to reliably validate an XML file against a variety of schemas. The most common schemas that you will use for XML validation are defined as constant URIs within the `XMLConstants` class:

- `XMLConstants.W3C_XML_SCHEMA_NS_URI`

- `XMLConstants.RELAXNG_NS_URI`

Begin by creating a `SchemaFactory` for a specific type of schema definition. A `SchemaFactory` knows how to parse a particular schema type and prepares it for validation. Use the `SchemaFactory` instance to create a `Schema` object. The `Schema` object is an in-memory representation of the schema definition grammar. You can use the `Schema` instance to retrieve a `Validator` instance that understands this grammar. Finally, use the `validate()` method to check your XML. The method call will generate several exceptions if anything goes wrong during the validation. Otherwise, the `validate()` method returns quietly, and you can continue to use the XML file.

■ **Note**   The XML Schema was the first to receive "Recommendation" status from the World Wide Web consortium (W3C) in 2001. Competing schemas have since become available. One competing schema is the Regular Language for XML Next Generation (RELAX NG) schema. RELAX NG may be a simpler schema and its specification also defines a non-XML, compact syntax. This recipe's example uses the XML schema.

Run the example code using the following command-line syntax, preferably with the sample `.xml` file and validation files provided as `resources/patients.xml` and `patients.xsl`, respectively:

```
java org.java9recipes.chapter20.recipe20_4.ValidateXml <xmlFile><validationFile>
```

20-5. Creating Java Bindings for an XML Schema

Problem

You want to generate a set of Java classes (Java bindings) that represent the objects in an XML schema.

Solution

The JDK provides a tool that can turn schema documents into representative Java class files. Use the `<JDK_HOME>/bin/xjc` command-line tool to generate Java bindings for your XML schemas. To create the Java classes for the `patients.xsd` file from Recipe 20-3, you could issue the following command from within a console:

```
xjc -p org.java9recipes.chapter20.recipe20_5 patients.xsd
```

This command will process the `patients.xsd` file and create all the classes needed to process an XML file that validates with this schema. For this example, the `patients.xsd` file looks like the following:

```xml
<?xml version="1.0" encoding="UTF-8"?>
<xs:schema xmlns:xs="http://www.w3.org/2001/XMLSchema" elementFormDefault="qualified">
<xs:element name="patients">
<xs:complexType>
<xs:sequence>
<xs:element maxOccurs="unbounded" name="patient" type="Patient"/>
</xs:sequence>
</xs:complexType>
</xs:element>
<xs:complexType name="Patient">
<xs:sequence>
<xs:element name="name" type="xs:string"/>
<xs:element name="diagnosis" type="xs:string"/>
</xs:sequence>
<xs:attribute name="id" type="xs:integer" use="required"/>
</xs:complexType>
</xs:schema>
```

Executed on the previous xsd file, the xjc command creates the following files in the org.java9recipes.chapter20.recipe20_5 package:

- ObjectFactory.java

- Patients.java

- Patient.java

How It Works

The JDK includes the <JDK_HOME>/bin/xjc utility. The xjc utility is a command-line application that creates Java bindings from schema files. The source schema files can be several types, including XML Schemas, RELAX NG, and others.

The xjc command has several options for performing its work. Some of the most common options specify the source schema file, the package of the generated Java binding files, and the output directory that will receive the Java binding files.

You can get detailed descriptions of all the command-line options by using the tools' -help option:

```
xjc -help
```

A Java binding contains annotated fields that correspond to the fields defined in the XML Schema file. These annotations mark the root element of the schema file and all other subelements. This is useful during the next step of XML processing, which involves either unmarshalling or marshalling these bindings.

20-6. Unmarshalling XML to a Java Object

Problem

You want to unmarshall an XML file and create its corresponding Java object tree.

Solution

Unmarshalling is the process of converting a data format, in this case XML, into a memory representation of the object so that can be used to perform a task. JAXB provides an unmarshalling service that parses an XML file and generates the Java objects from the bindings you created in Recipe 20-4. The following code can read the file patients.xml from the org.java9recipes.chapter20.recipe20-6 package to create a Patients root object and its list of Patient objects:

```java
public void run(String xmlFile, String context)
        throws JAXBException, FileNotFoundException {
    JAXBContext jc = JAXBContext.newInstance(context);
    Unmarshaller u = jc.createUnmarshaller();
    FileInputStream fis = new FileInputStream(xmlFile);
    Patients patients = (Patients)u.unmarshal(fis);
    for (Patient p: patients.getPatient()) {
        System.out.printf("ID: %s\n", p.getId());
        System.out.printf("NAME: %s\n", p.getName());
        System.out.printf("DIAGNOSIS: %s\n\n", p.getDiagnosis());
    }
}
```

If you run the sample code on the chapter20/recipe20_6/patients.xml file and use the org. java9recipes.chapter20 context, the application will print the following to the console as it iterates over the Patient object list:

```
ID: 1
NAME: John Smith
DIAGNOSIS: Common Cold

ID: 2
NAME: Jane Doe
DIAGNOSIS: Broken ankle

ID: 3
NAME: Jack Brown
DIAGNOSIS: Food allergy
```

■ **Note** The previous output comes directly from instances of the Java Patient class that was created from XML representations. The code does not print the contents of the XML file directly. Instead, it prints the contents of the Java bindings after the XML has been marshalled into appropriate Java binding instances.

How It Works

Unmarshalling an XML file into its Java object representation has at least two criteria:

- A well-formed and valid XML file

- A set of corresponding Java bindings

The Java bindings don't have to be autogenerated from the xjc command. Once you've gained some experience with Java bindings and the annotation features, you may prefer to create and control all aspects of Java binding by handcrafting your Java bindings. Whatever your preference, Java's unmarshalling service utilizes the bindings and their annotations to map XML objects to a target Java object and to map XML elements to target object fields.

Execute the example application for this recipe using this syntax, substituting patients.xml and org. java9recipes.chapter20.recipe20_6 for the respective parameters:

```
java org.java9recipes.chapter20.recipe20_6.UnmarshalPatients <xmlfile><context>
```

20-7. Building an XML Document with JAXB

Problem

You need to write an object's data to an XML representation.

Solution

Assuming you have created Java binding files for your XML schema as described in Recipe 20-4, you use a JAXBContext instance to create a Marshaller object. You then use the Marshaller object to serialize your Java object tree to an XML document. The following code demonstrates this:

```
public void run(String xmlFile, String context)
        throws JAXBException, FileNotFoundException {
    Patients patients = new Patients();
    List<Patient> patientList = patients.getPatient();
    Patient p = new Patient();
    p.setId(BigInteger.valueOf(1));
    p.setName("John Doe");
    p.setDiagnosis("Schizophrenia");
    patientList.add(p);

    JAXBContext jc = JAXBContext.newInstance(context);
    Marshaller m = jc.createMarshaller();
    m.marshal(patients, new FileOutputStream(xmlFile));
}
```

The previous code produces an unformatted but well-formed and valid XML document. For readability, the XML document is formatted here:

```
<?xml version="1.0" encoding="UTF-8" standalone="yes"?>
    <patients>
    <patient id="1">
        <name>John Doe</name>
        <diagnosis>Schizophrenia</diagnosis>
    </patient>
    </patients>
```

▓ **Note**　The getPatient() method in the previous code returns a list of patient objects instead of a single patient. This is a naming oddity of the JAXB code generation from the XSD schema in this example.

How It Works

A Marshaller object understands JAXB annotations. As it processes classes, it uses the JAXB annotations to provide the context needed to create the object tree in XML.

You can run the previous code from the org.java9recipes.chapter20.recipe20_7.MarshalPatients application using the following command line:

```
java org.java9recipes.chapter20.recipe20_7.MarshalPatients <xmlfile><context>
```

The context argument refers to the package of the Java classes that you will marshal. In the previous example, because the code marshals a Patients object tree, the correct context is the package name of the Patients class. In this case, the context is org.java9recipes.chapter20.

20-8. Parsing an XML Catalog

Problem

You need to parse an XML catalog in order to direct remote external references to a local catalog for security purposes, or some other need.

Solution

Utilize the standard XML Catalog API that is part of Java 9. In this example, a local catalog is read and parsed using the API.

```
public static void main(String[] args) {
        // Create a CatalogFeatures object
        CatalogFeatures defaults = CatalogFeatures.defaults();

        // Resolve using properties
        // System.setProperty("javax.xml.catalog.files", "catalog.xml");

        // Resolve by passing
        Catalog catalog = CatalogManager.catalog(defaults, "catalog.xml", "catalog-alt.xml");

        // Use CatalogFeatures to specify catalog files and/or additional features
        // CatalogFeatures catalogFeatures = CatalogFeatures.builder()
        //          .with(Feature.FILES, "catalog.xml")
        //          .with(Feature.RESOLVE, "ignore")
        //          .build();

        // Stream and filter to find the catalog matching your specification
        Optional<Catalog> cat = catalog.catalogs()
                .filter((c)->c.matchURI("calstblx.dtd") != null)
                .findFirst();

        // Do something with catalog
    }
```

How It Works

The JDK has historically had an XML resolver as part of its core. However, this resolver was private and utilized only by the JDK. As time moved on, the need to implement a public XML resolver became evident, so the private resolver was revamped into a new public API. The API allows one to manage the creation of XML Catalogs and resolvers, it implements the OASIS XML Catalogs 1.1 specification, and it implements the existing JAXP interfaces.

There are a number of key interfaces and classes that comprise the Catalog API. The Catalog interface can be used to represent an entity catalog. A CatalogManager is used to parse a Catalog by passing a CatalogFeatures configuration object, along with a variable argument containing the paths to the XML catalog files. It can also be used to generate CatalogResolvers. It is also possible to pass paths to one or many catalog files by specifying the "javax.xml.catalog.files" property, as seen in the example.

```
System.setProperty("javax.xml.catalog.files", "catalog.xml");
```

The CatalogFeatures object holds a number of properties and features, and a default implementation can be obtained calling upon the CatalogFeatures.defaults() method. To specify different values for a CatalogFeatures object, you can utilize the builder pattern to indicate values for each of the different features. These features can be seen in Table 20-1.

Table 20-1. *Catalog Features*

Feature	Property	Description
FILES	javax.xml.catalog.files	Semicolon-delimited list of catalog files.
PREFER	javax.xml.catalog.prefer	Indicates preference between public and system identifiers.
DEFER	javax.xml.catalog.defer	Indicates that delegate catalogs will not be read until needed.
RESOLVE	javax.xml.catalog.resolve	Determines action to take if no matching catalog has been found.

For more information on CatalogFeatures, refer to the JavaDoc (http://download.java.net/java/jdk9/docs/api/javax/xml/catalog/CatalogFeatures.html).

The Catalog.catalogs() method can be called upon to generate a Stream of alternative Catalogs using the nextCatalog entries within the current catalog. This parsing can used to match the entries that reside within the XML catalog.

The XML Catalog API is a nice addition to the JDK, making it easy to utilize local catalogs, rather than remote, when needed. Java has long had a resolver for catalogs, but it was not accessible for use outside of the internals of the JDK. The new API is a rejuvenated form of the older private API, and it is fully compliant with the OASIS XML Catalogs 1.1 specification.

20-9. Working with JSON

Problem

You are interested in working with JSON in your Java SE 9 application.

Solution

Add the JSON-P API as a dependency to your Java SE 9 application. There are a couple of options for adding the dependency. One can download the JAR and place it into the CLASSPATH, or if using a build tool such as Maven, simply add the coordinates of the project repository. The following lines are excerpted from the POM file (Project Object Module for Maven), indicating how to add the dependency.

```
<dependencies>
        <dependency>
            <groupId>javax.json</groupId>
            <artifactId>javax.json-api</artifactId>
            <version>1.0</version>
        </dependency>
        <dependency>
            <groupId>org.glassfish</groupId>
            <artifactId>javax.json</artifactId>
```

```
            <version>1.0.4</version>
        </dependency>
...
</dependencies>
```

How It Works

The JavaScript Object Notation (JSON-P) API was added to the Java Enterprise platform with the release of Java EE 7. JSON-P, also referred to as "JSON Processing," has become the standard way to build JSON objects using Java. Since Java 9 does not come bundled with a JSON building and parsing API, one must pull in the required dependencies to utilize the standardized JSON-P API. JSON-P is part of Java EE, but support has been left out of Java SE at this point. As such, it is easy to include the API by adding the downloaded JAR files to the CLASSPATH, or adding the Maven coordinates to the project POM file. In the solution, I covered how to utilize the Maven coordinates. However, be sure to update the version accordingly.

20-10. Building a JSON Object

Problem

You would like to build a JSON object within your Java application.

Solution

Utilize the JSON-P API to build a JSON object. In the following code, a JSON object pertaining to a book is built.

```
public JsonObject buildBookObject() {
    JsonBuilderFactory factory = Json.createBuilderFactory(null);
    JsonObject obj = factory.createObjectBuilder()
            .add("title", "Java 9 Recipes")
            .add("author", "Josh Juneau")
            .add("projectCoordinator", "Jill Balzano")
            .add("editor", "Jonathan Gennick")
            .build();

    return obj;
}
```

How It Works

The JSON-P API includes a helper class that can be used to create JSON objects using the builder pattern. Using the JsonObjectBuilder, JSON objects can be built using a series of method calls, each building upon each other—hence, the builder pattern. Once the JSON object has been built, the JsonObjectBuilder.build() method can be called to return a JsonObject.

In the example to this recipe, you construct a JSON object that provides details regarding a book. The JsonObjectBuilder.beginObject() method is used to denote that a new object is being created. The add method is used to add more a name/value properties, much like that of a Map. Therefore, the following line adds a property named title with a value of "Java 9 Recipes":

```
.add("title", "Java 9 Recipes")
```

Objects can be embedded inside of each other, creating a hierarchy of subsections within one JsonObject. For example, after the first call to add(), another object can be embedded inside the initial JsonObject by calling JsonBuilderFactory.createObjectBuilder() as the value to an add() operation, and passing the name of the embedded object. Embedded objects can also contain properties; so to add properties to the embedded object, call the add() method within the embedded object. JsonObjects can embody as many embedded objects as needed. The following lines of code demonstrate the beginning and end of an embedded object definition if we were to modify the sources in the example to break down the author by first and last name:

```
.add("author", factory.createObjectBuilder()
    .add("first", "Josh")
    .add("last", "Juneau"))
.add("projectCoordinator", "Jill Balzano")
```

It is also possible that a JsonObject may have an array of related subobjects. To add an array of subobjects, call the JsonBuilderFactory.createArrayBuilder() method, passing the name of the array as an argument. Arrays can consist of objects, and even hierarchies of objects, arrays, and so forth.

Once a JsonObject has been created, it can be passed to a client. WebSockets work well for passing JsonObjects back to a client, but there is a bevy of different technologies available for communicating with JSON.

20-11. Writing a JSON Object to File

Problem

You've generated or parsed a JSON object, and you would like to store it on disk in file format.

Solution

Utilize the JSON-P API to build a JSON object, and then store it to the file system. The JsonWriter class makes it possible to create a file on disk, and then write the JSON to that file. In the following example, the JsonObject that was generated in Recipe 20-10 is written to disk using this technique.

```
public static void writeJson() {
    JsonObject jsonObject = buildBookObject();
    try (javax.json.JsonWriter jsonWriter = Json.createWriter(new FileWriter("Book.json"))) {
        jsonWriter.writeObject(jsonObject);
    } catch (IOException ex) {
        System.out.println(ex);
    }
}
```

How It Works

The JsonWriter class can be utilized to write a JsonObject to a Java writer object. A JsonWriter is instantiated by passing a Writer object as an argument to the Json.createWriter() method. After that JsonWriter has been created, the JsonWriter.writeObject() method can be invoked, passing the JsonObject that is to be written. Once the JsonObject has been written, the JsonWriter can be closed by calling its close() method. These are the only steps that are necessary for writing a JSON object to a Java Writer class type.

20-12. Parsing a JSON Object

Problem

The application you've created requires the ability to read a JSON object and parse it accordingly.

Solution

Utilize a JsonReader object to read a JSON object, and then make use of a JsonParser object to perform actions against the JSON data. The following example demonstrates how to read a file from disk, and then parse it to display some content.

```java
public void parseObject() {
    Reader fileReader = new InputStreamReader(getClass().getResourceAsStream("Book.json"));
    JsonParser parser = Json.createParser(fileReader);
    while (parser.hasNext()) {
        Event ev = parser.next();
        System.out.println(ev);
        if (ev.equals(Event.VALUE_STRING)) {
            System.out.println(parser.getString());
        }
    }
}
```

In the example, the Json file named Book.json is read and parsed. When a VALUE_STRING event is encountered during the parsing, the String is printed. Each encountered event is also printed. The following output is the result:

```
START_OBJECT
KEY_NAME
VALUE_STRING
Java 9 Recipes
KEY_NAME
VALUE_STRING
Josh Juneau
KEY_NAME
VALUE_STRING
Jill Balzano
KEY_NAME
VALUE_STRING
Jonathan Gennick
END_OBJECT
```

How It Works

Once a JSON object has been persisted to disk, it will later need to be read back in for utilization. The JsonReader object takes care of this task. To create a JsonReader object, call the Json.createReader() method, passing either an InputStream or Reader object. Once a JsonReader object has been created, it can produce a JsonObject by calling its readObject method.

In order to perform some tasks, a JSON object must be parsed to find only the content that is desired and useful for the current task. Utilizing a JSON parser can make jobs such as these easier, as a parser is able to break the object down into pieces so that each different piece can be examined as needed, to produce the desired result.

The javax.json.Json class contains a static factory method, createParser(), that accepts a bevy of input and returns an iterable JsonParser. Table 20-2 lists the different possible input types that are accepted via the createParser() method.

Table 20-2. *createParser Method Input Types*

Input Type	Method Call
InputStream	createParser(InputStream in)
JsonArray	createParser(JsonArray arr)
JsonObject	createParser(JsonObject obj)
Reader	createParser(Reader reader)

Once a JsonParser has been created, it can be made into an Iterator of Event objects. Each Event correlates to a different structure within the JSON object. For instance, when the JSON object is created, a START_OBJECT event occurs, adding a name/value pair will trigger both a KEY_NAME and VALUE_STRING event. These events can be utilized to obtain the desired information from a JSON object. In the example, the event names are merely printed to a server log. However, in a real-life application, a conditional would most likely test each iteration to find a particular event and then perform some processing. Table 20-3 lists the different JSON events, along a description of when each occurs.

Table 20-3. *JSON Object Events*

Event	Occurrence
START_OBJECT	Start of an object.
END_OBJECT	End of an object.
START_ARRAY	Start of an array.
END_ARRAY	End of an array.
KEY_NAME	Name of a key.
VALUE_STRING	Value of a name/value pair in String format.
VALUE_NUMBER	Value of a name/value pair in numeric format.
VALUE_TRUE	Value of a name/value pair in Boolean format.
VALUE_FALSE	Value of a name/value pair in Boolean format.
VALUE_NULL	Value of a name/value pair as NULL.

Summary

XML is commonly used to transfer data between disparate applications or to store data of some kind to a file. Therefore, it is important to understand the fundamentals for working with XML in your application development platform. This chapter provided an overview of how to perform some key tasks for working with XML using Java. This chapter began with the basics of writing and reading XML. It then demonstrated how to transform XML into different formats, and how to validate against XML schemas.

The chapter also touched upon working with JSON. Although Java SE 9 does not ship with a JSON API, the JSON-P API can be easily utilized to generate, write, and parse JSON data. This chapter demonstrated how to perform each of those tasks.

CHAPTER 21

■ ■ ■

Networking

Today, writing an application that does not communicate over the Internet in some fashion is rare. From sending data to another machine, to scraping information off remote web pages, networking plays an integral part in today's computing world. Java makes it easy to communicate over a network using the New I/O (NIO) and more new I/O features for the Java platform (NIO.2) APIs. Java SE 7 included a few new features, enabling easier multicasting among other things. With the addition of these new features, the Java platform contains a plethora of programming interfaces to help accomplish network tasks. Java 9 introduces the new HTTP/2 client, which provides a simple and concise API, as well as performance improvements over the older HTTP/1.1 client.

This chapter does not attempt to cover every networking feature that is part of the Java language, as the topic is quite large. However, it does provide a handful of recipes that are the most useful to a broad base of developers. You learn about a few of the standard networking concepts, such as sockets, as well as some newer concepts that were introduced with the latest release of the Java language. If you find this chapter interesting and want to learn more about Java networking, you can find lots of resources online. Perhaps the best place to go for learning more is the Oracle documentation at `http://download.oracle.com/javase/tutorial/networking/index.html`.

21-1. Listening for Connections on the Server

Problem

You want to create a server application that will listen for connections from a remote client.

Solution

Set up a server-side application that makes use of `java.net.ServerSocket` to listen for requests on a specified port. The following Java class is representative of one that would be deployed onto a server, and it listens for incoming requests on port 1234. When a request is received, the incoming message is printed to the command line and a response is sent back to the client.

```
import java.io.BufferedReader;
import java.io.IOException;
import java.io.InputStreamReader;
import java.io.PrintWriter;
import java.net.ServerSocket;
import java.net.Socket;

public class SocketServer {
```

© Josh Juneau 2017
J. Juneau, *Java 9 Recipes*, DOI 10.1007/978-1-4842-1976-8_21

```java
public static void main(String a[]) {
        final int httpd = 1234;
        ServerSocket ssock = null;
        try {
            ssock = new ServerSocket(httpd);
            System.out.println("have opened port 1234 locally");

            Socket sock = ssock.accept();
            System.out.println("client has made socket connection");

    communicateWithClient(sock);

System.out.println("closing socket");
} catch (Exception e) {
System.out.println(e);
} finally {
try{
ssock.close();
} catch (IOException ex) {
System.out.println(ex);
}
}
}

    public static void communicateWithClient(Socket socket) {
        BufferedReader in = null;
        PrintWriter out = null;

        try {
            in = new BufferedReader(
                    new InputStreamReader(socket.getInputStream()));
            out = new PrintWriter(
                    socket.getOutputStream(), true);

            String s = null;
            out.println("Server received communication!");
            while ((s = in.readLine()) != null) {
                System.out.println("received from client: " + s);
                out.flush();
                break;
            }
        } catch (Exception e) {
            e.printStackTrace();
        } finally {
            try {
                in.close();
                out.close();
            } catch (IOException ex) {
                ex.printStackTrace();
            }
        }
    }
}
```

586

This recipe works in concert with Recipe 21-2, whereby this example initiates the server and this Executing this program will simply print "have opened port 1234 locally," but executing it along with the client that is built in Recipe 21-2 will result in the following output from the SocketServer:

```
have opened port 1234 locally
client has made socket connection
received from client: Here is a test.
closing socket
```

■ **Note** To run the two recipes so that they work with each other, first start the SocketServer program so that the client can create a socket using the port that is opened in the server program. After the SocketServer starts, initiate the SocketClient program to see the two work together.

■ **Caution** This SocketServer program opens a port on your machine (1234). Be sure that you have a firewall set running on your machine; otherwise, you will be opening port 1234 to everyone. This could result in your machine being attacked. Open ports create vulnerabilities for attackers to break into machines, kind of like leaving a door in your house open. Note that the example in this recipe has a minimal attack profile because the server is run through only one pass and will print only a single message from the client before the session is closed.

How It Works

Server applications can be used to enable work to be performed on a server via direct communication from one or more client applications. Client applications normally communicate to the server application, send messages or data to the server for processing, and then disconnect. The server application typically listens for client applications, and then performs some processing against a client request once a connection is received and accepted. In order for a client application to connect to a server application, the server application must be listening for connections and then processing the connection data somehow. You cannot simply run a client against any given host and port number combination because doing so would likely result in a refused connection error. The server-side application must do three things: open a port, accept and establish client connections, and then communicate with the client connection in some way. In the solution to this recipe, the SocketServer class does all three.

Starting with the main() method, the class begins by opening a new socket on port 1234. This is done by creating a new instance of ServerSocket and passing a port number to it. The port number must not conflict with any other port that is currently in use on the server. It is important to note that ports below 1024 are usually reserved for operating system use, so choose a port number above that range. If you attempt to open a port that is already in use, the ServerSocket will not successfully be created, and the program will fail. Next, the ServerSocket object's accept() method is called, returning a new Socket object. Calling the accept() method will do nothing until a client attempts to connect to the server program on the port that has been set up. The accept() method will wait idly until a connection is requested and then it will return the new Socket object bound to the port that was set up on the ServerSocket. This socket also contains the remote port and hostname of the client attempting the connection, so it contains the information on two endpoints and uniquely identifies the Transmission Control Protocol (TCP) connection.

At this point, the server program can communicate with the client program, and it does so using the PrintWriter and BufferedReader objects. In the solution to this recipe, the communicateWithClient() method contains all the code necessary to accept messages from the client program, sends messages back to the client, and then returns control to the main() method that closes the ServerSocket. A new BufferedReader object can be created by generating a new InputStreamReader instance using the socket's input stream. Similarly, a new PrintWriter object can be created using the socket's output stream. Notice that this code must be wrapped in a try-catch block in case these objects are not successfully created.

```
in = new BufferedReader(
                    new InputStreamReader(socket.getInputStream()));
out = new PrintWriter(
                    socket.getOutputStream(), true);
```

Once these objects have been successfully created, the server can communicate with the client. It uses a loop to do so, reading from the BufferedReader object (the client input stream) and sending messages back to the client using the PrintWriter object. In the solution to this recipe, the server closes the connection by issuing a break, which causes the loop to end. Control then returns to the main() method.

```
out.println("Server received communication!");
while ((s = in.readLine()) != null) {
    System.out.println("received from client: " + s);
    out.flush();
    break;
}
```

In a real-life server program, the server would most likely listen endlessly without using a break to end communication. To handle multiple concurrent clients, each client connection would spawn a separate Thread to handle communication. The server would do something useful with the client communication as well. In the case of an HTML server, it would send back an HTML message to the client. On an SMTP server, the client would send an e-mail message to the server, and the server would then process the e-mail and send it. Socket communication is used for just about any TCP transmission, and both the client and servers create new sockets to perform a successful communication.

21-2. Defining a Network Connection to a Server

Problem

You need to establish a connection to a remote server.

Solution

Create a Socket connection to the remote server using its name and port number where the server is listening for incoming client requests. The following example class creates a Socket connection to a remote server. The code then sends a textual message to the server and receives a response. In the example, the server that the client is attempting to contact is named server-name and the port number is 1234.

▓ **Tip**   To create a connection to a local program running on the client machine, set the server-name equal to 127.0.0.1. This is done within the source listing for this recipe. Usually local connections such as this are used for testing purposes only.

```java
public class SocketClient {

    public static Socket socket = null;
    public static PrintWriter out;
    public static BufferedReader in;

    public static void main(String[] args) {
        createConnection("127.0.0.1", 1234);
    }

    public static void createConnection(String host, int port) {

        try {
            //Create socket connection
            socket = new Socket(host, port);
            // Obtain a handle on the socket output
            out = new PrintWriter(socket.getOutputStream(),
                    true);
            // Obtain a handle on the socket input
            in = new BufferedReader(new InputStreamReader(
                    socket.getInputStream()));
            testConnection();
            System.out.println("Closing the connection...");
            out.flush();
            out.close();
            in.close();
            socket.close();
            System.exit(0);
            } catch (UnknownHostException e) {
            System.out.println(e);
            System.exit(1);
            } catch (IOException e) {
            System.out.println(e);
            System.exit(1);
        }
    }

    public static void testConnection() {
        String serverResponse = null;
        if (socket != null && in != null && out != null) {
            System.out.println("Successfully connected, now testing...");

            try {
                // Send data to server
                out.println("Here is a test.");
                // Receive data from server
                while((serverResponse = in.readLine()) != null)
                System.out.println(serverResponse);
                } catch (IOException e) {
                System.out.println(e);
                System.exit(1);
```

```
            }
        }
    }
}
```

If you're testing this client against a server that successfully accepts the request, you will see the following result:

```
Successfully connected, now testing...
```

■ **Note**   This program will do nothing on its own. To create a server-side socket application that will accept this connection for a complete test, see Recipe 21-1. If you attempt to run this class without specifying a server host that is listening on the provided port, you will receive this exception: `java.net.ConnectException: Connection refused`.

How It Works

Every client/server connection occurs via a ***socket***, which is an endpoint in a communication link between two different programs. Sockets have port numbers assigned to them, which act as an identifier for the TCP/IP layer to use when attempting a connection. A server program that accepts requests from client machines typically listens for new connections on a specified port number. When a client wants to make a request to the server, it creates a new socket utilizing the hostname of the server and the port on which the server is listening and attempts to establish a connection with that socket. If the server accepts the socket, then the connection is successful.

This recipe discusses the client side of the socket connection, so we will not go into the details of what occurs on the server side at this time. However, more information regarding the server side of a connection is covered in Recipe 21-1. The example class in the solution to this recipe is representative of how a client-side program attempts and establishes connections to a server-side program. In this recipe, a method named createConnection() performs the actual connection. It accepts a server hostname and port number, which will be used to create the socket. Within the createConnection() method, the server hostname and port number are passed to the Socket class constructor, creating a new Socket object. Next, a PrintWriter object is created using the Socket object's output stream, and a BufferedReader object is created using the Socket object's input stream.

```
//Create socket connection
socket = new Socket(host, port);
// Obtain a handle on the socket output
out = new PrintWriter(socket.getOutputStream(),
                            true);
// Obtain a handle on the socket input
in = new BufferedReader(new InputStreamReader(
                socket.getInputStream()));
```

After creating the socket and obtaining the socket's output stream and input stream, the client can write to the PrintWriter in order to send data to the server. Similarly, to receive a response from the server, the client reads from the BufferedReader object. The testConnection() method is used to simulate a conversation between the client and the server program using the newly created socket. To do this, the socket, in, and out variables are checked to ensure that they are not equal to null. If they are not equal to null, the client attempts to send a message to the server by sending a message to the output stream using out.println("Here is a test."). A loop is then created to listen for a response from the server by calling the in.readLine() method until nothing else is received. It then prints the messages that are received.

```
if (socket != null && in != null && out != null) {
    System.out.println("Successfully connected, now testing...");

    try {
        // Send data to server
        out.println("Here is a test.");
        // Receive data from server
        while((serverResponse = in.readLine()) != null)
            System.out.println(serverResponse);
    } catch (IOException e) {
        System.out.println(e);
        System.exit(1);
    }
}
```

The java.net.Socket class is true to the nature of the Java programming language. It enables developers to code against a platform-independent API in order to communicate with network protocols that are specific to different platforms. It abstracts the details of each platform from the developer and provides a straightforward and consistent implementation for enabling client/server communications.

21-3. Bypassing TCP for InfiniBand to Gain Performance Boosts

Problem

Your application, which is deployed on Linux or Solaris, needs to move data very quickly and efficiently, and you need to remove any bottlenecks that could slow things down.

Solution

Use the Sockets Direct Protocol (SDP) to bypass TCP, a possible bottleneck in the process. In order to do this, create an SDP configuration file and set the system property to specify the configuration file location.

■ **Note** The SDP was added to the Java SE 7 release for applications deployed in the Solaris or Linux operating systems only. SDP was developed to support stream connections over InfiniBand fabric, which Solaris and Linux both support. The Java SE 7 release supports the 1.4.2 and 1.5 versions of OpenFabrics Enterprise Distribution (OFED).

This configuration file is an example of one that could be used to enable the use of SDP:

```
# Use SDP when binding to 192.0.2.1
bind 192.0.2.1 *

# Use SDP when connecting to all application services on 192.0.2.*
connect 192.0.2.0/24      1024-*
```

```
# Use SDP when connecting to the HTTP server or a database on myserver.org
connect myserver.org    8080
connect myserver.org    1521
```

The following excerpt is taken from the terminal. It is the execution of a Java application named SDPExample, specifying the SDP system property:

```
% java -Dcom.sun.sdp.conf=sdp.conf -Djava.net.preferIPv4Stack=true  SDPExample
```

How It Works

Sometimes it is essential that an application be as fast as possible while performing network communications. Transfers over TCP can sometimes decrease performance, so bypassing TCP can be beneficial. Since the release of Java SE 7, support for the SDP has been included for certain platforms. The SDP supports stream connections over InfiniBand fabric. Both Solaris and Linux include support for InfiniBand, so SDP can be useful on those platforms.

You don't need to make any programmatic changes to your applications in order to support SDP. The only differences when using SDP are that you must create an SDP configuration file, and the JVM must be told to use the protocol by passing a flag when running the application. Because the implementation is transparent, applications can be written for any platform, and those that support SDP can merely include the configuration file and bypass TCP.

The SDP configuration file is a text file that is composed of bind and connect rules. A bind rule indicates that the SDP protocol transport should be used when a TCP socket binds to an address and port that match the given rule. A connect rule indicates that the SDP protocol transport should be used when an unbound TCP socket attempts to connect to an address and port that match the given rule. The rule begins with either the bind or connect keyword indicating the rule type, followed by the hostname or IP address, and a single port number or range of port numbers. Per the online documentation, a rule has the following form:

```
("bind"|"connect")1*LWSP-char(hostname|ipaddress)["/"prefix])1*LWSP-char("*"|port)&#x00C9;
["-"("*"|port)]
```

In the rule format shown here, 1*LWSP-char means that any number of tabs or spaces can separate the tokens. Anything contained within square brackets indicates optional text, and quotes indicate literal text. In the solution to the recipe, the first rule indicates that SDP can be used for any port (* indicates a wildcard) on the IP address of 192.0.2.1, a local address. Each local address that is assigned to an InfiniBand adaptor should be specified with a bind rule in the configuration file. The first connect rule in the configuration file specifies that SDP should be used whenever connecting to the IP address of 192.0.2.*, using a port of 1024 or greater.

```
connect 192.0.2.0/24     1024-*
```

This rule uses some special syntax that should be noted. Specifically, the /24 suffix of the IP address indicates that the first 24 bits of the 32-bit IP address should match a specified address. Because each portion of an IP address is eight bits, this means that the 192.0.2 should match exactly, and the final byte can be any value. The dash -* within the port identifier specifies the range of 1024 or greater because the wildcard character is used. The third and fourth connect rules in the configuration file specify that SDP should be used with the hostname of myserver.org and a port of 8080 or 1521.

Next, in order to enable SDP, the -Dcom.sun.sdp.conf property should be specified along with the location to the SDP configuration file when starting the application. Also, notice in the solution that the property -Djava.net.preferIPv4Stack is set to true. This indicates that the IPv4 address format will be used. This is necessary because IPv4 addresses mapped to IPv6 are currently not available in the Solaris OS or under Linux.

Although the SDP is available only with Solaris or Linux, it is a nice addition to the JDK for users of those platforms. Any performance booster is always viewed as a bonus, and the solution to this recipe certainly falls into that category.

21-4. Broadcasting to a Group of Recipients

Problem

You want to broadcast datagrams to zero or more hosts identified by a single address.

Solution

Make use of datagram multicasting using the `DatagramChannel` class. The `DatagramChannel` class enables more than one client to connect to a group and listen for datagrams that have been broadcasted from a server. The following sets of code demonstrate this technique using a client/server approach. The class demonstrates a multicast client.

```java
package org.java9recipes.chapter21.recipe21_4;

import java.io.IOException;
import java.net.InetAddress;
import java.net.InetSocketAddress;
import java.net.NetworkInterface;
import java.net.StandardProtocolFamily;
import java.net.StandardSocketOptions;
import java.nio.ByteBuffer;
import java.nio.channels.DatagramChannel;
import java.nio.channels.MembershipKey;

public class MulticastClient {

    public MulticastClient() {
    }

    public static void main(String[] args) {
        try {
            // Obtain Supported network Interface
            NetworkInterface networkInterface = null;
            java.util.Enumeration<NetworkInterface> enumNI = NetworkInterface.getNetworkInterfaces();
            java.util.Enumeration<InetAddress> enumIA;
            NetworkInterface ni;
            InetAddress ia;
            ILOOP:
            while (enumNI.hasMoreElements()) {
                ni = enumNI.nextElement();
                enumIA = ni.getInetAddresses();
                while (enumIA.hasMoreElements()) {
                    ia = enumIA.nextElement();
                    if (ni.isUp() && ni.supportsMulticast()
```

```
                        && !ni.isVirtual() && !ni.isLoopback()
                        && !ia.isSiteLocalAddress()) {
                    networkInterface = ni;
                    break ILOOP;
                }
            }
        }

        // Address within range
        int port = 5239;
        InetAddress group = InetAddress.getByName("226.18.84.25");

        final DatagramChannel client = DatagramChannel.open(StandardProtocolFamily.INET);

        client.setOption(StandardSocketOptions.SO_REUSEADDR, true);
        client.bind(new InetSocketAddress(port));
        client.setOption(StandardSocketOptions.IP_MULTICAST_IF, networkInterface);

        System.out.println("Joining group: " + group + " with network interface " + networkInterface);
        // Multicasting join
        MembershipKey key = client.join(group, networkInterface);
        client.open();

        // receive message as a client
        final ByteBuffer buffer = ByteBuffer.allocateDirect(4096);
        buffer.clear();
        System.out.println("Waiting to receive message");
        // Configure client to be passive and non.blocking
        // client.configureBlocking(false);
        client.receive(buffer);
        System.out.println("Client Received Message:");
        buffer.flip();
        byte[] arr = new byte[buffer.remaining()];
        buffer.get(arr, 0, arr.length);

        System.out.println(new String(arr));
        System.out.println("Disconnecting...performing a single test pass only");
        client.disconnect();
    } catch (IOException ex) {
        ex.printStackTrace();
    }
  }
}
```

Next, a server class can be used to broadcast datagrams to the address that multicast clients are connected to. The following code demonstrates a multicast server:

```
package org.java9recipes.chapter21.recipe21_4;

import java.io.IOException;
import java.net.InetAddress;
```

```java
import java.net.InetSocketAddress;
import java.nio.ByteBuffer;
import java.nio.channels.DatagramChannel;

public class MulticastServer extends Thread {

    protected ByteBuffer message = null;

    public MulticastServer() {
    }

    public static void main(String[] args) {

        MulticastServer server = new MulticastServer();
        server.start();

    }

    @Override
    public void run() {

        try {

            // send the response to the client at "address" and "port"
            InetAddress address = InetAddress.getByName("226.18.84.25");
            int port = 5239;

            DatagramChannel server = DatagramChannel.open().bind(null);
            System.out.println("Sending datagram packet to group " + address + " on port " + port);
            message = ByteBuffer.wrap("Hello to all listeners".getBytes());
            server.send(message, new InetSocketAddress(address, port));

            server.disconnect();
        } catch (IOException e) {
            e.printStackTrace();
        }
    }
}
```

The server can broadcast a message to each client that is a member of the group. The client should be initiated first, followed by the server. Once the server is started, it will broadcast the message, and the client will receive it.

How It Works

Multicasting is the ability to broadcast a message to a group of listeners in a single transmission. A good analogy of multicasting is radio. Thousands of people can tune into a single broadcast event and listen to the same message. Computers can do similar things when sending messages to listeners. A group of client machines can tune into the same address and port number to receive a message that a server broadcasts to that address and port. The Java language provides multicasting functionality via datagram messaging. Datagrams are independent, nonguaranteed messages that can be delivered over the network to clients.

(Being **nonguaranteed** means that the arrival, arrival time, and content are not predictable.) Unlike messages sent over TCP, sending a datagram is a nonblocking event, and the sender is not notified of the receipt of the message. Datagrams are sent using the User Datagram Protocol (UDP) rather than TCP. The ability to send multicast messages via UDP is one benefit over TCP, as long as the ordering, reliability, and data integrity of the message are not mission-critical.

Java facilitates multicast messaging via the MulticastChannel interface. Classes that implement the MulticastChannel interface have multicasting enabled and can therefore broadcast to groups and receive group broadcasts. One such class is the DatagramChannel, which is a selectable channel for datagram-oriented sockets. In the solution to this recipe, both a client and a server program are used to communicate via multicast messaging, and the DatagramChannel class is used on both sides of the communication. A DatagramChannel must be configured in a specific way if it is to be used for accepting multicast messages. Specifically, there are options that need to be set on the DatagramChannel client that is opened. We will discuss those options shortly. The following steps are required for creating a client that receives multicast messages.

1. Open a DatagramChannel.

2. Set the DatagramChannel options that are required to multicast.

3. Join the client to a multicast group and return a MembershipKey object.

4. Open the client.

In the solution to this recipe, the client application begins by obtaining a reference to the network interface that will be used for receiving the broadcast messages. Setting up a NetworkInterface is required for multicasting. Next, a port number is chosen, as well as a multicasting IP address. The group or registered listeners will use the IP address in order to listen for broadcasts. The port number must not be in use or an exception will be thrown. For IPv4 multicasting, the IP address must range from 224.0.0.0 to 239.255.255.255, inclusive. This port and IP address is the same one used by a server to broadcast the message. Next, a new DatagramChannel is opened using StandardProtocolFamily.INET. The choices for opening a DatagramChannel are StandardProtocolFamily.INET or StandardProtocolFamily.INET6, corresponding to IPv4 and IPv6, respectively. The first option that is set on the DatagramChannel is StandardSocketOptions.SO_REUSEADDR, and it is set to true. This indicates that multiple clients will be able to "reuse" the address or use it at the same time. This needs to be set for a multicast to occur. The client is then bound to the port using a new InetSocketAddress instance. Last, the StandardSocketOptions.IP_MULTICAST_IF option is set to the network interface that is used. This option represents the outgoing interface for multicast datagrams sent by the datagram-oriented socket.

```
client.setOption(StandardSocketOptions.SO_REUSEADDR, true);
client.bind(new InetSocketAddress(port));
client.setOption(StandardSocketOptions.IP_MULTICAST_IF, networkInterface);
```

Once these options have been set and the port has been bound to the DatagramChannel, it is ready to join the group of listeners. This can be done by calling the DatagramChannel join(InetAddress, NetworkInterface) method, passing the group address and network interface that will be used by the client. As a result, a java.nio.channels.MembershipKey object is produced, which is a token that represents the membership of an IP multicast group. Last, the DatagramChannel open() method is called, which opens the channel to listen for broadcasts. At this point, the client is ready to receive multicast messages and it waits for a message to be received.

```
MembershipKey key = client.join(group, networkInterface);
client.open();
```

The next lines of code in the client take care of receiving messages from the server. In order to receive a broadcasted message, a ByteBuffer is created and then eventually passed to the DatagramChannel's receive() method. Once the receive() method is called, the client will pause until a message is received.

You can disable this feature by calling the DatagramChannel configureBlocking(boolean) method and passing a false value. Next, the ByteBuffer is converted to a String value and printed out by repositioning the buffer index at 0 using the flip() method, and then pulling the text starting at index 0 to the last index into a byte[]. Finally, be sure to disconnect the client when you're finished. That wraps up the client code portion.

```
// Configure client to be passive and non.blocking
// client.configureBlocking(false);
client.receive(buffer);
// client pauses until a message is received... in this case
System.out.println("Client Received Message:");
buffer.flip();
byte[] arr = new byte[buffer.remaining()];
buffer.get(arr, 0, arr.length);

System.out.println(new String(arr));
System.out.println("Disconnecting...performing a single test pass only");
client.disconnect();
```

■ **Note**   In the example to this recipe, a single pass is performed, and the client is then disconnected. For extended listening, you would need a loop with a timeout and provide tests for an ending state.

The server code is fairly basic. You can see that the MulticastServer class extends Thread. This means that this server application could run in a thread separate from other code within an application. If there were another class that initiated the MulticastServer class's run() method, it would run in a thread separate from the class that initiated it. The run() method must exist in any class that extends Thread. For more information regarding threading and concurrency, refer to Chapter 10.

The bulk of the server code resides in the run() method. A new InetAddress object is created using the same IP address that the client registered with in order to join the multicast group. The same port number is also declared in the server code, and these two objects will be used later in the code block to send the message. A new DatagramChannel is opened and bound to null. The null value is important because by setting the SocketAddress equal to null, the socket will be bound to an address that is assigned automatically. Next, a ByteBuffer is created that contains a message that will be broadcast to any listeners. The message is then sent using the DatagramChannel's send(ByteBuffer, InetSocketAddress) method. The send() method in the solution accepts the message as a ByteBuffer object, as well as a new InetSocketAddress that is created by using the address and port, which was declared at the beginning of the block. Told you we'd get back to those!

```
server.send(message, new InetSocketAddress(address, port));
```

At this point, the client would receive the message that was sent by the server. As for the client that is demonstrated in the solution to this recipe, it would then disconnect. Normally in a real-world scenario, a different class would most likely initiate the server, and its run() method would contain a loop that would continue to execute until all messages have been broadcast or the loop was told to stop. The client would probably not disconnect until after a user initiated a shutdown.

■ **Note**   If your laptop or server is using a different network protocol other than standard IPv4, then results may vary. Please be sure to do a sufficient amount of testing before sending your code to a production environment.

21-5. Generating and Reading from URLs

Problem

You want to generate URLs programmatically in your application. Once the URLs have been created, you'd like to read data from them for use in your application.

Solution

Make use of the java.net.URL class in order to create a URL. There are a few different ways to generate a URL depending on the address you are attempting to work with. This solution demonstrates some of these options for creating URL objects, along with comments indicating the differences. Once the URL objects have been created, one of the URLs is read into a BufferedReader and printed to the command line.

```java
import java.io.BufferedReader;
import java.io.IOException;
import java.io.InputStreamReader;
import java.net.MalformedURLException;
import java.net.URL;

public class GenerateAndReadUrl {

    public static void main(String[] args) {
        try {
            // Generate absolute URL
            URL url1 = new URL("http://www.java.net");
            System.out.println(url1.toString());
            // Generate URL for pages with a common base
            URL url2 = new URL(url1, "search/node/jdk8");

            // Generate URL from different pieces of data
            URL url3 = new URL("http", "java.net", "search/node/jdk8");

            readFromUrl(url1);

        } catch (MalformedURLException ex) {
            ex.printStackTrace();
        }
    }

    /**
     * Open URL stream as an input stream and print contents to command line.
     *
     * @param url
     */
    public static void readFromUrl(URL url) {
        try {
            BufferedReader in = new BufferedReader(
                    new InputStreamReader(
                    url.openStream()));
```

```
        String inputLine;

        while ((inputLine = in.readLine()) != null) {
            System.out.println(inputLine);
        }

        in.close();
    } catch (IOException ex) {
        ex.printStackTrace();
    }
  }
}
```

Running this program will result in the HTML from the URL resource identified as url1 being printed to the command line.

How It Works

Creating URLs in Java code is fairly straightforward thanks to the java.net.URL class, which does all of the heavy lifting. A URL is a character String that points to a resource on the Internet. Sometimes it is useful to create URLs in Java code so that you can read content from, or push content to, the Internet resource that the URL is pointing to. In the solution to this recipe, a few different URL objects are created, demonstrating the different constructors that are available for use.

The easiest route to use for creating a URL is to pass the standard readable URL String for a resource that is located on the Internet to the java.net.URL class to create a new instance of the URL. In the solution, an absolute URL is passed to the constructor to create the url1 object.

```
URL url1 = new URL("http://www.java.net");
```

Another useful way to create a URL is to pass two arguments to the URL constructor and create a relative URL. It is useful to base relative URLs on the location of another URL. For instance, if a particular site has a number of different pages, you could create a URL pointing to one of the subpages relative to the URL of the main site. Such is the case with the url2 object in the solution to this recipe.

```
URL url2 = new URL(url1, "search/node/jdk8");
```

As you can see, the path search/node/jdk8 is relative to the URL that is known as url1. In the end, the human-readable format of the url2 object is represented as http://www.java.net/search/node/jdk8. There are a couple more constructors for creating URL objects that take more than two arguments. Those constructors are as follows:

```
new URL (String protocol, String host, String port, String path);
new URL (String protocol, String host, String path);
```

In the solution, the second of the two constructors shown here is demonstrated. The protocol, hostname, and path of the resource are passed to the constructor to create the url3 object. These last two constructors are usually most useful when you're dynamically generating a URL.

21-6. Parsing a URL

Problem

You want to programmatically gather information from a URL for use within your application.

Solution

Parse the URL using the built-in URL class methods. In the following example class named ParseUrl, a URL object is created and then parsed using the built-in URL class methods to gather information regarding the URL. After the information has been retrieved from the URL, it is printed to the command line and then used to create another URL.

```java
import java.net.MalformedURLException;
import java.net.URL;

public static void main(String[] args) {
URL url1 = null;
URL url2 = null;
try {
        // Generate absolute URL
        url1 = new URL("http://www.apress.com/catalogsearch/result/?q=juneau");

        String host = url1.getHost();
        String path = url1.getPath();
        String query = url1.getQuery();
        String protocol = url1.getProtocol();
        String authority = url1.getAuthority();
        String ref = url1.getRef();

        System.out.println("The URL " + url1.toString() + " parses to the following:\n");
        System.out.println("Host: " + host + "\n");
        System.out.println("Path: " + path + "\n");
        System.out.println("Query: " + query + "\n");
        System.out.println("Protocol: " + protocol + "\n");
        System.out.println("Authority: " + authority + "\n");
        System.out.println("Reference: " + ref + "\n");

        url2 = new URL(protocol + "://" + host + path + "?q=java");

    } catch (IOException ex) {
        ex.printStackTrace();

    }
}
```

When this code is executed, the following lines will be displayed:

```
The URL http://www.apress.com/catalogsearch/result/?q=juneau parses to the following:

Host: www.apress.com

Path: /catalogsearch/result/

Query: q=juneau

Protocol: http

Authority: www.apress.com

Reference: null
```

How It Works

When constructing and working with URLs in an application, it is sometimes beneficial to extract information pertaining to a URL. This can be easily done using the URL built-in class methods, which can call a given URL and return Strings of information. Table 21-1 explains the accessor methods available in the URL class for obtaining information.

Table 21-1. Accessor Methods for Querying URLs

Method	URL Information Returned
getAuthority()	Authority component
getFile()	File name component
getHost()	Hostname component
getPath()	Path component
getProtocol()	Protocol identifier component
getRef()	Reference component
getQuery()	Query component

Each of these accessor methods returns a String value that can be used for informational purposes or for constructing other URLs dynamically, as was done in the example. If you take a look at the results from the solution to this recipe, you can see the information that was obtained regarding the URL via the accessor methods listed in Table 21-1. Most of the accessors are self-explanatory. However, a couple of them could use further explanation. The getFile() method returns the file name of the URL. The file name is the same as the result of concatenating the value returned from getPath() with the value returned from getQuery(). The getRef() method may not be very straightforward. The reference component that is returned by calling the getRef() method refers to the "fragment" that may be appended to the end of a URL. For instance, a fragment is indicated using the pound character (#), followed by a String that usually corresponds to a subsection on a particular web page. Given the URL such as the following, recipe21_6 would be returned using the getRef() method.

```
http://www.java9recipes.org/chapters/chapter21#recipe21_6
```

Although it's not always needed, the ability to parse a URL to obtain information can come in very handy at times. Because the Java language has helper methods built into the java.net.URL class, it makes gathering information pertaining to URLs a piece of cake.

21-7. Making HTTP Requests and Working with HTTP Responses

Problem

You would like to initiate an HTTP request from within an application, and process the response accordingly.

Solution

Make use of the HTTP/2 client API and make requests in either a synchronous or asynchronous manner. In the following example code, a request is made to the Apress website. The example demonstrates a synchronous request, so the code will block until a response is received.

```
public static void synchronousRequest() {
    try {
        HttpResponse resp = HttpRequest.create(
                new URI("http://www.apress.com/us/")).GET().response();
        int statusCode = resp.statusCode();
        String body = resp.body(HttpResponse.asString());
        System.out.println("Status Code: " + statusCode);
        // Do something with body text
    } catch (URISyntaxException | IOException | InterruptedException ex) {
        Logger.getLogger(HttpClient.class.getName()).log(Level.SEVERE, null, ex);
    }
}
```

The output from running this example should be as follows, unless the site is down or there are network communication issues:

```
Status Code: 200
```

To perform an asynchronous request, simply call upon the responseAsync() method, rather than response(). Doing so will return a CompleteableFuture, upon which you can check status to determine whether or not the response has returned.

```
public static void asynchronousRequest() {
    try {
        CompletableFuture<HttpResponse> cf = HttpRequest.create(
                new URI("http://www.apress.com/us/")).GET().responseAsync();
        System.out.println("Request made...");

        System.out.println("Check if done...");
        while (!cf.isDone()) {
            System.out.println("Perform some other tasks while waiting...");
            // Periodically check CompletableFuture.isDone()
        }
```

```
                System.out.println("Response Received:");
                HttpResponse response = cf.get();
                int statusCode = response.statusCode();
                System.out.println("Status Code: " + statusCode);
                String body = response.body(HttpResponse.asString());
                // Do something with body text

        } catch (URISyntaxException | InterruptedException | ExecutionException ex) {
            Logger.getLogger(HttpClient.class.getName()).log(Level.SEVERE, null, ex);
        }
}
```

The output from the asynchronous example would resemble the following:

```
Request made...
Check if done...
Perform some other tasks while waiting...
Perform some other tasks while waiting...
Perform some other tasks while waiting...

...
Response Received:
Status Code: 200
```

How It Works

The HTTP/1.1 client had been a part of the JDK for years. In fact, it has remained largely unchanged since its inception in JDK 1.1. HTTP/1.1 has become outdated, and is no longer the preferred method of communicating via HTTP. The newer standard, HTTP/2 resolves many issues that have been around for years as part of working with HTTP/1.1. In Java 9, a new HTTP/2 client API has been added, allowing developers to easily make use of newer methodologies, while still remaining backward compatible.

Performance was oftentimes an issue with HTTP/1.1 due to issues such as head-of-line blocking and numerous request/response cycles. The HTTP/2 protocol was introduced in 2015, and it resolves many of these older issues. For instance, binary frames are now used when sending messages, reducing the complexity of parsing messages. Everything can now be sent over one TCP connection, rather than creating multiple TCP connections to send numerous messages. This only scratches the surface, and there have been many more improvements in HTTP/2...but this provides a sound understanding of why the changes were needed.

As mentioned previously, in Java 9 a new HTTP/2 client API has been added, making it easy to perform HTTP requests and receive HTTP responses either synchronously or asynchronously. In the first example, the synchronous API is demonstrated, invoking the HttpRequest.create() method, and passing a URI, followed by calling GET() and response() methods in a builder-style pattern. This returns an HttpResponse object.

```
HttpResponse resp = HttpRequest.create(
            new URI("http://www.apress.com/us/")).GET().response();
```

This is a blocking call, of course, as one will need to wait until a response is received before further processing can be completed. Once received, the HttpResponse object can be used to return the body, HTTP status code, and a number of other items. In this example, the HTTP status code is merely printed out, and in many cases the status code is used along with a conditional to determine how to perform processing.

Taking a look at the second asynchronous example, it is easy to notice the differences in code when the HttpRequest.create() method is invoked. After the URI is passed to the create() method, the GET() method is called again, followed by the responseAsync() method. The call to responseAsync() returns a CompletableFuture, and in this case generics are used to enforce that HttpResponse is returned. The CompletableFuture can then be checked to determine if the response has been returned by using the isDone() method. Appropriate actions can be taken to maintain a check again at a later time if the response has not yet been returned, or handle a received response accordingly. In this example, a while loop is used to continue looping until the response is finally returned. To make this code more production ready, a conditional could be used to halt the loop after a certain number of iterations have been completed.

The updated HTTP/2 client brings a more modern API for handling HTTP to Java. The updated API ensures that one can perform synchronous or asynchronous request/response lifecycles.

Summary

This chapter covered a few basic networking features of the Java language. In the recent releases, there have been some nice new features added, such as the SDP. However, much of the java.net package has been unchanged for years, and it is robust and easy to use. This chapter delved into using socket connections and URLs and broadcasting messages via DatagramChannel. Lastly, the updated HTTP/2 client was covered.

CHAPTER 22

Java Modularity

One of the most important new features of Java 9 is the modular system, which came to fruition via Project Jigsaw. Project Jigsaw may also be referred to as JSR 376: The Java Platform Module System. The purpose of the project was to construct a system that provided reliable configuration which would replace the classpath system. It also focused on providing strong encapsulation between different modules. The module system is composed of all modules that constitute the Java Platform, as the platform was reconstructed from the ground up and modularized as part of this project. Application developers and library creators can also create modules…whether they be single modules that perform a specific task, or a number of modules that together create an application.

In this chapter, the basic fundamentals for development and management of modules will be touched upon. Although Java Modularity is a very large topic, this chapter is terse, providing enough information to get started with module development quickly. I recommend reading more in-depth books and documentation for those interested in learning more details about Java Modularity.

22-1. Constructing a Module

Problem

You wish to create a simple module that will print a message to the command line or via a logger.

Solution

Develop a module so that it can be executed via the java executable. Begin by creating a new directory somewhere on your file system…in this case name it "recipe22-1." Create a new file named module-info. java, which is the module descriptor. In this file, list the module name as follows:

```
module org.firstModule {}
```

Next, create a folder named org within the recipe22-1 directory that was created previously. Next, create a folder named firstModule within the org folder. Now, create the bulk of the module by adding a new file named Main.java inside of the org.firstModule folder. Place the following code within the Main.java file:

```
package org.firstModule;
public class Main {
    public static void main(String[] args) {
        System.out.println("This is my first module");
    }
}
```

© Josh Juneau 2017
J. Juneau, *Java 9 Recipes*, DOI 10.1007/978-1-4842-1976-8_22

How It Works

The easiest modules can be built with two files, those being the module descriptor and a single Java class file that contains the business logic. The solution to this example follows this pattern to create a very basic module that performs a single task of printing a phrase to the command line. The module is packaged inside of a directory that is entitled the same as the module name. In the example, this directory is named `org.firstModule`, as it follows the standard module naming convention. In reality, a module can be named anything, so long as it does not conflict with other module names. However, it is recommended to utilize the inverse-domain-name pattern of packages. This causes the module name to become prefixed with its containing package names.

   In this solution, the module descriptor contains the module name, followed by opening and closing braces. In a more complex module, the names of other module dependencies can be placed within the braces, along with the names of packages that this module exports for others to use. The module descriptor should be located at the root of the module directory. Inclusion of this file indicates to the JVM that this is a module. This directory can be made into a JAR file as I will discuss later in the chapter, and this creates a Modular JAR.

   The other file that must be created to develop a simple module is the Java class file containing the business logic. This file should be placed inside of the org/firstModule directory, and the package should indicate `org.firstModule`. In this solution, the Main method will be invoked when the module is executed. Note that any dependencies that the module would require must be listed within the module descriptor. In this simple module, there are no dependencies. After setting up this directory structure and placing these two files into their respective locations, the module development is complete.

22-2. Compiling and Executing a Module

Problem

You've developed a basic module. Now you would like to compile the module and execute it.

Solution

Make use of the javac utility to compile the module, specifying the d flag to list the folder into which the compiled code will be placed. After the d option, each of the source files to be compiled must be listed, including the `module-info.java` descriptor. Separate each of the file paths with a space. The following command compiles the sources that were developed in Recipe 22-1 and places the result into a directory named `mods/org.firstModule`.

```
javac d src/mods/org.firstModule src/org.firstModule/module-info.java src/org.firstModule/
org/firstModule/Main.java
```

   Now that the code has been compiled, it is time to execute the module. This can be done with the standard java executable. However, the `--module-path` option, which is new in Java 9, must be used to indicate the path of the module sources. The -m option is used to specify the Main class of the module.

```
java --module-path mods -m org.firstModule/org.firstModule.Main
```

   The output from executing the module should be as follows:

```
This is my first module
```

If there were more than one module that was going to be compiled, they could be compiled separately using a similar technique to the one described previously, or they could be compiled all at once. The syntax for compiling two modules that contain a dependency is as follows:

```
javac -d mods --module-source-path src $(find src -name "*.java")
```

How It Works

As you know, before a Java application can be executed, it must be compiled. Modules are the same way in that they must be compiled before they can be used. The standard javac utility has been enhanced so that it can accommodate the compilation of modules by simply listing out the fully qualified paths to the module-info.java file and each subsequent .java file contained within the module. The d option is used to specify the destination for the compiled sources. In the solution, the javac utility is invoked and the destination is set the location src/mods/org.firstModule. Each of the .java files that constitute the module are listed afterward, separated by a space. If a particular module included many .java source files, then simply specifying an asterisk (*) wildcard in the path after each package, rather than the individual file names, would suffice to compile each .java file contained within the specified package(s).

```
javac -d mods/src/org.firstModule src/org.firstModule/module-info.java src/org.firstModule/
org/firstModule/*
```

The same java executable that is used to execute most Java applications can be used to execute a module. With the help of some new options, the java executable is able to execute a module with all of the required dependencies. The --module-path option specifies the path to where the compiled module resides. If there are a number of modules that comprise an application, specify the path to the module that contains the application entry point. The -m option is used to specify the path application entry point class, as well as its fully qualified name. In the solution, the main class resides within a directory named org.firstModule, and within a package named org.firstModule.

22-3. Creating a Module Dependency

Problem

You wish to develop a module that depends upon and utilizes another module.

Solution

Develop at least two modules, where one of the modules depends upon the other. Then specify the dependency within the module descriptor. The module that was developed in the previous recipes will be used in this solution as well, but it will be altered a bit to make use of another module named org.secondModule. This second module will accept a number and then calculate a room rate.

To start, create the module org.secondModule by creating a new directory within the src directory. Next, create a .java file named module-info.java and place it into that location. The contents of the module descriptor should look as follows:

```
module org.secondModule {
    exports org.secondModule;
}
```

The module will be making sources contained within the org.secondModule package available to other modules that require it. The sources for the module should be placed into a class named Calculator. java, and this file should be placed into the src/org.secondModule/org/secondModule directory. Copy the following code into Calculator.java:

```
package org.secondModule;
import java.math.BigDecimal;
public class Calculator {
    public static BigDecimal calculateRate(BigDecimal days, BigDecimal rate) {
        return days.multiply(rate);
    }
}
```

The code that was originally used for org.firstModule (Recipes 22-1, and 22.2) should be modified to make use of org.secondModule as follows:

```
package org.firstModule;
import org.secondModule.Calculator;
import java.math.BigDecimal;
public class Main {
    public static void main(String[] args) {
        System.out.println("This is my first module.");
        System.out.println("The hotel stay will cost " + Calculator.calculateRate(
            BigDecimal.TEN, new BigDecimal(22.95)
        ));
    }
}
```

The module descriptor for org.firstModule must be modified to require the dependency:

```
module org.firstModule {
    requires org.secondModule;
}
```

To compile the modules, specify the javac command, using a wildcard to compile all code within the src directory:

```
javac -d mods --module-source-path src $(find src -name "*.java")
```

Lastly, to execute org.firstModule along with its dependency, use the same syntax that was used previously to execute the module. The module system takes care of gathering the required dependencies.

How It Works

A module can contain zero or many dependencies. The readability of a module depends upon what has been exported in the module descriptor of that module. Likewise, a module must require another module in order to read from it. The module system practices strong encapsulation. A module always is readable to itself, but other modules can only make use of those packages that are exported from the module. Furthermore, only public methods and so on are available for use by other modules.

To make one module dependent upon another, a required declaration must be placed in the module descriptor, specifying the name of the module on which it is dependent. In the solution, org.firstModule is dependent upon org.secondModule since the module descriptor declares it. This means that org.firstModule is able to utilize any public features residing within the org.secondModule package of the org.secondModule module. If there were more packages contained within org.secondModule, then they would not be available to org.firstModule since they have not been exported within the module descriptor for org.secondModule.

Utilization of the module descriptor for Java 9 modules trumps the classpath, as it is a much more robust means of declaring dependencies. However, if a Java 9 module were packaged as a JAR (see Recipe 22-4), it can be used on older versions of Java by placing the JAR into the classpath, and the module descriptor will be ignored.

Modules can be compiled separately using the javac command as demonstrated in Recipe 22-2, or they can be compiled using the wildcard notation, as also seen in Recipe 22-2 and in this recipe solution. Execution of the module is the same, whether it depends upon zero or more other modules.

22-4. Packaging a Module

Problem

Your module has been developed and you wish to package it to make it portable.

Solution

Utilize the enhanced jar utility to package modules and also to make executable modules. To package the module that was developed in Recipe 22-2, navigate to the directory which contains the mods and src directories. From within that directory, execute the following commands via the command line:

```
mkdir lib
jar --create --file=lib/org.firstModule@1.0.jar --module-version=1.0 --main-class=org.
firstModule.Main -C mods/org.firstModule .
```

This utility will package the module into a JAR file within the lib directory. The JAR file can then be executed with the java executable as follows:

```
java -p lib -m org.firstModule
```

How It Works

The jar utility has been enhanced for Java 9 to include a number of new options, including a few that make module packaging easier. Table 22-1 lists the options of the jar utility.

Table 22-1. *jar Utility Options*

Option	Description
-c, --create	Create an archive
-I, --generate-index=FILE	Generate index information for specified jar files
-t, --list	List an archive's table of contents
-u, --update	Update an existing jar file
-x, --extract	Extract one or more files from a jar file
-C DIR	Change to the directory that is specified and include file
-f, --file=FILE	Name of the jar file
-v, --verbose	Generate verbose output
-e, --main-class=NAME	The main class or entry point for a module that will be packaged into the jar
-m, --manifest=FILE	Include specified manifest file information with the jar
-M, --no-manifest	Omit manifest
--module-version=VERSION	Module version
--hash-modules=PATTERN	Compute and record hashes of modules matched by the specified pattern
-P, --module-path	Location of module dependency for generation of hash
-0, --no-compress	Specifies that no ZIP compression shall be used

Looking at the table, there are a couple of options that are important for working with modules. Specifically, as seen in the example, the `--module-version` option allows a version to be specified. The other module-specific option is `--module-path`, which specifies the location of module dependence for generating a hash.

New options aside, creation of a JAR file using modules is not too much different than standard JAR file generation. Perhaps the most difficult part is ensuring that you are in the correct directory when initiating the command. As seen in the solution, simply specify the main class that will be executed when the JAR is invoked by using the `--main-class` or `-e` option. After that, perform a `-C` directory change inside of the module root, and then end the command with a "." to indicate the current directory.

Once a JAR file is created, the module will become portable, which means that it can be used on other systems.

22-5. Listing Dependencies or Determining JDK-Internal API Use

Problem

You would like to determine whether an existing application relies upon any of the inaccessible internal JDK APIs with Java 9.

Solution

Use the jdeps tool to list module dependencies from the command line. To see the list of dependencies for a given module, specify the --list-deps option as follows:

```
jdeps --list-deps <<your-jar.jar>>
```

Invoking this command will initiate output that includes each of the packages that the specified JAR file depends upon. For example, choosing a random JAR file from the GlassFish application server modules directory would produce something similar to the following:

```
jdeps --list-deps acc-config.jar
   java.base
   java.xml.bind
   unnamed module: acc-config.jar
```

There are also applications that may make use of JDK-Internal APIs, which are now inaccessible to standard applications starting with Java 9. The jdeps tool can list such dependencies, making it possible to determine whether an application will run on Java 9 without issue. To utilize this functionality, specify the -jdkinternals option as follows:

```
jdeps -jdkinternals <<your-jar.jar>>
```

Invoking the jdeps utility to review a JAR that contains dependencies upon JDK-Internal APIs will produce output such as the following:

```
jdeps -jdkinternals security.jar
security.jar -> java.base
   com.sun.enterprise.common.iiop.security.GSSUPName    ->
   sun.security.util.ObjectIdentifier                       JDK internal API (java.base)
   com.sun.enterprise.common.iiop.security.GSSUtilsContract ->
   sun.security.util.ObjectIdentifier                       JDK internal API (java.base)
   com.sun.enterprise.security.auth.login.LoginContextDriver ->
   sun.security.x509.X500Name                               JDK internal API (java.base)
   com.sun.enterprise.security.auth.login.LoginContextDriver$4 ->
   sun.security.x509.X500Name                               JDK internal API (java.base)
   com.sun.enterprise.security.auth.realm.certificate.CertificateRealm ->
   sun.security.x509.X500Name                               JDK internal API (java.base)
   com.sun.enterprise.security.auth.realm.ldap.LDAPRealm ->
   sun.security.x509.X500Name                               JDK internal API (java.base)
   com.sun.enterprise.security.ssl.JarSigner              ->
   sun.security.pkcs.ContentInfo                            JDK internal API (java.base)
   com.sun.enterprise.security.ssl.JarSigner              ->
   sun.security.pkcs.PKCS7                                  JDK internal API (java.base)
   com.sun.enterprise.security.ssl.JarSigner              ->
   sun.security.pkcs.SignerInfo                             JDK internal API (java.base)
   com.sun.enterprise.security.ssl.JarSigner              ->
   sun.security.x509.AlgorithmId                            JDK internal API (java.base)
   com.sun.enterprise.security.ssl.JarSigner              ->
   sun.security.x509.X500Name                               JDK internal API (java.base)
```

Warning: JDK internal APIs are unsupported and private to JDK implementation that are
subject to be removed or changed incompatibly and could break your application.
Please modify your code to eliminate dependence on any JDK internal APIs.
For the most recent update on JDK internal API replacements, please check:
https://wiki.openjdk.java.net/display/JDK8/Java+Dependency+Analysis+Tool

```
JDK Internal API                      Suggested Replacement
----------------                      ---------------------
sun.security.x509.X500Name            Use javax.security.auth.x500.X500Principal @since 1.4
```

How It Works

The jdeps (Java Dependency Analysis) tool was introduced in Java 8, and it is a command-line tool that is
useful for listing static dependencies of JAR files.

Java 9 encapsulates many of the internal JDK APIs, making them inaccessible to standard applications.
Prior to Java 9, there were circumstances that required applications to make use of such internal APIs. Those
applications will not run as expected on Java 9, so it is imperative such dependencies are found and resolved
before attempting to run older code on Java 9. The jdeps tool can be very useful for finding whether a JAR
depends upon these internal APIs by listing out the dependencies if they exist. If you wish to list the output
in the .dot file format, specify the -dotoutput option along with -jdkinternals, as follows:

```
jdeps -dotoutput /java_dev/security-dependencies.dot  -jdkinternals security.jar
```

The jdeps tool can also be helpful for determining JAR dependencies, in general. The tool contains a
--list-deps option to do just that. Simply put, the --list-deps option lists each of the modules a specified
JAR depends upon.

22-6. Providing Loose Coupling Between Modules

Problem

You would like to provide loose coupling between modules, such that one module may call upon another
module as a service.

Solution

Make use of the service architecture that has been built into the Java 9 modularity system. A service
consumer can specify loose coupling by specifying a "uses" clause in the module descriptor to indicate that
the module makes use of a particular service. The following example could be used for a module that may
have the task of providing a web service discovery API. In the example, the org.java9recipes.serviceDiscovery
module both requires and exports modules. It also then specifies that it uses the org.java9recipes.spi.
ServiceRegistry service.

```
module org.java9recipes.serviceDiscovery {
    requires public.java.logging;
    exports org.java9recipes.serviceDiscovery;
    uses org.java9recipes.spi.ServiceRegistry;
}
```

Similarly, a service provider must specify that it is providing an implementation of a particular service. One can do so by including a "provide" clause within the module descriptor. In this example, the following module descriptor indicates that the service provider module provides the org.java9recipes.spi. ServiceRegistry with the implementation of org.dataregistry.DatabaseRegistry.

```
module org.dataregistry {
    requires org.java9recipes.serviceDiscovery;
    provides org.java9recipes.spi.ServiceRegistry
        with org.dataregistry.DatbaseRegistry;
}
```

The corresponding modules can now be compiled and used, and they will enforce loose coupling.

How It Works

The concept of module services allows for loose coupling to be had between two or more modules. A module that makes use of a provided service is known as a service consumer, whereas a module that provides a service is known as a service provider. Service consumers do not use any of a service provider's implementation classes, rather, they utilize interfaces. For the loose coupling to work, the module system must be able to easily identify any uses of previously resolved modules, and on the contrary, search for service providers through a set of observable modules. To make the identification of the use of services easy, we specify the "uses" clause in a module descriptor to indicate that a module will make use of a provided service. On the flip side, a service provider can easily be found by the module system as we specify the "provides" clause within the module descriptor of a service provider.

Utilizing the module service API, it is very easy for the compiler and runtime to see which modules make use of services, and also which modules provide. This enforces even stronger decoupling, as the compiler along with linking tools can ensure that providers are appropriately compiled and linked to such services.

22-7. Linking Modules

Problem

You wish to link a set of modules in an effort to create a modular runtime image.

Solution

Make use of the jlink tool to link said set of modules, along with their transitive dependencies. In the following excerpt, a runtime image is created from the module that was created in Recipe 22-1.

```
jlink --module-path $JAVA_HOME/jmods:mods --add-modules org.firstModule --output
firstmoduleapp
```

How It Works

Sometimes it is handy to generate a runtime image of modules to make for easier transportation. The jlink tool provides this functionality, amongst others. In the solution, a runtime image named firstmoduleapp is created from the module named org.firstModule. The --module-path option first indicates the path to the JVM jmods directory, followed by any directories that contain modules to be incorporated in the runtime image. The --add-modules option is used to specify the names of each module that should be included in the image.

The jlink tool contains a bevy of options, as indicated in Table 22-2.

Table 22-2. jlink Options

Option	Description
--add-modules	Named modules to be resolved.
-c, --compress=<0|1|2>	Enables compression or resources.
--disable-plugin <name>	Disables named plugin.
--endian <little|big>	Specifies byte order of generated image.
--ignore-signing-information	Suppress fatal error when linked image will contain modular JARs which are signed. Signature-related files of signed modular jars will not be included.
--limit-modules	Limit the amount of observable modules.
--list-plugins	List available plugins.
-p,--module-path	Module path.
--no-header-files	Exclude header files from path.
--no-man-pages	Exclude man pages from path.
--output <path>	Output location.
--plugin-module-path	Custom plugin module path.
--save-opts <filename>	Save jlink options in specified file.
-G,--strip-debug	Strip debug information.
--version	Version information.
@<filename>	Read options from specified file.

Summary

This chapter provided a brief summary of the Java 9 Module System. In this chapter, you learned how to define a module, compile, and execute it. You also learned how to package a module and how to create modular dependencies. You learned about a couple of useful tools for working with modules for the purposes of listing dependencies, uses of JDK Internal APIs, and linking modules. Lastly, this chapter demonstrated how to create loose coupling via the use of module services.

Index

© Josh Juneau 2017
J. Juneau, *Java 9 Recipes*, DOI 10.1007/978-1-4842-1976-8

■ D

■ E

▓ N

■ O

■ P, Q

Get the eBook for only $5!

Why limit yourself?

With most of our titles available in both PDF and ePUB format, you can access your content wherever and however you wish—on your PC, phone, tablet, or reader.

Since you've purchased this print book, we are happy to offer you the eBook for just $5.

To learn more, go to http://www.apress.com/companion or contact support@apress.com.

Apress®

Made in the USA
San Bernardino, CA
25 January 2018